RAPHAEL

OSKAR FISCHEL

RAPHAEL

Translated from the German by
BERNARD RACKHAM

SPRING BOOKS · LONDON

G.D.R.
N.D.G.

First published 1948
This edition published 1964 by
Spring Books
Westbook House · Fulham Broadway · London
Printed in England by Richard Clay and Company, Ltd
Bungay, Suffolk

CONTENTS

LIST OF ILLUSTRATIONS

PLATES

Note—All the paintings and drawings reproduced in the Plates are by Raphael except where the title is preceded by the name of another artist in capitals. The references in brackets ("*R.Z.*") are to the volumes of the Author's *Raphaels Zeichnungen*, Berlin, 1913–1941.

vii

LIST OF ILLUSTRATIONS

LIST OF ILLUSTRATIONS

LIST OF ILLUSTRATIONS

LIST OF ILLUSTRATIONS

LIST OF ILLUSTRATIONS

LIST OF ILLUSTRATIONS

LIST OF ILLUSTRATIONS

PREFACE

FOR those who knew Oskar Fischel it is impossible to think of his life apart from Raphael.

Beginning with a dissertation on Raphael's drawings, he made it his endeavour, with an ever-growing knowledge of Raphael, to arrive at a comprehensive representation, and this he has left behind to us in this book.

It is evidence of ardent and painstaking efforts to solve the great miracle of this artist and at the same time shows clearly the happiness brought by admiration of Raphael into the life of his devoted advocate. What is said in these pages deserves to be carefully studied as a theme very near to the heart of the author. The illustrations gathered together by him over a period of many years were intended, in the selection here provided, to induce the reader to seek out the works of the artist in the original. In an age which follows entirely different paths in its own artistic productions, the author's desire was, in the face of indifference and prejudice, to lead the way to Raphael as the great creator and helper. Of the following that Oskar Fischel gathered round him at Berlin University, many are no longer alive.

As it is now in the English language that the book makes its first appearance, I should like to thank Mr. Bernard Rackham for his faithful work of translation; I have also to thank Dr. Otto Kurz for carefully revising the *Catalogue Raisonné of Raphael's works*. Acknowledgment is also due to the Publishers, who have brought out the book in so worthy a manner. It is not possible for me to mention by name all those who were associated with the life work of my husband and to whom he felt enduringly grateful.

MARGARETE FISCHEL.

London, 27th June, 1946.

TRANSLATOR'S NOTE

IN dealing with languages so different in genius, in spite of their kinship, as English and German, a translator is faced with a dilemma. He must be careful to render faithfully what the author wishes to convey, both statements of fact and metaphors, but he must avoid wherever possible anything that will seem to an English reader outlandish and foreign to an English way of thinking. I am conscious that I have not fully succeeded in this task, but what success I may have achieved is due in no small measure to the help and wise counsel of my wife and my son, Harold Rackham. I have also to thank Mr. K. D. Bundy, A.R.I.B.A., for help in connection with several points arising in the chapter on Raphael as architect, and Dr. Otto Kurz for undertaking the revision of the *Catalogue Raisonné* of Raphael's works. Finally, I am profoundly grateful to Mrs. Margarete Fischel for her ungrudging aid, especially for the pains she has taken in making clear her husband's intentions in certain passages where his words were open to more than one interpretation in English (he died on 27th June, 1939, before he had been able to make arrangements for the publication of the book).

In the *Catalogue* Dr. Kurz has inserted additional references (1) to various works of Dr. Fischel, where they contain information discovered after the respective volumes of his *Raphael's Zeichnungen* had been printed, and (2) to publications of drawings not included in the first eight volumes of that work.

BERNARD RACKHAM.

PUBLISHER'S NOTE TO 1964 EDITION

Although the vast majority of the paintings and drawings illustrated in this book are still to be found in the collections listed in the Catalogue and captions, it has not been possible to check on all of them. The same remarks apply to references in the text, which it has not seemed necessary to revise in any way and which is therefore the author's original version as published in the 1948 edition.

I

A REVIVAL

AFTER only a short obscuration the star of Raphael is to-day entering on a new aspect. He seems to have been out of sight for a period so brief as to be of no importance compared with the length of time his art has lived. Unless we had the right to get clear as to what has come about, it would scarcely be worth while to call to remembrance the reasons for the change in estimation of him which resulted in his rejection.

For three centuries after Raphael, society continued to live under the influence of a manner of living represented by those who look out on us from his portraits, and with which his figures, sacred and profane alike, seem to be imbued. In his time—in Raphael himself and in his circle, in the sitters for his portraits and the originals of his figures, in their gait, their bearing and expression—desire and aim had won visible attainment, the ideal of Renaissance society. In the *Cortegiano* of Castiglione the Aristotelian ideal of the "high-souled" man (μεγαλόψυχος) was brought in all its clarity to men's consciousness; and this form of *élite*, this type of a superiority setting the course for all mankind, was diffused over the world, tested, practised, taught and handed down in indescribable diversity by the powers, spiritual and temporal, of the Counter-Reformation. It was in the newly thrown-up ramparts of youthful Northern democracies, outposts of Protestantism with a growing bourgeois self-consciousness, that this organised force, outlasting centuries, first met with resistance. It was not destined to be shattered against those ramparts; though brought to a halt, it continued in existence, not without further effectiveness: held at a distance, yet too strong not to be felt, sometimes disturbingly, sometimes as a check, down to the present day, with an effect of admonition and even of antagonism.

Such a state of tension, still enduring to-day, need awaken no surprise. The *bourgeoisie*, in the last days of its strengthened power, could not but seek with a shudder to protect its consciousness of its own worth against something unfamiliar, that it could not comprehend, when it saw its own *ratio*, its delight in the realities of this world, confronted by that *gravità eroica*, that *terribiltà*. In justification, the question was asked as a matter of course what could be the meaning for us of the art of a bygone age, a foreign people, a distant climate!

RAPHAEL

Yet it was observed how in Germany Raphael's most famous work continued again and again to exercise its compelling power; it was a German poet who found simple expression for a highly significant idea, "He ever did what others wished to do." It was in Germany that the physiognomist Lavater, exploring Raphael's features to their very depths, called him with unconscious aptness the "man of all-embracing vision". We find Carus and Rochlitz, two critics who were very near to Goethe, drawing a parallel between Raphael and Mozart. It was the young German Romantics, the Nazarenes, who with their heart-blood gave a vitality, as pathetic as it was limited in effectiveness, to the cult of Raphael, frozen in academic traditions; Novalis perceived the secret connection, to be sensed yet hardly capable of proof, between him and the best of the Northerns.

In Germany, the pious Passavant laid the foundations for a knowledge of him with a biography carried out with a trustworthiness that is truly masterly; the completion of it, sterile but full of a spirit of devotion, was the work of a German prince, the Prince Consort, Albert of Coburg, one of the generation of cultured princes that came after the true connoisseurs among the royalties of an earlier age. He based his work on his exhaustive collection at Windsor Castle of reproductions of every stroke of Raphael.

The age of Goethe and the generations in which its influence was perpetuated divined in Raphael's creations the embodiment in plastic art of the imagination, perceiving that he was indispensable; no poetic quality of expression escaped them, they still felt themselves enriched by an influence from his character such as could come only from a great poet, a mature poet. For such things the younger generation had neither eye nor ear; in their search for what would profit and immediately further their art, they felt they went empty away. As men, they did not care "to listen to the language of the gods". Of course, it no longer fell on their ears from the mediating priests; in academic chairs the incessantly preached doctrine of Raphael's validity as a classic had become mere routine, for they could only talk of the master of religious art, the eternally youthful and divine Son of Urbino, the great draughtsman. This kind of stereo-typed, classicist estimate had its sequel in mechanised analysis of this classical art; it ended, in fact, with a painter of pictures devoid of colour. Thus it was possible for Raphael to become what might be called an object of ascetic enjoy-ment for a joyless, Epicurean age; this untroubled, "ever serene" spirit thus came to be suspect as shallow, like his great partner in the world of music, Mozart. In truth, the two great profound thinkers withdrew themselves from such devotees, and left in their hands nothing but masks and shells from which all life had departed.

The man of the Mediterranean—he could not be defined in the terms of the town culture of the North. The elemental quality of his expression of life, the basic foundation of existence continually exercising an influence

2

upwards, the equilibrium of spiritual and physical, were too remote from the controlling intellect of the *bourgeois* and his bodiless morality.

Here it was manifest that poetical creation, on the plastic plane also, could not be comprehended by the outward eye alone. An enjoyment of art that seeks to grasp everything at once is destroyed when confronted by an experience much less comprehensive but far more profound in its reach. The one barely touches the soul, the other demands creative response from within: instead of elucidation and the desire to be understood, reverence, just that sympathetic consciousness of the elemental, of germination and growth, of climate, blood and epoch in their effect on destiny, the master perpetually seeking revival from the powers of nature after the labours of creative activity, to the advantage of man's wellbeing. Only this aptitude for responsive vibration brings deliverance from the limitations of the ephemeral, of the passing epoch, from the accidents of frontiers and creeds, leading to that creative and emancipating power from which spring, in common, life and poetry alike. When therefore we turn back to the profoundest poets among the German masters, when the boundaries set up to fence off the Ancient world by Classicalism and by the mere ink and paper which its teachings have become, collapse before the impact of the younger generation, then, at that very moment, a path will be opened to Raphael's universal sensibility, to the daemonic character of his appearing and language, to that dominating and incomprehensible quality which, in his own time, was signified by the still current epithet *divino*.

II

ANTECEDENTS

DESTINY AND PERSONALITY

"Ueber Wolken nährten seine Jugend
Gute Geister zwischen Klippen, im Gebüsch . . ."

"Good spirits 'mongst the hills and woods
Fostered his youth above the clouds."

"THE sight of boundless distances and heights disappearing from view releases the spirit from the narrow sphere of the real and the oppressive captivity of physical life." Under no more favourable dispensation could the Man of Urbino have made his entry into life; no more fitting starting-point could have been found than Urbino for his path to "the sublime" (Plate 2*b*, 2*c*).

If the Italian is fond of naming his great artist after their birthplace, this proud custom, which we are apt to smile at, bespeaks among the people a strong creative power of living the past over again (in Germany only persons of education passing through the railway-stations of towns like Nuremberg, Aschaffenburg or Ratisbon, know them as places with monuments of art, surviving or not). In the South the birthplace, as the power that produced a genius, lives on, in the name given him by posterity and in their conception of him, even in cases where that place may long ago have ceased to be productive. Thus for centuries, through the consciousness of Italy and of the world, the MAN OF URBINO marches onward.

The heights on which Duke Federigo of Montefeltro delighted to found his castles and residences are characterized by views over the giant undulations of a high plateau. The voice of this landscape sounds clearly enough in our ears even to-day, with a poetry that is unique: these limestone levels, with their plantations of mulberry and olive among the ploughed fields struggling upwards into the rocky waste, were depicted, once for all, by the skill of Piero della Francesca in a manner which even we can still find satisfying (Plate 2*a*).

As if there were a mutual understanding between the ruler and his land, his merits, no less than a happy dispensation, were destined to attach to him just those artists whose works seem to be animated by the deep breadth of these mountain levels. The school of this region, known as the Marches, remained always

4

and everywhere true to the character of the country, with its vast expanses, even when the spirit of Italy entered upon its crisis.

The style of the Quattrocento ended in a state of general disintegration, wavering between chatter in commonplace prose and the phenomenon of a few interesting freaks. It is such groups that attract the eye to themselves and their confused performances, in Florence, Rome and Venice, to say nothing of countless local schools. Only where the *Marchigiani* appear amongst them do we find still prevailing, and not lost, the great unifying movement of poetry, which has nothing to do with merely registering observations of nature or new professional accomplishments; for great art is always strong enough itself to provide what it needs for expression.

To them, the Men of the Marches, it is not enough to understand the human body and to measure out space. Their aim is to make the sublime, disturbing countenances of their figures express, in a compelling vitality, beyond all that is earthly, the essence of the saintly and the spiritual. They are versed not in studio tricks of anatomy and perspective but in the sublime, the supernatural, the divine, the other-worldly. Their knowledge of the human body convinces us of the soaring flight of the beings they depict; their knowledge of space and light proclaims the charm of creation mysteriously waiting to be revealed in broad daylight, or of the luminous glory in which the Transfigured have their being.

PIERO DELLA FRANCESCA, SIGNORELLI, MELOZZO DA FORLI —these are the great masters who point the way to the beyond, and so to an art which again, as in Gothic and even as late as the first generation of the Quattrocento, was the servant of a significant content; it was an art that did not become entangled in that cult of the trivial to which we see the Florentines sacrificing their talents in the service of the Medici.

On the Arno, "the mind became accustomed to distraction", and we are spectators of a lamentably modern drama—Antonio Pollaiuolo, the darling of the Magnifico, unable through sheer absorption in anatomy to set up a single human being on his feet, and the fragrant and enchanting poetry of the Legends of the Saints smothered in the everlasting family gossip of a Gozzoli or a Ghirlandajo.

But the men of Piceno and the Marches stand among these belated adolescents as the only men of maturity. They remain always at a high pitch, and never bestir themselves but for a great purpose. Creatively—that is, without ever departing from unity of form and space—they add their inner concord with what is taking place to what was the common stock of the period—outward veracity; they prove, in the high sense, their simplicity, and as they thus recover that power of representing convincingly a sacred subject which for two generations had been lost, they stand there as the only worthy successors of the men of old. It was not in lifeless accuracies, executed in a manner of broad academicism, that the Renaissance consisted and the world of art was renewed; the true mission of the Renaissance and of Humanism was fulfilled, unbeknown, it may be, to the Humanists themselves and manifest for the first time to us of to-day, in their figures and groups, inspired, earnest, filled with a glow restrained but breaking forth: that mission was, to release the deepest in the human.

Compared with the sphere of the most vital of the old arts, that of painting, then effectively extant in the mosaics of the basilicas, what does the famous garden of the Medici signify, and the studies of the antiques there collected, of which the fame has been celebrated *ad nauseam*? Only a few misguided essays—naïve enough, perhaps—of the Pollaiuoli and Bertoldo. Nowhere do we find these mosaics extolled for the forcibleness of their vitality and power. But the figures of Piero della Francesca range themselves in front of the clear articulations of the architecture, in the axes of the building, and display anew the compelling force of the saints on Early Christian apses and walls.

No one in the early Renaissance came nearer than Melozzo to the marvel of Antique painting, known to us to-day but at that time almost undreamt-of; this is proved by the flashing, vibrant breaking-up of the fresco colours to represent the dithyrambic swaying of his angels of the SS. Apostoli and on the ceiling of Loreto.

To this Signorelli was destined to contribute the sublime inevitability of his proportions. For the first time since the days of Antiquity the nude speaks convincingly of life, and not of the model, it speaks of the soul, of the forces of nature in landscape, of the supernatural; in the PENTECOST at Urbino the Almighty—like a world on its course—bows down from clouds above; from a bank of clouds, at Loreto, a wrathful Christ blazes against the fallen Paul; demons and damned hurtle through space, archangels storm down to earth from their native element, their garments bellying in the air; in Botticelli, they merely dance and sing in a upper storey. The rout of Cupid comes raging on, a surge of bodies let loose, as on a Bacchic sarcophagus, the stillness of the fading moonlit night dreams in forms possessed. Where is there in painting anything, in all music made visible, to compare with the harmony of flutes that sounds in "the new foreshadowing of day"? And Signorelli's saints sit, filled with the godhead, for all their solidity and power, as if they knew that on earth they have no abiding place.

There was *one* however who made his appearance within the confines of the Italian scene, who does not need to be cleared of even so much as a suspicion of classicalism. This is that strange apparition, JUSTUS VAN GENT.

He has a place here not merely as representing the great style, rugged and free in its growth, of HUGO VAN DER GOES, to whom he stood near. He comes on the scene as ambassador of a veritable power of the first order, of the High Gothic of the North, still living and only then for the first time in new vitality. His effective contribution here is no less than the expression of the passionate, overflowing pathos of Germanic painting, which began once more, with Roger van der Weyden, to speak of the inmost depths of mankind; in his simple profundity, in his outbreaks of passion, we have always to be on the look-out for an assault that robs us of our composure. When Duke Federigo succeeded in enticing into his circle this very power, it was an action to which no other Maecenas of that time could offer a parallel. This force, so untrammelled in its greatness, could not fail to eradiate here an influence such as it could not have had in any other part of Italy. Can it be asserted that the oft-mentioned phenomenon of the Portinari altarpiece in Florence had any result in this generation on the Arno—in Ghirlandajo and Filippino Lippi, apart from a few bristly, unshaven heads and wrinkled hands or the interesting contrast with Michael Angelo?

At Urbino the Last Supper of Justus (Plate 228) has its effect as a single whole upon men who themselves in their own creative activity show a sensibility for the whole: structure within structure, space delicately receding in depth and casting a spell of solemnity, with the compelling, stately pattern of the figures; it is vaulted over by the group of angels forming a natural baldacchino, as earlier in the Monforte altarpiece of Van der Goes. The crystal-clear painting of the ground converges in the art of Melozzo with Piero's revelations of graduated light. There was a give-and-take of acceptance and stimulation between them in the studio and library of the Duke; the spirit of these apartments sweeps on its course with vitalising effect through the Italian world and finds fulfilment in the Vatican, in tasks which made of the Man of Urbino a monumental painter. Not much is proved for art by the fact that the Northern faces of Justus van Gent look dreamily out from the pictures of Giovanni Santi; the many who were given a corner in Giovanni's rhyming chronicle did not include the welcome guest from the North who found hospitality in the house of the Santi, but the painter-poet Santi must have looked with respect on his works, and so Justus must be counted among the influences of value in Raphael's paternal home. Those figures seen from behind, a thing unheard of in Italy, apprehended from head to foot, pursue their course through Netherlandish-German art from Roger van der Weyden by way of Schongauer to Kraft and Dürer: what could be the use of Van der Weyden, the great Northern master of tragedy, showing such figures to the Tuscans in the Year of Jubilee? It was only here in Urbino that the principle of their vitality was first understood, and thus they were, in fullness of time, once again brought into play; the master who composed the back views of figures in the Heliodorus and the Transfiguration unconsciously felt the compulsion of an impression received in his youth.

"As soon as we are born," says Goethe to Eckermann (11th March, 1828), "the world begins to have its effect on us—what can we call our own but energy, power and will?"

In the life of Raphael many a tributary influenced the stream of which the source was fostered, as if above the clouds, by good spirits, in the little city of Urbino; but the direction of that stream was never changed, nor could anything intensify its depth. Its onward-driving power only became more marked where surge after surge added to its flow.

Raphael grew up with Dante's verses ringing in his ears. We may well begrudge the elder Santi the reputation of being a better poet; it is undoubtedly of more importance that DANTE was for him the classic (Plate 4). The boy was environed by an atmosphere in which there lived, besides images and rhythms of the best, the spirit of the great Tuscan who, in the deeply significant phrase of Schelling, "dedicated modern art to its mission".

The genius of Dante, "obtaining its effect by sensual allegory", concealed within itself, in its exaltation above his age and its forms, the heritage of all creative power that gives shape to forms out of the abounding consciousness of the universe.

Thus in solitary paths Buonarotti meets Dante—no other was his kin— and greets in the Tuscan the Etruscan; they have motive upon motive in common. Michael Angelo enters, as it were, upon the inheritance that belongs to him; in his rendering, much of the conceptions and visions is now for the first time alive: the *Inferno* indeed took shape through him. In *Raphael* we feel how the poet helped his inborn pictorial sense to expand. Their contact offers an example, uniquely beautiful in its rarity, of the plastic sense stirred and excited by the voice of another art, an interchange and mutual attachment of disconnected elements; possibly we of to-day are the first to be impressionable enough to seem worthy of the experience prophetically suggested by the profound words of Schelling. Thus the poet helps the future painter to bring to birth what was peculiarly his, but as yet unborn; in the ST MICHAEL (Plate 8), with its landscape of Inferno, the seventeen-year-old youth was still painting illustrations; it is nevertheless significant that already he causes the groups from Dante to be lit through the night of Hell by the glow from the blazing city of Dis. In Dante was to be found by this reader something more than expressive groups. To the young Marchigiano his shapes, storming or gently wafted, make their appearance from far and near; horror, amazement, adoration become for him a vibration in space; he was inevitably inspired to pictorial presentation by a poet to whom Antaeus seemed "like Garisenda when the shade of clouds draws over it", or to whom the countless train of the damned comes hurtling behind waving banners out of scarce fathomable depths.

With Dante he created the heaven of the *DISPUTA*; with him, he beheld the tumultuous vision of the Queen of Heaven upon clouds, it was through Dante that he, and he alone, had true experience of the Epiphany in the Apollo Belvedere, and it is the very echo of the melody struck up by Dante when his angels look down out of heaven upon earth far below in such wonderful consciousness that they are worshipping. Here we have, applied to

8

what lies within, his great, reverent feeling for landscape. In like manner Fra Angelico, in the very midst of the disintegrating victory of the new perspective, had painted his landscapes, the loveliest revelations of Italian distances with all their colour, with his back to nature, in the pious seclusion of his cell; thus Raphael in his maturity depicted his perceptions of the wide expanses that stirred his imagination. What higher gift, comparable with that received from this, with his constant "ducae poeta", had Florence, with the scholarly wisdom of her art, yet to bestow on this painter of the beyond?

Dante lived in every painter of the Renaissance; but only Botticelli and Michael Angelo were fired by the idea of illustrating him. Through Raphael we gain a new approach to his world.

At that time the old Flemish painters visited many a princely Court in the South with samples of their art. They caused disquiet to every painter, at least at moments; rejection of what was alien came about for the most part as a natural reaction, the plundering of it, as a matter of course and almost always in a spiritless fashion.

At Urbino, in addition to that strange sojourner from Ghent, there were certainly a large number of works from the North, just as there were in the residences of the Medici at Florence. No one at that time absorbed with so much genuine understanding the exciting wonders of Hieronymus Bosch as this young disciple of Dante among the painters. He comes across one of the visions of Bosch full of bogies and witches' kitchens, and it was certainly not the "draughtsman" in him that was affected by the essence of this art—phantoms summoned up by an unbounded imagination out of the primal consciousness of the elemental in man and nature; immediately, as they coalesce with impressions from Dante, the horizon widens out for him into an endless scene of Hell permeated with darkness and glow of fire!

As a painter he begins his ascent to the "regions of an ancestry sublime" where stand the few poets of the other world. This was destiny; what do external influences signify, stages passed on the journey by his work, the procession of figures that go by? Perhaps one might speak of kings appearing to him in the mirror of history, in a succession at the end of which he was called to take his place.

9

III

RAPHAEL'S MASTERS

RAPHAEL'S first masters were the landscape of the Marches, the spirit of Urbino and Giovanni Santi. Until his twelfth year he was able to watch his father at work, and that means, in his case, more than merely learning the rudiments. He thus found himself as it were born into the ideals and craftsmanship of his native school, the traces of which no later impressions or development could efface or obliterate.

GIOVANNI SANTI was not only a painter, he was haunted by literary ambitions. There was in him perhaps something of the nature of a Vasari or a Pacheco. One who feels in himself the creative impulse has hardly leisure for rattling off heroic poems to be measured by the yard, or even a catalogue of the heroes of his own art. But the very fact that, though in painting he was not much more than an artisan, he belonged to a craft, and had the gift of being able to think and talk about it, makes the role assigned to him by nature unexpectedly beneficent. The high estimation in which his life and work were held by the great strangers who visited Urbino was passed on to the son; *he* mastered as a matter of course what his father had acquired with difficulty by his devout study. Throughout his life Raphael was ever conscious of an aptitude for valuing what he learned in deed and spirit.

One comes to love the old Giovanni Santi in his easel pictures—there is something that moves us in his pedestrian prosiness. His frescoes at Cagli inspire a deep respect for him. They have a remarkable power of conviction. A vital sense of spaciousness is woven around the enthroned Madonna and saints—these figures are alive and breathe; the pale colouring due to the drying of the limewash of the fresco gives charming effects recalling Piero della Francesca. The Resurrection above has an element of naïve display, with its bold foreshortenings; yet the forward-striding figure of Christ, with its suffering Northern type, well reflects the feeling of the great Netherlander. Its impressiveness is perhaps weakened by the fact that immediately below, the same figure has to appear again in the role of St John; yet this circumstance also has its importance for us, as it proves how full Raphael's father was of Hugo van der Goes and Justus van Gent; Melozzo too, on his own testimony, was especially dear to him, and Perugino, even as late as that, of equal rank with Leonardo!

Wherever the son went later in his *Wanderjahre* or had to work in his maturity, he came across works with whose merits he had been familiar from his youth. The influence and spirit of his birthplace affected him as something he could not lose or escape; as to this, we need to know the Italian's feeling of local patriotism.

Urbino was not destined to become, like Florence, the academy for all Italy, but it was before Rome "the arena of contending minds". It was in this atmosphere, full of spiritual tension, that Raphael breathed all his life long; this determined the beat of his pulse.

Vasari's description of the early youth of Raphael is no longer read with the emotion to which it stirred the Romantics. But one ought not needlessly to depart from his account of matters of fact. For the only facts relating to Raphael's beginnings that we have before our eyes to-day, his earliest pictures, prove that the artist-biographer was right.

§ The Question of Teachers

It seems that Giovanni Santi personally brought his son to the Master Perugino to be taught. That must have happened before Raphael's twelfth year, and it is at least not impossible; indeed, if we consider how early in those days under the guild system manual training in workshops began, and that Raphael had grown up in the home of a painter, so early an admission into the house of his master is by no means improbable. Dürer too was apprenticed to Wolgemut at the age of thirteen, and he also had certainly learnt the fundamentals in his father's house.

But out of this haze of conjecture there rises clearly to view what is shown by Raphael's earliest pictures—the innate attraction that distance had for a Picenian; this attraction he had occasion to meet with again in the art of Perugino, here too he must have felt himself confirmed in all he brought with him from his home and his father.

But Raphael himself and the Master of Perugia, now passing through his second maturity, belonged to a new generation.

§ Changes in Quattrocento Art

The last two decades of the Quattrocento were—not only in Italy—a period of concentration and spiritual tensions. In North and South alike possession of the worldly goods of life no longer seemed to make up all that the world was conscious of. City culture had been the vehicle of the so-called Renaissance; the period had sought for itself new forms of life, with the demands made on life by the merchant, with his outward-spreading horizon, the sense of his own new power, due to his own efforts alone; trusting to its own senses it had conquered the world—and filled with this victory it had created an art with a sense of reality and joy in existence. The spectacle of life tempted the eye of the artist ever anew to observations and imitation, but for generations the vividly conceived pictures borrowed from it no spiritual content; there was no beat of an angel's wings, no soaring, even the wandering figure of a saint was hardly rendered with success. The heavenly regions become the setting for a living picture, perhaps a performance in church, with charming child actors in whom the populace took a pure and harmless but quite irreligious delight, as in those who belonged to themselves. The devout had become spectators, the sacred subjects, stage representations; their mysteries were to be peeped at between beams and hangings and cords. Look into Filippo Lippi's heaven, or Jean Fouquet's, or at the Coronation of the Virgin, the Agony in the Garden, the Presentation, the Birth of the Virgin: on both sides of the Alps the same feeling. Bound to earth, the holy mystery is hardly capable of soaring, the spectator's gaze is distracted, not guided, and is unable anywhere to find exaltation; it reels along without direction on a level, close above the ground, filled with the commonplace and the material. To the descendants of the Van Eycks, of Witz, Masaccio and Donatello their inheritance had become no blessing; for the descendants of the founders of municipal freedom and civic self-consciousness, their joy in possessions and in the perpetual recurrence of carnival did not remain untroubled. The rift in life can be traced in the unconscious perplexity and helplessness of this art.

For two generations, by assault and struggle constantly renewed, the problems of the human frame had been so far overcome that hardly one of its secrets remained—save that of the heart-beat. Its freedom, displayed in all its freshness, strikes a note of serenity, but refuses to fit in with the ecclesiastical celebration of the holy mysteries. The figures stand firm on the ground of reality, and are surrounded by the commonplaces of space and landscape, with their effect of familiarity, in the presence of which every desire for the other-worldly, every belief in it, must of necessity fail.

Again, if in these generations the ever-widening emancipation of the profane led to the choice, in the South, of a humanistic subject from the vivid stories of Antiquity, in the North, of genre-scenes to which their underlying moral and biblical idea would hardly lend a note of solemnity, the art of both regions was completely lacking in a sense for the altered rhythm of the new theme. Mythological figures grouped as in a *Sacra Conversazione*, and light-hearted companies of chess-players in punctilious ceremoniousness, prove how this last generation, with all its observation and all its attention to externals, had lost the creative capacity of finding inspired form for the simplest as for the most sublime ideas. It knew only how to reflect impressions, and was thus able in the poorest period of the nineteenth century to win a reputation for being rich. It remained unfruitful in spiritual evocation until, imbued with dominant ideas, it learned once again to sift the media of expression and found, in broad movements of form and in colour deliberately chosen, a strong direction for sensibility.

These were the *Wanderjahre* for the masters of the High Renaissance! This was the generation to which destiny ordained that their teachers should belong.

§ Revived Gothic

Then, once more, it was Gothic that brought to "a grandiose end all searching and all complaining".

In the North, ROGER VAN DER WEYDEN was allowed to accomplish and bring to a conclusion his great mission. His art was given to the Northern hemisphere at the very moment when the mundane revelations of the Van Eycks seemed to be ushering in its falling-away from poetry. In his austere composure he stood ever at the side of all who were in earnest about serving high truths. If he was really "the man of destiny", destiny certainly had well in mind the art of his successors. Wherever something daemonic was achieved amongst the Netherlanders and Germans of the next generation, it was under his auspices. From Bruges to Nuremberg the deepest emotion assumed the form given it by *him*—in the stormy throes of his LAST JUDGMENT, in the sweep of his angels, wherever shoulders are bowed in deep submission or hands are wrung. Wherever the ungainliness of a figure carries us away through the spiritual agitation brought into play by its harsh lines, the world of his own and later ages had before its eyes a stimulating guide such as has hardly since been known, to the essence of creative construction. Perhaps Titian alone may have had the same stimulating effect, in quite another sense; Raphael himself perhaps exerted a similar power as creator of the heroic type.

In the works of Van der Weyden is clearly seen once more the product of Gothic art, fruit born of a period that has reached its consummation. The enchanting pattern of his groups so full of expression spreads over the surface of the picture into all the forms of the framework, the linear structures are filled with the simple unbroken colours; in all this the expressive power of the old glass-painters and illuminators of the Gothic period is renewed, nourished by the deepest sensibility, young, not yet far removed from *the* primordial, daemonic feeling. / All the new and personal sensibility of the townsman, then still bound up with the earthly, pours with vitalising effect into the old expressive linear language, and in their mutual influence content and form are strengthened.

This mighty resonance met with the most responsive echo in German art and was sustained in its mild, mystic strain. It was from the workshop of Van der Weyden that Memling, "Hans the German", absorbed into his less robust nature the fine feeling for line. Where the master narrates and announces, Memling gossips, but in his highest moments, in the Danzig LAST JUDGMENT, he is effective, in spite of all his garrulousness, through the sensitive significance with which the clearly outlined figures are set in luminous colours against the deep foil of boundless space.

13

The manner of Van der Weyden was communicated to a wider sphere by MARTIN SCHONGAUER as a most faithful, well-intending follower. In his pictures one seems to trace the reason why a people that kept to Gothic and practised glass-painting 150 years longer than any other, was of necessity devoted to this class of painting as the peculiar expression of their nature. A freely selected tracery of small trees or mullions divides up the surfaces, and the spaces so marked off are filled with the figures, beautifully outlined and restrained in their movements, as with delicate decorative patterns. The harmony of their contours contains and separates the great unbroken but not discordant surfaces of the colours. In the whole and in details the eye takes its fill of a music reminiscent of stained-glass windows—certainly not by accident. Both indeed derived their language from the same source, the poetry of the Church. How wide the influence of this art must have been when Schongauer, as engraver, found the means of speaking to the whole world! It is superfluous to ask whether the Colmar Master stands at the beginning or the end of an epoch. His contemporaries felt the Gothic he brought, which was nothing else than the *eternal law of unity*, to be a release from prosaic and therefore godless confusion. To follow the majestic sweep of his lines and their fine ramifications, which never get out of touch with the framework, the limits of the copper plate or paper, fills the consciousness with a melody which detaches it from the trivial, as compelling, within the narrow confines of the sheet, as in the gloom of a church filled with coloured light from its windows. Van der Weyden's disciple, as an engraver, with his gentler but more widely intelligible art, became his teacher's herald to the world; in this German Master, lovingly engraving on his copper plate lines of melodious pattern, there arose out of the Gothic goldsmith's workshop one who proclaimed to all, the greatest concentrated art. In his modest sheets the teaching of his profound forerunner made its way through the world; the greatest in North and South proved worthy to learn it.

For us to-day it is one of the most exciting moments in the history of art to see the young Michael Angelo copying Schongauer's TEMPTATION OF ST ANTHONY (Plate 5). Distinction by schools along the lines of racial temperament is forgotten; out of the chaos of diversity there suddenly arises, leaping together from North and South, one giant flame. It illuminates a wildly agitated spectacle in art: the two strongest natures of North and South, the "Men of Destiny", encounter one another here; out of the daemonic age of mankind creative power, unimpaired, in all its primordial force, becomes at moments visible and comprehensible as in a vision. This was the message, echoed back in manifold ways to Italy and across the Alps. When Van der Weyden himself had travelled through the peninsula in the Year of Jubilee, he found the time not yet ripe, in Ferrara, in Florence or in Rome, for the austere greatness of his style; but a generation later the Northern gospel of Gothic announced itself, in an altered form but none the less great on account of its medium, at Urbino, in the creations of Justus van Gent. It resounded precisely at the psychological moment. When the youthful Raphael passed from the sphere of his home to that of Perugia, he there met with the same style, but with a different religious tone; he heard the same melody in an Umbrian mode.

Pietro della Pieve became PERUGINO only in the second half of his life. His contribution prior to that, in Florence and Rome, to the common achievement of Central Italy was important enough to raise him above the others. Giovanni Santi was only expressing the general view when he extolled him as "equal in age and endeavour" with Leonardo. In the Sistine Chapel Perugino assumes the leading position, and not merely in the contracts, in spite of the fact that Botticelli and Signorelli are of the company. The most important theme of the Vatican, that of the DELIVERY OF THE KEYS, was entrusted to him, and he understood how to conceive it with dogmatic inevitability. *His* is the only picture among all the others capable of clear narration; *his* groups alone, in their stately and restrained movements, are permeated by the solemnity of the spiritual; even Botticelli side by side with this work seems garrulous and trite. The mission of the Umbrian himself was also that of bearing the keys. Wherever he appeared with his well-balanced compositions, their swaying rhythms and the quiet dignity and devout ardour of his exquisite figures, forced upon his contemporaries in the midst of their distractedness an awareness of a higher existence.

Throughout Perugino's lifetime a mental picture seems to have remained with him, from his home at Città della Pieve, of the lines of those heights dying away on both sides in a continuous and gentle sweep into the Tiber valley. It is almost tempting to trace to this source the principle of his creative activity; it is the epitome and image of a simple soul directed only towards an aim that was ever the same.

Amongst the provinces of the peninsula the title of honour, "the Heart of Italy", is borne by Umbria, that mountainous inland region, contiguous at no point with the sea that links nation with nation, and traversed by few rivers of any size; the title has a subtle twofold meaning. All the movements that stirred the busy world outside penetrated, it may be, the quiet Umbrian valleys and the mild air of those heights, but always, adapted to the spirit of the place. From the days of old, life goes on in these uplands of devoutness, undisturbed by the storms that rage in neighbouring tracts; and what was to surpass the enthusiasm that spread hence throughout the world, from the places around Assisi! From how many heights the influence of a shrine went forth with one of the countless relics which seem to have found a resting-place here in order to arouse and keep awake that devoutness in this tranquil land, until the rest of the world should find its way back from the confused dreams of reality to the truth!

Here only, all influences from without were traceable in uninterrupted enthusiasm; the soul kept itself in mystic readiness to receive and proclaim abroad the highest.

This is why it was possible for a beginning to be made in this region with the reconquest of the soul of Italy, as the "serafino in carne" hence began his flight. The effect in art of the figure, the teaching and the example of St Francis survived long after in Italy and in the world, and was to find realisation with renewed impetus even in the time of Perugino.

§ The new Umbrian Style

Out of its sufferings and its devotion during the Great Plague, this region created for itself endless votive frescoes, altarpieces and banners. In the paintings of the Umbrians the sacred figures continued, longer than elsewhere, to stand out in expressive outline alone against a gold ground. In neighbouring Tuscany, for generations, the saints had been shown standing in front of a marble framework with inlaid panelling of deceptively plastic effect, whereas the Umbrian seekers after God still are not allowed to come together in space, separated as they are from one another, as if in a monastic cell, in divided frames like the mullions of a window. What need had they for finite precincts made by human hands, when in the picture, as in life, their dealings were to be with the infinite? Such self-circumscribed isolation of the figure results in the development of a very telling outline; in its rhythm, not obliterated by the colour, not enveloped, but brought out more distinctly by the lighting, the figure expresses its otherworldly character. Even when in Umbria an earthly setting became customary for saints as for other figures, and the eternal gold ground had to make way for landscape, the principle of the strong line was maintained. Atmosphere, effects of light, distance, architecture, that in Tuscany became an end in themselves, were here admitted only as subservient to what was essential, the saintliness of the figures. They became an accompaniment to the leading voice, and against this foil the figure stood out with even greater strength, purity and refinement of expression. Thus arose a silhouette of wide effectiveness, full of life, stressed by a harmony, strong yet of the simplest, of colours acting and reacting upon one another. A cult of line began, and a new expressiveness of colour, as if Gothic wished to bring to remembrance its great, forgotten achievements. Perugino was to be the creative leader along this path; the significant figure of the Perugian master seemed chosen to make profession of this reformation before the world, and to live through the joy of creation, the sternness of artistic renunciation, the tragedy of the pioneer. In this life nothing seems to be chance, all seems to be a calling to a special mission.

The Umbrian had to learn from the creations of Piero della Francesca the enhancement given to saintly figures by light-filled space, and its power of adding to their essential convincingness, where the accents of architecture and landscape accord with the rhythm of the groups. Already at Perugia he had forced his school companions to fall into line with this principle, when they painted in concert the Legends of San Bernardino; how much he grew in significance when he dared to display this knowledge before all the world at the very See of the Pope, in the Sistine Chapel and in the choir of old St Peter's!

In Florence, ever the city of quest, the unmistakableness of his aim must have given him a peculiar authority. San Giusto, the monastery of the Gesuati, outside the Porta Pinti, was the place in which his transformations were effected, always with the same high poetic aim—sunny frescoes in the style of the San Bernardino pictures, with a crowd of figures, but raised to a higher order by means of dignified architecture, no longer the petty display of the timber stage-structures of Gozzoli, or distracting peeps into recognisable views, as in Ghirlandajo. The architecture in the picture served as a foil and framework to the figures, and forms as it were a free tracery; looking through the arcades of the cloister, the eye fell every time on a unified picture; from the arch of the vaulting to the foot of the wall the solemn harmony of the figures with architecture and landscape filled the surface—no more painting of "ground above sky", as in the old fresco cycles with their disposition in layers. In this manner the wall-painting gained an essential part of its effect. It occupied the surface from one architectural limit to the other, and in this framework the composition, to have decorative force, had of necessity to be carried out on broad lines. The colour must comply with this simplification, if it was to combine with it in effectiveness at a distance. And here we have the preliminaries of a most remarkable transformation which to-day we must needs regard as something more than accidental: the Gesuati had in their monastery a workshop for glass-paintings with which they supplied the whole of Italy, and Perugino raised the level of their productions by providing them for decades with the cartoons for them.

It is a curious contrast! The early Quattrocento had delighted in creating light, clear spaces, as had the late Gothic at the same period in the North; but hardly a generation later men liked to gather together for devotions, in brotherhoods. They sang the old *laudi*, and just as escape from reality was found on the wings of the solemn mediæval melodies, so, in the desire not to be reminded within the walls of the church of the world outside, the light of day was forbidden to enter by deep-coloured glass, and the eye glancing upon the window was turned back forcibly, compellingly, to its duty by the tranquil bearing of saintly figures.

The power that gathered the Florentines together before the pulpit of SAVONAROLA and constrained them to follow the prophet, was the same that filled them with a desire for worship amid the strains of ancient hymns in the coloured twilight of chapels and oratories adorned with stained-glass windows. The Umbrian brought with him from his home all the needful endowments for giving almost excessive satisfaction to such desires. To him had been given a sense for the figure exalted above the plane of everyday life; for his sensibility, every frame had to be filled in its entire extent with the expressive pattern that aided devotion. The secret was easily revealed to him of gaining an effect by means of figure-mosaic in large panes of glass, with their mineral brilliance as little broken up as possible, tuned to a simple and strong harmony of colour. He understood the captivating charm of Early Christian and Byzantine painting; its deep impression he had found vital when still on his quest in Rome and now consciously renewed, just as the strong, intimate effect of Northern engravers must have affected him when they filled the narrow limits of their plates to the full with gestures of devotion.

§ Glass-painting

All that was best in his understanding of glass-painting was communicated to his easel-pictures. He now became the Umbrian—the Perugian, in fact—that he was; the truth was now proved of the doctrine of space learned in his youth from Piero della Francesca, and of the training in highly expressive outline acquired from the hereditary school.

The Perugian landscape with its solemn twilight colouring in the hour before sunrise, and the deep tone of the sky above range beyond range of mountains of ever softer blue, is now combined with the coloured silhouette of the figure filled with a spirit of passionate or dreamy devotion. Undecorated archways of sweeping span or vaults upon plain pillars make a framework within the frame, or little slender trees divide the distance and give touches of vitality to the distant view on either side of the isolated figure; or saints in groups or often merely in rows stand and sway in the simplest rhythms in the foreground of the landscape. They stand out, in great passages of unbroken yet soft colour, in front of the wide zones of deep blue of the mountains and sky. There are compositions like the ASSUMPTION OF THE VIRGIN, from Vallombrosa, that have the effect of being divided, by invisible tracery, like one of the mighty *finestroni* of Gothic churches, or intentionally renew the overpoweringly sacramental austerity of Byzantine painting.

For a painter of the school of the Marches colour could never be without expression. Now—in this new phase—it gains such strength through purification of its elements that the harmony of figure and background, and of red, green, milky blue and violet against the azure of the distance, have their like only in the windows of Northern Late Gothic choirs. An altarpiece of Perugino in its original place even to-day has an effect of space opened up, and of reality captured by means of the melody of its lines and colours. Every other painting pales, in the most literal sense, before the VISION OF ST BERNARD at Munich.

It is symptomatic that an æsthetic based on impressionism, with its material interests, disparaged this phase of his art as reactionary; but for similar reasons the age of Perugino was responsive to the sacramental in this style as to an inward compulsion. It arose out of the deepest stirrings in the consciousness of a whole epoch. It was now no longer Florence or Umbria but a spiritually renewed humanity that created this style for itself.

Here the mature Perugino follows Perugino the youth; instead of the teaching of Masaccio and Piero della Francesca, the pious wisdom of ancient ecclesiasticism again holds authority. In the North, the arresting narrative of Roger van der Weyden had long been listened to instead of the matter-of-fact Jan van Eyck; Conrad Witz had been followed by Schongauer. And suddenly a universal conception of art opens up, strange and exciting. Out of the dimness of a distant past and of a tradition still incomplete the same conception takes shape, both north and south of the Alps, presenting itself in both regions as in a mirage. At Nuremberg, Albert Dürer the Elder has no other wish than to send his son "in die Lernung"—to be taught—to the great new Gothic master of Colmar, Schongauer; and however much Vasari's narrative may seem questionable in the light of sober examination, one thing remains certain: Giovanni Santi showed by his ideas and his words his reverence for Perugino, and five years after his death we find his son as the best assistant to the master in his reactionary attitude in matters ecclesiastical. Destiny intended that those who gave new life to art in North and South should receive their teaching from the revivers of Gothic— or rather, the creators of a new spiritual inwardness and inspiration in art. After half a century of confusion, forces rejuvenated and rallied give rise anew to the *monumental style*.

NOTE—Raphael's Teachers

The gap has to be bridged between Raphael's twelfth year, in which he lost his father, and his seventeenth, when we find him as trained assistant of Perugino.

Morelli (*Galerie zu Berlin*, p. 200 *seq.*) supposed that he had discovered Raphael's first teacher in the Bolognese, Timoteo Viti. No proof of this is brought forward; it is true that during this time Timoteo was settled at Urbino, but the pictures we possess by him (at Milan, Bologna and Urbino) are so badly preserved that conclusions drawn from them as to his style are very questionable. His NOLI ME TANGERE at Cagli shows him as being peculiarly weak and decidedly indebted to the ENTOMBMENT of Raphael (who had meanwhile come to maturity). Timoteo's Magdalen is slavishly borrowed from a study for the ENTOMBMENT which he perhaps possessed. He belongs to the race of those impersonal hangers-on who keep to the manner prevalent in the time of their youth and cannot profit even by drawings and motives of the great companions of their young days. If he really had a share, as Vasari reports, in Raphael's Roman works at Santa Maria della Pace and is to be regarded as the painter of the Sibyls above the Prophets, he can only have worked in the role of an assistant in the execution of the work, perhaps actually under the direction of Giulio Romano.

A just appreciation of his drawings was already shown by Vasari when he called him a *gagliardo disegnatore*. They are his most original work; vigorously carried out in stumped chalk and charcoal, they have scarcely their equal (cf. Fischel, *Zeichnungen der Umbrer*, p. 238).

Critics since Morelli have not as yet been able to dissociate themselves from his hypothesis, which makes Timoteo Viti the teacher of Raphael instead of his imitator, as Vasari relates.

Magherini-Graziani discovered the contract for Raphael's first altarpiece in the church of Sant' Agostino at Città di Castello; it bears, in addition to Raphael's signature, that of a hitherto entirely unknown Urbino artist, Evangelista di Pian di Mileto. As to the co-operation of this artist in the painting, the less can be said because the few badly-preserved fragments of the picture at Brescia and Naples only give evidence of the hand of one whose drawing and painting show him to belong to the school of Perugino, in other words, the hand of Raphael. The composition of the painting, which has been handed down in a copy, is undoubtedly Peruginesque, and each of the figure-motives can be paralleled in Perugino's workshop about 1500 (Fischel, *Jahrbuch der preussischen Kunst-Sammlungen*, 1921, p. 13). Nevertheless this name has been interpreted as that of the very first of Raphael's teachers, and a fictitious *œuvre* has been assembled for him in the *Arte* under the eyes of Venturi; as Evangelista worked in the role of *fattore* for Giovanni Santi, everything that seemed too feeble for Giovanni Santi was attributed to him. From this a conception can be formed of the work and effect of Raphael's supposed first master. It is indeed the pick of the store-rooms. In the history of art nothing is altered by this interpolated nonentity, for the separation of Evangelista's *œuvre* from that of Giovanni Santi only proved afresh that Raphael came to maturity, as an artist, under the influence of his father; and thus he was already under the influence of Perugino even before he entered Perugino's workshop. In view of this it is almost a matter of indifference whether, as Vasari relates, Raphael was committed by his father into the charge of the great master, or whether he did not enter his workshop until six years later. From the beginning of his career as a painter, from the first work of his own that we know, he is certainly following in Perugino's wake.

The only question may be whether Perugino could have had some part in Raphael's teaching, in spite of the fact that he was precisely at this time in the habit of being frequently away from Perugia for somewhat long periods. But the activities of a workshop in which the master took only a passing share even, were enough for lasting formative impressions; the atmosphere, the presence of his works, cartoons and studies, had a decisive effect. We underestimate also the mobility of artists, and the easy going and coming between the places in which great ateliers had to operate. It is very possible, indeed likely, that

Raphael accompanied his master even to Florence. Impressions of Donatello's figures of saints occur even before the authenticated stay of Raphael in Florence, in his drawings and in pictures by Perugino in which he collaborated. In a pen drawing at Lille he copied the motive of the St John of the Apocalypse in the Duomo of Florence (*Raphaels Zeichnungen*[1] I, 10); the KING SOLOMON in the Cambio, in the immediate neighbourhood of which he may be supposed to have been actively at work in 1499–1500, repeats the ST MARK of Orsanmichele, and the Archangel Michael in the Vallombrosa altarpiece Donatello's ST GEORGE.

In the Cambio of Perugia and in the altarpiece of Vallombrosa we can confidently seek for the share of Raphael, although in the case of the frescoes, the arbitrary exaggeration of Venturi's attributions should be a warning. On the wall with the subject of Fortitude and Temperance the FORTITUDO might be by Raphael's hand and the HORATIUS COCLES must be (Plate 10). One needs only to compare these organic heads—the marvellous, distant gaze, the opening eyelids modelled with a dark stroke on the under edge, the breathing plasticity of nose and lips, the chin jutting out from the neck—with the withered, lifeless faces to right and left by the master and the other assistants.

On the wall with the Sibyls the youthful KING SOLOMON stands out above the others by its breadth of look, its spirit and the noble freedom of its bearing; it is an interpretation of Donatello's ST MARK. We have here, of course, in simple unconsciousness, and without presumption, the influence, as it were regenerative, of the new spirit of the disciple and assistant upon Perugino's inventive power.

In the altarpiece of Vallombrosa the same reaction is repeated in the ASSUMPTION OF THE VIRGIN (Plates 6, 8): on the left, beside the principal figure, the angel is by Raphael, with the thoroughly musical gesture, from the enraptured gaze and the marvellous loveliness of the fingers on the strings down to the stance of the feet, unconstrained yet serving as a support for the harp. We need only compare the corresponding figure on the other side, with its frigid look, the lifeless bend of its fingers, and its impossible pose. But the head of the upward-pointing angel below this figure has again the "clear-cut purity and a little more" which, without being exactly beautiful, may be regarded as Raphael's signature. The St Michael to the right below (Plate 9*b*), and the cherub head to the left above him (Plate 9*a*), are again marked out by the organic lines that we know from Raphael's innate style of drawing in these early years. This is set beyond doubt by drawings such as the head of a youth at Lille, and the angel with a viola in the British Museum (Plate 16, *R. Z.*, I, 20, 22). In these as in the painting we have the peculiarities which he had no need to learn; he brought them with him from the Marches, as something in which he was superior to master and workshop.

[1] Hereafter cited as *R. Z.*

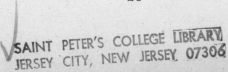

RAPHAEL

There is hardly need any more to dwell on the oft-mentioned dependence of Raphael upon Perugino's "foreman" PINTURICCHIO. The hypothesis of Lermolieff, established with the help of drawings of which hardly a single one is certainly by Pinturicchio, has broken down. The Venetian sketchbook certainly contains copies after the youthful Raphael by one of his fellow-learners.[1] Besides, the only motives to be found in Pinturicchio came from Perugino.

Greater importance seems to attach to the question whether Raphael can have had a share in Pinturicchio's frescoes in the Libreria at Siena. Vasari stated that he had: Raphael, he claims, provided his elder friend with designs for them. The still extant contract bound the master to make the drawings himself. Whether this condition held good at the moment when a Raphael was to be had at disposal cannot be decided. The sheet from the Casa Baldeschi, with the MARRIAGE OF FREDERICK III, is now more easily accessible in the collection of Count Contini at Florence; it entirely agrees with the drawing for the DEPARTURE OF AENEAS SYLVIUS in the Uffizi.[2] With its effect of sunlight on figures rendered with a feeling of freedom and roundness, the design for the MARRIAGE is, it may be said, the most beautiful of "Quattrocento Drawings". Nothing comparable is to be found in the wretched drawing and—so far as can be judged in their condition—the tedious brushwork of the wall-paintings with scenes from the life of Pius II. The oft-cited group in the CANONISATION OF ST CATHERINE supposed to represent Raphael and Pinturicchio themselves, has certainly a sentimental value, but in its meagreness provides no exception to this statement.

On the other hand, no notice has ever been taken, except by Crowe and Cavalcaselle, of the merits that distinguish the fresco outside, above the entrance door to the Libreria in the aisle of the Cathedral, with the CORONATION OF PIUS III (Plate 7). It is still in good preservation and possesses, in the group to the right of the empty middle space, from the relief on the pedestal below the Pope above down to the beautiful youth in the foreground, a freshness, a feeling of space, a plasticity in the figures, to be found only in the great preliminary designs, especially that in the Contini Collection. Nowhere in Pinturicchio, not even here in this fresco by his own hand, do the figures stand out with such movement and roundness as here, with so much atmosphere in them and about them, with such a breath of inspiration in the features. All other figures appear by contrast as if cut out and stuck on.

Added to this is the circumstance that, in front of the Triton relief, Raphael himself is unmistakably to be seen—whether besides Pinturicchio is still undecided—glancing up with a rose in his hand, and that the lines of the forefinger of the man to the left behind the dog and of the man seen from behind

---

[1] Fischel, "Zeichnungen der Umbrer", *Jahrbuch der k. Preussischen Kunstsammlungen*, 1917.
[2] *R.Z.*, I, 65 and 60.

to the right cross in this strikingly vital figure (Plate 284). This hitherto unnoticed self-portrait of Raphael would confirm and amplify the report handed down by Vasari of his participation. Thus we should have here, about 1503, to set beside the features of the fourteen-year-old boy in the drawing at Oxford, Raphael at the age of twenty, before the portrait at Florence of about his twenty-fifth year.

IV

APPRENTICESHIP

APART from the lively narrative of Vasari we are completely in the dark as to Raphael's apprenticeship, the period between the twelfth and the seventeenth year which particularly in those days was decisive for a young artist. Then there emerges suddenly no longer the pupil, but the skilled, fully-trained assistant of Perugino. About 1500 he is painting important parts in the works of the master and in the productions of the workshops, and himself takes on orders for altarpieces; it speaks for the early spread of his fame that major works were entrusted to the seventeen-year-old artist.

§ Perugino about 1500

At this time Perugino does not belong to Umbria alone; he is closely bound up with the life of Florence and had indeed civic rights and a workshop in the Borgo San Sepolcro. His studio is known to have been busily occupied, and in the years when Raphael was working with him, the master with his staff of assistants must be supposed to have enjoyed considerable liberty of movement in order to be active at one time in Perugia, at another on the Arno or at Siena, and to send round again and again—a habit in which he was becoming ever more confirmed—old cartoons that were kept in readiness, for execution in which he often had little share. In view of the useful aptitudes that Raphael already possessed in his master's eyes about 1500, there is no reason to doubt that he had taken part some years earlier in these journeys for professional purposes of Perugino and his people.[1] So he may well have seen Florence already, whilst still dependent and a learner; but this contact with the art of the Tuscan capital only becomes interesting when he was himself experienced enough to seek the fulfilment of his efforts, instead of merely observing with reverence.

Tuscan art moreover was not ripe for such mutual relations with the future perfecter of Central Italian painting until he began his travelling years again. Florence had in the meantime to attract to herself again her two great sons, Leonardo and Michael Angelo, and to set them in opposition in rivalry with one another.

We readily enjoy the charm of watching the rise, growth and maturing of a

[1] Cf. Note, "Raphael's Teachers", p. 19 above.

power that appeared for the uplifting and the happiness of mankind. But pious curiosity to know how it developed should never lead us to reduce the miracle to the commonplace dimensions of a school, and to seek to explain by influences what is really grace and revelation. Casual intercourse in the same craft explains nothing; the greeting of spirit by spirit explains much. It is not the *fact* that two geniuses must needs encounter and complement one another, that is illuminating on both sides alike, but the *reason why* this is so. Herder not Behrisch, Gluck not Mozart's father, throw a ray of light on those who come after them; it is worth while reconstructing the intercourse that took place between such great equals, but he who aspires to enter the sanctuary must leave the dust of the schools outside.

§ The Problem of Timoteo Viti

Worthless mediocrity has no place on the path of the great; if we wish to find our way back to Raphael, we must eliminate Timoteo Viti, whose pictures are fit for the storeroom.

The futility alike of the objects and of the problems that occupied the last generation since the bold conjectures of Lermolieff (who showed his love, and therefore at the same time his lack of it, by dwelling on the inessential) is revealed to us only when we comprehend how impersonal is the effect of Raphael's first independently undertaken work, in the fragments that have been preserved (in a condition that is admittedly deplorable).

§ Fragments of the first Altarpiece for Città di Castello

The seventeen-year-old youth who signed the contract had as yet, with his master's spell upon him, scarcely anything of his own to deliver; he painted his picture, the CORONATION OF ST NICHOLAS OF TOLENTINO, as if it had been ordered of Perugino and he had had to carry it out as foreman of the workshop (Plate 3). This example almost relieves us of the trouble of tracing the impersonal nature of his painting further back, into the period of four or five years when, with a brush in his hand, he was not yet Raphael. With crayon or pen he had of course, even in these early years, already begun to be himself, like Dürer.

It is indeed difficult, impossible almost, to prove that it is not a *self-portrait* that looks out with the boyish gaze of the Oxford drawing (Plate 1), seeking with amazement to drink in "what lies behind the eyelashes"; in which case the eyes must be those of the only one who "when he was a child", in the South and in this artistic environment, could have brought such a miracle to pass.

A child here looks out into the world with reverence for the wealth of creation and yet with a scrutinising instinct; at once humble and superior, he keeps his distance and, by contrast with the thirteen-year-old Dürer, who almost seems to be suffering under the impressions made upon him, he has an unconscious dignity of his own and the delicate, almost animal unapproachableness of young creatures. This boy seems to be born to be something more than the master of a workshop. "La maniera del disegnare e le belle maniere e costumi", Vasari tells us, fascinated the Perugian master, and he pronounced a judgment on the "*putto*" brought to him by Giovanni Santi that future events were to confirm. The complete painter is really contained in this chalk drawing—a wonderfully easy and yet energetic interaction of forms, up and down, to and fro, a feeling for movement and existence, that our eye enjoys in the play of the individual forms and in their slight foreshortening in nose, lip and eyelid, in the ease with which, apart from obvious mistakes, deliberate deviations from nature have been achieved for the sake of expression. A slight excess of means employed contrasts delightfully with that sure knowledge which makes a success as a matter of course of relief and spatiality. No portrait by Perugino, not even the beautiful boy with brown jerkin and blue cap in the Uffizi, can show this coherence of all the parts. The great Umbrian was able to attain his profound effects when, as he did especially at this period, he built up his figures and heads out of details that gave expression; his requirements in the way of expression were still—or once more—those of Gothic: they were satisfied by an almost needless emphasis on eyes, nose and mouth, and by merely indicating the bony structure and flesh between. Thus his figures also at that time were structures of draped attitudes, his fingers often mere members fitting into one another. Here, in this drawing of a boy, a breathing whole takes shape, full of life to the very hair. A universal sensibility, though as yet unconscious, distinguishes the young draughtsman from the master, preoccupied with the practice of his craft, whose experience and skill as a painter are nevertheless indispensable to him.

The writer of the *Lives* seems to have been better informed than his recent critics; for many of his statements about Raphael's youth have been confirmed almost by written documents. All he knew of Raphael's work of this period was the great altarpieces. We can understand that they seemed to him, especially for the uninitiated, to resemble those of Perugino in their painting, to the point of confusion. They are painted in accordance with studio customs and guild usages tested in their effectiveness for churches by the master—the beginner was perhaps bound by the commission in externals also to keep to Perugino's models. But even in these works he seems to show an innate independence and even maturity as soon as he designs and draws.

§ Drawings of the Coronation of the Virgin

The drawings that have been preserved of the CORONATION OF THE VIRGIN (Plate 22) are perhaps the most precious of all Raphael's drawings ($R. Z. I$); they are drawings of the figure in silverpoint on paper with milky white surface after fellow-students in costume of the period. The manner in which the pencil feels its way along the contours of the figures and the angel musicians are modelled

(Plates 12, 16), advancing with a gentle swell and dying-away of the outline, is something unprecedented in the Quattrocento and was never again surpassed by Raphael himself. It was a born draughtsman who painted the head of the doubting Thomas in the picture, with the Peruginesque convention of the upward gaze, but who in the study at Lille (Plate 14), in a few strokes lightly skimming the space, captured the tumult of the youthful soul, overcome by the revelation; foreshortenings play a part, a raising of the lips, a dilation of the nostrils, a throbbing in the hollow of the neck (the forward thrust of the neck is precisely the signature of Raphael, and continued to be so). The calligraphy is tumultuous, borne on the wings of his own sensibility, when he sets down with powerful strokes of the crayon the ecstasy of St James (Plate 15). Though always tied down to the same manner of composition in paint, as if under the eyes of Perugino, he knew how to render alike the sweet and the passionate, the bitter; this versatility of technique and behaviour was peculiarly his among the great draughtsmen. But it is never the outline or framework, always the expression in its entirety, of which he portrays on the paper the rhythms echoing in atmosphere and space. Being born, with these peculiar qualities, to be a *draughtsman*, he became one because he was a *born painter*.

§ The Painter of the Dramatic

To-day we have the good fortune, unknown to Vasari, of knowing Raphael's earliest little painting: the Painter of the Dramatic is there, complete, before our eyes. Here, in these small-scale works, there was nothing to check him, no model of the master to follow, no exactness of execution such as was required in large paintings; it may be that he did not yet consider himself professionally ripe for the monumental. Fra Angelico also often betrayed in predella pictures aspirations as a painter which he renounced in the devotional picture; in the former many a dream could be realised swiftly, as in drawings.

This compactness of pictorial narration, the indissoluble and indispensable interaction of colour and subject, the inescapable filling of the space with harmony of colour, Raphael only recaptured so arrestingly in the Second Stanza, after many a detour and even many a defection from himself. But the compelling power in the HELIODORUS and the MASS OF BOLSENA, in the DELIVERANCE OF ST PETER and the ATTILA, was only the sequel and the fruit of this new painting, already in early blossom, that conceives space and figures as linked together by colour.

He dared to believe himself capable of filling with life the narrow frame of a picture intended for a private apartment, in a manner which was already a matter of course to him in drawing, within the limits of the sheet of paper. And here, with these gems of painting a few inches square before us, dependence upon any other work as a model is unthinkable, or any kind of influence whatsoever.

RAPHAEL

§ Predella Panels for the Coronation of the Virgin

In the predella panels for the CORONATION OF THE VIRGIN (Plates 13, 17*a, b*) we find already a quality of colour of high dramatic significance utterly foreign not only to Perugino but also to every other contemporary of Raphael.

The only painters in Central Italy who displayed power of expression as colourists were the Sienese masters of the Trecento and their most faithful follower, Fra Angelico. In the fifteenth century colour harmony resulted "automatically" from the almost *pleinairiste* observation of light—and of this, these very artists of the Marches were unrivalled as examples, earlier even than the Venetians—or from the new convention of solemn harmonies of colour which Perugino made to dominate with a hymn-like grandeur the monotonous rhythm of his groups. But colour never became the expression of the entire mood of the scene as it did here, in the young Raphael.

§ The Knight's Dream

One is immediately struck by the contrast between the two women at the feet and at the head of the DREAMING KNIGHT (Plate 18), a bright little picture of which the colours have indeed been thought to display a Bolognese or Ferrarese quality; but there is nothing in these figures that would not fit in with the assistant in the frescoes of the Cambio—costumes, pose and movement: only *here*, on the small scale, everything is more controlled, every form is fuller and healthier, than in the laboured monotony of the master. Yet here, how much is conveyed by juxtaposition! Twice, at the confines of the picture, the eye is arrested—by the grave figure standing in contemplation, her head covered, her full robe some inches longer and many shades more sombre, in its neutral violet, than that of her partner, and by the facing figure, Voluptas, standing with the rhythm with which she must have come on the scene, still vibrating in her limbs. The wind plays with her veil, the light glints on her close-fitting sleeves, the little coral chains rattle on the yellow upper garment; she has gathered it up like a woman gardening, or a nymph, and in consequence, half unconsciously, half by intention, the shorter under garment exposes her dainty ankles. For sword and book, strength and wisdom, we have severe lines in sombre tones; for the world and its allurements, restless display, studied freedom in the alternations of contrasted colour. Between worlds so far asunder, the arms and hands that hold the tempting awards are extended towards one another in an airy region above the relaxed sleeping figure, as if in truth to suggest the cloudy fabric of a dream. This is the intention of the landscape, full of asymmetrical forms; the steep path to the mount of Virtue—the bridge leading to the road into placid vales. But in this bridge, and in the perpendicular formed by the little bay-tree, the immeasurable and imponderable qualities of a dream are forgotten.

The little frame is dominated, in a manner that cannot escape the eye, by this pattern of gestures, rendered in the most telling colours; is it too much to say that this born painter of histories amazes us here at the very start by his accomplishment? The means of expression came thronging to his hand; we already foresee the master who has the same means at hand later for his Plato and Aristotle, and who is also at ease, as here in the Dream, in a sphere above the earthly and capable of bearing witness to it. The monumental creator with his far-reaching influences, the visionary with his power of convincing, appears here before our eyes—and it is a young man of the world capable of seeing through the phenomena in society with an instinctively sure perspicacity and of controlling them for his own ends. Even before we know the theme, the essence of what is meant is there before our eyes. Even if it is true that the suggestion came from Sebastian Brant's *Narrenschiff*, this would speak for the painter's humanistic width of culture, natural to a man of Urbino; but it was this man of culture precisely to whom it was granted to give visible shape to the ideas of a highly cultivated society. This is true illustration—to bring into the light what is dark and wavering as a vague apparition by fixing it in living shape. Raphael no longer clings to the text; he transposes the thought, newly vitalised, into his own sensual world. And here he finds naturally that rhythm of narrative and presentment which alone is suited to this free realm of ideas. Whilst in the Cambio his teacher is laboriously using, for the sages of the ancient world, his cartoons that had before served for saints, and Signorelli introduces his Pan among the Shepherds into a group of the *Sacra Conversazione*, here the true painter of humanism arises. The theme is not one that is set for him, but innate, romantic as a fairy-tale familiar from the days of childhood onwards; and his creative power triumphs in a little panel like this no less than in later days, when he had to give form to the greatest ideas of Renaissance society.

§ The Three Graces

Thus he brought to the THREE GRACES also something more than a knowledge of the antique group (Plate 234). A chord of three ethereal notes weaves itself above the favoured earth, which floats under a whitish haze in terracotta and reseda. In this haze is poised the golden, living flame of the noble forms, dreamlike, void of desire; about their limbs plays softly the light-flooded breeze of the valley. Thrice this soft pale tone of the landscape is traversed by the warm colour of their bodies, the first bashful, the middle one full of dignity, the third easy and unconstrained in bearing; and just as in their surroundings the zones of colour border upon one another in gentle contrast—the sky, the blue-shaded terracotta of the mountains, the surface of the misty lake, the smooth green of the undulating ground—so there is a play of ever-repeated waves surrounding and traversing these limits: the gentle flow of the arms ripples from below against the pronounced pattern of the golden balls and the heads; below again, glide the dark contours of the torso, the undulation of the knees, the soft line of the feet treading the ground. The exquisitely clear, unconcealed outline of the individual figure is repeated in the entire group of sisters; forms open up, releasing the gaze, related to the flamelike tracery-patterns of Gothic windows, in the flickering interplay of the colour as well. And this is scarcely an accident, for we have here again the great media of this art; and its vital law, "In the beginning was pattern", fills the picture in every part with form saturated with the spiritual. These curves, scarcely touching the ground in their flow, unearthly, ethereal—the element that in ecclesiastical art gives an effect of sanctity—here convey the blithe tread of blissful beings. Even he, this young harbinger of the world of the gods, is not entirely emancipated from the conventions of centuries-old ecclesiastical art that dictated the forms of figure and gesture. At what prior period could there have been such a release? It is not merely that "in the South, what is great and beautiful is of itself sacred". Some people think that they see in Raphael's heads of the Madonna the only form known to the mystic when he desires to do homage to beauty. But the young humanist was a painter, and the same landscape that, on other occasions, with its grand lines in the evening twilight, is fraught with the solemn repose of nature as the setting of a sacred melody, here wraps in a sunny glow of consecration the three goddesses. To them belongs the daylight, their bright loveliness is in accord with the beauty of the mountain contours and this sunny atmosphere.

The Monte Subasio, by Assisi, was hardly conscious of the cult to which its exquisite colour-harmony of rose violet would one day provide a foil, but its beautiful lines are taken up by the lines of these figures just as if some temple of the Ancient world had to be built in congruity with the natural formation of the site.

This accord of form and landscape arises from the all-embracing sensibility which now for the first time adopted humanism as truly part of life and, in a select band of leaders, succeeded in harmonising it with their own existence. It was in the golden glow of this living heathen temple before the heights of Assisi that this happy equilibrium of spirit and form, in true accord with the dignity of man, first became visible. It was in a temple at Assisi, about three hundred years later, through Goethe speaking to Germans, that the meaning of the Classical again became clear: the Classical consists in what is sanctioned by the human senses, a natural growth ever breaking forth anew out of the Primal Cause. And what followed? A Greek temple was built among the pine-clad heights above the Danube, Classicism was taught beside the foaming Isar, and the figure was invented of the great "classical draughtsman", to be enjoyed in mere paper currency!

The humanistic backgrounds of these little pictures from a one-time diptych —they once belonged together—have been brilliantly interpreted as part of the survival of the Antique: a young Scipione Borghese, making his entry as a knight into the world, may have provided the occasion for this combination of the "chevalier délibéré" and the Three Graces, or rather, the Hesperides with the Golden Apples. This is sufficiently indicated by the pictures, rightly regarded as a single whole; it is confirmed by the knowledge we now have of the reason for the choice of these subjects. Raphael belonged already in these early years to that small, leading upper class for whom Antiquity supplied the models for their own vigorous manner of life; and their vigour showed itself in their aptitude for reconciling the demands of Christianity and Humanism in the only harmony worthy of man. Only in this manner does Humanism become more than an intellectual fashion. In this free association on parallel lines, and not in the profession of pure heathenism, lies the aim of that true Humanism which is superior to the fashion of a period: this aim is human dignity. It has an inherent capacity for lifting those who profess it to the level of the heroic. The diptych of ST GEORGE AND ST MICHAEL (Plates 20, 21), displays the entire scale from earthly sublimity to the heroic effect of the supramundane.

One of those young heroes that Perugino interpreted in the Umbrian manner after Donatello's St George seems to have stepped into the saddle—but which of them would one suppose capable of such a grip of the thighs, or swing of the sword, as alone is worthy of their forerunner at Or San Michele? Only the born narrator can achieve such an effect. There we have it all—in a rocky valley, remote, damp and gloomy, the monster has kept guard over his young victim. Hither rides upon the scene, out of the lovely other world, through the defile, the golden knight on the red-bridled horse with lance ringed in pink and white. He has startled the hideous creature out of the swamp. In the first onrush a deep, yet not deadly thrust; the lance has broken in pieces, all the more splendid the courage with which he urges his steed once more to the same spot, to bring the wild struggle to an end; the infuriated monster close at hand, the fleeing princess in the distance, paralysed in her effort to escape, convince us of the peril of the moment from which this sweeping lightning-stroke is to bring deliverance. On one side, convulsive rearing, on the other, a thrill of assurance; the hue of a toad and the splendour of gold! It was ordained that Raphael should have the gift of experiencing, with all the means at the painter's disposal, the tense feelings of his figures; and destiny intended that he should possess this gift in a lavish abundance that truly knows no limit.

For, perhaps as a pendant to the saintly knight, Raphael was at the same time achieving success with the heavenly warrior Michael—his first attempt to grapple with the world of the beyond. What is it that makes him supramundane? We are justified here in pointing out how the developing master keeps in step with Dante's visions and the primordial dæmonism of Bosch; it would be more important to recognise how it could come about that precisely this lurid hell-storm found its pictorial echo in a painter born for harmony! Already in this early work formula breaks down: we have here arising before us a power to which nothing was to remain unfamiliar in the three realms, from the infernal up to the heavenly. There was therefore a moment, as notable as the impact upon the young Buonarotti of that Northern combat of devils around St Anthony, when Raphael, full of the great Tuscan interpreter of the Inferno, felt himself stirred by the visions of Bosch to portray this glowing, blazing hell-night alive with a terrifying throng of whirring wings and phosphorescent eyes. Subterranean lava-masses, still uncongealed, out of the primal consciousness of man, here contributed their streaming glow to a painting of which the fullness of expressive colour continued to present to the eyes of generations—of centuries even—a second, even more incomprehensible miracle, a secret mystery.

But into this hellish region darts vertically down like a thunderbolt the glistening warrior, so devastatingly that there is a rearing of upward coils from the ground. The gleaming red cross on the bright shield has disarmed the adversary; the armoured heel was enough to hold him down. The saint has almost alighted from the course of the swooping downward flight which the next moment he is to resume; his body is still in its gliding rush through the air. It is a revelation, this sword-arm, not only for Raphael; it triumphs in the heights as if its bearer knew that weapons are not necessary to him—"afflavit deus . . ." It is alive with one of those ineffable but all the more telling movements of which the riddles suffer no solution in words, scarcely even in thoughts. But we may glance again at the St George; he brandishes his weapon against one of the emissaries of the evil powers that, according to the legend, seem to have stayed behind in the world out of a wild primeval age in order to give rise, in the champions of the Faith, to men with the gift of divine Grace. His sword circles round with a sure aim such as the young artist had opportunities of observing at the Court of his native city under the expert eye of Duke Guidobaldo.

But the heavenly combatant comes down like a thunderbolt on the archenemy, and his sword triumphs without a struggle. Everything here is a revelation: the arm flashing down as out of clouds, the shield that forms the centre of the whole, the flash of the cuisses traversing with its glint the enclosing coils. In this victory there are both weight and lightness; it could only have been depicted, at so early a stage of the painter's development, by one endowed with both these opposite qualities. The Nuremberg artist of the APOCALYPSE also speaks in him, through the symbol of the thunderbolt—and, as in the woodcut, Michael's lance raised aloft with both hands traverses with a blinding flash the clouds of darkness, revealing the infinite peril for the world below, and showing also the greatness of the moment increased by the greatness of the menace.

In Raphael the higher power is embodied in its winged messenger, in the flash of his weapons. In this figure, driving down upon the wind, the VISION OF EZEKIEL is here already anticipated. The painter of the Papacy and the *Triregno* was born, here, in this hour—for the second time.

APPRENTICESHIP

It is this Raphael whose career we have to follow, not the pupil of Perugino, whom Florence seems for a while to have diverted into its academic paths—perhaps the Marchigiano, who in his drawings never lost himself, and who found himself again triumphantly in Rome as a painter.

Vasari says, of the early works of Raphael done for Città di Castello: "chi non a pratica" could only too easily confuse them with those of Perugino. We must therefore acquire this *"pratica"*, so as not to be detained by futile talk of discipleship and influences; we must seek to pass from the attainments of learning to what is inborn, to the fundamental qualities that absorb everything they encounter and group all impressions in and around themselves; in the last resort it is these that triumph in all periods of his life—as what is really original in him. This is a duty we owe to him and to ourselves as well.

§ Pax Vobiscum, Brescia

In the small picture of CHRIST BLESSING, at Brescia (Plate 19), we certainly meet with echoes of the beautiful Gothic stained-glass harmony of Perugia: the olive-toned flesh-tints, the cherry red in the mantle, in front of the blue distance and the firmament passing upwards to a deep azure. But what use Raphael makes of these elements from Perugino's teaching! Has it really struck anyone before that Raphael is very ready to avoid the monotony of the legs in his devotional figures? In the CORONATION OF THE VIRGIN he introduces the sarcophagus slantways in the midst of the row of Apostles—where Perugino, the slave of Gothic, would show the lower limbs of a dozen figures. Raphael overcame the danger of unison, the hereditary weakness of the last generations of Gothic, which Perugino revived because he thought it permissible as an expression of religious faith, of orthodoxy even.

In this half-figure of the Redeemer he merely emphasised the rhythm of walking, the subtle outward bend above the leg that carries the weight of the body, the slackened play of the hip above the unburdened backdrawn foot— a counterpoise that is continued in the arms, one raised in blessing, the other laid across the body, also in the advancing and receding curves of the body; it extends even to the twofold slant of the head, forward and sideways. And emphasis of colour combines with this rhythmic vitality of the forms and the beauty of the enclosing lines to produce a ritual dance of forms; the deep red of the mantle surrounds the flesh-colour of the torso with a subtle ellipse of which the course is continued in the shadow on the disengaged shoulder and the arm; there is a similar echo of it in the oval of the face, and in the swelling form of the arm raised in blessing, emphasised by the cloak and the falling hair. Miraculously musical in its effect is this motive of the oblique rectangle formed by the red spots on the left hand and the wound in the side with the drop of blood on the temple and the *stigma* in the blessing hand—sweeping obliquely out of the vertical like the head, with its regular lines, almost Gothic in their

33

construction, inscribed within the oval. This threefold deviation from the straight line, combined with the harmony of flesh-colour, deep red, and blue becoming ever deeper in tone, gives an impression of balanced softness. Suddenly He is before us again, out of space, out of those blue depths, triumphing and gentle, still to bring his blessing to the world, from which nevertheless he remains apart—and this makes this small picture resonant with an indescribable majesty. What is schematic in Gothic has fallen away, what is really essential remains; a figure out of the beyond touches our world, and we may recall once more how closely Raphael is related—whether through actual contact or through spiritual affinity—to the Northern revivalists of spiritual expression through Gothic, Roger van der Weyden, Memling and Schongauer. The affinity extends even to the lovely subtle brushwork in the colours. One might say that Raphael alone in Italy is master of the reverent seriousness of the craftsman in spreading these enamel-like colours on the well-prepared wood panel; he alone carries the perfecting of technique, the final loving tribute of craftsmanship, to that degree of richness of expression which the world admires as a peculiarity of the old Flemish school, and then once again in Holbein. Adherence to the origin and purpose of art, the religion of a workshop-practice schooled only to express the other-worldly and for the service of the divine, and striving to attain a sphere that lies beyond the trivial, this is what gives resonance to the music of these representations.

Instigated by Perugino's retrospective nature, Raphael must have acquired a new, quite exceptional relationship to the religious art of the North. He was familiar with it already from his Urbino days as an art convincing in its poetic, devotional character. Now it was Schongauer, who as an engraver was able to exercise an influence beyond the Alps, firing this young Italian alone with an imagination for other-worldly expression and devout presentation.

We are not here concerned with details: a little cross in the halo, a cushion for the child Christ to sit on, just as they occur in Schongauer—what do such things signify beside a profound indebtedness in a work as a whole? What the Colmar painter derived from the Gothic sense for craftsmanship—adaptability to the prescribed conditions of material and structure, whether it were a wall for a fresco, a wood-block or a silverplate to be engraved, survives in Raphael as loyalty to the format of his pictures; every figure, every group is adapted to the great significant pattern, full of significance in the notes sounded by it. It was a favourite idea of Georg Dehio, who thought so highly of German art because he so well understood Italian art, that Schongauer was a Raphaelite before Raphael. Schongauer's angels in the LAST JUDGMENT cycle in the Cathedral of Breisach have lately reappeared out of the gloom and oblivion of centuries of whitewash. Nothing nearer than this to Raphael is to be found in German art before Italy began to make an impression on it. Take the angel to the right of the Judge of the World (Plate 232)—the movement of the figure flows with the lines of the fluttering robes from below upwards into the apex of the window and pointed arch; the oblique beam of the cross stands out boldly against the segment; the finely articulated hands twine about the stem, and with delicate emotion, conscious as it were of the suffering consummated on this tree, and of a feeling for those risen from the dead, the oval of the little head inclines towards the right hand corner—a new, more transfigured and passionless Bearing of the Cross! The oval of the head, wreathed about by the wavy abundance of the hair, ennobled by the beautiful, infinitely calm form of the outline, and divided by the lineaments of the almond-shaped eyes and the sweep of the brows continued without break of line in the nose, the draughtsman's delight in following this line over the bridge of the nose and the nostrils and in giving the clean-cut lips their rhythm and the chin its slight dimple—we have here revived the usages of Gothic glass- and fresco-painters. And now let us compare with this painting the half-figure of Raphael's St Sebastian at Bergamo (Plate 11). It divides the broad rectangle of the frame with the intense-coloured form of its cherry-red mantle and the oval of the face enclosed by brown wavy locks; the oblique pose fills up, towards the right, what remains visible of the landscape, out of which perhaps another small tree rose aloft. The less encumbered half of the landscape and sky is traversed by the feathered end of the arrow. That truly Gothic *horror vacui* that caused Schongauer to carry a kind of accompaniment of tracery into the space and framework round every group or figure, dominates also this small picture. We feel that here we have no mere adoption of those details with which Perugino aimed at an effect of orthodoxy; here we have the younger artist penetrating into the element of the elder, an intermingling of kindred spirits, that conspiracy, quietly growing and suddenly convincing and compelling all, which commonly makes its appearance at the beginning of a new epoch.

It is the delicate vibration re-echoed as in a dance by the graceful fingers, and the manner in which the picture is dominated exclusively by the subtle movement of the figure, that here make a saint of this youth (or, is St Ursula, patroness of Castiglione del Lago, indicated by the fine border of the vest and the rich chain?) and over all is the harmony, compellingly apparent at first sight, of cherry red in the robe, white, gold and black in the embroidered border of the vest, the olive tone of the flesh-colour, the brown locks set off against the firmament deepening upward to the most intense blue. The fundamental secret of glass-painting, with its exclusion of all that is commonplace, is found in these harmonious passages of colour with their grand contours.

The exclusive—it is this that calls the eye back again and again to the essential, even from the spaces within the frame left free by the figure, by means of an attribute, a touch of solemnity in the landscape, a gleaming gold-embroidered border. At no point can the eye stray into vacancy, it can lose itself in no spot void of inspiration: *horror vacui*—this is already the basic motive of

35

Raphael's first altarpieces painted under the eye of Perugino. In the CRUCI-FIXION in the National Gallery, from the Mond Collection, the majesty of the noblest figure, that of the Crucified, is dominant, with the clear olive of the flesh in front of the inescapable dark stem of the Cross. This arrests the eye as in Roger van der Weyden, in the *Pietà* of the MIRAFLORES ALTARPIECE. More compelling however, even if unconscious, is the effect of the circular rhythm with which, by virtue of this movement in the angels, the semicircle of the frame is repeated downwards, almost taking in within its scope the heads of the adoring figures; the eye is nowhere free from the movement prescribed for it, and even in the figures on the ground, part of the earthly solidity of their bodies is withdrawn from sight by their kneeling posture or, as in the case of the Virgin and St John, concealed by the kneeling figures in front. In a composition of this kind Perugino, in the same period, ranges in a row figures of which he is unable to fill with sensibility the lower extremities, thus leaving empty whole portions of the picture.

§ Coronation of the Virgin, Vatican

In the CORONATION OF THE VIRGIN (Plate 22) the twenty-year-old artist, with bold resolution, carries a really empty form like the sarcophagus across in front of the lower limbs of the Apostles, which he found not easy to render with vitality. Only two, flanking the stone structure, are allowed to be visible in their entirety; but how their bearing, even to the feet, is in keeping with the character and expression of the heads—James in a transport, even to the foot drawn forward involuntarily from the corner of the picture, John spell-bound with amazement in posture and gaze. And whilst here the colourless feature that dominates the centre, the sarcophagus, is framed about with coloured figures, above, where in the angels and cherubs the whitish element introduced in the colouring is still predominant, the strong colour seems to be reserved for the chief group. This group in its dramatic treatment, delicate but emphatic, is encompassed by the dancing and music of the angels; their stepping is confined by the melody within the line—easily completed—of a circular nimbus. In the angel with the tambourine and the viola-player the outer line of the leg performs this role; their companions, half hidden again by clouds, carry on this line in pose and gesture.

If Vasari, in his day, found it hard to distinguish these works of Raphael from those of Perugino, *we* have acquired this "*pratica*", as is our duty to him and to ourselves, and we shall recognise, at the outset, in this character of the lines and the manner of filling the space, the young genius by comparison with the mechanical Perugino. Most of all we shall recognise this in the colouring; for it is the Marchigiano who gives this milky tinge to the Umbrian stained-glass colours and thereby, to express the heavenly, makes them luminous—from the light grey sarcophagus to the whitish horizon below the blue, ever more intense, of the sky and the silvery layer of cloud. The angel on the left, in white upper garment with green sleeves heightened with lemon yellow, and the harp-player in white and green alternately, lead on, through the red sleeves of the latter, to the colour in the dress of the Virgin; the angel looking upward to the right, with white wings, is partly old-gold, partly green, the one with the viola on the right has parakeet-green pinions with high lights in whitish yellow, his yellow upper garment over a dress of variegated red—in a word, everything around the coloured central group is transposed into a tone of light, and even the cherub above the centre displays, upwards and downwards, white pairs of wings and thus completes the luminousness that is spread, as a perceptible nimbus, around the sacred event in Heaven. Only as a reflection is it re-echoed in the earthly group; in the row of Apostles, around the iconographic colours of St Peter and St Paul—blue and yellow and green and red—there is a rhythmic echo of white in the garments of the remainder.

For Raphael, it is impossible to sustain Perugino's never-varying scale of incense and organ-tones when his themes awaken in him variations of colouring. In the style of the altarpiece he may perhaps have still been struggling with the limitations of the conventional school colouring, yet all the time we trace everywhere, even in his veneration for his master, the enquiring, uncorruptible gaze of the boy in the Oxford self-portrait. In the predella-paintings, when colour and narrative become inseparable, this born painter speaks without restraint. Each time he captures the colour harmony that suits the key: in the ADORATION OF THE MAGI (Plate 13), a strain of luminous serenity and gaiety of hue—in the PRESENTATION, solemn gold and grey for the colouring of the stone of the Temple—whilst the ANNUNCIATION (Plate 17b) is the hour of the *Ave*, the hour of Perugia, when in the twilight the heights recede behind one another in ever more delicate ultramarine, the furthest quite close in tone to the whitish haze on the horizon; but from the horizon rise the heavens, in deepest tones of blue, like a dome, and all this, with the true architect's inborn feeling for landscape, he encloses within the cool twilight of a portico.

This "*Ave Maria*" may be hailed among his earliest dramatic narratives, coherently felt in its delicacy, and in its power to summon up external and inward visions, and already filled with that concord of figure and space in which at a later period we shall again recognise the greatest painter of Central Italy and the last dramatic artist in the visual art of the Renaissance.

§ *Sposalizio*, Brera

He brought his apprenticeship to a close with another such success; the world-wide fame of the SPOSALIZIO (Plate 23), might cause one to forget entirely that it is the creation of a young man of twenty who immediately afterwards, in Florence, believed that he must begin anew and learn all over again.

Colour harmonies in which coherence is obtained by means of the terracotta of the tiles and the sunlit stone of the runner-like strips of the pavement, and which are permeated with reflected and veiled lights, are interwoven with the happy play of the curves. For curves give an effect of lightness, and the picture is full of curves. We feel as if transported into the radiant atmosphere of a morning of Pentecost—truly, our feelings soar with the lark. The mystery of the rounded top communicates itself from the frame to the whole composition. The segment of the dome fits in, its circling movement is taken up by the drum of the temple, it is repeated in the sweep of the architrave in the peristyle; the arcades repeat the line of the dome in a dance of segments, and like a musical echo the line dies away correspondingly downwards, in the flight of steps, into the foreshortened radiating pattern of the pavement. And the outer basic line of the steps is taken up by the figures: the row of heads sinks, the row of feet rises in an undulating symmetry. Across the throng of figures the white hand of the Virgin—the altar of San Francesco was dedicated to her ring—floats towards the hesitating hand of St Joseph. The High Priest unites them, encouraging them with a slight nod of the head; they are causing him trouble new to his experience. The vexation of the band of suitors is revealed on the one side by the breaking of the wands. On the women's side the first bridesmaid, in unconscious agitation, is stroking her still ringless forefinger, not without an enquiring glance of the utmost delicacy at the unsuccessful suitors.

From observation to poetic creation, from charming figures taken from everyday life to saints! What is it that gives such nobility to the principal figures? St Joseph is no more the simple carpenter whose awkward gestures, in Northern art, speak to us so movingly of the common people. His deportment from head to foot, the gestures of his hands, which have no suggestion of plane and rule, the manner in which he wears his cloak, make him the first "*Cortegiano*", whose inward nobility of character must find outward expression also. Here we find revealed, as in the bud, what six years later will show itself perfected in the Aristotle of the SCHOOL OF ATHENS.[1]

In the Virgin we have again the Gothic rhythm, as in Perugino, but intensified through the drapery that now falls over her feet, and otherwise mysteriously enhanced; compared with the most charming of her companions, she seems to be swayed by a power which cannot be of this world. She floats over the ground. The old Gothic line has been realised anew and more sanely, and is yet as full of expression as when it was discovered. Here we have the beginning, perhaps in Raphael's contact with Signorelli, of a new heroic style of the human figure and of narrative. It resounds in the individual figure as in the melodious movement of the whole row, and casts its spell even upon the scene of the action; this had to be worthy of such figures. May we here be allowed to concern ourselves with detail? It will always serve as a guide to what is essential, as in a verse of Shakespeare; it will breathe the atmosphere of the whole and

[1] Ollendorff, *Raphael-Studien*.

thereby bespeak the truly creative artist—to him alone will detail ever be an indispensable organ for conveying life in its fullness.

A temple so complete in its parts coherently disposed around a middle axis and placed, with such calculation of height, width and extent, in this situation of lay-out and landscape, would be worth a day's journey and more to see. We should approach it with delight; we should make a halt on the last height before reaching it to enjoy the picture it makes in the landscape; we should walk round it, we should allow ourselves to be allured by these steps with their gentle ascent, wander in the portico, and for the rest of our lives we should never forget the view framed by the doorway, and the colonnade that attracts the breeze from this wide expanse—the most charming contrast of landscape and columns ever invented by Southern pantheism.

Here the complete artist of the Renaissance arose, out of a union of the senses; as painter and architect, as spokesman of the age, he builds up spatial form around the human form of his dreams. And because the architect was alive in him—although unconsciously, so far as practice was concerned—the painter arrived at this freedom in restraint by means of the prescribed semi-circular form of the frame, and at this condensation of narrative. Such was the feeling that now for the first time allowed him to inscribe his name on the architrave of the temple, in pure Roman lettering, RAPHAEL VRBINAS MDIIII—the Christian name with the "ph", as it was his wish that it should be written.

In the vicissitudes of fate chance has placed the picture in the Brera next to that MADONNA WITH SAINTS by Piero della Francesca from San Bernardino de' Zoccolanti at Urbino. This once stood at the first stage on Raphael's road— the austere saints in an austere court, a complete reminiscence of ancient Early Christian painting, a triumph of the new conquest of the world. Now the picture, with its apse inviting us to enter in and pray, appears as a concave counterpart to the wonderful convex effect of the *SPOSALIZIO*. In both pictures there is a marvellous harmony of figures and space, sublime bearing and digni- fied architecture, a happy symbol of Raphael's vocation, that of combining the best of Antiquity, Gothic and Revival with what was peculiarly his own. In the period of his apprenticeship he brought to fulfilment a mission enjoined upon him at birth, and now he was ready to carry hence the gospel of a new religious poetry through the art of the leading cities of Central Italy—Florence and Rome.

V

FLORENCE

EVEN before Raphael knew Florence, he had represented the Virgin of the SPOSALIZIO, that figure entirely filled with the spirit of the world above, as if floating over the earth; in the KNIGHT'S DREAM the two souls in man, as in *Faust*, take shape, created by a seventeen-year-old youth; in the ST MICHAEL, the sweep of the heavenly sword and the down-rush upon the subterranean enemy had become the embodiment of the three realms. What had Florence to give him? It brought him both prosperity and peril.

§ Tuscany. Florentine Mannerism

Tuscan selfpraise from the ready pens of Florentine writers has really won credence only with art-historians of the literary and antiquarian type of recent generations; artists had for centuries given their verdict in favour of Venice, Parma and Bologna. But one thing is already certain: even in art the Tuscan dialect maintained a certain universal validity. Apart from the amiable medio-crities now and again dominant, it was only in Florence that the truly poetical and therefore classical solutions were discovered, from one turn of the century to another: Giovanni Pisano and Giotto, Masaccio and Donatello, Leonardo and Michael Angelo. But in the self-complacent pride taken in these great artists, cleverly summed up in literary phrases, there was a danger of taking seriously those who made profit for themselves by following where these bold innovators led; the unprecedented means of expression discovered by the inward impulse of genius were regularly converted into cheap currency in merely talented hands. Florence was also in quite a peculiar degree the home of Mannerism. Even Raphael was to toy with it.

When he came into the atmosphere of Florence, the entire Quattrocento art of the second and third generation can hardly have had any existence for him, neither the animated dioramas of Gozzoli and Ghirlandajo, or the exercises of the Pollaiuoli and Verrocchio, nor the confused mannerism of Filippino, not even Botticelli's revival of Gothic. Of these beside many another impression, we find hardly an echo in his sketch-books.

§ The actual Prototypes: The early Perugino

As a painter he was naturally interested in his master Perugino, where he came across him. The frescoes in the monastery of the Gesuati outside the Porta Pinti, dating from the fresh period of Perugino's youth—"par d'etade e par d' amore" with Leonardo, were still there, undestroyed, for Raphael to see, and the bright sunny style of the pictures with scenes from the life of Saint Bernardino at Perugia; they appealed to the young man from the Marches as doubly familiar—for his teacher's sake and because they kept alive the truly brilliant example of the pictorial revelations of Piero della Francesca.

§ Signorelli: Leonardo, Michael Angelo

It came no less naturally to him to pay homage to Signorelli, whose traces he came across again and again in his years of travel, if he did not seek them out, of set purpose, in a spirit of piety which lasted from his youth onward. Through Piero's figures, as grand in execution as they were in their inspiration, he had his first experience of the heroic world, the expression of which was something worth striving after. His Virgin in the *SPOSALIZIO*, gliding out of the circle of her companions over the tiles of the temple forecourt, recalls Dante's first sight of Beatrice:

> Ella s'en va sentendosi lodare
> Benignamente d'umiltà vestuta
> E par che sia una cosa venuta
> Dal ciel in terra per miracol mostrare.[1]

In depicting her thus he may have felt that he had faithfully followed and yet surpassed the austere model set by Signorelli. The tensely bent figure to the right, of the young man breaking his staff in vexation, seems also to be descended from the Cortona master; but even the St Joseph with all his distinction, with his far too ample drapery, could not have seemed to the painter yet to have solved the problem of the robed figure as he had realised it in a few hasty touches, accomplishing in swift improvisation the figure as he would have it, among the priests in front of the temple in the background. A generation more full-grown and moving more freely was needed to carry the folds of such a mass of material—and these folds need to be filled out with breath less hesitantly drawn, and to be draped about a figure more definitely radiating energy, if they are to be an echo of heroic life. Like Raphael, many others stood before, and studied, the battle cartoons of the two great Florentines, who had then returned to the banks of Arno. With most, the result was *bravura*. He alone learned from the painter of the BATTLE OF ANGHIARI and from the creator of

[1] "In vesture of humility, benign
She goes, yet conscious of the praise she wins,
And like to something come from heaven to earth
She seems, as though a miracle to show".

41

the BATHING SOLDIERS and the marble DAVID how inadequate his own figures still were to lead a credible existence in the higher world. They needed to be shaped anew in order to be capable of discoursing and playing a part in the sphere of poetry and pathos to which this born dramatist among the painters aspired.

There arose for him the same conflict that Dürer had to experience in the same decade when he encountered Italian art. The occasion of it came rather from within than from without; in both cases it was more a struggle with self than a contest with the rival genius. For Raphael, the standard by which he tested himself was set by the forms and bearing of the greatest, Leonardo and Michael Angelo.

In times gone by Raphael's borrowings from outside sources were often made note of. At last, for a period of more than a generation, his art was thought of as a mosaic of derived motives, when the question should have been asked every time why it was that precisely such and such a master attracted such a creative genius, and arrested him in a given motive; nor have we any right to speak of "influences" when he makes some entry or other in his sketchbooks (*R. Z.*, II).

§ Sketchbooks: Impressions and Ideas of the Moment

Of these sketchbooks six are known to us; most of what is noted down in them by Raphael never occurs again elsewhere. Donatello's ST GEORGE, the motive of which was already familiar to him through Perugino's ST MICHAEL, from the time when, four years earlier, he had taken part in the painting of the Vallombrosa ASSUMPTION, may have appeared to him more knightly in character in the original at Or San Michele than in Perugino; Michael Angelo's DAVID, the BATHING SOLDIERS, Leonardo's COMBAT OF HORSEMEN and LEDA, fascinated him by the sweeping course or the convulsive flow of their powerful lines; all this he made secure note of with the strokes of his pen. He drew also nudes of his own composition, and strove to sketch their agitated gestures in the new style of Florentine art, with the accented dorsal furrow, the pronounced muscles, the taut rhythm of their curves, the *portato* of their stride, and that glance over the shoulder at the trifling things of this world which belongs to the *magnanimo*, the exalted mood of a man of the leading class, as ideally portrayed in Castiglione's *Cortegiano*. He seeks to discover the secret of this high spiritual bearing in a new outline, peculiar to himself—a single resonant stroke of the pen, swelling and dying away, never interrupted, as if he were drawing from a model in marble—for his inspiration for these figures comes from sculpture. Rubens in his early years had similar experiences in the presence of the antique in Italy.

Thus there arose a race of grave saints and young heroes (*R. Z.*, II, 81–102); they have been liberated from the everlasting Umbrian scheme of the backdrawn, unweighted leg and the minuet-step, and their pose, centred about the perpendicular, even though drawn only in the nude, guarantees that drapery and a hanging cloak would also be endowed with movement in every fold by the energy of the forms. FRA BARTOLOMMEO, to whom Raphael came near, at that time discovered the same forms, simultaneously with his young friend, when he began to paint again after a four years' interval in the monastery of San Marco. The progress of these years becomes perceptible when one compares the saints of the MADONNA OF SANT' ANTONIO, in the Pierpont Morgan Collection, and in particular, those of the MADONNA DEL BALDACCHINO, with the St Joseph in the SPOSALIZIO.

§ "Spirit to Spirit" instead of Influence

The noble, soul-possessed masculine type is now emancipated from the sphere of studio, robed lay-figure and draped materials; its inner character is worn outwardly. The poets of the PARNASSUS and the lofty spirits in the SCHOOL OF ATHENS are first made credible by Raphael. Leonardo, for whose comprehension we depend solely on the half-obliterated script of his ADORATION and LAST SUPPER, must have exercised the most profound influence on Raphael by his presence when he joined the circle of Baccio d'Agnolo. However strange it may sound, the far distant LAST SUPPER, with its dramatic association of so many heroic figures of no commonplace mould, left behind a deeper impression on Raphael than on anyone else; and we have no knowledge that Raphael was ever at Milan. It was spirit meeting spirit; that was Raphael's manner of absorbing influences. The principles of his DISPUTA and SCHOOL OF ATHENS derive from the LAST SUPPER and the EPIPHANY; the composition of the MASSACRE OF THE INNOCENTS and the PARNASSUS can be traced back to Michael Angelo's BATTLE OF THE CASCINA and Leonardo's FIGHT FOR THE STANDARD. Apart from a few odd scraps, what did others adopt from them? Raphael alone understood the sense of the whole, as did Titian shortly after and later still Rubens; their native language was adequate for an answer to this alien challenge. Raphael exchanges the power of orchestration and contrapuntal quality for the melody of the single voice. What remains here of the much-talked-of influence of Fra Bartolommeo? If we take account of the dates, the ideas they have in common were for the most part carried out by the Frate later. Perhaps the most we can say is that they hit upon their new solutions for old themes in common, and discovered together the means of enriching their inheritance of the music of the Church. They now caused the devoutness of their paintings to resound through the Church in more swelling tones in place of those of the customary hymns.

§ Drawn Compositions

The ideas that were absorbed in Florence by the young master that was to be, demanded to be made use of; they were poured out upon the paper in groups showing, in the manner of metopes, variations of the triad of figures:

young warriors stand round Donatello's St George; a satyr and two nymphs are gathering fruit; a woman plays an instrument between two naked youths—all pen-drawings at Oxford, the last-named on a sheet with studies for the Entombment (Fischel, *R. Z.*, II, 87, 88, 89). It is possible they found employment somewhere or other—perhaps between windows of a palace in *terra verde* or *sgraffito*—even so, they were no sufficient occupation for the growing self-consciousness of the born monumental narrator. At home in his adopted city of Perugia he is spoken of in a document, as early as 1505, as the "best painter" for works in the monastery of Sant' Antonio. Beside the Arno the Republic had no use for him, even when he was to have a recommendation to the Gonfalonier Soderini from the Court of Urbino. The Republic had enough artists of mature power of its own; it was only for private worship and civic self-consciousness that he seemed good enough in Florence. His commissions were: Madonnas and portraits.

§ The Painter of Madonnas

It was at that time that Raphael first became the Painter of Madonnas. One might think that the fifteen Florentine pictures of the Virgin reflected back his fame so dazzlingly on his Umbrian period that this earlier stage could be forgotten: in Umbria he was the painter of little pictures and great altarpieces after the manner of Perugino, and only four times did he depict the divine Mother with her Child.

Painter and client, at Perugia as at Florence, made terms with one another so strict that they would be quite incomprehensible to-day. Throughout his Umbrian period the Mother of God had been the mystic miracle, alien to everyday experience and withdrawn from the world. She can only be thought of in the figure of a nun who seems to have been called upon to hold in her hands the most sacred of vessels; there is hardly a sign of maternal solicitude for the child. Beneath the veil of the mantle that gives her the voluminous form of those dedicated to Christ her countenance, like an unopened bud, looks down with downcast eyelids on the child who, himself neither earthly nor childish, bestows upon the children of the world his benediction and a look as of dreamy compassion. Around this miracle, in the little Berlin picture, with three figures, the devoutness of St Jerome and the ecstatic emotion of St Francis compose a hymn-like strain, permeated by the harmony of blue and cherry red in the solemnity of an Umbrian twilight.

§ Umbrian Madonnas

In the Diotalevi Madonna (Plate 24) a reverently careful cleaning has in recent times released the most lovely play of colour, of olive, cherry red and milky blue, backed by the landscape which is of an azure rising to the deepest intensity; a popular element, important from the point of view of worship, is introduced by the young St John into the sacred group of Mother and Child. This is perhaps the earliest of his Madonnas. The small *three-figure picture* is followed next by the SOLLY MADONNA (Plate 25), of a more secular type by comparison, rendering homage to this chosen protectress of the holy Child as in a mystic love-ritual; the veil falls back from the clear, brown hair of her head and the slender neck, framing like a niche, and exposing for reverent admiration, her delicate build and the graceful pose of the hand with the breviary. At the same time, in the landscape, the world looks in upon the scene more distinctly—in these first productions of Raphael's own hand there are already traces of a totality of creativeness: figure and landscape are alive, full of feeling, in an atmosphere also governed by the same principles. In the CONESTABILE DELLA STAFFA MADONNA (Plate 26) it is a spring day, the branches already astir, snow still on the mountains, and the soft breeze playing over the surface of the waters, seeming to have invited this mother with her child to wander through the meadows. This exquisite circular picture, formerly in the Hermitage at Leningrad, painted on a panel out of which the frame with the flanking *griffoni* of Perugia (the griffins from the city arms), spreading out downwards, was carved at the same time, served of course, originally, to crown a shrine. The rhythm of the forms in the circular space, fitting in with the almost Schongauer-like sweep of the trees, was formerly more pronounced in its effect—too much so perhaps in the eyes of the painter, and monotonous also, when the Madonna held an apple instead of the book; this came to view in the groundwork of the painting when the picture was transferred on to canvas. Even so, everything, from the neck of the *penserosa* bowed in meditation to the pose of her arms and the lights on the fingers holding the book, contributes to the circular effect; the accord of the profile and the rhythmic pacing of the figure help to produce that delicate undulating movement which exposes for us to see a fragment of landscape, with its soft-flowing lines of mountain and lake, and seems ready with the next step to shut out from view what lies in front of her. In its lyrical quality also we experience an action which draws the eye to it and after it, and which must have been entirely convincing to those of a believing disposition.

Here the power of the later mysticism is once more alive, without the tendency to wander off into spasmodic reconstruction which we find in Crivelli and the Master of St Bartholomew and even in Botticelli, rather in all its purity, as in the self-composed masters of the North. In the case of Schongauer and Memling there was no need of their minor motives—the man on a white horse in the landscape, the masses of rocks grown over with bushes, and the pointed churchtowers, to remind one of them. The inward poetic surrender is entirely their own, as is also the faithful craftsmanship in the application of the colours which is inseparable from it. It is still operative in the earlier of the Florentine devotional pictures, when the forms are already adapting themselves to the wider world beside the Arno.

RAPHAEL

§ Madonna of Sant' Antonio: Ansidei Madonna

Under the influence of impressions and reminiscences two great pictures were produced, those painted for the nuns of Sant' Antonio and for the Chapel of St Nicholas in San Fiorenzo at Perugia, commissioned by the Ansidei family. They have the disjointed character belonging to a period of transition. The idea for the enthroned MADONNA OF SANT' ANTONIO starts off with an entirely Umbrian harmony, already genuinely Raphaelesque. In accordance with the destination of the work for this nunnery, not only is the Divine Child clothed; it was more important for the young painter to give a dark tone to the harmony. The blackish baldacchino over the throne is the starting-point for colours which are all broken up with black. It is the atmosphere of an early monastic Hour; the twilight of dawn or early Mass dominates the whole from the very beginning. The grave, almost gloomy Princes of the Apostles in the foreground are under its sway, although in them we have already figures standing firmly on their feet in the Florentine manner, and they seem to be breathing beneath their robes. The predella-pictures are more curious than convincing. In the centrepiece, the ROAD TO CALVARY (Plate 229c), the colours express the agitation of the start, if you will have it so; beautiful motives full of tenderness occur, among others quite devoid of feeling—the figure of Christ, in itself surprising in Raphael, because in its suffering it has not an effect of dominance, becomes more intelligible when we know that it was conceived under the stress of reminiscences of the strange central figure in the LAST SUPPER by Justus van Gent at Urbino. Among the scattered portions of the predella the only felicitous one is the ST ANTHONY in the Dulwich Gallery, carried out with free sketchy strokes of the brush, with all the charm of a drawing.

The style in which the MADONNA DEGLI ANSIDEI (Plate 28) is presented to us would decidedly be thought of as antiquated were it not that its date, on the border of the Virgin's cloak, must be read as MDV or even VI or VII (at the earliest, however, 1505). It might also be taken as a concave pendant to the SPOSALIZIO, and it is no accident that it recalls that altarpiece of Piero della Francesca from Urbino. Its whole effect was determined by the brightness of the shimmering reflections in the portico of white stone; the profound solemnity of colour is concentrated on the throne in the middle—blackish olive, bottle green, brown, leading up to the cherry red and blue of the dress; from this point it spreads in less intense but stimulating tones to right and left. The sunny chiaroscuro of Piero della Francesca contributes something to the alb of St Nicholas and to the hands; his pearl-embroidered mitre stands out in front of the whitish-grey of the pilaster, as well as his face, with silvery lights on brow, nose and the rime on his stubbly chin—a miracle of painting in Central Italy, not perhaps uninfluenced by Signorelli's altarpiece in the Cathedral at Perugia. In forms and expression the Baptist is, strangely enough, still almost inferior to the SPOSALIZIO; the Madonna and Child have closest affinity with that loveliest of Raphael's Umbrian charcoal drawings, the ·MADONNA DELLA MALAGRANA in the Albertina (*R. Z.*, I, 53).

§ Between Perugia and Florence

The commissions for these pictures followed him from Perugia to the Arno; their conception was still influenced by the Umbrian atmosphere—there is, as it were, an after-echo of its deep, bell-like tones. His Mother of God now derives a note of domestic intimacy and healthy ordinariness from the fact that, in Florence, only citizens of the middle class came to him with orders, requiring of him portraits to flatter their self-esteem and Madonnas for private worship.

It seems as if a native, homely element in him was now again released, for the first time after the Umbrian interval—a healthy trait from the Marches; perhaps it had received new emphasis from his more recent contact with Urbino, and his nature had been at the same time violently affected and then strengthened and brought to maturity by the undreamed-of greatness of Florentine form. Raphael came into the world with this powerful nature, only his years at Perugia had turned him aside from it to mysticism; but he showed himself always faithful to his inborn, native feeling for soundness of form where expression was allowed spontaneous course, unaffected by schooling—in the spontaneity of his drawings, in the predella paintings, and in the figures of his backgrounds, as in the SPOSALIZIO. This characteristic now comes to perfection. The preparatory work of Piero della Francesca, Melozzo and Signorelli, of endowing the sacred for presentation to the people with a certain rustic or provincial-town character, now for the first time had its fulfilment in the idyll of the Florentine Madonnas.

§ *Madonna del Granduca*

Nowhere in the whole Florentine domain at that time is this health-breathing type of figure to be found as it is the MADONNA DEL GRANDUCA (Plates 30, 31). Raphael composed it to begin with in circular form—this is the idea shown by the drawing in the Uffizi (*R. Z.*, III)—with the pure oval of the face seen from in front, the fullness in the cloak, and all the charming convexities of the Child's figure; but already in the sketch he has adopted the rectangular shape (it is a question whether in so doing he sacrificed the landscape, or whether it still to-day lies concealed underneath the truly surprising black ground). The severe angularity of the rectangle, however, intensified the sense of gentle convexity; how movingly, and therefore sacredly, are both hands of the Virgin occupied. The child is on the point of seeking refuge with his mother as he becomes conscious of the spectator, who at that time was the worshipper. No such moving contact with those who came to pray had been created since Luca della Robbia. Now the old popular note has been retrieved, in contrast with the vacillations between

47

triviality and refinement in the disintegrating age of the previous generations of the Medici. And Raphael discovered that *in art it is not the familiar but the monumental that is suited to the people*.

Everything deviates from reality in order to render truth the more simply. In the heads, those lines have been sought out which define essential forms; thus, in the most delightful head, in silver-point, in the Malcolm Collection (*R. Z.*, I, 51), in the British Museum, the bridge of the nose and the sockets of the eyes are embraced in one line, the tip of the nose and the nostrils in a kind of Gothic projection, which long remained Raphael's signature. These lines, almost Gothic in their decorative appeal, are faintly perceptible in the picture through the transparent glazing. The result of such stylisation is an indescribable aroma of expressiveness in the heads, and in the bearing of the Virgin—impersonal perhaps when compared with Leonardo's pictures, and yet, or perhaps for that very reason, everybody's unconscious secret ideal of motherhood. To tell the truth, we cannot to-day feel any immediate familiarity with Raphael's women—at least, not in the North—in Italy they are to be met with only on market days, when the country people come into town. Herder in his day already perceived by that these highest and purest exemplars of their kind are all country-girls, and Delacroix had quite a correct feeling about them when he called them healthy peasantesses; he thought that he met with their kind again in the South of France, where Maillol also found women to embody his sentiments, so simple in their grandeur. Far removed from the "sweet" type, they have about them a coldness of nature as if on the defensive; such austerity first made possible Raphael's later masculine style. That profoundest of poetic interpretations of the nature of women, of which he is for ever master, is just the outcome of his masculinity. If we wish to see her aright, and not to learn to see her in the manner sophistically commended for the last thirty years, there is one means of doing so; St Bonaventura in his *Meditationes* gives again and again this advice: "Form for yourself a correct conception," and Savonarola preached that "the Holy Virgin was a woman of the people, in simple raiment".

And now let us imagine that these figures out of Raphael's pictures were for once really there, in the same room with us and breathing the same air; what would be our impression if we had no longer to estimate them in the abstract and æsthetically, but to take up an attitude towards them, or on purely instinctive lines, to regard them and class them socially? We should find nothing of what, in women, occupies the great world to-day. But nothing more absolutely motherly will be found than the manner in which these women of Raphael's pictures deal with their child, hold him, watch over his life, are conscious of the happiness and sorrow that has come upon them, the unsuspecting, of all women the most unspotted. We should not however suppose that this way of looking at the matter concerns the care of children rather than the study of art. The Old Masters would not have moved a finger for our science, as it has now become. But it is once more time, and it is an obligation of history, to know wherein the value of a work of art consists as it was intended in its time. Here lies the intention of the artist. He made himself the spokesman of a generation of spiritual composure, such as Savonarola demanded. It is a generation with the great poetic power that shows forth the eternal in common humanity, and incarnates the power of love in this simple woman, exalted above the concerns of daily life, with her child. "In some place or other the queen as mother is mere woman, and the mere woman as mother, queen." For this reason Raphael's Madonnas are for ever everybody's mother, the "*Mütter Urbild*" ("archetype of mothers"), as Goethe calls the SISTINE MADONNA. And this is the only manner in which Raphael depicts the Madonna, in the apparel of her motherliness, in a red dress with a blue cloak, with at most a narrow gold border, as at one time in Northern Gothic; he is fond of setting her in the Tuscan countryside, where all seems as unspotted as she, with the Arno valley beyond, or a lake, perhaps a reminiscence of Lake Trasimene, with broad, gentle ranges of hills. The scene is like her nature and her dress, devoid of details, nothing but meadows with a few bushes and flowers; the ornament of this landscape is its grandeur and vast extent.

The High Renaissance has attained once again to the media of Gothic, by virtue of its inner composure: the great expressive figure against a neutral background.

§ *Madonna del Cardellino*. The Madonna in the Meadow

Raphael began his series of Madonnas in the open air with the plastically constructed group of the *MADONNA DEL CARDELLINO* (Plate 32). Those who believe they can get some understanding of art from "influences" may remark that, in this picture, Michael Angelo's Bruges Madonna was actually the model for the quietness of the contour and for the Child, who with one little foot still keeps close to his mother; but because this very character of inward plastic compression made the group too narrow to fill up the picture space, a beautiful Gothic motive was introduced, as in Schongauer: the delicate trees provide, in the distance, an accompanying tracery to the outline. In the final result, nothing remains of the prototypes but their life-creating spirit—from Michael Angelo the significant, self-contained character, from Leonardo the gaze of the three figures one on another and, with it, their mutual attachment in a common love. All is endowed by Raphael, as with something that is his very own, with the poetic feeling for space, around the group and within it; and exactly in the centre of the whole he gives play once again in no ordinary manner to his sensibility for space—in this little hand of the Holy Child shyly asking if it may stroke the cowering little bird and yet, arched protectingly above the helpless creature—a sensuous expression of all that is supersensuous. The whole composition is keyed, in all its parts, great and small alike, to this domed line—the contour of the Madonna's head, the line of her shoulders, her sitting posture. It was the age of imposing vaulting-schemes. In the distant plain, amid the buildings of a town, a church stands out, like that of the Consolazione at Todi, and the decisive line is repeated again to the left by the arch of the bridge! The picture has unfortunately been made to undergo the concealment of its expressive colour under coatings of varnish; the clean state of preservation of the MADONNA IN THE MEADOW (Plate 34) is all the more apparent by comparison.

One only of the many ideas for the mother with two children. As in the contemporary ST GEORGE, Raphael has sought to hold the eye by absolutely filling up the frame. The linking-up with the angles is rigorously carried through like an arithmetical problem. The painter seems to be in danger of becoming academic, and for this very reason did not escape the admiration of a whole generation of art historians in the presence of such a pyramid. But those who put invention above formal qualities can hear in his drawings the murmuring sources of his poetry. Two sheets from the Albertina in Vienna (R. Z., 115, 116) are covered all over, back and front, with sketches of the same group— three times side by side, the mother with her right foot stretched far out—it must be made reach the angle of the frame. She has let go the child from her lap, yet both her hands steady him; he is just making his first step by himself beyond her reach, with uncertain movement of his knees; Rembrandt could not have rendered more touchingly this feeling of sympathy with helpless infancy. The little St John draws near in an attitude of devotion; he is trying to make his obeisance, or he was intended to be saluting in the Oriental—present-day military—fashion (but this has been cancelled)—three motives in one. Underneath, the Madonna is repeated, St John is holding the cross, but hesitates to give it, and to the right, he is absolutely refusing to do so, whilst the Holy Child becomes aggressive.

The picture was originally conceived as cheerful and sunny, as witness a drawing at Oxford, washed with golden bistre tones and certainly genuine; a most cheerful note is sounded by the luminous original, with its light transparent yellow (R. Z., III, 118). All this preliminary play with movement and light is brought to an end by the finished picture in an almost ceremonious solemnity; so deep is the tonality of the colour, and a glorious cherry red, together with soft brown flesh-colour, stands out as a majestic form against the olive-green of the landscape and the soft, deep blue zone of the distance and sky. It is easy to overlook the delightful details of this landscape, the hazy view of a town in the distance and the shimmering lake with the mist on its wooded banks and heights. (Pl. 238.) The rare state of preservation gives an idea of the almost medieval Northern technique, especially in the head against the distant background (Pl. 229b); once again we are surprised, in an Italian work, by this enamel-like manner of laying on the pigments, the sharp, almost pattern-like prominence in the drawing of the brows and the bridge of the nose, the Gothic delight in the harmony of lines about the eyelid, and a loving adherence to remnants of the Umbrian manner: the direction of the gaze is indicated by three eyelashes rendered in exaggerated size; here we have Raphael's Expressionism!

§ *Belle Jardinière.* Holy Family with the Lamb

The enamel quality in the painting was to have its triumph in the "BELLE JARDINIÈRE" of the Louvre (Plate 35), perhaps the most complete, because the freest solution of the problem of filling the space and of allowing its form to be the guide and accompaniment. In completest accord with the craftsmanship of painting, the plastic construction is permeated with movements, surrounded by the intensified sweep of the distant landscape, and confined by the enclosure of the frame. In the inner part the lines of expression run from the back of the little St John across the hands, up the border of the cloak to the head of the Virgin, and back again from her face down her neck, along her arm to that of the Child, in the meeting of their hands across his gleaming body to the corner of the picture. The lines of their mutual gaze contribute to the figures an intimate spiritual association, as in Leonardo's MADONNA IN THE GROTTO. The same principle was certainly once carried through in the glazing, of utmost delicacy; this seems unfortunately to have fallen a victim to its celebrity, and has on the whole a disagreeably glassy effect. This and the blue cloak have been attributed to Ridolfo Ghirlandajo; anything unexpected—that is, anything that did not accord with the ideas of the Nazarenes—must always have been derived from others. But precisely in this period of search and experiment it is difficult to understand from a single point of view everything in Raphael that is surprising and strange. We recognise again and again how the young painter as he grew to maturity was stimulated by Leonardo—his spiritual richness and the glazing-technique, created to produce that effect, of the lively, almost breathing over-surface. Under such influence from without Raphael's later Florentine pictures were not always pleasing and coherent. We may admit the academic danger to which Florence continuously exposed him and in which he lived and worked. He would not have been Raphael if he had not overcome it. Take the Leonardesque motive of the HOLY FAMILY WITH THE LAMB, in the Prado (Plate 36), with the downright abruptness of its contrasting movements conceived while the work was in progress—the indulgent mother, the boy looking up, St Joseph approaching; we notice here the dramatic tensions of the ENTOMBMENT, and, as in that painting, the cold effect of the construction.

§ Canigiani Madonna

For the filling up of the frame a school example may be taken, the CANIGIANI HOLY FAMILY, at Munich. Groups of child angels in the upper corners formerly tempered the severity of the composition. In the nineteenth century it was completed by painting these in, in the twentieth, by leaving them covered up. It is impossible to say how much of the academic attitude in judging Raphael may have originated, precisely in Munich, with the maltreatment and subsequent misunderstanding of this composition, which has acquired only in modern times its coldly insensitive quality. But in spite of this frigidity and an inharmonious, unusually glassy colour, what growth of originating power there is in this young creator! The looks exchanged are the supreme expression of what is felt in the heart; every movement seems absolutely full of the spiritual; body and eye have the same inseparable aim.

The history of art, even the development of a Raphael, is apt to be regarded as a history of influences; but the destination of a man of genius seems to be more essential than the flowers plucked by him as he goes on his way to reach it. In these last years of wandering, Raphael perfected himself as the monumental creator of lofty ideas.

§ "The Monumental": Madonna under the Palm-tree

How may "the Monumental" be defined? If an attempt to explain it may be ventured, it is the power of presenting something so compellingly to the vision that the mind inescapably apprehends it and retains it so that it cannot be lost. Our concern would here be with the nature and destiny of the figures within the frame—and that means in the world—of the picture. Raphael at that time recognised, as his aim in every undertaking, this dramatic task of holding the spectator absolutely spellbound and breathless. He knew how to fashion his figures and forms for this purpose.

Leonardo's example and teaching required of the artist that the figure must be entirely and utterly possessed by the basic cause of its movements, by what is taking place in its soul; the demands made in Raphael's case were not otherwise. He had accustomed himself, from the marble forms of Michael Angelo, above all from the deep insight into nature exhibited in Leonardo, to cause the same feeling to course through every part of the body, from top to toe. In his great sketchbook belonging to this period, amongst the many pen-drawings suggested by designs of other artists, there is the most beautiful figure of a woman majestically advancing (Plate 38, *R. Z.*, II, 100). A comparison with one of the most famous figures of the Quattrocento, the Giovanna d'Albizzi of Ghirlandajo, will best teach us what has here been attained as contrasted with the much-praised forerunner. The wonderful detail from the VISITATION in the series of frescoes at Santa Maria Novella—a detail perhaps of greater merit than the composition in its entirety—seems unsurpassable, both as a portrait and as a record of fashionable dress. But, if the truth is to be told, she has the effect of being pushed in, tottering, by invisible hands on a disguised movable platform, stiff and, it might almost be feared, ready to fall over. In the Raphael drawing, one feels the indissoluble and yet relaxed, elastic connection of all the parts, from the look in the eyes, which seem to sweep towards a point in the direction in which she is going, through the supple neck to the gentle, forward-pressing motion of her feet. This unencumbered advancing movement in the rhythm of neck and feet had not been known since Antiquity—not even in Gothic. The precious drawing came to Oxford from the collection of Sir Thomas Lawrence, and we may imagine how the companion of his life, Mrs Siddons, looked at it, and what a fellowship of understanding may have grown up between the great tragic actress and this figure floating on a higher plane. And now we come to this same woman, or her sister, as the MADONNA UNDER THE PALM-TREE, in the *tondo* in the possession of Lord Ellesmere (Plate 27). With dignity and modesty she follows, with the whole upper part of her body, with her gaze and inclination, the playful movement of the child in her lap as she lets him go. St Joseph, all devotion, bows his forehead, neck and knee; both parents bend towards one another within the circular line of the frame. This line, with the vibration of musical logic, dominates the cloak of St Joseph, the little tree behind him, the canopy of the palm-branches and the light flecks of the flower-clusters and the feet.

Here one who was born to be a monumental painter is training himself for his vocation—without great circumstance, without pretentiousness, a king as yet uncrowned! And in this process, whilst learning refinement of means, his painting attains this profound delicacy of expression. The same delicate breath plays over the soft plaits of the Virgin's hair, interwoven and overlaid with a fine veil, as if glazed, over her bosom, in soft cherry-red bodice, her hand, and her sitting posture, dignified in spite of its intimacy. Domesticity and a profound inherent womanliness have not deserted her in the open air.

§ Tempi Madonna

This is also the chief motive in the half-length figures of the Mother of God, commissions executed entirely for private clients, of which the first was the *MADONNA DEL GRANDUCA*. The conception was typified, for the devout Florentine, in the countless plastic reliefs in the house and in the street, and it was doubtless no accident when Donatello's uncouth rusticity won the day with Raphael, in the TEMPI MADONNA (Plate 40), over so many sweeter and gentler solutions by Desiderio and Benedetto. The impressive quality of the intimate—the impulsive pressure of the abruptly bent arm with which the mother, stirred to a pitch of troubled forebodings, hugs the child to herself—has revealed its profound secret to the young Marchigiano; the Virgin towers up in a similar manner in the high frame, but she carries the boy, with his enchantingly superior look, through the bright landscape that wafts its springlike breeze around her, with a trace of anxiety in her face and in her hands as well. In the hang of her cloak as in the bending of her hips we fancy we see the swift step with which she advances.

By comparison with the CONESTABILE MADONNA (Plate 26) the clear, light tones in matt blue and pink, with the smoky yellow of the veil, indicate how much this most devout and contemplative of worldlings has developed in the interval as a painter.

§ Cowper Madonna

Whether or not in this instance a certain primness of form is to be explained from the prototype, the figures in any case do not fall short of the freedom of the motives. The small COWPER MADONNA (Plate 42) in the Widener Collection is a great work, with its full-face pose, and the marvellous arrangement of the oval curves of face, body and hips, with which the delightful interruption produced by the rounded forms of the child fits in; flanked by the serene landscape with the range of hills and the small domed church, the Virgin seems rather to be enthroned than seated. If it could be established that the little sanctuary on the eminence to the right represents Santo Stefano dei Zoccolanti outside Urbino, then the date round about 1505, could perhaps be made to agree with that of Raphael's stay in his native city. The picture is moreover reputed to have come through devious channels into the possession of Lord Cowper from that place.

§ St George with the Lance

Another small monumental work is, in any case, connected with Urbino—the ST GEORGE OF THE HERMITAGE, now in the Mellon Gallery (Plate 37). After the quiet Madonnas, this dramatic power would hardly be expected; and yet this little picture of most perilous combat, in the midst of the series of Madonnas, arose out of the same feeling for the essential and the same determination to fill every-thing within the sphere of the frame, beyond possibility of being overlooked, with an expression of energy. The eye is absolutely compelled to follow the line of the rearing white horse from the upper or lower right-hand corner, and again to take up the direction of the thrust downwards to the left, from the right arm of the saint. The Louvre ST GEORGE is more epic in its effect, with its narrative of the stages of the combat; this one, through its dramatic concen-tration, is a vital part of the great art of the city by the Arno. The first owner of this picture had a peculiar interest in seeing his patron saint so irresistibly victorious: "Our ancient word of courage, fair Saint George", the ally on Bosworth Field! Below the knee of the knight appears the blue Garter with, in gold, the word "Honi . . ." The little picture was intended by the Duke of Urbino, Guidobaldo of Montefeltro, for King Henry VII. It was to serve as a return gift; the Order of the Garter had been sent to him by the first of the Tudors in July, 1504. Eight months afterwards, according to the statutes of the Order, a representative of the new Knight was to appear in England; but owing to illness the emissary was detained until July, 1506—it was Count Baldassare Castiglione.

FLORENCE

§ The Urbino Circle

At least as early as that date therefore the perfect *Cortegiano* among courtiers, and the *Cortegiano* then attaining perfectness among painters, were acquainted with one another. In this same year the *"formator del cortegiano"*, as Ariosto calls the Count, was composing the conversations in the illustrious intellectual circle in the Palazzo Ducale at Urbino. Count Canossa was already an object of banter in the dialogues on account of his fondness for the Urbino Master, and we hear Raphael spoken of as in the same rank with Leonardo, Michael Angelo and Giorgione. The dialogue appeared as a book a decade later. Perhaps these observations were only interpolated in the intervening period, when the fame of the painter had reached its zenith. Yet they accord historically with the degree of esteem attained by Raphael in that select circle. He was at that same time called "the best painter of Perugia", and the pretentious Court of Urbino could find no one more capable of representing it abroad through a return gift worthy of the royal friendship. His art was thus placed on the same rank with the skill and dignity of the "Pattern of all *Cavalieri*". Raphael's entry into the great world will have to be dated at this period, and it has to be borne in mind that in those days the great world and artistic pretentions were still inseparable. Thus society early recognised in him their portrait-painter, and he in them the circle befitting himself.

The boy who already at the age of twelve looked at himself, in his unconscious superiority and distinction, was born to be interpreter of men and of their nature. To include him in the ranks of this leading class is more than a play upon the word *"cortegiano"*. His sense of the ideal, that made of him the poet of the Virgin Mother, gave him access also to the ideal figure of the circle that realised in itself, thanks to the beautiful illusion of "rebirth", the true recreation of man. It was rather a tremendous, self-conscious emulation of the Antique. A harmonious moderation here prevails over the grouping of the most diverse elements. The attitude towards the world is always receptive and always exclusive, ever outwardly balanced; in the man of this class, it is the dominating power in his contact with life, whatever quality in him may inevitably prevail. It causes him to appear superior, whether he be pugnacious or compliant, aloof or resigned; to seem at rest in himself, "not irritated without great occasion". All that gravitates about this mean conforms also with this principle.

§ Borghese Gallery Portrait. Francesco Maria della Rovere

This quality belonged to the young portrait-painter at the age of seventeen. It was a scholar or a sceptic, hardly an artist and certainly not Perugino, but surely a cultivated, self-cultivating humanist, of whom the character was faithfully interpreted by Raphael, at the time of the CORONATION OF THE VIRGIN, in that much-disputed PORTRAIT IN THE BORGHESE GALLERY—exactly full-face, severely fitted into the frame (Plate 45). There was much truth in the error by which the picture was attributed to Holbein. The quiet, not to say frigid, sense of superiority in his first independent step in this sphere betrays the artist, not yet twenty years of age, as born interpreter of a society to which he was hardly beginning to belong. The full-face portrait of a richly-dressed boy, in the Pitti Palace, came from Urbino—a youth with almost adult, mature features, coolness and energy in the look and mouth; seen in profile, the aggressive features would certainly be dominant. Gronau, who rescued this small panel picture from the indifferent name of Giacomo Francia, suggested FRANCESCO MARIA DELLA ROVERE, adopted successor to the throne of Urbino; thirty years later Titian painted him, in a state of physical and moral decay. Here already the sinister character of the features is rendered in the enamel of the painting with the delicate feeling for the rise and fall of the forms, so that the head sets a standard to which the pose of the arms is not equal. Indeed, the wonderfully noble harmony, metallic and gold-like, of warm brown, red, gold and white against the blue distance, and the free, mobile calm in the eyelids, nostrils and mouth, lead one to expect that the figure would rise up less stiffly in the space above the balustrade, and that the arms might be more freely developed. Can it be that these parts were completed by a less creative hand? As regards the lower part of the figure, it is not quite every inch the future ruler whose character is interpreted by Raphael; for in the effort to convey expression, Raphael rather went beyond nature than fell short of it.

§ The Budapest Portrait

The young humanist of the BUDAPEST PORTRAIT (Plate 116), in the violet-blue and red of his professional costume, backed by a distant landscape still conceived in the Umbrian manner, overcomes as a sitter every obstacle and displays his very self; with his intellectually refined nature, he goes on his way through the world of phenomena as if transfigured, with swan-like motion, and the forceful anatomy of the neck inevitably contributes to the triumph of the expression in the face. The same effect is indeed convincingly conveyed by the hands, which are not concealed from view; the one with the paper indicates that he is "appointed to be a writer", the other, in a motive that Giorgione hit upon in the same period, causes the bust to recede from the balustrade into the corporeal world which encompasses his shoulders and dark-complexioned head with its red cap. And so his character is summed up clearly in the fiery, facetious eyes and the sensual mouth. With his intellectual attractiveness, he goes as a favourite gracefully on his way amongst affairs and men. One is reminded of the role of the young Bibbiena among the *cortegiani* of Urbino—in the circle of the ladies, a forerunner of the abbés of the eighteenth century salons.

FLORENCE

§ Angelo and Maddalena Doni

The portraits of ANGELO AND MADDALENA DONI (Plates 46, 47) call us from the sphere of Court, Church and scholarship into the bourgeois class for which the young artist had now to work almost exclusively, during his years in Florence. It is a sign of the ripening maturity of the man of the world that he attained mastery over so wide a compass, and was capable of characterising with equal assurance the resolute stolidity of the citizen in the husband or the phlegmatic self-satisfaction of the wife. Nor is the future monumental painter for one moment disconcerted by such an incursion into an unfamiliar *genre*. He springs upon each model at the outset, as it were, with the only formula that is appropriate; the sound, forthright, even stately power of this Florentine citizen Doni reveals itself to the painter in a form that simply towers up from a broad foundation, in the strong harmony, still almost Umbrian, of the black doublet and red sleeve, passing on to the sonorous brown of the complexion and hair beneath the black cap; a silvery, cloudy sky, above the haze of a landscape recalling the THREE GRACES at Chantilly, throws up the silhouette into significance when seen from a distance. In all this, many a problem was presented for solution by his technique, which Florence had unsettled and not yet emancipated; energy of modelling is obtained in the brown flesh-tones by means of grey dashes. As if with a musical beat, the coatings of pigment on the cheeks, upper lip, nose and brows, and the obliquely-laid lights on the fingers, fall rhythmically, almost like rain.

Even in the *pendant*, it is already a new painter that seems to be presented to us; is this due to the greater delicacy of a female subject? It is surely permissible rather to recognise development in the course of the same commission, in the fact that here everything, from the rhythm of the composition to the tone of the colour, seems richer and more complex, absolutely hurrying over the tediousness of the theme, a quality however which he did not altogether fail to enjoy. For with almost cruel delight, he expresses here in the distinguished contours of his prototype, the MONA LISA, the early-acquired comfortable manner of living of the patrician lady; everywhere a dance of shapes as in Roger van der Weyden and Schongauer—even the little tree is there, giving like a delicate tracery the curves, or at least their direction, into which the empty space is to be divided as a frame for the figure. It is a play of pattern—mere ovals widening downwards, the face, in which the parallel forms of nose and chin are brought into prominence with almost refined humour, the cord round the base of the neck, the large pearl, the edge of the bodice, the interpenetrating lines of shoulders and arms, lastly also the patch of light formed by the hands. The shape of a pear has in outline mere size, but when it is resting on its centre of gravity, it is possessed of a certain immobility; and this is the form to which, in Raphael's eyes, the character of Maddalena Strozzi reduced itself: she cannot have appeared to him so lively in temperament as her relatives Marietta to Desiderio or Clarice to Titian.

RAPHAEL

In Angelo Doni's case Raphael's portrait of him means at least his vindication in the eyes of posterity, for this couple are of no exceptional celebrity. It seems, according to Vasari, that the husband found too expensive the *tondo* of the Holy Family painted for him by Michael Angelo. As to this, Jacob Burckhardt, who judged him from Raphael's portrait to be a man of generous disposition, expressed a suspicion that his wife had something to do with this "too expensive"; but confirmed bachelors, even if they are named Burckhardt, must not always be believed when they express their views as to the wives of their acquaintances. Nevertheless, from all appearances, Raphael was of a similar opinion; in the execution of this commission, at all events, he put forth his best efforts as a painter of female portraits. Delicate harmonies permeate the entire work; instead of the brown shading of the companion portrait we have here grey, suffused with luminous, silvery glazing beneath the chin; the little veil over the shoulders and corsage, the moire on the bodice, even the folds of the skirt, are rendered in little touches of transparent colour, and contrast is provided to this delicate colouring by the solid opposition of the sleeve material, with its lights laid on thickly on the ridges of the folds. The unlovely hands are done with the utmost care; bold fore-shortening gives them vitality, the fingers being touched with lights in pink applied as in a drawing. The whole is seen against the soft background of the landscape. It is an experiment, not yet entirely successful, but already definitely superior to the technique which meant, even for Raphael, an indispensable transition stage.

§ Louvre Drawing of a Girl

For he is a born painter, even where there are no colours. What paintings he can execute with a pen charged with bistre! This, and not the outline and the window borrowed from Leonardo's MONA LISA seems to be the essential thing about the little sketch in the Louvre (*R. Z.*, II, 80). The inscrutably captivating prototype seems actually to be surpassed, in breathing animation, by the little drawing, perhaps because the coming master of a younger generation was destined to intensify the innovations in Leonardo's miraculous work. The slight forward stoop, the small distance between the hands and the bust, the projection of the breathing body, the chin standing out free from the neck, the rounding of the shoulder in front of the window-seat near by and the hazy distant landscape, the secret which gives to this mouth a "fluidity"* in the Praxitilean sense, and the certainty that these commanding eyes can rove— all this is conveyed merely by the varying thickness of the penstrokes; one is kept constantly on the move within the bounds of the little sheet of paper.

We find him, elsewhere also, in drawings, as a "*Frauenlob*", one who extolled

---

*The reference is to the epithet ὑγρός (literally "moist") used by Callistratus and Lucian of the treatment of the human figure by Praxiteles.—*Translator*.

woman. The same girl, the so-called sister, of whom we know nothing whatever, was drawn by him in chalk, in her awkward youthful stage, perhaps when he was still in Umbria (British Museum, Malcolm Collection, *R. Z.*, I, 39), and a few years later, smiling, radiant and developed, in the small drawing at Lille from the Green Sketchbook (*R. Z.*, II, 75).

§ *Donna Gravida*

Once again in Florence reverence for women guided his hand, in the "DONNA GRAVIDA" of the Pitti Palace (Plate 48). Even after many injuries the picture still presents a rare concord of gold, red, black and white. The olive in the flesh-tones is surrounded by the hair-net shot with gold threads, with reflections on its border, golden-brown hair, reddish-gold transparence in the lobe of the ear; the lips and nostrils are pink, and the half-lights on the cheek. There is a more pronounced repetition of this harmony in the old-gold to deep brown of the bodice, the red sleeves and the flesh-tones of the hands, with the intervening green-shaded white of the apron and the puffs of the chemisette. Between the strong and the delicate zones of colour the white hem of the chemisette and the edges of the veil serve as a transition. In this figure, so beautiful in colour and sympathetically observed, there is no mistaking the character and condition of the lady. Much of the harmoniousness of the Second Stanza already finds expression here in advance.

§ Lady in Green

Finally, the consummation of such studies and experiments—the mournful LADY IN GREEN (Plate 49), formerly the riddle of the Tribuna in the Uffizi, now banished to Urbino, and even, since the time of Crowe and Cavalcaselle and Berenson, under suspicion as a representative of Raphael and accused of being by Perugino. Is it really necessary at this time of day to defend the picture against this charge? Perugino is apt to make his figures falling over backwards, through a deficient constructive sense of their organism, as for example even in the renowned GIOVANNI DELL' OPERE in the Uffizi. This woman keeps her balance with complete freedom, like the young girl in the Paris drawing and like the COUNT CASTIGLIONE of a few years later. One stands before the painting puzzled afresh absolutely every time by its uniqueness; the technique also, entirely objective and almost without a trace of a "signature"—simply perfect both as regards its composition as a whole and in every detail—compels the judgment that Raphael is the only Italian with Northern characteristics. May we call these advantages? When the picture still hung in the Tribuna, one sometimes found oneself, completely baffled, turning suddenly with a question towards the SIR RICHARD SOUTHWELL of Holbein. Holbein's LADY WITH CHILDREN at Basle, and his DERRICK BORN at Windsor, executed almost thirty years later and in another climate, really offer the only points of comparison.

The colour-harmony is as follows: olive-brown flesh-tints with lights in yellowish dashes on the bridge of the nose, the collarbone, and hands, and the wrinkles of the sleeves, and deeper olive green, with golden lacquer-red velvet borders and purer red, in the girdle, traversed by the white of the embroidered chemisette on the bust, of the sleeves and the apron, in light and dark tones spanned by the gold of the jewellery. The colouring has the same effect of sustained repose as the disposition of this grand, pure form in the frame, and of the more restricted forms produced by the thin, illuminated face, the chain running down to a point, the puffed chemisette, and the delicate hand. The character of this *malinconica* has a look of forbidding haughtiness, as if something surprised her. Reflections flit over her nostrils, as if she were sobbing; something like a tear lurks behind her eyes; her self-contained pose extends majestically over the space of the picture, filling it to the right, whilst the decisive lines of the hands with their air of resignation point to the left corner. They lie foreshortened, full of vitality and lightness; we are conscious, on a small scale, of a sense of landscape in the charm underlying the lines of the knuckles, the jutting thumb, and the back of the hand as a whole; the rise and fall within the space gives an assurance of animation to the figure; note the still-life in the little chain with its twist, providing with its glint and shadows the only means of giving projection to the gently breathing bust, and in the cross that seems to be twisting as it hangs down—thirty years before Holbein, a century and a half before Terborch!

Fortunately for those who leave the Doni portraits and pass on, these musical traits are not to be found here only; the picture is to be estimated only as a link in the chain of undoubted works. It leads from the drawing in the Louvre (p. 58), to the CASTIGLIONE (Plate 120).

Nearest to it comes the head for the youthful ST PLACIDUS at Oxford (Plate 53) (*R. Z.*, IV, 210), for the fresco of San Severo at Perugia, which does not need to be cleared of any suspicions; the slightly melancholy saint looks out from a drawing full of elements taken from the art of Leonardo, from the anatomical study of an old man's head to the BATTLE OF ANGHIARI and the vicious horses. The close approach of this drawing to the mysterious PORTRAIT OF A WOMAN indicated the nearness, at that time already, of its young author to Leonardo —who was probably resignedly content with this pupil who adhered to his teaching as a firstborn "son of nature".

§ Raphael's Portrait of Himself

What was the appearance of this man who understood so well how to interpret the nature and destiny of man? What did he look like to himself? His PORTRAIT OF HIMSELF (Plate 44), in the collection of painters in the Uffizi, questionable as it is generally reputed to be, does not, in its state of preservation, resolve our doubts. Certainly it has suffered many injuries, particularly in the outlines which mark off the figure in the space. To encroach on the outlines of Raphael is to put one's instrument out of tune, and it may be doubted whether the Velasquez-like greyish gold of the background can be trusted. However this may be, the resemblance to the self-portrait at the border of the SCHOOL OF ATHENS (Plate 285), arrests our attention in our devotion to the artist and should sharpen our eyes to look for its spiritual quality. We find in him the sympathetic Italian type, that mixture of modesty and irony, reserve and superiority, which Lorenzo Lotto knew how to render so charmingly. This however remains unaffected. Over and above the typical, what are the personal characteristics? Lavater, the physiognomist, thought there was nothing "osseous"—*beinigtes*—in the head, "only a soul of art"—*Kunstseele*. Perhaps it was restoration that first took the bones out of it, so that it became possible to find the picture suspiciously sentimental, even indeed to be a copy of a model for an angel by Botticelli, or that it could be asserted that the features had been transformed by over-painting in accordance with the Raphaelesque conceptions of the Nazarenes in the nineteenth century. But many portions of Raphael's painting and even of his "handwriting" were preserved in decisive passages, particularly in the eyes, nose and mouth, also the ear set amidst the chestnut-brown of the hair, in translucent pink as in the "*GRAVIDA*". In the face, the modelling is carried out with transparent tempera streaks over whitish under-painting; the rhythm of the brush-strokes can still be observed on the brows, and the shape of the eye was entirely in his style, with the firm line for the edge of the lids which deepens so finely the small area below; so also are the red dots in the corners of the eyes. This gives the look in the eyes its mingled sweetness and bitterness—we are arrested once again by the significant phrase of the physiognomist Lavater, as to the "man of all-embracing vision". Such will be the gaze of a discoverer of the three worlds that we found in his St Michael; he will have another, deeper look in his eyes, even when seeing himself in a mirror, than a "matter-of-fact" painter of the nineteenth century: it will be a marvelling, sweeping look—"in a fine frenzy rolling", not the gaze of one taking aim, full of hate, as of a hunter's eye, by which self-portraits can often be recognised.

Desire and reality, on the evidence of this portrait, were at that time one in him; seeing and looking coincide. In these portraits of persons of consequence, he was above all things master of his subject and of himself as painter. This may have given him the feeling of assurance, the freedom for action, that was readily conceded to him, even in the "keen air" of the Arno. Even under the shadow of the Titans he was so much respected that recollections of this fact were handed down even to the generation of Vasari. The artist-biographer relates how artists and other quick-witted spirits gathered on winter evenings at the *bottega* of the architect and woodcarver Baccio d'Agnolo, in the Piazza della Trinità, for "dispute d'importanza", in weighty discussions. Even Leonardo was accustomed to drop in, and now and again—"ma però di rado"—

even if as a rare visitor, Michael Angelo. It was with a circle having such important intellectual claims that the young artist from Urbino joined in, with his ready wit and acumen, when disputes arose and sides were taken about the perennial Florentine theme, Dante. We know that he was equipped for this from the days when he lived in his father's house; it was a theme that for him too was to prove immortal! Perhaps he was actually witness of the oft-related encounter, when Leonardo, in a discussion about Dante, pointed to Michael Angelo, who came in just at that moment, as the man with the deepest knowledge of the subject, and was obliged to take as a man of breeding should, from his suspicious and irritable fellow-artist, a challenge of unparalleled offensiveness.

Raphael lived in the tension between two such poles, and he had to suffer from it before this new experience could be turned to his inner profit. For the ferment in him had not yet subsided. From the Madonnas, and from the clarity of several of the portraits, he might be supposed to have arrived in port, but every major commission, every composition of a number of figures, seems to have driven him out again on to the high seas. In these intimate groups of mother and child, in the inevitableness of colour and form in a portrait, he attained, after a brief period of indecision of which we had evidence in the MADDALENA DONI, the right colouristic filling of the frame; inspired by Leonardo, and then out of his own resources, he succeeded in discovering, adequately and even happily, with the media of his Umbrian period, the harmony of the Mother of God, and the colour-formula for his sitters with a landscape background. But as painter, when he turned to the Holy Family, he must already have been confused by the accession of the figures of St Joseph and St Elizabeth, with their colours stereotyped by iconographic convention; the hopeless traditional Florentine polychromy must have suggested itself. The mastery with which the Venetians adjusted to their calculations of the colour of a picture the yellow of a cloak, for example, was not to be attained in Florence, especially by a painter struggling with problems of form; Fra Bartolommeo was at that time faltering in similar difficulties; Andrea del Sarto was not yet mature. In the poetic amplitude of his motives and in all the wealth of his expression, we learn not to be exacting in this one point of Raphael's colouring. The fact belongs to the history of painting—but only because its surmounting belongs to Raphael's peculiar title to fame as "painter". It was to be his happy lot to fulfil the injunction "Be what thou art" as a son of Urbino, and what he was destined to become as an artist was, after the purgatories of Umbria and Tuscany, precisely his role as a Marchigiano.

§ The Entombment

After all the progress he had already achieved, the commission for the ENTOMBMENT confronted him with the new problem of a dramatic subject;

or as it seems, he himself decided upon the dramatic procession to the grave, instead of a lyrical *Pietà* which he had at first intended. In doing so, he brought upon himself all the bitterness that falls to the lot of the beginner, the struggle with an unfamiliar task.

The noble and unhappy Atalanta Baglioni of Perugia wished to lay her own sorrow at the feet of the sublime Mother of God, as an expiation for the bloody wedding in which the youth of her house fell as victims in murderous mutual entanglements. These alone were the ideas that were to be embodied in the commission for the altar of the church of the Franciscans. The long series of studies begins in a purely lyrical strain, and still, following the precedent of Perugino, with the lamentations over the body of the Redeemer lying extended on the ground; sorrow is the content of the great pattern that fills the drawings at Oxford and in Paris (*R. Z.*, IV, 164, 168). Raphael was already drawing from the naked model single figures in the composition—those of the group surrounding the mourning St John. He made a pounced tracing from the perforated nude study on a larger sheet—now in the Louvre (*R. Z.*, IV, 166, 168), and threw draperies round the figure. It is possible that at this stage Mantegna's engraving of the Entombment, was brought to his notice or suddenly occurred to him. That this print was known in the Umbrian studio is proved by the so-called Venetian Sketchbook, which originated in the near neighbourhood of Raphael; Dürer also knew the engraving, and Mantegna in his turn saw Roger van der Weyden's WEEPING WOMAN, and the Antique tragic masks, and used them for the wailing companions of the Virgin. Such influences are not the essential thing; nor was the circumstance of any importance that Raphael, in the final form given to his ENTOMBMENT, was thinking, in the group of women, of Michael Angelo's *tondo* painted for Angelo Doni. The decisive fact, however it may have come about, was that the PIETÀ was converted for him into the Carrying of the Body to the Grave. This marks the victory in him of Tuscan drama over Umbrian lyricism! Now he was stirred by the theme of the physical energy of the bearers and the attendant train of sorrowing women (in the British Museum, *R. Z.*, IV, 171). Then as a true dramatist, he conceived a moment of tension in the *ritardando* on the steps leading to the sepulchral cavern; and in this purely corporeal group the convulsive cry of parting breaks forth—the Magdalen, in a transport of emotion, as she was once before at the feet of the Lord as he sat at meat, and again at the foot of the Cross, has left the group of women in order to touch his hand once more before the dark tomb receives him. Among the bearers striding with effort under their burden she seems to glide as on wings; perhaps her figure, in the precious drawing in the possession of Dr Lugt (Plate 39, *R. Z.*, IV, 117), who first conceived this idea, was derived from an Antique relief—as if to prove that all high dramatic art, even in painting, is a kind of dance, and that dancing only becomes art when, as here, it is the heart by which all is prompted. The languishing turn of the head, the elastic step of the foot, and even the fluttering robe, all have the same derivation!

Finally, out of all these studies there emerged a number of sublime and touching motives for groups expressing friendship and devotion and for what is, after all, only a cold picture. The dramatic pattern is disposed correctly in the frame, but all the parts operate in unison or reciprocity with the exactness of a machine. Noble figures and noble movements are enveloped in stiff plastic drapery-motives; their flesh-tones seem pallid, and modelled with exaggerated softness. The great sculptor and the great painter who refined the mediums of his art, were not here a blessing to their pupil. He hovers in danger of losing his individuality in eclecticism. The depth to which indigenous Florentine mannerism could fall is nowhere exhibited more clearly than in this glassy flesh-painting, and in the smooth greyish-violet draperies, abruptly changing to yellow or even orange in the lining; here and there a harsh madder red absolutely shouts. One can hardly speak of the colour as expression; it serves only to keep the mass of limbs distinct from one another. The skin is modelled over with glazings, as in the Mannerist followers of Massys at Antwerp and in Leonardo's degenerate pupils. It is only in the lovely landscape with its softly graduated distances that the eye recognises Raphael once again.

The unhesitating acceptance of such a work made it possible for the idea to develop of the "great draughtsman", whose colour was of no consequence. Even more!—the early nineteenth century derived from this, for whole generations of painters, the right to be incapable of painting; to it can be traced, at the end of the century, among historians of art, the justification of their practice of writing-table study with the help of photographs.

The predella-painting shows what a strong propensity Raphael had at that time for sculpture; designs in gold on an indigo-blue ground, with sporting *putti* and griffins (now in the Gallery at Perugia) separated the little green-and-grey pictures, in the Vatican Pinacoteca, with *tondi* deceptively painted to simulate reliefs of the Cardinal Virtues, flanked by angels whose gestures tellingly illustrate Faith, Charity and Hope. Perhaps the stone- and gold-colouring was continued on the frame and provided something in the nature of a transition from the vivid colour of the picture to its architectural surroundings. This is a factor which should console us for many a disillusionment, as regards colour, in Central Italy. Even Fra Bartolommeo's colours must have had a less garish and shiny effect among the pillars in the dimness of a church than they have to-day in the indiscreet light of a gallery.

§ St Catherine

Is it permissible to talk of Raphael's colours at all, in the present condition of his works? The picture of St Catherine, in the National Gallery (Plates 33, 239), is among those that are quite well preserved. It dates from the period of the Entomb-

MENT and provides solid grounds for our judgment; her attitude, standing and leaning with feet crossed, comes from Classical sculpture, presumably from a sarcophagus with figures of the Muses, and the lines of the folds are plastic, flowing in conformity with the twist of the body. But the robust proportions and the fresh expression of purity are entirely those of the "noble peasantess" of whom Delacroix spoke. A remarkable feature is the almost Spanish coolness in the harmony of the olive and blue of the landscape with the delicate grey-blue and olive green of the clothing and the ivory-toned flesh, with bluish shading—a harmony certainly, so long as one hides from view the red cloak and its twisted yellow lining. We do not know for whom the picture was commissioned; perhaps, surrounded by Tuscan architecture in *pietra serena*, it would have had a monotonous effect without red and yellow, not plastic enough for a Florentine eye and therefore lifeless. Perhaps it was a matter of concession to instructions and environment—or had Raphael for the moment lost himself? We know that as a painter, already in these years, what he had to lose was everything that is of the best—the picture tells us this, even here; for was it, after all, no "painter" who produced such a landscape, with the softly-flowing stream and the floating reflections of banks and trees? One must not for this reason make of him an Adriaen van de Velde, a Solomon Ruysdael, or even a Corot. But responsively, as he discovered these things, they needs must be adopted by him—above all, the phenomenon of the heavenly vision, that light breaking forth from the clouds, towards which the saint is raising her gaze! This is something that is absolutely without parallel in the whole circle. Since the time of the ST MICHAEL such a thing had not occurred in Raphael, nor does it appear again until the DELIVERANCE OF ST PETER (Plate 110), in the Second Stanza, and in the VISION OF EZEKIEL (Plate 223). This "painter"—it should be written with quotation marks and a note of exclamation!—was then learning more and more to look upon the world of phenomena as his instrument on which he sounded chords to express this mood or that.

§ The Red-stained Sketchbook

The more he was matured by his years in Florence and the more rapidly, so much the more sincerely and freely he emancipated himself from the synthesis to which he seems to have fallen a victim in the period of the ENTOMBMENT, with its coupling of newly-acquired forms and colours not yet mastered; for "synthesis" was still ever the symptom of crisis and stagnation, even with Raphael. But he found the way back to his starting-point, as painter; colour once more became the vehicle of poetic expression, and—as before his Florentine bewilderment—inseparable from the poetry of expression. Anyone who knows how to read the handwriting of drawings will find this in the leaves from a Sketchbook of his latest period by the Arno, and in the drawings of the days of his removal to Rome—pen-sketches in yellow ink on red-stained paper, in strokes with intensifications or a few broad hatchings in one direction, without cross-strokes; Perugino drew in this manner, just with the pen only, when he was young and daring. The effect is quite that of sunlight, as though every form were brightly circumfused with light, right up into the shadows. There we see the Virgin seated suckling the Child, at their ease in the sunshine (Plate 50*b*, *R. Z.*, III, 153); nowhere connected outlines—they are broken up as if by dazzling reflections on the convexities of the forms. The young mother stoops, with both legs drawn in, like a console figure, listening to the contented sucking of the boy. The left leg is represented as stretched out; the frame—here, the edges of the sheet—had at all costs to be filled up. On other pages the motive is varied with the child becoming roguish—the discontinuous contours are all the time expressive of waywardness and light.

The same critical generation for whom Raphael was of no account as a painter disputed his claims as a draughtsman to these precious evidences, on account of the "intermittent line" (Plate 50*a*, *R. Z.*, III, 150–158). In consequence Léon Bonnat with his taste for Old Masters was able to acquire them without competition. In this style of drawing he goes the round, as a painter also, of the last, brilliant group of Florentine Madonnas; the unfinished but sunny-tone ESTERHAZY MADONNA, the COWPER MADONNA (the larger one from Pans hanger, in the possession of Duveen, New York), the COLONNA MADONNA and the MADONNA WITH THE BALDACCHINO belong to this group.

§ Colonna Madonna

When Raphael looked round him, after his self-effacing acknowledgments of the new Florentine marble form and of the improved manner of modelling by means of glazing, he may possibly have found that there had been capable painters already, in earlier times, by the Arno, and he discovered his master from Perugia. For the COLONNA MADONNA (Plate 41), so full of radiant cheerfulness in mother and child, shows an acquaintance with the light-suffused, early works of Perugino in the monastery of the Gesuati outside the Porta Pinti. They were not destroyed until twenty years later, when Florence was besieged in 1529. With these works before him, Raphael had once again come into contact with the great luminous style of painting and the transparent chiaroscuro of Piero della Francesca, *painting proper* as it was in Central Italy. It was handed on by the young Perugino, Verrocchio and Leonardo to only a few in their generation; to few only was it indeed intelligible. The last of them, Piero di Cosimo, may have been still at work at that time as a genuine eccentric. The style also affected Boltraffio and Lotto; it anticipated many of the miracles of Vermeer. The COLONNA MADONNA, with its sunshine inward and outward, is not quite finished—glazings are wanting in places; but they would only have produced variations in the brilliance of the picture, they would not have altered it. The brocade cover of the breviary in the left hand of the Virgin should have cast reflections out of the half light such as are found in the pictures under the name of Verrocchio and his circle, which are connected with the "Master of San Bernardino" of Perugia and thus with the early works of Perugino.

§ Trinity of San Severo

Thus the evolution as a school of the best Central Italian painting and of its unexplained but close relations with the art of the Marches is brought to a close here, in Raphael. He attracted others and was himself attracted; Fra Bartolommeo was then beginning to paint again, and his influence on Raphael has been unduly emphasised. It can certainly be recognised in that heavenly semi-circle of saints in which the fresco of San Severo at Perugia takes suggestions from Baccio's LAST JUDGMENT in Santa Maria Nuova. Bartolommeo set the austere assessors of the *"Giudizio"* in their exalted position in two recessed, curved ranks; in Raphael, the light-robed monks are enthroned, full of lofty aspirations, in a rarer atmosphere above the world. In the DISPUTA, the semi-circle is enlarged, in transfigured repetition. We must be satisfied with knowing that the two were acquainted, the young aspirant and the elder, resigned master, and Vasari must be admitted to be right after all in stating that they associated with one another; but in summing up, the most that can be said is that they arrived simultaneously at the new solutions which they some-times shared in common, such as the angel musicians among the clouds at the top of Raphael's study-drawing for Alfani (Lille, *R. Z.*, III, 161) and in the ASSUMPTION OF THE VIRGIN by the Frate, in Berlin.

§ Madonna of the Baldacchino. The "Painter" as Draughtsman

The MADONNA OF THE BALDACCHINO (Plate 29) of 1508 certainly appears at first sight to resemble the celebrated composition of Bartolommeo in Paris and Florence—but it is quite independently conceived, and came into existence a year before the first *Sacra Conversazione* of the monk known to us, in the church of San Marco, with the beautiful light-encompassed St Mary Magdalen in the foreground.

Only Raphael contributes to the motives they share in common the life in a realm above the earth; Bartolommeo puts earthly life into heaven; his floating figures remain statues without a base, his angels seem to hang in the air, and their motion is that of running, at best gliding, as if on skates, through the clouds—whilst Raphael's figures have breath in them and space, in its height and profundity, about them.

The MADONNA OF THE BALDACCHINO, incomplete as it has come down to us, has the effect of being among the best of works as a painting. A niche in the best style of Brunelleschi, absolutely overflowing with light, encloses the Virgin, the throne and saints. The dark bottle-green baldacchino embraces the mother with her radiant child in its gloom as a foil to the red and blue that stand out in the light. The accompanying figures participate in this transfiguration on earth. In the St Bruno, a light figure, the spiritual grace of Ghiberti's Gothic is revived. The studies for this figure at Lille show the upper part of his body in silver-point, the floating figure of a visionary, his head illumined by reflections on an ochre-yellow ground. And yet another revelation of the painting manner can be put to the credit of Raphael; amongst the drawings in the reserve collection at the Uffizi was to be found the wonderful Tiepolo-like improvisation, with brushwork in bistre in the transparent half-light of the shadows (Plate 243, R. Z., III, 148).

This draughtsman remained to be rediscovered, like the "painter", for a new generation. The sunlit pages with golden washes and applied white were almost all unrecognised as his. Here we have the most charming Madonna with the Child in a landscape (Paris, Plate 242, R. Z., III, 144), quite near to Leonardo; he elevates this group on a throne, in the preliminary drawing at Chatsworth, and makes a study for the robe round her knees in drapery that breathes the very spirit of Praxiteles, in silver-point heightened with white on an ochre-coloured ground (Plate 43, R. Z., III, 145, in the École des Beaux Arts). On the back of the same sheet there are attempts at rendering the sun-illumined contours of children's bodies, in the style of the Bonnat sketchbook (Plate 51, R. Z., III, 146).

If we turn back to the almost finished work, after being ourselves prepared by these preparatory studies, it gleams with a vision of space of unparalleled radiance; this can no longer be regarded as a summing-up, a convergence, of elements from Leonardo, Bartolommeo and other sources. No, it becomes the manifestation of a single elemental force, the power of the born painter who seeks what is sublime in the earthly and in what is above the earth. Here he is on the point of passing beyond the mark and attaining perfection.

If it has always been repeated that the fresco of San Severo is a preliminary trial for the heavenly hemicycle of the DISPUTA, this picture, with its sublime figures harmonising with the consecrated space in which they are set, may be hailed as the prelude to the SCHOOL OF ATHENS.

We do not know how or when Raphael came to Rome and to his great undertakings in the Vatican, nor which of the traditions that have become legendary we should believe. This also remains a miracle—that the young artist of twenty-five, still without experience of work on a large scale, should have been called upon to undertake these mightiest of all schemes of the Italian Renaissance. What had the Pope seen of him? Had he, on his campaign against Bologna, stood before the ENTOMBMENT, in the house of his own Order, the Franciscans, at Perugia? We may well believe the fiery instinct of Julius II capable of recognising in anticipation what we, looking back, think we can see in Raphael's drawings of that period—the Oxford combat-sketches, the latest made by him in his travels (Plate 52, R. Z., IV, 194, 195). Among these Oxford sketches there is one that is nothing but vigour, permeating individual figures and group alike, throwing itself into the action of the narrative, full of an innate force, inescapably compelling, which captures all the senses and makes them respond to the rhythm of such poetry. This power is not conscious of the frame as a cramping boundary, either on the wall-surface or on the sheet of paper, but only feels that a field has been marked out for it, a space offered in which to exercise itself. The possessor of such power knows no external constraint, only the one elemental impulse to fill the prescribed area to the limits with the rhythm of passion and exaltation. This power made of Raphael the monumental painter, in these drawings already, even without a wall to paint on! The miracle of the First Stanza is consummated between Raphael and the Pope, those two mighty poles of force, like a great natural phenomenon.

VI

ROME

STANZA DELLA SEGNATURA

FROM time immemorial Rome has been held to be the arena of the talents—and so, as regards Raphael's time, Urbino may be regarded as their melting-pot and Florence may be called their academy. Rome has seldom produced anything peculiarly its own throughout its entire history, but there has always been inherent in its very soil the power of lifting above themselves those already formed and mature. Even Titian and Velazquez could not but excel themselves in their portraits of Popes, the highest commission that could then be given to a portrait-painter.

To-day it is hardly within our powers to imagine how much a commission means, or rather, how much it meant in those days when every work of art was still the outcome of an order. It can be spoken of as "ordered", because the artist knew one thing: his theme was common to himself and his contemporaries, and to a society that was acquainted with all the sublime matters to be depicted, whether sacred or secular, and felt about them as he did. If the artist had the gift of poetical creation—and after the prose in which the Quattrocento had expired there were poets once again—he could invent a form for what was unconsciously stirring everyone, and could set before the eyes of all—*interpret*—the indwelling power of the spiritual. *He* was the chosen prophet to display to others the object of veneration as a higher power ruling with decisive sway over man and his life, in the image of which, as in a conception full of sublimity, they found the measure and aim of their life, "in the realm of the ideal"! And Pope Julius II was the man who, by his creative nature as by the physical force of his politics, filled the thoughts of Italy, among adherents and adversaries, with a great content, with the idea of a power exercising on its environment an influence that was no other than dæmonic, "il papa terribile!"

We do not know whether Raphael was called to Rome by the Pope for his great commission, or whether perhaps he merely followed in the steps of his fellow-countryman Bramante. It is also possible that the young master and *familiare* of the Palazzo Ducale had a recommendation through the new princes of Urbino of the House of Rovere, the Pope's kinsmen. And lastly we may be allowed to suppose that he felt in himself the impulse to visit on his own account the Eternal City, and had lived there, for a while without any commissions, since the beginning of 1508. His name is not mentioned among the artists who were at work in the Vatican in 1508 and the beginning of 1509. An oft-quoted letter of Raphael to Francesco Francia at Bologna, about his activities at the Vatican, is irrelevant, as an old forgery of a sentimental kind.

Certainly his entry into Rome remained among the great impressions of his travelling period. At Loreto he made the acquaintance of Melozzo's ceiling in the Sagrestia della Cura and of Signorelli's CONVERSION OF ST PAUL; the figure of Christ breaking in chastisement out of clouds remained with him until the period of the tapestries. He was soon after to stand again in the presence of Melozzo's art and once more to admire the familiarity with another world shown in his countryman's painting. At Orvieto he saw for the first time a huge vaulted area filled by a forceful creative will. The mighty movements of Signorelli's figures had long been familiar to him at Urbino and Perugia; now, in the Capella di San Brizio, he was granted the experience of seeing how the master carried this significant pattern of human figures, over the arched wall-spaces right up to the crown of the vault, and how, the more narrowly he was confined by the horseshoe arches, the more he utilised this confinement as a means to dramatic vitality; the other-worldly is forced upon the faithful as physical experience, without impairing the sublimity which is its due, through the marked objectiveness of the frame; this art of dominating space so as to make it the more obedient to the laws of poetry, is here displayed well-nigh to perfection. Not since the time of Masaccio had perspective been made thus subservient to narration. Here it is precisely through perspective that the apocalyptic visions come to life.

The studies of the young Raphael on his journey towards his exalted destination abound in sparks of the passion of these first liberated bodies, the symbol of true rebirth in classical detachment. His drawings of this period, the large pen-sketches of heroic combat and obsequies, at Oxford, display bodies in the style of Lysippus; it is the style of a youth, even for his age, impulsive and resilient. And this young man is now introduced on the scene of the Vatican by the Pope, who still retains his youthfulness. He gives him full power to do as he will with the walls and, if anything has already been painted on them, authority even over the artists and their works.

It is not known what paintings Raphael found already in existence there, or what he was allowed to suppress by the injunctions of the Pope. If this were known, we should perhaps gain information as to the original destination of the apartment when Julius II had this upper series of rooms fitted up as a residence. This was already decided upon in 1507, because he did not wish to remain for ever condemned, in the Appartamento Borgia, to be reminded everywhere by the walls of that "Maran", his deadly enemy Alexander VI, and his infamies.

§ The Commission

When the present-day visitor to the Vatican comes into the Stanze, as into a gallery, to see pictures, there awaits him, after several rooms, nothing but yet another suite of saloons with paintings. He does not as a rule say to himself that, in combination with this room, they have, in their position, some peculiar significance, nor does he think of asking why here in particular this must be the case. We shall need first to investigate again, and acknowledge anew, the inward inevitableness of the art of the past; we shall have to reconstruct this room as it was in Raphael's time in compliance with the wishes of the Pope who gave the commission, and we shall not penetrate to the vital nerve of these pictures and hear the stimulating accents of their language until we know what message they were meant to convey. Art in ancient interiors has always a purpose; the form and purpose of the room were inseparably bound up together.

The lining with intarsia-work by Fra Giovanni da Verona on the dado below is part of the original effect. From the shaded colours of the woodwork in the ancient sacristy cupboards of Santa Maria in Organo, in Fra Giovanni's native city, we can still get an idea of what was lost, in warmth of tone and the beautiful framework below Raphael's paintings in this room, when the coloured woodwork, fitted together with such ingenuity, was destroyed by the bivouac fires of the Imperial soldiery in 1527. The present imitations and the bronze-coloured pictures amongst simulated architecture, painted in chalky fresco by Perino del Vaga, offer no substitute for the original warm harmony with the wall-paintings. In front were stands with books, as surviving to this day in the Laurenziana at Florence—not shelves, but desks for the richly-bound and illuminated volumes, relics of the great minds of the past; from the walls above, these great ones looked down facing one another with lively impressiveness! Raphael was familiar with such libraries; at Urbino the collection of Duke Federigo was formed on the humanistic plans of Nicholas V, like most of the book-collections of the Renaissance. There, above the intarsia bookcase, sat the sages and poets of ancient and modern times, painted probably by Melozzo and Justus van Gent in concert. Raphael's father knew these apartments, and so therefore did Raphael also. Dante's portrait there (Plate 4) left an abiding impression on him; it is the work of Justus, and for depth of character and insight into the nature of the poet, it can be compared only with Rembrandt's Homer; here a Northerner showed understanding for the great Italian—it is well known that we have here the first, but far from the last, evidence of the esteem in which he was held on this side of the Alps. The Libreria of the Cathedral of Siena had also been known to Raphael, since the time of his collaboration there, with its beautiful *ensemble* of stands in wood, still preserved, and the decorated antiphonals, and the frescoes by Pinturicchio above, with their effect of great miniatures. Here were dominant on every side only those personages connected with the one great friend of books, Enea Silvio, Pope Pius II.

In well kept-up Baroque libraries it is still customary for busts on the book-cases to indicate who are the thinkers entombed, as it were, in the ancestral vaults of the compartments. Here, in the rooms of the High Renaissance, in the living-quarters of Julius II, above the spot where at one time books stood or lay, everything is full of life; we see the great minds, the men of the writings, going to and fro in the flesh, in fruitful intercourse, among one another.

§ Purpose of the *Stanze*

But was it after all really a library? The question as to the former purpose of the saloon has been much discussed.[1] To begin with, the name "Camera della Segnatura" has been variously interpreted; it has been pointed out in this connection that the highest Papal Court of Justice consisted of the *Signatura Justitiæ* and the *Signatura Gratiæ*, and that once a week it transacted Affairs of Grace here, under the presidency of the Pope. Against this we have the assertion that the very themes of the pictorial decoration point to a library; everywhere on the walls, wherever one looks, are books and authors (Plates 54, 55).

Now the name "Camera della Segnatura" occurs already in the *diario* of Paris de Grassis, Steward of the Papal Household, in 1513, in Raphael's time. The dilemma can only be resolved if we reflect that in the Vatican the apartments changed their names with their destinations; this room may have served several purposes at once or in quick succession. It was intended and fitted out as a library, and the Pope used it as a study.

However this may be, the scheme of decoration comprises the four spiritual provinces of the Renaissance; so it might be said, if this had not been already the structure of ecclesiastical doctrine as unalterably laid down by Scholasticism. There sat the Pope, in sight of the four great activities that are ordained to give inspiration to the spirit of man, all serving the highest endeavour after the perfect life; they looked down on him, from them he might derive illumination and power, whether administering justice or signing his decrees, to be published to the world. Raphael was here permitted to give visible shape to the claim of the dæmonic Pope, for himself and his office, to reign and to live as supreme Head of Christendom, counselled by all the highest wisdom. And this Pope was no scholar; he thought simply, as a political genius. The spiritual, in life as in art, took its place as part of his great purpose.

§ The Question of Programme

In this he was at one with his painter. The great artist can only give shape to what he has experienced, and therefore it is a matter of indifference to him whether men of learning stood at his side when he planned the execution of his painting. With the help of a programme one can paint like Delaroche or Kaulbach or Stevens, but in order to express what great minds mean to his age and therefore to himself, the artist must vitalise that programme anew from within himself. Only so will images come into being that can be set in convincing

[1] Pastor, *Päpste* III (3, 4 ed.), 849 ff.; Klaczko, *Jules* II, 245; Wickhoff, *Jahrbuch der preussischen Kunstsammlungen*, XIV (1893), p. 49 ff.; Künstle, *Ikonographie der christlichen Kunst*, I, p. 153 f.

relationship with one another, vital—not "living"—pictures. If Raphael conversed with the scholars of the "Sapienza" and of the Vatican, we must reflect that what to them was paper, book or doctrine, became to him immediately conception and animated image. What he brought with him from Urbino, from the home of his father, and from his relationship with the Ducal Palace—that which made him capable of impressing others as a peculiarly lively thinker in those "dispute d'importanza" and in the expositions of Dante in the most exacting circle of Florence—had here an opportunity of being translated into artistic action; he stood on a footing of equality, certainly, with the leading minds of the Vatican.

The essential thing, therefore, about the decoration of these Stanze is not the programme, but the fact that they are vitalised and spiritualised into a pictorial symphony in four movements, the notes of which have continued to resound down to our own time; the titles in the play of allegory and symbolism are given by the pictorial decoration of the ceiling.

§ Ceiling (Plates 56, 57, 60)

Naturally, this is where the work of decoration must have begun. It had been started by Sodoma; much of his painting Raphael was able to preserve—the *putti* with the Papal arms in the middle area, the small trapezes *en camaïeu*; and perhaps the entire disposition of the whole can be traced to the Sienese master; we cannot even begin to conjecture what had at that time already been begun by other artists, or how much of their work was obliged to make way for the paintings of Raphael. It is remarkable that the subdivision of the ceiling into *cassette* is based upon a Roman mosaic pavement; thus Renaissance feeling for life, far removed from the erudite and bookish classicalism of later days, understood how to make good an absurdity perpetrated in Late Alexandrian Antique, and to restore framework and *cassette* to their peculiar rights, on the ceiling, where alone they could sensibly find a place.

Perhaps it was Raphael who first made the gold-grounded borders of the framework to suit the imitation-mosaic ground of his figures. The *tondi* with the allegories serve as titles to the wall-pictures; the latter are connected with one another by the significant content of the stories in the obliquely-set rectangles: between Philosophy and *Justitia*, the wise judgment of Solomon, between Theology and Righteousness, the Fall; Poetry (Plate 57) and Theology have as connecting link the punishment of the presumptuous Marsyas by the god Apollo, and the Contemplation of the Starry Firmament is suspended between the "Poetry", inspired by the Godhead, and the "Knowledge of Things" in the Creation.

Only one who as a man of education is master of the world of ideas can intertwine his threads so unerringly as he brings these ideas into play; it was not humanism that first created such a chain of connections. Teaching and education for such achievements were, from the Middle Ages onwards, entrusted to every spiritual personage, and Raphael carried within him a consciousness of this, the sole legitimate, vital union and intercourse of the Faculties, as something obvious and indispensable, more surely than it could have been communicated to him by a *humanist* scholar, perhaps by one of those who had, then already, lost their power of vision.

The ceiling-paintings are extraordinarily different in effect from one another; even in their proportions the figures of the *tondi* do not correspond with one another. The same can be observed also, as work progressed, in Michael Angelo's ceiling in the Sistine Chapel. Justice sits, slender and graceful, on her throne, and for the accomplishment of her stern duty with scales and sword she requires the four *putti* with their humour to give to the frame its due compliment. Poetry with her wings, inspired by the Godhead—*numine afflatur*—fills with vigour, almost by herself, the extent of the *tondo*, and the *putti* crouch. The children on clouds beside the delicate figure of Theology are dancing, but almost with constraint, whilst in the powerful figure of Philosophy and her boys the Roman sense of form breaks through.

For this reason it would be irresponsible and arbitrary criticism to seek to attribute one of these paintings to some alien hand or other, without any understanding of the process of creation; as an artist proceeds with his task he grows in competence for it. This is proved even by the example of Michael Angelo—indeed, we who are unproductive have this experience; who does not know, when he has finished a book, how he *ought* to have written it!

In a "full-blooded" young master, abounding in creative force, the task to be carried through releases at the outset his spiritual powers, and his competence grows from picture to picture; his style will be apt to alter from week to week. The very contact with the lime on the wall arouses his sensibility, and with it, his capability of expressing himself. He brings to his task nothing ready-made; everything is snatched out of a ferment that is perpetually being renewed. How at that time Raphael lived in his imagination through everything! What creative impulse urged him on, driven by force from within, spurred on by his task!

When he designed the Theology, he had before him the image of a figure upon clouds, the Daughter of Heaven, clothed in white, green and red, in the favourite symbolical colours of Gothic; this was the aspect of Dante's vision, Beatrice:

> "Sovra candido vel cinta d'oliva
>   Donna m'apparve, sotto verde manto
>   Vestita di color di fiamma viva."

> "Guardami ben; ben son, ben son
>   Beatrice."[1]

[1]"Wreath'd with olive above a veil of white
  A lady I beheld; 'neath cloak of green
  The hues of living flame her robe display'd." *Purg.* XXX 31
"Look at me well; 'tis I, 'tis I, Beatrice." *Purg.* XXX 67.

RAPHAEL

§ Parallelism of Ideas

And these words "*Guardami ben . . .*" inspired Raphael's pen with the loveliest drawing at Oxford, with the countenance revealing itself to the gaze (Plate 56); she steps unawares out of her other-worldly sphere into the region of human sight, and as she showed herself suddenly to an astounded mortal, she awakened in Raphael a new vision: the same sheet was entrusted with the transfigured RESURRECTION OF THE VIRGIN. The commission of the nuns of Monte Luce outside the Perugia for an *Assunzione Mariæ* followed him to Rome. At the moment when he began the Stanze, *her* glorification presented itself, consummated and incarnate before him, liberated by the figure on clouds and the Dante vision—the Virgin on clouds in the light of the beyond, raised aloft into the semi-circle of the frame, her way made ready for her by angels. Around the sarcophagus the Apostles start back, blinded, as at the Last Supper, and as in Leonardo, in the ADORATION, one on the left beats his brow against the ground. An immortal figure!—Donatello created it, in his bronze relief in Sant' Antonio at Padua; thence it was handed on to Leonardo, now it flashed upon Raphael; next, it took its place among those risen from the dead in the LAST JUDGMENT of Rubens, and finally we have it in Rembrandt's TOBIAS, in Paris.

Here allegory and drama arise simultaneously; out of the abstract theme "Theology" is born the loveliest of the visions among Dante's verses—and through Dante again allegory received anew vitality of colour—recovers it, one may say. They are the old colours of Theology that Dante brought to life: above the red and green, the white veil waves in the wind of the heights. This touch is Raphael's very own; it springs from his universal sensibility; the air of the other region is for him inseparable from the figure out of the beyond, and at that time already the radiance of the other-wordly was beginning to give him power to express those spheres. For him, light and lightness coalesced. Thus was born and consecrated the illustrator, elect above all others, of Dante's "*Paradiso*".

Raphael, the narrator, makes everything a source of vitality, even the restrictions imposed by the frame. What trouble he had had in filling the wide square of the ENTOMBMENT! Now, the narrow rectangle with the JUDGMENT OF SOLOMON is filled to bursting point (Plates 60, 61). The stage is completely occupied —no scenery but a ground of gold mosaic, which imposes dramatic play in the highest degree. Every gesture upon which the action depends makes of it an action that takes the breath away—the arm of the executioner, the attempt by the real mother to parry the stroke, in an essential line following the diagonal of the rectangle. A new feeling for the human body, revived by contact with Signorelli and gaining audacity in the atmosphere of Rome, raises the scene to a heroic plane. The HORSE-TAMER of the Monte Cavallo is roused to life again, and the fresh beauty of the women bears witness to a knowledge of the world, of the feminine world also—mature, new and enduringly young, a "vita nuova". The charming deceiver to the right, throwing herself on her knees at the foot of the throne, might have caused a less wise judge to waver. As it is, her figure, like one on the pedestal of a monument, cannot fail to heighten the impression of his wisdom as he looks straight in front of him. She is shown as if before the footlights, with deliberately coquettish plastic effect on the light from the window below, in the "*Justice*" wall. The real mother is real because we become witnesses to the overmastering of her fear in the presence of the king by her fear for the child. It is her terror that brings her into the focus of light in the picture, and thrusts her body and her arm into the diagonals.

The dramatic idea here dominant in the appointed theme gave rise to variations of the motive that were no part of the commission—the studies for the MASSACRE OF THE INNOCENTS, famous through Marcantonio's engraving (Plates 58, 61). On a single sheet of paper in the Albertina we find a first study for the composition of the JUDGMENT OF SOLOMON (Plate 60), for the man pursuing one of the mothers of Bethlehem (Plate 59), and for the ASTRONOMY of the ceiling (*R. Z.*, V, 236–237). The connection of the various sheets can almost be described as physical; a sheet with rough drawings for the central group is improved in a highly ingenious manner in red crayon, and its outlines have been pricked and traced on a new sheet; this became the finished red drawing at Windsor Castle (*R. Z.*, V, 233, 234), and on the back of this red drawing this invention of his phantasy survives in a new transformation; the border of a dish is sketched with a pen—tritons struggling with mermaids they are pursuing (Plate 190, *R. Z.*, V, 235); the fleeing mother dragged back by the hair also occurs here. The technique is as varied as the conceits are exuberant—pen-drawing both hasty and finished, silverpoint, white chalk, red crayon in a bold sketchy manner and carefully worked up. This example might teach us what a spectacle of ripening creative power is forfeited by false, self-complacent connoisseurship when it condemns as not genuine every unfamiliar-looking stroke (*R. Z.*, V, 232–237). The separate drawings connect one with another in an unquestionable crescendo of animation (*R. Z.* V, Text, p. 251f.). The executioner on the left seems flabby, to begin with, in the Vienna drawing, more muscular in the Vienna red-crayon study, more ferocious in the London pen-drawing, all tension in the latest red-crayon sketch, at Windsor. The final conception in the Marcantonio engraving gives to the confusion of the turmoil concentration of form and content, through the arched shape of the Ponte de' Quattro Capi. This role was certainly assigned deliberately to the famous bridge by Raphael; the engraver cannot possibly have contributed it out of his own imagination, for the bridge provides the heroic setting for an action which first acquired from it its concentration. Its curved line re-echoes again in the feet below. A great oval is set transversely in the rectangle of the sheet, accentuated by the towers which carry their lines insepar-ably from the protagonists upwards and thus give rhythm to the whole—a pattern, one might almost say a dance, of menace, flight, and maternal love, reverberating like music, with the figure of the mother rushing distraught into the turmoil as centre; her face is set like a mask or a blossom at the focal point of the scrollwork, like those of the frenzied men in the BATTLE OF THE CASCINA. The MASSACRE OF THE INNOCENTS seems the best proof that in the Holkham cartoon or in the replica in the Palazzo Albani at Urbino we perhaps have, faithfully handed down to us, the copy by Aristotile da Sangallo and thus the entire, lost, old composition of Michael Angelo. Confronted by him, as by Leonardo, Raphael masters the spirit, not the details, of monumental arrangement; there is no other manner in which creative spirits can pay their respects to one another, and how conscious of creative power the young painter must have been, who had but just before composed, however laboriously, the ten interlocking figures of the EMTOMBMENT, and who was now, through the papal commission, free, in his new scene of operations, to make a beginning with the ceiling pictures! An allegorical figure on clouds grew into a conception of Transfiguration that dominated his life right up to the end; from the theme of the Judgment of Solomon three pictorial compositions eradiated. The stream of his inventiveness flowed in the same tempo as the wishes of such a patron (R. Z., V, 229–235); between this Pope and Raphael there was no obstacle.

Raphael had yet, it may be, to come to terms with himself, as *painter*. Here on the ceiling the colours are still not appropriate to conveying expression. In the JUDGMENT OF SOLOMON, it is true, the real mother stands out by her light, whitish-grey colouring among other characteristics, but the PUNISHMENT OF MARSYAS displays the same arbitrariness of colour as did, at an earlier date, the ENTOMBMENT; THEOLOGY, being restricted to the triple chord of her iconographic colours, red, green and white, has a thoroughly discordant chromatic effect owing to the blue tablets held by the *putti* (this is perhaps the fault of a restoration in relatively recent times); as regards this blue, one is reminded involuntarily of Maratta, but even apart from this, the colours are pleasing only where, as in the ASTRONOMY, they have become thin and pale, with grey flesh-tones. Possibly this was Raphael's intention—to keep the ceiling-pictures keyed in light tones to the gold mosaic, more vague, as it were, in between the rigid framework of the *cassette*; in any case this effect failed of attainment, and perhaps here the chromatic intentions were not yet operative which were to control the wall-paintings below, in new or revived colour-expression.

§ Sequence of the Frescoes: Painting and Themes

Scientific research in its endeavour to be critical and its sense of devotion to chronology has considered itself justified in asking which of the frescoes is the earliest. As a rule the *DISPUTA* has been placed at the beginning of the series, because of the similarity in disposition of the figures to the TRINITY OF SAN SEVERO. But the SCHOOL OF ATHENS might with equal justification be connected, on account of correspondences in figures and architecture, with the *MADONNA DEL*

BALDACCHINO. Even where art is concerned, there is a tendency to think in the categories of mediocre research; but those who suppose that one work of art can be traced back to another, are apt to forget that jumping over intervals is a sign of artistic, as of other kinds of genius. Not even in rational, scientific literature, does a book come into existence without the chapters being taken into consideration simultaneously.

In this case there was such simultaneity: the pictures are the occasion and the complement one of another. Now and then an idea that has been worked up in advance has been transferred to another wall, from the PARNASSUS to the SCHOOL OF ATHENS, or from the *DISPUTA* to the *JUSTITIA*.

In the First Stanza, when it fell to Raphael to interpret the content of the knowledge and consciousness of his time, it was a case, as it were, of a symphony in four movements which must sound as a single whole. They had therefore to be attuned to one another. This is where the painter came into play; and now he threw himself into his themes as he had shown himself capable of doing in the portraits at Florence It is marvellous how clearly he succeeded every time, in all four cases, in seizing the fundamental chord: radiance and other-wordly light, as of a transfiguration, for the *DISPUTA*; the grave, sublime, human task of Philosophy, in the tones of grey of the SCHOOL OF ATHENS; the soft, rarified air of the heights on PARNASSUS; the clarity of the judicial virtues above the flaunting red and gold of the robes and vestments on the walls of the JUSTICE.

Certainly it is not easy to-day to discover how to get at the pictorial quality, the peculiar chromatic language, of these frescoes; they have faded into the plaster. The ultramarine has coagulated and lost its limpidity, forming great disturbing patches, massive islands in the floating transparency of the remaining colours. Pious copyists have destroyed the lower parts that are within reach, by using oil-paper in the process of tracing. Added to this, there has been that plague of recent centuries, the host of restorers. Carlo Maratta may have contributed greatly with his *vino greco* and his thoroughly ordinary blue to the dissolution of the original colour-harmonies.

§ Pictorial Designs

There is only one way of knowing Raphael's original intentions, that is, from his designs! But are these drawings genuine? Scarcely a single sheet has gone unquestioned in the period of criticism since Lermolieff. The great collectors of former days, true amateurs, believed in them, for they competed for them as artists, or as laymen with an artistic training, and themselves still worked more or less in the traditional craftsman's style of the old Accademia, like the great masters with their workshop; and they found these sheets of drawings desirable possessions because they seemed to them indescribably precious as examples to be imitated; they based upon them their conception of Raphael as the great *inventor*. More recent criticism, with the irreverence of the age of Impressionism, applied as a criterion a notion alien to Raphael or even to art as a whole; works of art must be criticised, classified, dated and commented on, instead of being allowed to speak for themselves—this was its only creed. Art history as a Last Judgment! And in this judgment were classed among the damned all the precious sketches of Raphael for his compositions, especially the drawings for the *DISPUTA*. Since Lermolieff's time those of them that are washed with bistre have been attributed to Perino del Vaga, the more delicate chalk drawings to Penni or the school of Michael Angelo. It did not occur to anyone, when these sketches were under discussion, to enquire into their invention, or their wonderful poetic ideas. They make possible an infinitely more profound conception of Raphael as a poet; and since poetry and colour are in him inseparable, they afford an entirely new idea of him as a *painter*. It was worth while to enter the lists against the clever Lermolieff and his over-clever followers in defence of Raphael as an artist of deep sensibility and rich inventiveness. In so doing, one could feel oneself to be in the good company of the greatest connoisseurs, from Jabach, Mariette and Richardson, from Reynolds and Lawrence to Léon Bonnat and J. C. Robinson.

§ *Disputa* (Plates 62, 63)

The *Riconquista* has resulted in the assembly of forty-five drawings for the *DISPUTA* alone; half of them at least had really to be won back again.

Thus we have well-nigh half a hundred studies for one and the same picture; this must be considered a unique case in the history of art, and yet we may feel convinced that there were once four or even five times as many, and whole portfolios with designs belonging together must have perished. But in any case, we have enough to allow us to follow the development of the ideas in this fresco, from the first pictorial conceptions to their execution in unison with the architecture; the great pattern, of such high significance in its fixed framework, grew out of a painter's musings over phenomena of light, but the way was a long one.

"Pinxit Raphael in Vaticano cubicula duo ad Præscriptum Julii pontificis" —Raphael painted two rooms in the Vatican after the prescriptions of Pope Julius, says Giovio. . . . Here it was a matter of embracing the most comprehensive ecclesiastical and liturgical themes; in those days the abstract in corporeal shape never appeared so strange as to modern times. For this there existed, in Central Italy as in the North, on both sides of the Alps, a rigid tradition; the Spanish Chapel, the ancient chapterhouse of the Dominican monastery of Santa Maria Novella, like the Ghent altarpiece and Dürer's *ALLERHEILI-GENBILD* ("Adoration of the Trinity") provided for the devout without trouble a picture of the *Ecclesia triumphans* in a dogmatic pictorial homily—the Ghent altarpiece in the lovely mingling of ritual dignity with an animation of earthly vivacity.

ROME

§ Theme of the *Disputa*. Dante

If experienced theologians had to elucidate to the young artist the programme of his painting, if some scholar such as Thomas del Vio of the "Sapienza" referred him to Thomas Aquinas and his teaching or to Bonaventura, Raphael was able to recognise, as he listened, always with docility and certainly not with mere courtesy, that these teachings of sublime wisdom had long been familiar to him through the living doctrine of the greatest theologian he could meet with, the poet of the *Divina Commedia*. Dante's picture of Paradise had been waiting for two centuries to be given visible form by an artist in sympathy with it. The chosen artist was Raphael.

At first, the painter of the ENTOMBMENT and of the fresco of San Severo must have been oppressed by the breadth and height of the wall. Two series of twelve figures had to be distributed over it. In the ENTOMBMENT there were only ten bodies, but at that time still seven legs too many for him. In the new composition, in the tier above the ground, there are on all sides long sweeping robes which fill the space better and with greater dignity. Yet in the first well-known sketch at Windsor (Pl. 64, *R. Z.*, VI, 258), one of the washed bistre drawings, he seized on the expedient of the architectural wing; it was of course intended to be repeated on the opposite side. From this, the heavenly figures of the Trinity, and of the saints in three zones one above another, detach themselves in the clearest of heavenly light, almost incorporeally radiant; below are the earthly seekers after God, in the brightest effulgence of earth, beautifully illumined in their palpably corporeal character, in front of the distant lines of an Umbrian horizon. One can recognise the Fathers of the Church sitting at the altar and, behind them, groups passionately pressing forward, seeking, hesitating. Leonardo's ADORATION—not merely the picture but also his studies for it—must have been familiar to Raphael. What, one asks, is the solution of this riddle—in the ENTOMBMENT we still have figures visualised plastically, then the *MADONNA DEL BALDACCHINO*, and now, in this drawing, a rarified atmosphere which Titian was to be the first to render in painting in his "GLORIA"! The answer is given by the figure on the left, with the carriage of one wont to walk on clouds:

> "Con atto e voce di spedito duce
> . . . al ciel ch'è pura luce"[1]

Beatrice!

Here Raphael is no longer illustrating words, as at an earlier stage, in the ST MICHAEL. The painter poet, Dante, inspires the poet painter. The first conception, at Windsor, was carried further in the great design from the former Mariette Collection, now divided, the upper region at Oxford, the earthly groups

---

[1] "With voice and bearing of a ready guide
. . . to heaven that is pure light." (*Paradiso*, XXX 37)

at Chantilly (Plates 66, 67, *R. Z.*, VI, 259, 260); Raphael thought that in this he had found the final solution, for he divided it up into squares for transferring to a larger scale. We recognise the "tre rimoti giri", the furthest circles in the Heavenly Rose:

> "... tanto bianco
> Che nulla neve a quel termine arriva"[1]

In the study for the figure of Christ, at Lille (Plate 69, *R. Z.*, VI, 289), one is reminded of Tiepolo, so translucent is his body, so blinding the radiance in which his garments appear; the light rests on them as on a glacier-field. Here Raphael felt himself entirely indebted to Dante; the drawing at Chantilly sets the poet in the conspicuous position in the middle, almost in the same rank with the Doctors of the Church. And now the lower half takes shape, in the series of studies, almost dramatically before our eyes. From the beginning the figure of St Gregory was there, firmly established; his gaze is fixed on the Holy Ghost above the Sacrament—even in the first sketch, at Windsor, he is shown raising his countenance towards it. The next step is represented by the old Louvre copy after a lost original in which two separate drawings are combined—only feeble copies, but invaluable as evidence of the conception and for the stages of the composition (*R. Z.*, VI, 262, 263). The groups in the drawing from the Vaughan Collection in the British Museum (Plate 65, *R. Z.*, VI, 267) appear already nearly finished and draped as in the painting; their movements suggest the company in Leonardo's LAST SUPPER risen to their feet and striving to reach the Salvation in their midst; out of a lifelike picture has grown a picture *full of vitality*. A profusion of ideas amongst the kneeling figures come from Leonardo's designs for the ADORATION—and now it is the line formed by the heads, with which our painter is not yet satisfied—the stream of "viatores" of Thomas del Vio, pilgrims to the Love-feast, did not seem sufficiently devoid of interruption; he sensed as a gap the side of the marble throne of St Gregory. It was now essential that there should be rhythm in the flow of the arrangement, and rhythm demanded the whole apartment, to hold the pictures on the four walls in a relationship to one another.

In the PARNASSUS wall, division into parts was provided by the window cutting into it; the lines of the jambs are continued upward in the figures of Homer and the Muse seen from behind (Plate 73). In the SCHOOL OF ATHENS the shadows of the pilasters give the same accents in the same positions. Raphael linked up the *DISPUTA* with the other pictures by inserting here also this cæsura. Thus, in a study in the Loyd of Lockinge Collection (*R. Z.*, VI, 270), the figure of the new convert comes behind the place taken by St Gregory, whose head in its raised attitude is sketched like an antique helmet. But in

[1]"... so gleaming white
That never snow their purity attains".

this pose of astonishment he was rejected for the DISPUTA, his gesture is assigned as that of "holy dread" to the Pope in the SISTINE MADONNA. In the glorification of the Sacrament he becomes the man tardily becoming conscious of his conversion, a figure full of lofty emotion. Astonishment is more suited to the youths; the man does not alter his pose, and in his intense agitation he has a more agitating effect. Thus he now steps towards the altar. But in this case the youths have to make room for him; in the Vaughan drawing (Plate 65) they are seen scattered over the steps of the altar; now their movements become several degrees more restrained, we are witnesses to the astonishment that is just beginning to overwhelm them and has not yet quite brought them to their knees. In this there is more significance! Thus this group, now restored, is shown by the great drawing in the Albertina (*R. Z.*, VI, 273). It has unfortunately been ruined; used on the spot whilst the work was being executed, passing from hand to hand, it suffered even more when a raw hand restored the white of the high lights; the unmistakable traces of Raphael's crayon lines remained however undisturbed in the beautiful youth to the left and the priest by the altar on the right. The sheet was divided into squares, for transferring. As the composition now stood, it seemed to Raphael to be finished. Now the row of heads leads surging on towards the Sacrament. Yet there remains a gap behind the newly-converted proselyte; the eye does not pass easily from the head to the mitre. Then, in the fresco, another mitre is inserted beside this one, and the great guiding line is restored. Finally, on the extreme left, a retarding group is introduced instead of that stepping forwards, an eddy, as it were, before the breaking wave—the heretics with the portrait of Bramante.

Of the opposite side, beyond the altar, we hardly possess preliminary designs. Here very much must have been lost. But symmetry must have resulted with a certain musical necessity; the rhythmic flow and the points of emphasis must inevitably have been repeated here.

For the upper part also a great deal is missing that might have enabled us to participate in the development from that first Dante-vision, dissolved in light, to this rigidly-arched semicircle of the picture.

There are separate studies for the sacred figures at Oxford, Milan and Florence. They are carried out in chalk, with high lights in white; the white often envelopes the blackish-grey shadows so that the figures seem to float in light as if transfigured. A study for the angels (Plate 74, *R. Z.*, VI, 297, 298) on both sides of the sheet in the Malcolm Collection comprises the most charming of visions. These beings live in higher spheres—or rather, they come from thence, with unencumbered step, in flight that we can believe in, wafted through endless expanses. The middle angel gazes down from almost dizzy heights and points towards still further heights, a figure like those of Milton. Their outlines are firm and hazy, as their element; their bodies seem all light and lightness.

Raphael was then conscious of his capacity for making heavenly regions credible; his heritage from the Marches received fresh sustenance in Rome—he cannot have seen, without being moved by them, Melozzo's angels in the SS. Apostoli; he had just been awakened enough to be aware of every appeal from the beyond. When he drew the Adam for the *DISPUTA*, on the large sheet now in the Uffizi (*R. Z.*, VI, 293, 294), he made a note, on the back, of the unburdened hip and slender upper thigh of the BELVEDERE APOLLO (Plates 70, 71). It was in 1511 precisely that the statue was transferred from San Pietro in Vincoli to the Belvedere. Others, too, saw it and made drawings of it. This was the first understanding acknowledgment of it. Only Raphael was alive to the quality of *epiphany* that makes it unique among all Antique figures of divinities; the god comes from above to make his appearance in the world! The dictum of Winckelmann—"he walks as if wafted onward"—conveys an echo of this idea; he wrote it shortly before the sacred precincts were invaded by the matter-of-fact rationalism that must needs find the pathos of this figure theatrical, or misunderstood its idea and thus failed to derive exaltation through the god.

§ The Other-worldly

It came to pass that two stars met on their courses in the most memorable way. Raphael was just on the point of discovering the path to the heavenly regions when the god appeared; and to the posthumous or reborn Goth it was granted to give to his age what was given to his own by Leochares, the creator of the Apollo—the vision of the godhead descending from his realm on high. The feet of the Apollo which bear no weighty burden, and the Sixtina advancing over the clouds, are both the result of a similar revelation. There is something of this already in the rustling robes of the angels of the *DISPUTA*. One has to go back as far as Roger van der Weyden to meet with figures so unquestionably dwelling in the heights.

But if we are to understand the final aim of all such preparatory work, the composition of the *DISPUTA*, one reflection remains: it is no "dispute", it is rather an exchange of ideas, in the Italian sense, with a view to mutual understanding. The theme in view is the great unity of the Faith in heaven and earth. For the North, this mighty theme had been solved by the Ghent altarpiece; for Italy, it had been delineated by Cavallini in the great fresco of Santa Cecilia—the LOVE-FEAST, with the faithful introduced by angels stepping down on either side and, above, the Trinity between saints on their heavenly thrones. The picture has only quite lately been disclosed to view again—Raphael must have known it. Yet all this does not explain, any more than the learned programmes, or Fra Bartolommeo's heavenly semicircle, the miracle which genius here brings within the field of our experience—a painter filled with a sense of the sacredness of the liturgy being inspired by the poet of the beyond, and his sermon in light and colour acquiring from poetry *colour and light* in the true sense of the words.

The physiognomist was right in discovering in Raphael's face the "poetic painter"; otherwise Raphael would not have been so profoundly affected by the painter poet. For cases of such complimentary reaction are rare; Raphael illustrates not the word but the sense, and throws "illustrative" light on the verses, in the literal significance of the word. From individual lines of the poet, to which he was still adhering in his ST MICHAEL, he advanced to the situation in its entirety. Let us look comprehensively at the *DISPUTA*, and our most distant recollection of it will be one of light and lightness, as of Dante's Paradise.

Passing through the pronounced rigidity of the vault with its archivolts and *cassette*—an element in gaining an effect that had already been employed before Raphael by Melozzo and Signorelli—the eye suddenly comes upon movement; crossing the threshold of the framework, the gaze is met by a scene of gliding, flow, effort. The ring of clouds sinks down, in conformity with the semi-circle above; the groups open to disclose the Sacrament. All the lines of the pavement below and the segments of circles from above lead to this central feature of the picture, towards which all the figures on the ground are striving and around which all those in the heavens gravitate. All the time the Holy Sacrament, like a magnet, attracts the gaze. In the drawings we witness the gradual progressive architectural restraint of what, to begin with, was an unconfined roaming in light-filled space. But even now, in the final solution in the fresco, the best remained of that first vision, derived from Dante—the sense of lightness in the heavenly sphere, inseparable from light. The draughtsman has at last taught us to understand the painter, independently of all the injuries that have defaced his work. It was the painter who gave to each wall in this room its chromatic and linear pattern as a significant decoration.

§ School of Athens (Plate 72)

We need only transfer our gaze from this vision of light to the SCHOOL OF ATHENS, which is placed opposite to this revelation of the divine, as the supreme revelation of the mind of man. As in a Gothic altarpiece the side exposed to view on ordinary days with its grey colouring seems to contain a promise of the interior, whilst the side reserved for festival days displays gold and colour in fulfilment of this promise, so the radiant glorification of the Sacrament is placed opposite to the grey tones of Philosophy. All that gives, in the *DISPUTA*, an effect of oscillation and suspense is, in the SCHOOL OF ATHENS, at rest; a stratum of heads and figures appears like smoke above the ground. Thus the painter strikes his chords: in the *DISPUTA* a uniform movement is dominant, here we have a throng of disputants, even though there is no lack of clarity, for the ideas are full of sublimity that are being explored and discovered beneath this proudly soaring vault. And they are sublime figures that have been built up on such conceptions; in their bearing they resemble noble vessels to hold the noble content of their ideas. It is Dante's "filosofica familia" of the wise, in the *Inferno* (IV, 131), that here streams over the tilework steps:

RAPHAEL

"Vidi il maestro de color chi sanno
Seder tra filosofica familia
Tutti l'amiran, tutti onor gli fanno . . ."[1]

They form themselves into groups, gather in clusters, exploring, discussing, construing, writing. But suddenly, in the midst of all the throng, one group becomes clearly dominant to the eye. They line up, where a space opens down to the ground in front of the sublime pair that come stepping forward out of the recess, attending only to one another and both full of the loftiest ideas, Plato and Aristotle.

Here also it has been asked to whom Raphael was indebted for the scheme. Yet whoever this may be, Raphael's achievement in giving pictorial form to philosophy could only have been the result of a culture innate and developed. From childhood up, he was a familiar figure in the Ducal Palace at Urbino, and to Italians of the Renaissance such as he, these great philosophers signified not authors of books but creators of a way of living. Thus everything that furthered *humanistic* cultivation of life, which then meant cultivation with a view to the dignity of man, was here consummated in this pair of figures as they went on their way unimpeded beneath the lofty vaults of the hall.

Plato, we read in the *Farbenlehre* (II Abt. "Ueberliefertes")—"Plato directs his movements towards the heights, in his yearning to participate once more in the origin from which he sprang. Aristotle on the other hand stands facing the world like a man, and a man who is an architect. At the moment he is here, and this is to be the scene of his creative activity." In him we see the perfect *cortegiano*. They step forward, seen against the background of the great open arch; everything leads the eye towards them—the lines of the pavement, the cornices of the vault, the gaze of the disciples, just as in the LAST SUPPER Christ, in front of the window, draws every line towards himself. Clear above all the seekers stand out these two discoverers of what can make men noble and good, that is, fit to be exemplars and dignified in their attitude towards life. No learned adviser could have communicated to Raphael the inspiration for the sweeping stride of Plato and his heavenward gesture, nor for the bearing of Aristotle, to whom belong life and earth, free and bold and noble-minded, and yet mindful of the appearance he presents. Let us ask ourselves what this hand signifies—no seizing of what is earthly, but rather the gesture of the conductor of an orchestra when as "master" he checks the swell of a crescendo—"*halt Mass*", "keep within compass", the favourite motto of Renaissance man and so even of its "architects". There he stands, body and mind in equilibrium, even to his garments, the masculine ideal of those times, ancestor of many a later

[1]"The master I beheld of those who know
Seated amid the philosophic band;
All do him honour, on him with wonder gaze."

86

type in life and art. Hence comes the *galantuomo italianizzato*, the "italianised gentleman"; but hence also is derived the man, insufferably "beautiful" because lacking in contrast, who, since the Counter-reformation and especially in the nineteenth century, again and again makes his appearance in religious art as saint and hero, and for whom it was reserved to disseminate in art also the emptiness of ideas prevalent in matters of religion.

Simultaneously with the vital rhythm of these figures there arose before Raphael's eyes a housing worthy of them, the scene of their existence; here he became the consummate architect, even if the design of the hall was to be traced back to Bramante's ideas for San Pietro. But here we have certainly no church interior; when measured literally it is only five times the height of a man. It may rather be thought of as the platform in front of a hall, the true Renaissance stage! Its façade is dominated by the groups with their inherent rhythms; they are vitally and inseparably interrelated, whether human figures or architectural members; they form flanking wings and a projection in the middle. This interpenetration of figures and building was certainly carefully worked out in advance. The cartoon in the Ambrosiana already shows that this is so. Indeed, how could such wisdom in the achievement of effect have been attained otherwise than by long reflection and intelligent thinking-out? Unfortunately we have no single study for the whole composition, as in the case of the *DISPUTA*, and only a few studies of details have come down to us. The greater part must have been destroyed.

§ Cartoon

The cartoon tells us little of the preliminary work (Plates 75—77). The mighty figure of Democritus is lacking; as one peculiarly marked out to be the prey of the devotee it has been cut out. It is impossible that here, in this stage of the composition, it should "still" have been lacking; without it the whole hangs in the air.

We recognise from the cartoon, as from the principles of the composition, that Raphael must at that time have been very near to Leonardo. For the very reason that they have been used and effaced, cartoons always appear "smoky", and therefore like one another. But the Pythagoras group in the left foreground was actually introduced direct from Leonardo's ADORATION into the first sketches for the *DISPUTA*, and from these it was adopted here amongst the philosophers. The softness of the modelling no less than the motive recalls the master of "*sfumato*"; yet this impress of the older prototype must not be allowed to distract us from the entirely new and personal element in Raphael's art, or from his complete mastery of the inspired figure. An immense range covering all grades from good breeding to the heroic was at his disposal, according to the role filled by them; thus beside the dignified scepticism of Zoroaster we have the young, kingly Ptolemy (Plate 77) with the gait and the lithe, turning movement of a noble animal, like a roebuck seeking cover. The decisive and determining element however is the union of all the persons in the group in a single sublime sentiment! To this group the young master felt himself to belong (Plate 285); on the right, he joins in with the school of astrologers, full of understanding for their knowledge of the spirits that rule over the life of men from their birth onwards, and, with the others, linked up in the fixed terrestrial system of measure in thought and structure.

§ Parnassus (Plates 73, 82, 83)

How airy by comparison, how free and imaginative, is the movement of the figures and groups in the pattern of the PARNASSUS around the window, which provides an area in the shape of a horseshoe for the decoration to fill between the window-frame and the arch. Idle talk about the unfavourableness of the space on this wall originated in the period in which art withdrew further away from life and was therefore regarded as "difficult". For the old masters there was only *one* circumstance favourable to their tasks—the opportunities afforded under given conditions for their powers to be brought into play, as in a marked-out arena. This was the view of the situation taken here, and thus it was apprehended. The top of the window provided a kind of podium out of which Mount Parnassus was formed. This was imitated by disciples in later times in an infinitely tedious manner, and Nazarenes working on Roman soil repeated it with even greater affectation. But as a dramatic painter Raphael never confines himself to the filling of the space; for him the mountain is not only the seat of the god, or the stage for a living picture; this rather is how he sees it—the mount, the spring, the laurel grove draw the poets on, and they surge, in an unconstrained, lovely troop, across the slopes through the soft air and the gentle wind that "blows from the blue heavens". The tones of Apollo's viol resound, constraining the others to linger in silence and with halting step. Only Homer sings, and behind him Dante follows Virgil, his poet and guide—"tu duca tu poeta"! Pacing forward, with the beloved book, he is rendered in a drawing at Windsor Castle (Plate 78, *R. Z.*, V, 247). The figure without the head is just comparable with the full-length portrait of Ghirlandajo in the intarsia door by Benedetto da Majano for the Sala del Giglio in the Palazzo Vecchio; in making such a comparison we shall be profoundly aware of the points to be noticed in the juxtaposition of Quattrocento and Cinquecento, of High and Early Renaissance; then the "Classical Art" of the High Renaissance will not seem so out-of-date as it often appears in the books of its opponents and its champions. The poets were in good hands with this poet painter, who so beautifully "dismissed them wreath-crowned thence", and the lovely Sisters never received more graceful homage than here. In assigning to them, under the impulse of his earliest enthusiasm for Rome, motives derived from the Antique sculpture, which seemed to have been retrieved from the rubbish-heap specially for him, he felt he was bestowing on them a character, refreshed by the Castalian spring and aflame with divine fire, peculiarly appropriate to Parnassus. Euterpe, on the left of Apollo, shows the pose of the thighs and the drapery of the so-called CLEOPATRA, the ARIADNE of the Vatican; the Muse on the left, sitting up, came from the sarcophagus with Achilles in Scyros, from which also are derived the sisters leaning against one another (Plates 80, 81). Melpomene, swaying to the tones of the viol, comes nearest to the Antique; it is precisely she who is a quite personal invention of Raphael's own (Plate 79, R. Z., V, 249); originally she was turning back her face, as seen in the precious drawing at Oxford—as Tragedy looking towards Mythology. Then the profile view in this group remained reserved for the head of Dante.

It was not without effort that Raphael overcame the danger of producing an assemblage of beautiful motives. Marcantonio's engraving of course hands down to us only an approximate reproduction of an earlier stage; the powerful rhythmic accent given by the Muse on the right, as a *pendant* to the figure of Homer, is still lacking. The copy of a workshop drawing with nude figures, at Oxford, shows the composition essentially complete (R. Z., VI, p. 259). On the right we still have the man standing with his arms pointing towards the middle, as in Marcantonio's version; for this figure there was already a finished nude study, now in the British Museum (R. Z., V, 238, 240). Finally came the figures of Sappho and of the aged poet, like volutes beside the window, fitting in to the great, arresting pattern, truly Muse-inspired character in its grace, which Heinrich Bruhn found comparable with Antique acanthus-scrolls.

The PARNASSUS was perhaps the composition which, in the fluctuations of the designs for all four walls, was first the subject of a final draft. It retains the most rigid arrangement, the most Umbrian in character, with much of the precision of the ENTOMBMENT, but perhaps also owes its peculiar compactness as a pattern to its format. It is possibly here that Raphael first invented that great rhythmic accent pervading all the walls, when he took up into the composition the lines of the window-jambs; Homer and the standing Muse form in a measure the borders of the central projection, from which the wings jut forward right and left.

As regards colouring, the free and lightly swaying composition is, in its present condition, at first sight disappointing, with its many moribund patches of opaque blue in the draperies; and yet, in some portions, as in the figure of Dante backed by silvery atmosphere, in the matt-grey mantle, we feel we can still trace the effect once intended to be produced by these regions filled with divinities and spirits of genius. Chromatically however, something of the perplexity of the ENTOMBMENT seems to have prevailed even from the beginning; heavy tones such as the bronze-coloured drapery of the Muse seen from behind and the blue cloak drawn over yellow of the Homer, must even from the outset have been out of keeping with the brightness of the fresco tones, which however had still not been taken full advantage of, as on the other walls, and which required more frequent retouching in tempera.

The numerous detailed studies in Lille and London show the dominant note of light and mellowness that was intended. All are still executed as usual with the pen in bistre, as they had been in his Umbrian and Florentine periods; likewise in the Gothic and Umbrian manner, garments, hands, feet and heads in particular are rendered with studied care, copied from the model or from actual draperies with such exactness as to give rise to the idea that they betray the carefulness of one who in his inexperience is determined, in his new monumental creations, to proceed with absolute security (Plates 78, 79, 88, *R. Z.*, V, 239–253). All have in common a delicate light carried right in to the half-shadows, with a light strip along the ridges between the folds of the draperies. When transposed into fresco-painting, this could not but produce a softness of light in the lime-wash which would have been very appropriate to figures moving, remote from earth, in this transfigured sphere. In the words of Gluck's Orpheus: "How clear the heavens that overspan this place."

§ Raphael's Many-sidedness

Up to this point the ceiling has given us the impression of a ceaseless ferment of creativeness, alike in the preliminary studies and in the painting—it is all the same thing. What versatility the artist shows merely as draughtsman, as we pass from figure to figure—for the PARNASSUS, light pen-studies, for the SCHOOL OF ATHENS, fully detailed silverpoint drawings with a pink ground, and then, the boldness and softness of the charcoal drawing in the cartoon; in the case of the *DISPUTA*, the unearthly brightness of the high lights washed in with the brush in white, the studies in a mixture of chalk and white body-colour for the celestial hemicycle, pen and charcoal for the earthly groups—everything in its expressiveness allows of conclusions as to the original intention of the *painter* on the walls.

§ Justitia

The theme of the *JUSTITIA* has not, for its exponents, like the other Faculties, God-possessed spirits or soaring seekers after truth and interpreters of life. The painter had recourse to allegory and representation, and thus achieved sublimeness and dignity here also.

A pattern of the utmost freedom fills a flat upper segment above the window, with the Judicial Virtues; the unequal narrow portions to right and left remained for historical state documents, the foundation of ecclesiastical and civil law—the Pandects and Decretals.

In the allegorical painting, the pattern of the PARNASSUS was raised to a degree of airy freedom. There is a play of lines and gestures, advancing and receding, in an even rhythm throughout the lunette; one might compare it to a melody for two voices. These figures impersonating abstract conceptions move in a new, ultimate freedom. Here we have the Roman woman with her full figure and the noble suppleness of her limbs. There is no need to recall even, unless it be to forget it again, Vasari's account of Raphael's secret visit to the still-closed Sistine Chapel to see Michael Angelo's ceiling frescoes, then just completed. There is a Roman quality in the marvellously healthful and unconstrained pose of the PRUDENTIA, sitting in the middle, with the Janus head. The TEMPERANTIA perhaps shows us for the first time the features of the Fornarina; she makes even the restraining bridle a thing of loveliness, just as she seems rather to dance than to be sitting. The FORTITUDO, robust, with the branch of an oak-tree, "the Rovere badge ever with beauty fraught", was surely the favourite figure with the *Papa Terribile* (Plate 275). Through her the *virago* finds expression, a feminine ideal of the High Renaissance. This ideal, intellectually realised, was known to Italian history at that time in many a great lady such as Caterina Sforza. The type was given shape by Ariosto in the *Orlando Furioso*. This figure should always be called to mind in reading the verses about Bradamante and Angelica, and between Ariosto's lines will be met the figure of Raphael's warlike virgin. The poet himself was to be found not far away from this spot; Raphael has a place for him on Parnassus—the figure to the right with his finger to his lips shows the intelligent, bold sweep of profile perpetuated by Titian some five and twenty years later (Plates 83, 280, 281). As ambassador and in the train of Alfonso of Ferrara the poet must have met Raphael. His precipitous flight from Rome with the Duke as "nobile mascherato", before the threats of the Pope, engrossed men's minds; even here a secret seems to hover over the figure.

§ Allegory

It is too easy to forget the *painter* in seeking the *inventor* of the themes; at this point least of all are they to be disconnected. The frescoes of this wall have suffered in the lower part through the dampness of the lime-wash, as in the case of the JUSTINIAN, or through restoration, as in the DECRETALS subject. The lunette with the JUDICIAL VIRTUES (Plates 84, 86) has been entirely preserved owing to the fact that its situation kept it from the hands of restorers; it is radiant in the original brilliance of its matured painting. There is the brightness of sunshine in the reflections on the draperies spread over the stone-grey plinth, and with it, a serene background of sky with silvery clouds; Fortitude in cherry red with soft violet-grey lights, Prudence (Plate 85), old-gold, white and light-green, light-green also the sleeves of Temperance, with a whitish-grey sheen on her pink and greenish-grey robe. Every colour is broken up into unison with the stone grey, but the flesh-colour, kept light and shaded with grey, of the *putti* plays through all as the most lively of the tones; the grace of their figures is wonderfully attuned to this tone of silver. We ought not to attempt to make of Raphael a Paul

Veronese, but neither ought the latter painter to be ranked as an abstract draughtsman, far from it. Andrea del Sarto himself did not at that time create anything comparable in fresco. His contemporaneous ARRIVAL OF THE THREE KINGS, in the Annunziata, has an effect of arbitrary colouring without being rich—it seems almost garish and over sweet; his *MADONNA DEL SACCO*, not unlike this fresco, was not painted till 1525 and is thus half a generation later in date.

The allegory was once intended to have an effect in combination with the other paintings; this is why the treble here soars in golden yellow from the blonde head of the *putto* on the left, by way of the shoulderpiece on the cuirass of the Fortitudo, to the curls of the little clambering boy, the wings in orange mixed with white of the child holding the mirror, the sleeves of Prudentia and the whitish-green lemon-yellow of her bust, from the torch and its bearer to the orange in the veil of Temperantia and in the curly head of the *putto* on the right. Below could be seen the Emperor, all in gold, and the pluvial of the Pope in the midst of the purple gowns; amid all this stood the throne of the Apostolic Justiciary when, once a month, he presided over the supreme chamber, that is, the *Segnatura delle Grazie*, with above their heads, the three JUDICIAL VIRTUES.

§ The Decretals

The fresco of the PRESENTATION OF THE DECRETALS shows against the grey, richly-shaded background of the architectural niche above green and grey floor-tiles, the red tones, mixed with grey, of the watered silk of the Cardinals, Camerlenghi and notaries; amidst them, the Pope in white-and-gold tiara and pluvial with much gold upon it. Unfortunately the blue of the brocade pattern, with oaktrees and insignia, originally doubtless the soft ultramarine that has remained out of sight in the shadow to the right, as in the cuirass of the Fortitudo, has been transformed into a blue of an atrocious dead, milky tone. The picture in its former splendour must have been one of the utmost sumptuousness, a perfect ceremonial picture, for the first time after a lapse of two hundred years. Probably it has its source in one or other of the dedicatory illustrations from the Vatican Library. Four Popes have been counted in it; by the right side of the enthroned figure the young Cardinal Giovanni de' Medici, then still Camerlengo, scarcely two years later the successor of the great Julius; on his left, Cardinal Farnese, twenty years later Paul III, a generation afterwards immortalised with his long white beard by the hand of Titian. Standing at the left border is supposed to be Cardinal del Monte, but it is Cardinal Antonio del Monte, rather than Giovanni Maria, the one-time Pope Julius III, whose villa outside the Porta del Popolo shows the Renaissance as brought to its zenith by Raphael. The master here introduces the series of those to come, as in Banquo's mirror. Unfortunately there are serious injuries just where the Pope's head comes, and this was doubtless the last portion of the paintings in the Stanza to be executed. Julius wished to see himself painted with the beard which, to the horror of Court and clergy, he had allowed to grow—in accordance with a vow such as we read of in the Old Testament—when Bologna seceded. This action appeared sufficiently important; the Ambassador of Ferrara reported it in July, 1512, to Alfonso I. We must take, instead of the ruined features, Raphael's portrait study at Chatsworth (Plate 90, *R. Z.*, V, 257). It is drawn with the same breadth as the heads in the cartoon for the SCHOOL OF ATHENS, in a grand, sweeping manner like the Zoroaster (*R. Z.*, VII, 343, 344), for Raphael had now become the fresco-painter in the truest sense, and with red chalk in hand he thought *al fresco*, and on broad lines also, because the Pope was not in the habit of taking much time or leisure for sitting still. In spite of all that complacent or petty-minded doubters may say, the mark of genuineness is set—or enthroned—on this forehead, with its rock-like structure, and around the eyes with their bushy brows there lurks something of the vital character of a heroic landscape—steeps and chasms overhung by storm-beaten trees. This study from life probably served for the PORTRAIT OF THE POPE painted for his favourite church, the shrine of the Rovere family, Santa Maria del Popolo. The attitude given him by Raphael has been supposed to signify a moment of dejection or repose; it does not seem to be exactly characteristic of this volcanic life. Weakness is the one quality that should not have been attributed to him, as by the Orsini, when they proclaimed the Republic from the Capitol as he lay sick. For this attitude still has in it the capability of a menacing outburst; in a word, when we see the action in the hand, the Jove-like form and expression of the brow, as of a ruler over wide dominions, the deep-set eyes, we can believe him capable of springing up and pushing his chair far back in his impatience. What his contemporaries called *terribiltà* flashes and rumbles like thunder from this similitude of his *physical* form as forcibly as from his *spiritual* portrait, the Moses of Michael Angelo, on his monument.

Unfortunately, we are by no means certain as to the original of this majestic interpretation of a dæmonic nature. Among the extant versions, that in the Pitti Palace deserves the prize as the most fiery; but it is certainly none other than the copy painted by Titian for the Duke of Urbino as *pendant* to his restored portrait of the other Rovere Pope, Sixtus IV. In the case of the Uffizi picture, the pedigree seems to be better than the state of preservation. It is hidden beneath such a thick coat of varnish and restorations that in the absence of any trace of "handwriting", belief in it is more difficult than doubt. It is remarkable that the example in London, at the National Gallery (Plate 91), presents a feature, not shown by either of the Florentine pictures, that may have been added by a copyist; at the second button of the *mozzetta*, the red tippet, hairs of the fur trimming show through. Without drawing too favourable conclusions from the circumstance, we shall find here much else that has more the effect of Raphael than in the Uffizi picture, in its present condition.

RAPHAEL

Raphael had come from Florence to Rome as a good portrait-painter, fully formed as regards conception and colour; he now takes his place among the rare historical portraitists. There are not many of them, however numerous the portraits that have come down to us. This is a distinction only to be attained by a great narrator, for to become a great narrator is within the power only of those who understand how to concentrate on what is most essential, and therefore how to show forth and enhance what gives vitality to the action. In this succession, Roger van der Weyden was followed first by Raphael and by Holbein also, then unquestionably by Titian.

Raphael attained this concentrated power as the fresco-painter of Julius II. The great subject and the great scale, the task in itself and the pulsing vitality of the Pope, the breadth and speed of the required technique, all contributed to develop in a few years to the utmost degree of freedom and power the inborn gifts of the narrator in paint.

The pontificate of Julius II was Raphael's time of destiny also. The spectacle, and even more, the impetus of this mighty life made of him the great historical painter of the Second Stanza.

VII

RAPHAEL AS DRAMATIC PAINTER

"In everything, a bold attack, a good grip, are essential to mastery."
GOETHE. Letter to Herder, July, 1772.

WITH the Second Stanza the "poetic painter" entered on the domain of the dramatist. We are fully conscious that, even as the pupil of Perugino and as the mature master of the First Stanza, his paintings, his delineations of men, groups and situations, have the vital, compelling force of poetry, not dwelling on mere imitation of life but penetrating into the depths of existence so as to interpret it to us out of those depths. The mere ability to dramatise the dogmatic theme of the DISPUTA, or the abstraction of the SCHOOL OF ATHENS, or the humanistic vision of the PARNASSUS, would inevitably cause one endowed with it to feel in himself—even if unconsciously—the impulse to be a dramatist.

What is the justification for calling the painter a dramatist? The dramatist is recognised by a peculiar manner in narrating events; for not everyone who has to paint an occurrence has a claim to this name. Ghirlandajo does not rise above mere gossip; Gozzoli is never more than an illustrator. They divert, instead of holding the attention. Where are we to find the criterion? Shakespeare and Mozart in modern times provide us with examples of the classic drama—drama, that is, that carries one away. Invention in an unceasing stream, the tense situation perpetually renewed, the capacity of raising the elements of a plot to such a pitch of intensity that the spectator, whether in the literal or a metaphorical sense of the word, goes away with the feeling of a profound personal experience, and participation in the character and destiny of the hero is stamped indelibly in his consciousness—all this lies within the power of the dramatist; his name comes from the Greek word for doing, for action and occurrence. It has been defined by a Roman: "quidquid in medium profertur ad animos commovendos." This rapt absorption in temporal occurrences was known to Gothic art in forms as yet unsurpassed—in Giovanni Pisano and Giotto; in the early Renaissance it was possessed again only by the great pioneers, Masaccio and Donatello. With them it seemed to die away; Ghirlandajo marks the nadir of this decline. In Botticelli a trace of it occasionally peeps out. Raphael brings it with him, as something to be taken for granted, from Melozzo and Signorelli, and in his mastery of the dramatic he coincides with Leonardo and Michael Angelo. We have seen in the First Stanza, from the ceiling to the walls, his capability of irradiating with action the scene within the frame, in every frame. He understands how to introduce, even into the great assemblies of elect spirits, an animation, in which whatever unites them and brings them into relation with one another and with a purpose, has the power of kindling in us, from the moment in which we set eyes on the paintings, a sense as of something taking place by an inward necessity. The eye is compelled to return again and again to this action, guided by the lighting, the landscape or the architecture, of which the lines seem to participate in the movement. Human figures and space, and therefore light and colour, were also compelled by the painter to subserve in equal measure this vital purpose.

§ Assumption of the Virgin. Plan for the Resurrection

Even while at work on the First Stanza, he was occupied, beyond the original limits of the theme, by the dramatic conception of his subject, a subject which perhaps derived its first inspiration from himself. The commission of the nuns of Sant' Antonio for the CORONATION OF THE VIRGIN accompanied him from Perugia to Florence and from there to Rome. He seems to have transformed the theme into a GLORIFICATION (Plate 94) when he conceived the Apostles as standing round the empty sarcophagus; their amazement, and the Coronation, beyond their range of vision, would have provided two separate scenes, as in his youthful works. Instead, when he pondered over the Theology among clouds, like the transfigured Beatrice, in the Oxford drawing (Plate 92), he conceived the notion of the Virgin wafted away whilst the Apostles remained behind, bound to earth below. And this idea accompanied him through the heavenly region of the *DISPUTA* and was revived, in new vigour, when he came across the Belvedere Apollo. In the guise of the RESURRECTION OF CHRIST (Plate 95) this motive of a serene manifestation on high, that is, in light above the confusion on earth, occupied him when he passed on to the Second Stanza (*R.Z.*, VIII, 381–392). We do not know of any such commission, but to judge from the sketches and studies of detail, it must have existed if it was worked out to such an extent. With Raphael there were at that time certainly no uncommissioned works.[1]

At the head of the series, as a first tremendous project, stands the great pen-drawing from the Lawrence Collection (Plate 97). Modern expert criticism declined to accept it as genuine, and so the portrait-painter Léon Bonnat, as a fine connoisseur of organic construction, was able to acquire it. In the invention which creates for itself the "handwriting" he found the stamp of originality, and thus he collected the precious sketches belonging to Raphael's most fertile period which are to-day at Bayonne.

The Risen Christ soars from the tomb with the winged step of the Apollo, and blesses the earth while he leaves it. The brightness of his realm finishes upwards

[1] *Jahrbuch der preussischen Kunstsammlungen*, 1925, p. 191.

in a semicircle with the nimbus that surrounds him. Angels like a living glory round about him prepare with ecstasy a pathway through the clouds. Thus a circular form is cast in the mould of the frame; it can still be made out, indicated in lead pencil. The guards below start back from the sarcophagus as if in an explosion; the light from the angel of the Lord floods over them, striking terror into them and blinding them completely. Two drawings, full of temperament, for this scene of confusion on earth, are preserved at Oxford (Plates 93, 95)—in one the angel on the sarcophagus in a blaze of glory and the guards parting asunder; the other has the effect of a second solution for the lower portion. We seem to trace, in the flow of all the movements, even to the pen-strokes, the proximity of Leonardo, who appeared in Rome from time to time in the years 1513–15. The second sheet, with studies for the right lower corner, is even more reminiscent of him; in this the composition was already rounded off in the figures to correspond with the upper semicircle—the Northern Late Gothic rule for composition of pattern. Roger van der Weyden had adhered to this principle as an unfailing means of dramatic effect, and it was respected by Raphael, as a reborn Gothicist, right on to the period of the TRANSFIGURATION, whenever it was a question of embracing actions taking place in widely separated spheres. This had indeed become a vital principle in his art.

From the tangled throng of figures one can make out a falling Roman soldier, overthrown by the same blast against which a standard-bearer is struggling to hold fast the staff of the wildly flaunting banner. The collapsing figure is drawn a second time on a larger scale, and his contorted grimace separately alongside. In the middle, the standard-bearer is repeated more distinctly, standing. The motive of this figure becomes clearer from an engraving by Marcantonio after a nude study for it, which was often copied; it was introduced in Titian's TRIONFO DELLA FEDE as St Christopher, and in a drawing in the Louvre in the manner of Della Bella or Guercino we actually find the date 1513 in old numerals, very well authenticated.

To the left below are two angels out of the uppermost region sketched in the most cursory manner, but their gaze, full of wonder, into the depths beneath them is distinct; they appear to be scattered in the light like puffs of shrapnel— a painter's drawing! In the upper part of the sheet are figures hit by the blast, falling over or starting back. In the violence of the conceits the artistic "hand-writing" observes none of the rules of modern criticism; in some of them, which are drawn in angular blocks, one would be compelled, according to current notions, to "guess" at Cambiaso.

For most of these figures there are finished nude studies at Oxford, Windsor Castle and Chatsworth, and in London (R. Ž., VIII); none of these drawings has been accepted without question: many of them have been attributed to the School of Michael Angelo. Some in fact, show an uninteresting elaboration of finish which may perhaps be explained as due to another hand working over the original with the intention of making it more clear. It may be that Raffaelle dal Colle had a share in it; he used these figures, with all the life taken out of them, in San Sepolcro, for his patchwork composition of the RESURRECTION. Raphael himself gave up this idea; but the other-worldly character of such a phenomenon of lighting, and the radiance cast by it over mortal beings, survive in the TRANSFIGURATION. The earthly, human motives of terror and collapse are transferred to the stirring pictures of the Second Stanza—the HELIODORUS and the ATTILA and to the cartoon with the PUNISHMENT OF ANANIAS—and finally to the RESURRECTION in the second series of Vatican tapestries.

§ The Second Stanza as a Victory Memorial of Julius II

From such ideas during Raphael's earliest years in Rome we recognise the rhythms in which his imagination moved, and what forces were released by the commission of the Pope when he set him to portray on the walls of the Second Stanza the memorable changes of fortune in his own life—pictures of those wonderful deliverances in which Heaven revealed itself to the Faithful for their beliefs.

Thus the apartment of Julius was conceived as a memorial of victory. This Pope could discover in his own personal activities nothing but a strife in defence of the Church. In his own victory he saw the triumph of the Faith. He is counted as the founder of the States of the Church, and the world of that age held that the establishment of the States of the Church was a glorious undertaking; it was considered even to be a religious act; everything that the Pope undertook served this idea alone. His artists—Michael Angelo, Bramante and Raphael—felt themselves—unconsciously—to be fired by a spirit like his. The physical and moral impetus of his policy had told with full effectiveness upon their spiritual world. From the great perils and successes of this mighty Shepherd of the Peoples they learned how to recognise the heroic life in the real world, and how to understand the great past. His dæmonic fire communicated itself to them; the MOSES and the Heliodorus frescoes became in some degree *the royal dramas of the Italian people.*

§ Historical Painting

Historical pictures in the highest sense—histories! This means something more than record, or narrative and illustration. It is a question of interpreting a historical occurrence, and emphasising its importance for present and future in a loftier human sense. The Greeks discovered for this their type of symbolic art; in the Temple of Aphæa at Aegina the combats of their forefathers with the Trojans under divine protection stood for the victory of Salamis. On the altar of Pergamum the overcoming of the barbarian Galatians by the Attalids is celebrated as a victory of ordered, over uncontrolled, forces under the figure of the combat of the Gods with the Giants.

Thus the victories of Julius II are here immortalised by him as those of the Church. The Godhead himself participates to protect those who believe. In this the Pope combined pride and piety in his mental attitude no less than the Ancients; this also is characteristic of the Rebirth—the Middle Ages knows only humility, not this self-consciousness coupled with proud humility.

The Rovere Pope had driven the Venetians out of the possessions of the Church; this recalled to him the punishment that overtook the Temple-robber Heliodorus. Apostate priests, his own Cardinals, had dared to call together a council, that "conciliabulo" held at Pisa, and had attempted to depose him; the doubting priest in the MASS OF BOLSENA was a telling hit at them. The Pope was rescued at Bologna from imminent danger and threatening imprisonment as if by a miracle; he had offered up his thanks for this to his patron saint in his own former titular church of San Pietro in Vincoli; he saw himself again in the miraculous deliverance of St Peter from chains and the Mamertine Prison. The threatened incursion of the Northern sovereigns into Italy was frustrated; in the same manner the flood of Attila's destroying hosts was brought to a standstill by the Princes of the Apostles; this illustrates the papal battle-cry "fuori i barbari"! The ceiling-paintings provide titles, as it were; all have a basic theme in common—the intervention of the Divine power. Above the HELIO-DORUS, the Almighty appears in the burning bush to Moses, Jacob's dream of the ladder to Heaven is above the DELIVERANCE OF ST PETER, Abraham's offering above the Sacrifice of the MASS OF BOLSENA, God's message to Noah above the Princes of the Apostles dispelling the forces of Attila.

§ Ceiling-pictures as Tapestries

For these ceiling-pictures Raphael chose the form of trapeze-shaped tapestries; they have the appearance of velaria stretched on the somewhat paltry grey framework of Peruzzi which Raphael had spared from destruction. For more than a generation no one has had anything good to say about them, and they have been assigned to very mediocre artists. But it seems as if modern criticism is more ready to call in pupils than the master was himself. For when he began to paint the Second Stanza—and naturally he had to begin with the ceiling—Raphael's consciousness was absolutely taken up with invention and execution. The ferment still continues to work in him, and invention takes a hand again and again in a most amazing way—how splendidly, can be seen in the picture in which the Almighty appears to Noah. We need only call to mind the words in the Bible to which this vision of his relates: "Then . . . be fruitful and multiply upon earth" (*Gen.* VIII, 15–17). God, unapproachable, above all that is earthly, benevolent and commanding, sweeping out of the Infinite towards this little product of human workmanship and this group of dwellers on earth; Noah simply carried away, in a transport, from the seam of his robe to his finger-tips (Plate 100). The objection is obvious that little of this

99

is to be seen; the fresco colours have decayed, even the drawing has suffered. But the principal consideration is, what still remains effective. Here it is as with a good actor—his body is all mime, and Raphael knows only actors of this quality, like this patriarch Noah and this motherly woman, who has enough to bear, and now has to bestir herself with bringing out of the Ark her self-willed second boy, who *will* stay behind amongst the animals. In the OFFERING OF ABRAHAM there is, about father and son, something of the greatness of the Laocöon; the angels sweep down out of the beyond—one of them as if it were a case of holding up a bolting horse; the other swoops to earth with the ram, in an airy *contraposto* which is quite new in its audacity. The sketches for the ASSUMPTION gave opportunity of testing such ideas as these; they are echoed again and again—in the SIBYLS and in the completion of the *MADONNA DEL BALDACCHINO*; the complementary rhythms of the angels on the wings of the wind, in the BURNING BUSH (Plate 101), with their ethereally convulsive movements, also took shape for the first time in these drawings.

The prototype of the sleeping JACOB AT THE FOOT OF THE LADDER TO HEAVEN might perhaps be looked for among Michael Angelo's Ancestors of Christ, but in vain; it is rather the style of the Pope that was here the common element.

§ Condition of the Frescoes: Original Colouring

Unfavourable criticisms could not be made independently of the bad state of preservation of these frescoes. The surface has parted in exactly the same manner as the wall with the JUSTICE in the First Stanza. It may be that in both cases a new composition of the lime coating was tried which proved disastrous to the pictures, at least to the shadows. In addition to this there is the hideous blue ground that a restorer at some time or other has painted round the figures, venturing in so doing to impinge on Raphael's contours—a veritable *crimen laesae majestatis*. The effect here intended was that of fabrics hung like velaria, here allowing the vaulting to be easily seen. This is shown even by the choice of colours; in the BURNING BUSH, violet-grey, olive, and reseda-colour heightened with gold stood out, against the original soft ultramarine of the background, on the draperies of the Almighty and Moses, on the wings of the angels, and the ground. In the OFFERING OF ISAAC the shadows on the figures are of a golden hue, the garments and the flames on the altar are gold-orange, the wings reddish-gold, the ram yellowish-gold; there are also violet and reddish grey and matt blue in the draperies. These colours of course harmonised with the old, soft ultramarine, though they do not with the new blue.

In the picture of the ALMIGHTY APPEARING TO NOAH the old colour-values can still be recognised, in spite of the fading of the shadows; the ark, in golden ochre-yellow, is a magnificent foil for the violet, grey-green and matt blue of the figures.

In Jacob's Dream there is much matt green, purple broken up with grey, heightened to red in the angels, the Almighty in purplish grey against gold.

Everywhere there was the same soft blue ground, not obtruding itself but rather maintaining that pleasant balance in the colouring which belongs to outspread tapestries. To-day the figures have the effect of being cut out and stuck on, owing to the surrounding heavy blue and the loss of vitality in the contours—the only reason, in fact, for thinking of Peruzzi as their creator.

Raphael brings into play with absolute freedom the Grand Style of figure-painting, pictorial composition on every scale, and the idea of a ceiling-filling of an original kind; indeed, as the figure of the Almighty in the Burning Bush still proves, he made experiments even with a new kind of tapestry: all the colours from the broken grey, shot violet and matt purple, lead up to the fiery gold and red with which he brings out the miraculous nature of the occurrence. Here we have at last tapestry style; we have a conception of the effect of harmony and splendour the Vatican tapestries must once have had before they lost the greater part of their gold high-lights. And apart from this, these ceiling-paintings are alive with a new heroic determination. There was a promise of it already in the *Fortitudo*, amongst the Judicial Virtues, and the progressive growth of it can best be gauged by tracing its course back to the *Justitia* in the ceiling-medallion of the same Stanza, or even only as far as the figures of the Parnassus.

Those who look round for explanatory reasons instead of believing in the growth and liberation of a dæmonic talent, may turn to the studio gossip of Vasari; according to this, Bramante is said to have used the key of the Sistine Chapel in order to show Raphael Michael Angelo's ceiling, which had not yet been unveiled, and after that, his *protégé* altered his style.

One thing is certain: Raphael had all his life long to contend with a good memory; but if this must be mentioned, it can only be to his credit—he was good at forgetting also. He was obliged again and again to counter extraneous impressions with his own intrinsic creative power. To Raphael himself belongs the credit of becoming the *dramatic painter* and to no one else. From his Urbino days onward we have watched in him the steady growth of this capacity.

§ Treatment of Walls: Mural Style

The choice as a scene of action of the walls of the Stanza of Heliodorus is proof at the outset of a new and assured mode of conception. The space is confined between the arches and the floor-line. The pilasters on which the enclosing arch rests, here reach only as high as the hips of the figures; in the *Disputa* and the School of Athens their capitals are placed at the height of the heads, and the action of the figures, thanks to this fact and to their greater vigour and solidity, forces itself more upon the eye. The players dominate the scenery, and the stage provides no more than what is essential for the explanation of the action, like a musical accompaniment to the human voice. Thus in these frescoes, in spite of all the perspective, the picture always remains a wall; the painting does not, as so often in the Early Renaissance, seem to knock a hole in the wall, or to throw open a window. Rather, at every instant, the action remains a pattern, the event depicted always appears in its effect to exceed reality. The interior of the SCHOOL OF ATHENS at all events could be regarded as beautiful building "in itself".

§ The Heliodorus (Plates 102, 114)

Here, in the HELIODORUS, the temple has quite a different part to play. What is here brought into the forefront, *ad animos commovendos?* Let us imagine ourselves in front of a stage when the curtain rises on the scene; the first impression is that of a temple interior, or of what is most essential to a temple—the view of a Holy of Holies, with gold-gleaming domes on proud grey pillars and columns above a violet and grey tile pavement; to right and left, dimly-lit side-aisles. There is a crowd of people, but in front of the steps leading to the altar-area, the space is empty—it must have only just become so, for the women are still pressing back, and the middle pavement is still dark from something that was hovering over it a moment ago—the shadow of the angel with the rod who, with his companion and the heavenly horseman, pursues the plunderers—the temple robber with the confederates who aided him swept like rubbish into the corner, utterly brutal and devoid of dignity. The space before the Holy of Holies has now been cleansed of them, and facing them, calm and victorious, the Pope with his train, carried ceremoniously on the *sede gestatoria* into the midst of all this commotion, Julius II himself. We seem to hear him, clearing his throat with deliberation and making some magnificently unceremonious pronouncement upon what is taking place before him, quite in accord with his manly dignity, to which pose of any kind is unknown, needing no display, nothing but what he had it in his power to imbue with his own personality. Thus Raphael has succeeded in depicting him. The red of his *mozzetta*, the red and black of the Secretary, the old-gold and brownish-violet of the bearers, are ceremonial enough, by contrast with the duller tones of the populace in a whirl of confusion and of the robbers; the agitation of these figures is surpassed only by the luminous effect of the golden horseman and the gold and pink of the angels. Here, in the figure of the prostrate Heliodorus, the eye can still estimate what transparence and what significant luminosity this painting can have possessed when its colour merged directly into the light limewash of the wall, and the clear effect had not been disturbed in its uniformity by retouchings *al secco*. (Plate 103.)

The charger is perhaps not worth much in the eyes of horse-experts, but it seems to be capable of throwing down the lusty evildoer with its hoofs—a recurring motive ever since the time of the Attic funeral relief in the Vatican and the Alexander statues of Lysippus. It was revived in Leonardo's Sforza monument, and Raphael succeeded in exalting it from the imposing to the miraculous. Every note is sounded in the wide scale from the noblest heavenly wrath to the depths of Caliban-like contortion. There are here an echo of the BATTLE OF JOSHUA in the mosaics of Santa Maria Maggiore (Plate 221), and the same dramatic motives that occur in the soldiers guarding the sarcophagus in the RESURRECTION. (Plate 95.)

§ Self-portrait in the Heliodorus

It may have been a consciousness of such new self-assurance that impelled Raphael to introduce his own portrait in this Stanza also. Vasari says nothing of this; he merely mentions that the foremost bearer is Marcantonio. The woodcut portrait of the engraver as frontispiece to his biography, and the long hair in the manner of Dürer, support this assertion. The second bearer, beneath the Pope's left hand, was said to be Peruzzi, because the ceiling was supposed to be by him. Which can be Raphael? An attractive suggestion was once made that the young man on the extreme left in front was he, in the red and black official costume of the *Scrittor da Camera*. The name, Giovanni Pietro di Foliari, on the letter in the hand of the Secretary, was soon disposed of: it appears to have been painted in later. So the intelligent head was supposed to show Raphael's features, for the painter had at that time been for years holder of the prebend of which the office gave him his place beside the Pope. In the picture of St Luke by Giovanni Francesco Penni in the Accademia di San Luca, which is reputed to have been founded by Raphael himself, it was supposed that the same features could be recognised in the youth behind the patron saint of painters.

The search for portraits is a highly dangerous occupation. The *Scrittor da Camera*—it must be admitted—looks intelligent enough for Raphael, too intellectual, perhaps; yet the second *parafrenier*, below the Pope's left hand, is really looking out of the picture as if from a mirror, and with Raphael's eyes and turn of the head, as we know them in his own portraits. If this is so, we have here the fourth such portrait (Plate 286). Self-portraits apart from the mirror-painting, portraits, that is, with eyes roaming at large, began first in Venice, with the use of large glasses and two mirrors. Titian's famous late portrait in Berlin offers the best-known example.

Oxford possesses a glorious double-sheet drawing for the group of women in front of the Pope—back and front views in grey chalk; the woman starting back seems as if the whirl of her movement, the rhythm of her terror expressed, as it were, in a dancing motion, had been rendered in the "hand-writing" of the shading; the manner in which the movement dies away and becomes more indistinct in form and lighting as it recedes is quite wonderful (Plate 96). The mother with her children provides an abundance of motives, terror, anguish and love intermingled—the great figure of a Roman woman, with her vibrant, rhythmic freedom.

It is this flow of movement that draws the figure, from head to foot, forward towards one goal, the goal of her spirit, as in the red-chalk study of a nude woman, at Chatsworth, perhaps for the group of worshippers in the MASS OF BOLSENA (Plate 98). It is a movement that the creative master alone can infuse into his creations with the breath of life: he communicates to it animation, blood and a beating pulse. It is possible that this is the last of Raphael's studies from the nude in red chalk. His pupils never succeeded in it; they remain always in some way dependent on the master's motive or on their impressions of the model, hence perpetually burdened and hampered. He alone has an idea of his own, and is free, constrained only by it. This follows from the principle of his method in detail, as in the work in its entirety; in composition on the wall, it is just this that makes him a dramatist.

It was on the wall and by means of the wall that he attained this style of historical painting, and only this decoration, bound up with the wall-surface, seems to keep within its lines a performance that takes the breath away.

§ The Mass of Bolsena. Luther in Rome

The MASS OF BOLSENA (Plates 104, 106–109) remains perhaps unrivalled as an example of a great pattern of this kind "written", as the Chinese say, in clear lines from left to right; beginning with the upward-soaring woman, it rises to the white surplices of the choristers, the alb of the priest, through his arm to the holy wafer, and then down again from the hands of the Pope—surge and cascade. Did the wall, which is here cut through by the window, really present difficulties, as writers have told us again and again? Its narrow limits certainly gave Raphael freedom—release from everything subordinate and from an excess of figures. In it, his desire for a limited arena was met. This is immediately perceived from the colouring. On the podium there is white and gold, of the purest and most rich; altar and sacramental vessels and the priest are white and greenish-gold, the ministrants white; apart from these, among the populace, there are everywhere restrained colours, mingled with soft green. On the further side of the bright velvet-red of the Pope, the scale descends, through matt purple with grey shading in the watered silk of the cardinal, to the red, old-gold, black, green and gold lacquer of the Swiss Guards. Immediately the eye is drawn upwards again, by the priests in golden green alone. Vatican eyes saw more, they cannot but have looked with amazement upon the spectacle; can it be that there, on the wall above, the thousand-year-old ceremonial has suddenly become uncertain and indecisive in its consecrated agent? An officer faltering on the ship's bridge? Instantly, the ministrant becomes uneasy, the candles of the choristers waver and flicker, the congregation forget to hold back reverently before the tribune. But on the opposite side ritual and edifice remain undisturbed. Facing the hesitant priest kneels Peter's Vicegerent (Plate 108), steadfast as the rock on which Christ built his Church, and not less immovable the representatives of the Church (Plate 107), down to the chair-bearers of the Swiss Guard (Plate 109). For them it is no disturbing miracle that is taking place up there; they know that in the moment of transubstantiation the wafer is becoming the Body of the Lord.

This is the story of the Miracle of Bolsena: a "sacerdos teutonicus", really a Bohemian, had doubted the truth of Transubstantiation; he made the pilgrimage to Rome to overcome his scruples. On the way, at Bolsena, at Mass, he saw the wafer in his hand covered with blood; the blood saturated, in the pattern of a cross, the corporal in which he sought to wrap up the wafer. The miracle of the presence of the Lord in the Mass was bruited abroad. The Bishop of Orvieto obtained for his diocese this very treasure, the consecrated cloth with the sacred bloodstains on it, and it was then deposited in the gleaming enamelled silver shrine dedicated to receive it. The ancient cathedral was no longer adequate for the stream of worshippers. A new cathedral, the wonder of Italian Gothic, rose with its vault above the relic; the mosaic-decorated facade of the church flashes afar across the country, itself like a giant reliquary, on the highest point of the rock. The Feast of Corpus Christi was instituted to celebrate the miracle. When Julius II marched against Bologna, he visited Orvieto to adore the holy cloth. The legend of the doubting priest became for him a living fact. Undutiful, vacillating priests, doubting the Anointed of the Lord, had attempted to depose him at Pisa. Now this picture becomes a symbol of his victory over the threatening schism of the Church, a remarkable memorial of victory at the moment in which the greatest crisis of the Church had already appeared on the horizon. It was almost that very year that Luther was in Rome.

Raphael's style keeps moving on in step with that of the Pope; his touch became sure, in grouping, form and colour alike. The figure remains the decisive factor for the pattern on the wall; in the accompanying space poetic licence prevails. It would be vain to try to find a place for this *tribuna* in a church—this follows inevitably from Raphael's monumental manner; he admits into the picture only so much of nature and life as is needful for clear narration, no more! The "handwriting" of the painter is as bold and comprehensive in its formation as his procedure in the main scale is summary: the most profound interpretation of the inner life, and simplicity in form. The group of Swiss officers, as straightforward as could be in its vitality of portraiture, is set down like a transparent watercolour on the limewash ground of the steps, with the economy imposed by the technique.

In the virtuosos of the brush nothing bolder can be found than these trusty-looking defenders of the Papacy, nothing, in the masters of the quiet style such as Lotto, Veronese, Terborch and Degas, that seems so convincingly to be alive and breathing. Their pure Alemannic racial type tells us how accurately they were interpreted. Are we to call Impressionism, or Expressionism, the manner in which the immediate attendants of the Pope are portrayed, with their individual temperaments (Plate 107)?—the aged friend, at this time no longer living, of the Rovere pontiff, Gabrielli, Cardinal of San Prassede, and the Chamberlain, Raphael Riario, much spoken of as Cardinal of San Giorgio; he is mentioned in this connection by Vasari, and the portrait medals of this head of a pampered favourite support the biographer. Raphael again immortalised the builder of the Cancelleria and friend of Erasmus, shortly before the end of his magnificence under Leo X, in an arrestingly true and typical portrait. This art will avail to cure us of the employment of catchwords; whether realistic or monumental, it remains poetic painting, absolute and timeless, a handling of the mediums with complete sovereign power.

§ The Deliverance of Peter: Effect of the Window (Plates 110, 111, 113)

In like manner Raphael makes play with the wall and his subject in the DELIVERANCE OF PETER. The picture may have been very near to the heart of the Pope. To contemporary history, and in Italy and France, he had been known for decades as "San Pietro in Vincoli"—by the title of his advowson—not as Giuliano della Rovere.

The window in the wall provides a platform for the prison, but it also dazzles the spectator; confronting the daylight, the eye becomes unsure of itself, and

"'tis now the very witching time of night . . ."

It is like a prison in a mystery-play or in Shakespeare—all gratings and pillars; from it gleams forth a terracotta-hued light towards the angles and embossments of the rusticated work, and even beyond these to the deceptively painted soffit of the framing arch. It is not superfluous to remark that everything which has such a plastic effect in this archivolt-frame is painted on the flat, perpendicular wall. In the light the grating looks even more inexorable, and the masonry even stronger. Thus the eye becomes sensitive to the light in darkness which is too much for it. Delivered from the chains by which he is fettered to the guards, Peter is seen hand in hand with the angel, stepping forth like a sleepwalker over the legs of the slumbering watch. The triumphant aureole of the angel here is contrasted with terror and alarm on the opposite side. The scene is Rome, the city lies asleep, and clouds drift across the sickle of the moon. The soldiers start up, scared by the footsteps and blinded by the torchlight, shivering in their armour. Even the colours are chosen to give the utmost impressiveness of effect; "Lux lucet in tenebris"—the globe of light like a miracle in the sheer austerity of the scene, warm terracotta light of Redemption in the *mandorla* of the angel-guide to freedom, a cold harmony of slate, blue and silver to render the disillusionment on the opposite side. Three scenes in a single picture, as in mediæval art or—what amounts to the same thing—in sacred drama. The High Renaissance led art out of bondage when confronted by nature, back again to the freedom of the essential; thus it succeeded in attaining the supramundane, the world of the beyond. To the Quattrocento this was a closed book.

§ Attila: Narrative in Colouring (Plate 105)

The last wall is devoted to the deliverance of the fields of Italy from the incursion of Attila. Pope Leo I has encountered him near Ravenna, and the King of the Huns sees himself with his hordes threatened with swords by the Princes of the Apostles, appearing out of the clouds.

The arch with its heavy shadow undoubtedly helps to make intelligible the ethereal nature of the heavenly visitants. Suddenly they appear, sweeping down in their wrath and, with an ease that is unearthly, threatening the foe with their great swords. The fierce soldier-king advances at the head of his fierce hosts, trumpets sound in the van of the fire and smoke they leave behind them, the blood-red banner waves above the column, like a raging stream. They are met by the gentle train that advances out of the evening landscape of the Campagna. Heaven has taken up arms in their defence. In front ride the Pope on his palfrey, his hand raised in blessing, and gentle cardinals behind him on cream-coloured mules; swerving to one side, the Cross-bearer, the bearer of the silver mace, and the Marshal of the Household. Attila recoils, like the guards at the tomb of Christ, at sight of the heavenly swordsmen; the white horse amongst his retinue shies and the piebald of the Dacian bolts. Here the colouring is made to convey almost more of the narrative than in earlier pictures. But this fact has been overlooked because it has been considered important to seek out contributions made by pupils—but quite wrongly: the colour composition is novel and audacious: the yellowish-gold cloak of Peter (prescribed by iconography) has its counterpart in the golden scale-armour of the horseman on the right. The blood-red banner is balanced by the red of the cardinals. The vast medley is broken up with golden strands—the cream-coloured mules, the cope of the Pope, the yellow of the *Parafrenieri*, the breast-plates of the warriors in the middle, the helmet of the man on the white horse, the breastplate of the rider of the piebald on the extreme right.

Indifferently painted heads by the hands of pupils do occur, it is true, in this fresco, though only distributed here and there through the middle distance as if to fill in gaps; but the papal group in red, white and gold foiled by the Campagna landscape with its tapestry-like evening hues, a harmony of grave solemnity, and, to the right, in front of Attila, the silver rider on the white horse against the ground of grey mingled with reseda-colour, are among the most beautiful passages in Raphael's paintings. They are perhaps the last pieces of fresco-painting done entirely by his own hand.

The supernatural element has been called insignificant, the composition inferior "in formal values"; but where else is to be found anything to match the irresistible, cloud-like onward sweep of the Apostles? They have just appeared from afar, accompanying the Pope above his head, and the ease with which they threateningly brandish their swords as if they were sticks, is marvellous.

The intention was to show the Rovere Pope going to meet Attila on the *sede gestatoria*, in full pontificals, with his retinue. We possess only the very weak replica at Oxford of the sketch for this; Peter goes threateningly, with his keys, in front; among the retinue beside the Pope a boy stands out, through his self-conscious bearing—certainly the young Federigo Gonzaga (then hostage for the loyalty of his mother, Isabella of Mantua), whom as especial favourite of the *Papa Terribile*, even Raphael was obliged to paint. It is not owing to any vanity on the part of the Medici that the Pope now wears the features of Leo X; in the interval, the son of Lorenzo had succeeded to the great Julius. He is riding the palfrey which a year earlier, at the battle of Ravenna, had been of no avail to rescue him from imprisonment, and had just carried him, in occupation of the Holy See for the first time, from the Vatican to the Lateran. A harmony of white, red and gold—it is an entirely honest portrait and yet flattering too—with its well-tended musician's hand so gracefully raised to bless (Plate 112). Such a thing was simply unthinkable in the case of Julius! But Raphael was now become a man of the Court—*cortegiano*—and could hold his own with the great ones, fully conscious of his relations to them, of their strength and of their weakness. The great interpreter of historical events now becomes, by virtue of the same power, the great portrait-painter.

§ Development of Raphael's Colour

It has been supposed, on utterly superficial grounds, that this man of the Marches, now grown assured of himself, must have learnt his expressive colour from Sebastiano del Piombo. When under the influence of Giorgione's colouring, the Venetian came to Rome, and through Michael Angelo very speedily became one of the first victims of Mannerism. The free, unconstrained painting of Raphael should have been recognised in these heads of the Attila fresco. They have about them something timeless. Coming across them in isolation, many an expert would be perplexed as to the century they belong to, or even the school. How different they are one from another! Both Cardinals were first sketched in with contours scratched in the limewash; the outlines are still to be seen—even the invisible birettas and the ear are indicated under the hat (Plate 115*a*). But then one of these figures was painted with liquid colour on the wet lime, including the ermine cape and the strings of the hat with their shadows. The Cardinal on the right, certainly as he now is and no less genuine, was gone over *al secco*, perhaps only because a new portrait had to be superimposed over one already there. We see that we should have formed our ideas of Raphael's manner from his works, so as to spare ourselves the confusion of applying our prejudices to the criticism of his work.

§ Portraits of Cardinals

We will yield to the fascination of dwelling upon these Court portraits. Of these two Cardinals, one seems to be Amadeo Berutti, from April, 1514, onwards Governor of Rome, the other perhaps Giovanni Francesco della Rovere, Archbishop of Turin and Governor of the Castel Sant' Angelo.[1] Their military rank gives them a title to this special place in the picture. Otherwise they become just types of their order. One could imagine them in conversation with the versatile young artist of whom an anecdote in the *Cortegiano* relates as follows: two members of the Sacred College criticised the heads of the Princes of the Apostles as being of too red a flesh-colour, and Raphael answered: "Perhaps they are ashamed at having such deputies in the Church." A ready rejoinder, but not quite so gracious as might have been expected—if it had to be accepted as true! It is more likely to have been, in allusion to the words of Peter (Dante, *Paradiso*, XXVII, 19–21): "Trascolorato in rosso per la vergogna del loro malfare."

§ Portrait of Paris de Grassis

We know, about this papal Court and the Court of Leo's illustrious predecessor, a great deal that provides us with the atmosphere surrounding the works of art. We may look with grateful remembrance upon this group of the papal retinue—good, simple, trusty men, the middle one, especially, beautifully painted, in full sunlight (Plate 115b) the head proves what can be attributed to Raphael, as a draughtsman in water-colour, and what he intended to express with his washes of bistre tones. There was no need, throughout a whole generation of critics, to trouble Perino del Vaga with this. In the case of this head one might speak of Impressionism, if it were not that there is exceptional expressiveness in the eye, hanging with the look of a trusty hound on his papal master. The staff he holds shows that we must recognise in him the Vatican Majordomo, and at this time it can have been none other than the excellent Paris de Grassis. We owe to the journal of this pedantically correct man, who was obliged patiently to pass over so many incorrectnesses of Julius II, many a lively detail concerning the careers and everyday life of Julius II and Leo, and also about their artists.

[1] Hill, *Italian Medals*, Pl. 142, No. 891 and Pl. 121, No. 726.

VIII

ROMAN PORTRAITS

§ Historical Painter and Portrait-painter. Likeness and something more

THE great historical painter and the true portrait-painter both spring from the same stock; both titles alike are deserved only by one capable of abstracting from events and from men the sum of their spiritual significance, and of knowing how to reduce them to a simple, comprehensible, impressive formula. He will track out what is important in the phenomenon of the individual as in the historical process; he will disclose in them the higher power that was embodied in this particular living form and no other, or evoked this rhythm of occurrences, exercising an influence on this particular individual or course of events so as to reveal itself in them. In both cases the greatness of the interpreting artist consists in perceiving and making visible the essential.

The real portrait-painter cannot possibly stop short at mere likeness, even when a model has been set for him. For him, the outer shell in his subject is less important than the shaping, motive power; he divines in the given form how its basic material has been transformed by life, and how it was the spirit that fashioned for itself this embodiment and no other.

Speaking of himself, Raphael acknowledged, in that much-quoted letter to Castiglione, that in moments of creative inspiration, a "certa idea" gleamed before him; he might thus have applied to himself the words of his "duca e poeta"—"ficca diretro agli occhi tuoi la mente"—"direct thy mind towards that which lies behind the field of vision". This idea therefore may possibly impart to his portraits, however convincing the likeness that speaks in each individual, a factor in common which causes all the cardinals, humanists and ladies to appear like kinsmen of a *single family*.

§ Subjectivity

It is generally not considered a compliment to the faithfulness of a portrait-painter if he himself is constantly being recognised in his works; this was disastrous to Rubens's portraits, and Van Dyck's great power ends in his own gallant snobbery. Raphael does not possess the objectivity with which portrait-painters are commonly supposed to approach their work. He belongs through and through to the class of subjective painters who impart to the model what is in themselves, but he understands at the same time how to sum up and para-

110

phrase, in a conclusive statement about the particular human being, what he or she in the outward appearance, character, type and aspirations, actually presented to him.

The Vatican circle, to which he now actually belonged as an official of the palace in the entourage of the Pope and whose members he had to portray, so to speak, as part of the ordinary routine, brought before his easel essentially clerical types. In these planets of the Vatican solar system with their hierarchical ordering, a selection or breed was exhibited before his eyes in a uniform sublimation like that presented by the aristocracy of the Burgundian Court to Roger van der Weyden, the only portrait-painter in the North comparable with Raphael.

The personal comes to light only in the convention of a clarified form; inward power and vital impulse appear only as if cooled on ice. All the more harrassing and stimulating therefore is the task of interpretation, the revealing of a spiritual landscape which lies hidden under such a uniform atmosphere and which the artist whose life is surrounded by the same ceremonial is only allowed to divine.

§ Stylisation

In the course of this process a kind of sublime interpretation will develop along lines that bring into relief only what is essential, and this essential element will, in a circle of society tuned to so high a pitch, be the form to which that circle aspires; the painter may sense from type and demeanour what kind of men his sitters would like to seem. Hence arises in Raphael this nimbus of the "idea" around the persons represented; they all have in their eyes that look of the Burgundians, who did not desire to behold anything of the world outside themselves—but in the eyes of these Mediterranean people, even lowered eyelids cannot veil the glowing brightness, nor even the practised reserve of the cleric. Thus there remains only the lofty aloofness, a gaze as it were into another world, compared with which a man's own life appears almost like the gliding past as of a swan on a stream. Or should we reflect how many of these chosen beings believed themselves to be influenced by the dæmonic motive forces of their star, and looked upon ordinary life around them as if their own world swung past it on a more exalted course?

In the YOUNG SECRETARY, at Budapest, we already see Raphael at one with his sitter as regards this expression of lofty character, perhaps a survival of the Urbino atmosphere; this quality was alien to the bourgeois Doni and his wife, but it weaves a peculiar charm about that entirely melancholy WOMAN IN GREEN. Julius II with his look of thunder breaks through every cloud, but something of the quality in question enlivens every portrait from the enigmatic CARDINAL at Madrid to the *VELATA*, the CZARTORYSKI MODEL, the BIBBIENA, the Two FRIENDS of the Doria Gallery, and from Raphael's own portrait in the

Uffizi to the late SELF-PORTRAIT WITH A FRIEND in the Louvre. This is the demeanour, in the fresco of the DECRETALS, of the younger Cardinals as they gather round the throne of the Holy Father (Plate 87). Like a permanent mould, it was, and still is to the present day, in ecclesiastical circles, filled almost as if *de rigueur*, again and again with new life. It presented itself to Raphael, when he entered the Vatican circle, as something long familiar which it was quite natural, a matter of course even, to experience.

The enigmatic portrait of a CARDINAL, at Madrid (Plate 117), can perhaps be traced to the first sensation of such states of tension; such profound experience is in his look that it might be doubted whether one may say "of a young Cardinal". Even the date of its origin is uncertain; only the peculiar enamel quality of the colour permits the surmise that it was executed before Raphael's hand was freely accustomed to fresco-painting. The Florentine portraits have made us familiar with the absolute completeness of colour-harmony that has now been reached. Note the red tones of the biretta and the watered silk of the mozzetta—brilliant and shaded off till it dies away in the olive-green background—in between, the pale face with lips keyed in colour to the red above and below, the whole presentment gaining a convincingly plastic quality by means of the white sleeve and the set of the hand (it is possible that the finishing-off below is here wanting). It is contrary to Raphael's custom for a motive to conflict with the frame. Everything in the plastic movement seems to follow the lines of the prominent nose and to provide the framework for the uncanny composure in the face, with its far-away, ardent eyes and the grace that hovers over the narrow lips.

No finality has been reached in conjectures as to the identity of the subject; Alidosi, the favourite of Julius II, Cardinal Schinner, and Bibbiena have been suggested. It is most probable that we are here looking into the eyes of Cardinal Ippolito d'Este, of which he was so proud. He has the profile of the Este, especially of Ippolito's father Alfonso I, and Castiglione gives in the *Cortegiano*, I, 14, a literary portrait of his "grave autorità" in his younger years that would be peculiarly appropriate to the character here depicted, in its dæmonic, tragic mysteriousness.

We see that Raphael discovered the style for stating the same things as the "formator del Cortegiano"; he himself had ripened into a man of the world, and had observed the individual phenomenon in this solar system of the Vatican that came within his aspect, with the serene superiority of a member of it. Besides the Princes of the Church, consumed with wordly passion, we have the easy-going, witty Prebendary TOMMASO INGHIRAMI, called *Fedra* (Plate 118). In the part of the queen, in a performance of Seneca's *Hippolytus*, he had once improvised endless verses in Latin, to the rapturous delight of all humanists, when the curtain failed to function at the end of an act. To this man of refined taste in several domains at once the Vatican Library owes its arrangement; he is the author of the funeral oration, so rich in magnificent similes, over Julius II before the College of Cardinals. In moments of like inspiration Raphael may have hit upon such a formula, of an almost Northern intimacy, for the accomplished man of learning. One thinks of Holbein and Massys, and may perhaps also recall that Erasmus was at that time an esteemed guest at the Vaticana during the régime of this Prefect. For all that, it will be well to reflect that about the middle of the second decade, when this picture must have been painted (the sitter died in 1516), Raphael was in advance of all others in this mode of interpretation. The diptych of Massys with Erasmus and Aegidius dates from 1517.

The favoured humanism of the Vaticana, consecrated by the Purple, finds expression in this concord of the madder red in the biretta and gown and the cherry red of the book-edge with the broad passages of pink in the flesh-painting, which is laid on as in the Swiss Guards in the fresco of the MASS OF BOLSENA, with cloudy grey for the shadows and the shaven chin. As long as the second example at Volterra was known only to a few, no one ventured any more to enter the lists in defence of the picture in the Pitti Palace. Morelli had the strange notion, as so often in other cases, of seeing in it a Netherlandish copy. Even since the picture in the family palace at Volterra was transferred thence to the Gardner Collection at Boston, the question has not been decisively settled in its favour; it shows the head a little more *en face*. The Pitti Palace picture is unquestionably related to the contemporary wall-paintings; it falls within the period of Raphael's freest fresco style.

As regards two famous members of the Sacred College we have, it seems, only reproductions to inform us that they were painted by Raphael and how he conceived them. There is an unusually exciting picture in the Naples gallery that shows CARDINAL ALESSANDRO FARNESE, the future Pope Paul III. Visible as far as the knees, with a letter in his right hand, he walks past us in the foreground of a bright landscape towards the dark walls of a hall. It was surely Raphael who gave the head its poise on the neck, the eyes their look, and the hand with the letter its foreshortening; and Titian's portrait of the aged Pope at Naples assures us, thirty years later, that the thin-fingered left hand is faithfully portrayed. This delicate hand shows still the same habit of self-representation—but the painting is out of keeping with such profound interpretation of character. It is certainly noteworthy that from 1587 onwards this picture in the possession of the Farnese family always bore Raphael's name; it would be better if it showed more consistently the Raphael touch, without the structureless, oily colour, and without the disturbing, obtrusive landscape and the clumsy folds of drapery. The narrow upright format, the strong relief, which do not occur elsewhere, may have been thus chosen by Raphael for the first time; but in that case the question would still remain whether he could really have left the lower portion so lifeless.

The portrait of CARDINAL BIBBIENA in the Pitti Palace has to contend with similar justifiable doubts. It must be taken as certain that Raphael painted the faithful counsellor and companion of Giuliano de' Medici throughout his banishment and the short period of his princely splendour; Bibbiena had shown favour to the artist since his Urbino days. The "Cardinal of Santa Maria in Portico" was faithfully devoted to the Medici, their diplomatic representative, Secretary of State and most graceful jester. He had destined his niece to be Raphael's bride, at that time certainly a proof of high social esteem. This interesting portrait also owes its vitality to Raphael's genius; none other than he can have seized, in the imposing attitude of the Prince of the Church, this subtle sense of the hue, "sicklied o'er", of the man of irony. But the commanding quality of a genuine composition is lacking in this head, with so much space above it and lifeless masses of white below; above all, the fitting of the arm into a parallel with the frame makes one miss precisely that sense of being at ease in the handling of space which is Raphael's peculiar signature. The colour is applied in brushstrokes, this way and that, in a somewhat arbitrary fashion; it is laid over the forms in an unintelligent and tell-tale manner. The right hand, with the letter, shows an easy animation and was certainly conceived by Raphael, but even this remains nothing but oily pigment. Here we can have only a workshop replica that misrepresents Raphael, from the hand of Giulio Romano. Even so, it is still of value, because it perpetuates one of the most interesting types of the circle in which Raphael had to pass his life.

Bibbiena was for years the inseparable friend and associate of his master, GIULIANO DE' MEDICI, the youngest of the sons of Lorenzo—through the favour of his brother the Pope, Duke of Nemours; this scion of the House of Medici was a man of much promise and small fulfilment. Giuliano's portrait as a child was painted at Florence by Ghirlandajo in the fresco of the CONFIRMATION OF THE FRANCISCAN ORDER, in the Church of the Trinità; he attained transfiguration as *Capitano* of the Church in Michael Angelo's famous sepulchral monument. Leonardo was for long his companion, Raphael was one of his household when by his marriage with Filiberta of Savoy he founded a princely establishment. This tired man's portrait dates from the last years of a life declining into infirmity. It may well be due to Raphael that the bearded head, with its delicate grey shadows below the biretta, which looks so monumental above the gold-embroidered skull-cap, is placed high in the picture above the tremendously effective substructure of the gown. One must regard as an addition completely foreign to Raphael the Castle of Sant' Angelo, with the corridor to the Vatican and the ramparts, in reference to the Capitano dell' Ecclesia, which is thrust into the picture, bursting through the neutral curtains. Only in this painting, when we look at the lethargic head with its majestic gaze upon the world, as if in a dream, do we conjecture what Raphael could have made of a typical layman's portrait. But not everything that is lacking here can be explained by bad preservation.

The unlucky star of the House of Medici seems also to have influenced Raphael's portraits of the last representative of the dynasty. We feel most acutely the loss of the picture of the young LORENZO DE' MEDICI, Duke of Urbino, Michael Angelo's "Penseroso"; for Raphael finished it in February, 1518, that is, when his painting was at its zenith. All the portraits in the family series go back to the single type which is perhaps best handed down in the great replica in the corridor between the Uffizi and the Pitti Palace. But here the figure is out of keeping with the frame, and in the costume at the level of the knees there are such serious voids that it may be questioned whether the original by Raphael can have been composed in this manner. The statue of the Virgin, after Michael Angelo's figure in the LAST JUDGMENT, also speaks against the view into the room; it must be an addition of the copyist. In any case, Raphael's arrangement can still be traced from the biretta, of which the spreading pyramid is repeated in the collar of the gown and in the bulging sleeves, down as far as the hips; the manner in which the collar clings to the slightly bowed neck is one of those inventive touches which are denied to school-painters. Another example at Colworth shows a more sensitive expression, but the figure is cramped and ill-adjusted to the frame. The Junian look in these true Medici faces, to which the beard especially imparts an element of fatalism, can now only be conjectured; it may be that this eye, and the highly imposing ostentatiousness of the figure, provided Raphael with a way of escape in his divided allegiance between the hereditary Montefeltro-Rovere dynasty and the new one appointed by his master the Pope; he immediately had to work for the new ruler of his home country, and we know of a design for a coin with Lorenzo's portrait which was required and obtained from the artist. The expression of the young prince handed down in the Colworth replica is sufficiently remarkable; Francis I of France seems to have been present to his mind as the ideal of his aspirations in bearing and expression, and his daughter Catherine was actually to ascend the throne of the Valois. Is it perspicacity, or foresight, in the great historical portrait-painter?

§ Castiglione: the *Cortegiano*

We learn, from the COUNT CASTIGLIONE in the Salon Carré of the Louvre (Plate 120), the effect of a portrait fully worked out on a basis of personal experience by the fresco-painter of the Stanza of Heliodorus. The "formator del Cortegiano", as Ariosto calls him, had been known to Raphael since his Urbino period, from the days when he had to paint the ST GEORGE, as patron of the Order of the Garter (formerly in the Hermitage, now in the Mellon Collection) for Castiglione's embassy to England. We know of a correspondence between them in which Raphael reciprocates the praises of the fastidious connoisseur with intimate, profoundly significant professions concerning his creative activity. They visited together the ancient ruins to which, with a poet's subtle melancholy,

Castiglione felt himself attracted. We have an account in Bembo's letter to Bibbiena, of an excursion they both made to Tivoli in company with the poets Beazzano and Navagero; once again, at a later time, Raphael painted his distinguished friend, who was then staying in Rome as Ambassador of the Duke of Urbino. The picture was apparently intended as a present for Castiglione himself; one of these two portraits inspired the Count to poetic paraphrase in a sonnet—an imaginary dialogue of his wife with this counterfeit which had to do duty for her absent loved one!

Doubts have been expressed as to whether the portrait could possibly represent to us the man whose intelligence fulfilled the unexpressed aspirations of Renaissance society for harmonious completeness, discussing and outlining them in his book of the *Cortegiano* by means of the dialogue form. Not only did the conception of a man of the Renaissance in all its nobility receive from him its literary form; his book, translated into many languages, may really also have given a practical import to the trend of the North towards the classical Italian land. How many travellers first found in that country fulfilment on the lines of these teachings! It is simply impossible to say how great was the enthusiasm kindled in the international Court circles of those times by the type of a manliness complete both outwardly and inwardly. In places where the term "society" was still something more than an empty phrase, its ideal survived effectively till the verge of our own times.

This man of a profound influence that spread far and wide was conceived by Titian in a vein of intelligent alertness better suited than its subject to the eulogy of Charles V at the time of his death: "uno de los maior caballieros de mondo." When we seek in vain for this elegant versatility of the courtier in Raphael's painting of him, one point has to be taken into consideration: at least a hand's breadth is lacking from the bottom of the Paris picture; the chair-arm on the front part of which the left arm rests was more widely visible, and the hands also stood clear above the lower frame; at least, Rembrandt drew it so with a special white spot when he saw the picture in 1639 at the Van Uffelen auction sale in Amsterdam. He joined with enthusiasm in the bidding; beside him sat Joachim Sandrart, who went up to 3,000 guilders. But they both had to see the picture carried off by the Spanish Ambassador for 3,500 guilders. Thanks to his notes on the hastily sketched sheet in the Albertina, Rembrandt retained from it the motive for his self-portraits. A copy by Rubens exists, with hands, now in a private collection in Vienna (Plate 121).

According to current views of Raphael's art and of the Dutch artist's relation to it, a work to which Rembrandt took such a fancy about 1640 that he wished to possess it must really have been quite unlike Raphael. Yet Rembrandt thoroughly understood the Italians, especially when they painted well. The noble congruity of the colouring with the imposing contours awakened in him a response. Thus, it seemed to him, this dignified man once looked out on the world from his exalted station; such was his character, finding expression even in the choice of colours. The black velvet with grey shading stands out against a greyish-golden ground—the grey of the sleeves with slate-coloured shadows and cool golden reflections. Such refinement of dress, with its materials carefully chosen to match one another, may be found elsewhere only in Romanino's warriors in the frescoes at Cremona. This, then, was "l'elegante Castiglione", as Ariosto called him in his forty-second Satire. He himself voices the opinion (*Cortegiano*, II, 27) that the *cortegiano* should not wear bright-hued clothes but more sober colours—black, brown or grey; he should, in fact, show the "riposo" of his inner self, a superior calm, in his outward appearance also. Castiglione himself appeared on a mission to the French Court dressed in the Spanish fashion, which at that time meant in discreet colours. These fashionable shades were a foreshadowing of the "Spanish costume"; a century later they are an indication of the Puritan taste of the Northern *bourgeoisie*. For this reason the light in the greyish-gold of the velvet sleeve and the wealth of shades of black and brown could not fail to make a deep impression on the republican Rembrandt, and to strike in him related harmonies. In this connection it is always well to recollect that Rembrandt saw the picture without the Louvre varnish of two and a half centuries, and that perhaps he found it less "golden" or "Rembrandtesque" than we do to-day. But in any case, however hasty his sketch may have been (and nothing else in it really corresponds), he left in reserve, from memory, a special light to represent the colourless reflection on the folds. Let us be glad of this trustworthy witness for Raphael as "painter"—in this age of ours that for long believed, in its cautious reserve, that it had done enough if it conceded to him value as a "draughtsman".

The CASTIGLIONE was transferred from wood to canvas, thereby forfeiting some of its original character. A picture belonging to the same period, the DONNA VELATA, and another somewhat later, the DOUBLE PORTRAIT OF TWO FRIENDS, the two Venetian poets Navagero and Beazzano, have preserved in a wonderful manner the canvas style of the fresco-painter. The two friends, so unlike one another, in the picture of the Doria Gallery, are known as the Venetians ANDREA NAVAGERO and AGOSTINO BEAZZANO (Plate 19b). The bearded Navagero, precisely at that time—at the beginning of 1516—entrusted with the office, as honourable as it was important, of Librarian of San Marco, in his native city, stayed in Rome with his poet friend; Bembo mentions them as taking part in that excursion of March, 1516, to Tivoli with Raphael and Castiglione. We must therefore imagine, at a time when Raphael's interests belonged to architecture, and to antiquarian research as inseparable from architecture, an inner bond of the two poets with the artist, that made him capable of a portrait so intimate and bearing every mark of his own hand; a consonance of strength and refinement. Perhaps no picture leads us so far into the circle of this humanist society, with its claims to a balanced harmony of the outer and the inner; there is a hint of the multifarious play of genius when men of no commonplace stamp are brought together. And Raphael understands how to suggest the trend of their desires in their bearing and attitude towards the world. The very absence of colour in the dress gives the picture an exclusive character, and forces the eye to immerse itself quietly in the subtle variation of tone, and this again is inseparable from the essential character of the two men thus brought together. The seated Navagero (Plate 122) turns round, boldly and proudly; the line of his cap stands out, like his profile, nose and frontal bone; his powerful neck towers up superbly in an uninterrupted line from the silhouette of the body. Confronting him, standing, as it seems, is the squat figure of Beazzano, mild but intellectually proud. They gaze upon the world as if with a single pair of eyes. One turns towards us, in penetrating scrutiny, his clear right eye; the other, with more of a gaze, casts on us the spell of his soul expressed in his left eye, retaining also in his mild contours an imposing simplicity. No imitator has been at work here, but a creator who has carried into the very folds of their garments the rhythm inherent in his models; in the left-hand figure the high-lights forming the confines move, as it were, with an irresistible *forward leap*, in the other the whole character of the form from the cap and the hair to the set of the shirt and even down to the folds below, is one of *horizontal repose*, in conformity with the broad contours. Expressiveness of colour is inseparable from such observation of life: "in quietate mobile." In Beazzano (Plate 123) the vitality of the colour advances from the bronze-olive of the background to the chestnut brown, with its lively reflections, of the hair and the light copper tone of the face, with the pink lips and a heightening of brick red in the eyelids; the flesh-tone is mingled in the shadows with a greyish olive that forms a transition equally to the bronze-olive ground and to the high-lights on the sleeve. One may almost feel here a foreshadowing of the tones of Rembrandt. In the figure of Navagero the brush has been used in bolder strokes. His beard has been laid on as if in fresco; the cheek and the shadows round the eyes are drawn in greyish brown, in a coarser chiaroscuro moreover, with the strokes of the red-chalk sketch at Chatsworth for JULIUS II; the yellow lights on brow, eye and nose, and the reflections that follow the course of the folds, are done absolutely as if with the free strokes of fresco on a wall. All this gives an effect of improvisation in the application of the colours, as in the VELATA. Perhaps the ST CECILIA was once conceived in this manner, before her figure disappeared under the thick layers of the over-paintings; in the Cartoons, many passages still show this manner of laying the pigment. The CASTIGLIONE was the product of similar inward promptings.

With this beautifully balanced adjustment of the two figures before us, we might almost reject as ungracious the surmise that they may once have been each separately composed, in the Roman mode, and then brought together in this Venetian format. There appear to be insistent traces of remnants of a landscape with a tree and tower seeming to lie in the background between the figures, and of a balustrade on the right. It is also possible that the hand of Beazzano, now indispensable to the composition as a counterpoise to the heads, may have been shortened in its form afterwards. It remains remarkable that in this masterpiece, as in the CASTIGLIONE, there seems to be something lacking at the lower border in the motivation of the figures.

§ Raphael's last Self-portrait

May we venture to introduce here a problem of which the solution is not yet ripe for pronouncement, so long as the picture eludes the examining eye through its high position, the other works by which it is surrounded, which destroy format and composition, and the almost impenetrable condition of its surface; it is that of the double portrait in the Louvre, which is little regarded under the romantic title of RAPHAEL AND HIS FENCING-MASTER (Plates 124, 125). To connoisseurs of recent times it has merely offered a tool for the exercise of their critical powers; it has been attributed successively to such mere free-booters as Sebastiano del Piombo, Pontormo or Polidoro. For fifty years no connoisseur has worried any more about the question whether Raphael himself, as he was in figure and bearing in his latest period, looks out upon us from the countenance of the figure standing behind in the picture. His own contemporaries knew for certain; this *is* Raphael. Thus Giulio Bonasone engraved after this painting the miserable print with the bearded head. Doubtless he must have had before his eyes this figure, with its frilled shirt, before the picture was enlarged by some two inches. These are the features of Raphael in the medallion set among those of Dante, Petrarch and Marsilio in the vaulted ceiling of a room in the house of Baldassare Turini da Pescia, who was Raphael's friend and executor, in the Villa Lante on the Gianicolo. Giulio Romano is reputed to have painted him there, and he must have known his master's features. They are the features in the lost self-portrait of the old Vendramin inventory, which seem also to be perpetuated by Hollar's engraving (Plate 127, Parthey, *Hollar*, 1486; T. Borenius, *The Picture Gallery of Andrea Vendramin*). He is given thus in the "promptuaire de medailles" of 1581. We must accustom ourselves to the artist with a beard, the "manly" Raphael; whether we must also accept him as the painter of this picture remains an open question. Until it is settled, our vision may be sharpened by reflecting whether it is Raphael who here directs his scrutinising gaze upon himself, and whether we have here his figure standing completely without constraint, his neck airily girt with the shirt-border, rendered as in a still-life, behind the chair of his companion, on whose shoulder he lays his left hand, lightly detaching itself from the background; his associate sits before him, in a shooting-tunic with facings of which the reflections towards the lower border of the picture give once again a touch of vitality; the fencing-master points in front of him with boldly foreshortened hand, and this movement lightly echoes through the picture-space. His martial bearing, almost that of a bravo—and the wild but not ignoble Roman type, will seem at the very first sight unfamiliar; they have indeed caused the airy delicacy of the group in the space to be over-looked, and its harmoniousness, subtle but rich in contrasts.

But no portrayal of Raphael's features should be passed over with indiffer-ence, nor that of any of the master's intimates, whatever may be the first impression. Even men of the world—we saw a case of this in Navagero—did not all look like æsthetic humanists and refined clerics. It is exciting to learn on whom Raphael bestowed the distinction of such trustful intimacy. Curiosity on this point will perhaps bring us back to the intimacies of a manner of painting that with broad, tentative brush rendered masses, lights and angles in the material, in the shirt and on the shoulder, with wonderful facility. And we shall not omit this in our admiration of the unique, free, irresistible movement with which the group distributes itself over the space; it is something that has no equal in the second decade of the sixteenth century, not even in Raphael himself, on a large scale in the tapestries or, in narrower limits, in the portrait of LEO X (Plates 128, 129).

§ Leo X

It must have been between 1517 and 1519, within the period of the short cardinalate of Ludovico de' Rossi, that the commission was given for this official portrait. It has often been compared with the portrait of Julius II, to the glory of Raphael as a painter of historical subjects. Here we have the mighty Ligurian, with his far-away look of a peasant, in his dæmonic loneliness above the world, the high-climbing son of a bourgeois city in the milieu which was the foundation of his strength—family connections, wealth and education. There he sits, amid his beloved collection of books (it is still supposed that the saloon of the old Vaticana which is to-day the Floreria can be recognised in the pillared architecture), flanked by the most trusted confidants of his household, his nephews, Cardinal Giuliano de' Medici and Ludovico de' Rossi, son of his sister. The former was Secretary of State to the Holy See, and after Bibbiena's departure, the most important diplomatic personage; soon, after the intervening reign of Adrian VI, he became Leo's successor as Clement VII, the "Pope of the Downfall". Ludovico de' Rossi, with that passionate temperament which especially appealed to the painter's powers of representation, had little time to turn his attention to politics.

§ Free Relationship to Reality

Raphael now transfers the monumental style to portraiture. In this class of composition, nothing corresponds any more to reality, in the relationship of the persons either to the architecture or to one another. An artist, or a portrait-painter, was never more free in his attitude towards nature. We make this assertion to anticipate any further question as to Vasari's absurd admiration for the reflecting globe on the chair-back. For the picture is full of expression, at the very first sight, even in the colour. Note the splendour of the triangle of red velvet between the two softer triangles of watered silk with a matt sheen and the table-cover of dull red cloth. The richly shaded white damask and the light passages provided by the Medici ball of the armchair and the hands of Rossi, the reflections and the ermine edging on the Pope's *mozzetta*, his hands, and the still-life of book and bell—everything is arranged, and the arrangement conforms in direction with the lines of the apartment. Even on a superficial examination of the picture, splendid colour is seen to be characteristic of the person portrayed in it, a man who understands how to combine exalted rank and intellect with enjoyment, wearing his ugliness with dignity and grace and making his epicureanism sympathetic. He is not in solitary dependence on himself—his dignitaries are at his disposal, the prudent heir to the family sovereignty, Giuliano, with a look of superiority but melancholy and repressed, De' Rossi clutching familiarly at the chair to which he owes his career, but even apart from that, a speakingly genuine type of clerical breeding.

The monumental painter here becomes a man of the world and a courtier; he follows up with peculiar love the singularities of the model. The Pope was proud of his well-cared-for hand; we have seen an acknowledgment of this in the ATTILA picture. The Medici shortsightedness suggests to the portrait-painter a moment of intimate enjoyment with the magnifying-glass. Whatever comes into these hands, even down to the utensils of daily life, the bell for the soon-exhausted temper of the master, must be of the most substantial description. The illuminated book on the table is well known—it is a Naples Gothic Bible; it passed from the Vatican Library into the hands of the newly-converted daughter of the Church and of Gustavus Adolphus, Queen Christina of Sweden, then into the possession of the Duke of Hamilton, and from the Hamilton Collection into the Berlin Kupferstichkabinett. The open page on which the Pope's hand rests helps with its soft medley of colours and its shape to guide the eye further in the main general direction. We feel that detail is under control, and is compelled to serve the monumental structure of the whole. This picture shows, even in its painting on wood panel, the grand sweep of the frescoes; all the brush-strokes follow in the material structure, for instance, the lights on the nose, and on the temples and under the brows. The shadows in the shaven face of Leo seem as if drawn in underneath in grey; it is the same in the case of Giuliano, whose figure has suffered somewhat, whilst Rossi, done with a copious flow of pigment, can be compared with the Swiss Guards of the MASS. Drawing technique is apparent in the lights on the hands, as in the LADY IN GREEN at Urbino; in the magnifying-glass they follow the direction of the reflections. The Pope's collar has bold red streaks on the wrinkles, as in the Julius II in the MASS; in the fur there is the same broadness as in that painting and in the Chatsworth STUDY OF A HEAD—and as, after all these astounding observations we turn from the work, the eye carries away a vibrant accord of deep purple and cherry red, and soft purple shot with gold in the watered silk, harmonised with white and gold! Magnificent, and at the same time intimate.

§ Valerio Belli

And at this point, after a glance at the refined dilettantism of the Pope, the little picture in the possession of Sir Kenneth Clark may be introduced (Plate 119a). A rare case of miniature by a monumental painter, it is perhaps the lid of a small round box a few inches in diameter; it bears the portrait of the medallist and crystal-carver VALERIO BELLI. To complete the sport of paradox, this miniature on a tiny scale is executed with the customary methods of the wall-painter. The blond, bearded head fills, almost indeed bursts the frame, leaving room in addition only for the hand raised fairly high towards the eye, with a delicate example of Valerio's workmanship. Related in the brushwork and in the free methods of characterisation to the heads of the Cardinals in the ATTILA fresco, the shape of the head, the line of the neck, the contour of the fur, and the hollowed hand fit magnificently and, as it were, obviously into the space; there is a refreshing vitality in the way in which the flesh-tones stand out against the cool blue of the background. In the eyes of Raphael the "principe degli incisori" was no prince, but a doughty master of a small but precious handicraft. We may well be curious about the society that, with a view to its own enhancement thereby, provided the means for a style of life with such luxurious passions.

§ Bindo Altoviti

Bindo Altoviti was closely associated with Raphael, as also at a later period with Benvenuto Cellini and Vasari, and the oft-quoted passage in the *Lives of the Painters* (ed. Milanesi IV, 351) . . . "e a Bindo Altoviti—fece il ritratto suo, quando era giovane . . ." will certainly have to be interpreted as evidence that there was a portrait of the banker by Raphael's hand. It is certain that the Munich picture comes from the possession of his descendants, but also unfortunately that it does not show the Raphael touch. Whom it represents is less certain. The question whether it is Altoviti could have been settled long ago if Cellini's bust had only been photographed from the same angle as this head. The painting has at all events little in common with Raphael himself. The state of preservation is good, yet we feel the absence of any congruity between the green of the background and the violet gown, the black cap and golden-straw-coloured hair, and the hot red flesh-tones. At no point has the colour been successfully dematerialised; it displays everywhere a uniformly viscous and oily quality. There has been talk of Giulio Romano, also of Peruzzi. The impression cannot be dismissed that we may here be concerned with a self-portrait painted by one of Raphael's followers in Rome. But Giulio Romano, who might be taken into consideration on account of the colour, had black hair; Penni had gentler features.

ROMAN PORTRAITS
§ The Portrait of Chigi lost?

Our curiosity to see a portrait of the "gran mercante della cristianità", Agostino Chigi, remains unsatisfied. Beyond a doubt Raphael must have painted him. The works he did for him, the dome in Santa Maria del Popolo, the SIBYLS of the Pace, and the Farnesina frescoes, show in what a profound spirit of friendship he entered into Chigi's desires. We should then possess the portrait of a man who felt his actions and existence to be astrologically determined for him, combining with this trait the life-affirming sensuousness and the grandiose manners of a man of widely influential power in the world as a citizen. But not a trace of such a picture has come down to us, and only the distorted profile of his medals gives an idea of the subject that must in this case have presented itself for Raphael's interpretation.

§ *Donna Velata*

Cardinal Bibbiena, trusty servant of the House of Medici, who sang the praises and enjoyed the benefits of its magnificence, writes as follows: "To complete its proud splendour this Court lacks only one thing—a garland of beautiful women." This would also be sadly lacking in the series of Raphael's Roman portraits if the artist had not taken up this theme for himself. The DONNA VELATA of the Pitti Palace (Plates 130, 132) is the result of a commission of his very own, in the midst of the great frescoes and orders for altarpieces; it is a love-prompted improvisation on the most charming of themes—the innocence and womanly dignity of a young Roman woman of the people. The colour echoes this harmony of character. The painting on canvas has retained in a delightful manner the style of the fresco-painter. The warm flesh-tints are laid on the grey ground with brush-strokes structurally following the movement of the forms—for instance, in the ravishing curves of the upper lip and the delicately modelled pit of the neck, the ear in transparent pearly tones, the contour of neck and nape vibrating against the cool tones of the dim recesses in the veil. The contrast of the deep chestnut brown in the hair with the softer surroundings is mitigated by the transparency at the crown of the head; a transition is provided by the fine wisps of hair astray on the temples and the red, blue and gold of the clasp with a pearl. The shadows are laid broadly on the flesh-tones, without toning-down, in the fresco method; on the amaranth necklace the stones are grey-green flecked with red where they remain dull, glazed only over the flesh-tone, the gold mounting thickly outlined. The eyes, lips and black-and-gold laces on the border of the chemise add to this improvised harmony of pale pinkish-yellow and green on the skin, the only stronger colour, a delicate parallel to the lifeless greyish white of the veil. The painting on the damask of the sleeve and the golden trimmings has an impasto effect, as though in a different sphere, with a somewhat mannered, decorative play of the brush, as if it were by a rougher hand and the poetry of the conception displayed in the head needed to be made clearer for us; we feel that this modish display seems out of keeping with the essential refinement of a woman of the people. She herself also responds by her look to the whim of her painter, feeling strange in the dress she is not really *wearing*, half gratified, half embarrassed, asking, "what does he find in me?"; that intimate charm of the most personal avowals wafts over her which we find again in Titian's " BELLA", but not so filled with sublimity.

The longer we dwell upon this picture and the wonderful construction of its forms and lines, the more a feeling of estrangement is forced upon us by the presence, with so much perfection, of certain dead passages. The space between the top of the head and the frame seems rather too wide to allow of the complete dominance of the proudly carried head, and the left hand ought to be holding something between the thumb and forefinger in such a pose. The mass of the veil on the left has a clumsy and monotonous effect beside all the subtle mobility of the hands. We have a right to the highest anticipations; faults in the execution such as we find here could hardly be Raphael's. Information on this point would perhaps be given by the example formerly in the Arundel Collection; we know it only from the engraving by Wenzel Hollar (Plate 131, Parthey 87). Here the space above was filled by the nimbus, the line of the veil over the bust was broken by the palm, the fingers of the left hand were laid on one of the spikes of the wheel. On the left, at two-thirds of the distance between the line of the veil and the frame, the palm may perhaps still at the present day be visible in the Pitti picture.

This lovely being would thus here for the first time be described as a saint. Whoever she may have been, she was doubtless called Catherine. This is more certain than that she was a baker's daughter from the Trastevere, as legend will have it, and that her name was Margareta, as is supposed to be provable. At a later time Raphael's pupil Giulio Romano seems to have profaned her in the well-known picture from the Barberini Gallery, now in the Borghese Gallery; in a school painting in the Strasburg Museum her features are recognised again in a coarsened version, and a wheel has been inserted beside her as St Catherine. Her features are borne by the Magdalen in the St Cecilia (Plate 244), and they may be assumed to occur in the entirely ruined picture in the gallery at Hanover, combined with wonderful remnants of Raphael's own painting on the neck and bust. But these uncertain and questionable facts fail to attract attention. We know that the master found the purity of her young features, with the dark, beaming charm of her look, worthy of the other-worldly revelation of the Sistine Madonna. Years ago it was supposed that her still dazzling features, although quickly coarsened, might be recognised in the picture in the Czartoryski Gallery at Cracow (Plate 133). Once there was a much-disputed idea that it might be a self-portrait of Raphael, also that it perhaps represented the Duke of Urbino or, finally, the Fornarina. Sebastiano del Piombo was mentioned as its painter, and so were as many other artists as there were experts who stood in front of the picture when it was at Dresden during the last war. The hair with its locks reluctantly breaking loose on the temples, and the deep-cut thumbs, warrant the conclusion that it is a woman who is here represented; also the secret of the bosom is rather betrayed than guarded by the fur cloak, not put on, but thrown as if on the spur of the moment over the shirt. This négligé has a poetic significance only if it is a woman who is in question. The right forearm seems to rest on the bottom of a lute. The white of the chemise, the gold and brown of the gown with its fur collar, the greenish-golden cover on the table, form with the gleaming flesh-tones a boldly conceived harmony, gorgeous to a degree, which is gathered together within the grand, free form of the silhouette. The painting can be compared for triumphant power with the group of the Pope in the ATTILA; like this fresco, it is of inestimable value as the last evidence quite incontestably from Raphael's own hand of his most personal chromatic expression.

For evidence of this nature is rare, at this time when the master was so fully occupied. Even tempting commissions from influential patrons, such as the portrait of JOANNA OF ARAGON, which went to France, were carried out by pupils, often of course with the tacit intention on Raphael's part of going over them again personally. In the case of this gift of Bibbiena to King Francis I, the cartoon at Naples was drawn by a pupil, certainly Giulio Romano. With the gorgeous red tones of this picture glaring at us we have the impression that nothing whatever about it betrays Raphael's participation. All the forms and movements fit in with Giulio's unpleasant relief style; spatially the picture fails to achieve anything more than background effects. The composition of figure and environment in their relation to one another—Raphael's most personal sign manual—is completely lacking. He did not pass on the secret to his pupils.

§ Interpreter of Renaissance Society

If there is one thing that makes Raphael a great portrait-painter, it is the experience he makes possible for us of a humanistically—which at that time meant harmoniously—cultured society majestically interpreted in accordance with their own desires. So long as this culture was dominated by an ideal, until the triumph of the new bourgeoisie in the French Revolution, Raphael was accepted as its painter, without any question. It embodied itself in the symmetrically developed man, full of poise and spiritual energy, and in the fact that these figures gave outward effect to the inner moderation of their character. Herein lay Raphael's prolonged influence, peculiar and ennobling, on life. It was not until the more recent, Nazarene appreciation of him, in the nineteenth century, that he was regarded as "the Painter of Madonnas". His creative nature, with its ennobling of everyday life, found its fairest consummation of that capacity for setting even maternity also before the eyes of mankind with a halo of virginity like that of Paradise.

IX

ROMAN MADONNAS

THE Blessed Virgin appeared to the boyish painter as a nun, to the roaming youth as a beautiful soul; to Raphael the man she became woman in her perfection as mother.

At the outset he may have been prevented, to begin with, by the great new Vatican commissions from going further in his confession of this mystery, a mystery which he had so young become a master in proclaiming; indeed, it seems as if he never carried through to completion any paintings of the Virgin he may perhaps have taken with him from Florence, with the intention of finishing them in Rome; yet they included some that were very near to his heart. Such was the ESTERHAZY MADONNA at Budapest, of which only the underpainting is finished. He had done the preliminaries for it in one of his freest Florentine pen-drawings, in the Uffizi, which at the same time served as cartoon for the little picture a few inches in dimensions (20 × 25). In a motive taken from Leonardo, the Virgin turns on one knee and, with a charming gesture, holds the Child as he reaches from a mound of earth towards the little John the Baptist; the saint crouches on the ground with his inscribed scroll, like a Cupid drawing his bow. This elastic kneeling pose was transferred to the Albertina drawing of children playing and the little torch-bearer who, five years later, crowned the central niche in the fresco of the SIBYLS in Santa Maria della Pace (Plate 195). The delightfully conceived landscape in the drawing, with a little chapel on a height approached by a row of cypresses, gives way in the painting to a view of the Tiber with the ruins of the Forum of Nerva—the only part of the little picture that appears to be entirely carried out; there is a truly Roman atmosphere in the soft terracotta tones which Poelenborch might have envied the master. Everything else retains the unfinished charm of the rough sketch and of the visible underpainting.

The MADONNA DI CASA COLONNA of the Berlin gallery, still in many places unfinished, also certainly belongs to this transitional period. Full sunlight is provided as a harmonious accompaniment to the inward bliss of mother and child; here Raphael succeeded in painting in colours what he had in view in the pen-sketches with contours broken by excess of light—the profusion of light of Perugino in his early days, with sunny half-darkness in the shadows and in the brocaded breviary in the Virgin's hand. But the very forms and attitude point beyond any observation of nature; the great *contraposto* that begins in the head and neck must die away downwards, although out of sight, in the leg hanging down at full length. It is the freedom of the First Stanza, before the true Roman forms had yet been mastered.

The riotous profusion of such intimate ideas could not be entirely suppressed by the monumental undertakings. At the time of his arrival in Rome Raphael began a little sketchbook, to the pink-ground pages of which he committed with silverpoint his inspirations for his favourite theme of mother and child. It has been possible to identify as belonging to this book eleven sheets, by their technique and by the linking of their motives with one another—at Lille, in London, and among former possessions of the Granducal House of Tuscany, now in a private collection at Basle. They surround early Roman compositions (*R. Z.*, VIII). Amongst them there recurs, on several sheets, a child lying down, reaching out towards the left, just awakening or else saucily playing; as he does so, he looks up at his mother in a delightfully animated *contraposto*, like the BRIDGEWATER MADONNA (Plates 134, 136), in the possession of Lord Elles-mere, in London. In this picture the child with his disordered hair looks like a brother of the *putti* that help to fill with charm their grouping round the figure, naturally not very alluring, of Justice, in the small ceiling pictures of the First Stanza. It is perhaps no accident that this composition has its only parallel, as a self-assertive outbreak, among German sculptures of that period, such as Gregor Erhart's KEISHEIM VIRGIN, or in Veit Stoss, one of whose graphic works may have derived a spark of inspiration from this source. Beside the window in the semi-twilight of a room the boy is being watched over by the tenderest of mothers, with melancholy joy in her child, who is trying to have his way without her and her guidance. The finest glazings are employed for the in-expressible quality in her emotion. Thus the figure, one of the profoundest of tributes to the divine mother, stands out, half in the shadow of the room, in alluring *sfumato* against the background; the tenderness of the figure indicates, in the artist who had the sensibility to perceive it, the maturity of manhood.

§ Pink Sketchbook: Questionable Execution of early Roman Madonnas

The comrades of this child in the pages of the pink sketchbook had, it seems, to await their summons to life, to awakening and continued existence in pictures by the master's hand. Yet it was hardly an accident that they were employed for compositions of which the ideas could only have arisen out of Raphael's very own imagination, but of which the execution in painting is often doubtful; frequently several examples compete for a privilege which nevertheless cannot be conceded to any of them. Thus, the child of the MADONNA WITH THE CARN-ATION occurs on a sheet from the sketchbook at Lille (*R. Z.*, VIII, 352); of this composition examples are continually turning up with the claim to be the lost original, and perhaps there was no such original. In the same manner, the MADONNA WITH THE SLEEPING CHILD, of which the motive occurs on these pages, appears in examples belonging to the Duke of Westminster, to Prince Wied, at Munich, and in Budapest. The composition of the ALDOBRANDINI-GARVAGH MADONNA, in the National Gallery, we find carried to quite an advanced stage in these pink pages. It is the great Roman theme of the Madonna crouching with thigh drawn high up, on a stone pedestal in front of the pier of a window; the Child turns from the left down towards the boy St John, who is reaching up from the opposite side. The Virgin gathers the group together, with the protecting folds of her cloak on one side and her arm on the other, with an effect of monumental grandeur (*R. Z.*, VIII). But the execution has about it something of a glassy, Florentine quality in the pink and blue, almost reminiscent of Lorenzo di Credi; the artist seems to have bestowed all his pains on plastic effect alone, and none on colour expression. Unusual though the manner is in which the headdress, in blue, green and gold, the hair, and the oval face, with refreshingly austere look, are set off against the background, yet they must be allowed to pass for Raphael's ideas as regards colour; but for all that, in this picture there is nowhere any echo of the harmony and breadth of the fresco-painter. It seems as though a final outer surface were lacking which would have given to this theme the vitality of colour worthy of him; here if anywhere it would be permissible to think of early works of Raphael's pupils. The choice would lie between Penni and Giulio Romano, though in favour of Penni one could adduce nothing but the semblance of a Florentine character, and for Giulio only a certain *bravura* indifferent to refinement. The issue is similar in the case of the *VIERGE AU VOILE*, in the Louvre, which is made up of elements belonging to different periods. The striking landscape seems, with its vertical form, to have nothing to do with the composition of the figures, in which everything fits into a square. Nevertheless these pictures, even without being carried out by Raphael personally, contributed to the reputation of their composer; the Child of the ALDOBRANDINI MADONNA—whether through the original or through a study for it such as that in Vienna (*R. Z.*, VIII, 359)—was given the peculiar distinction of being awakened to new, radiant life through Rubens in a picture of the child Christ in the act of benediction (Plate 137).

Raphael's thoughts circled in the pink sketchbook around the sleeping and awakening boy. The Madonna lifting the veil from the recumbent Child is found in the magnificently grouped ADORATION OF THE SHEPHERDS of the pen-drawing at Oxford belonging to the period of the *DISPUTA* (*R. Z.*, VIII, 361). A ruin serves as a stage for the animated scene; shepherds peer in from the sides and over the walls; Mary kneels as she lifts the veil almost shyly from the miraculous babe, who turns his opened eyes towards the eldest and devoutest of the shepherds. A cape, the long divided beard, the strongly-formed brow, and his especially humble bearing make him recognisable as the "servus servorum", the servant of the servants of God, Julius II. It might be conceivable to see in this group crowded with persons the sketch for a picture for his favourite church, Santa Maria del Popolo. That it is the Pope who is kneeling here seems to be proved by a finished drawing for a tapesty, in the Louvre, by Thomas Vincidor, which shows his successor, Leo X, doing homage in the same position. We have no knowledge of a picture with this subject, only of a tapestry which has been lost, woven after Vincidor's design, for the bedroom of the Medici Pope. In the time of Julius II the only work done by Raphael for the church at the entrance-gate of Rome was the Virgin that later acquired the name of the MADONNA OF LORETO. To the "People" he gave a popular and intimate theme—an ordinary bed, with the Child just awakened and taking as a game the lifting of the veil by his mother, whilst Joseph looks on out of the half-darkness of the back of the room, with the solicitude of the fosterfather, at her enraptured hesitation and, as it were, aloof enjoyment. The boy's attitudes are continually introduced anew, with all the intimate charms of his little figure, on the pages of the *taccuino* (*R. Z.*, VIII, 345–355); we should dearly like to have seen rendered in paint this tenderness so much in accordance with the rules of Leonardo. How near Raphael came to them is shown by the head and pose of the Virgin, who looks like a sister of St John in the LAST SUPPER. But if there was an original, which must have been contemporary with the earliest ceiling-paintings, the *JUSTITIA*, for instance, it has not been preserved; it has disappeared, or is as ruined as the example discovered in the possession of the Russian family of Demidov-San-Donato, in the Urals, which even Raphael's signature does not avail to bring back to life and repute.

Among the other leaves from the pink book we possess the delightful study of a head and the laughing child's head in London (*R. Z.*, VIII, 349) belonging to the MACKINTOSH MADONNA (Plates 135, 138*a*); also ideas for her pose seated on the pedestal, at Lille. The study of the head was at one time considered to be a Franciabigio, at another a forgery; the cartoon preserved in the British Museum, broadly executed in charcoal, which comes quite near to the previous fragmentary study for one of the *putti* beside the POETRY (Plate 140, *R. Z.*, V, 229) in the same collection, was attributed to Brescianino soon after it was bought. The picture in the National Gallery is only a wreck that has become unrecognisable, apparently as the result of a fire, from which it can hardly be seen whether it ever was a work of Raphael's own hand. But many replicas, from the first by Domenico Alfani in an altarpiece of the year 1518, to one of Sassoferrato's time, speak for the celebrity of the original. The Roman *tondo*-pictures, which perhaps came into existence when the artist was pausing to take breath between the two Stanze, are the first to show an equal balance between conception and painting; for these also, the earliest ideas are to be found in this sketchbook. On one of the leaves with the awakening child three times repeated, there is a boy's head entirely finished in fine strokes which gives an idea of the glazings intended for it after the example of Leonardo's BENOIS MADONNA; side by side with this there one is astounded to find a female nude drawing—the Fornarina crouching on the ground with her left knee drawn up high, and her head bowed slightly forward and looking outwards, seemingly an idea for the attitude of the MADONNA DELLA SEDIA (Plate 138*b*, *R. Z.*, VIII, 354). On another little sheet there is a preliminary study, although disfigured by lines added afterwards, for the child St John of the ALBA MADONNA.

Into these circular pictures Raphael at last introduced the sublime features of the Roman type; in the consummate creation of that type, the Roman woman, he found them capable of expressing what is highest in purity, maternal dignity and grace.

This was the moment when, on the sheets of studies for the DISPUTA, among laudatory sonnets addressed to a fair recipient known only to him, there came to the draughtsman's pen the loveliest conceptions of woman, in the nude sketch for the reclining PRUDENTIA, in the lunette of the fourth wall (Plate 86, *R. Z.*, VI, 280.) The strands woven in Michael Angelo's DONI TONDO thus taken up by Raphael resulted, here and there on pages of sketches, in crouching groups of the Virgin with the child St John, in the pink *taccuino*, at Florence, (beside a figure from the SCHOOL OF ATHENS), in Vienna, and at Cambridge. The double sheet at Lille (*R. Z.*, VIII, 364, 365, Plate 144) outshines them all; it is the triumph of all draughtsmanship, not of Raphael's alone. One side shows the first circular design for the ALBA MADONNA, in red chalk—the motive of the Child carried out further below with the pen; above, hastily jotted down with the pen in bistre, the scheme for the MADONNA DELLA SEDIA, and in the quadrangular frame a similar pictorial idea—Mary with the Child and the little St John against the background of a waving curtain, an idea that ended in the MADONNA DELLA TENDA at Munich.

The reverse of the same sheet comes nearer to the execution of the idea of the composition; here we have a nude study for the pose of the ALBA MADONNA, slightly draped and now set down with red chalk, in curving, plastic half-shading. The seething profusion of ideas at this period, between the First and Second Stanza, is revealed further by the plan and elevation of a building adorned with statues which even the admiring gaze of architects has found incapable of interpretation.

In the design, the supple movement of the Virgin is in complete conformity with the rhythms of the circle, the mountain range, the little trees, the base of a column beneath her arm. From the grace of the leg with the sandal-adorned foot we can imagine how divinely she must walk who could look thus when at rest. Here also, as in the angels of the DISPUTA, the motive really comes from the BELVEDERE APOLLO.

In the circular picture the landscape with its gentle features, the lines of the houses, the growth of the trees and herbage, is not only an accompaniment to forms disposed in it with the utmost freedom; it also encloses the group in all its harmony spatially within the wide sweep of its curve, beyond the limits of the design, as the stars ranged themselves in order to the strains of Amphion. The deep space encircles the figures as its centre; throughout all the lines, forms and sentiments, the circle repeats itself again and again significantly as the means of concentrating vision and mood on the message so mysteriously proclaimed by the figures. With her child and her book, the Virgin has given herself up so completely, in this spot remote from men, to quietness and devotion, that the little crossbearer who approaches out of the landscape is of course kindly greeted, as a fond playmate—but a mother's instinct causes her to look at his significant plaything with a trace of anxious questioning as to the use of this gift for her child. Quite a new profundity has been introduced into the familiar theme: the pious imagination traverses in an instant a tremendous course at the beginning of which, still obscure, are tender care and childish play, and at the end the sign of sacrificial death, with the fulfilment of a destiny of which even this mother has hardly a foreboding, at the foot of the Cross. This course seems also to sweep through the liquid blue of the overarching sky and the harmony of blue and red with the enchanting flesh-tones which these spaces encircle as the centre round which all gravitates. With all her charm, it was through her free and heroic bearing, that the vehicle of such conceptions had to speak; the Roman type, absolutely breathing grandeur, made so convincing an impression on the poet-painter that figures and space are composed as a single creation. If the group were suddenly to appear before us, with this bending and stooping figure—this knee, foot and drapery, it would demand none other than this circular frame, and the earthly world would be suffered to approach it only thus at a distance, so as discreetly to encircle it.

Even here, in a lyrical theme, it is the historical painter who speaks, compelling our attention to the essential in every inch of his picture. Environment is becoming for him more and more inessential in its details. In the frescoes of the Stanza of Heliodorus a few beats are enough to give the tempo; now space becomes for him a category of thought instead of an object of observation, and the artist has yielded place entirely to the poet—his painting exists solely for the sake of its poetry.

The MADONNA DELLA SEDIA (Plate 142) derives its vitality only from the figure in space—one might say, the figure as space. A green curtain intercepts the eye that might otherwise pass beyond into the depths of space, and compels it to concentrate on the group, as in former times the gold background had done, in Gothic art. And the figure with its boldly foreshortened members creates space in itself. These majestic Roman women are accustomed to walking on historic soil that witnessed on its hills the rise and fall of the historic destinies of peoples; they have grown up among pedestals of columns and stone steps, and their bearing in repose is as free as their gait.

Thus the Virgin supports herself, leaning back in her chair, her left foot

131

raised high on a step; in the hollow thus formed by her lap the Child seems to be ensconced like a pearl in its shell. In fact, everything in the frame gives a sense of concavity—even the little St John comes under its sway; thus every motive in the picture recurves outwards, even to the impression of exuberant splendour in a child, and of a life that brings blessings to every worshipper. In the life and aspirations of all such this mother, wearing as she does the dress of a Roman woman of the people, seems to participate; it is to *them* that she wishes to speak in their own dialect, as it were with her very nature.

§ The Architect as Painter

The lines and forms gravitate in a circle about the rounded contours of this boy with his tremendous vitality, as if one stood on the diagonal within the compass of a cupola; so real is the attraction for the gaze of the *opaion*, the fascinating eye of the Child in which all the circles and curves have their centre and come to rest. We must bear in mind that at that time the painter was thinking as architect on the lines of vaulted compositions such as this, designed to concentrate devotion; the Cappella Chigi and plans for St Peter's were simultaneously in progress.

The excessive gorgeousness of the gold baroque frame, it is true, makes it impossible to-day to take in the rhythm of this most famous of pictures; it is the falsest architecture for the composition and colours. Thanks to the coloured fringes and gold lace, the green cloth with the soft red sleeve, even an unfortunate yellowish gold in the Child and the blue of the cloak, are keyed to the neutral ground and are intended really only to enhance the lively rounded forms of the divine Child; the colours are not laid thinly, but in large brush-strokes as free as could be, the flesh-tones with a wonderful fineness of surface that seems to breathe.

The MADONNA DELLA TENDA has been preserved as a miracle of painting, though less admired than the picture we have been discussing—indeed, since the verdict given by Lermolieff at Munich in favour of Giulio Romano, now almost disregarded; its condition has given excuse enough to critics of the last half century for no longer attributing this precious piece to Raphael (Plate 148). The conception for it began at the same time with the ALBA MADONNA (Plates 143, 144) in the lovely Lille drawing; it is all but circular. The upraised leg brings the line of the blue cloak and of the neck into a sweeping curve with which the contour of the Child and even his feet fit in and conform. The colour is laid by the brush with an effect of fresco-painting, very various in rhythm; in the hair it is in rough short strokes, then again in tones applied in the manner of Ribera, on the shoulder and upper arm of the Child, as in the fragment of FRESCO IN THE SAN LUCA GALLERY and in the portrait of Leo X. The little hand on the soft-red cloak of the Madonna is a miracle of transfigured colour—an improvisation of transparent red in the shadow of the fingers, with lights giving an effect of vibration; it is the same on the nose and round the eyes—a juxtaposition of diaphanous roseleaf and mother-of-pearl which is otherwise regarded as the signature of Titian. The conventional red and blue colours of the Madonna are attuned to the whole more delicately than in the MADONNA DELLA SEDIA; chromatic transitions of colour to the whitish light on brow and cheeks are provided by the wine-red, gold-striped kerchief, passing through the gold-worked veil and the ochre-brown hair, with straw-coloured lights on individual shining strands. The gleam here and in the eye is almost the same—the white reflection on the iris of pale bluish tone. The child's head, blooming, alive, beams forth in front of the cold blue of the cloak and the green of the curtain, among the warmest tones—the red of the dress and the brown of the head of St John—which are a triumph for the artist through the fluid quality of the painting.

Those who wish to know why Raphael was held in repute as a painter in such a vital period should join the ranks of the worshippers before this picture in the Pinakothek.

When this picture came into being, Raphael had familiarised himself with mothers of the people in the MASS OF BOLSENA, and the other-worldly had revealed itself to him. The world of his thoughts was in perpetual intercourse with the things of the beyond, which he had scarcely had new opportunities of painting since the DISPUTA. The vision of the heavenly world revealing itself to the earthly never forsook him again after those first designs for the apparition of the Virgin above the Apostles beside the sarcophagus. The studies for the RESURRECTION had once again summarised in a condensed form this effect of an apparition upon earth; its last appearance was to be on the Heliodorus ceiling, in the ALMIGHTY ANNOUNCING HIS PROMISES TO NOAH, and in the BURNING BUSH; it is also the vehicle of the convulsion, caused by the figures of the Apostles, amongst the hosts of Attila. But the elevating and consolatory clearness of the vision when Heaven opens and the mediatress of Heaven's love was to appear before the eyes of earthly men, was still withheld.

To conjure this into solid form out of the chaos of ideas was reserved for a commission. It seems that the merit of providing Raphael with the first opportunity to express himself in this strain belongs to the Papal historian and friend of Julius II, Sigismondo de' Conti; it was he who gave the commission for the Madonna for the High Altar of the Basilica of Santa Maria in Araceli, behind which he wished to find a burial-place. His family two generations later allowed the picture to be brought to San Francesco at Foligno. Then it received its name, when it came to the Vatican after the Paris interlude of 1797–1815.

Conti died in February, 1512, a year before his Papal master. Raphael will thus have conceived the composition of the MADONNA OF FOLIGNO (Plates 145, 146) at the time of the First Stanza. In actual fact, the revelation of the Virgin, in a truly other-worldly guise, is to be found with a drawing for the SCHOOL OF ATHENS, in charcoal, in the boldest of strokes. Angels sweep down to earth with her as she looks benignly down, whilst the Child takes shelter at his mother's neck as if shuddering at the nearness of the world (*R. Z.*, VIII, 368). This poetical conception is carried further and consolidated in the grandiose chalk drawing at Chatsworth (Plate 141): the Virgin looks into the distance as if she felt herself suddenly withdrawn from the clouds, with halting foot and the boy pressed protectingly to her; her gaze is directed almost as in a swoon down towards the earth, which nevertheless it greets with blessing. The old copy of a lost pen-drawing in the Uffizi (*R. Z.*, VIII, text p. 380) discloses the fact that this idea must already have acquired more definite form; but it was then converted into the group seated quietly on clouds. At one stage, as Marcantonio has handed it down to us in his engraving (Bartsch 47), the Virgin looks downwards, with the Child on her knee; and finally the finished chalk drawing on North Italian greenish paper already approximates to the group in the painting (*R. Z.*, VIII, 370), only here there was still some indecision in the case of the Child—he was originally thought of as reclining on his mother's lap, then he came to be standing. Only in the picture did the conception first obtain its final expression, connecting it with the worshippers below.

§ The Araceli Virgin: its Antecedents

One who had to paint the picture for the High Altar of Santa Maria in Araceli could not well fail to pick up the traditions that are associated with the name of the ancient basilica and are present in the consciousness of its congregation. The Virgin Mother on the Altar in Heaven had appeared to the Emperor Augustus. For this reason Raphael necessarily gave the preference to the apparition of a sovereign lady on her heavenly seat over this figure suddenly revealing herself in his sketches. Nevertheless she seems just to have floated upon clouds out of the blue firmament, to favour the world with her regard; in this aspect she rose up, visible from afar in the gleaming yellow of her nimbus, out of the niche filled with a dim blue cloud of angels, in front of the apse of the church. Everything circles, above, behind, beneath her; for as she inclines herself towards her faithful adorers, she takes with her, into the circle of her airy sphere, which is closed upwards by the arched form of the frame, the heads below lifted in the rapture of worship. The line of the figures rises in the direction pointed out by the Baptist, and leads the eye upwards from the angles, where the lifeless folds of the garments have acquired their soaring vitality, through the hands swaying in adoration on either side, to the Child who, half in dreamy playfulness, takes an enchanting part in the scene.

This dependence of the earthly participants on the spectacle of the Child gives to the heavenly group an enhancement almost above that of their original appearance by themselves on the Altar in Heaven. They are all there with a view to this effect—the Forerunner with his beckoning hand, more compelling in its appeal than his head, which is foreign to Raphael's world; St Francis, who approaches on his knees, entirely fascinated by the cross that he holds before him as his goal and above which his gaze now carries him away; St Jerome, all devoutness in his bowed shoulders, to which his kindly, spiritual hands lead up, as if preparing the way; and the unfeigned emotion of the donor. The *putto*, beaming upwards in rapture, may possibly, when the tablet he holds still bore the words of praise now obliterated, have impersonated the first sermon of a child preacher in honour of the heavenly boy, a sermon that has remained the custom in this church to the present day, from Christmas to Epiphany. The beginning of its wanderings from the place for which the altarpiece came into existence was to another Franciscan church, at Foligno; then it was transferred from wood on to canvas in Paris, and after the injuries it suffered in transport thither, it was falsified by French restorers in its colouring and in the expression of many of the heads. Thus the yellow with a heavy instead of a light effect was introduced into the nimbus surrounding the Virgin, also the lifeless, thick brown mass in the hair coat of the Baptist, and the ecstatic expression, baroque in its nervousness, in the St Francis. Raphael's handiwork has been preserved in the peach-coloured skin of the Virgin's face, as well as in the harmony ranging from the chestnut-brown hair and pink flesh to the bronzy gold of the borders, one of which, on the red sleeve, gleams like the diaphanous inside of a fruit. Behind all this refinement of detail the yellow of the nimbus must once have had a softened effect by the quietness of its form, in the twilight and the wide dimensions of the church.

As regards the landscape, with a meteor on its enigmatic flight, of which we know nothing more than that Raphael understood how to make marvellous use of it for the rhythm of its sweep, the vista displays, in a remarkably good state of preservation, a touch in which it is hardly credible that Raphael's hand is to be recognised. Thick silvery high-lights are laid over washes of warm tones. It has been believed that one of the Dossi might be inferred, though we possess no clue to prove such a conclusion; we do well however to keep clearly in view the fact that much yet remains to be disclosed with regard to Raphael's attitude towards nature.

§ The Sistine Madonna (Plate 147)

To Roman eyes of that period his work doubtless seemed more bound up with tradition than to us; the group of the donor with the patron who presents him had been a constant feature for more than a generation, since the time of Perugino's fresco in the apse of Old St Peter's, in representations of the Pope as worshipper. Such groups were repeated on the sepulchral monuments of the two Piccolomini, Pius II and Pius III alike, in Old St Peter's, now in Sant' Andrea della Valle. The deceased was depicted kneeling *in pontificalibus*, presented by the Prince of the Apostles, whilst the Child on his mother's lap bends down towards him.[1] It was the great Pope, whose commissions and temperament had made Raphael a monumental painter, who called on him as if from the grave to capture the heavenly, for the space of an hour of solemn devotion, for mortal eyes to see. All the mystic legends as to its origin have not availed to explain the miracle of the SISTINE MADONNA; equally unavailing has been the interpretation of it, piously deduced from liturgical arguments, as a funerary velarium to be set before the coffin at the obsequies of the great Julius. For Raphael this commission was decisive. He was now allowed to bring within the range of experience, purely for its own sake, the dream of the Epiphany of the Godhead that he had committed to paper in studies for the CORONATION OF THE VIRGIN and the RESURRECTION; also the conception in the *DISPUTA*, of the appearance of the Godhead out of the Infinite before the eyes of the world, which only the architectural setting had compelled him to tie down to an earthly plane. The spectacle of this revelation out of another sphere separates us from all that is finite; for a few moments we can believe that we look into the beyond, and here is the beginning of all that remains ever inexplicable in the other enigmas which beset this vision.

Vasari relates, it is true, that the picture was painted for the High Altar of the Black Monks of San Sisto, at Piacenza. But it was never an altar *panel*; from the outset it was painted on canvas, never even transferred from wood. Canvas style is rigidly adhered to throughout, the colours are laid on very thinly, entirely without that plastic effect of the panel picture which at that time an altarpiece required in order to hold its own in the church amid all the severe stonework. Even Rubens was still aware of this. Canvas was used for painting on only to meet special occasions, for transient decoration or to cover something up, coloured ornament being given to the envelope.

§ Interpretation

After long intervals in pronouncements as to the Sistine Madonna, Hubert Grimme reinstated the tradition of piety, and discovered a new approach which seems to lead right up to the threshold of devotional experience.[2] So much has been written about the picture without any notice being taken of the brown strip on which the two *putti* are leaning; it did not occur to anyone even to ask why St Sixtus, who is at home among the clouds, has had to put down his tiara on this earthly object of wood. St Sixtus was regarded by the Della Rovere as their patron; his name was adopted by the first Pope of the family, Francesco della Rovere, Sixtus IV. St Barbara is revered as the patroness of the hour of death; her gaze is directed towards the spot where the Papal crown with the Rovere acorn is placed. This armorial badge of the family, the acorn, is repeated in the brocade pattern of the cope. The look of the Virgin, as of the Child, is of

[1] Fischel, *Zeichnungen der Umbrer*, figs. 31, 32.
[2] "Das Rätsel der Sixtinischen Madonna", *Zeitschrift für bildende Kunst*, 57, 1922, p. 41 *seq.*

compelling seriousness, strikingly majestic and solemn as in no other instance. Only in the Good Friday painting of Botticelli from San Francesco, in the Kaiser Friedrich-Museum, do we find anything to hold us equally spellbound. The unusual gesture of the hands with which the Virgin bears the Child, as if to present him, contributes to this result. Thus the Prayer for the Dying, "Salve Regina", seems truly to find echoing fulfilment in look and gesture ... "eja advocata nostra, illos tuos misericordes oculos ad nos converte"—"Come, Thou then, our Advocate, turn upon us thy compassionate eyes that we know so well"—"et post hoc exilium"—"and after this vale of tears", that is, at our death, at our entry into bliss—"ostende nobis Jesum, fructum benedictum ventris tui"—"and show us Jesus, the blessed fruit of thy body". This present-ation of the divine Child, and the turning of eyes towards him, provide the motive for the figure. Riemenschneider was also full of it, at the same period, in the wood figure of the Mother of God, in the Deutsches Museum; we see that it was accessible to other faithful souls also within the Church, but this is the beginning of Raphael's role, leading into untrodden spheres. The curtain has separated the world, with the coffin on the lid of which rests the crown of the Pope, from the sphere beyond, which is now to receive the departed; now we see it gathered up by unseen hands, parting and swirling aside—the rings still shake on the swaying rod—so suddenly has it opened before the Queen of Heaven as she comes to fulfil the prayer for the Dead. This unexpected meeting between the earthly and the heavenly becomes clear through the uncom-promising mass of the coffin with the crown, which has provided an unaccus-tomed place to rest on for the winged messengers of Heaven, and through the fluctuation of heaviness and lightness in the figures. The saints, in the brocade of the cope or in trailing earthly draperies, kneel half sunk in the clouds, as if wading; but up above, the feet of the Virgin bear the sublime Figure as, with her veil blowing out and her swaying garments, she has swept, a moment before, out of spaces filled with billowy blue clouds that become ever lighter and more luminous behind her, like the cherubim and their song.

Line and colour are inseparable: the green of the curtain, the brown of the coffin-lid and the crown are the only heavy things, belonging to this world; in the radiance above, the lightness dispenses with lines and tones; the heavy borders of the Papal vestments and the gathered-up cloak of St Barbara trail stiffly by comparison with the flowing blue mantle about the ankles of the Virgin. In the wind of the realm on high and waving in front as she steps forward, it flaps back, whilst in the same breath of wind her smoke-grey mourning veil flutters down. No weight rests on these feet, and the knees are unaware of the corporeal burden they have to carry. The figures are to be looked at on two axes of vision: the Virgin, although near at hand, seems further back, and though smaller, yet over-tall. Only the fringe of a cloud beneath her foot bears witness to the starry distances that she has left behind her, in a majestic vast

137

vision of space and remoteness; such is the poet's handling of space—as in Dante: "Dove la legge natural nulla rileva." And in the human intimacies we note the lifelike ease of the movements, the foreshortening to the utmost degree of freedom in the forward-stretching right hand of the Pope and beneath the hand on his breast.

The eye is allowed to experience this rich and fascinating upward and downward movement. Even to-day, in spite of all injuries and worse rumours concerning the picture, the SISTINE MADONNA is among the best preserved examples of Raphael's painting. The faces of mother and child were slightly rubbed and touched up in the last restorations, one hundred years ago, the St Barbara even more so, but her hair retains undisturbed the fine brush-strokes of the golden high-lights; the *putti* below, applied on the ground quite lightly and transparently, make their contribution with the slight rustle of their pinions, wine-red and green, and the mother-of-pearl shimmer of their eyes, set down with a freedom equal to that of the most expressive passages of his fresco-painting of that period; their wings, in colours from another world, are stirred by a quivering rhythm, immediately above the rigid brown wood that serves as a welcome support as they keep watch at their ease over the coffin and listen to the earthly choir singing the Office for the Dead in the earthly sphere of the church. Above, the other pair of eyes, of the Divine Child, supported on the hands of his mother; he directs his gaze into the depths in front of him, not in order to see or to hear—nor does he look into endless space—it is another kind of immensity this eye embraces, in his future realm, the world of suffering, for the sake of which he was sent down to earth. Yet all this interplay between the spheres only makes the more incomprehensible that revelation of eternal motherhood that Raphael suggests in the consecrated expression of knowledge through suffering, of goodness and distance, happiness and presentiment, and that Goethe described in a similar blend of austere exaltation:

> "Der Mütter Urbild, Königin der Frauen
> Ein Wunderpinsel hat sie ausgedruckt.
> Ihr beugt ein Mann mit andachtsvollem Grauen,
> Ein Weib das Knie in Demut still entzückt."[1]

Everyone who has retained a sensibility for the poetry of the other world has always remarked the unusual character of the Sistine Madonna and its unsuitability for an altarpiece; and the canvas-painting style inseparable from its formal lightness and from the undulation of all the lines, has even occasioned the surmise that the picture may have been conceived as a processional banner. But

---

[1] "Of mothers primal type, of women Queen,
By magic brush portrayed for eye to see,
A man in holy dread, a woman meek
In quiet transport, to her bows the knee."

any desire to produce an effect with curtains on a fluttering cloth would have involved an unseemly trick. The vast difference between this picture, with its other-worldly character, and the others, particularly those for private devotion, only becomes clear when it is borne in mind that they were created by a painter whose thoughts at that time, as already an architect, were filled with the vitality of architectural members, with columns and half-columns enhanced by pedestals, with groups of pilasters permeating and dominating every flat surface. The masterbuilder was bound to give energetic direction to the hand of the painter in the altarpiece. He knew the demands of his building. In spaces divided up by members in such strong relief, with such a well-calculated and often triumphant influx of light in the choir, a picture could only hold its own if he gave a particularly emphatic structure to its painted surface. The lines of the SISTINE MADONNA would have proved too delicate in their modulation, its forms too slender. In the new, pronounced instrumentation of these buildings other means were demanded—a great diagonal in the composition, contrasts of chiaroscuro, of form and lighting, of heavy and light. The architect Raphael had first ventured to make use of these means as a painter, earlier almost than the Venetians—and again we may recall that these principles had already been mastered by Melozzo, a native of the Marches. This apparent interruption of architectural symmetry to secure for architecture decoration by means of painting in particular, denoted for the period, and in view of the derivation of Central Italian painting, an audacity without parallel. The plastic qualities of light in his construction enticed the architect, in his role as painter also, to new shores as yet unexplored.

The pictorial MADONNA WITH THE FISH (Plate 149) displays this new style in the Spartan simplicity of the forms and setting, the solidity and power of which make themselves felt only in the austerity of the fully mature architecture. The two steps of the dais and the knob on the arm of the throne are decoration enough for the seat of this sublime mother with her child; the mighty sweep of the curtain serves her as nimbus—set against the surging oblique lines of the folds, she seems even more sure of herself, in her inviolable purity. No braid or ornament is allowed to be seen on her dress. The devotion shown by the youthful Tobias is hardly adequate to such majesty, scarcely even that of the Archangel, the breath of whose inspiration seems to be continued in the curtain. In this hallowed sphere St Jerome, who faces them, can only look on with quiet emotion out of his inner sublimity; even his lion is banished uneasily to one side. The sketches we possess for the picture lead up to the entire grandeur of this composition. A study from models, in red chalk, is preserved in the Uffizi (Plate 150, $R.$ $Z.$ VIII, 371)—on a studio dais with a single step, a Roman woman wearing the kerchief of the peasant costume, with a bundle in her arms in place of the child; a bearded studio assistant as St Jerome, hastily sketched and, as it seems, clumsily touched up to make it clearer by another hand; above, a youth and a boy in contemporary costume.

The fiery inspiration of the painter has taken possession of their deliberately arranged poses. The youth is drawn by his emotion in shy reverence towards the centre; the head, hurriedly sketched and schematically outlined, made to tell by means of a few strong shadows, has its counterpart in the youth above the balustrade in the MASS OF BOLSENA; the bearing of the boy, full of veneration from head to foot, is paralleled in the kneeling of the Swiss Guards.

The large drawing for the entire composition, in a wash of sunny bistre over a chalk sketch abounding in *pentimenti*, belonged to the very select collection of Sir Thomas Lawrence (Plate 151, *R. Z.* VIII, 372). Almost all the figures have their place and their motive just as in the picture; the Child seems more pathetic, in his faltering movements, the young Tobias, already so close to Our Lady, is in the act of bending hesitatingly the knee, and there is a turn of surprise and shyness in his face; he is presented by the Archangel, a messenger from another world, whose air of veneration does not belie the element in which with these wings he is wont to soar; on the pious Tobias, love from above has in truth bestowed itself; and the Virgin looks down in delight over the homage paid to her child, yet without losing her austere composure concerning the things of earth . But if all this detail presents itself to us so that we feel its impress with greater freshness, yet even so the picture in the Prado denotes a still higher attainment. Again Raphael summons himself from revelation of the spiritual to a more majestic coherence in the architectural structure. Mysticism and dogma combine.

In the design, which Raphael divided into squares for enlargement and therefore regarded as the finished solution, the Madonna sits against the curtain, on the chair above the step, like an exalted mortal, *par inter pares*, as it were. The Archangel reaches with the crown of his head as high as her cheek; the face of Tobias is level with her lap. And there is something fascinatingly instructive about the manner in which these intimate touches are made to conform and harmonise with the coherent and unescapable majesty of the picture. The throne becomes steeper and narrower; instead of the chair with a round knob, the side of the throne is given its curving profile, whilst to the knob upon it is added another small knob with a gleaming high light. The baluster form distracts the eye from the quality of mundane indifference in the folds, and stresses the unparalleled nature of this woman who may in this manner look down from on high on her worshippers; for the Angel's face is now set the width of the shoulders away from her throne, and his back-thrown head remains below her shoulder; Tobias feels himself constrained to kneel, so that he remains, as if in humility, below the level of her hip, and is obliged to look upward to the point above from which the Lady with her grand and sublime gaze deigns to receive his homage to the Child. All is now subject to her, everything compels worship for her. The step, which in the drawings was placed as if by accident beside the studio dais, has become the block with its simple broad lines seen exactly from in front, which here also, from the inanimate zone of the picture, inescapably forces gaze and devotion in her direction. And this vitality concentrated in the centre of the composition is constantly being renewed; the curtain becomes two handbreadths wider at the top, its folds fuller of sheer energy in their sweep. They take up, as it were, the *aspiratio* of the Angel and proclaim through the whole church a "numine afflatur" and "sursum corda"; the line of the folds forms a nimbus for the oval of the head gleaming in front of them, with its moonlike stillness—an accent of unprecedented architectural power, yet entirely free from the massiveness of stone. Everything earthly is here suddenly raised to the degree of the heroic. Architecture sends out its challenge to painting and awakens the sublime style.

X

RAPHAEL AS ARCHITECT

BUILDING AND PAINTING

---

§ Union of the Earthly and the Heavenly

IF it is true that the challenge of architecture to painting awoke in Raphael the sublime style, his passage through the school of architecture will have offered him more than merely a glance at the new calling in which he had not yet tried his hand. Here also he must have undergone an upward progression from the earthly to the other-worldly, from the attainable to the desirable, from pious exaltation to heroic flight. Grown to maturity, he found in *architecture* the means of uniting both worlds, this world and the world of the beyond. The building of St Peter's, combined with the disposition of the great Pope, determined the destiny of Raphael in this sphere also; even before he himself became director of the Fabbrica di San Pietro, he was already under the spell of the great purpose that, thanks to the Pope and Bramante, the architect after his own heart, sought expression for the highest aspirations of the time.

§ Raphael's Training as Architect

His whole career was merely a road towards this destination. His dedication to architecture began already in early youth. He grew up with the Palazzo Ducale of Urbino before his eyes, and in veneration of its creator, the Istrian LUCIANO DA LAURANA, from Lovrana near Abbazia, whom old Giovanni Santi celebrated in his rhyming chronicle:

> "L'architetto a tutti altri sopra
> Fu Lutian Lauranna, huomo eccelente
> Che per nome vive, benchè morte el cuopra."[1]

Thus from the very beginning he was under the influence of the Late Antique Baroque at Spalato, with that irresistible trend of composition towards comprehensiveness that Palladio acknowledged anew, as we know, under the influence

[1] "The architect who all his peers excelled
Was Lucian Lauranna, man of worth,
Whose name lives on, though from us death him hides."

142

of Raphael's architecture. It was in this form, not the Greek, that he learned to venerate the Antique; it was not the organic refinement of the Greek architectural members but the Roman will to spatial expression, subordinating to itself all articulation, that he first of all recognised, and in his maturity felt as a claim upon him which he discharged. Here also he was a renovator in Plato's sense. He awakened a "forgotten antiquity" and thereby became the leader into a new land.

§ Buildings in Pictures: Temple in the *Sposalizio*

"The child is father of the man"; everything in the way of architecture that occurs in his youthful works, still under the eye of Perugino, shows situations fully thought out. The hall in which Mary receives the Angelic Salutation—in the predella of the CORONATION OF THE VIRGIN, in the Vatican—already presents an interior carried out in detailed structure in complete maturity, and the impulse towards a comprehensive whole which alone makes the true architect, is betrayed by the fact that the relation of this beautiful structure of masonry to the landscape, of the fashioned building-material to the soil whence it sprang and to which it returns, can be so happily sensed.

Then at the end of his apprenticeship he devised the temple in the *Sposalizio* (Plate 152). Here there was little to learn from his master Perugino. This painter's temples in the DELIVERY OF THE KEYS, in the Sistine Chapel, or in the *Sposalizio* at Caen, have nothing but a profile; his cupolas fit as badly as the hats of his figures. Raphael's figures with the breath-inspired soundness of their limbs require for their existence, even in these early works, a spacious environment of landscape and buildings. In this, reminiscences of the architect's dreams of Luciano speak as a legacy from his home country. In the house of the Santi more was known of these dreams than was ever realised or left for us to become acquainted with to-day. A favourite idea of the Renaissance, the focussing in a round temple of a wide view over a clearly articulated open space, is here brought to preliminary fulfilment. Spalato is the site of Diocletian's mausoleum. Laurana would have been no architect of the Renaissance if he had not adopted such a monument, an ideal type for his time, a building dating from Antiquity constructed round a centre. This suggestion was seen, revived, in the *Sposalizio*. The young painter-architect of twenty years sets his temple in a landscape; his imagination chooses for it the most beautiful of situations: the lines lead from a wide valley to gentle elevations. Into this setting he builds a broad-paved terrace like the Mercato behind the Palazzo Pubblico of Siena; the drama seems as it were to be played on a stage with a wide prospect—and he carries on the pavement into the hexagonal stepped platform and thence up into the temple. Thus the building with its halls develops out of the lines of the terrain and reverts vitally into the wide landscape. Palladio did not show a more beautiful understanding of giving back to the earth its own in the fashioned stone, and making the stone as a product of art to return again to the soil, by discovering the harmony between structure and site, and by creating this pantheistic accord of columns and landscape. This temple anticipates the note of Palladio's Villa Rotonda on the Monte Berico near Vicenza.

§ At Florence, Intercourse with Architects: Enthusiasm for Vitruvius

It cannot have been otherwise: in Florence, intercourse with the architects CRONACA, ANTONIO and GIULIANO DA SANGALLO in the house of BACCIO D'AGNOLO must have had the same importance for Raphael's world of architectural forms that the spectacle of the figures then being magnificently revived on the banks of Arno had in painting and sculpture. His interest was certainly aroused by the enquiry into the new proportion in relation also to architecture and the more exact knowledge of the theories of Vitruvius. The discussion raged like a conspiracy through Venice, Urbino, Perugia, Florence and Rome; it is impossible that the subject would not be touched upon in those "dispute d'importanza" among so many who were concerned with building and were investigating style; nor could anyone fail to hear it spoken of who already, in his early years, had been in contact with the spheres of Francesco di Giorgio and Piero della Francesca. He assimilated with eagerness all that had materialised in Florence on the basis of such doctrines. When the Dei family commissioned him to paint an altarpiece for Santo Spirito, the apse in which the Madonna's throne stands beneath the baldacchino became a tribute to the great builder of this Renaissance basilica, Brunelleschi, whose proud austerity was to be the environment of Raphael's picture. The great reviver of "buona architettura" had discovered in Rome, from among the ruins, his rules for a stately architecture, and had brought them to life in Florence. Now with Raphael they return again to Rome.

§ Architecture in Frescoes

There BRAMANTE, born like him in the Duchy of Urbino, awaited him. He will have brought to Bramante a new wave of inspiration from his birthplace. Laurana and the Antique traditions handed down from Istria and Dalmatia must have been revived anew. All this contributed to the pulsing life of which he was witness in the Vatican; he was soon to take a part in it, indeed to become its driving force. When the ideal setting had to be created for the SCHOOL OF ATHENS (Plate 72), in which the sublime spirits, the Titans of Antiquity, had their existence, Raphael was certainly not unaffected by the aspirations of the age, which Bramante was about to embody in symbolical form in the dome of San Pietro. Their thinking, their speech, the rhythm of their footsteps even, —in a word, their sense of sublimity, needed the noble members of such walls as a background for their utterances, the high-vaulted ceiling to re-echo them. Such a conception, in its harmony with the mood of these figures, could not have been derived from anywhere, not simply from Bramante's ideas for San Pietro, nor from the arch of Janus Quadrifrons on the Velabrum which was at that time repeatedly adopted by Fra Giocondo, Peruzzi and Giuliano da San Gallo. Certain passages in the form of a Greek cross are there to be found, between pillars similarly articulated. Ghiberti's relief of SOLOMON AND THE QUEEN OF SHEBA on the doors of the Florentine Baptistery are also supposed to have given Raphael the suggestion. Yet we know his works could not consist of mere additions; every suggestion had to be converted into his own experience; there everything, from whatever source, became a harmonious interweaving of voice and accompaniment in figures and space. The hall which he constructed for himself was a stage for Peripatetics, and for these sublime minds it could not be sufficiently spacious and light, high or majestic; rather lofty than real. For however clearly thought-out it may appear—and Theobald Hofmann drew a section and ground-plan of it—it is nevertheless nowhere finished off. The only similarity to Ghiberti's hall would be that both are unreal, one might say theatrical—not in the nowadays disparaging sense of the word, but in its true sense, that of making visible the heroic. Halls like this were at that time constructed by architects on the stage for *sacre rappresentazioni*, as for celebrations of the Mysteries, or for profane classical representations. In this manner they could regard their dreams of a monumental architecture as being realised, for festal occasions, at least in perishable materials and in approximate proportions. This was their share in the festivals, as contributors and recipients. Raphael also toyed with his art, as we know, on such occasions.

Comparison with the Temple in the HELIODORUS fresco (Plate 102) sets before our eyes the scale at his disposal, as in a short span of time he learned to acquire it. It is like the background of a mystery-play, almost a Shakespearean stage—a strongly accented central structure, at once façade and interior, and laterally receding unlighted spaces. They are enough for the action. We feel how greatly Raphael's architectural—or rather tectonic—energy has increased, in pace with that of his forms, since the stage of the hall in the SCHOOL OF ATHENS. All the merely superficial enlivenment of the walls there seen, with arrangements of pilasters and recessed niches, has now given place to a pervading and resonant articulation of the entire compact structure. Everything has been set in motion: the structural forces appear to flow and to swell—pilasters with columns set in front of them, vistas into lateral aisles, energetically articulated by means of pillars; in place of supporting walls we have architectural members alternately pronounced and less pronounced, and cornices and abutments coming at unequal levels, and the rhythmical undulation and interchange of light and shade —all overborne and stressed by the tremendous projection of the central part. We feel that the effects of what we have been accustomed to call Baroque are here being prepared in advance; indeed, the Baroque seems to be anticipated in the breaking up of the structure into members that absorb the vision. In the

MASS OF BOLSENA the *tribuna* seems to be completely transfigured; it is so, in fact, even in the preparatory stage in the Oxford drawing (Plate 146). This conception of an apse in dissolved light streaming through it can only be traced to Raphael's invention; it cannot have occurred to the bad draughtsman of this sheet!

Such ideas thronged his mind at that period, at the time of the death of Bramante and Fra Giocondo, in the architectural backgrounds of his pictures; the fact has been overlooked that they followed the same course of development as his painting. In his painting also, a prominent part is taken by the play of the human figure in the "articulation" of the picture-space; here also the sphere of the frame becomes ever more and more imbued with the function of figure and limbs. It is no accident that background, space and landscape are lost in the pictures of this period, the MADONNA DELLA SEDIA and the MADONNA DELLA TENDA, and the play of the limbs in their action occupies the eye of the beholder.

It is quite in accord with Raphael's custom, and is one of the peculiarities most deeply rooted in his nature, that he should transpose into a spiritual element the promptings of architecture, perceptions derived from his own structural creating as a painter. Up to this point conclusions as to his unrealised constructional ideas had to be based on the spatial setting in his pictures (they were certainly no mere backgrounds); now, when he was entirely taken up with building and architectural planning, it is noticeable that his imagination as a painter moves in the same categories that direct his creative activity in the sphere of building also.

§ Office of Works of St Peter's: Ideas for the Dome—Radial *v.* Oblong Plan

And what plans they were that then engaged his attention!

Since April, 1513, immediately after Bramante's death, Leo X had entrusted him provisionally with the Clerkship of the Works of St Peter's. From September, 1514, he was assisted by Fra Giocondo, with his practical experience; and when the latter ended a life of activity and inventiveness, Raphael remained alone, from 1st July, 1515, onwards, the first architect of the *fabbrica*.

In the present church of St Peter's hardly anything of Raphael is to be found. The condition of the central structure that had grown up in its might under his direction behind the old Basilica, and was then at a standstill, has been handed down—from a date a few years later—by the Netherlandish painter Marten van Heemskerck, in his Berlin sketchbook. Heemskerck wandered round it and, with the pious amazement of the pilgrim in the presence of a ruin that was strange to him, sketched it from several sides: there are the pendentives and the mighty arches on the pillars of the dome that were to carry the drum (Plates 153a, b, 154). It is known that Raphael had to spend much of his time and resources on making secure the pillars and foundations. This sounds as if his share in the building was "only" technical; just as if, in the true artist, there could be technique not subservient to the impulse of invention! Fra Giocondo's experience of statics derived from the Pont Notre Dame in Paris and from the Ponte della Pietra at Verona came in opportunely for this very purpose. Just this preoccupation with the pillars shows clearly that he was conscious of the duty of strengthening them, because his aspirations were already reaching out very energetically towards the vaultings and the dome. The ambition he had in view was to rescue their dominance over all parts of the building—Bramante's great, sublime plan; for other plans threatened this proud solution. The clerics wished to see the many consecrated spots of the old Basilica still included in the new building; this must be effected by means of a longitudinal nave. The Eastern arm of the Greek cross originally planned would not have sufficed for this purpose. Raphael acknowledged the necessity of the nave for the requirements of worship—but he wished to give it a moderate extension so that there should be no possibility of impairing the dominant effect of the cupola in both interior and exterior of the structure (Plate 183). He retained for it the profile of Bramante, externally the calotte of the Pantheon, raised up by a drum permeated with light. The apses of the arms of the cross and the ambulatories of the choir lead up gently with their vaultings to the great central cupola. There are some drawings which we may believe to hand down to us in fairly true reproduction his own designs. They show the walls opened in vistas, ideas from the Pantheon, but now applied to light, adapted to this new manner of introducing light—a harmony of curved, light spaces opening into still lighter, to be overborne by the tones of the lightest of all, the central structure, flooded with radiance.

§ Lightness and Light: Sant' Eligio degli Orefici: "Palladian Motive"

This conception of the cupola space, with its weight diminishing and its abundance of light increasing upwards, occupied in a special manner the painter of "lightness and light"; two smaller chapels show how he learned to master it. The little church of Sant' Eligio degli Orefici (Plate 156) is supposed to have been built by him after 1509, inspired by one of the lateral cupolas of Bramante in St Peter's. The conception he may well have brought with him already formed, from San Bernardino de' Zoccolanti at Urbino. Raphael's building stands to-day in rather a dilapidated state on the Lungo Tevere Tibaldi, parallel with the Via Giulia, that is to say, in the neighbourhood that had lately won the favour of Julius II, opposite Agostino Chigi's villa on the Lungara, the country house afterwards called the Farnesina. The Baroque reconstruction must have deprived the delicate work of much of its original character, together with the lime-wash. Even so, the moderately elevated drum, and the dome above a severely restrained console-cornice with stopped profile, still show the delicate vitality given by a gentle projection and recession of planes, evinced also in the stepped window-soffits, which may be remotely attributed to the builder-painter. It is claimed that we have here for the first time an example of the so-called "Palladian motive"—an arch of which the archivolt appears to be buttressed, as it were, by two upright structures. Can this really be accepted as an invention of Raphael's (Plates 157–159)? Moreover, we may recall that it is to be found already in the forecourt of the Mausoleum at Spalato; from that time on, a perpetually enduring motive! In the interior, the cupola is seen at its junction with the drum and vaulting encircled with a delicate cymation and bead-and-dart ornament (Plates 159, 166); it almost calls to mind the classicalism of the Brothers Adam. The cupola opens in the eye of the lantern; round the circle, in purest Roman lettering, runs the inscription:

"ASTRA DEVS, NOS TEMPLA DAMVS, TV SIDERA PANDE"

"Thou, O God, gavest the stars, we the temple,
Spread thou above the firmament."

The humble vault beneath the dome of heaven! For this, colour was certainly intended, if not pictorial decoration.

§ Cupolas and Tondi: Cupola Conceptions in the Pictures

His imagination was dominated more and more by the idea of the dome during his life in Rome; it exercised its power over the master-builder even when he was painting pictures. The results of sensibility can hardly be dismissed as mere imagination; the habit of thinking in cupolas and of seeing masses and forms arrange themselves in rounded shapes released in the painter a peculiar aptitude for composing *tondi*. The great new, expansive form—achieved in the second Stanza—adapts itself to the round shape—in the ALBA MADONNA, still encircled by the landscape under the protecting vault of heaven, in the *MADONNA DELLA SEDIA*, itself circling, not unlike a cupola-painting filled with a throng of figures, in which also there is not lacking a veritable *opaion*, a shifted focus for the astounded upward gaze, in the arresting look on the countenance of the Child.

In the great design for the ASCENSION, from the Bonnat Collection, the luminous *calotte* composed of cherubs' heads sweeps above the Risen Christ. The SISTINE MADONNA steps forward as out of a light blue *tribuna*. The comparison appears to perfection, unknown perhaps to Raphael but to us inescapable, in the ST CECILIA (Plate 244): the figures stand around the saint in a formal arrangement like pillars—the sky opens in a semicircle irradiated with streams of light the upward progression from solid to ethereal, from colour to light, a chapel come alive. The same mind is revealed in picture and building; this altarpiece has the power of communicating to the worshippers in the church the spell of communion and composure, the result achieved otherwise by a domed space. The guiding spirit employs the same medium. From that time onwards this power belonged to Raphael!

RAPHAEL AS ARCHITECT

§ Cappella Chigi: Unity of Building and Decoration

Once Raphael had the rare good fortune of being able to conceive and give final shape to such a space for worship as a single whole together with its pictorial decoration—just as Michael Angelo had in the family chapel of the Medici at San Lorenzo. This was in the sepulchral chapel for Agostino Chigi in the church of Santa Maria del Popolo. The building, with the sweep of cornices and niches in the wall, the pyramidal tomb of the founder, gently expanding and melting away again into the wall, the lighting, which entices the eye and leads it on to the reflections on the pictorial mosaic decoration of the ceiling, make of the little room one single *sursum corda*.

It is difficult to give an idea of the interior effect (Plate 160). Photography fails; architectural diagrams lack spatial quality, and nothing else is here important. An impetus is communicated to the eye, starting with the lower storey. The pillars of the dome have niches with statues between pilasters; even these adapt themselves with their absolutely audacious recession to the lines of the space. The tomb-pyramids stand in the great intervening arched recesses. Raphael was the first to use them, though not yet in their present baroque forcibleness, as an interruption of the classical line and yet bound to the wall-surface—a form with a mystic intention, the symbol of eternity. The spherically trapeze-shaped spandrels carry the cornice of the dome, and here the energy of the circular movement is renewed in its sweep. The eye feels itself carried on from the fixed cornice into ever more ethereal regions—from the inert stone to the light-interwoven sphere with its dazzling effect before the dome, causing reflections on its mosaic decoration; the play of light that, in the DELIVERANCE OF PETER, confronted the gaze towards the window in the picture, is here repeated more boldly and deliberately (Plate 161). The confusion of the eye in the presence of the miracle on earth here becomes a dazzled attraction towards the luminous spheres of the upper and highest region. A soft atmospheric blue gleams between the strongly profiled cornices and ribs; in front of it advance the figures of the Planets, who of old set the starry firmament in motion, the deities of the Greeks, guided in their course by angels of God. And beyond their sphere the gaze passes irresistibly, through an ever lighter framework of gleaming gold, up to the *opaion*, and sees God the Father through the ethereal, fiery air, wielding sway with unapproachable hands over the universe and the stars, overpoweringly threatening and yet immeasurably vast, just as a cloud passes above the "eye" of the Pantheon (Plate 302).

It was the heart's desire of Agostino Chigi and the most intimate wish of the "gran mercante di christianità" to know himself to be, in his life, under the sway of the dæmons that guide the stars. It was with this in his mind that his villa on the Lungara offered hospitality to the gods of Antiquity; in his thoughts of death, he wished to feel himself and the stars that ruled his life to be in the hand of the Most High.

This involved for Raphael more than a commission; here he was concerned with the conception of the universe of an entire circle, the élite of his time, amongst whom he was allowed to reckon himself. This view of an Olympus ordered on a Christian basis had already become part of his experience through Dante. This it was to which he succeeded here in giving shape.

§ Architect, Painter and Poet: The *Marchigiano*

Those who wish to comprehend Raphael as painter and poet must spend an hour of contemplation in this chapel, beneath this dome. For the sense of transfiguration evinced in his painting has nowhere been preserved in such purity as here. It is certain that the mosaics were inserted after complete coloured designs by his hand. Nor could the mosaicist Alvise del Pace as a Venetian have produced, about 1515, these sunny effects; he would never have found them at that period in his native school, in Giorgione, Titian or Palma Vecchio. If these luminous half-shadows melting in blue atmosphere came from any source other than Raphael's intuition, we have here a revival of the prototype inherited from another son of the Marches, Melozzo da Forlì, and therewith of the great colour tradition of Early Christian mosaics. Melozzo's ceiling in the Sagrestia della Cura at Loreto shows a similar sub-division with openings through which the angels glide in, above the heads of the Prophets reclining on the cornice, with that objectivity of the Quattrocento which succeeded in conquering reality. Raphael keeps gods and angels on the further side of the windows and so of what is earthly, and from his predecessor's colour-scheme he introduces for his purpose only the transfiguring brightness, with soft lights in gold, against the soft blue background of the sky. Melozzo's Apostles and angels accompanying the Ascension of the Redeemer could still be seen by him, in the choir of the SS. Apostoli; they were at that time still preserved intact. Their radiant fragmentary remains in the Vatican still tell us what the *Marchigiano* round worthy of his acknowledgment in his fellow-countryman.

§ Raphael's Ideas as a Painter perpetuated in Mosaic and Weaving: Calculated Scheme of Colouring

At that period Raphael had to conceive his greatest pictorial schemes—this Planet ceiling and the history of the Apostles—in a gleaming material, in mosaic and tapestry work, shot through with gold and bound up with the principles of architectural decoration. Where the high-lights were to have their most powerful effectiveness in gold, there resulted a scale of bright colours leading up to the metallic gleam. It thus came about in his case as in that of his master Perugino, more than a generation earlier, in his work for the glass-painters, that his chromatic style acquired from these higher principles of decoration an impulse of its own.

The mosaicists seem to have understood him better than the Flemish weavers, and to have felt his directions more compelling. We feel that it is no arbitrary choice, but a calculation giving its character to the colouring, that places these figures, with colours of such a kind, precisely thus in a setting of light. Eight times over these ancient deities that set the stars in motion, with their guiding attendant angels, echo in ever new colours the same harmony with the background of sky, and every time the colours exert their expressive power (Plate 161). It is impossible in the Jupiter, not to believe in the "bright god", in his matt purple with pinkish-grey lights and white hair; the angel raises aloft his arms, pointing towards the Creator, in pink drapery gleaming with gold in front of the grey silvery shadow of his wings. Yet what can the grey of the eagle avail, and the golden thunderbolt, against the gold-shimmering drapery of the Almighty?

In the firmament of fixed stars we find the harmony of gold, white and green, as in the Czartoryski portrait. In the wings there is a flood of white, gold, green and red; in the heavenly sphere there is a progression of intensity from the white of the inscribed scroll to the deep blue of the background; all its reflections are intermediary between the colours and the luminous blue atmosphere. In the other axis appear the deities of light, Apollo and Artemis, bright, and particularly light and airy in their movements—the goddess (Plate 290) holding her bow with arms, light grey shaded with pink, emerging from a mantle shot with green and gold, the sun-god with gold-flaming nimbus, his arms taking aim, wonderfully light and ethereal, yet turning towards the maiden who undrapes herself to his gaze and takes no heed of Cupid with his torch, her flesh-tones shaded with grey, the boy browner. Opposite to her is Saturn, in yellowish-orange drapery; his light has its complement also in the crocus-colour of the angel, whose pinions, in red and blue, rise proudly and at the same time with the function of providing a transition in front of the background of sky. Mercury, in red cloak shot with grey, his flesh-tones with gleaming shadows; the angel, born of the air, truly mercurial, with grey pinions steeped with pink and bluish drapery near in colour to the atmosphere. At the other end of this axis we have Mars, in breastplate flashing with greenish-gold, his flesh shaded with grey, violet and crocus-colour; his angel especially overpowering, a restraining, not an impelling force, in red, pink and violet besprent with malachite-green. Above all, in his quiet, rich framework, the Creator, with soft blue mantle—so brilliant in the upper arm that it would fade away in air if the golden highlights did not outshine the heavens—and out of this mantle the creating arms protrude in fiery glowing red with shadows like gilt lacquer, spotted with reflections that glisten round about him with a golden lustre on the wings of the attendant angels also. Through this *fortissimo* of light the green fold of the mantle below the breast weaves a seemingly fortuitous descant—but certainly of set purpose, for the Classical deities float in a harmony eight times repeated, and only Jehovah moves exalted on high above them; it is this green that mingles in the chord of almost all the other compartments, modulated by one means or another to the angels. In most cases this gives an appearance of greater massiveness in the lower portion of the compartment, so that the ascent into the ethereal becomes inevitably apparent in colour also.

Once again we may recall the foreshortenings of Melozzo, and his sunlit colours, of the brilliant effect of which a delightful impression can still be gained from the fragments from the SS. Apostoli, with the pale gold spots of the haloes forming a gentle transition into the blue. The *new* feature in Raphael's work was this: *an entire architectural conception was allowed to culminate in a luminous picture, and all the soaring motives arising out of the space below were made to culminate their upward sweep in the vision of the Most High—*

"Quasi di val andando al monte" (*Paradiso*, 31, 120).

§ Dante and Beethoven

Once again we are listening with Raphael to the echo of the dome of the Pantheon. Dante's verses ring in our ears; the words of the Psalm come to life, in the very rendering given to them by Dante in his *Convito* (Canzone 1, Tratt. 2, Cap. 6), but the whole of literature does not explain how Raphael came to be blessed with the power of discovering the ascent from the earthly materialism of architecture to the serene regions of the gods, of making credible in colour the harmony of the spheres, of causing their ordered ranks to move gently forward in obedience to the commands of the Lord, and finally of giving to God all the might that resounds from the words of the 19th Psalm:

"The Heavens declare the glory . . ."

Fortunately for us, much in the higher realms of art remains incomprehensible; so also does this. How close is the gesture aroused in Raphael's imagination by the rhythm and pathos of this text—the uplifting alike of arms and voice—to that which Beethoven must have experienced, in his sphere, at the words:

. . . "ihr Klang pflanzt sei—nen Namen fort".

§ Latest Style

We feel that neither Michael Angelo nor Melozzo had anything to do with the style and rendering of these visions; they represent the maturity of all the conceptions that display in the earliest works of Raphael a genius already independent and familiar, as none other was, with the other world. Unfortunately, in Raphael's case, by the decree of fate, we may not speak of the style of his old age, but this, his latest style, which characterises the lustre of his creativity before the end, was the style of consummation. Figure, form, space with varied recession and lighting—he has now complete mastery over all; he is attracted solely by the employment of these means in the manner that seems good to him for his higher purpose.

The great "draughtsman" has become painter and architect in one. On the paper for his studies the "hand" had to be transformed. The sheets of drawings for the Chigi Chapel (Plates 162–164) are evidence of this new phase; in the passages of sunlit shading in red chalk, with which up to that time he had hardly been so familiar, he gives form, almost without contours, to the luminous foreshortenings; in the rough surface of this crumbly material a medium offers itself for substantialness in figure and gesture. The angel above the Jupiter (Oxford), expressing with his uplifted arms the command "Hear, O world, the word of the Lord", is washed in, as it were, in loose strokes almost without contours. The first idea for the figure of the Almighty is full of force, with the heavy pressure of the red chalk on the paper. No better example will be found of the late style of the artist, in which a peculiar majesty, as of the common people, is inherent: Goethe called him at this period "the virile" Raphael.

This "virile" Raphael will scarcely be included in a history of painting. He needs to be seen as the sum of his faculties, through all the obstacles that have heaped themselves between him and us—time that has destroyed so much, the one-sided worship of the divine son of Urbino as a young man, as religious painter, as draughtsman divorced from colour, as an architect who deserted painting. This man of the Renaissance, in his all-round perfection, would have smiled at the complaint that he pursued aims that were alien to him, or that he neglected the art of which he, as no one else, understood the practice.

§ Manifold Scenes of Activity

In all the scenes of his labours at that time—whether the architect's office at St Peter's, with the soaring archivolts of the choir apses, the open halls of the Loggie with vaults sweeping like a canopy or giving a deceptive foretaste of the open air, the garden saloons of the Farnesina, the villa of Agostino Chigi, where the ceiling seemed to perpetuate, under the sway of the gods, a festal improvisation of arbours and awnings, or his studio in the Piazza Scossacavalli, where the TRANSFIGURATION awaited its completion—everywhere his planning for the totality was dominated by the desire to press forward from the material to air and light, from the earthly to the beyond, from affliction to transfiguration.

It is this *mature* Raphael that we have to rediscover in his latest style. In the presence of his creations nothing is more important than to come up against the impelling purpose; for this guides us, through all digressions of research as to the share taken by pupils, to what alone is genuine—*his own power of invention*.

§ Vatican Loggie (Plates 168, 169)

Raphael, as architect and painter, here in the Loggie of the Vatican conceived a single whole: in him were united the power of the architect, the decorator, the great narrator in pictures. However much his gift may be reflected in his assistants, few or many—the glory remains *his* of the invention displayed in the provision of the decorative designs, of the seriousness of the architecture and of his application of it, of his respect for the Antique and of the deliberate humour which caused him to intersperse its motives among those of his own devising; to him is due the credit of employing the picture to set a key of religious seriousness, and of providing the tenour for the heroic rendering of these biblical stories.

Some time after 1514 Raphael had brought to its termination the Loggie range of Bramante; the whole must have been completed in 1519, in the summer (at all events, the date MDXIII is found distinctly in the twelfth arcade, under a seated Victory).

§ To Air and Light

Everywhere during these years we come across his most personal trait—progression upwards and outwards into air and light.

To-day these galleries, formerly open to the breeze, are closed with glass; once again, art historians can give themselves up to contemplation of the paintings as comfortably as in a picture-gallery. Thus they have spent much time also on the study of detail and have conducted inquiries into influences, pupil's work, and motives. This may certainly be necessary, but in the process one ought not to neglect reconstructing to one's self Raphael's intention, in this building of an entirely novel order. This remains more important than anything else! It guides us to *his* imagination in its elemental creativity.

§ Architect and Decorator: The Loggie as Façade of the Palace

Here also, we have architect and painter in *one* person—we see him conceiving and arranging everything, from the main theme to detail. He built a shady and airy promenade alongside the Papal apartments with an outlook, unique in the world, upon a landscape of beauty and dignity. Up here once again he knew the significance of arcades when they have to frame such lines of hills and forms of landscape. In these stages the building formerly rose, confronting anyone coming from the Borgo, as façade to the whole Vatican Palace—above Bramante's Doric arcades a storey with Ionic pilasters, and above that, as termination, a lighter loggia with raftered roof casting deep shadows, in the manner of the Florentine Palazzo Guadagni.

In the inner corridor, instead of the simple, flattish pilasters of Bramante, he introduced the rhythmic alternation of reinforced pilasters, that is, broad pilasters combined as a unit with narrower set in front of them, and niches on the wall facing the arcades; antique statues, favourites of the Pope, were to have their place in front of them.

Such an alternation of varied shadows and lighted portions, even without painting, of itself produces on the eye, as it feels its way over the surface, the effect of painting. In this case there was in addition the rhythm of shaded painting. Against this background stood out the antique figures in the niches, happily and with room to breathe, and those standing opposite in the arcades answered them. Between them, with his gaze on the blue of the sunlit distance which restored new life to them, the strolling visitor walked from pillar to pillar, with ever-changing excitement. His eye was greeted ever afresh, from the pilasters, by antique motives and pictures of sheer *joie-de-vivre*, as by familiar melodies he listened to with delight.

Twelve times over from bay to bay the manner of the vault-decoration changes; but all the while the sky looks in upon the airy gallery, and sheds its light through the larger openings of the vault-surfaces upon the landscapes with a few biblical figures. The gaze is enticed and directed away from the angles and pendentives to the airy summit—it is the light-motive of the Chigi dome in endless variations (Plate 167).

The sectroids or spherical trapezes of which the vaults in the individual bays are made up, are in each case interrupted by a picture—spherical rectangles, some of them curved at the top in the segment of the arch; in the first and last (thirteenth), he gave the pictures the form of oblong hexagons. In most cases, from out of the rigidly architectural or playfully fantastic decoration of the ground, they open up a view into a landscape with figures from the Old Testament. Only in the last bay are there four scenes from the Life of Christ. Thus the pictures are not the essential part of the decoration; only as parts of the whole they contribute, to the interplay of the profane motives, a certain devotional composure.

§ The Bible of Raphael: Grotesques

The nineteenth century thirst for pictures, in the presence of "Raphael's Bible", has caused its wealth of phantasy to be forgotten; here, with amusing drollery or compelling seriousness, he spoke to the visitor wandering amongst things profane of those eternally sacred things also which he must take into consideration if he was to give to humanistic subjects a sense of true human dignity.

The term "grotesques" in itself allows us to divine how a lover of the Antique with Raphael's aptitude for assimilation and re-composition must of necessity have made himself master, in the true sense of the phrase, of the Antique mode of decoration that had just been discovered in the "Grotte", the remains of Nero's Golden House brought to light just below the ground. According to Vasari it was his assistant Giovanni da Udine who rediscovered the secret of marble stucco. The essential feature of the style was the intermingling of coloured plastic elements that are continued in colour on the flat surface— scrolled stems terminating in the bodies of animals or human figures and once more dying away in scrolls—plants, still-lifes, little pictures, *amoretti*, birds, trophies of music and the chase—in short, that richly overflowing and yet architecturally ordered medley that has given to the term *grottesca* the underlying sense of "drolly whimsical", "scintillating with the unexpected".

At the outset Raphael must himself have indicated the main direction, so that in the interplay with the serious themes his guiding will is certainly to be recognised. He also gave suggestions for detail, to leave his assistants, at a later stage, a free hand for designs as well, when they had grown equal to the task.

§ Raphael's Share in the Designs of the Pictures

None of the designs for the Biblical pictures (for the decorative work we know of hardly any preparatory sketches) has a claim to be regarded as entirely by Raphael's own hand. But it can hardly be believed that any one of his pupils, who were nothing but the premature offspring of Mannerism, could have evoked from the lines of the Old Testament anything like these figures of the Creator, or Jacob's Dream, or Moses on Sinai; if the drawings for them that have been preserved are certainly original designs, not copies, then there can be no doubt: these motives can belong to no-one but Raphael; at the very least he sketched them with a lead-pencil or in chalk and then had them carried further on the paper—first of all on paper, then on the ceiling, always with the tacit reservation that he would himself in due course get to work on them himself if time offered. This did not often occur—only, at the beginning, in the first bay, do we find his hand; amid the rigid simulated framework surrounding rhombic compartments (they enclose like antique coffering the scenes from the story of the Creation) the angels of the Heavenly Hierarchies are wafted in the sunny air.

§ The Heavenly Hierarchies (Plates 172*b*, 224)

The hovering of these angels and cherubim in veneration of the acts of Creation recalls Melozzo—some in quiet ecstasy with arms laid submissively on their breast, some in wild agitation carrying the banner of the Cross to earth, others again with soft steps moving forward around the Creator. We have here an echo of the verses in which Dante has rendered the vision of the Angels of Dionysius the Areopagite (*Paradiso* 28, 127):

> "Questi ordini di su tutti rimirano,
> E digiù vincon si, che verso Dio
> Tutti tirati sono, e tutti tirano."[1]

Here Raphael himself filled in one or two of these frames, with the motive ever newly employed, for his own delectation and as a model for his assistants. These

[1] "These Orders all their gaze on high direct
And downward from above extend their sway
All drawn towards God, and drawing all to Him."

figures, where their spontaneity has not been destroyed by over-painting, have preserved the charm of his freest handiwork in all its expressiveness; they hover gently but vigorously in contrast with the rigidity of the framework. In several there is a Bacchic element, as in the tambourine-players of Melozzo; others again are in soft blue against the sunny ether, or in red, violet and grey on the luminous background of the heavens. Above are Cherubim in yellow, blue and violet on gold, in the manner of mosaic. Here, actually in the Vatican, it is possible for a loving eye to discover unknown works of Raphael. Even where he was not himself the painter, the main motives go back to him; their luminous power betrays the nearness of the sun.

In the *pictures*, landscape is brought into prominence for the sake of atmosphere; this can be the only purpose he associated with it, for at the same period, in the tapestries, he abandoned landscape in favour of the figures. Giovanni da Udine has been suggested for these pictures, as a specialist in representations of nature. Certainly, wherever the landscape remains accessory and mere background, he may have painted it. But where the landscape is a vehicle of narrative, where it provides a heroic expanse for the action, and breathes a mythical virginity in which the few figures set against a distant horizon have their being—alone in the world, as it were, and here for the first time—it must be Raphael, and only Raphael himself, who struck such a new note. He alone, out of his profound feeling for space, could have created a presentation of the earth, far, far beneath, embodying Dante's words in the *Paradiso* (XXII, 151), such as he gives in the painting of God the Father dividing the waters and the earth:

"L'aiuola che ci fà tanto feroci
tutta m'apparve da colle alle foci."

"The threshing-floor that maketh us so proud
Was all apparent made from hill to harbour."
(*Trans.* Longfellow).

For these hallowed themes he discovered a solution which was valid as long as his art found an uncontested echo in society. Even when the epoch of the intellectual class which arose with him came to an end, at the time of the French Revolution, his ALMIGHTY DIVIDING THE LIGHT AND DARKNESS (Plate 170) exerted an influence that confirms in a most striking manner the law of the Conservation of Energy. Two great spirits hailed one another across the centuries. The drawing for this figure of the Creator was in the possession of Sir Thomas Lawrence, in London, and this picture appears on the title-page of Haydn's *Creation*. The profoundest preoccupation of the peoples in Raphael's time found its favourite and most vigorous expression in the visual arts. In the

RAPHAEL

eighteenth century the powers of the imagination were mostly attracted to music. Thus Raphael's conceptions of the Creation broke forth into new life in *The Creation* of Haydn.

§ Authentic Composition of Raphael

In their present condition, after so many restorations through the over-paintings of which the old *craquelures* are once more becoming visible, the pictures all but entirely baffle criticism. Yet who else but Raphael could have confined within the astounding diagonals of the hexagon the tumult of the First Day of the Creation? The drawing in the British Museum shows it still less disfigured. Or God the Father sweeping above the earth and dividing the dry land from the waters (Plate 171)—his movement, the soaring line of his mantle blown by the wind, sweeping marvellously within, and in unison with, the frame and around the streaming hair of his head?

In the Promise to Abraham and in the Command to Isaac we still sense the power of invention in the onrush of the Deity and in the helpless shrinking of human strength before him. As the heavenly messengers come to Abraham, he in his lowliness is approached by a delightfully rhythmical triad—in its grace we have indeed an echo out of another sphere above the earth-bound figure.

The sleeping Jacob slumbers, with limbs relaxed, transfigured by the unearthly brilliance of the ladder to Heaven—he also forming a pattern with inevitable lines within the frame: the heroic dreamer! How often, in fact, the attitudes—striding, recumbent or parleying—take on the form of the dance or the ceremonial gesture. Such is the rhythm that pervades the hall in which Joseph interprets the dreams to Pharaoh. Here narrative becomes history, and near by, the idyllic is revived—in the scenes in Paradise, in the Building of the Ark, where we have glimpses of landscape through the ribs of the ship, in the nocturnal Amours of Isaac and Rebecca in the house of Abimelech, also of course in the scene of Jacob and Rachel at the well, in the menacing group of the brethren when Joseph relates his Dream, and especially in the delightful chatter of maiden voices in the Finding of Moses. And in each case there is the effect of the surrounding ceiling, fanciful, archæological, wantonly profane—yet again and again filled with the echo of serious rhythms. Then we have the simulated architecture built up vertically out of the groining—the corner of a palace court with two rows of columns one above another, the solemn splendour of the Tuscan Order with bronze capitals, or the angle of a hall of which the beams rest on pilasters set diagonally, with beautifully profiled cornices and marble incrustations (Plates 172*a*, 173*a*, *b*). We must accept these architectural dreams as substitutes for what the master in his early consummation owed to posterity, or for what posterity and, unfortunately, our own contemporaries believed themselves at liberty to destroy of the buildings he actually carried out.

Even apart from this, an attentive eye may succeed in detecting much more besides that allows us to draw conclusions as to the world in which he had to live and for which he had to create. It will be interesting to notice what remained from Antiquity, in the way of beautiful and lively motives, for Raphael and his circle to see, to be awakened to renewed life in the stuccoes and decorative paintings. A precise archæological inventory of these is given in Hofmann's *Raphael als Architekt* (Vol. IV). But we are grateful for the information afforded as to the mode of life in the Vatican in Raphael's time. Thus on the fourth window-pier there is actually a small stucco medallion telling us of an intimate ceremonial scene in the house of the owner of the Loggie himself: in the vista of a corridor with a series of cross-vaults on Tuscan pilasters His Holiness Pope Leo X himself gives his blessing to a man kneeling with a roll in his hand. Is it a Cardinal, and if so, who? Perhaps Pucci, whose commissions were so lovingly to be immortalised in these very apartments? And what is the scene of the incident—is it the lower Loggie, or the Library that was so especially dear to the heart of the owner? In a medallion on a pillar of the fourth bay appears a necromancer and astrologer, perhaps the Genoese Ceccotto, who amused the Court with his astrological conjurings.

§ The Assistants

On the first pillar on the right we have before us, in a frieze-like stucco relief, the workshop, on this, its site of operations: to the right, before a suspended drapery, an assistant sits at a folding table with a sheet of paper before him; whether he is drawing or pricking the sheet cannot be made out. Next in order, to the left, follows a bearded dwarfish assistant, who holds ready the pots of colour on a board. A third is busy laying a long cartoon against the wall, so as to apply the drawings on to the freshly plastered wall, whether by transferring them with the help of *spolvero*, that is, pounced tracing, or by impressing their outlines with a stylus in the wet plaster; beside him a mason appears to be preparing the plaster, and on the extreme left sits a young painter—the gracefulness of his pose distinguishes him clearly from these "banausii" as the creative designer—applying his art, lovingly yet with ease, to the wall of the pillar.

In the circular medallion above, an assistant is grinding colours on a table, and on a *pelta* above this is the painter, sitting on the ground with a block, drawing—whether Raphael himself or a pupil cannot be determined: perhaps it is Giovanni da Udine or the young Perino. We feel that here, in the provision of recreation, the whole content of life was in a wonderful manner brought into play—from the artist to the Pope, the master of the house, from architect to painter, from building to landscape, from art to nature, from artistic seriousness to ironical self-contemplation—and at the very moment in which this exuberance of fancy was gushing forth with such wantonness, the Ferrarese ambassador is reporting to the Duke that Raphael is, like most people of genius, "malinconico".

> "Viel muss ein solcher Geist von solchen Gaben
> Wenn er um Leichtsinn buhlt gelitten haben."[1]

The humanistic *magnanimo* in Aristotle's sense suffers much under the crazes, peculiar to the period, of the intellectual élite amongst whom society has long counted him, just as they reckon him as one of their own number. Without losing his own creative self, he met this society with understanding; he shows it in their portraits—as also in the ideal figures, the visions arising out of his "idea". Thus he was able, starting from the same means and in obedience to the same central will, to become their spokesman as architect also.

§ Architectural Ideas in the Ceiling Paintings

In precisely the same manner as the backgrounds of his frescoes, the imaginary columns and structures reared into the air, in the paintings of the Loggie vaults, are enough in themselves to betray the fact that, at the height of his career, Raphael had become the great architect so much in request among his contemporaries that little time was left to him for painting.

With the exception of AGOSTINO CHIGI, all his patrons—from the King of France and the Duke of Ferrara to the nuns of Sant' Antonio, had to see their hopes disappointed for pictures from his hand. The Ferrarese Ambassador, perpetually spurred on by Alfonso I, was obliged on account of a commission remaining for years unexecuted to pester the master, who knew how to evade him with elegant courtesy, and in his report to the Duke regarding the fruitlessness of his reminders, dated 17th September, 1519, he writes: "I met Raphael on the site for St Peter's—*fà il Bramante*—he is playing the part of Bramante."

He was playing no part, he was profoundly in earnest; it was indeed a matter of the deepest inward compulsion! He felt the office of architect to St Peter's to be the height of good fortune. Posterity has regretted that his time for painting was thereby curtailed—in the same way we are less grateful to Goethe for his *Farbenlehre* than for his poems. In taking this attitude we forget that the finest work of art speaks to us in the fulfilment of a personality, and that it contains within itself the faculty for richer creations.

§ Architect as Spokesman of his Age

Painting was not always, among the visual arts, the language most easily understood by the generality of people, as it became later. Architecture has often presented itself as the mirror and expression of all the strongest forces of the age; it is so, really—in a more or less adulatory manner—even to the present

---

[1] "A mind thus gifted needs must suffer much
When in frivolity 'tis called to vie."

day. The architect, in a creativity bound up with life, in his manner of affirming existence, sets himself up as the herald of a generation; its peculiar mentality is embodied in his works.

What was vital in these men, whether unconsciously hidden within them or consciously externalised, was expressed in Raphael's buildings; this is what breathes in his compositions in stone.

§ Palazzo Vidoni: New Motives of Articulation (Plate 174)

The Palazzo Vidoni, next to Sant' Andrea della Valle, is the expression of dignity, "pondus" and "gravitas"—the dwelling of men for whom "grave nel andare"—gravity of demeanour—was something to be commended, a place for those serious *cortegiani*, in their dark clothing, wide and voluminous, who thus gave visible evidence of their "magnanimità". From the proportions of this palace one might think of Castiglione, as we know him from the Louvre portrait, approaching this façade—or the dark nobleman from Brescia, by Moretto, in the National Gallery, painted six years after Raphael's death; then you may picture to yourself Moroni's slim *cavalieri* in their Spanish costume, as they step out from one of the façades of Palladio at Vicenza. The mutual proportions of man and building, or rather, their relationship and harmony in character, would then be convincing in its effect.

Raphael had come to fulfil the ideas conceived by Bramante. He gave stronger instrumentation to the motives of his teacher. Instead of applied pilasters on the façade, three-quarter columns; instead of a single accent, two. The eye tentatively feels its way more gently over the convexities of the two colonnades; it is not a mere alternation of light and shade, there is a softer tone between the dark window-openings. The painter as architect aims at the same transitions in the stone as on the canvas. The strong shadows of the cornices, the pedestals of the double columns brought together in a broad block, the transverse stripes of the rustication—all these combined give to the stone structure a recumbent character and to the general proportions the weight and heaviness of the horizontal. As painter also, he abandoned the norm of Lysippus for the dignity and compactness of the Apostles in the tapestries. Only, if we are to form an idea of the true effect, we must rid the composition of additions and alterations made to the building in later times. Originally the façade was composed in seven bays: at one point in the Via del Sudario one has still superficially, undisturbed, the impression of strength, stability, and free, soaring dignity. We could only wish to know more of the owner, Bernardino Caffarelli, who is said to have given the commission for this building in 1515 (according to Vasari[1] it was Lorenzetti who carried out the design), so that we might be acquainted with the man whose manner of life, Raphael felt, had to be embodied with so much dignity in his dwelling.

[1] *Le Vite*, ed. Milanesi, Vol. IV, p. 579.

For undoubtedly an artist who understood how to create in building the form and expression for every mood, for every life's desire, for each fluctuation between display and relaxation, even for persons of all states of affluence and for every situation, felt himself to have a mandate from the society amongst which he could count himself.

§ Suburban Palazzo Pandolfini: Changing Mood in Facade and Garden Front

The Prelate Giannozzo Pandolfini (Plate 176), one of the trusted fellow-countrymen of Leo X, required a house near the Casino Mediceo in the garden suburb. The fine distinction made, or at least stressed, in England between a palace and "house" seems here to have taken shape. The design of Raphael provides for both—exclusiveness and intimacy in a delightful blend, two stretches of different height on the Via San Gallo, the mean between an official residence (one might say between a *palazzo*) and a country house. The higher, two-storey building shows pronounced cornices on both floors, and on the surface as background there is a plastic alternation of the angular and curved pediments of the *aediculae* round the windows, with a plastic effect by turns sharp and gentle; rustication at the angles gives to the building the aloofness of a distinguished bearing. In order to enjoy this transition from the urban to the suburban, this facade must be seen in its entire extent together with the roadway space, which miraculously enough has been preserved to the present day: earlier views of it possessing some feeling for a single whole give this even better than the realistic modern illustrations. Architecture does not come into being until there is this harmonisation of building and setting; if this is lacking, we have humourless class-work from a technical school, and strange as it may sound, it is precisely humour that here plays its part, in many different veins. The haughty aloofness on the outside is given up in the interior, and on the garden front (Plate 177) there is a gentle flow of planes and lines that invites one to relaxation—a deliberate change of tone which surely belongs to Raphael and is his authentic invention, even if Giuliano da San Gallo carried out the construction and brought it to completion only after Raphael's death.

§ The former Palazzo Antonio da Brescia

An acute-angled corner in the Borgo was assigned by the Pope as a building-site to Jacopo Antonio da Brescia, Leo's Surgeon in Ordinary, together perhaps with a subsidy for the costs of building. The plot of ground had belonged to San Gallo. On this site was erected a small palace, full of dignity (Plate 178), in the Via Alessandria, now the Borgo Nuovo, where the Borgo Sant' Angelo opens obliquely into it, composed after Raphael's plan at the sharp-angled junction of the two streets. Its proportions on the narrow site are slender; it shows a relief full of energy through applied pilasters and half-pilasters and alternating window-pediments. Hardly any flat surface remains—everything has the appearance of an architectural member, including the brick ground and the freestone articulation set off in chromatic contrast with one another; this latter feature was inseparable from the vitality of a building right on into the eighteenth century, the sense for it being lost to modern times in a false abstraction, in just the same way as a feeling for site. Here we have it triumphant: the front on the narrow angle, with the segment above the cornice, had the effect—to one coming from the Vatican—of a kind of tabernacle for the arms of the Pope, and so of a compliment to the patron who had made the building possible. Heemskerck's sketch (Plate 179*a*) perpetuates for us the old state of the building, in all its courtly dignity. In this dignity we have evidence that the occupant belonged to the narrower circle of the Palace, the "gentry". It was not carried in a *crescendo* right up to the Papal habitation; the palace of the Chamberlain Giovan Battista Branconio d'Aquila, at the entrance from the Borgo to the Piazza San Pietro, had a gayer effect.

§ The former Palazzo dell' Aquila

The façade was treated in the "grotesque" manner, customarily employed at a later date by the Baroque as the fashion for garden fronts, decorated with stucco, with three-quarter columns on the ground floor; in the other storeys there is an alternation of *aediculae* or niches with statues and stucco decorations. We are indebted to Parmegianino's admiration for an illustration of the façade (Plate 175). Among the reliefs of the attic there was presumably a CUPID WITH THE EAGLE OF ZEUS as a play on the name of the patron; Raphael made a sketch of it in the wonderful little red-chalk drawing in the British Museum (Plate 179*b*). There was thus a further throb of vitality in the horizontally-set rectangular projections of the attic storey, which had a ribbon-like effect in combination with the squat windows. A frieze of festoons and medallions is also carried along above the windows under a strongly accentuated cornice. The eagle appears again as a heraldic supporter: two, of the same antique form, guard the cartouche with the arms of the Papal patron. The palace was demolished; it had to make way for Bernini's colonnades. The exit from the Borgo thus lost a superb, beautifully profiled cornerpiece, which died away with a projecting ramp into the unevenness of the site. From the drawings of Dosio and Heemskerck, which are to-day, since the destruction of the entire Borgo, absolutely priceless, we see that this was the last corner of the Borgo.

We must find consolation in the enduring effect of these motives in later buildings. In the Palazzo Spada they occur afresh, and in many a Baroque garden front we have proof of an enduring stream of energy inevitably inherent in Raphael's ideas, the notions that *he* was the first to conceive. Nothing of this was lost, even when the originals disappeared.

§ Villa Madama: Conviviality, Building and Landscape

Even more unfavourable were the stars that shed their influence on the fate of the Villa that was erected after Raphael's plans on the slopes of the Monte Mario, above the bend of the Tiber at the Ponte Molle (Plate 180). Cardinal Giuliano de' Medici, the all-powerful Cardinal Secretary of State to Leo X, was here the Patron, the later Clement VII. The project must surely have been, from its inception, on so large a scale that a pontificate was scarcely adequate for its realisation; it seems to have been condemned to remain a ruin before it became a reality. Its destruction began even before it was finished, at the time of the *Sacco di Roma* in 1527; Clement, shut up in the Castle of St Angelo, could see from afar the catastrophe that befell his favourite spot. His old enemy, Cardinal Colonna, believed the moment of revenge had come, and had the Villa blown up. It must nevertheless have been re-erected when it came into the possession of "Madama", Margaret of Austria, as her residence. It was from her that the Villa got its name. To obtain an idea of what was demanded by the patron for whom it was built or by Roman society, or of what formed part of such a many-limbed creation, made to be occupied on days of Southern relaxation, will hardly be possible any longer, with the help of art histories, unless one is alive to the freedom with which Raphael peopled his Parnassus with men and women walking, reclining and gathering in circles, on the ups and downs of the hill. This may give us a condensed picture of that life in a *villegiatura* of those times, or in the *giardini letterarii*; such diversions made it worth while to create an *ensemble* of separate, individual scenes and precincts. Precisely this site, on the slopes of the Monte Mario, the landscape of which even to-day has not been entirely destroyed, alongside the Tiber, seems to have had attractions for the building patron and the painter architect.

The theorist Serlio derived his *Regole Generali*[1] for the *unity* of landscape and architecture from the example given by this builder-painter.

§ The Loggia as Expression of *Villeggiatura*

The Casino, without losing any of the imposing splendour of the *palazzo* form, conforms in its contours with the outline of the hill; formerly, with the dark shadows of its three great openings, it must have fitted into the landscape with less heavy effect and more picturesquely. The part to be played is not so suited to the living-rooms, concerned as they are with the individual, as to the saloon; this belonged to the company that passed gaily into it from the garden. Anyone in the habit of strolling out-of-doors in the wide spaces of the garden could take with him into the interior something of the pleasant sense of being in the open-air, glad to feel himself, here also, in out-door surroundings. Thus the facade opened, with three arches rising almost to the cornice, into a saloon;

---

[1] Venice, 1537, p. VIIIa; compare Golzio, *Raffaello*, p. 285.

the garden front thereby acquired a powerful shade-motive. At the time of the last restoration it had scarcely been opened up when it was again destroyed by glass walls. In its earlier state of neglect, that lasted for centuries, it long delighted the eyes of painters of ruins—down to Hubert Robert and Chays (Plate 184a). The mighty opening is continued inwards in the three magnificently wide sweeps of the cross-vaulting on slender soaring pillars. Anyone stepping beneath the span of these vaults has even to-day a sense of breathing freely; the architecture itself seems to communicate something of the lightness of the ethereal element outside (Plates 181, 182). The great niches are repeatedly broken into by smaller ones, and even as a decorative pattern on the pillars and archivolts overlaid with stucco, there is a succession of *aediculae*, cupolas and niches in plastic foreshortening. What we find here is no less than a collection of the motives with which Raphael was busy for architectural ideas that remained uncompleted. But there is here an extension, in a playful mood, of that propensity to overcome gravity, to progress from solidity to air and light-suffused clarity, that is evinced, in great seriousness, by his projects of that period for St Peter's. It is a motive of gardens and halls in which the air can be freely breathed, refreshingly cool spaces of greenery or stonework in endless variation.

In pursuance of Raphael's idea the Casino became the arena for the mutual emulation of a whole host of talents devoted to a uniform plan. On the showing of Vasari, Giulio Romano appears to have assigned to himself somewhat too large a share in the architectural conceptions; the paintings by him—the first to be carried out by him independently—are unfortunately unmistakable in their crudity. In and below the beautiful vaultings of the saloon, on archivolts, pillars and walls, have been preserved the whitish-gold stucco-decorations, at many points interspersed with green, yellow or red, with which GIOVANNI DA UDINE accompanied, in a spirit of charmingly unobtrusive playfulness, the architectural themes of his master. The wanton explosions of the year 1527 destroyed a portion of the lay-out; the original scheme can now only be conjectured. Heemskerck has handed down to us motives of the garden, the entrance to a hippodrome and the much-admired Elephant Fountain, a faint echo of an amazing *ensemble* (Plates 185a, b). Here Raphael may have followed the model of Bramante for the building-over of the Vatican demesne; he had to vary it in the open landscape and for the purposes of the place, and he introduced into his architecture the lines of the declivities, the contours of the hill, and the convexity of the site. Or better—he adopted from the movements of nature the principle by which his terraces and, as being inseparable from them, the relationships of his buildings should be governed. With a painter's sense for landscape and a feeling for the indispensable accord of all parts handled and accommodated one to another, he here composed the setting for the noble, stately and good-humoured forms, so richly diversified, of conviviality in the Roman countryside; in spite of all destruction he thus became the standard for later times as long as the style of this society was maintained. The background even for Watteau's ITALIAN COMEDIANS is provided by the entrance-niche of the Villa Madama; everywhere indeed in his pictures, a prospect of niches, and of spaces that, contrasted with everyday scenes, seem to withdraw themselves as if in sport from the eye, recalls the mysteriously dream-like lay-out of ancient *nymphaea*. The architects Gutensohn-Thürmer (Plate 184*b*), Geymüller and Th. Hofmann have essayed to reconstruct at least on paper these lost architectural landscapes and garden-structures.

§ Ceiling in the Garden Hall of the Farnesina: Festal Motives

Nymphaea, splashing waters, statues of gods, were scattered throughout this villa; the true humanist conceived the rural world, a beneficent nature, relaxation from the duties of everyday life, in the guise of primeval powers holding sway over the existence of mankind—the Olympians of the Greeks. Agostino Chigi had provided himself with reminders of an insistent dependence on these deities in the ceiling-spandrels of Baldassare Peruzzi in the garden saloon of his Villa on the Lungara. In the neighbouring gallery Raphael succeeded in capturing the very spirit of recreation. He caused the gods, with their life of sportive unconcern, to participate with men in their festivities. For this he did not limit himself to the role of a decorative artist. The architect Peruzzi had already had his say before the painter set to work. The hall, formerly open on to the garden, rose in Peruzzi's reserved, somewhat arid style to a flat-vaulted, level ceiling with sectroids, as in the Sistine Chapel, the walls articulated by means of combined pilasters—delicate, yet anything but cheerful. Then the painter, in a mood of humour and lightness, completed the building of the second garden saloon, a veritable wreath crowning the festive conviviality that the master of the house loved to conjure to this spot. Above Peruzzi's cornices, along the edges of his vaults, Raphael carried an arbour-like trelliswork of garlands like a decorative setting for a fête, just the right motive for Renaissance *festajuoli*. The development of this motive was worked out from Mantegna and Correggio to the "*joyeuses entrées*" of Henry II of France and Marie de Médicis, and so right on to Poussin; arcades in the form of spherical triangles sweep aloft, framing the pendentives of the ceiling with their resilient play, and the slight concavity of the ceiling surface gives the effect of tapestries as *velaria* flapping and bellying. Here also we have the leading motive employed by Raphael during these years—the passage from the massive and solid to the light and airy; and in the aether, that was designedly intended to enter with a look of friendliness and sunshine, the Olympian gods weave a light-hearted fable about the love and sufferings of a mortal woman, the story, as related by Apuleius, of the Soul with whom Love comes down from above to sympathise—the ROMANCE OF CUPID AND PSYCHE (Plates 205–211).

We do not know what was the original aspect of the lower walls before the incongruous decorations of the seventeenth century were introduced—whether tapestries hung there or whether there was actually a fresco design of Psyche's earthly pilgrimage, as has been surmised. This design will hardly have been so trivial as the compositions in the engravings of Michiel Coxie which have been thought to reproduce it. In any case the ceiling was intended, by an effect of space opened up in contrast with the walls, to set free the eye and feelings from the rigidity of the walls; as in the dome above Agostino Chigi's tomb, here also the pale blue of the sky looked in. Any such ethereal quality was entirely lost under Maratta's rage for restoration. We have to picture to ourselves that the luminous figures of the gods once moved and had their being against this bright background of sky, like the angels improvised by Raphael himself in the *cassette* of the Loggie (Plate 224). The much-admired garlands of Giovanni da Udine provide the more substantial framing, but even their network of lines, last remnant of the earthly, sways aloft with an airy swing, penetrated by the wantonness of the fluttering *amoretti* with the attributes of the mighty divinities above and below (Plates 208, 209). It was already noticed with approval by contemporaries that the heavens here retain their infinitude, and the supernal beings go on their courses without any foreshortening due to being seen from below from a human standpoint. Serlio commends the peculiar poetic seriousness in this treatment of the ceiling. All the more profound is our regret that here, in the case of this wonderful scheme, the architect-painter was obliged to leave its execution to pupils, burdening the work with the material burden laid upon them, instead of carrying it out with the ethereal quality that was in his dreams, "die Täuschung, die er schafft, aufrichtig selbst zerstört".[1] According to the opinion of many contemporaries the design never had the light effect he dreamed of. In this connection it may be of interest to connoisseurs of pictures to ascertain the shares in the work taken by pupils, and certainly as a matter of art-history the great division of labour in it is worthy of remark. The essential feature is the poetical treatment of an entire apartment, of which the ceiling-design was on exactly the same plan as that of the Sistine Chapel, as a sphere of humanist festivity, and this could only be the invention of the painter and architect in a single person who here succeeded, out of his own all-perceiving, self-conscious experience, in bringing into play anew the powers of the Antique. It was this same all-percipient self-consciousness that made RUBENS the great narrator of the North. Thus it was no accident that the two were here on common ground; we know how the imagination of Rubens was fired by this very ceiling (Plate 292). This relationship seems absolutely to have been foreordained between these two artists, creators, each for his own nation, of heroic form.

Again, it appears equally to be no accident that the Fleming and the Urbino master alike strove to create for themselves, for their pretensions as regards

[1] "The illusion he creates by itself in sooth destroyed."

RAPHAEL

their mode of living, an architectural setting for their own daily life. Their universality urged them to introduce into the whole of existence, in a form of similar clarity, their inward bearing: their life, their creations and their buildings should be of a single spirit!

This was the enduring element in Raphael as he appeared in the eyes of his contemporaries and posterity; this is the purport of Vasari's words.[1] As Raphael's renown as a great man grew in pace with his wealth, he desired "lasciare memoria di sè"—to leave a memorial to posterity: he wished to have a like standing with future generations also. He therefore built himself in the *borgo nuovo* in Rome a palace that Bramante "carried out for him in concrete".

§ Raphael's palace

This desire of Raphael's for a memorial of his life was fulfilled in a strange manner. Destiny sported with it in a thoroughly Raphaelesque fashion. Of the palace nothing is left, but about a generation after the master's death Palladio perpetuated it, with an understanding due to kinship of spirit, in a sketch sparkling with life (Plate 186); certainly we have Palladio to thank for the echo, as it were, of this creation that can be perceived wherever there is a desire to produce an effect of dignity and grace coupled with the expression of social importance. PALLADIO, SANMICHELI and VIGNOLA were indebted to him, and through them, the architecture of their followers in the North far into the eighteenth century. The stone structure of the building has disappeared from our sight; the spirit and the rhythm in which it took shape continued to survive, entirely in Raphael's sense. His *Palazzo* was erected in all probability on the south side of the old Piazza di San Pietro, where the Borgo Vecchio opened out opposite the Porta San Pietro; the narrow block formed by its eastern angle had to give way to a widening under Pius IV in 1565, just as a hundred years later the Palazzo dell' Aquila was crowded out by Bernini's colonnades.[2] It stood at the point, more or less at a tangent to the present-day circle round the obelisk, where the ground slopes up with a gentle rise to the steps of Old St Peter's, as indicated also by Palladio. Still at the present day one is conscious in walking of the swell of this ascent on which Raphael had to build. The head end of the Palazzo met the eye of those coming down the Borgo Vecchio; the façade with its five axes presented itself to anyone entering the Piazza through the Porta San Pietro (about where the Porta Angelica now is) or turning out of the Via Alessandria from the Borgo Nuovo, destroyed in 1937, into the great opening of the "Forum Sancti Petri". It appears that Raphael intended it as a studio, so as to have a

---

[1] *Vite*, ed. Milanesi, Vol. IV, p. 353.

[2] Th. Hofmann's investigations concerning Raphael as architect (*Raphael als Architekt*, Vol. II—2nd ed.) have shown this very clearly; compare the plans of Bufalini (1551) and Nolli (1748), drawn one above the other, reproduced in Hofmann, *op. cit.*, pp. 99–101.

scene of operations for his workshop and assistants near the Vatican. His residence was still on the Piazza Scossacavalli, in the house that Bramante had occupied and that he had taken over. It was here also that he died.[1] The site was here, on the Piazza San Pietro, in the extended axis of the south wall of the old Basilica, approximately between the southern fountain and the middle passage through the south colonnade of Bernini.

The solution was thus given of a building that gave emphasis at once to the side of the piazza and the angle: it could not be other than distinguished. It was carried out for Raphael by BRAMANTE, according to Vasari's narrative in the *Life* of the latter: "lavorato in mattoni e di getto con casse" ("in bricks and blocks of concrete")—"columns in the Doric Order and the dressing in rustication, a very beautiful work and an innovation as regards the invention of concrete." An innovation also, in any case, the invention of the entire scheme. We have no right to think only of Bramante's idea for the composition of the palace; his part was only that of carrying it out. It is to be attributed to the young master who had at that time already achieved success in the architectural compositions of the HELIODORUS fresco and the MASS OF BOLSENA.

Certainly he gave effect to his own idea when he made it his aim "lasciare memoria di se". Thus there stood in the immediate neighbourhood of the seat of supreme power, there at the corner of the Piazza San Pietro, the Forum Sancti Petri, this first palace of a painter who felt himself to be one of the *Cortegiani* and desired to leave evidence of his mode of life to contemporaries and the future.

This house has an effect of importance and at the same time of graceful buoyancy, whilst his Palazzo Vidoni, for all its similarity, in its heavy, recumbent, horizontal character, represents more the later, masculine style.

§ Relationship to the Palazzo Vidoni

Above the rusticated storey with fairly narrow pillars, narrower at all events than the openings between them, the upper storey is set back with a perceptible recession, giving greater lightness. The pairs of columns appear even more slender because each column has a pedestal to itself. They are not, as in the Palazzo Vidoni, combined by a single plinth for each two columns, stressing by its breadth the horizontal quality in the façade and thereby the weight that binds it to the earth. Here everything was made to serve the slender upward movement; even the triglyphs of the entablature continue it, as do the narrow balusters of the balcony-railings. Thus arises, above the vaults below and the mezzanine, a superstructure with high, light rooms. One of the

[1] We can here follow the loving researches and expert conclusions of Th. Hofmann; in his second volume he has cleared up the question of the various sites in which Raphael owned plots of land.

ceiling coffers and some balusters were still preserved a few years ago as relics in the Palazzo de' Convertendi, where Raphael's residence was. On this site the building cannot have had any depth; on the upper floor it can have contained only a few large rooms.

The solution of the corner was provided of necessity by a column projecting almost full circle between the last two semi-circular columns of the two fronts; it was brought out with particularly pleasing effect by Palladio in his sketch, and is worthy of the architect-painter who seeks out intermediary transitions and strives to harmonise colours and forms; certainly columns, entablatures and window-frames stood out in lighter tone—at least through the smoothness of their form—against the duller surfaces (they were, of course, as cast stonework, a substitute for stone). Vasari speaks of this "getto con casse"—"blocks of concrete"—as a remarkable innovation, a dignified invention for a reality worthy of endeavour. Even this suffices for the citizen painter, who as a true courtier, builds his *palazzo* so near the seat of the supreme power in forms appropriate to it. As in his figures, Raphael here discovers the means of expressing the ambitions of a society in the cultural development of which he had already, as friend of the "formator del cortegiano", had a share at Urbino; this society he passed on to posterity in his creations, whether as painter or architect, as an ideal that can never be lost.

Precise theorists in the nineteenth century have supposed they could find, in this use of concrete for genuine stone forms, the beginning of a decadence, a divorce of the material from its original form, something "clumsy", like a "bourgeois posing as nobleman"; and in this they were not by any means greatly mistaken. Throughout the whole period there runs a tendency to give nobility to the form of living; in the Spanish *sosiego*, in the *sprezzatura* of the *magnanimo* and *Cortegiano*, the self-centred nature of the man of self-reliance seeks for itself a dignified expression. Here the intention of the aggressive rustication, of the soaring classical columns, is none other than to bring into play the heroic form; for neither the ashlar nor the free-standing columns nor the triglyph-entablature are essential to this building as a dwelling. But it meant running to death the demand for "organic" character in architecture, in the most up-to-date academic arrogance of the new objectivity, if it was ever to be made of any account at all as compared with the earlier architecture. Even the Hellenic Doric temple with its triglyphs and coffering fails to meet organic requirements; it would be the negation of art and the denial of the happy relationship between architecture and music, indeed of all genuine arts whatsoever one with another, if the use of forms for effect were excluded from building. For if any art brings into play images of support and burden, elements communicating an atmosphere, rhythms of life-awakening significance, it has been architecture, and in this sense Raphael, when he builds, demands to be regarded as the interpreter of the mood of his time. In so far as this palace and the spirit it expressed were really his memorial, even though it stood for hardly half a century, his energy was preserved for posterity.

§ Raphael for his Contemporaries an Architect

In the eyes of his contemporaries this painter, in the last lustre of his life, stood as the great creative architect, the director of the building of St Peter's, who gave the Papal residence its form. The profound impression made on the period by his personality as architect cannot be sufficiently estimated. In his time the eyes of the world were directed towards the building of St Peter's, of which he was in charge, either in devout admiration or, as we know—in Northern countries—in critical disapproval, everywhere, in fact, among the world of the Faithful. His problems were debated with equal excitement among artists and clerics. But *urbi et orbi* he had the same standing, as regards his widespread influence, in his other spheres of operation as an architect. Everyone who at any time came to Rome found himself under Raphael's spell, whether consciously or not, when he entered the City of Leo, the *civitas Leonina*. The most vivid conception of this is given by Lafreri's plan of 1577 (Plates 188, 189). In the Borgo, on the Piazza Scossacavalli, facing the Palazzo Giraud-Torlonia, stood at the corner the house taken over by Raphael from Bramante, now absorbed in the Palazzo de' Convertendi. In the Borgo Nuovo, at that time the Via Alessandria, to the right of the oblique entrance of the Borgo Sant' Angelo, arose the palace of the Surgeon-in-Ordinary, Giovanni Antonio da Brescia; next, the Casa Battiferro and yet another house with frescoes on the façade after a scheme of Raphael's. They have disappeared, but not far from them, in the Vicolo del Campanile beside Santa Maria Traspontina, a *sgraffito* façade of his school still survives. At the exit from the street to the left, on its ramp, was the Palazzo dell' Aquila, with grotesque designs of an absolutely novel kind. At this point however, the eye is already drawn onward by the Piazza of St Peter's; above the Basilica consecrated of old, the amazing arches were already rising that were to serve the new cupola. Heemskerck made a drawing of them (Plate 153*b*) half a century after the death of Raphael, who had done so much for the support of their piers, to make possible the mighty vaulting on high. And this view of the old and the newly growing sanctuaries was flanked by impressions of the new architecture. There on the left side of the Piazza stood the palace of the Pope's painter-architect, entirely new-fashioned in the aristocratic bearing of its *single* magnificent main storey—the *piano nobile*—and this was the palace of the master who had provided the Vatican with its main front. There in the Vatican the range of the Loggie arose, dominating or masking with its tones the mediæval confusion of the Quattrocento structures; it soared aloft with its gracefully energetic alternation of light and shade, of the light supports of the arcades and their dark openings, imposing in the estimation of the masses as the residence of the Pope and woven over with the fabulous novelty of its decoration of grotesques. These belonged to the renovation of Antiquity and of the Eternal City; their fame brought lustre to its name.

When the severe baroque palace of Clement VIII (1592-1605) had not yet deprived this view of its cheerfulness Raphael's Loggie building was the real main front of the papal residence. It dominated also the sacred places; already however, under Raphael's own impelling direction, rose the beginnings of the mighty cupola, that dome which was to readjust once more, on this consecrated spot, the relationship of secular and sacred.

§ Raphael *Maestro di Strade*

Of profane and sacred not at this point only; his plans related to Rome in its entirety. We know little more than the warrant of nomination tells us as to Raphael's activities as *Maestro di Strade*—Master of Street Planning, to which he was appointed by the Pope; but this warrant contains Leo's instructions for the reduction to an ordered system of the three streets from the Piazza del Popolo—straight on, the Corso, the upper street as yet hardly in existence (the present Via Balbuino) beside the gardens of the Pincio, and the street on the right leading to the Tiber which was called "Leonina" and which, in accordance with the Pope's wish, was to have an aspect "more worthy of his name". The commission contained neither more nor less than the provision for the capital, the secular City of Rome, by means of this radiation of streets, of an impressive accent at its very gate of entry from the North. We may regard Rome's most famous, though forgotten, Superintendent of Highways as being immortalised in these three great axial lines. It is fascinating to realise how he provided secular Rome with its entrance, and the goal of all pilgrims, in the Vatican and its environment, with its form.

In Raphael as architect as well as painter lived the great motive ideas of that period of which he was privileged to make himself, by his buildings and pictures, the harbinger to his own and after ages.

XI

RAPHAEL AND AGOSTINO CHIGI

§ Raphael's great Patrons

THE records offer us little in the way of personal touches relating to Raphael's life; it is almost with a sense of shame that his biographer, in spite of this, attempts to describe the circumstances under which these great works came into existence. Yet there is a very gracious and thoroughly Italian chapter in the story of his life which makes amends to us by records founded on fact—that of his relations with three great Maecenases in addition to Pope Leo X—the Duke of Ferrara, King Francis I of France, and Agostino Chigi.

The artist's connections with ALFONSO I must have begun already under Julius II; Ariosto was often entrusted with the role of intermediary when he visited Rome. But the Pope's painter had no need of such an advocate. He was at that time working on the portrait of Alfonso's nephew, the little Federigo Gonzaga, in armour, with a plumed cap—certainly by the desire of the boy's mother and to please the Pope, to whom the little Prince quickly became a favourite instead of a hostage. Isabella d' Este had been obliged to give him up as surety to the victorious Julius; the boy's charms soon converted this political action into an idyll that brightened in the most agreeable manner the pauses between the peals of thunder of the mighty Rovere, and also may have mitigated the menacing reception in Rome of his uncle the Duke of Ferrara. One day, when Alfonso seems to have been detained for an unpleasantly long time in the palace, the young Prince took upon himself the liberty of showing the Ferrarese suite "the apartments of the Pope and the rooms painted by Raphael". As to the Duke, we know that at that time he climbed up to join Michael Angelo on the scaffolding in the Sistine Chapel; he must then have met the master of the Stanze, and the portrait of his nephew by Raphael may have originated at that time. Alfonso loved mythology; Bellini, Titian, and the painters of his own territory, the Dossi, decorated his palace with Bacchic scenes. On the occasion of that visit to the scaffolding under the vault Michael Angelo had to promise him a picture; it was eighteen years before that promise took shape, in that LEDA that was lost to the Duke through the bungling of his ambassador.

In the case of Raphael the Duke's patience was sooner exhausted. The first mention of the Duke's commission was three years later. At that time Alfonso commissioned the Roman *Chargé d'Affaires* Paulucci to ask Raphael, as Conservator of Ancient Monuments, to procure medals, busts and statues. It appears that a mythological subject was agreed upon, when Leo X, and Raphael presumably in his suite, came to Bologna in 1515; a visit to Ferrara, or a new meeting of Raphael with Alfonso at the interview of Francis I and the Pope, would have been possible. In April, 1517, the Duke, after many a fruitless letter, sent another reminder to his plenipotentiary Paulucci: "Raphael must at last put the finishing touches to our pictures, and with all possible speed; Raphael certainly is in close relations with His Reverence Monsignore Cibo, so I wish that you should visit His Highness in our name and urge him to press for the delivery at last of this our picture, in accordance with the promise made to us when His Highness was in Ferrara—it is to-day precisely three years since he pledged himself to it."

The ambassador was in a difficult situation, between the energetic notes of his master and the courteous manners of the artist when he was permitted to see him. In February, 1519, he succeeded in obtaining access to the workshop; he extols to the Duke the beautiful sketches shown him by one of the assistants, a "MELEAGER HUNTING" and a "TRIUMPH OF BACCHUS". Nothing more was yet finished. But Raphael personally promised solemnly that both pictures should be dispatched at the following Easter; in any case up to now there was nothing further to be seen but the sketches. For the moment moreover Raphael will have been entirely occupied with the stage decorations for Messer Ludovico Ariosto's comedy (*I Suppositi*).

Meanwhile the artist learned that the Duke had already ordered a TRIUMPH OF BACCHUS of one of his painters, Pellegrino da Udine. His own sketch had already been sent off to Ferrara. Now he proposes another theme and obtains a payment of fifty ducats. In the meantime the cartoon for the fresco in the Stanza dell' Incendio representing the OATH OF PURGATION OF LEO III went to the Duke as a present, as from one potentate to another. The potentate bestowing the present knows well enough that in doing so he is giving something to which at heart he attaches no great importance; for the master can have had hardly any share whatever in sketch, cartoon or execution of this composition. Then we read: "Raphael begs to be excused for the delay; he will not have finished the picture for Your Highness before Easter." "The Pope and his lord, the Duke of Urbino, keep him entirely taken up with portraits and designs, so that he cannot work connectedly on the painting of the picture. At the moment he is deeply involved in work on a life-size ST MICHAEL which His Holiness has commissioned as a present for His Majesty the Most Christian King. This picture must be finished as soon as ever possible. But in spite of all, I persevere in refusing to let him off and reminding him again and again as well as I can."

Raphael however had grown to be the equal as opponent of the cleverest diplomat. He offered the impatient Duke the cartoon for the St Michael; the princely answer ensued in the form of a payment of twenty-five ducats. Thereupon Paulucci wrote as follows: "The artist politely (*delicatamente*) refuses to accept the money; he only offered the cartoon as a token of his attachment and respect for Your Person; and at this point such was his courtesy that words failed him, and he declared again and again how much rather he would be at the service of Your Highness than of this entire Court. At last however he accepted the money with much gratefulness towards you." Now the Duke desired to have also the cartoon for the portrait of Giovanna of Aragon—he was present when the painting arrived in France—and he obtained it. But the Ambassador was not allowed to lose sight of his two pictures. A tragi-comical drama began. When Paulucci visited the artist at his residence, the latter made his excuses at the doorway: Count Castiglione was just then with him, sitting for his portrait. The poor envoy made the best of it; he pretended to believe it and waited till the next time. When he came again, Raphael must have seen him; it appeared to the Ambassador as if he had left the house by another door. Then he met him on the site of the building of San Pietro, where he "fà il Bramante"—perhaps the best explanation of all Raphael's procrastinations in painting—and whilst the Duke, accustomed to break down opposition with artillery, fired up at this behaviour towards a person of high standing, and threatened withdrawal of his favour, his representative was so captivated by Raphael's accommodating graciousness and inward invincibility that he suggested he would rather win him over with the customary forms of friendliness—"vincer con l'humanità consueta"—for men with such excellences are for the most part inclined to melancholy—"homini di questa excellentia sentono tutti de melencolico".

And so a dreaded ruler like Alfonso of Ferrara had to be satisfied with courtesies. The Most Christian King received as a present from the Pope only studio works, almost entirely by Raphael's pupils. The strong personality of this unique painter eluded the Pope himself; his various services forced him to distribute his powers in different directions.

Only one magnate of an exceptional order, the banker AGOSTINO CHIGI of Siena, understood how to use Raphael's most peculiar accomplishments to his own advantage; it remains a question what it was precisely that availed to bind the artist to this man of finance. The "gran mercante di Christianità"—as an Oriental addressed him, certainly did not captivate Raphael by his wealth, nor by the power with which money endowed him. His keen intelligence balanced by his *magnanimità* caused him to appear one of the most cultivated men of the time. The alliance of capitalism and humanism has so often falsified intellectual values and disintegrated spiritual and moral values; in Chigi it may for once have desired to make justify itself. Here the talents of the artist seemed to have chanced upon a neutral region of forces.

§ Raphael stimulated by Chigi's Themes. Attitude towards Mythology: Astrology

No-one among the other patrons gave Raphael orders for themes of such dignity or so stimulating, themes in which the possibilities of his art were extended, to work themselves out with full effect only in the future. These monumental profane subjects received their consecrated form from Raphael; they certainly aroused the strongest echo in the sensibility of his wealthy friend.

Agostino loved to promote with his unlimited means what seemed good to his expansive spirit. He had a private printing-press in his house. Here he, the μέγα εὐπρεπὴς, the *magnanimo* and *magnifico*, brought out, for the first time in Rome, printed in Greek characters, Pindar (1515) (Plate 226) and the *Idylls* of Theocritus (1516). Thus in life as in death, the gods of the Greeks soared above him, on the ceiling of his summer *salle de fêtes* as on the dome of his mortuary chapel in Santa Maria del Popolo. And these Olympians signified for him not sensual pleasure, still less humanistic vanity; they were rather a pious sporting with the idea of dependence on the unapproachable powers from whose cult, for ever renewed, Christianity had broken loose, whose heavenly bodies with their dæmons, guided by heavenly motive forces, never ceased in the firmament to circle over and sway the life of mankind. Expression was thus found in him, as one of the élite of the time, men of a deepened sensibility, for an inner relationship with the Antique. To him the gods were dæmons of the stars that held sway over his existence, within the eternal ordinances, in the firmament. Raphael gives us evidence of these trains of thought, of their wide range and deep reverence; indeed it was perhaps through his imaginative interpretation that they first acquired for us life and breath, and by this means such astrological conceptions with their temporal associations were maintained until an impulse made itself felt to find the way back to the depths of their essence.

In him Raphael was sensible of something to which he gave shape; in him, that is, he perceived the fusion, as a cultural unity in the consciousness of the Renaissance, of the living present and the past, of contemporary and ancient, as it were in a lofty mood of playful reverie that gave charm to life when it found itself reflected in the mirror of these great conceptions and beautiful forms.

Agostino Chigi's first commission already gave to the young painter of the Stanze, just appointed by the Pope to his great task, an opportunity of co-operating in such a transfiguration of life. According to a contract of 10th November, 1510, the goldsmith CESARINO ROSETTI, a native of Perugia, was to make two bronze dishes, "grandi quattro palmi", with many flowers— "con molti fiori"—in half relief, after the pattern which "maestro Raffaello di Giovanni Santi da Urbino dipectore" would give him. It was certainly no mere floral-design that was then expected of Raphael, but a frieze of figures among scrolls. We may thus regard the Oxford design and the Dresden drawing as substitutes for the lost dishes—especially as they agree approximately in their measurements (42 cm.) with those stipulated in the contract. The Oxford sheet (Plate 300), a design of a half circle, begins in Raphael's own hand and is finally carried through by another, which does not seem to be that of any of the known assistants. The Dresden circle shows traces of preliminary drawing in red chalk in many places, but is carried out by the hand of a pupil and gives Raphael's brilliant motives in a less inspired hand, perhaps that of the young Giulio Romano. The sketch on the back of the Windsor drawing for the MASSACRE OF THE INNOCENTS (Plate 190, *R. Z.*, V, 235), very likely represents the first idea for such a subject; by its closeness to the ceiling of the Stanza della Segnatura and to the School of Athens, and on internal evidence also, it belongs already to the period denoted by the contract.

These show dishes were certainly intended for one of the famous banquets of Agostino, and this is entirely appropriate to such a company, saturated in Antique ideas and, in a full-blooded manner, fulfilling with its vitality the classical conceptions; so we may well imagine how this Bacchic *thiasos* was taken as an allusion when the host, who had once said to the Pope that he had a fleet of a hundred ships sailing on every sea, had fruit presented to his guests on these dishes encircled by the powers, surging in wild conflict with one another, of that element which he knew to be tributary to himself over as wide a range as had once been traversed by Dionysus in his progress over the sea.

Of Chigi's much-renowned art treasures we know little more than that he possessed antiques, medals and gems "like the wealth of the *Imperatores*"—and we surmise what inspirations were bestowed from this sparkling abundance upon the artists who shared and augmented his delights.

§ Birth of Venus

"Hic Venus orta mari et concha sub sydera fertur" are the words of Blosio Palladio in the poem *Selva*; it appeared in Rome in 1512, and sings of the Farnesina when it was not yet finished. Thus the verses could not refer to the GALATEA, even if we could see in this a TRIUMPH OF VENUS; this fresco came into existence hardly before 1514. It must therefore have been another picture of the foam-born goddess that the poet had before his eyes. Perhaps one of Raphael's drawings puts us on the track of the lost painting that belonged to Chigi. Among sketches for the DISPUTA and early Roman Madonna-compositions on a sheet in the Uffizi (*R. Z.*, VI, 264) there is one of the rare schemes for pictures already entirely framed in a vertical rectangle—Venus rising from the sea, in the consciousness of her revealed beauty, conceals herself in the attitude of the Aphrodite of the Capitoline and of the Medici Venus; in this case she is transposed into the mode of Ariosto, in masculine triumph: his fair ones fettered to rocks would here greet their sister. Drawn with pen-strokes swelling in crescendo and diminuendo, the solid, magnificently compact forms of the figure stand out before sea, mountains and clouds, with flights of birds hovering round about, whilst the shell beneath her feet seems to communicate to the goddess the sense of swaying on the waves. The frame tells us that a picture was to be made out of this sketch. In any case, in his early Roman days, the painter of the Madonnas and the DISPUTA was busy with an Antique pictorial idea, at the same time as with these dishes. Form and gesture gain nobility in the unaccustomed Roman atmosphere; impressions derived from the Antique are mastered and brought into play in a new, individual style. With Peruzzi, in the garden saloon of the Farnesina, the same motive was frittered away in pedantry. Only Raphael is able to repay his debt of gratitude to the Antique on terms of free equality.

§ Chigi Chapel: Sibyls

Even before Chigi had had erected for him the mortuary chapel near the monastery of his patron saint in Santa Maria del Popolo, he seems to have had in mind another spot to remind him of death, the first chapel on the right in Santa Maria della Pace, with Raphael's Prophets and Sibyls. We do not know how the niche was once adorned, before the Baroque rebuilding, or whether it ever provided a place for a tomb. In connection with an old restoration in the seventeenth century there is talk of a fresco above the altar; perhaps it contained a *Pietà*. The inscription on the scrolls and tablets above could refer to the dead Redeemer. There would then be nothing contradictory about the circumstance that, whilst here, in Santa Maria della Pace, the idea of death and resurrection is dominant, the burial-place was already under construction at Santa Maria del Popolo, the favourite church of the Rovere family, whose arms were borne by Chigi, and near the monastery of St Augustine, his patron.

§ Damaging Restoration: Original Architectural Background

This frescoed wall has been under the sway of an unlucky star (Plates 194c, 196–203); the master was obliged to leave the grandly conceived upper part with the Prophets to be carried out by others after his design. As regards the Sibyls, their harmony has certainly always been admired, but the composition has not come down to us as it was conceived. Arbitrary restorers have had their way with it, first in the sixteenth and seventeenth centuries, then in the nineteenth, when Palmiroli proclaimed to the world his belief that he was the right person to renovate the SISTINE MADONNA. Whether before his time, and if so when, the Sibyls lost their architectural background and were provided with the utterly unspatial curtain before which their movements, springing as it were like flowers from the ground, appear as if on front stage between the acts, we do not know. On the occasion of a restoration in 1618, that is to say already a hundred years after they came into existence, there is still mention of the *sky*. Agostino Chigi the younger, who founded the fortune of Fabio Chigi (later, Pope Alexander III), writes in his *Commentarii*:[1] "Under the eyes of Giovanni Lanfranco and the Cavalier d'Arpino they have begun to clean the fresco with a little moist farmhouse bread and a touch of white-of-egg to liven up the colours, and to make up certain unimportant parts such as draperies and sky." At that time the most beautiful of the Sibyls was already seriously damaged by tracing with oil-paper. They moved therefore against a background at least as deep in tone as that retained by the Prophets; perhaps the vistas were more open than in the upper part. At all events one can recognise, from lines scratched in the green curtain, that the architecture, of which remnants can be made out on the right at the head of the angel surging forward above the aged Tiburtina, must have extended into a hall; only so could the movements of the figures have had any sense, from the *putto* with the torch (Plate 195) to the angels, who require for the beating of their wings as they sweep above the earth more atmosphere than is afforded between the green curtain-hanging and the cornice beneath the feet of the Sibyls.

For in Raphael a background is not a foil for the figures; he can entirely dispense with it, as is shown by his MADONNA DELLA SEDIA and MADONNA DELLA TENDA. But otherwise the space repeats the rhythm of the movements; the ALBA MADONNA is not merely composed in the round—she is also encircled by the landscape in a wide sweep. Thus the attitudes of the earthly prophetesses and heavenly messengers are also unthinkable except against a receding background. The æsthetics of our classicism took a delight in this design, which had taken on a flavour of *style Empire* with its flat ground—but Raphael's *horror vacui* would never have tolerated such lifeless surfaces above the figures; they were pervaded by architectural members of which the lines can still be recognised, and the perpendicular setting of their pillars provided the animated forms with a kind of framing. An angular niche of which the cornice and hollow passed behind the heads and, with the charm of alternating light and shade, gave vitality to the background, once formed as it were a common circumscribed space; thus one was put in mind of a cavern-scene in the manner of the Shakespeare stage, serving as abode for the solitary prophetesses. For solitude is what belongs to these forthtellers of profound visions. Against the architectural setting each of them must surely once have appeared to stand forth, as from her own special sphere, to receive the tidings of the messenger from above; the more rigid the structure of beams and pillars, the livelier their emotion, the more sweeping and airy the flight of the angels, interrupted by the straight lines of the framework. And taking their place as they do on the top of the arch, the Sibyls seem still to belong all the while to the air, even though they bend towards the regions of earth. To-day the figures, with their abundance of soft red and yellow, with the green and grey and the golden flesh-tones which, on

[1] Cugnoni, *Archivio della Soc. Romana* IV, 1881, p. 64, No. 9.

the right of the arch of the niche, they have retained more or less as they came from Raphael's hand, stand out somewhat too brightly against the unbroken green. When here also, as in the case of the Prophets, the architecture still extended rhythmically behind the figures in tones of bronze shaded off in perspective on pillars and entablatures, the whole undoubtedly had such a splendidly harmonious appearance that it had no need of Palmaroli with his "harmonising" devices.

Such a harmony of colour was for Raphael inseparable from linear resonance; the sonorous pattern in which this series of women, *putti* and angels traverses the rectangle broken by the niche and arch has long been admired. Compared with the lunette of the Segnatura, with its linear pattern of the JUDICIAL VIRTUES, it has a more complex effect, and with its one-time architectural setting it pervaded with powerful and pathetic rhythm the space to be filled. If the period of *Aufklärung* found the solution of such a problem difficult and therefore worthy of admiration, Goethe commended its "secret symmetry" as something that came as a matter of course to the master. Raphael here wove a legacy from Gothic into his new style, with its play of atmosphere and space. A similar procedure was adopted by Roger van der Weyden, the "last of the Gothics" before him, when he set his great DESCENT FROM THE CROSS, in the Escorial, in a golden, angular niche as if in an altar shrine; the feeling of space in the figures fits in with the confined position, yet the gold ground produces the affect of a shrine. In Van der Weyden two epochs were locked in conflict; Raphael consciously reverts to the adoption of methods from the times of the ultimate concentration of expression. In this employment of the arch for the glorious motives of seated figures we may also recognise an acknowledgment of the Antique, as for instance of the reclining VICTORIES in the spandrels of the triumphal arches, or the BACCHUS AND ARIADNE in the Casali sarcophagus, now in Copenhagen. Yet Raphael comes nearest to the Antique where he is independently inventing. The angel to the left on the arch, as by his upward-pointing finger he gently suggests reconcilement with death, of which the Sibylla Persica is writing, remains in movement as he sits, having no need of repose; he is as buoyant as the nimble Messenger of the Gods, resting for a few moments, in the delightful bronze at Naples, with which however Raphael was not acquainted (Plate 203).

There are obvious dangers in all this beauty of form—with Raphael we ourselves are always in danger of misunderstanding him, because we do not believe him, with his facility, capable of deep thinking. Certainly Michael Angelo's solitary figures have descended with greater passion into the untrodden region; here, heavenly love has had a part in them—the wings of the *putti* flutter like butterflies amongst them, and the predictions that they take up out of the urns at their feet are answered by the angels, the *amori*, with comforting gestures pointing to the heavens, or they bear the tidings of Resurrection triumphantly to all the winds—for the flanking angels seem to have snatched up the palm-leaves of Cumæa. Her uplifted arm can never be a mere dancer's phrase; it lets go the sheet with which the angel will soar up, and his companion, like an eager messenger, once more looks back as he sweeps down; "into the All Strive ye in ecstasy through nearer zones to press". This hymn of Death and Resurrection must therefore be taken as a single whole.

§ Prophets (Plates 194a, b, 196)

Up above, among the wonderful pillars of an open hall, all is whispering, in masculine animation: with great gestures the PROPHETS receive their promptings from above, throned on their seats or standing like statues. A youth-like angel behind Hosea points upwards to the heavenly Power of whom the prophet bears witness with his tablet: "Suscitabit eum Deus post biduum die tertia" (I Cor. xv, 4)—God will raise him again after two days on the third day. Jonah, in intense agitation, looks up at the winged boy who points out of the narrow worldly bounds towards the airy heights—one of Raphael's most beautiful inventions. David is a mighty, priestly, standing figure, almost like one of Claus Sluter's Prophets, with the words "Resurrexi et adhuc sum tecum", and his angel, in the act of departing, has a look of emotion at this promise of divine support, whilst Daniel, shaken and transported, follows with his gaze the child angel who withdraws above the hall with his companion. Much here, as in the preparatory stage in the Stockholm collection (Plate 193), is reminiscent of Michael Angelo's design for the tomb of Julius II, especially the figures sitting enthroned. The red-chalk study for DANIEL AND THE ANGEL in the Uffizi (Plate 165) belongs to the examples, as rare as they are precious, of Raphael's most individual, late draughtsmanship. Powerful forms, dæmonic, and showing an endless wealth of vitality in their varying degrees of mood. When Rubens made a copy of this very group of David and Daniel, in a broad drawing in the Regteren-Altena Collection (Plate 191), he felt to whom he was here indebted, and for what. Where recent speculation concerns only the question of authorship, this kindred genius knew how to recognise the magnificent conception —in fact, the inventiveness—of figures like these, in their lofty setting in front of this superb pillared space. Vasari was still hearing, from persons who pretended to have been present, that the Prophets were painted by Timoteo Viti. In reality little is known of this alleged teacher and obvious imitator of Raphael; enough nevertheless to show that his hand is not to be discerned in these paintings. The coarsely turgid forms in the heads, the snaky folds and shot colours are reminiscent much more of the later style of Giulio Romano, if it is permissible to recognise this assistant of Raphael at so early a date. The curtain caught up in loops, as in the niches of Quattrocento tombs, doubtless took shape only when the restoration was carried out. The inscriptions below the figures were certainly renewed; in the process, the Prophet on the extreme left was given a wrong name.[1] The prophecy on his tablet—"Suscitabit eum deus post biduum die tertia"—can only belong to Hosea; there is no possibility of determining how much of his appalling unconcern is attributable to Raphael's satellites. Here the "harmonising" restorer is perhaps not guilty; in a sketch of the group, which is an early example of the participation of the youthful Giulio, the expression of this Prophet is not exactly in keeping with the great Moses-like motive of his attitude; one is conscious of the classical relationship of pupil to master, as of Van Dyck to Rubens—greatness of form and the emptiness at heart of the pupil.

§ Architectural Composition of the entire Wall

The entire wall was conceived by Raphael on architectural lines; twice over, one above the other, the intrusive openings—window above, niche below— were united with the architecture in the picture to form the Palladian Motive. Here on the wall a painted structure was erected which in Sant' Eligio became reality in stone (Plate 192). The lower surfaces on either side of the niche up to the cornice were intended to be decorated in circular medallions. Perhaps the circular composition in the Uffizi, with Christ in a nimbus, belongs here, and its counterpart preserved in the design secured for Cambridge from the Wilton House Collection, and in Caradossi's bronze relief—the Risen Christ with Thomas among the Disciples. Above the arch is a somewhat recessed space in front of flanking pillars airily standing to right and left, in which the old architecture of the church, before it was stuccoed in the Baroque period, may have been continued. Then, above this, came the pillared hall, interrupted by the high window, as a setting for the Prophets, with the open coffering seen from beneath; their figures somewhat larger in their proportions than the Sibyls, to conform with the distance from the eye.

Taken as a whole, these Prophets and Sibyls should not be compared with the solitary seers and harbingers on the Sistine ceiling; these latter have their place in the gigantic area of the Old and New Dispensations, and gaze into remote distances of time that extending unconsolingly around, with sinister purport for their country and their contemporaries, for whom they seem to have no relevance and therefore to be almost hostile in their mood. Raphael's Sibyls really plant hope above the grave, and bring tidings of salvation to the world, and where one of them, with the loveliest of arms, is about to inscribe an announcement of death, the angel already counters her comfortingly with tidings of resurrection; she is obliged hesitatingly to stay the stroke of her pen, in order to hearken to him (Plate 203). The genius on the keystone carries, in the sketch two flaming basins, here a torch; this may be the torch of death, but in such charming, almost roguish hands and with such a peculiar,

[1] *Viz.* HABACVS. The words are actually an adaptation of *Hosea* VI. 2—*Translator.*

flickering glow, it may also signify that other flame which is not extinguished even above the grave (Plate 195).

Amore was Chigi's theme in life and in his festal celebrations.

§ Chigi's Garden Loggia on the Lungara

In his garden loggia the line of life extended from Venus and Amor to Mercury soaring into space; to a certain degree they govern the axis of his world and his life. In the midst of all this, we witness the fate of the helpless soul in pursuance of the decrees of the Olympians. Its suffering at the hands of Venus is perhaps expiated through Mercury.

Who knows what understanding may have prevailed here between the master of the house in his pleasures and the painter's flights of imagination. Legend has woven itself about their intimacy: Agostino Chigi is said to have had the Fornarina brought to his villa, with no intention of releasing her; only thus did he believe he could reckon with certainty on the attendance of the painter.

§ The Assistants: Raphael's Invention acknowledged by Rubens

The omnipotence of the "magnifico" among the bankers and the humanity of the "divino" were thus kept alive for contemporaries and posterity. Would such an anecdote have survived about Giulio Romano? And yet we hear his name, and those of Penni and Giovanni da Udine mentioned here by professional historians and guide-books more often than Raphael's. It was not always so; three hundred years nearer the time than we are, not yet three generations after Raphael, a judicious visitor from the North, a man possessed of ideas of his own, was of a different opinion: Rubens lived with Raphael's ceiling decoration; it appears that he copied it in its entirety and retained the essential character of these groups of deities right up to the end, through his great mythological periods. This seems more important as a mark of discernment than the participation of pupils, which could only spoil what was great and novel in the invention; and therefore the greater, posthumous pupil, by virtue of his own lofty character, outstripped the petty company and caught the essence of him by whom he found his own tumultuous creative spirit affirmed. Stylistic criticism perhaps has to make a beginning with the painted surface, but it can have no right to interfere with delight in great, new discovery. It did not enter into the thoughts of anyone but Raphael to make the mighty figures of the gods go about their affairs so unconcernedly upon clouds; he alone had the vision to conjure away the dark vaulting above by means of gleaming bodies in the light blue heavens. And this freedom of fancy coincided with the mood of assurance of the man of the world; it asserts for itself the right to turn away from a merely sensuous and irresponsible heathenism and bring on the scene powers and figures to whom, in their sublime abode to which duties are unknown, life below also seems no more than a game.

§ Raphael's own Ideas

These were the ideas of the builder-painter—the overburdened architect hindered the painter not in his inventiveness but in his execution. The studio was therefore obliged to get to work on carrying through the scheme according to his instructions. It can only be surmised what general lines he gave them to work upon; without question the audacity of the arbours composed of festoons and the bellying tapestries on the surface of the ceiling were constructions of *Raphael*, perhaps due to the fact that he was conscious that he had beside him, in Giovanni da Udine, one competent for still-life art of this order. To make the Olympian groups loll in such godlike manner within their pendentives—as Jupiter, for instance, in the scenes with Venus and Cupid, was only possible for one with a superior sense of humour; the employment of the curve of the pendentive on the narrow side for the Vergilian leap of Mercury could have occurred to none but *his* universal sensibility, or the scene where, in the midst of this jubilant pattern, Psyche with her air of a Victory is entrusted to the messenger of the gods to conduct her, as if to a dance, into the Olympian regions (Plates 205, 208, 210).

To whom but Raphael alone can be attributed such telling use of space to convey a narrative as in the scene where Psyche emerges meekly out of the depths with the ointment, at the feet of the haughty Venus; in a sketch in the Oxford collection, enchantingly rich in happy conceits, he has dashed off in quite a small space, with the pen and red chalk, this relationship of the two one to another—Psyche in three different positions that bespeak her charming timidity, Venus with the ill-natured humour of a pampered woman. With uplifted arms she makes an excessive display of amazement, leaving the outstretched hand of Psyche with the cruse of ointment to wait for a moment. This only extant sketch from Raphael's own hand was afterwards worked up into the famous red-chalk study of the group in the Louvre (Plate 215)—the nude figure of the goddess studied after the model, over a preliminary pen sketch with *pentimenti*, the beautiful massive forms nevertheless already made materially heavier by Giulio Romano; only the master who conceived them is capable of filling them with the vitality of his own beating pulse. Thus it is *his* hand which intervenes here with the chalk, giving an effect of bold resilience to the emerging figure with a few segment lines; it is he who brings out the humility of the arm laid on the breast, the expression of cajolery and entreaty in the upthrown head. He conceived and passed on the preparatory work, stepped in here and there with a helping hand, and was at last obliged to see his most enchanting ideas surrendered to uncouth minds, eyes and hands, always in the hope of being able once more to take a part in the work. For this studio, destitute of ideas, is only able to copy and fall short, in fact to spoil. Who but the master should have invented this COUNCIL OF GODS on the ceiling (Plate 206), in which once again he sets up the principles of tapestry composition for the feigned velarium, the relief-like train of figures with a free frieze above, in which the rhythm of the heads inscribes as it were a continuous band? Certainly Giulio and Penni had a part here in these Olympian deities; but the idea and rhythm of the whole, the irresistible course and flow of the narrative from left to right, the reception of Psyche through Hermes, as it were on the threshold, the animated group of gods looking on in their celestial ease, standing out one before another with the expressive outlines of their figures, the impulsive forward movement, in step and look, of Venus as complainant—whoever may have had the task of executing all this, he was painting Raphael's conception.

§ Wedding of Cupid and Psyche

In the WEDDING FEAST (Plate 207), what a gulf still separates the composition and the Mannerist assembling of individual *bravura* figures! The Stanze of Leo X, even the renowned FIRE IN THE BORGO, show the pupils left to themselves, fallen entirely victims to this danger. Here in the long frieze, the graceful lines of Hebe and the kneeling form of Ganymede seem to provide a setting, as for a jewel, for the group of the major gods. Connection with the lateral portions is provided by the highly ingenious expedient of the opening angles: on the left, the arm throwing blossoms of the last of the Hours and the club of Hercules, the connection on the spiritual plane with the dancing mother of the bridegroom by means of her not altogether enraptured spouse Vulcan, and the all but actual participation in the dance of the delightful Hebe; on the right, the lines repeat themselves in similar manner in the wings of the Hour and the dorsal line of the *putto*. Above the group of the bridal pair in their self-sufficiency the fragrant blessing of the Graces descends like a thalamus-throne or the canopy of a couch; of these figures of the Graces also there is a nude preparatory study, with livening touches of Raphael's own hand, at Windsor (Plate 214).

§ Motives from the Antique. Raphael's Humour

Raphael and no one else can be credited with the initiative when the Antique is called in here to justify divine nudity, so that it once more becomes vital. Only he is able to complete these torsos so that they seem to wake up again. Where the pupils get to work on them, they become classicists. When the pupil who does the preliminaries for the group of Mercury and Psyche with the cup sets an antique head of Hermes upon the torso of a youth from the Casa Galli (Plate 213*a*), we find traces of the inorganic character of the completion (Plate 212). The figure in the painting is a rare case of superiority to the study. The master composed a head of his own instead of the Antique head, and the head imprisoned in the marble is awakened to vitality by the living fire. In the WEDDING FEAST OF THE GODS the back view of Hebe is imitated from the "*Letto di Policrate*",

185

a Late Antique relief at that time much extolled, which Raphael recommended in a letter to the Duke of Ferrara. It was held to be the work of Polycleitus ("Polycrates!") This divine back, originally doubtless a Nereid, starting from Pompeii, goes on its progress through the world as Venus in Adonis subjects from Titian to Rubens; here for the first time it is completed, with gloriously naïve unaffectedness in the position of the feet, and coupled with the BELVEDERE TORSO (Plate 213b). Thus paired they represent Hercules and Hebe. But no classicism explains the profound and free humour in the figures of the pairs of major deities that come next: Pluto in gloomy self-absorption, in an expressive foreshortening such as would be possible only to the greatest of draughtsmen, who made space a medium for his themes; enthroned beside him, Proserpine, touchingly youthful, clinging to life and restrained in her gaiety. All animation, the group of Neptune, Amphitrite and Juno beside the Father of the Gods, girt with clouds, who in the midst of his remote meditations reaches after the cup of Ganymede; immediately next, infinitely aloof in the union of their souls, the bridal pair.

Vasari knew that Raphael himself had drawn all the cartoons and carried out much of them. To-day it may be difficult to forget all the injury these poetical conceptions have had to suffer, from the moment of their origin to their restoration by Maratta, then in the nineteenth century through criticism impervious to poetry, and most recently through the renovation of the background, which was restored as a *triste*, Hyperborean, commonplace grey-green instead of a gleaming blue.

§ Galatea

A few steps further on, the GALATEA (Plate 204) attracts us into the second garden saloon, with the peculiar charm of entirely personal execution; it makes a complete and enchanting certainty of what, on the ceiling with the gods, we were only able to conjecture through the veil of pupil's work. Here the sublime style assures us of the presence of superhuman beings. Their elemental life fills the space so astoundingly that the representation of landscape, sea and distance is almost superfluous. There is a bare suggestion of the shimmering green of the sea between their limbs, rather as a foil than as an accompaniment, like the grey-blue sea atmosphere behind and above them. Here pictorial ideas originating in the sketch for the BIRTH OF VENUS, on one of the sheets with designs for the *DISPUTA*, were brought to maturity. The figure in its vital warmth, set against the zones of water, horizon and air, has now acquired with the passage of years a more complex instrumentation. In the light and air of the sea, the yearning nymph stands on her shell, facing the wind, that blows out her golden hair and her cloak, red, shimmering with silvery grey, and makes of them a foil for her fresh loveliness. Around her in her ecstasy is gathered the winged troop; the lustiest and most wanton of them all has taken on himself to guide the shell chariot; he is borne by his wings on the liquid element. Three others disport themselves and twang their bows about the heads of the nymph and her wreath-crowned companions. They need only to aim their painless missiles, and triton, centaur, nymph and seahorse tumble lasciviously to the sound of conch and trumpet. But the arrows that inflict wounds that smart are kept in a sheaf for the lovelorn Galatea by the genius with the dark locks who, shrouded in sombre, sinister clouds, holds aside from the sport and threatens trouble in earnest.

Here also, above Chigi's festivities, it seems as if we are not allowed to escape a presentiment of the cloud that hardly two years later was to darken the sunshine in the lives of the most splendid participants in these festal hours.

The sepulchral chapel of Agostino was raised under Raphael's own direction; in its luminous dome he had appointed, for the heathen powers that hold sway over life, their place and their course according to the will of the Creator. Those who had felt themselves, here in the villa, to be like the Olympian gods, were soon to take their places in the great Dance of Death of the year 1520–1— the great Papal patron, who had always bestowed his peculiar grace on this house of pleasure, the like-minded Cardinal Bibbiena, the great merchant and hospitable master of the house, and he whose art had provided the imaginative accompaniment for his joyous festivities, the Divine Painter himself!

XII   RAPHAEL AS HUMANIST

Motto: "The torch of life is kindled and kept alight only in the combined employment of all the senses and organs."

HERDER.

NEITHER Raphael nor we ourselves can claim to appear as humanists because we can attribute to him some hundreds of borrowings from Antique works. Like the true masters of the Renaissance, he always acknowledged his indebtedness to Classical art when it seemed to provide him with a formula for his own sublime mood, or if he lighted upon a particularly vital motive from that quarter to encourage and confirm him on his way to find the highest and most widely valid expression.

This experience of a similar impulse, an awareness of kindred origins in those forerunners in Antiquity who were in those times looked upon in Italy as heroes, made him sensible that, for them in their day as for him now, "the torch of life is kindled and kept alight only in the combined play of all the senses and organs".

§ True humanistic Culture

A new type, among artists and laymen alike, not previously experienced, is present in this creative man who with every fibre and in every pore enters into, and fashions his life in conformity with, nature and tradition—and is blessed with the power of finding form and shape for this susceptibility; thus he lives to impart his own culture to countless others, and causes it to re-echo through his works in distant regions of time and space.

For recent generations the artist was a mere man who could paint; as for the humanist, the century that, in literary matters, "believed in the written word", agreed to picture him as a thinker wrapped up in his study-table mentality, with overdeveloped brow and undernourished physique. Raphael also, in his time, encountered a certain number of this type; he was able to find it in such illustrious visitors to Rome as Erasmus, and in the classicists of that circle, even then already devoid of vision. But his lofty ambitions were directed towards the powers that school men to an equilibrium of the inner with the outer, through the cult of the Ancients and through the secrets wafted across from the "regions of an ancestry sublime"; through his symbolical figures he gave to humanism the interpretation of harmony and, therewith, of human dignity.

Whenever he lingered in homage before the Antique, he did so because it was this very appeal in response to which his nature opened out, by reason of an inward state of unity with the ancient work; he alone was capable of taking it as a pattern, not for imitation but for creation, because only he had within him the same creative powers, to make vocal again the life that had in this respect been dumb for centuries, and to bring it once more into play.

The archæologist may be captivated by a list of the works Raphael saw, for such a list could not fail to teach what was then extant in the way of ancient art. But it is sufficient to note that hardly more than a generation after Raphael's death, Heemskerck took some trouble about this question: apart from the catalogue of pictures of Roman antiques presented to us by his sketch-books (Plates 213a, b), there is not much worthy of note even in Raphael, and if we had even the much-admired collection of Antique gems in which his friend Agostino Chigi seemed to have gathered together before Raphael's eyes the treasures of all the Roman emperors, there is *one* obligation we should not be absolved from: with regard to his cult of the Antique, it is not the *fact* but the *reason* for it that we have to en-quire into, because this yields the only consideration worthy of him and of our-selves. For discussion of Raphael's *manner* of adopting a motive, and of what it kindles in him, leads us away from archæology to the artist himself, to his poetical nature and thus to the ever-impelling forces of creative genius.

§ Cult of the Antique at Urbino: The Library in the Palazzo Ducale

To one who grew up in the circle of the *Cortegiani* of Urbino, who was per-mitted to awaken there to intellectual life, and already through his father be-longed to the familiar circle in the palace of the Montefeltri, the Antique was to be seen in a totality quite other than that presented by it to the Florentines in the famous garden of the Medici. At Urbino, through the works of Laurana, the tremendous baroque space-composition of Diocletian's buildings at Spalato and Aquileia, magnificently put into practice, had entered vitally into the studies of the Vitruvian Francesco di Giorgio, familiar and counsellor of the Duke himself.

Here "the spirits of the Titans of Antiquity" rise before the eyes, conjured up pictorially above the bookshelves of the library through the friend and guest of Giovanni Santi, Joos van Gent; since the time when Federigo of Montefeltro made studies of the tactics of Livy and Cæsar, for which FRANCESCO DI GIORGIO had devised the engines of war, a lively interchange of reverence for the ancients and actual practice had been traditional.

The thoughtful Sienese master had learned from experience that it is useless to begin by following the old works "senza ragione regulare"—without a principle based on rules, and he was entitled to say of himself that "he had himself seen most of the ancient remains of buildings and sculpture in Italy, and had compared them with the words of VITRUVIUS"; in all learned arguments about Vitruvian questions his Duke and he were regarded by contemporaries as the ultimate authority.

This was the inheritance into which the young Urbino master grew up; he remained faithful to it until his end, for it was in his house that the learned Fabio Calvi was required to translate Vitruvius "a sua instantia" into Italian, the *volgare*; he added to it marginal notes (Plate 283) and, what is more, he "argued against Vitruvius and confuted him"—a triumphantly free and respectful attitude towards the Ancients worthy of the true humanist who has to preserve the self-consciousness of his own time and personality.

§ Raphael's early Education: Borrowings from Antique Art

It is a thankless task to investigate what other elements of education were at his disposal to this end; it would be peculiarly thankless in the presence of one of such creative power. A "*semierudito*", as strangely enough a modern Italian of all people must needs call him, he certainly was not. Even scholars simply could not—and still cannot—follow the theoretical arguments of Vitruvius. Moreover it is almost a matter of indifference whether one whose father was a painter at this Court and author of a rhymed chronicle, as Giovanni Santi was, knew any Latin; it can hardly be doubted that he did. Latin was then learnt *before* Italian; in the States of the Church and in that part of the Marches called the "Vecchio Piceno", this was the practice in schools as a matter of course far on into the nineteenth century. As the idiom and language of the Liturgy, Latin certainly cannot have been unknown to him, even if we may not suppose the Latin grammar printed at Urbino in 1494 "ad uso de fanciulli" to have been in the hands of the young painter-boy. But the fact that the book was published in that city restores for us the background to the language of the figures and personalities who conveyed to him in a more intelligible manner the real Ancient world. The expressive ancient forms and the poetry of realms above the sphere of everyday things, with its nimbus of the heroic, opening up to one born in the Quattrocento worlds undreamt of, could not but be, to this child of imagination, a call to new aims.

We can figure to ourselves his excitement, in untrammelled veneration, in the presence of the multitude of ancient remains of architecture, sculpture, paintings, poetry and learning which he met at successive stages on the road of his life—Urbino, Florence, Rome. Himself full of ideas, in ceaseless striving occupied with thoughts about his own development, at one point he struck a chord as on the strings of an instrument, at another he seized a harmony that would fit in with his fancy as he created. And in one who remained so remote from becoming a classicist, there was room for a wide diversity of motives.

Sometimes it was a mere borrowing, a design adopted for the sake of its note of nobility, appropriate as it were for the life of a society whose existence was saturated with the use and enjoyment of ancient languages and passed amongst fragments and ruins, a society that drank wine amongst the greenery of its *vigna* at Roman capitals instead of a table, drawing water and listening to its plash as it dripped from sarcophaguses serving as fountains. Thus his *putti* bear the inscriptions, above the POETRY and in the *MADONNA DI FOLIGNO*, on a *tabula anziata*, he makes thrones out of herms, gives the feet of antique altars to the sides of the chairs of the Fathers of the Church, in the *DISPUTA*, fits the Diana of the Ephesians into the seat of the PHILOSOPHY.

§ Roman Impressions: Life instead of Archæology

Overwhelmed by the wealth of Roman impressions, surrounded by an exacting environment of learning, he may often have felt a temptation to give his personifications of ancient themes the halo of "genuineness". For the Apollo of the PARNASSUS, if we are to believe that Marcantonio's engraving has handed down to us an earlier stage of the composition, he introduced the Antique Orpheus with a lyre from an Early Christian sarcophagus; but to the annoyance of the learned world, he decided in favour of the more lively anachronism of the fiddle whose notes, with their wider range, could be wafted with effect among the groups surrounding the god—the dynamic of experience instead of archæological correctness. In the Muses beside Apollo there is a note of actuality combined with reminiscences of the Vatican ARIADNE, and of the maidens from the relief on the sarcophagus of Achilles in Scyros (Plate 80), with their figures beautifully supported against, or leaning away from, one another in airy freedom. He remains the *painter*, even when dealing with sculpture, when he appropriates the very unconstrainedness of such motives for the bright environment, profoundly and happily felt, of the god and the Muses. Lastly, by secret attentiveness to the true powers in Greek art, he discovered, to express the interpenetrating tones of a society thus dominated by harmony, that delightful acanthus-ornament to the soft musical constraint of which this poetry with poetry for its theme owes the effect that most peculiarly belongs to it.

§ Sense for the Aesthetic

In his mood of creativeness, where the Antique is in question, the "genuine" means precisely light and lightness, and to this interpretation he still remains true in the Farnesina. In the COUNCIL OF THE GODS (Plate 206) it was certainly not a case of the pupils having recourse, more or less out of a consciousness of their own insufficiency, to the rich heritage of Antiquity; by themselves they would here have invented only false and lifeless amplifications, as did Giulio Romano, who in his drawing at Chatsworth for the HERMES WITH PSYCHE set an ill-fitting head on the torso from the Giardino Galli (Plate 212). In the fresco, the master gave it organic completion—a rare case of a finished work that may be regarded as more full of life than the study!—in marvellous harmony with the godlike body and the situation: slightly bent, with a profound look of understanding encouragement towards the lovely, hesitating creature to whom he offers the

RAPHAEL

draught of immortality. In the same garden of antiques, not far from the torso so beautifully interpreted anew, crouched the sphinx on which here the aged figure of the Nile is based. Heemskerck copied both when they were still in immediate proximity to one another (Plate 213*a*); he also saw, still lying in the Belvedere, the much-admired torso (Plate 213*b*) from almost the same angle as Raphael now completed it for the Olympus, a torso which could be equalled, among gods of the Elements, only in the Parthenon pediment. Above, he adopted the relaxed line of this mighty back once again, for the resting Hercules, thereby anticipating the interpretation of recent archæology and the manner in which it is at present set up in the Vatican. In the WEDDING FEAST OF THE GODS (Plate 207) he again introduces the torso, revived as Hercules, wedded to the graceful line which he adopted for Hebe from the famous "*letto di Policrate*", the much-copied relief that Raphael was to acquire for the Duke of Ferrara; Titian also was indebted to it in his VENUS WITH ADONIS. Torsos seem to have been for Raphael sources of energy, accumulators, so to speak, from which he released the indwelling power for giving life to new bodies. The Apollo as leader of the Muses is a new derivative from the back, with its deep, tense furrow, of the torso in the court of the Casa Galli; an Aphrodite of the Medici type awakes to new life, in a drawing at Windsor, as one of the Graces, naïvely conscious of her nakedness, for the glorious trio of loveliness that forms the right-hand termination of this WEDDING FEAST.

In the group of Poseidon and Amphitrite embracing one another, which it would be impossible to blend more delightfully with the characteristics of the two other pairs of major deities, there is an echo of the motive of that bowl of red *terra sigillata* which Vasari saw in the house of his grandfather, the aged Lazzaro, at Arezzo, and which came as a gift into the possession of the Medici.

We feel that it was, first, vitality and then "genuiness" that prompted the seizing of these motives. Fancy was also served and intimate chords were struck when, in the tapestry of the HEALING OF THE LAME MAN (Plate 256), the situation was dominated by the Late-Antique twisted columns. Everyone knew them in the venerable *Tribuna* of the Basilica of St. Peter; according to the teaching of the old guidebooks for pilgrims, no-one could doubt that they came from Solomon's building. Thus at the first glance they directed the imagination towards the scene intended by the artist, the Temple at Jerusalem; it was an aid towards a similar transportation into the ancient world when the Holy Family was made to rest under the oak in a distant land and a distant age, at the foot of a hill with ruins including the circular structure of the Temple of Minerva Medica, and beside the broken foot of a candelabrum, the Grimani "*triangolo*" in the Doge's Palace, at that time in the Palazzo Vescovile at Tivoli (Plate 219*a*). This was certainly an object admired by the illustrious excursionists Bembo, Castiglione and Raphael in April 1516.

RAPHAEL AS HUMANIST

§ Sense for Antique Harmony: Cosmic Feeling

The harmony of form sounded by Raphael like a familiar melody certainly often outweighed every other interest. In the theme of the Graces—he may have seen the group at Siena, or perhaps only in some medal or gem—he filled with new content, so to speak, the given capacity of a beautiful vessel; and this rejuvenated vitality spread itself over their forms, above the lines and tones of the landscape, to produce the most radiant of harmonies with the figures. In none of his later works did this born humanist among painters achieve a more profound feeling of pantheism and therefore of Antiquity. And in the same cosmic spirit a feeling for environment is expressed by the attitude of sunny, delighted expectancy of the *putto* in the Gallery of San Luca,[1] repeating the motive of the APOLLO SAUROCTONUS, which has been called the most beautiful rendering of landscape in Antiquity. A similar absorption in the bliss of creation breathes in the figure of Jacob dreaming of the ladder to Heaven; in his cult of the most expressive lines Raphael was here consciously indebted to the ancestor of the figure, the sleeping Jonah from an Early Christian sarcophagus, because the relaxation of soul expressed in the limbs precisely fitted his feeling for, and his enjoyment of, the tranquil environment, and the release of the spirit from reality. Something of this sense of the universal also animates the river-god in Marcantonio's JUDGMENT OF PARIS.

And this seems to disclose one of the most profound reasons for the strong attraction the world of the Ancients had for Raphael, an attraction entirely personal to him; he shares it with many a contemporary and predecessor in the Renaissance, but he leaves them all far beneath him in the number and degree of his obligations, in their force and the spirit in which he incurred them. The Quattrocento was already susceptible to this freedom of the Antique, a freedom that broke violently away from its matter-of-fact study of the model, as being, so to speak, of a more distinguished order. The elemental character in the "*pathos*" of a hurrying figure, with draperies fluttering about a winged stride, if it gave the supple limbs expression and a foil as well, put life into Botticelli's nymphs and Ghirlandajo's young maidens; by way of Ghirlandajo, who here played only the role of an intermediary, it descended to Raphael. His wild Magdalen in the ENTOMBMENT, so important for the dramatic expression of the composition, is alive with such an echo of the Antique, seizing the figures and lifting them above the level of the commonplace.

§ The Heroic

His inner being was long acquainted with the attraction of the heroic; in drawings of his years of apprenticeship and travel, and frequently in the independently painted predellas, the heroic ventures to assert itself—encouraged by

---

[1] A related drawing at Haarlem is reproduced on Plate 99.—*Translator.*

the Antique he emancipates himself. Only thus do historical and mythological themes come to life—only thus are they released from the commonplace; then only does the divine become credible, and the touch of the Godhead, only then can the teachings of the beyond be perceived.

The St Catherine (Plate 33) in London stands leaning on her wheel and receives in a beam from heaven the call from above that makes of her, the innocent earthly prince's daughter, a mighty heroine; it is the attitude of the Muse in the Chatsworth drawing (*R. Z.* IV, 206), even more conspicuous among the divine sisters, Euterpe the melodious, and resting too, released from heaviness, near to the heavenly ones.

The bearing of Ancient figures is suddenly animated with a deeper breath—however well-known they may be, they seem through him to receive new life, and bring with them only so much of their divine origin as, by ennobling narrative to make it history. In the Judgment of Solomon (Plate 60), how the dramatic situation girds itself to the highest degree of perilous tension through the brisk stride of the executioner as he comes on the scene. The introduction of one of the Dioscuri of the Monte Cavallo, by the pathos of his godlike figure, raises this scene, which in the sketches was still little more than a child murder, to the level of fiery passion, sublime and significant.

§ Intensification of Pathos through the Antique

Whatever the channel through which he may have become acquainted—and in his early period—with this oblique line of movement, for his St George (Plate 20), the pathetic quality in the horse's head thus thrown high simply leapt to his mind as fitting a situation of extreme danger, of which man and beast alike are conscious. Again, in his period of maturity, it was the bolting horse of the Roman rider in one of the Trajan reliefs on the Arch of Constantine that, by its *furia* absolutely took by storm his imagination when, in the Attila fresco, he had to depict chaos let loose stemmed by the power of the Princes of the Apostles (Plates 105, 216, 217). Thus this Antique motive of panic broke violently in beneath the enclosing arch, following the diagonal of the picture, truly spreading rebellion among the ranks; his fantastic rider in scale armour, peculiarly menacing to European eyes, was taken from the Dacian reliefs of the Trajan Column, rather to create an atmosphere than as an archæological borrowing.

§ Raphael's Susceptibility to Ancient Religious Sentiment

For it was through such a process of purification that, in Raphael, every extraneous motive gained admission to the sphere of his poetical invention. If the representation of animals was rejected by him, as a Central Italian, in favour of that of man, this deficiency was made good not by mere borrowing from the Ancients—his plagiarisms are rejuvenated by the creative manner in which he adapts them to his own inventiveness, or recover something of the divine elemental power with which they were first conceived by ancient religious sentiment. The overflowing humour of the Antique BOY WITH A GOOSE is converted into the group of Cupid striving to bridle the eagle of Zeus (Plates 179b, 218a). But this companion of the son of Chronos from the APOTHEOSIS OF TITUS, or from the angle of an altar tomb, is powerless with his mighty wings and talons to do anything against the brutal little god but suffer himself, with amorous look, to be harnessed for his triumph; with the same expression, in the TRIUMPH OF GALATEA, the horse of the Dioscuri is compelled to join with his neighing in the jubilation of his love-smitten entourage. In Raphael these motives invented by Antiquity plunge every time, as it were, back into the element of their mythical origin; as a last supreme example, when the bull of Mithras, or one of the sacrificial oxen beneath the knees of Niké at the Palazzo della Valle or the Casa Sassi, raises his head lowing to the Lord as symbol of St Luke in the VISION OF EZEKIEL, and to the accompaniment of this sound, himself presents his throat to him as if to be sacrificed, this creation of Antiquity is here once more brought to new life (Plates 219b, 223); what we see of it has a share, through the homage thus paid, in the elemental power of what is happening; and what was once conceived in a spirit of worship returns to worship again, and helps to lift it above the level of the earthly. For it is out of the fullness of his own soul and his sense of worship that Raphael borrows from Ancient art. To him alone was perceptible a sound from the beyond in the Antique mode of expression, because he himself was on the point of making the same discovery.

Pathos now overleaps the bounds of nature and ordinary life: Laocoön's face of anguish as he cries aloud to the gods provides the expression, in the PARNASSUS, for the ecstasy of the blind singer Homer, as he receives inspiration from above and "sopra gli altri come aquila vola"—soars above the others like an eagle. This flight above the earth out of the sphere of the ordinary raises the young maiden in the MASS OF BOLSENA above the women of the populace with their children; she alone is admitted to the miracle, and must needs follow the compelling force of the higher power. It is the magic of the Medea in her upward flight, on the sarcophagus in the Mausoleum of Augustus, which Giotto at an earlier time had found appropriate in his SPES, striving after light and warmth, in the Arena Chapel.

Melody and the call of the divine determine the main lines of the composition of the SIBYLS; only figures filled with the Godhead could thus recline, set free from the trammels of earth, on the airy arch, like the Victories in the spandrels of the triumphal arches of Septimius Severus and Constantine, or even more, in the manner in which, on the Casali Sarcophagus at Ny Carlsberg (which at that time may well have stood "in giardino", in one of the "gardens of antiques"), Bacchus and Ariadne feel themselves drawn towards one another across the intervening space. And those who may have been prone to regard Raphael as being in this instance more or less trammelled by his classical knowledge may recognise, in the angel pointing heavenwards of the PERSICA, that the painter derived his powers from the same element as Antique art. The RESTING HERMES from Herculaneum in the Naples Museum certainly cannot have been known to him, and yet *his* divine messenger, in this painting, is alive in conformity with the same laws; he belongs to the air, even if for a few moments he sits down on an earthly seat; and the mercurial fluid that imbues him gives this angel his posture as he sits, as it does to the god resting lightly, and as if only till he hears the summons to return.

§ Antique *Amoretti*—The Holy Child

Raphael seems to have lived as if in an electrically charged atmosphere; from every side he must have felt its tensions. Where others saw mere themes he felt the call of the divine. The Renaissance turned the troups of Antique *amoretti* into a design of "*putti*," essentially without any other significance than to be pleasing; on tombs however, they doubtless had an allusion to the promised Heaven. But Raphael, in the Palazzo della Valle, comes across the oval sarcophagus on which *genii* in wayward exuberance play the part of deities of the Seasons (Plate 218*b*). One of these sprawling children's bodies he exalts to be the Divine Boy of the ALBA MADONNA; and now the child seems to be ranging with free dominion over the lap of her that has been ordained to be his mother. The unconstrained movement occurs yet again in the ALDOBRANDINI MADONNA, and in the Child in the act of benediction in a study-drawing in Vienna. This more than earthly superabundance of life of the Divine Child (*R. Ƶ.* VIII, pl. 358) inspired Rubens three generations later, for his figure of the BOY CHRIST IN BENEDICTION in the Goudstikker Collection (Plate 137).

§ Raphael an Admirer of Antique Painting

Where the language of the heroic was uttered by ancient art it found in Raphael an echo. Certainly he was not guilty of the great *misunderstanding of the Antique* as an *art of colourless marble* bequeathed as a disastrous inheritance by the High Renaissance to the following century. From his youth up he was attracted by the marvels of Antique painting; the art of Melozzo da Forli was based to a large extent on an understanding of the shimmering breaking-up of the colours in the old mosaics, whose strong forms and rhythms had already provided Piero della Francesca with his schooling. Archaism had been consciously aimed at in the studio of Perugino; the scheme in the great two-dimensional compositions of the ASSUMPTION OF THE VIRGIN (Plate 6), painted for Vallombrosa and the Cambio frescoes, in which Raphael may well have co-operated, was chosen with the intention of recovering an effect of orthodoxy and of avoiding spatial dispersion, thus attaining assimilation to the rules of Early Christian and Byzantine art. It has been thought that Perugino's stained-glass style can be seen foreshadowed in the *Rabula Codex*, which nevertheless can be only an echo of greater lost originals; and here also we have a case of recourse to media for giving an other-worldly effect. A sense for this must have remained awake in Raphael when the new age supposed itself to have left Perugino behind. Only this pupil of Perugino had anything vital to learn from the mosaics of Santa Maria Maggiore, a message more living even than that of sculpture. In the CHARGE TO THE APOSTLES, of Santa Maria Maggiore (Plate 220), he met with the sublime bearing with which the figures stride forth in their white togas, their carriage as they move, swathed in drapery, with the grand sweep of the folds from knee to hip which gives such a sense of high purport in the wearer; this bearing was bestowed by Raphael on one of his favourite figures, the figure in a high light, of a youth showing the way, in the *DISPUTA*.

And he alone perceives the peculiar passionate appeal of ancient painting as expressed by these mosaics—their dramatic force when seen as a whole, in detail the mime effect of the rolling eye—when he has to compose the group of the HELIODORUS(Plate 103). The chief motive of the BATTLE OF JOSHUA (Plate 221)— the heavenly power sweeping its adversaries before it like rubbish into a corner —was adopted and transformed by him in the freest manner; and when this theme became bound up in his imagination with the scenes of terror of the watch over the tomb of Christ, the original of a warrior collapsing with his shield, at Oxford (Plate 95, *R. Z.* VII, 393), is to be found in this mosaic immediately beneath the charger of the victor. But he seized the peculiar quality of this ancient painting, its power of permeating the scene with terror, and turned it to account to provide the rhythm of the entire composition of the HELIODORUS fresco.

Raphael's enlistment of the Antique river-god motive for the collapsing figure of the predatory treasurer, or for Ananias smitten by the judgment of God (Plate 251), was due not to any Manneristic sense of pleasure in the beautiful pose; it was rather that, for him, there was inherent in this relaxation of limbs a dying-away of movement which could not fail to be welcome to the true dramatist as an opportunity for a tense *ritardando*. A great actor and master of the stage could not have proceeded otherwise; one thrown violently to the ground is struck out of the field of vision; as he falls, the last tension is prolonged in the stratum above the soil that still belongs to life, and the divine power that has here taken effect seems to hold up the figure as an example to the world by showing him in the act of falling, not by depicting his end—even in his nothingness he is still exalted as an instrument of the higher power.

§ The Breath of the Beyond

Only *Raphael* took in such a breath from the beyond—"numine afflatur"— in his intercourse with the Antique. His Almighty sweeping down before the eyes of Ezekiel (Plate 223) appeared to contemporaries "a uso di Giove"—but no Antique Jupiter is upheld by such a power of movement; he felt the possibilities in the fragments of Zeus-sculptures, statues and heads, just as he was aware of the concentration of divine power in the BELVEDERE TORSO (Plate 213*b*). He completed the torso as Poseidon in his "QUOS EGO" (Plate 222), and in doing so awakens the powers of the superhuman so that they permeate the head and limbs with their might, and even the horses of the chariot and the elements; this became the mythological counterpart of the dynamic force of that vision of the Lord of the Universe before Ezekiel.

Only one endowed with creative power can achieve the representation of the Creator; around his God the Father, in the first days of the world, "the jubilant choir of the Sons of Light" circle through the airy rhombic coffering (Plate 224); this loveliest passage of the Loggie decoration, full of a sublime poetry communicated by the artist himself even to the assistants, was adapted from a mosaic of Victories swarming in the framework of the coffering, of which a remnant, or perhaps rather a related design, is now preserved in the Museo delle Terme (Plate 225). Flight through the heavy, earthly framework becomes for him visions into the pure realm of the Beyond, of the first days of Creation, and combines with Dante's angel hierarchies to make up the significant decoration of the Papal promenade.

The wonderful movement of the genius gliding by, in the APOTHEOSIS OF THE EMPRESS SABINA, the relief in the Palazzo dei Conservatori which he surely saw still in place on the arch in the Via Lata, the "Arco di Portogallo", provided Raphael, familiar as he was with the region of angels, with the turning movement of one of the heavenly messengers floating down from the left in the DISPUTA; the light, elastic tread of a Niké, more revealed than concealed by her close-fitting raiment, is revived by him when he has to depict, in the Louvre painting, St Margaret in her purity breaking forth out of darkness and temptation as if out of clouds; and the heavy hand of Giulio Romano, in carrying out the design, did not avail to disguise such a truly supramundane revelation.

§ Impressions produced by the Belvedere Apollo

Everyone in those days had stood in the presence of the BELVEDERE APOLLO (Plate 71); for centuries it has been copied—only Raphael proved himself inwardly capable of understanding its sublime idea, *Epiphany*, rare in Antiquity also, the appearance of a god upon earth when he wills to reveal himself in his pride, beauty and power. The occasion of his coming upon the god coincided precisely with the psychological moment in which the artist was pondering over the heavenly sphere of the *DISPUTA*; the first rays of the illumination kindled in him by the statue break forth in studies for the angels, in the pathos of the St Stephen turning round at the rustling of angels' wings (Plate 68, *R. Z.* VI, 295). This inspiration did not die away, and when he has to paint the apparition of the Mother of God out of the luminous depths of heaven, the stride of the Apollo as he steps into the world is revived in the pacing of her feet, accustomed to tread the clouds. Antique epiphany and Christian vision coalesce with happy effect. One of the sublimest conceptions of Antiquity became the most personal possession of the painter of the Beyond, and in the course of the centuries was unconsciously perpetuated among thousands as he revived it.

We can hardly expect it would be otherwise with the architect Raphael. According to the narrow, current notion of renaissance, he seems more firmly tied down to the individual motive of his originals; yet how much it rests with the artist himself whether he feels himself to be the spokesman of his time and seeks unswervingly the expression of its way of thinking, or whether he apprehends on broad lines this way of thinking and is constrained to fix in lasting form the ideas, aspirations and unconscious urge of his contemporaries. No detail will turn him aside from his course in pursuit of the great and the essential, however welcome each lovely fragment may be to him, because he knows how to make it serve him as a means to a whole.

§ The Architect and the Antique: Revival at Urbino: Pacioli at Perugia

Already at an early stage Raphael has shown himself to us as heir to the architecture of Antiquity. He was sent out equipped for such a mission by his home country, where Laurana had had an influence, with the doctrines of his prototypes of the age of Diocletian, and Francesco di Giorgio had reduced to rules the "wherefore" of the operation of the great examples he had collected, and had interpreted Vitruvius. This school traces the source of its revival at Urbino right back to the Baroque of the ancient Empire; Brunelleschi and his Florentines derive from Gothic, and their art, in the light of the book of Vitruvius, retains a suggestion of scaffolding, something meagre—rather members assembled to form a complete building than enclosed space. But one brought up as Raphael was, comprehended whatever monuments lay in his path more clear-sightedly, listened with more eager attention to every initiate that crossed his path among the architects of the time who were sworn devotees of the Classical and its proportions. Precisely Perugia was visited, during the year 1500, that is to say in Raphael's most susceptible period, by LUCA PACIOLI; his treatise on the Proportions, and his inheritance from Piero della Francesca, the teacher of Perugino and fellow-countryman of Raphael, must have made a great impression on the young beginner. In Perugino's workshop he came in contact with esteem for the youthful, truly revitalised architecture of Brunelleschi; but that which, in the Umbrian master, was perverted in bald imitation into papery stage scenery, became in the young Raphael the sublime setting of the *MADONNA DEL BALDACCHINO*. In this light-flooded niche, in its rhythmical columns and pilasters, the high-mooded figures of the saints find a halting-place and a foil. In this apse, carrying on the influence of Brunelleschi's building of Santo Spirito, Raphael sounded a new note by which he gave consecration to the radial plan in building; wherever an opportunity offered, Raphael pursued this conception with ardour. In the temple of the *Sposalizio* it was already solemnly adapted, as an exterior, to the sacred scene and landscape. In this guise old Giovanni Santi had seen the Temple of Fame in his poetical vision of the rhymed chronicle.

§ Enduring Sympathy with Vitruvius and the Theorists

Certainly Raphael continued in lasting sympathy with the *teachings of Vitruvius*. For whom but such as he could all those commentaries otherwise have appeared —for example, those of Giovan Battista Caporali, son of the painter Bartolommeo Caporali, of Battista da Sangallo, brother of Antonio, of Genga of Urbino, in whose studies of Vitruvius his fellow-subject Giovan Battista da San Marino has a share, of Cesare Cesariano, who at the turn of the centuries worked for Bramante, Raphael's most immediate teacher in architecture, of Falconetto, who took advantage of two long sojourns in Rome to make a thoroughgoing study of the teachings of Vitruvius, and lastly, of the great and deep-thinking Fra Giocondo, who with his venerable experience was appointed by the Pope as adviser of Raphael in the building of St Peter's, and whose editions of Vitruvius appeared about the middle of Raphael's lifetime; they were dedicated to two of his patrons, Julius II and Giuliano de' Medici. Whilst he went open-eyed on his way by remains of Roman monuments, he was so to speak surrounded by Vitruvius, who "gave him much light, but not enough"—as he writes to Castiglione.

§ The Idea of the Cupola

It would be wearisome to relate all that he acquired, on the plane of mere craftsmanship, in the way of motives from the monuments How much of the originals that were still extant before his eyes has since disappeared! But we can conjecture infinitely more when, as recently, in the newly uncovered Forum of Nerva, in the alternation of *aediculae* with angular and segmental pediments as window-frames, a motive comes to light again, designed to add vitality to the façade-surface, that was turned to account by Raphael in palaces for Bishop Giannozzo Pandolfini, or in the rare beauty, only recently destroyed, of the Palazzo Bresciano. It would be of more essential importance, as pointing to the most personal direction of his life, to investigate the cupola-idea as revealed to him again and again anew in moments of inspiration as expressing the highest degree of concentrated self-communion. We see it appearing shyly, yet already mastered, in the temple of the *Sposalizio*, half fulfilled in the niche of the *Madonna del Baldacchino*, realised on a small scale in the sepulchral chapel of Agostino, with its sweeping circles and its upward spring all converted into light by the miracle of the mosaic painting; in Sant' Eligio it softly hovers, and in the plans for the central upthrust of the building of St Peter's it seeks almost passionately to attain the luminous heights. His knowledge as a painter of "lightness and light" in its highest degree of intensity, prompted him then, in the secular sphere, once again to make cupolas opening out in pantheistic manner into landscape, above the pierced and ornament-fretted pillars of the soaring halls of the Villa Madama. Finally, his last wish, for a tomb under the vault of Pantheon (Plate 302), revealed the same acknowledgment of the Beyond that guided him in the presence of Antique sculptures and never abandoned him. The conception of a last resting-place beneath the unequalled solemnity of this dome dedicated to the sublime heavenly beings, has provided subsequent ages with the architectural idea, and often the name, for their cult of heroes. Raphael was followed in the Pantheon by less immortal beings, but the conception of a consecrated asylum provided in death for the genius of a nation and for its great sons, a conception that has been adopted since that time by all nations, goes back in the last resort to his interpretation of the Beyond in architecture. His desires overleaped the limits and earthly laws of the building; he saw only transfiguration. "Vom Dust Zu den Gefilden hoher Ahnen."[1]

§ Raphael's Draughtsmen of the Antique. The Reconstruction of Rome

The two souls of Faust dwelt in the breast of him of "all-embracing vision"; no stranger in the heights and the depths, he strove after his sublime ancestors; it was part of his nature to look back towards his origin whilst striving to attain his aims. Only so can be explained his propensity, creator and originator though he was, for an ever closer acquaintance with, and devotion to, the art of the Ancients. It sounds quite credible when Vasari, with a sense of awe in the presence of the greatness that set in motion forces with such an aim, records "Era tanta la grandezza di questo uomo"—so exalted was this man's disposition—that he kept draughtsmen employed throughout Italy, at Pozzuoli and even in Greece; their duty was to copy and report to him whatever there was of value in the way of Ancient art. He offers the spectacle of an enduring power of attraction and readiness to accept what presents itself, whilst nevertheless reserving all the time to himself, in his high conception of his own dignity and mission, the choice of what he willed to make his own. More important however would seem to be what the productive genius gives in return, his masterpiece (in Leonardo's sense)—the searching out of the archetype, with a view to creative activity in emulation of it. And so, to the astonishment of his contemporaries, he is impelled to undertake that *reconstruction of Ancient Rome* of which no vestige has come down to us unless it be the report, tinged almost with horror, as though it recorded a raising of the spirits of the mighty dead.

§ Conservator of Antiquities

After Fra Giocondo's death on 27th August, 1515, Raphael was appointed

[1] "Out of the mist To regions of an ancestry sublime."

by Leo X Conservator of Roman Antiquities, and his commission expressly laid upon him the particular duty "of opposing the destruction of ancient fragments of marble bearing inscriptions". Fra Giocondo had made complaints about this; more than 7,000 columns and fragments were reported to have been utterly destroyed or employed in recent buildings of Rome. Bramante, to begin with took as much as he needed; it was at the cost of such noble material that the Palazzo Giraud came into being. In the instructions to Raphael there was nothing about the preservation of works of art in the sphere of sculpture or architecture, and one might be tempted to lay the blame for this preference given to inscriptions upon eyeless *literati* of the Papal Chancellery; but Raphael himself seems occasionally to have stressed, and made use of, his right of turning to account remains of Antique works in his buildings. Sentimentalism over ruins seems always to have been remote from creative and, especially, constructive men, in Renaissance times indeed completely so. In spite of all proverbial admiration for them, ruins were at that time regarded practically as stone-quarries. An architect of the next generation, Pirro Ligorio, found the best lime could be extracted, by pounding them to dust, from the ancient marble statues that were every day being brought to light. Cardinal Ridolfi obtained from the Thermæ of Caracalla the material for his *palazzo* in the Borgo; Cardinal Farnese satisfied his requirements in building materials for his palace from the Trajan Column, the Arch of Titus, and the Temple of Faustina; fragments of sculptures went to the lime-kiln. They may have believed that new works of equal rank thus came into existence. What mattered one or several bays of the Basilica of Constantine, if their admired coffering was revived in the vaults of the new basilica of St Peter's? Raphael himself came into conflict with the "*Conservatori*" on the Capitol when he wished to have brought away a few antiques secured as a bequest from the Patrician Gabriele de' Rossi. He based his demand on the Papal commission; but the magistrate appealed in the name of the Will of the testator and of the "rights of the People" to the Holy See itself, and the master was obliged to abandon his claim—but not to the spiritual possession of the objects. In the collection of this Gabriele de' Rossi there were a *Diana of Ephesus* and a *Sacrifice of a Bull*[1]. Even though he did not possess them, Raphael immortalised them in his works.

§ Plans for the Mausoleum of Augustus: The Memorial to Leo X: Castiglione's Participation

In these questions he may already at an early stage have been thought capable of judging. Bramante called him in as umpire in a competition; three sculptors had to make copies of the Laocoön group, and Raphael gave the prize and the execution in bronze, for Cardinal Grimani, to the young Jacopo Sansovino. The confidence of the Pope had now appointed him to be judge over

[1] Later on the garden front of the Villa Medici in Rome, now in the Uffizi.

the fate of all Roman antiquities; by office and affection alike he was wedded to a great object, the old and the new Rome. When an Orsini wished to pull down the Mausoleum of Augustus, and a beginning had already been made with the removal of the remnants of the marble facing, Raphael proposed to the Pope that the two obelisks should be transferred to the Piazza San Pietro; but the project broke down on account of the cost, 90,000 ducats. The obelisks now stand respectively in front of the Quirinal and near Santa Maria Maggiore and in this location also Raphael's idea is perpetuated (Sanuto, *Diarii*, col. 470–1).

A memorial to Leo X has come down to us concerning the antiquities of Rome and their preservation. It has always been argued that it might be attributed to Raphael; and if cogent reasons have been brought forward in favour of Bramante, even so this does not take us far from Raphael's own ideas as to these matters. Castiglione has also been considered as author, and it would perhaps be no unsatisfactory solution of the question if it could be assumed that this highly-cultured aristocrat and master of verbal expression had lent his voice and pen to the ardour of his younger friend. By parentage moreover, Raphael was himself no stranger to letters; his sonnets prove it. Vasari mentions notes by him, together with those of Ghiberti, as sources used by him in his *Vite*. Doubts have been raised as to whether such notes by the Urbino master existed. In support of them it is enough to say that he was credited with them by contemporaries, and in the next generations that were under his influence. And a glance at the manner of that co-operation in the plastic arts for which, as a living reality, peculiar credit is actually due to Raphael, should make us more careful also in seeking to find in literary quarters the sole author of a memorial expressing the opinion of so many like-minded friends who were to a certain extent secret conspirators. Let it suffice us that there is much that speaks for the immediate circle of Raphael. In Bramante's favour the fact would be conclusive that the author, by his own admission, had for twelve years been compelled to look on at the lamentable destruction of irreplaceable monuments. The writer has also at his disposal great technical experiences, and the proposal, at that time quite novel, to raise monuments with the help of a compass, sprang from his inventive brain. But Raphael also was technically experienced, as is proved by his correspondence with the Duke of Ferrara about the correct construction of chimneys; he had not been entirely useless in this respect in his dealings with Leonardo. Moreover every great architectural conception such as those he cherished for St Peter's, was implicitly taken as involving an acquaintance also with the means of carrying it out. In no art were imagination and technique at that time divorced; rather they depended inseparably upon one another. Alongside these ideas of an ingenious brain there speaks also in the *Memoriale* the pain of a lover and patriot: "vedendo quasi il cadavero di quella nobil patria, che è stata regina quasi del mondo così miserabilmente lacerato"—"when I see as it were the corpse of this our noble country, once Queen of the World, now so wretchedly mutilated" ... And we recall the verses of Castiglione on the death of Raphael:

"Tu quoque dum toto laniatam corpore Romam
Componis miro, Raphael, ingenio
Atque urbis lacerum ferro, igni, annisque cadaver,
Ad vitam, antiquum iam revocasque decus . . . ."

"Thou thyself hadst to die, just when thy lofty spirit was on the point of re-awakening to life again, in her ancient beauty, Roma, mutilated in every limb and ravaged by war and fire and the lapse of centuries" ... Let it remain an open question whether Castiglione was here referring,

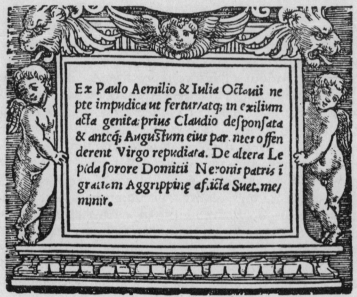

Fig. 1

years afterwards, to himself or Raphael, or whether these phrases are not one of the formulas of secret understanding that, like motives in music, are generally the common property of contemporaries with a bent for production. They only show us that the intellectually gifted Count, the creative artist, the skilled author of the Memorial with his ready pen, who could not have spoken thus without official authority, were essentially at one. The artist however was not satisfied with complaining and writing; he *acted*, and acted *constructively*, and thus made himself the spokesman of his time, and one of the chosen company whose ideals, desires and longing for the lost paradise of the Antique, the sublime object of an ancestor-worship, he felt an urgent need of fulfilling; what was in reality no longer possible, the restoration to life and to its former beauty of the "noble mutilated and violated corpse", was the task undertaken by the poet-painter on paper; before the astonished and, as it were, dazzled eyes of his contemporaries appeared the miracle of Ancient Rome, "not as it is, but as it was".

§ Reconstruction of Rome as it was: Dispute as to Raphael's Work

What this reconstruction was has been the subject of so much research and writing that it only remained for classical and archæological science at the end of the nineteenth century to doubt whether it ever existed. In this connection, speaking *unscientifically*, it should be pleaded, that with great figures of history the attribution to them, quite early, soon after their death, of deeds and words of especial importance, is often inseparable from their fame, interwoven like a ray in the nimbus of their glory. "Tanto era la grandezza de questo uomo",

Fig. 2

says Vasari, and relates an unconfirmed rumour. And *scientifically* we are fully confirmed, by voices of the period itself, in our belief that contemporaries knew and testified of Raphael that he was at work in his last years on a pictorial reconstruction of the aspect of Ancient Rome. In the laments over his death there is everywhere a note of grief that Roma the sublime has lost her restorer. Besides all other achievements, amongst which his buildings in the Vatican and in its surroundings were of course what aroused the greatest excitement in the world at large, these plans of his were also admired as a bold, indeed a dæmonic undertaking. His friends of high standing knew about them; the man was living who had worked with him on the raising of the monuments of Ancient Rome; Raphael had been for some time in touch with the scholar ANDREA FULVIO, who a few years before had published the *Antiquaria* of Rome (1513) and the *Illustrium Imagines*, conceived as a collection of historical portraits, with somewhat fanciful illustrations (Figs. 1, 2). The painter is supposed to have borrowed much from this book of portraits for his PARNASSUS—but no head among the Muses or poets has anything in common with the work, which appeared somewhat later (1517). But certainly in the last years of his life the artist worked in collaboration with the antiquary. How are we to suppose the work was divided between them? As a producing architect Raphael was certainly able to give the learned writer a conjectural interpretation of many a fragment of ancient building; the antiquary with his literary knowledge would doubtless follow out the trails from the sources for their work in common. Looking out over the city from the Seven Hills, he could pride himself on having rediscovered the partition of Ancient Rome under Augustus into fourteen regions. In the preface of his *Antiquitates Urbis* (1527) he expressed the opinion that he could rescue the ruins from decay and make them good in accordance with the written sources; without the light thrown on them from the writings of the Ancients they would still lie in the darkness of oblivion. "Priscaque loca per regiones explorans observavi, quas Raphael Urbinas (quem honoris causa nomino) paucis ante diebus quam e vita decederet (me indicante) penicillo finxerat." "I have visited the ancient sites of the Regions and explored them thoroughly, and Raphael of Urbino (whose name I mention for the honour's sake"—we do not know on whom the antiquary here intended honour to be bestowed, whether himself or him who hardly had need of it—) "made a pencil (or brush?) drawing of them after the indications I gave him, only a few days before he departed from life." A stimulating communication! What a picture: the topographer going on in front into the fields of ruins—like a well-informed steward, perhaps in eager delight at finding confirmation in the monuments of what his sources have disclosed to him, he shows Raphael the ruins and is actually able to mention them by name; and the artist, thrilled by the proximity of the Ancients, comes, sees and conquers, whilst he re-establishes the connection of the fragments one with another, creating anew in his constructive imagination out of a foundation wall the core of a building, a hall from the stump of a column, a vault out of its stone springing; indeed, he converts the information and intuitions of his companion into a dream of reality. And whilst their eagerness spurs them to mutual emulation, the draughtsman as he creates his reconstructions is carried away in self-forgetfulness—perhaps to catch the germ of the destroying fever that sets a limit to this as to so many other hopes. At the time of his death he can hardly have completed the study for the First Region: "pictis mandare tabellis", in order to expand it in painted panels, are the words of a panegyric of the time by Caio Silvano Germanico. Even more do the elegies upon his death reveal what a work it must have been that was cut short, what great expectations must have attended the universal interest in this plan. First and foremost we have the opinion of CASTIGLIONE:

"Tu quoque dum toto laniatam corpore Romam
Componis miro, Raphael, ingenio
Atque urbis lacerum ferro, igni, annisque cadaver
Ad vitam, antiquum jam revocasque decus,
Movisti Superum invidiam, indignataque mors est,
Te dudum extinctis reddere posse animam."

"Thou didst excite the jealousy of heaven, when thou didst with thy marvellous mind reconstruct Rome, her body all violated; when thou didst call back to life and to her ancient beauty the corpse of the sublime city, wasted with war, fire and age, death was angry that it should have been granted thee to restore to the departed life extinguished."

In a poem that probably has for its author Raphael's admirer, the Apostolic Protonotary Celio Calcagnini, we read, obviously from the most intimate acquaintance:

"The ancestors and centuries that went to the building of Rome are equalled in multitude by the enemies and races that have destroyed it; and now—

"Romam in Roma querit reperitque Raphael;
Querere magni hominis, sed reperire Dei est."

"Now a Raphael seeks in Rome for Rome, and finds it;
seeking belongs to an exalted mind, finding, to a God."

It is the same CELIO CALCAGNINI to whom we owe, in the prose of one of his letters, the truly poetical, because sculpturesque portrait of Raphael in the perfection of his last years; we read there that he superintended the Office of Works of St Peter's—but also that "ipsam plane urbem in antiquam faciem et amplitudinem ac symmetriam instauratam magna parte ostendit"—he has undertaken to reinstate the former appearance of the Ancient City, its splendour and its great beauty in relation to its individual parts, and he has already a large portion of it to show.

He was thus seen to be making discoveries, and it was known that the Pope was favourable to his venture. The remains should be investigated thoroughly down to the foundations, and the finds should be made secure in pictures:

"et pictis mandare tabellis
Sed tanti artificem monumenti in limine primo
Sustulit ac claris mors obstitit invida cœptis."—

"Yet the master of so mighty a monument death snatched
away at the first outset, jealously opposing so glorious
a beginning."

207

Everywhere there was talk of a beginning, and initiated persons actually knew what the method was to be; it seems to have been the same proposed in the Memorial, found worthy of mention also by PAOLO GIOVIO in his short sketch of Raphael's life—the compass:

"Raphael died in the flower of his life, just when he had undertaken to measure the remains of the buildings of Rome; he had devised a new and wonderful means of doing this, so as to present the city as he saw it, as if new, before the eyes of the architects":

"Id autem facile consequebantur, descriptis in plano pedali situ ventorumque lineis, ad quarum normam sicuti nautæ ex pictæ membranæ magnetisque usu maris ac litorum spatia depræchendunt, ita ipse laterum angulorumque naturam ex fundamentis certissima ratione colligebat."

"This however could easily be followed from the site and the lines of the winds drawn on a flat chart, by the help of which as a norm, just as sailors by using a painted parchment and a magnet make out the distances of sea and shores, he himself deduced from the foundations of the buildings (the remnants of walls) the nature of their superficies, sides and angles, in accordance with an unfailing principle."

The Venetian art-lover Marcantonio, in his report of Raphael's death five years later to a fellow-countryman in his birthplace, comes even nearer to the indubitable truth that, far beyond all copying and measuring, the master's artistic imagination went straight to the formulation of the results and made reconstruction intelligible:

"Raphael . . . died, to the sorrow of everyone—but scholars have most of all reason for sorrow; after them, painters and architects. For just as the geographer Ptolemy described the world, so Raphael intended to represent in a book the ancient buildings of Rome, and in this work he showed their proportions, their forms and decorations so clearly that everyone who saw these pictures—*che averlo veduto haria iscusato ad ogniuno aver veduta Roma antiqua*—could justly say it was as good as if he had seen ancient Rome— He had already finished the First Region. In this he showed the plans and situation of the buildings, which he had copied with the greatest care and devotion from the ruins themselves but he drew also the exterior aspects (*le facia*) with their decorative members in a very expressive manner, as he had learnt from Vitruvius and in accordance with the rules of architecture (*delle regole de la architectura*) and from ancient traditions, where the original aspect was no longer retained by the ruins.—Now death has interrupted these beautiful and glorious schemes and jealously carried off the master still in his youth."

§ The planned Book: Single Sheets

Amongst initiated persons therefore, in circles in close touch with the artist as with the Vatican, it was known that the publication of a book was planned, perhaps of plans in book form. By the methods of the period this could only be with engravings on copper or with woodcuts; but the original by Raphael, which had to show so large an area, will have been, if not a painting, certainly a wash-drawing. Even in print it must have presented a fairly substantial appearance. Twelve years after Raphael's death the Mantuan ambassador Fabrizio Pellegrino reported on it to his Duke: he is sending him a "disegno di Roma", "which has just appeared, showing the aspect of Rome as it once was in the time of the Ancients, with its buildings". And three weeks later: "in a few days another print will appear"—of Rome, "che fu disegno di Raphael da Urbino e è bellissima cosa e molto copioso"—it was drawn by Raphael of Urbino and is a very beautiful and comprehensive undertaking.

Sheets of illustrations in woodcut for a book were in existence, therefore, or copperplate engravings for a series to appear in book form, like the later sets of Lafreri, which there was reason to regard as originating with Raphael, that is, made after his drawings. We can suppose that whatever had at any time been privileged to come within the circle of his influence claimed to be part of his activities, then as in later times, just as his pupils also invoked his name for their tedious compositions in the Sala di Constantino. This report of the Mantuan's therefore is certainly no conclusive proof—but where did traces survive of a work so much noticed and admired, of the beginning of which, in the First *Regione*, so many persons closely connected with Raphael have given evidence? Would Andrea Fulvio, in whose preface to the edition of his *Antiquitates* of February, 1527, no trace of false modesty can be observed, have failed to notice the already existing manuscript of Raphael redounding to his own glory? The book came from the press by Papal licence dated 15th February, 1527, a month before the *Sacco di Roma*; the only known copy of this edition is to-day in the possession of the Biblioteca Vittorio Emanuele in Rome. It would not have been impossible that the entire stock was destroyed in the storms of that catastrophe, when still in the hands of the publisher Ludovico Vicentino. The second edition of 1532 (published in Rome, at the house of Valerius Doricus of Brescia) contains nothing but fairly primitive woodcuts with which the shade of the great master must not be taxed. Simultaneously with the *Antiquitates* of Fulvio a plan of Rome appeared—*Antiquæ Urbis Romæcum regionibus simulachrum*—and was dedicated to Clement VII, by Fabio Calvi of Ravenna, who in those years shared Raphael's house and was his classical adviser in his Vitruvius studies. One would have thought that, having been produced almost under Raphael's eyes and drawn up in accordance with the principles of the Regiones of his closest collaborator, Fulvio, it would show traces of the master, at hand with his powers of conjecture; it contains only childish plans with plastic structures that betray not one trace of an artistic hand, let alone the hand of the greatest of artists.—And yet, uneasiness and passionate curiosity refuse to be allayed, peering into the gloom in which anything whatsoever seems to throw out a ray of light. LAFRERI, the publisher of engravings on copper to whom we owe many sheets that acquaint us with the aspect of the ruins of Rome in the Cinquecento, is reputed to have had in hand, and himself to have drawn on linen, a "Cartone di Raffaello"; so the enthusiastic investigator of antiquities Giovan Antonio Dosio relates, some fifty years later, to his patron Niccolo Gaddi of Florence, who was a collector of drawings.[1] ARETINO also tells of a "Carton" with a picture of Ancient Rome "come ella era, non come ella è", in his *Dialogo sulle Corti* (*Ragionamento nel quale M. Pietro Aretino figura quattro suoi amici . . .*, 1538, p. 100).

Once when Leo X and many Cardinals and dignitaries of the Vatican were seated at table, a "gentile intelletto"— a refined and intelligent man—unrolled before them a large, wonderful cartoon, the result of much research, on which Rome was represented as once it was and not as it is to-day. And whilst this person, with growing ardour, pointed out on it the seven Regions, the scenes and monuments of heroic events, some wax dropped from the candles in the hands of the servants upon the precious work; he did not notice it, even when the cartoon caught fire in one corner, and whilst he in his enthusiasm was dwelling on the past, the company, clerics and laymen alike, made a joke of the terrible present, into which the Court seems only to have been waiting to find its way back again, and burst into laughter that swept all before it. A surmise has been expressed that this "gentile intelletto" must be intended for Raphael. It might also apply to Fulvio or Calvi, however little what we know about them may appear "mirabile". The situation will not precisely fit in with the consideration in which Raphael was held at the Palace, but what all-too-human occurrence was not possible amid the frivolity of this Court?

§ Fate of the Copies

We may ask what can have become of the copious number of drawings Raphael must have made in his zeal for copying. Among the property left after his death by Giulio Romano at Mantua, and afterwards in the house of Perino del Vaga's widow, the antiquarian and dealer JACOPO STRADA found a quantity of architectural drawings; amongst them were "le più belle cose que havesse Raffael d'Urbino già stato suo maestro", the finest pieces that Raphael, once his instructor, had possessed; apart from drawings by his own hand, they were mostly drawings of architectural subjects, ancient as well as modern—and the

---

[1] Bottari-Ticozzi: *Lettere pittoriche*, p. 308 f.

ingenious Strada combined all this with the materials of Serlio, as he himself relates in the preface of his edition of Serlio of 1575. It may be that, in this multitude, traces of Raphael may still to-day be lost from sight, or have been lost long since.

§ Ideas based on Raphael's Reconstruction: Plan of Pirro Ligorio

Here and there however a feature crops up, in the half fanciful, half pedantic plans of reconstructions of the Imperial City, that reminds one of Raphael's ideas. In the plan, dated 1561, of Pyrrho Ligorio, who was a pupil of Bramante and Giulio Romano, a plan also drawn up on the lines of the fourteen Regions of Augustus, the Temple of *Mars Ultor or Bisultor* in the Forum of Augustus shows almost the same form that Raphael gave to the sanctuary of Ares in the tapestry of ST PAUL PREACHING AT ATHENS. The "Forum Transitorium" recalls Peruzzi's architectural phantasies, and the Septizonium looks like the building of the Loggie. In any case it is difficult to regard this as accidental, and one can scarcely imagine that nothing except these few miserable woodcuts of the two learned antiquaries was destined to survive to later ages as the outcome of an energy that left contemporaries breathless with the audacity of its schemes for reverent reconstruction.

§ Stage Designs of Raphael at the time of the Reconstruction : Raphael and the Theatre: Echoes

When Raphael was occupied with this reconstruction, he had to give up much time to the staging of Ariosto's comedy *I Suppositi*, for a performance in the residence of Cardinal Innocenzio Cibo in the Castle of St Angelo, a task also possessing a special architectural interest. The new theme gave him no breathing-space. When the Ferrarese Ambassador pressed for the completion of the pictures promised by Raphael for his Duke, the master repeatedly referred in reply to the work on this scenery. Once he comforted him by claiming that this delay was to the advantage of the picture for the Ambassador's sovereign: he had just lately made exceptional progress and gained experience in perspective. We see that he was acquainting himself with the manner, current in those times, of representing scenes in half plastic form of buildings and streets in the flat as if modelled, so that with the slanting, ascending lines of their bases and their descending copings, they presented to the eye a deceptive appearance of more or less great recession, thus giving it an anticipation of foreshortening. The Urbino artist had succumbed from his youth up to the charms of such play for play's sake. In his native city he must have seen such things from the hand of Francesco di Giorgio, for by his pictures with their rich palaces rhythmically disposed round a central structure, that dreamy master of architecture discloses himself as an adept at stage scenery also. Perhaps Giovanni Santi also provided scenery of this kind for his allegorical poetical play at the Court, of which we have knowledge;

in any case, from his youth up Raphael was familiar with the custom of Renaissance architects of themselves giving a fête on festival occasions, so as to concede the honour of realisation, for once in a way, to their own ideas and dreams. On these occasions they were allowed for once to see before them in deceptive reality, for their own enjoyment, palaces that they would fain have built, squares and town plans that they felt an insistent desire to lay out on the grand scale; they could really project out of themselves, and construct in wood and stucco and correct proportions, and put to the test, projects for which reality denied them the means. These magnificent perspectives and dreams of palaces and temples were not confined to the stage; they assert themselves everywhere in creative fantasy. The Theorists, Serlio for instance, perpetuate the heroic and the comic scene in woodcuts, and there are drawings by BALDASSARE PERUZZI, in closest proximity to Raphael, of Roman stage settings (Plate 187); round a triumphal arch in the middle are grouped arches, halls, temples, the Torre Milizia di Nerone, the Colosseum, the Pantheon, the Column of Marcus Aurelius—in short, as Shakespeare puts it, "the scene is Rome"; and ideal piazzas, rarely destined to be carried out in real life, occur on paper as structures to which great architectural ambition aspired. This new form of stage began with Bramante; Raphael's pupils, and their pupils in turn, such as Peruzzi's son and SERLIO, continue them and hand them down. In the secret power that gave them their impetus one is obviously put in mind of Raphael, who created his stage scenes *Urbi et Orbi*, as the link between them and Francesco di Giorgio, Laurana and Bramante. Actually, in the time of his fullest maturity, he gave a setting thus sympathetically felt to the great narrative subjects of the tapestries. " . . . representavasi bene per mia fè Ferrara de prospective"—"Ferrara was seen in true reality in prospective" is the report at that very time of the Ferrarese Ambassador concerning Raphael's settings for the *Suppositi* in the Castle of St Angelo in 1517 (Golzio, p. 94).

§ Architectural Backgrounds in the Tapestries

In the St Paul Preaching, the square of the Areopagus appears as half of an architectural stage scene disposed symmetrically about the circular temple that already usually occupied the central position with Francesco di Giorgio, Laurana and Bramante; and in the Sacrifice at Lystra a series of selected buildings is displayed, the hall with coloured columns and niches filled with statues, the niche-decorated circular temple, the beautifully profiled palace with its row of pilasters, forming the side of a square—easily completed on symmetrical lines with the eye fixed on the statue of Hermes, to form one of his favourite heroic settings. From this earliest decade of the High Renaissance onwards, in stage constructions a circular building like the Colosseum perpetually occurs again and again as a second splendid feature within the recession of the streets. One feels instinctively that this motive must derive from one of the greatest and most admired masters, namely, from an idea of Raphael's. Here was preserved, in perishable material, but in the indescribably conservative tradition of the festival stage, an echo of what was destined to be lost in actual structure.

It can hardly be doubted that the imagination that created such a background for the heroic career of Paul as he went on his way through the world of the Roman dominions, worked along similar lines when it was completing the remnants of Ancient Rome. Ancient and modern combine in receptive productivity in this style that aims only at grandeur of effect, unencumbered and free from any search after correctness. "The buildings of the Imperial period," says the author of the Memorial, "the most glorious of all, carried out in beautiful taste, which alone I intend to represent, were all, even the later ones, erected in a *single* style. When other arts declined, architecture maintained itself longest on an equal level of taste. It was the last of all to be lost."

What was it then in this attempt that had such a dæmonic effect for his contemporaries? Certainly not the raising up of spirits of the mighty dead; it was rather the fact that a unique individual could believe himself capable of constructing anew, out of the remains of the world of ruins, all the various motives— the halls, forums, arches, basilicas, temples, *thermæ*, and *nymphæa*—and so to speak, of creating a paraphrase of these individual themes out of the abundance of his own architectural imagination. "His zeal as architect was so unhampered that he planned and carried out schemes before which even the most inventive intellects had to admit defeat."

§ The Reconstruction: its Value artistic rather than archæological.
The Pantheon reconsecrated

Archæology therefore least of all was the loser, from a purely material point of view, when this ingenious reconstruction of Ancient Rome was lost in oblivion; architecture and the history of imaginative construction were deprived of an example of plastic creation of untrammelled magnificence and of formative power in many moods—a performance with great motives that a sublime mind was pleased to exhibit to the world only for a few moments, merely to take it with him to the grave, that grave which he himself chose under the dome of the *Pantheon* (Plate 302); and thereby the *most glorious relic of Antiquity was consecrated to a new phase of its existence*—this also an idea worthy of the creative humanist whose intention was to call Ancient Rome to life again; in this transfiguration of death he succeeded spiritually in fulfilling what fell to the lot of Michael Angelo, who gave fixed outward form in a plastic vaulting to the splendour of this supreme Roman architectural conception, thereby making it, as the dome of St Peter's, a new symbol of the Eternal City.

§ The constructive Humanist: Raphael's Aptitude for high Culture

The constructive humanist—it was granted to him to feel himself called upon to represent what was vital in the best men of his time. It did not remain un-expressed, for there was abundant discussion of what pertained to the perfecting of man in the stream of life; in the circle of the *Cortegiani*, at the Court of Urbino, and already during his years of travel in his meetings with Bembo and Casti-glione, Raphael was occasionally witness of such debates; he had already dis-tinguished himself in the "bellissimi discorsi e dispute d' importanza" in the house of Baccio d'Agnolo. Afterwards, in Roman circles, in the "giardini letterarii", he became a valued guest. It must have been felt, when the con-versation was conducted in Latin or Greek, that in his way he was capable of contributing by his silence something more essential than clever talk; in his own language he had already given the answer more plainly, and would continue to give it with ever greater clarity, to the question of the nature of the human ideal—that ideal which they all wished to attain, and which they were un-wearied in debating and picturing to themselves with a cleverness that was already becoming almost academic. In these beautiful periods of discourse and intellectual phrases there stood before his eyes, as if between the lines, that figure in which this ideal in its entirety was shown in consummation. "So perfect a man," it was said at the Court of Urbino, "a *Cortegiano* such as we here desire and describe, has never been, does not live, and never will be"—and yet, in Raphael's figures he was already there, in process of consummation.

It may well be that these conversations and opinions brought the creator in him to maturity; it was as if he gathered up in himself the aspirations of the age—listening, reading, in thoughtful observation—the "man of all-embracing vision"; and from his experience of life, outward as well as inward, the moving form in which all these desirable properties took shape, presented itself to his spiritualised bodily sense. When he painted the portraits of the men of this society, there arose before him a vision of what they *desired to be*. He would never have attained to this interpretation if he had not brought with him to the task a standard inborn in himself. His intercourse with them and their intellectuality gave him assurance and, as it were, loosened his tongue. He had scarcely taken his place, as painter of the Pope, enjoying the privileges of this society, on a footing of equality with its choicest spirits, when he had already become their spokesman.

§ Herald of the Humanist Ideal

All the thoughts and aspirations conceived under the impress of the great fashioners of humanity in Ancient times, Plato and Aristotle, in the Florentine Academy of Marsilio Ficino and at the Court of Urbino, here found before the eyes of all, both contemporaries and posterity, their most vital herald. One who discovered for loftiness of mind such expression as was conceived by the painter of the "filosofica familia" in the SCHOOL OF ATHENS must himself have had exalted aims. Only one acquainted with the nature of these greatest of teachers and guides could have dared to give it lasting shape in these representations of

PLATO and ARISTOTLE, in the individual figures no less than in their parallelism, the contrasts and the conformities of the two (Plate 227).

§ Innate Education: Sense for ideal Tensions: The Aristotelian Ideal

It was said in the nineteenth century that education begins when you have forgotten everything you have read. As we know, education makes its appearance even before one has begun to read; education signifies a condition, a stratification of intellectual and spiritual powers that must be antecedent to all teaching. The gaze of a child of fourteen already comprehends a universe of knowledge as to essentials. In Raphael there was a capacity for discerning and experiencing mysterious tensions between ideal powers. That which seems for the seventeen-year-old painter to hover between the two women in the KNIGHT'S DREAM, the conflict between the ideal and life, is here, in the SCHOOL OF ATHENS, successfully emphasised by him in the dominant group of the two great thinkers —but now it is no question of alternatives, but rather of a complementary relation. Great and creative men are creative because their powers grow out of antagonisms which they master in unceasing struggle; they have as a rule not a single significance only but a wealth of complicated attributes. They are familiar with heights and depths, and seem to be in league with incomprehensible, primordial forces. The two souls of Faust, the cleavage of impulse in the earth-affirming soul and the soul that strives towards the heights that Goethe was perpetually impelled to confirm and to formulate, were equally familiar to Raphael. As child of the society that, from a social point of view, produced him and reared him, he clung to Aristotle and modelled his character and his heroes after the character of Aristotle's man of lofty mind. "Their lofty disposition consists in lofty aims, just as beauty depends upon lofty appearance. Towards honour and renown their attitude is one of moderation. Their nature is to be composed in the presence of life, in the fleeting spectacle of which they observe the mean. Thus it belongs as of right to the man of lofty mind to look down on others; he strives after a position of superiority. He shows restraint in his movements; his voice is deep, his speech measured. Towards the great masses he adopts an attitude of irony, and his serenity is the mark of an active mind: *majestas gravis et requies decora*."

§ Plato's Idea

Raphael's ARISTOTLE embodies in a lively manner, yet with human dignity and poise, all that the artist found—in isolation, or perhaps in groups, but rarely collectively—in the society of his high-mooded friends, the *magnanimi*; he fashions his heroes as masters of things that can be grasped, in fresh, vital consciousness of self combined with moderation. In the case of PLATO's figure however Raphael shows himself conscious of that other power, that dwelt in himself— and he reverently pays homage to it—the power of directing the gaze beyond what can be seen and grasped, upon a higher aim. There we see a figure beckoning towards heights above even the ideal figure of that society, and presenting itself as lodestar of the unfulfilled strivings of the human race: "to regions of an ancestry sublime", as the poet has it, and it was Goethe also who in this Plato, "recognised Raphael's yearning to participate once more in his origin". Here Raphael found himself prepared in advance through his inborn sense of beauty, which was nothing else but the impulse to seek, for his high visions, the worthy, the convincing form. And Plato answers him with the "idea". "Because real beauty is rare to find, I follow a certain idea that hovers before me (a conception of beauty), living in my mind," Raphael himself says in the letter to Castiglione.

§ Parallels to Dürer: The Canon in Vitruvius and Thomas Aquinas

The same striving filled the existence of DÜRER, and in his need, Vitruvius had to be enlisted in order to find a doctrine of canonical validity for what is astir above the sphere of everyday life. The Middle Ages could still take their stand on the rule of St Thomas Aquinas—"Beauty is composed of three elements: '*integritas sive perfectio*', flawlessness or perfection, '*debita proportio sive constantia*', the appropriate relation of parts to one another or unity enduring in plurality, then, '*claritas*', for what shines with a brightness of its own is called beautiful."

§ Plato and Aristotle

Between the dimensions of Vitruvius, which for the Renaissance in its strivings after harmony were an object of perpetual research, and the Gothic, pattern-like melodiousness in countenance and bearing, the difference for a follower of the "idea" was not so great that he should be accused, on the score of his cult of Antiquity, of a "decline into heathenism". For the twenty-six-year-old Raphael perceived Plato, with the *Timaeus* under his arm, as affecting the superterrestrial and terrestrial cosmos of the *DISPUTA* on the opposite wall, and in Plato and Aristotle it was precisely their *accord* and their *indissoluble unity* that he comprehended by his sensibility; in the same manner, in his maturity, it was granted to him to feel himself to be between life and the beyond, at the centre of the universe. He was allowed to think of himself as being in its "eternally vital ordering" because, like Wilhelm Meister, at the time of his maturity, he was likewise conscious in himself of a glorious mobility, a revolution about an absolute centre.

For that reason Raphael was conscious of the power in himself, at one and the same time, of summoning up the Olympian deities in the Farnesina, so that in serenity and irony their irresponsible sway could be seen in its progress high above the world, then of showing the gods once more, circling above the tomb of Chigi, as dæmons of the heavenly bodies ruling over earthly destiny, yet in accordance with the will of the supreme Power—and finally, in the "Feed my lambs" tapestry, of discovering the sublimest and yet most gentle of figures for the Son of Man.

§ The *Cortegiano* surpassed: The Son of Man

In order to penetrate to the solemn calm in these heights, Raphael had first to surmount the sphere of the *Cortegiani*; their aspirations after perfection in this world he left beneath him. The flame that Goethe set up as an image of Plato's figure leaps up like a flame of sacrifice towards this height. But the nobility in Raphael's figure of the Redeemer in the *PASCE OVES*—"Feed my lambs"—derives from other worlds; its sublimity does not soar above those that remain on earth— it has stooped to their level only to return again to its own proper sphere. The presentiment of the world in the look of the Mother of God and the Child in the Sistine Madonna, and in that vision preserved at Chatsworth (Plate 141), found confirmation in the horrors on earth and victorious fulfilment in the Passion; in this look and this backward turn of Christ, the Divine Leader takes his leave and— gently—delivers his ordinance, in profoundest human understanding.

For the first time this painter of things heavenly, almost against the wishes of humanism—certainly not in accordance with the intentions of its exponents— here grants their most intimate desire for the purest *human dignity*, a desire as for something impossible of attainment. Even their choicest spirit, Bembo, could declare that he was little troubled by the thought of a beyond. His friend the poet among painters, who saw himself ranged amongst the circle of humanists as they proudly counted him as of their number, stands there in solitary loneli- ness, with this work filled with his confession of faith, presenting Our Lord in this and no other guise, in the presence of his circle and of his age—indeed, of all ages; he makes perceptible the gulf between the now and the beyond, between heights and depths; but he also displays that power of purest humanity, of the true *humanitas*, to which nothing is alien, not even the sense of what is higher, and to which the divine reveals itself even if it does not enter into association with it.

In Raphael there lived something of this power that seemed to reach out beyond the bounds prescribed for earthly existence. His contemporaries, con- scious of their own disability, were sensible of the drama of this self-perfecting life as a presentiment of the beyond, as a gift of grace from above. They could name it none other than "divino".

XIII

RAPHAEL AND GOTHIC

"We retrieve the treasure of piety for a new age and to take noble form."
C. F. Meyer: *Huttens letzte Tage.*

FOR centuries Raphael has been looked upon as the master who achieved perfection of form; we see him fulfilling the strivings of three generations of the Renaissance, he gives embodiment to an ideal that may perhaps in favourable moments have floated at times before the eyes of humanists, but was only seldom attained by artists apart from him. In the new canon, his figures animate the space in which they freely breathe; they appear to be released from every confinement, delivered from the dusty classicalism of literary culture, called only to lend new life to the Antique myths that are the happy possession of everyone. One can believe they are alive and breathing in their airy element; now for the first time the style seems to have been discovered in which to tell over again pictorially, in an adequate manner, the vital stories of the Hellenistic circle. And just as, to Raphael, the kindred creatures took shape between the lines and verses of classical texts, so his age in astonishment saw him evoking speech from the stones when he took upon himself to reawaken Ancient Rome, and gave life to Antique motives and rules of architecture the influence of which we can trace right down to our own day.

§ Apollo and Dante

And yet, with reference to this happy inheritance from the Ancients, we may venture to speak of "*Gothic*"; indeed, as we survey his work, we are almost entitled to call one of the most essential chapters "Dante and the Belvedere Apollo". So deeply grounded is his call to interpret the divine, and his impulse to fashion into tools for this mission the powers operative in himself, that wherever he met with evidences of the beyond, it must have stirred him as a greeting of the spirit and a new summons to aims he had early foreknown. In fact, a propensity for the world of the soul operates with excessive force in this Southerner, who seems from birth to have been consecrated as a "disciple of the Greeks"; in him this propensity may perhaps have arisen out of a peculiar blending of blood that fairly often betrays itself in many stocks of the peninsula from their contacts with the peoples of the Migration period in their freshness; it is as if it were communicated and promoted through a community of primordial beginnings that can merely be divined.

218

RAPHAEL AND GOTHIC

§ The Northern Element in Raphael

We feel something like embarrassment from the abundance of inward vision, an inescapable compulsion to arise out of the world of the real and measurable into a more spiritual sphere, to "regions of an ancestry sublime", to seek out even in earthly figures signs of a divine mission; if we may compare this tendency with Gothic, if we may call it mystical or think of its effects as transferred out of the dreamy, yearning world of Northern atmosphere into the clearer air of Southern expanses—however and from whatever source such immortal energy of soul may have transplanted itself—as primordial kinship of enduring generative power or as a newly perceived challenge—it has in all peoples passed over the threshold of consciousness at times of more profound revolutionary convulsion.

He who is called to be spokesman of his epoch, and knows as a seer how to unite in his breast past and future, will reveal to those who live with him their inner depths; he will direct on the path to the heights, through the bewilderments of the present, that impulse within them towards the light which operates from the beginnings of time. Before such a spirit, in such a consecrated moment, there is no old and new, no alien or indigenous; in him and his creations there will only dwell that energy of promise fulfilled which springs from a higher prompting, and which knows how to greet as an innate idea of its own every great impression it encounters, whatsoever its source—Dante's visions and the self-revelations of the gods of the Greeks.

§ The Law of Pattern

This was and ever became the style of youthful peoples, of a god-possessed period; hence, out of "*Sturm und Drang*", arose its necessities: "in the beginning was pattern"; every given area must be filled to leave no breathing-space, every frame must reverberate to its utmost limits with the rhythm of lines that produce an atmosphere. This law derives from structure, whilst nevertheless eternally giving expression in the clearest possible manner to sentiment. The builder's workshop makes a custom of this rule: in every sphere and volume, from the block to the outline of a tower, the material should be transformed into a highly significant pattern of figure or natural form, the shape evoked should be imposed imaginatively upon the volume of the piece of work in hand and should be released from the material, the outline of the part of the structure in question should be left to the material, but the play of lines within the limits should be allowed free course and should be called upon to convey the general air of the structure. This sense of the coherent block was of course known to the Ancient World in its early period, as late as the metopes of Selinus and Olympia, on one of which are to be read the significant words: συν θεῷ. It consecrates art to the service of the godhead. But it first triumphs once more, all-conquering and all-captivating, at the time of the mighty Northern art, when devotion discovered anew how to fit together great stones and small—as by the strains of Amphion. And with this ordering power it controls glass window and pendentive, the polychrome decoration of the building—even the painting of altarpieces takes from this sense its origin and rules. Always, when the godhead is present, near at hand to the artist, the law asserts itself again; it arises consolingly, every time and everywhere, when in art the sense of the origin and destination of the soul threatens to be lost.

§ The Gothic Law revived at the Close of the Middle Ages

When the VAN EYCKS and CONRAD WITZ, bourgeois masters with the townsman's selfconsciousness and factual sense, open up to realism access to the holy spheres in order thus to glorify the Creator in the contemplation of Creation and its newfound wonders, a spectacle is presented as if all the conceptions of evolution and progress that became current in the nineteenth century must, for art, be refuted. For the youthful bourgeois selfconsciousness there arise suddenly the noblest interpreters of its inward life; they discover expression for it in the rapture of the figure in pursuit of a spiritual goal. And in the same instant that ancient law asserts its sway—the prophetic insight of the soul becomes the essential thing instead of knowledge of the corporeal world, dominating once again picture-space and field of vision. We may recognise in this a retrogression, or a revival or effective continuation of Gothic, or an eternal law renewing itself out of mystic depths; however it be, the Van Eycks gave place to ROGER VAN DER WEYDEN, Conrad Witz was succeeded by SCHONGAUER—and in the midst of the group of scattered Quattrocentists attached to the first MASACCIO arise FRA ANGELICO'S visions of Paradise, and PERUGINO'S *hymnlike colour harmonies* re-echo the entranced devoutness of his figures. Finally out of the whirl of contending sensibilities there emerge gothicising eccentrics like Botticelli, and, on opposite sides of the Alps, Crivelli and the Master of St Bartholomew could have hailed one another as kindred spirits experimenting in the orthodox style; indeed, stars seemingly so worldwide apart as RIEMENSCHNEIDER and MICHAEL ANGELO appear by virtue of these self-renovating powers in the same aspect; the DEAD REDEEMER from Münnerstadt in the Deutsches Museum, and the late PIETÀ at Palestrina move one to devotion by the same, old, eternal means. The treetrunk in the North and the block of marble in the South become pregnant, and are given new meaning, to appeal with the same compelling force to our feelings; and the breath-taking power of a pattern that becomes a gesture of deep poetical significance, goes on its way as a new gospel through the art of the peoples and of the ages.

§ The Blessing of Constraint: Influence of the North on the South

This it is that moves the devout most profoundly in periods of upheaval. It is not the freedom of the figure, attained after toilsome studies from nature; it is rather its constraint when it is dependent on a higher power than the Law of

Gravity; not the space that envelops it and of which the foreshortenings are explored—the figure lives in a sphere above the earth—"dove la legge natural nulla rileva"—where the Natural Law can have no validity.

In this higher, this poetical sense Raphael may be compared to the great men of the Gothic age. Where he came across them, what he owed to them, what it was in his blood, or derived from his feeling for his native home, that responded to their call, it is difficult to say succinctly. One may rather conjecture some inescapable dæmonic power. It is almost a matter of indifference whether he actually saw works of Roger van der Weyden; in many of his early works Raphael already shows himself under the spell of that painter's principles, and certainly he made himself receptive to him, as to every stimulus from the North. Any work from that quarter is enough to fire in him a kindred spark. A glance at the LAST SUPPER of Justus van Gent (Plate 228), which after the first impression it made on him as a youth will always have been sought out by him when visiting Urbino, a print of Schongauer coming wafted over the Alps, cannot have failed to communicate, to one receptive and prepared for life, knowledge of the secret powers by which one learns to acquire a spirit of devotion; these powers became law for him. They had already once penetrated beyond the Alps, to help the Italian world of the Dugento towards a break-through of its own selfconsciousness. Whatever of these forces continued to operate, or became operative once again, in the Netherlands and Germany, now found in the few poet-artists of the South men of allied sentiment; and just that silent conspiracy sprang up which in times of spiritual stress ever overstrides the boundaries between the peoples, and then prepares in advance the inward upsoaring that is common to the strong and bold spirits among them. Then arises the struggle to attain sublime form for the language of the soul.

More than this can hardly be said in substantiation of this phenomenon as a stimulating influence in Raphael. But it can be overheard at many points in the course of his life, can perhaps actually be illustrated, without necessarily thereby verging upon the pitiful game of seeking after "influences". With masters of creative power, what they borrow is converted into their own property, and— beyond the meagre fact of copying—one has to recognise that the moment in which Raphael paused before the work of another artist, or a strange motive flashed upon him again, will have revealed to him something more essential in his great predecessors than mere isolated features.

§ Spiritual Influence of Justus van Gent and Roger van der Weyden

When he transplanted from the LAST SUPPER by Justus van Gent at Urbino into his early BEARING OF THE CROSS (Plates 229c, 233) just that uneasily balanced figure of Christ, he was surely conscious as we are of the very terribleness of the spectacle as an opportunity for unrestrained expression. But apart from this, he was long haunted—to the very last—by the delicate music in the composition of the figures which, themselves a spatial group, are converted from space into breadth and height. For a true unison is set up between the angels and the vaults, between the overtowering of the group of figures by their wings and the high-vaulted space of the choir; it is as if even the dish in the foreground provided to the eye a prelude to the circling movement to which it has to surrender itself when it follows the rapt figures of the Apostles. Never again, right up to the time of his late works, was Raphael able to set himself free from these lessons learned in early life. Rather, he was impelled to multiply out of himself and to condense in himself their effective qualities. Even the Transfiguration still derives vitality from this kind of constraint of pattern, from this fitting of lights and spots of colour into the dynamic lines of a structure of figures.

He seemed to be called by this happy mission, everywhere, in each phase of his life, to be welcomed by it, at all times and places, at every stage of his journey through life, continually to hear its voice, to measure his own growth by the degree of profoundness with which he understood it, by the extent to which he was able to make his own its revelations.

What was it but revived Gothic that he met with in Perugino? His father before him had esteemed the master of Umbrian devoutness as highly as the universal inquirer Leonardo; his interest can have been enlisted only by the deep harmony of passages of colour quietly rounded off, by the sweep of the hem of a garment from above the gently-moving foot upwards to the head, and the heaven-seeking gaze—by the curve in which the movement from earth away into the beyond had already found expression before, two hundred years ago

§ The Inheritance of the Marches: Mediums of Gothic renewed

In Santi's country, the Marches, a disposition for passionate worship and a readiness for the influence of mystical powers existed from time immemorial; Northern carvers of images, in whole colonies, here and in the Abruzzi served the needs of religion with their arresting art, in Pietà groups. And now it appears as a dispensation of Providence that none other than the youthful Raphael should have been guided by destiny to Perugino, or that the aged Santi, according to Vasari's account, in his concern for his son, must needs take him to that master and no other. In these circumstances the boy's native disposition was confirmed in him; he opened himself to the message of Northern mysticism, wherever on his path it may have been revealed to him—in Justus van Gent at Urbino, in his LAST SUPPER and his portrait of Dante (Plate 4), of such uncanny profundity, in the Duke's library; at Florence, in the presence of the ENTOMBMENT by Van der Weyden, in the Villa Careggi (Plate 230),[1] and of the PORTINARI ALTARPIECE of HUGO VAN DER GOES; in a print of Schongauer; in the teachings of NICHOLAS OF CUSA, or in SAVONAROLA'S claims for art—then actually being realised—as one of the ways to true devotion; in the appeal of Dante, who was familiar to him from

[1] This painting is now in the Uffizi—*Translator.*

the days when he lived in his father's house and was ever anew becoming his "duca e poeta". And thus, on his path to the beyond, he must have been filled with enthusiasm and uplift by the god appearing from above in the Belvedere (Plate 71). But the revelation of the SISTINE MADONNA gains its convincing power not only from the light tread, nor from the sublime gaze out of another sphere; the unearthly character of the figures becomes clear first of all in the line that sweeps from the crown of the head to the soles of the feet, as in Gothic, when the saints float across the scene as not of this world. Whence it came about that these inborn ideas in Raphael could find themselves in unison with Northern art,

"state contenti humana gente al quia" . . .

For us, as for his poet when he looked back from Paradise to earth, source and outflow coalesce.

§ Properties common to North and South

The distinction between Northern and Southern art is stressed often enough, and clearly recognisable. But one who, stimulated and refreshed by an alien nature, turns back to the indigenous and becomes aware, by a responsiveness that is all the greater, of what belongs to himself, will thus be ready to greet related features in the alien type. For the most part we discover strong personal qualities separating us from what is alien; yet the power revealing itself in what is common is stronger. To become conscious of this power seems to us the higher duty; it leads to brighter spheres of knowledge.

Those who see the true elements of beauty belonging to art north of the Alps precisely in the fact that the pattern of line and colour is entirely dominated by inspiration, those who have been struck by the manner in which this devotion to expression suffers every personal touch of the brush to become fused in the enamel-like quality in the application of the colours, will be struck by one fact as by a miracle; it will seem to them miraculous that this unison of pattern and expression, this fidelity to craftsmanship, of the most refined late Gothic painters such as Memling and Schongauer, is to be met with beyond the Alps only in Raphael, whose art represents precisely an epitome of the Italic type and of that majestic quality which belongs to the South.

The points at which his path crossed the tracks of Northerners in Italy would soon be counted up if we were concerned only with the game of seeking for borrowings, which however can never be allowed to signify "influence".

§ Raphael's organic Response to Northern Art

The circumstance must be taken into account that the veneration for Northern art already awakened in him at Urbino, in the presence of JUSTUS VAN GENT and, it may well be also, of HIERONYMUS BOSCH, was fostered still further at Perugia by Schongauer's engravings, and followed him in Florence when he stood before the Portinari altarpiece; it caused him to gain access to Van der Weyden's DESCENT FROM THE CROSS, which was in the chapel of the then deserted Medici villa of Careggi. But it is more important that only *he*, broadly speaking, at that time responded organically to these promptings from the North; and they grew in him into something individual, like the teachings of his masters, that he could not but develop further in an unsuspectedly personal sense.

§ Perugino and Schongauer

In the midst of all the distractions of the Quattrocento Perugino represented an orthodox art. It is little noticed that he consciously "archaised"; quite part from his Early Christian, Byzantine elements, he certainly thought he was approximating more closely to orthodox art when he adopted many non-material features from the engravings of Schongauer and the young Dürer. They may have appeared as the solemn expression of a consecrated existence of which in Perugino's eyes these Northern Late Gothic artists were still capable. From the Colmar master Perugino adopted a minuet-like step; this he found also in Dürer's early engravings, and a tube-like drapery about the thigh that creases above the knee and gives rise to a pattern-like play of folds, involved in his favourite motive of the pose with the "*Spielbein*"—the unburdened leg—drawn up. The young Raphael understood, more completely than his teacher, Schongauer's delicate lyrical quality in the interwoven lines of the compositions. They went profoundly to his heart; he could not but transfer and extend the pattern-motives to his entire figures—a devoted discipleship which, however, is nothing else but an awakening of spiritual kinship.

In recent times only, the frescoes uncovered in the Minster at Breisach have revealed the inner spiritual nearness between the "*best painter in Umbria*", as Raphael was then already called, at the age of twenty, and the *best painter* in the *Sundgau*, and thus also, as a natural necessity, Raphael's affinity with Roger van der Weyden, whom Nicholas of Cusa, the great adherent of both zones, called "maximus pictor". The men of insight of the time—they were the "Faithful"—used the superlative only of the art that satisfied their pretensions to be endowed with a gift profound poetic interpretation.

§ Raphael's inner Relation to Schongauer also

Raphael's ST. SEBASTIAN, the lovely half-figure at Bergamo, seems like an echo of the angel bearing the Cross in the Breisach LAST JUDGMENT (Plates 11, 232). The melody of its lines, the harmony of the oval freely enclosed by the mass of hair echoed in counterpart by the shadow at the base of the neck and by the chain, the sweep of the interior drawing—the eyebrows curved with obvious delight over the forehead, the stereoscopic accentuation of the bridge of the nose and the nostrils in the manner of the old glass-painters—all these features are clearly observable, in a sufficiently striking manner, in the Breisach fresco, in spite of all injuries, whether its painter is Schongauer, or one of the artists who followed his lead. Formerly the kinship between the fervent lute-player above the balustrade at Breisach and Raphael's heavenly fiddler in the Coronation of the Virgin was undoubtedly even clearer (Plate 22); both have downcast eyelids, listening to the tones of their music echoing within them. The submissive face, slightly bent forward, is softly outlined, and this outline is continued, as in the loveliest calligraphy, in the inner drawing of brows and nose down to the bud-like mouth. This is the manner in which the youthful Dürer still draws his designs for glass-paintings. On both sides of the Alps it is nothing else but a perpetuation of Schongauer when, in the small, delicate cartoon by Raphael in the Berlin Cabinet (*R. Z.* I, 39), the lovingly studied hands of St Peter, converted almost into pattern, have the effect of a print by Dürer in the period of his travels; in either region we have a conscious and inwardly inevitable reversion to the style of essential expression. And there is no room for doubt that the manner of the German engraver (who was a crafts-man in the precious metals), with its joy in line, was to the Italian—akin to him where form is concerned—like the sound of a sacred orthodox melody. The stylised folds of the drapery, the delight in pattern shown in the locks, the sweep with which the rim of the eyelid is outlined, the expression of the eye beneath as if arrested in its wandering, with its exceptionally dark accentuation, these present as many points of relationship as they betoken a common striving for inward conversion; one side needed of the other only to be made aware of this fundamental fellow-feeling, through any such hint as a sheet of drawings wafted across the Alps might bring, and both together made the same step forward in common into the new age. Such Gothic conformity may be recognised in the manner of outlining a figure, in the contraction of the hips, stressed like a formula, the delight in undulating lines with which the play of muscles is ren-dered. This conformity existed already between Perugino and the invasion from the North. It would never have obtained validity in the South without that propensity for profound devotion for which Umbrian and Tuscan art took on new forms; indeed, the sympathy with the rare visitors from the Far North had certainly sprung from the same spiritual source, interest in Van der Weyden's Descent from the Cross. The commission for the Portinari altarpiece, even the invitation extended from Urbino to Justus van Gent, also played a part.

Raphael in his youth borrowed from German prints motives from that animal world which was apparently unattainable by the Central Italian—in-stances are the horseman from Schongauer's engraving of the Crucifixion (Bartsch, 25), for the Aeneas Sylvius in the Uffizi drawing (*R. Z.* I, 62), or the swine from Dürer's Prodigal Son for the Jousting Children at Chantilly (*R. Z.* I, 42); this circumstance is less revealing than the fact that he immersed himself in this art at all. From a single one of these prints he was able to derive corroboration for his own efforts. These masters of the North had had no compunction, as had Jacopo de' Barbari towards Dürer, about "explaining clearly" to others "the principles" on which they went.[1] They allowed the message in their engraved sheets to go on its way all over the world. It could be said that a head like that of St John beneath the Crucifix in Schongauer's CRUCIFIX-ION, or the secret, perceptible circle upon which, and in which, the angels swing and sway around the Crucified, was enough to re-echo, and continue to echo hymnlike, as unending music of curves, in the susceptible sensibility of the young Raphael, who was seeking, and was on the point of finding, the most compelling expression of devotion.

This remained the dominant note in all his doings after he met with the art of the North. That which makes it possible for these late Gothic artists to take possession of block, wood and frame once again, in the turmoil of feeling and conscience at the turn of the century, as a means of entirely securing devotion, in Raphael makes equally inescapable his humanistic profession of faith as shown in his youthful work of the THREE GRACES (Plate 234). Their surging rhythm, the undulations that in perpetual repetition permeate the row of heads, the arms, hips, knees and feet, the gleam of the vista seen between the pale limbs in a kind of *flamboyant*—in a word, the element of solemnity in their nature, is based on employment of the same means as the mystical homage felt in the presence of the inspiration and grace of the sacred group by MEISTER GERHAERT of the VIRGIN AND CHILD WITH ST ANNE, in the Deutsches Museum in Berlin (Plate 235). The prescribed volume of the square block of stone has the same life pulsing through it, overflows with the same undulating lines, that fill up with their spell-binding power the small square of the frame in the little picture at Chantilly—the row of heads, the airy region of the arching arms, the frail bridge of the knees of mother and grand-mother, the spread of the hems and folds on the ground.

§ Consecration of Line in Raphael and Gerhaert

This delight in curves, by reason of a similar character of suspended beauty, raises the productions North of the Alps, as in Raphael's case, above what is commonplace in nature. What else is it but this weaving about a spiritual centre, of marvellous clarity, in a circumference as tranquil as a crescent moon—Stephan Lochner in his time was already conscious of it—that gives to Raphael's VIRGIN IN THE MEADOW (Plates 34, 229b) that peculiar quality of consecration to her maternal occupation apparent in the face? It may be the symmetry of balance in the shoulders, the eyebrows, the arrangement of the hair, the contours of the figure, the eyelids, the bordering shadow of nose, lips and chin, and also the edge of the garment on the bust, all vouchsafing such a sense of one who is elect and remote from earth. But it is this symmetry and nothing else that gives such ravishing beauty to *Nikolaus* Gerhaert's BÄRBEL (Plate 229a), so diametric-

[1] "Dan mir wolt diser . . . Jacobus seinen grunt nit klerlich anzeigen" (W. M. Conway, *Literary Remains of Albrecht Dürer*, Cambridge, 1889, p. 254).

ally opposite in type. In these two women there is almost a hint of a canon such as Dürer sought to find for his heads—so strange and certainly devoid of immediate connection, even if not accidental, is the conformity of these qualities of beauty in South and North.

We are sensible of an element in common, indeed we have an inkling of the power that was having an effect this way and that; we no longer believe in an accidental meeting and influence, and await with alert attention an explanation worthy of the artist and of ourselves, arising out of subconscious, as yet imperceptible connections; for the present it suffices that they must have existed.

But where there was a possibility of Raphael coinciding with the great masters of the North, what happened was the same, so far as he was concerned, as in the case of the mighty Italian exemplars: there was no stimulation except such as was changed into conformity with his own mind, to spread its influence there with lasting and powerful effect.

§ Figures seen from behind in Van der Weyden and Justus van Gent

The back views of figures by Justus van Gent in the LAST SUPPER (Plate 228), at Urbino, had made a lifelong impression on him, producing a deep effect through the inescapable significance of their gestures; there is no face to draw the attention away from their spiritual force. He must have lingered all the more understandingly, in his Florentine days, in front of Van der Weyden's ENTOMBMENT (Plate 230), the altarpiece in the chapel of the Medici house in the Villa Careggi. The Magdalene, here with her back turned to the worshipper, now that she is confronted with the spectacle of the dead so recently alive, at the moment when his arms are being extended, seems almost to be received by the ground; no life in her eyes, her mouth open, her hands recoiling, she helps us to experience the horror of the event more deeply than could be achieved by any expression of face whatsoever. Years later Raphael had before his eyes this picture of terror in its most unmitigated aspect when he had to paint the panic-filled temple in the Heliodorus fresco. The young woman completely possessed by horror on the left, in front of the clean-swept central space, radiates once again, in splendid concentration, what had in the past been discovered on Italian soil only by this great dramatist from the North (Plate 231); the concord is even clearer in the Oxford sketch, where the bare soles lend peculiar impressiveness to the language of the figure convulsed from head to foot (Plate 96). Could there be clearer proof of the deep inner kinship of the two great dramatists among the painters, so widely separated by time, race, country and style?

§ Tracery in the Heliodorus

To dwell on details may seem petty in the presence of revelations so much more sublime. It remains essential to make one's self clear on this point: we see here only part of the totality, of that creative quality that in Raphael comes under a new law, or rather, a revived law, *the* law which of old had been put to the test. For precisely in the HELIODORUS (Plate 102) he proves himself to have true mastery over space, thrusting it back, allowing it to join in the harmony only in order to subordinate it to the great force of the figures. Across the self-appointed boundaries of the planes he pours the pattern of their limbs; indeed, he frames each of the groups like pictures within the picture by bringing the arches into play. Like a secret tracery, they span in half circles the separate circles of figures; even the empty space in front almost comes within the scope of their attraction. The temple, with all its convincing spatiality, remains only a suggestion; it cannot have been intended realistically, and is meant only to point the imagination in the direction of the essential, like a musical accompaniment. Everything comes back in semicircles to the great significant pattern which has to convey the story of the cleansing of the Temple court. The highest dramatic power of the Holy Word become Flesh rules over the simplest of stages; yet this Word exercises its compulsion only through the rhythm made visible. If gesture is to be *dominant*, then the inanimate, space, can serve only to lend it fullness by closely confining it.

Now that we know that Raphael arranged his Sibyls, in Santa Maria della Pace, in a short, rhythmically articulated pillared court, in which they and the angels, without losing any of the freedom of their limbs with their space-permeating pattern, preserved the sense of a wall (Plates 192, 194*c*), the painter seems to us even more closely allied to the manner of *Van der Weyden*; this master's altarpiece of the DESCENT FROM THE CROSS, in the Escorial, fills the eye with its undulating pattern; its curves traverse every inch of the surface and, bridging over each corner, draw together top and bottom into a single compact form; the whole gathers itself together in perceptible but reticent plasticity in the shallow space of a simulated altar-shrine.

§ Acknowledgment of the Poetic Victory of the Idea

Only a conscious, in fact, an enthusiastic employment of the fascinating play with the reality of space can condense what is in itself essential to such a degree of poetic energy. In Raphael at the final height of his career the same conflict with his own generation was renewed, the same contempt of the established stock of artistic media, and the profound acknowledgment of the ancient poetry of devotion, which *Roger van der Weyden* had already taken upon himself to accept, almost a hundred years before. In such a victory of the *idea* over the material we see Raphael completing his course.

In the TRANSFIGURATION (Plates 236, 268), the sublime height of Mount Tabor becomes a hill near at hand and yet remains in all its mysteriousness worthy to serve as the scene of glorification, remote and elevated above the everyday world. For what is taking place there on high in the Beyond catches up in its rhythm the swaying figures, as it does the chosen few on the ground of the mountain summit—exactly as in Giotto (Plate 237) [1]—and the same force compels also the passion-charged groups below to conform with the tremendous sweep of its curves: a single mighty, overpowering pattern arises, binding heaven and earth, this world and the Beyond, into a unity of place and action.

§ Power through Renunciation

Thus Raphael at the end of his days, like the poet of *Faust*, was sensible of the "beneficently restraining form and solidity of mediæval art"; and in its confinement he felt the freedom to exercise the highest poetical power, diverted by nothing from the essential. Now again, as in Gothic, there was revealed to the great new interpreter of Christian doctrine, the language of the mystery in *renunciation*; and by this last "Stirb und werde"—"through death to birth"—he for the first time attained the power of soaring to the highest spheres and therewith, when he quitted this world, the true title to the name "DIVINO".

[1] This painting is generally attributed to Taddeo Gaddi—*Translator*.

XIV

RAPHAEL'S FEELING FOR NATURE

§ The Gifts of his Home

THE Urbino master brought with him from his home country, the Marches, that benign universal sensibility which makes perceptible in every picture an enhancement of nature, the *essential*, an effective existence. When the first conscious gaze sweeps across the endless expanses of the high plateau, when the first breath inhales the rarefied mountain air and the first steps are taken up and down the stair-like streets and slopes, a buoyancy of the hips as the breeze blows round them, and in the supple knees, communicates itself to the body, giving alacrity to the eye; it is a lightness, an alacrity, to which those who were born in the mountains usually remain faithful to the end of their lives, receiving from it a sense of free superiority, physical and spiritual. Men of creative nature, but only they, will inevitably communicate something of these favoured natural surroundings to their creations; under their hands figures grow after *their* image.

§ Animal Instinct: Sense for Totality and Space

Raphael's youthful look in his self-portraits betokens, besides spiritual sublimity, this type of superior freedom also. His bearing, like that of his figures, betrays this animal instinct for the surrounding world; the self-assurance of his last days in his intercourse with equals and superiors in Rome has the same foundation. *One* essential trait of his art derives from the same source—the sense for totality! It pervades his creative power and his existence, and consecrates him as the perfecter of that humanistic ideal of equilibrium of inward and outward bearing, of exalted being, in the image of the man of the world after the teaching of Aristotle. Perhaps this was the closest link between him and the Antique; attempts have been made to point out this connection in so many details, yet it could lead to success only by virtue of a general sensibility. One power alone is of interest to us as furthering our enquiry, the power of giving concentrated shape in the picture to the environing world, to the outflowing force of nature, of embodying the influence of nature, the elemental waves of its energy, in the vitality of a figure, and of causing these waves to be re-echoed by it; whether the figures be those of saints or of mythical beings, they come alive through the surrounding landscape, and the landscape through and for them. Raphael's wonderful sense of space, a secret gift of nature to him in his cradle, was manifest from an early stage upward, on the grand scale in the sympathetic relation of his figures to the landscape, in fine detail in every little subtlety of modelling—an outcurved lip, the throbbing pit of a neck, an overhanging strand of hair; it becomes an element in the tone of the language of gesture, whether in a lyrical or in a dramatic context. In Raphael's early painting, down comes St Michael swooping in circles—in the late work, out of a remote distance the Archangel has followed in pursuit of the foe; from on high towards the earth the Almighty descends, in menacing course, before the eyes of Ezekiel.

We may feel amazed to note how uniform is this sensitivity in the whole of his creative life—from the touching detail of the little hand of the Child in the MADONNA DEL CARDELLINO, that arches itself protectively above the goldfinch, to the master's last wish, to find his resting-place in the Pantheon. There is always an intentional grandeur about his figures; we feel how something all-embracing, something encompassing them, is wafted about them; they seem to be at once qualified by it and exalted. This quality they contribute out of themselves, to Perugino's stereotyped Gothic; it gives the St Michael in the Vallombrosa altarpiece, the part of it painted by Raphael, (Plates 6, 9b) its superior freedom as compared with Perugino's St Michael for the Certosa[1]; it is the same with the angel with the supple fingers on the strings of the harp, in the same picture, as compared with the neighbouring figure with the viol (Plate 8); it is found in all his drawings from his youth on. This vitality is radiated by the figures upon the landscape, and by the landscape upon them. Hence surely comes, as the fairest, self-multiplying inheritance of his native home, the purely pictorial sense for harmonies and their compelling mood: in the AVE MARIA (Plate 17b) the evening tones that come wafting in to the twilight of the court, in the PRESENTATION, the greyish-gold of the Temple, in the ADORATION, the gay splendour, and for the first time quite triumphantly, in the SPOSALIZIO, the all-encompassing Pentecost-morning with its festival accords. Thus the great, sonorous touches are being prepared of the First and Second Stanze, the instrumentation of entire wall-surfaces. Here a great "*painter*" exceeds his aim. We now feel clearly that he has passed from being an observer to vision. The man "of all-embracing vision" has been stirred also by Dante's "diretro agli occhi . . .", what takes effect behind the eyes.

§ Impressions of Nature poetically introduced

Impressions of nature become fixed in his memory, in all their differentia-tion, until he puts them poetically to his account. The DISPUTA is dominated by light; already in the design for it (at Windsor, Plate 64) there is a *crescendo* from the pale gleam above the earthly seekers after God to the luminous flood of light in the heavenly region, and thus inseparably from this *crescendo* the char-acter of the figures progresses, from walking and sitting attitudes, full of dignity,

[1] Now in the National Gallery—*Translator*.

to life above the earthly sphere, enthronement, floating on high. The eye is caught up in this tension between the earthly and the heavenly by the angel looking with the tremendous depths below him—a gaze from dizzy heights to earth; in the study of St Paul for the DISPUTA (Plate 70) a blinding by ineffable light. St Stephen hears the rustle of wings from above (Plate 68). Raphael was the solitary artist among them all who was sensible of this coming from out of the beyond—epiphany—in the presence of the APOLLO. For him as painter, *light equals lightness*—forty years before Titian!

§ The Allegorical

Here the *Allegorical* is dominant, the impression derived from nature remains quiescent in him until it is transfigured as symbol; fact is turned into simile. In the SCHOOL OF ATHENS it is the sublime activity of man which is astir—knowledge of things, as opposed to the splendour of the Sacrament in its vibrant radiance—like a film of smoke above the ground; the building is confined in extent; all the pacing and high debate is perpetually reverberated from the vault back upon itself. In the DISPUTA, there is a rising, a soaring upwards as of a smoke-offering. In the HELIODORUS, above the pavement in the Temple—(it seems to have been swept clean)—the shadow of the heavenly avenger hovers like the pinion of an eagle. St Michael sweeps down upon Satan like a lightning-flash.

On the COLONNA MADONNA the sun pours its light, inwardly and outwardly, and in the charming drawing in the Louvre (Plate 242); again, in the last, supreme work, the Chigi cupola, the Creator passes by, like a cloud above the "eye" of the Pantheon.

§ Power of the Impression received from Nature as dynamic Element

What Nietzsche says of music—"it renders the will of Nature"—holds good with just the same cogency of this painting. The forces and rhythms of impressions received from nature are here revived as a dynamic element. Only when thus poetically consecrated does the detail of what is observed seem to be admitted, in order to subserve the narrative, the action in process, the lofty existence of the figures in their sphere above the real.

§ Arrangement of Figures and Pattern: Landscape and Structure

For the figures in Raphael immediately separate themselves from the world of the tangible and, even in early pictures, arrange themselves into the great significant pattern that fills the world of the frame. Only in the great early altarpieces in which he was still under the sway of Perugino has the landscape a life of its own as something accessory. In a predella such as the AVE MARIA it has the effect of being inseparable from the action, with its "when even was now come". The small pictures of the earliest period are already dominated as a whole by space and pattern. In the KNIGHT'S DREAM the rock and the gentle path are conceived as forming, with the figures in front of them, a universe in themselves, in the same way as, in the Northerner Jan van Eyck, in the Ghent altarpiece, the citadels and town-halls, the gorges and distant lands, with knights, judges, hermits and pilgrims!

In the THREE GRACES of the Ancient World, we have the sense of sunny well-being in the nude figures played upon by light and breeze—in the ST MICHAEL, the blazing valley of Hell; the ST GEORGE charges against the monster on the dank ground; the Conestabile *Penserosa* meets us on her first spring walk, with the snowclad hills behind; the Brescia *Salvator* has suddenly appeared from out of the universe. The wedding-group in the *SPOSALIZIO* seems imbued and enveloped by the solemnity of the hour, awaited with such excitement, in the forecourt of the Temple over which a spring day sheds its brightness; and this is not all—the Temple hall, opening to the expanse, breathes in the landscape. Here we have the vitality of the great, the genuine architect, who cannot do otherwise; he can only fit the fashioned stone once again on to and into the ground, the climate even!

§ Raphael an Observer of Man

As he matures, the creator of form gives expression to his sensibility more and more in the region of the human figure. In the Florentine Madonnas we are held by the coherent relationship between the figures of mother and child, arresting us still on the physical plane but now psychically as well; we observe, for instance, how the motherly hand of the *MADONNA DEL GRANDUCA* fits itself to the round form of the *bambino*, and the readiness of the child to flee from this world to the other world of his mother. The tension is here already vital, in his almost perplexed child's look, as of an animal scenting a trail, and her mildness that seems not to be of this earth, but if it is so, then a mystery of heavenly sacredness in the midst of this tangible world!

A similar motive of the child clinging at the feet of his mother, or of the boy free to wander within the limits of a garden—even if not of the *hortus conclusus*—with its peace of greenery and sunshine, far from the city, fills the charming Madonna compositions of the Florentine period—a piece of untouched nature, as if coming from the hand of the Creator, with the simple young mother, to be touched only from above, the mystery of the "*immaculata*" as popularly imagined. If we extract any detail from the background and take it by itself, we are amazed at its beauty as landscape, and at the deep emotion with which here the young composer of the concord of man and nature must have carried his impressions home with him from out-of-doors, in unforgettable freshness. For the prize in this respect, the view of Lake Trasimene, behind the MADONNA IN THE MEADOW (Plate 238), and the flowing course of the river, may contend with the reflection in the stream in the ST CATHERINE, in London (Plate 239), almost as in Adriaen van Ostade or Corot.

RAPHAEL

§ Raphael as Imitator of Nature: Poetry of Space

When the artist turned back from nature to his studio, the essence of his impressions lived on so powerfully here—"diretro agli occhi"—that it guided him still when he was composing; his creation seems to come to life—quietly set in motion and animated by the artist himself, like every one of his figures.

In this sphere, the means he employs to guide the eye along the lines and curves that charm him are a matter of indifference. Whether it is the form of a hill-top with the haze of the valley behind it, or the line of a shoulder set off against background and distance, or a foreshortened hand beyond the knuckles of which one can imagine the whole back of the hand, it is precisely the perceptible delight in sounding these depths in things great and small alike that should be regarded as *his most personal signature*—the droop of an eyelid, the quiver and set of the nostrils, the projection of a lip, a forearm or a hand stretched out towards us, the ease with which, in a portrait, the body draws in and bends forward, the way in which, in the portrait of a lady in green (Plate 49), a necklace with its shadow models the rise and fall of the collar-bone, the little cross above the bosom seems to move as she breathes: "ecce pictor!" The greatest masters of utmost tranquillity do not know how to do better—Lotto, Terborch, Vermeer, Chardin! The vitality of a form rises gently and as if fleetingly out of the depths—mobility, not motion, the last, Praxitelean freedom of Central Italian art—for foreshortening, depth, space, landscape always appear in his picture-area solely for a purpose, never for their own sake; they remain subordinate to the greater vitality, to form, expressive and wholly animated—and whatever in the way of colour incidentally plays around and over the figures serves only to give intensified, concentrated expression. In whatever direction nature has it in her power to allure him, she finds in him her master and her son—her son because he loves her, her master because he knows her.

§ Figures "Possessed"

If the celebrated epitaph speaks of him as *Victor over Nature*, it can only signify that there stand, as it were, at his command, tones from the world of reality which he in his poetic sphere causes to resound in harmony with one another, where figures and objects seem to soar in a stratum above the ground; but everything has previously passed through his experience, through his all-perceiving sensibility. The step of his heroic personages has been conceived out of *his own* innate feeling for the human figure; from the same source, the gravity of any given model is overcome so that mobility is attained above the ordinary, without which there is in art no appearance that is convincing, or capable of beguiling us into the beyond. He traverses, as it were, with his figures the space through which they seem in sentiment to reach out towards a goal; their motion resembles a perpetual gentle impulse to press forward, seen already in the drawing, at Oxford, of a woman walking (Plate 38); in his dramatic figures there is the striving of one possessed, as for instance, in his angels with their violently beating pinions in the HELIODORUS, or in the quiet, flowing movement in the compassionate figure of the young apostle in the TRANSFIGURATION (Plate 268). In his creations, the subconscious world of man comes out, and thus he stands already on the threshold of that realm into which the Belvedere Apollo was able to guide him as his *Musagetes*.

§ Light as Expression: Supersession of the Material

And at this point he rises to complete eminence through the power of light. Having grown up in the school of Piero della Francesca and Melozzo da Forlì, he repeatedly paid his respects to their works when staying in his native place; in Florence he was fortunate in finding a reflection of them in the luminous frescoes of Perugino, in the monastery of the Gesuati outside the Porta Pinti. Soon he pressed on from observations of the effect of sunlight that give solemnity to his *MADONNA DEL BALDACCHINO* and a happy note to his COLONNA MADONNA, to mastery of light; the DELIVERANCE OF PETER owes its effect to the contrast between the unearthly glow and the earthly lights of moon and torch—but the true miraculousness of this night scene derives entirely from the dazzling effect caused by the window below. The actual, common daylight gives its own radiance—as in Rembrandt's *Faust* etching—to the apparition out of the beyond, and the spectral is exalted into the heroic by a touch of nature which makes itself felt in the picture—the drift of storm-clouds with the half-veiled crescent moon above the city of Ancient Rome.

Here too it becomes clear how the material element begins to be done away with—it withdraws more and more into the background in the presence of the conception of the Deliverance of Peter. The scene of the incident, the Mamertine Prison, becomes simply an abstraction, "prison bars" between two pillars of masonry built as if for eternity. The enduring features of great stage drama, as in the mounting of the mystery-plays, and in Shakespeare too, come into play also for this dramatic painter, the essential, and nothing else—and the essential is that which is capable of showing the way to the imagination. The practice of the Dugento was not different from this, in representing the prison of John the Baptist.

§ Selection of Essential Traits in the Portrait

It is just this which makes of the secret Gothicist in Raphael the most profound of interpreters in painting portraits; thus in a task that seems pledged to the closest adherence to nature, it commits him at the very outset to observation in the presence of a given model. Here the passion with which he attacks characteristic traits instead of becoming subservient to the prescribed form, his peculiarly poetical nature, can be most clearly perceived. In actual life, anatomically, one would never find the subject of the portrait in such an attitude—nowhere such a turn of the head to full face on a neck seen three-quarters front; thus already in the Budapest youth, the feverish eyes appear excessively large, the neck three-quarters as high as the face for the sake of this majestic turn. Here for the first time the select quality of this society is revealed in the way it glides swan-like past, taking cognizance of the profane world only as something strange, and as if keeping it at a distance. The admired vitality of his portraits depends, as in his kinsman in temperament, Van der Weyden, on this power of selecting those traits from a condensation of which the upper orders of society formed their ideal figure. Accessories are excluded—at the ultimate height of his attainment, in the portrait of BEAZZANO AND NAVAGERO, landscape seems to be positively suppressed. Where representation was not to be avoided, owing to the requirements of the patron who gave the commission, as in the LEO X WITH THE CARDINALS, the portrait-painter boldly takes in hand the material: the figures appear as the heavy red note of a triple pyramid against the architectural background, which is restrained in colour and also curtailed in volume. It is just here, where one would have expected him to be tied down to real life, that his impulse towards emancipation from the material comes out most clearly.

§ Transfiguration of Colour through Reflections

Finally it may be asserted, even where so much of the colour has been destroyed, that painting retired more and more into the background in favour of light; "in this bright-hued reflection"[1] the painter discovered in his onward progress the new beauty of colour; it was this that first helped him to give a suggestion of a higher existence. We can comprehend how he must have been captivated, in his efforts to attain this, by architecture, with its means of expression. The path to the other world passes from the solid to the imponderable, the airy, the luminous. Play with forms here offered him possibilities of the clearest symbolism; it would hardly have been possible for him any more, as a painter, to accomplish the same purpose. But from the heavenly visions of the Chigi cupola, with its reflections of light on limbs and draperies against the pale blue, we can form some conception of his intentions in the Olympian deities of the Farnesina ceiling; they were to lead their bright, untroubled existence in elemental light.

§ The Popular made Monumental. Pattern as Expression of the *Horror Vacui*

The tapestries with the ACTS OF THE APOSTLES were conceived as similarly "transfigured". The technique of the cartoons made allowance for this with the tone of the paper; the woven tissues were able to supply for this very purpose the enhancement of the broad lights in gold. And this "bright-hued reflection", heightened to sheer light, enhances with its play of radiance the fullness of power in the Apostle figures, raised from the level of mere men of the people which they occupy in the Gospels to the height of sublimity. The setting of the scenes contributes to this,

[1] "Am farbigen Abglanz haben wir das leben" (Goethe, *Faust*, 2nd Part, Act 1).

with their elements of ancient architecture, condensed, and conceived as *heroic*; this setting was perhaps found by Raphael on the stage of the period, and was destined to represent for after times the "*scena tragica*". It was with the nobility of such architecture as background that the company of Raphael's Apostles, true vessels for receiving the Gospel teaching, moved as if floating in the light-enhanced tone of the paintings. A new language, as if in verse!—carried beyond all prose and exalted by rhythm, *reflected light in place of life*. In the TRANSFIGURATION, with the reflected splendour below, and the glorification above, shining with a radiance of its own—as if this light had been born of the storm—the chosen participants are snatched up into a sphere which gives them wings; in the rush of the winds Moses and Elias float as in more than earthly rapture; and the earth-bound disciples on the mount feel themselves suddenly gifted with a mobility above the ordinary, as if caught up in an ecstasy. It is impossible to interpret their gestures otherwise than in the manner of allegory. But just as it has been given to each of these figures individually to express bliss, sorrow, terror, devotion, rapture, or a state of superior exaltation, so it is borne in upon us again and again that their convincing vitality takes effect only as part of a whole; here, in the composition as a whole, the power comes into play that raises each figure above reality—the great, significant, tone-giving pattern in which all is disposed. We have here also a highly expressive dance of lines and forms, in which the individual detail is compelled to take its place—figure and structure, the lines of movement, the landscape with all its details, the mountain, trees, flowers (Plate 240). So that *horror vacui* will have it which dominates this art, just as formerly it gave to Gothic its unsurpassed, compelling power of effect.

Since the time when Perugino revived before the eyes of his great pupil those mediæval features, the S-curve of saintly figures and the profound harmonies of unbroken passages of colour, the true character of Gothic must have sunk deep into Raphael's soul. Only so do we understand what a strong and unforgettable impression must have been made upon him by the language in the LAST SUPPER of Justus van Gent, and why the expressiveness of the back view of the figure, in the Ghent artist and in Roger van der Weyden, was inevitably revived in that dance of expression of which one is conscious in the women in the EXPULSION OF HELIODORUS and in the TRANSFIGURATION. We have here the rhythm that makes of every flight of angels an ascending and descending stream of movement, and that converts pictures of life into winged images, visual perception into interpretation, to end at last in a presentiment of the beyond.

§ Symbolism in Architecture

Raphael's mastery in architecture is hardly to be understood otherwise. It is not merely that in varying social mood he complies with the desires of his patrons, with the purpose of the building in question, and with the just claims of the landscape setting, thus transposing its nature into the symbolism of the building; we also apprehend his achievement in bringing his figures under the hallowing sway of the mysterious creative law of that life imbued with spirit, which he learned to detect in the world of the human body.

§ "The Idea"

It was granted to him to embody in portrait and architecture the "idea", that goal of aspiration for which he strove and which he shared with the choicest of his contemporaries. In these spheres he made himself, compellingly and with supreme mastery, the spokesman and leader alike of a society of men of noble temper.

The examples that, out of his own sensibility, he derived from life and created as ideals for life, were really the "bright-hued reflection" in which he and his class at that time discovered the life which alone they found worth while, an ideal of such alluring power that it could not remain without influence on contemporaries and posterity.

§ Creator of another World

Already in *his* generation men had an obscure and grateful sense of this, his vocation; and they felt that they themselves had a vocation through him. To express this they found the word "divino". Vasari paraphrases it in saying that he feels himself tempted to regard Raphael not as a man like the rest of mankind, but as a "mortal god". Goethe repeatedly calls him "dämonisch", dæmonic, and in the same breath with Mozart. In this definition the impression, not easily to be grasped, takes shape, of a power in a sphere beyond this world, that extends its influence into it and exerts an almost irresistible attraction to itself.

XV

THE LAST FIVE YEARS OF THE PAINTER

R APHAEL had become an architect. This meant that he could not but feel the impulse to reduce to formulas the dominating sentiment of his time.

§ Religious Crisis of the Time

If he thus, as architect no less than as painter, took his place among the great spiritual poets and interpreters of the soul, one thing has to be borne in mind: this decade to which he owed his maturity inevitably chose him and no one else as its witness when it was preparing for the fateful crisis of the Church. A generation with a deep longing for self-communion felt itself called to confession. Consequently it is hardly to be wondered at that it was possible, precisely at the beginning of the conflict of the Faith, for the SISTINE MADONNA and the TRANS-FIGURATION to come into existence, simultaneously with the plans for the dome of St Peter's, whilst beyond the Alps the strain and stress of the time were finding expression in Grünewald's Isenheim altarpiece and Dürer's *ALLERHEILIGENBILD* ("All Saints"). For the same spiritual powers give the impulse to the far-reaching schisms that disrupt and turn upside down the whole of life and yet show the Northern and Southern worlds to be at one in a single point: faith, devotional collectedness, men's capacity for meditation about the origin, purpose and aim of life, were common to all, before material, political, national and commercial forces reduced this higher unity once more to their own limitations and shattered it in fragments.

Times of inward tension and of great vitality of sentiment accentuate in art the phenomenon of man as the repository of the soul and the vehicle of expression, and they have little feeling for the accidents of external nature that are operative around them. Gothic offered to all artists of deep religious feeling an example ever new, not because of its peculiarities from the standpoint of the history of style but rather by its essential characteristic, the isolation of the figure, making it an inescapable guide to the eye searching for aids to the devotional mood. Raphael was already an adherent of Gothic in his training period with Perugino; now in the moment of completest independence, when his forms seem in their power to be furthest removed from Gothic, it proclaims itself again in him with the same principle. Perhaps one ought to call it the state of one possessed rather than Gothic. For Raphael's figures appear to attract to themselves the whole of space for the free gestures in which their inner being discharges itself. Their environment has no longer any dimensions and is entirely subordinate to the figure. All earthly measurements are discarded for the occurrences on Tabor and at the foot of the Mount.

A tendency to other-worldliness is common to all his creative work, painting as well as building—the ascension from the earthly to the supramundane, from the corporeal to light. The *new* style of figure—his latest—arises out of his own depths, stirred by inward storms; and out of the native elements of his descent from a lineage in the Marches there are awakened in him also, more and more, the healthy provincial traits that belong to Piero della Francesca and Melozzo da Forlì. The figures take on that impressive character of the peasant almost simultaneously with the rustication in his buildings. We shall have to look for the prototypes of his Apostles *no longer in the circle of the Cortegiani*—they have their place in a region beyond those social forms whose plastic creator or interpreter Raphael, more than any other artist, had become, for centuries to come, with the higher classes. *The place of these Apostles is to be found among the simple beings to whom they feel themselves to have been sent forth.* What meaning for them could the methods have of the philosophers against whose cleverness the doctrine of the "New Man" surges in vain? It is not the style and bearing of these philosophers, carefully chosen, with beautiful folds of the cloak, to make an outward show, of which these gladsome harbingers have need. These disciples of the "poor in spirit" feel themselves to be "ministers of Christ and stewards of the mysteries of God", and "moreover it is required in stewards, that a man be found faithful". Only "to the least of all saints is this grace given" (*Eph.* iii, 8) and "base things of the world, and things which are despised, hath God chosen, yea, and things which are not".

We have long been in the habit of recognising in the great manifestations of the Renaissance the revival of the man of the Ancient World, in the equal balance of physical and spiritual powers; we have been wont to feel a sense of beatitude in such a confrontation. The deeper the insight permitted us beneath the surface of this movement by its plastic interpreters, when they constrain us to follow their vision of the holy things, the clearer the light that falls on their serious, profound humanity. Their attachment to society explains much; from their loneliness of soul the higher side of their nature can be surmised.

Their intention was not that of idle *literati* for whom it was enough to crown their humanistic work with the glory of a true Ciceronian style. The endeavours of these few truly great ones to attain a fitting human dignity through humanism could only be directed towards a perfection that included heart and soul as well. For them the *New Man* was no longer the revived heathen man of Antiquity; before the eyes of the twenty-seven-year-old Raphael Plato was already wandering upon the scene side by side with the boldly-advancing Aristotle—Plato, with his hand guiding us upward away from earth;—and how symbolically does his uplifted finger point in the same direction which Raphael assigned to the gesture of the Archangel of the *DISPUTA*, and in the mosaic cupola of the Chigi Chapel to the motive powers of Jupiter and Mercury.

But how different is the effect of even Plato's gait compared with that of the Apostles. His "relationship to the world is that of a blest spirit who condescends for a while to lodge in it"; the harbingers of the Gospel walk amongst the people with the irresistible bearing of men who can say of themselves: "we labour night and day, because we would not be chargeable unto any of you." They have no mind—because they have no time—to think about the folds of their cloaks, and stand with firm feet and sturdy back in the midst of their congregation, their "loins girt about with truth, and having on the breastplate of righteousness". For they come as disciples of the Master who has revealed himself to the world in the form of a servant. The "New Man", whom they have put on, asks for nothing according to the wisdom of this world, for "if I yet pleased men, I should not be the servant of Christ".

The story of Salvation had not been told with such inexorable evangelical earnestness on that side of the Alps since the time of Masaccio; only the Evangelists of Piero della Francesca, Melozzo and Signorelli represented with equal power this apostolic race. Was it an accident that the imagination of the Urbino master, in this last span of mature life still remaining to him, harked back to his native sphere among the peasants of the Marches as the source of his creative power?

He felt himself attracted with the best to this new experience of, and pondering over, the Gospels. He gave testimony of it, earlier and more illuminating than they by their word and doctrine, in his renderings of the Apostles and in the figures in his latest works.

Times of such mighty tensions, of such religious and ethical, economic and social upheavals in Society bring a chosen few characters to maturity. These truly significant leaders in the advance into a new age therefore appear to us, as it were, with the features of a head of Janus. What is fruitful out of the past suddenly gains power to tread the path into the unexplored regions of the new age, and over its revolutionary doings there often gleams the inspiring torch of great ideas out of remotely distant times.

The teaching of NICHOLAS OF CUSA and SAVONAROLA had been nothing else but what was now being revived in that circle of the best minds with which Raphael stood in close relationship through chosen friends.

The spirit of Savonarola, cleansed from the dross of his political aberrations and fanaticisms, lived again among these aspiring seekers after purity. "When there were not as yet so many books or so many arguments from reason and discussions, belief grew more speedily than it has grown since." "The clerics—why do they not teach, instead of so many books, the *one* book in which the law and life are contained? The Gospel, O Christians, you should ever carry with you;

I mean however not the book, but the spirit. For if thou hast *not the Spirit of Grace*, even though thou didst carry with thee the whole volume, it would profit thee nothing." (*Predica* II, 208–210.)

By the wish of Julius II or with his consent, Raphael had himself set the preacher of repentance, whose aim was again receiving recognition in its creative, inspiring purity, among the saints and teachers of the Church in the *DISPUTA*. Savonarola's trial was thereby revised *urbi et orbi*, but his spirit revealed itself as an undying force in the life of the soul of this generation, as guide in their conversion and self-communion, when he set true culture in opposition to the mechanical and vainglorious wisdom of the schools. With Savonarola's teaching Raphael remained familiar from his days in Florence on. It was precisely in 1514 that Fra Bartolommeo's visit may have revived anew, for the first time, their common recollections of those hours of spiritual interchange of ideas. The preacher of penitence had become the man of destiny not only in the life of the Frate; he had long had an influence on Raphael, as on all natures with any depth of character, strengthening their creative power by the self-communion he demanded.

In a similar frame of mind the artist was able to assimilate the teachings of NICHOLAS OF CUSA also; he had become acquainted with them from the Florentine Academy gathered round Pico della Mirandola; perhaps when he was at Urbino he had already felt the influence of this far-reaching spirit. The ideas of this teacher of half a century earlier had just been diffused with new vitality in Rome through appearing in print, from 1514 on. The last wish of this world-embracing thinker seems symbolic: he desired with his bones to rest before the shrine of St Peter's Chains in the church of his cardinalate, San Pietro in Vincoli; his heart was to find a place where he was born, at Cues on the Moselle. Thus his words reached all responsive souls on both sides the Alps, North and South, and through the most receptive of all, the artists, they could not fail to have the strongest influence on the multitude of the devout.

"Except by seeking it with the most intense yearning we do not walk on the right path to attain wisdom." " . . . those proud, presumptuous men, wise in their own conceit, acquainted only with their own understanding, regarding themselves in their proud exaltation as equal with the highest—they are all in error. They have barred for themselves the path to wisdom, because they hold nothing to be true but what they have measured with their own understanding. Their vanity is their ruin; they have embraced the Tree of Knowledge, but the Tree of Life they have not attained. But those who have learned that man can obtain wisdom and the everlasting spiritual life only through *the gift of Grace*, these all are blessed—so great is the goodness of God that He hears all who call upon His name."[1]

It was this "holy, fruit-bearing, indispensable wisdom, this precious stone," that Contarini "brought out after the Church had long kept it half forgotten",

---

[1] From *De docta ignorantia*.

as Cardinal Pole writes. It brought all receptive spirits under its spell—as if in a conspiracy. The Church by its secularization had disturbed that immediate relation of man to God; now a silent understanding attracted many in this circle to which friends of Raphael belonged. The art of his last years seemed to have a vocation to reflect this immediate, pure humanity as a new power, in contrast to a humanism that had become artificial.

If it remains true that an artist needs patronage in order to give concrete form to his visions, yet it is not the will of the client alone that helps to release great ideas; the client's demands also seem to be merely prompted by a higher power. In the case of the Medici Pope it may have been a craving for display that caused him to desire these tapestries, shot with threads of gold, after Raphael's designs; but he was called to give the kindling spark for the fuel, garnered up and now ablaze with a far-reaching glow, of these passionate witnesses to the story of Salvation;—Agostino Chigi's astrology and cult of personality, magnificent in its sentiment above his tomb, through the splendour of the mosaic material, was destined to release the sublime conception of the open cupola, with a vision of figures of unearthly power in the light of the other world; and thanks to the lasting quality of the technique, these mosaics were to help in preserving undimmed for centuries the lustre of this vision.

It was the mark of Raphael's last maturity that every wish of his patrons was to be fulfilled far in excess of the specified bounds, to be converted into Raphael's entirely personal gift as a thankoffering and legacy to his own and the coming generation. No artist has ever quitted his labours and the world richer and more blest in giving than the painter of these last five years; he had discovered the style of his consummation.

Since in Raphael's pictures the setting had to give precedence to the figure, his men and women, as embodiments of divine inspirations, absorb with their expression the entire scope of the picture within the frame. Heavenly powers reveal themselves in them; they have taken possession of them, body and spirit, and unfold their deepest nature. Through them the supramundane is brought before our eyes; it descends as a vision, and constrains us to gaze into higher worlds, or through consecrated figures it carries its power amongst men, working miracles.

During the last span of his life every religious theme is lifted for the painter into this hallowed sphere; it was a new profundity of contemplation and experience by virtue of which a man in his maturity here pondered over the things of the other world. With other chosen spirits of the time, united by tacit consent, he felt himself allured or called by an inner compulsion—indeed, bound in duty and by responsibility—to rally devotion by means of his language, that is, by art, so that along this path he could guide it on high.

His thoughts as a painter circled in zones above the world. In painting historical subjects, he adopted from this world just so much in the way of impressions as he needed for these transcendental purposes. Even then it must have happened to him that his eyes were opened for the strong elemental play of atmosphere and water; or was it only then, and at no other time, that his sensitiveness was for the first time strong enough to make itself accessible to the sway of higher powers in those awe-inspiring moments when nature rests from her labours? It may be that his distant views over hill and dale and the calm surface of lakes had disclosed themselves with such lyrical beauty from the very beginning, even in Umbria and Tuscany, as an accompaniment for the tranquil scenes of motherhood or the movements of the Graces; yet it was only now that the dramatic play of the elements came over him, and clouds and breezes are alive with the same breath that quickens the heart-beat of his figures. In the presence of nature he is transformed, in Leonardo's phrase, "like a mirror", into as many colours as appear before him; in his own intensity he apprehends the secrets of nature that are conformable to him. Under their impress also he remains creative, "like a second nature" (Leonardo, *Trattato della Pittura*, 57).

He had long since adopted a more popular rendering of the accustomed theme of the Mother of God; from the character of the women of Rome he adopted, with entire understanding of the simplicity of domestic devotion, the noble bearing of the MADONNA DELLA SEDIA, the MADONNA DELLA TENDA, and finally, of the MADONNA WITH THE FISH, in which an effect of sublimity is attained by the manner in which a breath of the air of heaven blows out a simple curtain— "numine afflatur". Now he might well find it essential, in the altarpiece for the parish church, to set before the eyes of the congregation Grace rather than maternal bliss. So the Virgin with the Child becomes for him a vision, as she is wafted down on clouds into the sphere of the altar, above the mediating saints; after the SISTINE MADONNA we have the MADONNA OF FOLIGNO and that sublime conception, in a large folio drawing at CHATSWORTH (Plate 141), of the Mother who brings the divine Child to the abyss of the world and seems to shudder on the clouds before the depths upon which he is bestowing his blessing. Here we have, unexpectedly revivified, a bit of Renaissance, yet another revival of the Antique mode; the element of life that fills the universal space in and around humanity is concentrated in significant figures; incomprehensible powers that have influence on mankind are seeking to embody themselves in symbols. Michael Angelo knew how to sum up in figures the phases of the day. Ten years before him, Raphael renders, in the ST CECILIA, the revelation of the "inner" voice—a vision, but only for the eyes of those who "look not at the things which are seen, but at the things which are not seen: for the things which are seen are temporal; but the things which are not seen are eternal."

§ The St Cecilia

In the ST CECILIA also (Plate 244), the glory that is above her is not presented to view; her eyes, it is true, look towards the sky but they are not aware of it, for her senses live in supersensual worlds. Earthly music has proved to be temporal; the sound of its instruments as they lie on the ground has died away—even the pipes drop down of the little hand-organ that sounds no more.

The *Legenda Aurea* tells of the vow of the saint on her wedding day: "Cantantibus organis decantabat dicens: fiat cor meum immaculatum. Cum esset symphonia instrumentorum illa in corde suo Domino psallebat." Here, as a reminder of the sublime tones that offered to her as it were a ladder to the other world, the organ hangs down humbly in her hands; in the tradition of the legend nothing transpires as to the saint having played herself. But for Raphael also the tones of the organ formed the transition between this world and the next, from the perishable earthly things on the ground through the zone of the sacred to that sphere in which the heavens open and answer; from the heavy, substantial brown on the ground, through a stratum full of extreme vitality, in the figures and reflections on the brocade of the saints, the violet-pinkish lustre in the drapery of the Magdalen and on the red cloak over a green garment of St Paul, towards the horizon softly permeated with the light on the busts of St John and St Augustine; over all, in the radiance of transfiguration, upon a bank of passing clouds with gleaming sunlit lining, the heavenly choir in a concord of shimmering gold harmonising with the soft pink, yellow and matt green draperies. We pass from the obtrusively earthbound, through the zone of agitation and effort, to the soaring transfiguration of light: it was the calculated poetical effect of an architect who had to think in terms of cupola spaces. The strength of pillars disposed in a circle is concentrated at the place where, above the cornice of the cupola, the daylight streaming in bestows upon the structure in all its power the airiness of light.

Space and pattern had however long been one for the painter of the Stanze. Just as the countenance of Cecilia gazing on high broke the row of bowed heads, filling them again with ecstasy, so the line of back-drawn feet rose, the movement in the girt waists followed in accompaniment, whilst the harmony was repeated by the course of the bank of clouds, the arms of the heavenly singers around their music-books, and the trio of their heads (Plate 278). The circumstance that the loosest of the pipes on the hand-organ lies exactly in a diagonal direction may also be taken as contributing to the architectural cohesion; thus for the painter this presentment of the sublimest of earthly instruments deprived of its power was important enough to be given a decisive position in the picture.

The original commission may have had in mind a *sacra conversazione* in the Bolognese style of Francia and Costa—a row of other saints disposed about a principal figure on a slight eminence. We do not know what determined the lady who gave the order for the picture in her choice of saints. Elena Duglioli dell' Oglio, a lady of Patrician family at Bologna, owned a relic, as a gift from the Legate Alidosi; obeying the promptings of supernatural voices, she felt herself called upon to build a chapel in honour of St Cecilia in San Giovanni at

Monte Oliveto. Her relatives Antonio Pucci and his powerful uncle the Cardinal of SS. Quattro Coronati, Lorenzo Pucci, Grand Datary of Leo X, undertook to superintend the fitting up of the chapel. The Prince of the Church communicated the order to Raphael; whether he himself gave the commission is not certain. For it was the voices from the other world and from her inner being by which the foundress was guided, that were decisive in the choice of saints, not the ineffective voice of the Cardinal, of which we know from Paris de Crassis that it prevented him from conducting High Mass, "quia cantavit ita, ut omnes riserint."

It would be impossible more convincingly to set five individuals thus isolated, as it were, beneath the dome of a spiritual impression produced by unearthly voices, sounding out of the beyond. So many pictures were painted of the *Sacra Conversazione*: seldom indeed does it establish an unexpressed and yet indissoluble understanding, on the deepest and most essential plane, between five saintly figures. The defeated music of humanity has to provide a pedestal, as it were, for these elect souls, whose perceptions seem to live in a remote sphere high above the world. So a surging movement pervades their feet, their waists, their row of heads, which formed originally a circle like a diadem, as of the choicest jewels, for the entranced head of Cecilia. Out of this harmony of lines and rhythms there breaks harshly forth, precisely on the diagonal, the lowered organ—transient, this also, when Heaven opens and bestows on its elect upon earth, with its transfiguring light, the harmony of other worlds. But the inward music of these profoundly responsive souls is not distracted by a single upward look; the eyes of St Cecilia even take no heed of that light. With the resonance of music from above, a great concord seems to fall over them all, and as they each feel themselves to be directed towards their own selves with their individual sensibilities, the mightiest of powers is summoned up in them all—determining their movements upon earth, in each different and in all the same—and that power is love!

Doubtless we have here already ideas deriving from that circle of the Oratorio del Divino Amore that later led to the dedication of the oratory of St Cecilia in the Campo Marzo to the Madonna del Divino Amore.

The reasons that may have existed for the choice of the saints surrounding Cecilia have remained hitherto completely in the dark; and yet their relationships to the person of the lady who gave the commission and to the place of its destination were not unfamiliar to Raphael. At that time nothing of the content of a devotional picture can have been left to the artist; only in Raphael did every commission work itself out as a self-chosen theme, thanks to his free and dominating imagination and to the profound culture by virtue of which he adopted everything and caused it to become part of his own vital experience.

The significance of these saints precisely to the donors of the picture can scarcely be surmised. Only St John (Plate 245) is adequately explained, as patron of the church of San Giovanni in Monte—the "disciple whom Jesus loved" and upon whose countenance seem ever to shine forth the words: "He that dwelleth in love dwelleth in God, and God in him." (I John iv, 16.) He exchanges a glance of tearful radiance with the Doctor of the Church, St Augustine, who with a gesture of embarrassed rapture, as if overcome by the heavenly strains, feels the joy of accord with the beloved Disciple. The emotion in his features reflects the words in his own writings: "Quantum flevi in hymnis et canticis tuis suave sonantis ecclesiæ vocibus commotus acriter"—"How often have I wept at thy hymns of praise and chants, filling thy Church with soft strains, and have been stirred by its voices to the very depths." "Domine, tu nos ad te creasti, inquietum est cor nostrum usque requiescat in te Domine!" He too is a confessor of love: "Lord, Thou has created us for Thyself, and our heart is restless until it rests in Thee." St John seems to come from St Paul; he understands the sublime Apostle—in the book on which the eagle stands there is a sign with the word "Corin"; here, then—from I Corinthians xiii—we have the explanation of the connection between St Paul and the Magdalen. The Apostle mighty in speech acknowledged of himself: "Though I speak with the tongues of men and of angels, and have not charity, I am become as sounding brass, or a tinkling cymbal." There at his feet lies the allegory—but at this point St Mary Magdalen may come in; she that "loved much" goes "in peace". (Luke vii, 36.)

How greatly Raphael's profoundest sense for beauty is misunderstood if this figure is taken as a purely external tribute to womanly charm. From her turning gesture to the very soles of her feet she is encompassed as with a glory by the kindliest words of the Bible.

§ St Paul: Raphael and the Apostle

Reverence for such a poet imposes a closer scrutiny also into one of his favourite creations, this figure of St Paul. Is it enough to explain it from the allegory mentioned above? Is there nothing further in the melody-flooded sphere of this picture that arrests him to whom the visible is nothing—nothing more than he can behold at his feet? It is to him precisely that Raphael acknowledged himself to be indebted, by him attracted. In the early CORONATION OF THE VIRGIN it is his dark head alone, as he looks into the blossom-filled tomb, that evinces a profound, devout emotion. In the DISPUTA, although the Prince of the Apostles sits on a throne to the right, at the end of the heavenly circle, it has been suggested that the honour of his name belongs to the newly-converted in front of the youths surging forward on the left of the altar; and truly, the hesitant cry and the emotion of this man in his maturity, consciously undergoing an inner conversion, bear witness that the painter of the figure was no stranger to the character of the great preacher of Conversion. Raphael at that time lived with the words of St Paul. When, in the course of his work on the DISPUTA, the pages of his sketchbook were being filled with ideas for the figures, a hasty sketch was made for St Paul with his sword, upon clouds, on the back of the great study of Adam, in the Uffizi; his hand shields his eyes, as if blinded by a more than earthly radiance (*R. Z.* VI, 294). And then, on a drawing, at Oxford, for the *DISPUTA*, line after line is set down for a sonnet (Plate 89, *R. Z.* VI, 278, 279, 280); out of an overflowing sense of bliss, occasioned by an incident by night which must remain for the world in obscurity, Raphael discovers that his tongue is bound, in a sudden kinship with the Apostle who, caught up into Paradise, "non podde dir d'arcana dei"—"cannot bear witness to the enrapturing wonders that he has seen and to the unspeakable words that may not be spoken."

And now, as the Apostle stands beside Cecilia, these ineffable hymns are re-echoed from above, and the hand of the Apostle is laid like a clamp upon his chin, checking every word, in that state of frustration and emotion that makes us so mysteriously familiar with this mighty man. His fingers merely play about the pommel of his menacing sword; more important for him seem to be the letters, the Epistles they are clutching. Thus Raphael conceived the character of this Roman Knight—as a warrior thrown out of his course, he was relentlessly assailed by the convulsion that had converted him—a perpetual combatant; here and perhaps also in the SACRIFICE AT LYSTRA, he appears on the scene for the last time in such a noble form; in him Raphael embodied his ideal for society, the "*cortegiano*" perfect in his power, in an equilibrium of essence and semblance. The lofty bearing of his inner being is shown and intensified with dignity in outward appearance; in the cast of his cloak, in his slow, serious pace, even more when he is stirred to the very depths, it is always the same. Yet when this manly dignity vibrates through and through with a sudden upwelling of emotion, then its human impressiveness becomes irresistible for anyone who is allowed to witness it, through the unexpected violence of the onset. Only the greatest dramatists have been happy in giving such a human radiance to the heroic without impairing its majesty. From Odysseus, who awakes in his home but does not recognise his native country, from Peter weeping after the cock crew thrice, to Coriolanus—"I melt, and am not of stronger earth than others" —to Sarastro's resignation in the presence of Pamina—"Thou lov'st another dearly"—or to the Count's "Contessa perdoni", "O Countess, pardon"— finally to Goethe's "Das strenge Herz es fühlt sich mild und weich"—"The doughty heart, it tender feels and kind"—a marvellous series; in all, a tragic irony is alive, and we are stirred every time by the spectacle of proud dignity melting into simple human grief. Thus by the moving power of the back view of this figure, who has with sweeping cloak just entered the circle of the elect, the worshipper is, as it were, carried along with it into the region of other-worldly happenings—seized, with St Paul, by a sense of the vanity of all action "that has not charity"; and a bridge is thrown across to link him with her who "loved much" and therefore, her sins forgiven, may enter in before many. The painter gave her the earthly features of the *VELATA*, in whose portrait at Florence he had just made avowal of the bliss conferred on his soul by a simple and rich child of the people. In the SISTINE MADONNA he exalted her character to that of "the pattern of motherhood, queen of women", presenting her to the world and future generations, and here as the Magdalen her beauty, now mature, is allowed to appear in the blessedness and freedom of innocence renewed.

§ The personal Element

How much personal experience underlies for the painter this sublime spiritual poetry. From the great Apostle whose mighty, speechless trance in an hour of blessedness never before experienced became for him an allegory, he passes to the humble, precious flower beside the path of Him on whom much love was bestowed, that blossom in whose cup a last secret of the creation of motherliness unlocked itself to him, to the disciple whom Jesus loved, and to the enquiring interpreter of divine revelations who found, to express his own self-surrender, the words: "Lord, Thou hast created us for Thyself." Upon this group Cecilia has called down by her music the participation of the higher world, and a glory of transfiguring light combines with the glory of their strains to build upon the pillars of faith the vault of a true "oratory of the Divine Love"; no work of devotion was ever more profound, more personal and of more universal validity in its conception. What a creator, out of whose own life such soaring religious poetry could arise!

§ Colour

The architect-painter could be relied upon sooner or later to pass from the tenderness of the SISTINE MADONNA to this concord of the group of saints in a harmony of colour. It is possible that St Cecilia occupied the middle place in the accord of gold, black and reddish flesh-colour; now that her face has lost its spontaneous foreshortening in false reflections on eyes, nose, chin and neck, and her drapery, in which the tunic below still has a vibrant resonance, no longer appears to be set in motion by her limbs, as it still is in Calvaert's feeble but unselfconscious copy at Dresden, the expression in the painting is hidden beneath thick layers of varnish and pigment. The red and green of the St Paul have been completely renewed in accordance with the customary, oily, academic practice; only in his head with its growth of hair boldly sweeping round it, and in the figure of the Magdalen, has anything been preserved that gives a notion of Raphael's own brush-strokes; they are clearest where the veil, with the bluish white of its folds, shot through with gold threads, leads up to the flesh tones, or comes as a transition to the pinkish violet of the dress and the grey of the cloak, from which, in its present state, the blue reflection on the metallic folds of the sleeve stands out so as to destroy the harmony. For this picture must have had an arresting effect by its harmony and with the resonance of its colouring. The original frame is still preserved at San Giovanni in Monte; Formigini treated it as a delicate, flat relief, as befitted the mature style, still architectural, of the composition. Spatial and plastic qualities certainly did not appear so obtrusive, when emphasised by colour for its own sake; the precious work, for which even in this condition there has been a chorus of commendatory and explanatory opinion from Goethe to Carl Justi[1] and Burckhardt, fell a victim to the false worship of Raphael. It may have been restored already at an early date in the manner of Domenichino; the years of its sojourn in the Musée Napoléon, with its transfer from wood on to canvas, seem to have sealed its fate as a painting. It lost that harmony without which a picture cannot have been conceived, least of all this one, in which the mind of Raphael showed itself capable of giving to such figures unity through equality of power.

§ The Tapestries

It was this power that broke down other barriers for his imagination. Not without deep emotion must he at that time have apprehended the sense of the Gospel that came as a message to the poor. When themes were set him for the tapestries taken from the *Acts of the Apostles*, he was seized by the intense seriousness of inner self-communion that was preparing to gain a sway over him, as over other men of the time who were discovering their souls anew; this seriousness caused him to experience the text of the narrative with simple emotion and passionate sympathy. That which in this story was being spread abroad ever afresh by the word of God throughout the world and had once proclaimed to a wearied culture its birthright, could have no use, as its bearers, for heroes like the *cortegiani*, in whose type society found a basis of agreement. Here it was a question of struggle and revolutionary change through powers that rose fresh, elemental even, out of unexhausted depths. The text for the elucidation of which he felt himself called by the seriousness of his mood, made of him the most creative illustrator of the Bible.

For Raphael as a painter the commission for the tapestry cartoons involved more in the way of superficial obligations than he may otherwise have been accustomed to undertake in his pictures.

Not only was the format tremendous, of these oblong rectangles; Raphael had also to take into account that his picture in another technique had to be effective when seen at a distance. And this technique of weaving required clear and simple forms; fine details would inevitably be lost in it. In the transposing of the effect, the clearer and broader the surfaces, and the less complicated the presentation of the pictorial elements, the greater the certainty of attaining his forms. What the sublime contents—the history of the Apostles—demanded must be related with the fewest possible figures, shown as large as possible and visible without any obstruction. In the low situation in which the tapestries were to hang, far from the inlet of light on the other wall and with a dazzling row of windows above them, the effect had to be obtained in bright colours,

[1] Justi, *Zeitschrift für christliche Kunst*, XVII, p. 138.

even by means of the reflections thrown back by the wealth of gold that had to be introduced for the high lights; this use of gold was an idea that did not simply fall in with the Pope's craving for magnificence, but would also enable this tapestry cycle to assert itself. The series was indeed intended to give from far below a confirming answer, with the last echoes of the story of Salvation, to the pictures of the Creation, Paradise Lost, and the prophecies of the Messiah, on the ceiling. Here the problems involved for Raphael in this work were strained to the utmost. In the space dominated by the heroic style of Michael Angelo to the exclusion in oblivion of all other masters, Raphael had to measure his strength with the dæmonic energy of such a rival. His figures must assert themselves against the aristocratic, rustic strain of the Tuscan; here there was no question of a striking effect in the "Buonarotti *maniera*". But Raphael found the answer to all these requirements in the simplicity of the Gospel and in the force of the new Confession; for this he was doubly prepared in advance, for whilst he had drawn nearer to that group of men of the Oratorio del Divino Amore who were living out anew, with earnest zeal, the problems of the Faith, there could be no lack of self-communion in the depths of his own being. The mind now grown to manhood became conscious of all the sources of strength most intimately his own that came to him from his home *in the Marches*; a powerful type of figures that Piero della Francesca, Melozzo and Signorelli had already consecrated to be the exponents of the dæmonic mode of existence of the saints, arose once more, in Raphael's mind, for these new, unaccustomed dimensions. How much the scale is of consequence when chosen for his purposes by this fashioner of poetic conceptions is mostly left out of consideration, as also the rare, inspiring spectacle of forms such as these, filled with sublime vitality.

In Leonardo's LAST SUPPER the eye is still arrested, in spite of the harm inflicted by centuries of damage, by the mere exceptional dimensions of the figures. Out of the dim haze of colours a gigantic race of majestic men takes hold of our very souls by the unmatched energy of their impressiveness in common and individually. The lines of the composition carry us away into this valiant band of table companions. The same creative mastery, with more than life-size figures—vessels filled with an upwelling ferment—was repeated on Michael Angelo's ceiling. Now in the tapestries, the final instalment of the decoration of the Sistine Chapel, Raphael takes his place as the third of these chosen poets of the heroic. It is permissible to speak of the large dimensions; they were chosen by him because he knew he would be able to give to the figures of more than ordinary stature that intense, breathing vitality which is their due as vehicles of the story of Salvation.

As a painter he was here under restrictions, and yet singularly well equipped for this task. The rich gold of the high lights in gleaming threads permeates figures, groups, landscape and architecture. The compositions are keyed, as regards colour, to these reflections playing over the strongly-modelled figures.

In many passages this superb effect is still displayed in the series of tapestries in the Vatican, also in the Berlin series since they were cleaned. The scale of colours originally intended can be seen most clearly on the still unfaded reverse side of the weavings; the effect was that of the most costly Burgundian hangings. If the harsh juxtaposition of the colours is thought of as being broken up by the middle tones interwoven in between, if the emerald green, which now that the yellow has been lost appears as a heavy blue, is reinstated and the portions that now look dull and dirty are heightened with the once golden reflections, it suddenly becomes clear how these woven pictures were entirely keyed to the dominance of their reflections and to their harmony with their light environment, the stone of the architectural setting, the yellowish ground, and the delicate colours of the landscape, to die away at last in the pure monochrome gold-relief style of the lower borders. Raphael had already employed this subordination of local colouring to the dominating brilliance of high lights in his conception of the painted velaria on the Heliodorus ceiling; the mosaics of the Chigi Chapel with the durable material of their technique have handed down to us a similarly calculated colour effect, and the TRANSFIGURATION was originally alive with the harmony of the local colours dominated by reflections, below, with the obvious source of light from above, before they disappeared beneath the clumsy over-paintings of pupils and restorers.

In this case also the commission with its peculiar demands engaged in the artist powers that had insistently sought for expression even whilst he was in the stage of development. How much more must his matured dramatic power have become concentrated within the technical limitations of this work; the metre of verse was, as it were, prescribed for him—the narrative, setting forth the ACTS OF THE APOSTLES, had to run like a frieze in several sections round the lower part of the walls of the chapel; or the economy of means and his familiarity with architectural discipline induced him to acknowledge, not reluctantly but of his own accord, the restrictions imposed by the laws of weaving technique; and in this submissiveness he had his reward. He came to be the profoundest of all biblical narrators. The true biblical note had not been struck in this manner since the time of Giotto and Masaccio, nor indeed since the mosaicists, thoroughly familiar to him, of the earliest Christian art that was still not far removed from the times of the Evangelists. Out of inexhaustible sources—the atmosphere of the time, the development of art, his own self-mastery, the task set before him, the technique, and lastly the place—an elemental force seems here to have sprung into being of which the effects belong to what is dæmonic and inexplicable.

The groups in the tapestries are arranged as if in friezes; the earthly comings and goings of the Apostles find eloquent expression in the series of heads, always similar, that is everywhere poised almost at the level of two-thirds of the height of the picture-space, just as was the case at an earlier period with the earthbound character of the philosophers in the SCHOOL OF ATHENS. Only where the other-worldly breaks in upon worldly happenings is it otherwise; in the CON-VERSION OF ST PAUL, the figure of Christ forms the apex of the groups—and St Paul, in the sublime office of witness to the Unknown God, dominates the congregation from the height of the steps, standing entirely alone before an alien world.

It is not merely the great cycle of the doctrine of Salvation represented by the entire Sistine Chapel that has its conclusion in this broadly unfolding pedestal-frieze; its author comes to an understanding with the thinker who devised the first chapter, on the ceiling above, with regard to the style in which such mighty themes should be brought near to the faithful, thereby reducing their Quattrocento forerunners on the walls to the role of unimaginative, colour-loving miniaturists.

Contemporaries, it is true, talked only of the splendour of the weaving, with its gleaming gold, and whispered about the fabulous sums spent upon it by the Pope. But in such expressions of amazement we still hear across the centuries something of a shudder at the unaccustomed, the unprecedented. The cost caused an age with its senses wide awake to be clearly aware, without being able to see it in any other light, of the power that was strong enough to put such resources in motion. Those belonging to Court circles, and the next following generation, were trivial-minded enough to express this in figures; but there remained nevertheless an incomprehensible element, as with everything new and unexpected. Even figures like this weave themselves into the radiant diadem of the great dæmonic master, the "divino".

For us, who survey all that has been developing for centuries out of the style of these biblical narratives, from the Mannerists and Eclectics to Rubens, Poussin, Prud'hon, the Nazarenes, Couture, Feuerbach, and the mechanised ecclesiastical painting of recent times, for us, to whom Raphael seems to be a link in this chain, it is difficult to feel conscious of that *originality*, belonging to what is seen for *the first and only time*, which must have thrilled his contemporaries.

In the tone of these narratives he represented to them their own feelings, which had not yet taken shape in themselves. These Bible illustrations throw a light, in the true sense of the word, upon the Holy Scriptures, on persons and occurrences, the significance of which for the Faith they bring out again on a gigantic scale. They appear full of the Holy Spirit, of that spirit which at that time made the best men of a shaken world, in things of the Faith, serious and inexorable even.

This inexorableness here contributed to the formation of the style; there is nothing that could assert itself beside such embodiments of such a faith—land-scape, space, seem to be there only to accompany, with a few notes struck here and there, the sublime recitative of their voices. Such is the theme unfolded through the picture-space, words and gestures inseparable and indispensable.

That the cartoons, the originals by the artist himself, were given up by the Pope without a thought, can well be explained: what for us, as the share in which Raphael's own hand participated, is the most precious part of all, was for his contemporaries put in the shade by the costliness of the materials used in the execution. The copy was regarded only as an intermediate stage; the thing aimed at, for Raphael also, was the finished picture, in the place for which it was destined, in the colours and splendour for which it was designed, in the grand combined harmony he intended it to prodúce. It is conceivable that our admiration for the copies on paper, as contrasted with what he had before his mind, would have surprised the artist himself, with his clear consciousness of what he had in view.

For this reason we may yet consult the cartoons, as relics of infinite value, as to his intentions in his heart of hearts. Their answer however is difficult to comprehend; by their condition we conjecture what they have suffered in the weavers' workshops, where for centuries they must have served repeatedly as copies. We know that a hundred years later Rubens found them, sadly neglected, at Brussels and brought them to England for Charles I. They were punctured, cut in strips, and used afresh again and again, in English workshops also, and carried about from palace to palace. We can understand that, having been mounted on canvas and restored under William III, they exhibit almost more obvious traces of these wanderings in the paths of affliction than of their original production. The false conception of Raphael of the academic world through the centuries has been at work on them; not everything can be traced to the share in them of pupils—Giulio Romano and above all, Penni—as handed down by Vasari, when we are conscious of disconcerting crudities in the forms and colouring at which only those feel no surprise who do not regard the "master of line" as a painter.

The weavings diverge in several places from the colours of the cartoons. If these were intended to serve as copies, this means that as good as nothing was left to the weavers. Either the tapestries or the originals have changed. If the tapestries—*the* set, in the Vatican, and also the Berlin series—often have an unharmonious effect, the fault lies with the dullness spread over the surface by the gold that in large portions has turned black where it ought rather to stand out as a gleam on the high lights. Originally the colours were keyed in light tones to these reflections; where a heavy blue comes next in the tapestries to red, the yellow of the original green threads has for the most part faded, as often in textiles of this period. Green, yellow, gold, red, was the dominant scale, leading to the sand-colour of the ground. The technique of the cartoons, size-pigment on paper, with brown underwashes, originally came fairly near to this effect which was aimed at in the weaving technique; this is still shown in a well-preserved piece such as that with Ananias thrown to the ground. We find in the cartoons, besides signs of the lack of colour-sensitiveness of academic times,

impossible things that have been taken for insensitive over-painting. In the
MIRACULOUS DRAUGHT OF FISHES, the white cloak of Christ has now a red
reflection in the water, and it is shown red in the tapestries in Rome and Berlin.
The madder, in the drapery, has with the passage of time been consumed by the
white admixture. But to what lengths of audacity must the restorers have gone
to whom undoubtedly must be attributed all the crudities in the expressions and
muscles, the vulgar assertiveness of the added high lights.

Here also we must attempt a reconstruction; it remains always more worth
while to seek out the *great* masters instead of the *little* masters, in the manner of
the last generations. For over these mighty tributes to the Book of Books there
ruled supreme a star that in passing hence compelled all lesser lights to follow in
its track. Here, however large the share that Raphael may have left to his
workshop, it was *he* who provided the plan of the designs; but nothing so convincing could ever have resulted from collaboration if everything from start to
finish had not been controlled by *his* will.

Nor does Vasari, when he mentions Giulio Romano and Penni, teach us
anything as to the process of production of these cartoons. We possess too little
in the way of preliminary studies; the solitary study unquestionably by Raphael's
own hand shows the Apostle Paul in the SACRIFICE AT LYSTRA—the "wet"
drapery in silverpoint over a bold drawing of the nude, vigorously heightened
with white body colour on the head and on the light side. This is what Raphael's
own designs looked like, which it remained for his assistants to enlarge and
translate. Nevertheless, the deviations therefrom in the cartoon seem like
additions, not deletions. The flat surfaces are more in conformity with the
requirements of weaving technique, the edges and lights with those of the gold
heightening, on the green sleeve and the red cloak of St Paul. On closer
inspection of the cartoons we are conscious everywhere of these transformations
under the eyes, under the hands even, of the designer and conceiver of the compositions.

In the PUNISHMENT OF ANANIAS the fallen figure seems to be still completely
preserved as from the hand of the great fresco-painter and water-colour
draughtsman. The head (Plate 253) provides the clearest example of a design
in charcoal and a wash-like under-painting in tones of brown; throughout we
have a paper style—slight, with the ground left almost in reserve, on the brow
with its charcoal strokes, on the nose, on the upper lip; the original hand-strokes
have remained likewise on the foreshortened left calf and foot, and in the
drapery on the shoulder, in white and shaded raspberry red. The figure of
St John by the balustrade to the left above, still shows *pentimenti* in charcoal on
the edge of the cloak; the light yellowish drapery is laid on over shading in
sepia-tone. The Apostle with eyes upcast presents in tempera colour the same
features as the Oxford red-chalk study for the ALMIGHTY of the Chigi Chapel
(Plate 162).

RAPHAEL

The rare sheets of studies that have been preserved give scanty, but all the more welcome, information, and more important too, as early ideas for the MIRACULOUS DRAUGHT, with the mothers on the shore and the two boats in the distance, are attributable to pupils, and the coarse, mundane Giulio Romano. They indicate intermediate stages. It seems that the master allowed the pupils to carry through a design, for a time independently, until later, at a given moment in the intervals of other work of his own, he himself took a hand, with "a cheering but forcible word", gathering together the scattered ideas that were trailing on earth and catching them up to fit them for his purpose.

The Windsor drawing for the "FEED MY LAMBS" (Plate 247), introduces us to just such a dramatic moment. The Louvre possesses a study of a youth half in studio-costume, with left arm raised, a fragment of a group of Christ and the Apostles (Plate 270). We know this from the counterprint at Windsor, which shows the entire group of Apostles. The figure in the Louvre drawing is sketched as a nude with the stylus; the intensified white lines of the preliminary drawing can still be recognised throughout through the shading of the red crayon; they are to be found precisely reproduced on the counter-proof at Windsor. In the other figures also we can recognise these colourless outlines of the nudes throughout. It is possible that the hastily sketched indications of the nude figures are the work of Raphael himself; in the heads there is much that gives the impression of tedious studio work from the model, as if uninventive hands had been at work on the drawing. Even in the counter-print the lack of rhythmic energy is traceable in expression and attitude—in the central group there is a sudden intrusion of red chalk. Among the impressed, incorporeal, non-plastic coatings, in the middle figure that divides the group, there is conspicuous a pronounced, broad stroke with an effect of plastic modelling, that gives it a spatial setting, atmosphere and life; the figure, tense and full of vital energy through the accentuations in the hair and face, and the turgid sweep of the contour, especially in the hand, thrusts itself to the fore among the phlegmatic, trailing and standing figures around it.

One has here the impression of an assemblage of nudes slavishly following the model and of feebly-set heads superimposed upon a first hasty sketch of the group by the master himself with the stylus. From the sketch, which is in the same direction as the cartoon, a proof had to be taken to show its effect when reversed in the tapestry. The resultant feeble copy is even more uninteresting; then the master takes it in hand, and with two or three strokes makes, of the figure looking round, the pivot of the group; the mechanically off-printed repetition of a lost study becomes an original drawing full of plastic creativeness and rhythmic movement. Now the motive of the arm pointing towards heaven—the "Verily I say unto", is converted into the gentler "Feed my sheep", and the studio, with the course thus prescribed for it to follow, may have carried out, in the main, the execution. Then the master again intervenes, in order to set

256

the rhythm of the draperies and to leave no uncertainty as to the sublime spirit in the figure of the Redeemer and, again, the dæmonic force of the Paul-like central figure with his glow of zeal for the flock. So from beginning to end this creative process kept on its course. It is impossible to exaggerate the artist's inward sense of responsibility towards this work, for all his busy activities. It was not, merely from a religious point of view, his confession of faith; it signified for him as man and architect in full maturity the essence of spacebound, grand, monumental hieroglyphics, in the sublime ancient sense; this revival also became for him part of a newly understood renaissance.

As an immediate result, we have in this "FEED MY LAMBS" a work displaying a quite new boldness (Plates 246, 248, 249). Beside the Sea of Gennesaret the Risen Lord has awaited the Disciples at the landing-place, as they come from their fruitless fishing (*John* xxi, 4). "But when the morning was now come, Jesus stood on the shore; but the disciples knew not that it was Jesus." But after they had at his bidding cast their net once again and had taken the great draught of fishes, John speaks to Peter: "It is the Lord ... So when they had dined, Jesus saith unto Simon Peter, Simon, son of Jonas, lovest thou me more than these? He saith unto him, Yea, Lord; thou knowest that I love thee." Jesus says to him: "Feed my lambs", and a second and third time he says to him: "Feed my sheep." ... But Peter turned and saw following him the disciple whom Jesus loved. . . . When Peter saw him, he said to Jesus: "Lord, and what shall this man do? Jesus saith unto him: If I will that he tarry till I come, what is that to thee? Follow thou me." Whilst Peter fervently embraces his new office, as guardian of the keys and shepherd of the flock before the others, the overflowing soul of John will scarcely allow his bodily self to hold back, and it is just dawning on the grey-haired Andrew that it is the Lord who is appearing to them and is already departing again; two others strive to approach, irresolute. Then an especially fiery disciple—he would be a worthy representation of St Paul—takes up the leadership of those that are holding back, who are slow of heart to believe. His passionate nature resents their lukewarmness, or is his soul in that state of perpetual glow that gives at every moment to head and bearing the expression of one possessed, *terribiltà*? His backward turn looks like that of a leader who is disillusioned as to his followers—we can hardly fail to recognise that the feet of these five cleave to the ground; slow of heart to believe, in *their* attitude there is no exaltation. They whisper among themselves—there may be an allusion to the preference given in the command to John (*John* xxi, 22, 23). But notice how, in spite of this lack of unanimous acclaim, this whole throng is linked to earth and one to another, a group which, even if not without dignity in detail, is almost like the lengthy, beautifully articulated building of a church by the side of which, but separated from it, rises the campanile. And here, with an entirely novel daring, a single figure at one end of the beam holds the entire remaining mass in equilibrium: it is the scene of Masaccio's TRIBUTE-MONEY turned about through a quarter of a circle. But in this transformation, for Central Italy, the critical change consists, for the customary architectural symmetry. It had begun already in the audacious diagonals of colour in the ATTILA; here it becomes the element that gives dramatic effect: the whirl and simmering of emotion express the tension of the eleven towards the chief figure who passes by, a guest from the other world. They are all in profile, in planes one beside and in front of another, like figures in a relief; only he is revealed, completely disengaged—and as he stretches out his arms in gentle and yet unhesitating command, he resembles a temple seen in foreshortening, built into the landscape, shaping itself to it and with it. The range of hills that dies away into the plain towards the disciples seems to rise only for him. And this decides the question—the composition was conceived in the direction of the tapestry, running from left to right. It begins hesitatingly and yet already with a trend towards the right, then surges in a wave of passion, and ends with the last words of Christ, "Feed my sheep—follow thou me!"

There, before a train of simple, almost coarse men of the people he stands, an appearance of compelling perfection, heroic in figure and bearing and yet, as he turns out of his course to come upon the scene, with a dispassionate and distant look which defies every comparison with what is earthly. Thus what Raphael divined as their aspiration in the models who sat for his portraits may have found in this figure its consummation—the Archimedean point. The Risen Christ appears as if he had attained this point from whence he sets the universe in motion. By this scene Raphael illustrates profoundly and, for all sublime art, significantly, the words of Savonarola: "So long as Our Redeemer still lived together with his Apostles, they in their subjection to the senses loved what was visible in him too much to allow of their rising to his spiritual stature. It was necessary for him to disappear into Heaven, so that their spirits might soar up to him above the world of the senses."

The iconography of this group of Disciples has its enigmatic aspects. Raphael knows the Bible narrative so accurately, syllable by syllable, that he can give it visible form out of his own inner experience of it. In this place however there is mention only of seven disciples to whom Jesus revealed himself—Peter, Thomas, Nathanael of Cana, the sons of Zebedee, John and James the Elder, and two other disciples. That is to say, the group extends as far as the figure standing in amazement; the four last remain unexplained. Peter and John are recognisable with certainty; the doubter Thomas may perhaps be identified in the seventh. Where everything is so profoundly characterised nothing can be regarded as arbitrary; the curiosity is excited all the more when such significant figures as that with curly hair (Plate 252) and the one in shadow turning as if to go away remain unexplained; for Judas is excluded by the sequence of time, although in Perugino, in the DELIVERY OF THE KEYS, he also appears recognisable by his look and the money-bag. Possibly this figure would be the somewhat envious-toned spokesman of the group amongst whom the saying went forth about John: "This disciple should not die."

The disciple turning away in wrath is filled with indignation, even to the eyes and hair; more than life-size, he displays in every way an uncanny power of expression that would be worthy of a Paul. It is possible that here Raphael may have derived his inspiration from the Antique, direct from the paintings and mosaics of the first apostolic centuries; here if anywhere it breaks through, with truly happy effect.

How much the landscape with its accompanying lines contributes to give the figures their role and tone! In the tapestry of the MIRACULOUS DRAUGHT OF FISHES (Plates 250, 262) the expanse of water and the shore that are incidental to the narrative are enhanced as a foil for the highly expressive gestures of the human figures, through the largeness of surfaces and forms at once a monumental medium and purest tapestry style. This chosen group has suffered itself to drift far away from the other shore; from afar is wafted over the waters the Spirit who illumines the occupants of the two boats (*Luke* v, 4): "Now when he had left speaking, he said unto Simon, Launch out into the deep, and let down your nets for a draught. And Simon answering said unto him, Master, we have toiled all the night, and have taken nothing: nevertheless at thy word I will let down the net. And when they had this done, they inclosed a great multitude of fishes: and their net brake. And they beckoned unto their partners, which were in the other ship, that they should come and help them. And they came, and filled both the ships, so that they began to sink. When Peter saw it, he fell down at Jesus' knees, saying, Depart from me; for I am a sinful man, O Lord. For he was astonished, and all that were with him, at the draught of the fishes which they had taken: And so also was James, and John, the sons of Zebedee, which were partners with Simon. And Jesus said unto Simon, Fear not; from henceforth thou shalt catch men."

Between the two lines of shore the surface of the water gently gleams, serving as a foil to the highly significant, bold pattern of the figures. The meaning can be read only in the direction of the tapestry, from left to right: all the bodily toil and all the eagerness of the series of figures is directed to the drawing of the net by the steersman, who has to exert himself to keep a straight course for the young fishermen, the sons of Zebedee; they toil hard, but in that rare transfiguration of the commonplace which in the physical sphere indicates something heroic; yet already we perceive in the younger of the two—it is John—that he is listening, his attention is held by the other boat. There the old fisherman—Andrew—comes on the scene, towering up, with the carriage and poise that come of dealings with the unstable element, overcome, carried away by the miracle of the overflowing catch that has brought his brother Simon Peter to his knees. Impulsively Peter's hands and voice are lifted up out of the depths of his contrition towards the blessing Redeemer: "Depart from me; for I am a sinful man, O Lord." And gently and commandingly the hand beckons, of him to whom nothing is impossible and who therefore can make his throne of the stern of this boat: "Fear not: from henceforth thou shalt catch men."

Along heads and shoulders the line runs, as in a tremendous chain of mountains, rising with an irresistible curve in the Andrew, to descend boldly and to end in a gentle rise—the eternal law of the monumental. The striking and the enduring, so often employed as externals, are here endowed with soul and spirit in the service of the narrator, or rather of the dramatist. And this dramatist was a painter who dictated his rules to weavers also. How we feel our attention held by the turning attitude of John, through the definition given to the shape of his head by the detail of the foreshortened back and to this in turn by the red cloak! How arresting the eloquent hands of Andrew, one in half light against shadow, the other dark against the surface of the water—the speaking silhouette of Peter, and the holy, hovering calm in the figure with which the line dies away, counterpoised against the strenuous steersman with whom the row of figures begins on the opposite side. It is as if the birds were specially intended by their flight to direct the eye away from the empty spaces above to this most tranquil among the figures. What is here taking place had its peculiar significance precisely in the palace chapel of the Pope; it was he who wore the fisherman's ring—and *his* was the dominion over heaven, earth and the depths that are here shown.

It was at this time especially that Raphael's eyes were opened to the play of the elements. At the same time the FINDING OF MOSES, in the Loggie, came into existence, with its scene of fishing in the idyllic evening light; in the "*QUOS EGO*", Neptune rides on, upon waves lashed to fury, against the rebel winds, in a plastic framing like that of the tapestry compositions, and in the GALATEA experience of the watery element is almost wholly concentrated in the delicate seagreen around the deities conceived as embodiments of primeval force.

Here in the tapestry the effect of the ground is obtained with the matt blue that had become almost conventional for water; probably the yellow has faded out of the originally green thread. For we have continually to take into account such changes of colour when we seek to picture to ourselves the old colour harmonies. At every point this great narrative poem needs to be read as if out of different manuscripts. The cartoon of the MIRACULOUS DRAUGHT OF FISHES has been so senselessly over-painted in many places that, for example, the drapery of Christ has become white whilst its reflection in the water still remains reddish, as the tapestries show it. The expression of the figures, especially in the principal group, appears in the Vatican tapestry more refined than in the Berlin example, even than in the cartoon itself. The first version, for the Pope, obviously kept more carefully to the design of Raphael; it was indeed woven under the responsible care of his pupil and intimate, Thomas Vincidor. The cartoon has in the meantime suffered many injuries, particularly in the faces through clumsy handling. As regards both its material and spirit it was treated in a rather arbitrary manner in Brussels. Good as the Berlin version may be—it was probably woven for Henry VIII of England—touches can be found here already that are foreign to the original design. Below the figure of Christ a great, rugged oak-branch with withered leaves of beautiful colour rises up, a good example of weaver's work, but the Vatican tapestry here follows the entirely Raphaelesque recipe—scattered clusters of flowers and grass, dandelions, coltsfoot and reed sparingly distributed, so as to make a telling pattern.

But above all such questions, which nevertheless were intended again and again to lead on from small details to the great whole, the guiding conception in all these telling patterns inscribed within an identical format stands forth every time triumphantly dominant; indeed, from time to time the artist seems to pounce upon what is essential in the narrative and fixes it in a compelling formula before the eye.

The DEATH OF ANANIAS (Plates 241, 251) has been treated with something of the equilibrium of a balance. Pronounced rectangles divide up the picture-surface—the balustrades, the space occupied by the Apostles, the window, the staircase building on the opposite side; the narrative is based upon what fits into these divisions and what deviates from them. After the healing of the lame man the Apostles preached to their followers—"and when they had prayed, the place was shaken where they had assembled together; and they were all filled with the Holy Ghost, and they spake the word of God with boldness. And the multitude of them that believed were of one heart and of one soul . . . for as many as were possessors of lands or houses sold them, and brought the prices of the things that were sold, and laid them down at the apostles' feet: and distribution was made to every man according as he had need. . . .

"But a certain man named Ananias, with Sapphira his wife, sold a possession, and kept back part of the price . . . and brought a certain part, and laid it at the apostles' feet. But Peter said, Ananias, why hath Satan filled thine heart to lie to the Holy Ghost . . . why hast thou conceived this thing in thine heart? though hast not lied unto men, but unto God."

"And Ananias hearing these words fell down, and gave up the ghost: and great fear came on all them that heard these things." (*Acts* iv, 31–35; v, 1–10.)

Raphael's living presentation of the scene is based not only on these words— he had before his eyes also the twelve messengers from *Acts* ii, 4, when "they were all filled with the Holy Ghost, and began to speak with other tongues"— "Then Peter, standing up with the eleven . . ."

Something of the divine light hovers above their brows, and their eyes seem not yet to have become re-accustomed to look at earthly things; only John with heavenly gentleness attends to his charge—the rest stand like an unapproachable court of justice, and the shattering occurrence which they see taking place below cannot but confirm them in the knowledge which they have just acquired amid the rushing wind from heaven. From the right hand of Peter the punishing ray descends upon the man who has lied before God—and if we follow the train of the people bringing their gifts, we see him suddenly prostrate in the way, broken down, before the feet of the bearded man in a turban and the youth who with wonderful quickness comprehends what is happening. He points up to the tribunal, standing there so unswervingly firm from head to foot and in whose pronouncer of judgment, Peter, all the lines converge, from the pavement as from the folds of the curtain. The middle of the scene is left clear by the onlookers shrinking back in terror, as if there were a surge and ebb of unrighteousness and passion in front of the steps. Leonardo would have found here with satisfaction corroboration of his teaching: "In a historical painting the dignity and bearing of the prince or sage is to be strictly observed. It is attained in such a painting if the chief figure is kept apart, or entirely separated from the tumult of the multitude." (*Trattato dell' Arte della Pittura*, II, 247.)

The aged master was able to witness this living triumph of his endeavours at the hands of the fortune-favoured younger artist, and in Rome of all places, before he finally quitted that Italy by which he had so often been disillusioned. In him he could see "a son, not a grandchild of nature", after his own heart. For every inspiration, in Raphael's case, had of necessity to be converted, in the tumult of elemental discovery, into something that was his very own. One might believe, with regard to this group with the youth, that the artist had in mind a mosaic from Santa Maria Maggiore, with the Apostles at the moment of parting. That he was acquainted with this mosaic seems to be proved by a figure in the *DISPUTA*[1]—but in that instance as in this the original is altered in conformity with his spirit; it can serve only to confirm him in the course he has discovered for himself. Here we have suddenly before us the true "history"— men of the common people, the chosen leaders and the led, both after their own manner stirred by an unearthly happening.

Perhaps the visionary character assumed for Raphael at that time by all religious feeling makes its effect most strongly felt in this tapestry; an echo of it continued right down to the deep impression of which Goethe gave proof on his second stay in Rome (*Italienische Reise* III, *Zweiter römischer Aufenthalt*). In the cartoon Raphael's personal participation can be traced at its clearest, although the head of Peter in particular was perhaps already impaired by Giulio Romano. The apostles on the left of Peter, the one looking upward and another, with downcast eyes and half-raised hand, looking down, show all the refinement of Raphael's forms, and in their expressions, gentle and strong respectively, a breadth of difference which none but he could command so completely in the final execution (Plate 254). Along the cloak of Peter an outline, still visible, is drawn in charcoal, modelling it in just the same manner in which sometimes an element of vitality is introduced by a correcting line in the red chalk sketches of the pupils. In the head and the left calf of Ananias the personal

[1] *R. Z.*, VI, Text p. 288, pl. 243.

touch of Raphael has for once remained surviving in its entirety (Plates 253, 264). The bold foreshortening of the face, laid down in charcoal, is lightly set off in brown; the lights are left in reserve—the style, out and out, of painting on paper, this insertion in water-colour manner, of the shadows on forehead, cheek and upper lip, over a preliminary drawing in charcoal. The drapery has also survived, in delicate cherry- and raspberry-red tones with lights in white, on the foreshortened shoulder. The drapery of John, leaning over the balustrade towards a pauper, was done in light yellow, with washes of sepia over hatching and charcoal *pentimenti* in the outline. His eyes, as he looks at the recipient of his alms, become even kinder through the lashes that, after Raphael's manner in his own handiwork, give them an expression almost of radiance. The artist's most personal participation can be recognised with exceptional clearness in this head (Plate 255).

One might imagine that this method of producing an effect with the paper ground was an original element in the style of the designs, which were intended to be translated in resplendent colours shot with glistening gold.

The tapestry with the HEALING OF THE LAME MAN (Plate 256) would be worthy of taking the central place in the series, so strongly is the symmetry marked by the framing of the principal group between the columns. *Acts* iii, 1–11: "Now Peter and John went up together into the temple at the hour of prayer, being the ninth hour. And a certain man lame from his mother's womb was carried, whom they laid daily at the gate of the temple which is called Beautiful, to ask alms of them that entered into the temple; who seeing Peter and John . . . asked an alms. And Peter, fastening his eyes upon him with John, said, Look on us. And he gave heed unto them, expecting to receive something of them. Then Peter said, Silver and gold have I none; but such as I have give I thee: in the name of Jesus Christ of Nazareth rise up and walk. And he took him by the right hand, and lifted him up: and immediately his feet and ankle bones received strength. And he leaping up stood, and walked . . . and all the people saw him walking and praising God . . . and they were filled with wonder and amazement at that which had happened unto him."

Acts iii, 11: "And as the lame man which was healed held Peter and John, all the people ran together unto them in the porch that is called Solomon's, greatly wondering."

Acts iv, 1: "And as they spake unto the people, the priests, and the captain of the temple, and the Saduccees, came upon them. . . ."

Raphael succeeds in spanning, as with an arch, the whole extent of the narrative through several chapters, and in a truly popular manner he gave his contemporaries a peep into the "porch that is called Solomon's"; no-one at that time knew any better, or regarded it as impossible that these celebrated twisted columns, which in the old St Peter's carried the *Confessio* over the tomb of the Apostle, should have come from Solomon's Temple. Here, with the splendour

263

of the central pair and their serried ranks lost in the dimness of the background, they represent alike the "Beautiful Gate" and Solomon's Porch; indeed, the sense of contracted space between them multiplies even the number of persons, hardly a dozen in all, to "all the people". In the midst of this commotion of coming and going, calm reigns only where something supernatural is taking place. How Peter and John fill out the grave folds of their cloaks with their vigorous vitality! With what a wonderful physician's gesture the shoulders and hand of the Prince of the Apostles seem to say: "But such as I have give I thee", and with what sympathetic participation the look and hand of John accompany the words: "Rise up and walk!" Compared with the simple power of these men of the people the "interesting" heads of the onlookers seem truly commonplace. To the boy in his exuberant energy the amazement of his grandfather seems even to have lasted too long; he wants to drag him away, after his playmate with the doves. For those on the opposite side the miracle is in vain; to the beggar it means hopes unfulfilled, to the Captain of the Temple amazement, and to the Sadducee annoyance.

This clear language has been wonderfully preserved through all the working-over of the cartoon and the rough treatment at the hands of the weavers. Nor could the participation of pupils do much to spoil the design; they were here held in check by the power of the designer to an extent which has no parallel in the Borgo Stanza, where the studio assistants were often left entirely to their own devices. The two principal figures, especially in the heads, have been deprived of all original quality, under the respectful attentions of the centuries, ever renewed and renewing—even to the turns and gestures; in their amplitude and compactness, these figures must have been carried out by Raphael himself. The free manner in which the gesture of John traverses the space, combining forward and upward movement, is one of his original ideas in these last years. Where you come across anything of *this* order, there you have Raphael! Where the cartoon has remained without over-painting, as in the young mother in a green dress suckling her child, it has been supposed that a good, obsequious pupil's hand could be recognised. Yet in the figure as she passes by, no assistant could ever have achieved, even to the look in her eyes, this blend of sympathy, fear, and unswerving devotion to a mother's duty (Plate 259). In the multifarious expressions of the subordinate figures, particularly those between the columns, we meet all the time with the master himself (Plate 258). In the head of the beggar on the right the manner in which it is put in, in charcoal and fluid lime-pigment, recalls the manner of rendering the younger Cardinal—Riario —in the fresco of the MASS OF BOLSENA—vitality given to the forms by cloudy shadows, the hair clustered in curling lines about the contours of the skull.

This St Peter series formerly extended along the Gospel side, the wall on the left of the entrance in the chapel; thus anyone entering followed the course of the narrative in the right direction. The MARTYRDOM OF STEPHEN comes as the last incident, leading on to the epic of the second Prince of the Apostles. In this, the young Saul looks after the clothes of the stone-throwers.

Is it really because we no longer possess the cartoon for it and only have before us the woven version, that the first subject in the St Paul series, the CONVERSION ON THE WAY TO DAMASCUS, seems to us weaker? The original design is supposed to have disappeared; in 1521 it was already at Venice, in the possession of Cardinal Grimani, just at the right time to give some ideas to Titian for the BATTLE OF CADORE—the foreshortened group of the horse with the flowing mane, the falling figure with arms extended, the youthful head looking upwards. Such an acknowledgment of the original composer should have imposed a fitting check on the search for the participation of unimaginative pupils. Acquaintance with such a work meant more than this to the painter of the PESARO MADONNA and the TRIUMPH OF BACCHUS. He was conscious of sanction from the direction of Rome for his liberating plunge into space, extending far beyond the mere boldness of the motives.

Here, where the other-worldly makes itself visible, Raphael broke away from the frieze-like disposition which is dominant everywhere else. A ray of glory upon which Christ is suspended raises the centre of the composition. To him the great pattern leads up, taking its effect from the two diagonals. In these dramatic figures the artist brought to consummation many ideas for that RESURRECTION which he never carried out; the guards of the tomb, starting back and striving to escape in the very act of falling, are combined into the figure of Paul: "And as he journeyed, he came near Damascus: and suddenly there shined round about him a light from heaven: and he fell to the earth, and heard a voice saying unto him, Saul, Saul, why persecutest thou me? And he said, Who art thou, Lord? And the Lord said, I am Jesus whom thou persecutest: it is hard for thee to kick against the pricks. And he trembling and astonished said, Lord, what wilt thou have me to do?" (*Acts* ix, 3–6.)

The Apostle lies with arms stretched irresolutely out, as if ready for death on the Cross; so suddenly has the light thrown him from the saddle at the head of the column that his troopers have already almost ridden over him—and along the beam Christ comes down out of the clouds, just as the thunder follows the lightning, with tremendous, threatening finger. Once again the master in his maturity gives proof of a profound impression received in his youth at home in the Marches—from Signorelli's fresco at Loreto, one of the rare other-worldly revelations in the Quattrocento. This gesture of the "Contra stimulum ne calcitres" had remained alive in his memory throughout the whole course of his life.

Compared with the other tapestry of which we have no cartoon, the STONING OF STEPHEN, the CONVERSION OF PAUL thus shows fully the quality of something complete in itself which it was intended to achieve. In the death of the Proto-martyr, a few wonderfully free motives raise the trivial to the level of the heroic by their spatial momentum. The manner in which the two men on the left put all their fury into the swing of body and arm is all too sharply contrasted with the figure of a man gliding past in profile behind Stephen, and with the inept twisting attitude of Saul. Moreover, the heavenly region in the composition may well have been put together from misunderstood sketches of Raphael's; the ecstasy of the young martyr could not have been so entirely lacking in the power of affecting those who witnessed it if the master himself had designed it. Raphael was at that time familiar with the realm of the visionary; it was certainly he who designed these passages in the Stephen. The saint prays with his right hand, recommending his persecutors to forgiveness: "Lord, lay not this sin to their charge!" We feel that his left hand already expresses a sense of collapse, and his eyes look up "stedfastly into heaven" and see "the glory of God, and Jesus standing at the right hand of God". (*Acts* vii, 54–60, viii, 1.) One who could conceive so tragic a figure in communion with another world would surely have been able to devise, in the upper region, some other response than this.

The narrow supplementary tapestry with Paul in prison at Philippi seems to be similarly the outcome of indications given by Raphael and the breakdown of his assistants. For the earth-demon there is a detailed, not quite certain, drawing from the Grahl Collection; the fleeing jailor, in boldest foreshortening, may still be based on one of the terrified guards of the tomb in the Resurrection. The pupil who, in the "*Pasce oves*", introduced the washing in the landscape above the heads of the Apostles, may have been responsible for making the "tremoto" thrust his elbows through the masonry border of the tapestry, and for the literal representation, above, of the Mamertine Prison in Rome; it would be worthy of Giulio Romano.

In any case the real epic of the great convert and writer of the Epistles, the wandering founder of congregations, begins for us only where beyond doubt Raphael himself takes a hand with his favourite hero. We should not allow it to be regarded as an accident that this creative force, or his wanderings through the Roman Empire, should have appeared to Raphael as inseparable from a concrete background of monumental buildings. Thus Paul confronts Elymas before the Tribunal of the Praetor of Asia, Sergius Paulus, "a prudent man", in Paphos (Plate 257, *Acts* xiii, 6–12). The same called before him Barnabas and Paul and "desired to hear the word of God. But Elymas the sorcerer . . . withstood them, seeking to turn away the deputy from the faith. Then Saul (who also is called Paul), filled with the Holy Ghost, set his eyes on him, and said, O full of all subtilty and all mischief, thou child of the devil, thou enemy of all righteousness, wilt thou not cease to pervert the right ways of the Lord? And now, behold the hand of the Lord is upon thee, and thou shalt be blind, not seeing the sun for a season. And immediately there fell on him a mist and a darkness; and he went about seeking some to lead him by the hand. Then the deputy, when he saw what was done, believed, being astonished at the doctrine of the Lord".

The contest between faith and imposture takes place in front of an architectural composition entirely befitting the figures that are to occupy the space, with the nobility and compactness of its contributory members; it is as if there were a summons before a temporal tribunal. In the dignity of office, with a golden wreath and green toga, raised above the multitude by his place above the steps and in front of the tribune, Sergius Paulus has taken his seat on the throne when Saul stretches out his right hand like a rod of heaven against the stricken impostor who has dared to intrude with his Eastern sorceries under his eyes. This simple man, with the strong shoulders of the artizan and firmly taking his stand, seems to be the one amongst all the others who has "put on the new man", "full of the Holy Ghost". And the judge, who has them both brought before his judgment seat, is nothing but a harassed mortal. In sympathetic fear, his lictors recognise that the temporal force of their arms is not needed where the judgment of heaven is being executed. The one next to the Proconsul, thrusting his arm from his toga, draws the attention of the doubters behind him to the proud man who has been smitten from heaven. He is answered by the gesture of the woman full of foreboding; she has recognised the power of God sooner than other onlookers, who in their dullness are merely clever, whilst the men round Elymas have not yet got over what is actually taking place, the transformation in his eyes. The attention, as one looks at the picture, is centred on the great thing that is happening within the narrow compass of a pair of eyes, as if in some play of circling balls worthy of Leonardo. But from the smitten shoulders of the victim the line is carried on, through the companion who gropes after him with seeing eyes, to the terrified Praetor, along his arms to his head—and from the opposite direction also he is the focus. The chastising hand of Paul is directed at his adversary, but at the same time every fold of his garment, ending in the high light on his hand and threatening finger, points undeviatingly towards the Praetor. And here history-painting becomes world history; in this Praetor the Roman *Imperium* is shaken, and the judge himself becomes the tongue of the scales of justice, inclining towards the "new man" when the old man proves to be too light. All that was in him depended on equilibrium. This judge on his tribunal resembles the priest in the MASS OF BOLSENA who falters at the spectacle of Transubstantiation. The focal point of vision of the whole space, of which the construction is shown with great exactness, lies to the left of his head. In the dramatic undulation of the row of heads, from the praying Barnabas to the deaf mute on the right-hand margin, he is dominant, not merely through his golden crown. The axes of the occurrence in the foreground meet at an angle in him; they cross in him, and diverge into the distance in the architecture behind him. He forms the centre of this composition, spiritually and spatially and aesthetically. A semicircle opens in front of him, rises up and descends towards him, sweeps around him. The entire architectural symmetry is dominated by a polyphony of vertical rhythm and pattern vibrating throughout the great space which can only be compared with the musical quality of Baroque façades. Jutting lateral wings flank a central structure of which the projection is plastically graduated, and almost as a matter of course, in the tapestry, another niche-ornamented pier, behind the powerful bodily presence of Paul—lacking in the cartoon—forms a pendant to the figures on the border and in the wings opposite. Indeed, it seems as if the vertical band of light in the architecture above his figure becomes thereby an even more impressive pointer from the inanimate region above to him as the source of all the vitality in this throng. We recognise here the monumental intention of the architect-painter.

Paul appears as the focus of all the animation in the picture in the SACRIFICE AFTER THE HEALING OF THE CRIPPLE AT LYSTRA (Plate 260, *Acts* xiv, 8–15). "And there sat a certain man at Lystra, impotent in his feet, being a cripple from his mother's womb, who had never walked: the same heard Paul speak: who stedfastly beholding him, and perceiving that he had faith to be healed, said with a loud voice, Stand upright on thy feet. And he leaped and walked. And when the people saw what Paul had done, they lifted up their voices, saying in the speech of Lycaonia, The gods are come down to us in the likeness of men. And they called Barnabas, Jupiter; and Paul, Mercurius, because he was the chief speaker. Then the priest of Jupiter, which was before their city, brought oxen and garlands unto the gates, and would have done sacrifice with the people. Which when the apostles, Barnabas and Paul, heard of, they rent their clothes, and ran in among the people, crying out, and saying, Sirs, why do ye these things? . . . And with these sayings scarce restrained they the people, that they had not done sacrifice unto them. And there came thither certain Jews from Antioch and Iconium, who persuaded the people. . . ."

Raphael shows the multitude, quickly stirred and quickly lost again, as they rush vehemently forward for the sacrifice towards the place where the Apostles stand, surging as it were against the altar at the feet of the latter. They hasten to discharge their duty to the supposed deities. The first beast for the sacrifice has already been wreathed with a garland, consecrated out of the casket in the hands of the boy beside the glowing altar. The second steer is being brought up by garlanded priests, for whom there cannot be haste enough (Plate 266). Behind them press the multitude. The speed of their onrush is perceptible in the cloak of the kneeling priest, still sweeping out with the double movement as he comes forward and sinks on his knee, and in the bellying garment of the bearded man, a physician who, with a not very dignified bearing, runs up, keeping pace with the cripple that has been healed, and must needs clumsily examine the leg that has now dispensed with a crutch (Plate 265); the youth full of foreboding is only just in time to check this relapse into heathenism and to stay the axe of the sacrificing attendant, as he rushes headlong with a haste more than precipitate, an isolated figure among the crowd as it surges onward like a rolling flood. Already a wreath-crowned temple-servant is dragging in from the left a new victim, a ram; and the Apostles are horrified at the new declension from "the living God" to "these vanities". Paul, still raised on a step, full of sublimest spiritual dignity, directs his indignation against himself and rends the garment on his breast, and Barnabas rises on tiptoe to master the throng, begging rather than adjuring them, as if it were incumbent on him to be as unlike as possible to the god Jupiter for whom he is being taken. The sacrificing attendant (Plate 263) looks up in amazement at this gesture of the presumed deities, whilst a group of veiled men, veiled also in their thoughts, unmoved and sceptical as between heathenism and Christianity, stands aside—the Jews of Antioch and Iconium. Ancient heathenism is rampant once again among these temples—houses "made with hands". What takes place here must be tangible; the time is not yet fulfilled for the word of God, and where the higher power is being revealed through a miracle backsliding still lurks. Even the divinely consecrated Apostle has to meet with these oppositions, with shattering agitation of soul, as his severest trial. What a grand conception on the part of the poetical creator of this figure, to concede to him this spiritual martyrdom before reaching his bloody end! Here for the last time he gives his hero the aspect and bearing of a Roman knight—the character unforgettably presented to us standing beside St Cecilia. In a precious silverpoint study at Chatsworth he essayed to render the power and resilience, the dignity and passion of the figure; in the cartoon the drapery became even more statuesque. Perhaps this composition preceded the others, for in the presence of the Praetor Sergius and on the Areopagus this character of the knight and *cortegiano* has given place to the "new man", the preaching traveller, whose dignity consists not in the way his cloak is folded but in the spirit with which he is filled.

As in the "Pasce Oves", the single figure is here balanced by a throng. Everything relating to him points towards him—looks, praying hands, the arm commanding a halt in the proceedings, the action of sacrifice even to the up-lifted axe—and the scene has a truly Shakespearean setting; the slavish amazement of the attendant beside the principal figure could only find suitable expression in the idiom of the common people; on the opposite side, the well-groomed physician, who would like to detect a professional blunder in this fateful competitor—"By this the learned gentleman I note, All that you touch not is from you remote".[1] He is himself "the common people", in spite of all the dignity in his jealousy.

The colours are distributed with careful intention: Paul, in his green robe, with a red cloak tempered by broad golden high lights, gains emphasis from the

[1] "Daran erkenn ich den gelehrten Herrn—
Was Ihr nicht tastet, steht euch meilenfern"

green of the columns above him, the gleaming colour of which is repeated on the opposite side and breaks out several times in the crowd; these isolated passages of green have their central, focal point in the green drapery with gold shimmering through it of the man swinging the axe. The terracotta in the clothing of Barnabas is continued in the coppery flesh-colour of the figure of the temple servant, and has its pendant in the figure of the inquisitive onlooker. It breaks through the centre in the garment and sleeve of the youth. Through all the spatial undulations, that solemn effect of distance which Raphael found indispensable for wall-decoration is restored again and again with the harmoniousness of an ornamental hanging. His knowledge as architect and archæologist was also brought into play to contribute its effect to the poetry of distance. The dignity of ancient architecture as understood by Bramante and Raphael himself encompasses the scene. The "*Tempietto*" of San Pietro in Montorio appears as the second member, in the range of buildings, and from that time forward a circular structure was always introduced in all settings for heroic scenes in the Renaissance. It was just at this time that Raphael was priding himself on new observations of perspective, and in the Carneval of 1518 he constructed a stage for the performance at the residence of Cardinal Cibò, from which perhaps, by way of Peruzzi and Serlio, an echo was to reverberate for a long period through all theatrical experiments in scenic construction.

With these great innovators, new structures which were destined to prevail with fruitful results for generations, and to have an effect for centuries, had their birth in the beautiful delusion of having discovered the authentic Antique. And it was something more than an idle playing with historical fidelity and with his knowledge of the Antique—his picture of the Late Classical world was interwoven, as it were, in his state of tension between outward ceremony and inner experience when he designed this altar as an imitation of an antique *cippus*; he achieved archæological accuracy in the ceremonial, and in the sacrificing attendant with the bull, from the relief of the Ara Pacis, now in the Uffizi, which he could still see, before it was brought to the Villa Medici, in a Roman garden of antiques. All this was woven into his constructions no less than into his culture, with happy natural inevitability; the line of the bull's back combines to produce an effect with the upper arm and face of the youth, giving rise, when counterpoised with the sacrificing figure, to the substantial central pattern which holds the picture together, in line no less than in the balance of the colour-rhythms. For in historical painting this is the true secret of monumental quality—to give to the subject an all-pervading vitality. The working-out of the narrative from left to right, as in the tapestry, also has to do with this. We notice this with the cartoon before us, exactly as if we were swimming against the stream; in the tapestry, wave upon wave surges towards the right as we look, and the young convert, like a swimmer, outstrips the impersonal element of the crowd with his gesture.

This art still produces its effect only by symbols; it plays upon pictures from natural life, introducing them without effort to represent the results of profound intuition. Thus it discovers a language of its own with which history is not narrated, but interpreted. Raphael already excels Leonardo, the greatest of those who gave profundity to the media of art and their teaching; in PAUL ON THE AREOPAGUS (Plate 261) the painter of space is triumphant in his new style.

(*Acts* xvii, 16): "Now while Paul waited for them [Silas and Timothy] at Athens, his spirit was stirred in him, when he saw the city wholly given to idolatry. . . . And they took him, and brought him unto Areopagus, saying, May we know what this new doctrine, whereof thou speakest, is ? . . . (For all the Athenians and strangers which were there spent their time in nothing else, but either to tell, or to hear some new thing.)

"Then Paul stood in the midst of Mars' Hill, and said, Ye men of Athens, I perceive that in all things ye are too superstitious. For as I passed by, and beheld your devotions, I found an altar with this inscription, TO THE UNKNOWN GOD. Whom therefore ye ignorantly worship, him declare I unto you. God that made the world and all things therein, seeing that he is Lord of heaven and earth, dwelleth not in temples made with hands; neither is worshipped with men's hands, as though he needed any thing, seeing he giveth to all life, and breath, and all things. . . .

"And when they heard of the resurrection of the dead, some mocked: and others said, We will hear thee again of this matter. . . . Howbeit certain men clave unto him, and believed: among the which was Dionysius the Areopagite, and a woman named Damaris, and others with them."

The Hill of Ares, from which the sublime words were uttered, Raphael transformed into a splendid terraced structure. The gilded statue of the god gleams in front of his circular temple; his head adverted, it does not seem to him yet the time for listening to the message that this man, his one-time champion in arms, now armed with the Word, has to proclaim. The latter however is standing not in the presence of the group of hearers, doubters and a few faithful, nor in opposition to the heathen god. He stands before the universe, through which his words resound on high. There is no parallel to the effect here achieved by Raphael, of a single human being feeling himself sent to confront a multitude, indeed, countless communities in regions immeasurably remote. The entire new method of handling space, the balancing of the power of such a figure by a void, was a tremendous idea. We may not, of course, speak of "the style of his old age", but something of the unexpected dæmonic quality which, in popular phraseology, is spoken of as showing "his end is not far off", is operative in the boldness with which a painter of poetical bent here steps out on untrodden paths. A preacher such as this, thus raised up on a top step where he cannot in his agitation approach nearer to his hearers, cannot help turning involuntarily this way and that, and describing the full circle that takes in each of them in his turn, sweeping beyond them to the remotest distances; for He whom he proclaims, "hath made of one blood all nations of men for to dwell on all the face of the earth . . . that they should seek after the Lord, if haply they might feel after him, and find him, though he be not far from every one of us. . . ."

Thus, with the lofty range of his words, we number these hearers as only one, which happens to be the first, of countless circles around him and before him and after him, in space and time, to whom his words reach out in their sweep. Between his hands hovers the eternal In-comprehensible; he himself— "il gran vasello dello spirito santo" (*Paradiso*, XXI, 127) towers there aloft, vying with the pillars, gaining from them power and intensity in his amplitude by contrast with the void opposite through which the throng is seething. In the cartoon we follow his words into space—in the tapestry we strive in amazement with Dionysius and Damaris to attain his altitude, we see him towering up, and the thunder of his words rolls forth over us also.

As regards colour, formerly the red of the trailing cloak and the gold on the light green sleeve glowed out above the softer, as it were more undecided green, yellow and pink of the congregation. They diminish in size as also in colour before his sonorous chords.[1] He gains force from the stonework. The height and bareness of his pedestal on the steps makes him appear to soar almost superhumanly, and his "lifting up", this "sursum corda", is intensified by all the soaring lines of the buildings behind and beside him; the lines of their abutments and cornices intersect higher up, above the point of vision of the steps and pavement. This is how Raphael employs his media; where the word is to be made visible of the Unknown God who is "not far from every one of us", all earthly measurement can only serve the immeasurable. The creation of Raphael in his consummation lived for the good of mankind, in accordance with laws of its own.

§ The Otherworldly

Or are there iron laws that reveal themselves at the turning-points in the history of man, to warn him, as with a trumpetblast, of eternity? Raphael's language appeals to stout hearts; only such does he seem to desire to guide to the heights. This was *his* translation of the Bible!

It is hardly an accident that four times in his latest works this force of uplifted hands seems to preach a "sursum corda"—in Paul bearing witness to the Unknown God, in the menacing Jehovah of the VISION OF EZEKIEL (Plate 223), in the Creator, of the Chigi dome, and lastly in the transfigured form of the Redeemer. Each time the gesture reaches out into the beyond; one renounces the attempt to follow with words the greatest interpreter of life into such exalted spheres.

For "the hand of the Lord came upon him", as upon Ezekiel (*Ezekiel*, i, 4).

---

[1] In the cartoon much has been over-painted; in the tapestry of the Berlin series the green has turned almost entirely blue, and gold high lights are missing.

"And I looked, and behold, a whirlwind came out of the north, a great cloud and a fire infolding itself, and a brightness was about it, and out of the midst thereof as the colour of amber, out of the midst of the fire. Also out of the midst thereof came the likeness of four living creatures. And this was their appearance; they had the likeness of a man. . . . And above the firmament that was over their heads was the likeness of a throne, as the appearance of a sapphire stone: and upon the likeness of the throne was the likeness as the appearance of a man above upon it. And I saw as the colour of amber, as the appearance of fire round about within it, from the appearance of his loins even upward, and from the appearance of his loins even downward, I saw as it were the appearance of fire, and it had brightness round about. As the appearance of the bow that is in the cloud in the day of rain, so was the appearance of the likeness of the glory of the Lord. And when I saw it, I fell upon my face, and I heard a voice of one that spake." (*Ezekiel* ii, 1) "And he said to me, Son of man, stand upon thy feet, and I will speak to thee."

For the painter the word of the prophet and the word spoken to the prophet were one. He had no need of the theological interpretation which sees in the visions of Ezekiel the forerunner of the "Revelation". He felt as Dürer did when, in the unearthly terrors of the Apocalypse, he shows the heavenly powers high above the tiny world that is being warned by threatening storms of its fate in the great day of change.

At such moments of creation his inward experience was present before the eye of his divining soul; into it streamed out of his recollection the shattering force of the elements at play, the wall of the rainstorm overmastered by the power of light breaking through, the massive thundercloud above the earth, the giant tree smitten by tempest and weather, the angry shaft of light flashing down against the puny child of man below—all this turmoil of earth merely prepares the way for the overwhelming upheaval from above.

Thus Michael Angelo's Ezekiel may have seen it,

"With wind approaching, and with cloud and fire,"

"Venir con vento, con nube e con igne" (*Purgatorio*, XXIX, 103).

For Raphael every vision now becomes inevitably a living experience. Impossible to escape this downward flight on the wings of the Four Beasts, that has now for a moment been halted and brought them to their knees. That the inescapable oblique line is along the diagonal intensifies the convincing sense that they have just suddenly descended. But the power of the arms, the gesture of the hands, remain unexplained, and let them remain so. And yet, their first effect on mortal eyes is that of an allegory; it is something above the ordinary. Here a primordial gesture appears, in elemental form; an Olympian deity thrusting down Titans, his own rebel creation—the triumphant arms still held aloft—thunders after the downfall of the defeated foe; or a Cyclopean, Centaur-like being, still looking down at the block of stone he has hurled, as if to add to its effect. In the manner of Zeus—"a uso di Giove", Vasari expressed it. Doubtless it is the Creator who must needs menacingly warn his creation, now in anger, now in pardon; and that he appears in this guise may be a warning to the world of the Day of Judgment.

But "as the appearance of the bow that is in the cloud", there seems to be a sound as of pardon from angel choirs above; securely sheltered beneath the shoulders of the Most High, the winged children support his mighty arms, and in humble rapture the Beasts raise their tremendous voices. In the bull, bellowing without restraint, we are hardly conscious of the fact that his throat has really been stretched out by a Nike, or by Mithras, to receive the mortal stroke—it is the magnificent motive from the Antique that Raphael may perhaps have seen at the Palazzo della Valle (Plate 219b). Here the creature is offered in sacrifice by himself.

The dynamic force put into such a vision by the painter seems immeasurable, and nothing ought to be accepted with indifference, as it has been by criticism in the most recent generations—whether it be the power of the gesture, or the play of colour bursting forth out of the beyond; it is impossible to attribute to some landscape specialist of the studio the vitality of atmosphere that is here enlisted in the service of things so sublime. Every dramatic medium—the fore-shortening of the limbs, the light breaking forth—is only a poetic expression of the great, *unique* composer who undoubtedly designed the picture; possibly an assistant, to us unknown, perhaps the enigmatic Thomas Vincidor of Bologna, had a share, with his broad strokes in the mode of the Netherlandish Mannerists. But we ought not to attempt to hazard the recognition of his part in the work until we have made our acknowledgments to the master who thought out these tremendous pictorial conceptions, and surrendered ourselves to the impetus of his rhythms from another world.

The power of his decisive pictorial vision did not perhaps suffice to give guidance to the pupil who executed the work—the small picture in the Pitti Palace, in spite of its greatness, of intuition, is now disappointing by reason of a certain oily vividness of colour, and one secretly admits to one's self the expectation that a more worthy version might possibly come to light, perhaps that which was at one time in the Orleans Gallery. Once again, school work shows itself to be separated by a gulf from the master, at a distance that cannot be bridged. The heavy blue clouds contrasting with the strident yellowish gold of the glory, the flesh tones a hot red, with slate-grey shadows and straw-coloured high lights in the hair—we recognise here, and also in the red robe, shot with silver grey, of the Almighty, and in the powerful flesh tones, how much of the colour indications given by Raphael may have been misrepresented by an insensitive hand.

THE LAST FIVE YEARS OF THE PAINTER

§ St Michael

We never know to what extent in these last years Raphael had set down in enduring conceptions his pictorial visions when he was obliged to leave them to his pupils to carry out. Yet throughout their banalities of colour and form, we can often trace the impetus of his imagination. The essential ideas in the pictures painted for the King of France, the ST MICHAEL and ST MARGARET, could only come from him, out of his familiarity with otherworldly spheres. Only from such a source could such convincing and triumphant representations have been derived of Satan in combat, twice over, with a male and a female antagonist.

The patron saint of Their Very Christian Majesties appears to have pursued his enfeebled foe over mountains and seas out of remotest distances, in conformity with the legend which has it that the contest in the skies raged from Mont St Michel in Normandy to Monte Sant' Angelo near Naples. The victory seems almost more like a great act of purification, as these glorious arms wield the spear, to thrust down the foulness before him; the air quivers in his wings, the sweep of his cloak still tells of a pursuit out of far-away regions. Now, as the chasm opens in the earth, the moment of decisive victory has come. One single, perpendicular, downward swoop—from the closed, gliding pinions to the triumphant tread of the heel. There is miracle enough in these wings that, with the shoulders and arms, disclose an energy of their own. They have their complementary action in the wings of Satan which, with their amphibian colouring of a toad, are compelled to return from the heights they have usurped to the subterranean element which seems already to be licking at them. The Son of Hell, a veritable monstrosity, is descended, in his posture of undignified subjection, from the company of guards in the RESURRECTION, and in him have been united the mediaeval animal attributes, horns, claws and tail, that are traceable to the Satyr of Antiquity. For the three zones through which the combat has raged Raphael has enlisted his feeling for landscape—the radiant skies around the rustling splendour of the wings, the expanses of a view of the Sabine Hills, and the ancient Chaos of the *Inferno*, known to him from Dante since the days of his youth. Unquestionably all this is attributable to his inventiveness and his alone. All that seems organically out of place in these elements —the thigh of the angel that has the effect of being overburdened, and his sword —are earthly remnants contributed by the pupil who carried out the design.

§ St Margaret

Since it has become the custom to look for the Little Masters in Raphael's activities instead of the single great master, the ST MARGARET in the Louvre, as a work of Penni or Giulio Romano, has ceased to attract much attention. Yet it is one of the rare works that proclaim the triumph of maiden purity. With the Sign of the Cross she has exorcised her adversary into his degrading shape, and now, with the symbol of her victory, the palm, she treads under foot, like a Nike, his jagged wings, between his powerless coils and menacing jaws. And her virgin spotlessness is not without its lovely imagery, like the chaste light of the moon issuing from clouds—wholly triumphant, from her serene brow, through her delicate wrist, as she gathers up her robe so as not to touch the unclean thing even with its hem, down to the foot that supports this vessel of purity. It is a grand, poetical conception, to which every line is made to contribute. She exerts a constraint of her own; in this easy poise, apparently amazed at itself, we desire to be allowed to participate.

§ The Bearing of the Cross

The commission for the BEARING OF THE CROSS (Plate 267) came from a distant quarter; the Olivetan monks, of Palermo, of the monastery of Santa Maria dello Spasimo, requested this altarpiece for their church. We may recall the wanderings of the picture. It suffered shipwreck on its first outward voyage and remained undamaged. It reached its destined place at Palermo; thence it went to the Alcazar in Madrid; from the burning castle it was rescued and taken to Buen Retiro. For six years in the hands of the French, it went to swell, from 1813 to 1819, the series of works by Raphael in the Musée Napoléon; there it was transferred from a wood panel to canvas. It was brought back to Madrid to the Palace, and finally exhibited in the Prado. After this, much cannot be expected to survive of the painting in its original state.

Criticism fluctuates accordingly from mystical admiration and the legend of rescue unimpaired from the surging billows, for which Vasari serves as witness, to doubt as to the origin of the painting as a composition of Raphael's, in our age of formal criticism and impressionistic standards.

Actually, the chief groups are dominated by that compactness which belongs to Raphael's late style, in the tapestries, combined with that dispersion of individual motives for which as a rule his assistants in the execution alone have a sense. His own architectural feeling was accustomed at that time to an articulation productive of rhythm. Thus in this picture also a dynamic element arises out of the multitude of human forms crowded together. The dramatic painter uses the space of the composition only as a sphere that ensures free mobility to the figures and allows the eye to sweep in the direction of the focus of spiritual interest; he portrays only gestures that clear a space around them, not space itself.

This feature becomes the very signature of the master in the medley of late works turned out as the regular business of the studio. And so, in the case of many a false note of colour, in many a figure that fills up space, or over-fills it even to the degree of superfluity, in a detailed landscape that tells nothing about the theme, the name of one or other of the pupils of whose peculiarities we know little, may be invoked. The vitality of the chief group in this work, in spite of all injuries, belongs so certainly to the great religious composer that, in the presence of the exaltation it expresses, every misgiving as to the remaining portions should subside into the background. The central group of the PRO- CESSION TO GOLGOTHA has the movement in the grand style of the ACTS OF THE APOSTLES—a strongly undercut relief, with a row of heads at almost the same level. Here everything that is essential is told—the horsemen and the standard-bearer, as well as the commander beneath the gateway, appear to be inserted without any connecting links; but in this train of figures modelled in high relief a gap opens, and as it is bridged over from group to group, we experience the violent emotion of the figures in the tragic scene. The Virgin, sinking on her knees, is encompassed by her attendant women as by an aureole, and out of her heart all her overpowering love for her afflicted son streams into her eyes and into her hands as he breaks down under the burden of the hard beam of the cross. Too late the powerful arms of Joseph of Arimathea seek to grasp it; they can only restrain the cruel impulsiveness of the spearman, who curses like a dray-man. The beautiful human wrath in his eye is here of no avail, for the leading executioner, under the eyes of the commander, will brook no delay; with elastic step he snatches up the halter slung round the girdle of the Saviour. Sinking down, toilsomely supported on his knees as he moves forward, the victim is thereby robbed of his own hold, and yet, thus cruelly torn between weakness and compulsion, his body seems rather to be in suspense than to suffer. "Inclin-ation" is the word uttered, as by five voices, by the shoulders of this group of women—only the mother breaks forward among them. Her love had followed as it were on his heels; as he is dragged forward, he seems to swing away from her. In the midst of his tortures, he is already hardly of this world any longer, his soul has again entirely resumed its participation in the divine, that causes him to think more of love than of suffering. His features, unspeakably sublime, and streaming with goodness, would fain reciprocate the maternal love that seeks to reach him. It is impossible to attribute to any other than the master himself such a turn in the direction of the sublime as the gesture in the arms and hands of Mary, to be explained only by the Italian character; the same is true of the bold manner in which the groups turn one towards another, from the executioner to the head of Joseph of Arimathea and from him to the group of women.

The drawing, in the Uffizi, for the Virgin and the kneeling girl, must have been suggested by Raphael; in the picture he may well have reserved for him-self the principal figures, and to a large extent have carried them through —and if, in the press of many another activity, the assistants may have been allowed to finish them, he certainly intervened again himself in the figures of the Redeemer and of the Arimathean, as also in the expression and hands of the Virgin.

The pupils when left to themselves were not capable of further mastery in this exalted style; they lost their way in bravuresque painting of cuirasses and landscape—so that it looks as if they had inserted in the incomplete composition motives such as they were capable of understanding—the shouting shield-bearer with his obtrusive thigh, the unconvincing horses, in which they have misunderstood the bold indications of an extant study in red chalk. But if sketch and execution often diverge from one another, it must be considered fortunate that, in the head of Christ, we discover in the brush strokes that give the expression, the same structure that is so creatively triumphant in the double portrait of the Doria Gallery, and that made of several head studies for the TRANSFIGURATION the last and supreme revelations of the draughtsman-painter.

§ Transfiguration (Plates 236, 268, 269, 271–277)

One approaches Raphael's latest work, the TRANSFIGURATION, with twofold, enhanced veneration. Not only do we know that with it, an ascent of scarcely two decades, such as cannot be described in words, is abruptly broken off; the idea also forces itself on our consciousness of what is meant by the vivid popular expression "His end is not far off"; we are also constrained to feel that this Transfiguration was conceived by a sublime spirit who was drawing near to transfiguration himself—his latest work may be likened to his own "Requiem".

§ The Commission: Choice of Theme

By commissions of Cardinal Giuliano de' Medici, Archbishop of Narbonne, Raphael and Sebastiano del Piombo had been called upon to paint altarpieces for the cathedral of his see, St Just at Narbonne; the order to the Venetian was for a RAISING OF LAZARUS. Whether intentionally or not, there arose in the impassioned atmosphere of Rome of those days a spontaneous rivalry, fostered by the great multitude of intellectual onlookers without occupation of their own. It led at last to the triumph of the dead over the living. Sebastiano's picture was taken to Narbonne and went finally to the National Gallery. Raphael's last work remained in Rome, first in the palace of the Cardinal, the Cancelleria; then it stood on the High Altar of San Pietro in Montorio; since 1815 it has been preserved in the Vatican.

We are acquainted with the external occasion for the choice of theme; this commission for Narbonne, a city particularly affected by the troubles of the time, arose out of the excitements of an age that saw Southern Europe in standing danger from the attacks of unbelievers, the African pirates and the Turkish fleets, and had the experience of witnessing once again a summons of the Christian Powers by the Pope to a Crusade. The liturgy for the 6th August had, since the time of Calixtus III, comprised the Mystery of the Transfiguration, the Feast of the deacon-martyrs, SS. Felicissimus and Agapetus, and thanksgivings for the victory over the Turks at Belgrade in 1453. Thus there arose out of the solemnities that were to inaugurate the new Crusade against the Turks the conception of this picture, for a city whose history, past and present, was identified with peril from the Saracens; the basic idea of the painting was to be that of the Redeemer transfigured above the distresses of this world and coming again.

But however closely the painter was bound by this theological and historical decision to the liturgical life of the Church, even down to the introduction of the kneeling martyrs of the Feast-day of the Transfiguration, this in no way explains the miracle of a particular event exalted by an inspired poetical soul into a universal, sacred validity; the tribulation which may have been in the mind of the believer and of the donor, in celebrating the mystery of the Transfiguration, namely, the Turkish peril, is extended and interpreted as the suffering of humanity in the gloomy vale of earth, above which the Redeemer is already by his Transfiguration proclaiming the divine Grace. For whatever the thoughts underlying the commission and the Biblical words inherent in the theme—Raphael's idea, at the end of his days, could only make visible and interpret in paint the mysteries to be revealed. This is his Bible commentary, his manner, as a true "illustrator", of throwing light upon the text of Holy Scripture. Thus his imagination hovers at large over the narratives of the Synoptics. It will ever be highly profitable to keep in mind the words of the Gospels that found an echo in him. It is the winged power of his imagination that sets up, out of the sequence of the narrative, a juxtaposition, a superposition—in fact an interpretation; its order of the day is simultaneity. So, for him, the work of Salvation, which his painting was to depict, is in its supreme manifestation to be found at the moment of deepest affliction, of bodily and spiritual suffering, of helpless subjection to the earthly, with the despondency it involves. For him, now that the doctrine of Grace had come to him as a vital experience, this work of Salvation could not remain a theological conception, as in the pictures of his forerunners. Grace is granted to those who put their trust in the divinity of the Redeemer—thus through doubt and despondency as to their own earthly powers, the Apostles point to him whom they "have not seen, and yet have believed". And he appears—overwhelming in his radiant presence and figure, in light and grandeur!

(*Matthew*, xvii, 1-6) "And after six days Jesus taketh Peter, James and John his brother, and bringeth them up into an high mountain apart, and was transfigured before them: and his face did shine as the sun, and his raiment was white as the light. And, behold, there appeared unto them Moses and Elias talking with him. Then answered Peter, and said to Jesus, Lord, it is good for us to be here: if thou wilt, let us make here three tabernacles; one for thee, and one for Moses, and one for Elias. While he yet spake, behold, a bright cloud overshadowed them: and behold a voice out of the cloud, which said, This is my beloved Son, in whom I am well pleased; hear ye him. And when the disciples heard it, they fell on their face, and were sore afraid."

(*Mark* ix, 6) Peter "wist not what to say; for they were sore afraid. . . ."

If it were permissible to sum up visions in words, how would one seek to explain the power of these gestures? The figure of Christ raised aloft by the breath of heaven, blowing through his cloak and hair, seems to endure submissively the experience of the moment, and yet around that figure, rising for the first time from life on earth to the new element destined for it, there is wafted a fullness of power of its own. The gesture reaches out quite definitely into the beyond! The withdrawal from the world expressed in his arms becomes a sign of benediction, as if he must needs share with the world his bliss. From his rapt figure Grace flows streaming forth so overpoweringly that Moses and Elias seem to be caught up wildly into his sphere, and the three chosen disciples, "overshadowed by a cloud", throw themselves down: they "were heavy with sleep", and when they awaked, James falling humbly on his face, in utter irresolution, Peter, smitten with the unbearable light and deafened by the voice out of the cloud, merely stammers the words "Lord, it is good to be here", whilst John, "overshadowed" beyond expression, is as if on the point of fleeing in terror from the beam of light and yet held fast within its radiance, in an almost dithyrambic rapture and moving as in a ritual dance (Plate 269). In the wild, joyful swaying of the figures, in the harmony of these rhythms, otherworldly in their movement, with the utmost brightness, Raphael's earlier motive of "lightness and light" here takes on a new significance. The contrasted opposition, in the DISPUTA, of transfiguration above and illumination below, is here transformed into a final, dramatic tension before unknown. Raphael's poetical imagination sweeps in rushing flight over this narrative, and interprets the related meaning of its various parts to the eye of the faithful in a *single* picture in which its significance is literally shown in a condensed form; the beams of such literal illustration dispel the nocturnal spectre of rationalism, which could see here only two fortuitously combined pictures, and thus feared a relapse into the habitual methods of the Primitives. The style of the "Primitives" appears to us to-day as the enviable style of what is essential, and this painter of Renaissance forms and of space comes nearer to them than nineteenth-century Classicist or Impressionist estimates might suppose; he approaches them through renunciation, or rather perhaps through mastery of his mediums. One who penetrates like Raphael into the sunlit heights of these late visions comes to know well that in those regions "la legge natural nulla rileva", the natural law has here no currency. The summit of Tabor is there, close at hand and small; but it is Raphael's desire that we should perceive in it a mountain, and we acquiesce. For around this summit are wafted the airs of the far mountain region, and around this little flock, exalted above the life of the lowlands. There we see them, lying small and impotent, thrown down by the radiant light, below the overwhelming grandeur and splendour of the Redeemer; and so, like satellites round a star, Moses and Elias circle round him, smaller and yet more than life-size—all of them, in the proximity of the region of the Holiest, distinctly visible in their gestures, whilst there below, the teeming throng of the common people has the effect of a troubled stranger on the dark earth.

> [1]"Ist er in Werdelust
> Schaffender Freude nah
> Ach an der Erde Brust
> Sind wir zum Leide da!"

How indispensable this radiance of Grace appears, above the confused, gloom-encircled human throng; a chasm of impotence and misunderstanding cleaves them into two sections, both pitifully helpless, one in agony of soul, the other marked by physical suffering. Their repose interrupted, as they wait and meditate, the gathering of Apostles meets in alarmed sympathy the multitude pressing forward with the maniac, just as in ancient tragedy the Chorus bear the sufferings of the people before the steps of the royal palace. The parents have brought down their boy; at the very moment of a seizure, they present him, half entreating help, half reproachfully. The father simply holds up his son, who is torn asunder by the convulsion; his roaming look seems to be changing into one of terror. Here also no help is forthcoming, at the moment of this fresh access of horror; once more the case is merely referred to one who is away! The sister stooping forward in entreaty pleads for the sufferer, Is what you see not enough to call for your help? And her eyes are ready to fill with tears. The young woman in the foreground—surely she must be the mother!—is already on her knees, beside the child and his father, to support the tottering boy. Now she turns round almost ferociously, in a fresh access of alarm and wrath; merely to be put off with consolation, her eyes rolling, she points with both hands to the epileptic: "See, this is what we live through daily—and you wish to turn aside!" Slightly frowning, in the act of drawing herself haughtily up, she looks like a leader of the Chorus, menacing rather than suppliant. In her, personal participation is expressed at its utmost intensity; in the others, there is only a fullness, an excess, of entreaty, lamentation, weeping, crying. This foremost group has an effect of isolation, for now a storm has broken among the Apostles; utterly shaken, the old man in the centre seeks to ward it off with terrified hands; as if fascinated by the eye of a serpent, the young man beside him approaches, clutching his bosom, giving way to his feelings of sympathy almost like a woman. A kindly man with long hair and beard—wearing like Paul a red cloak over a green robe—feels himself called upon to speak; and

---

[1] "Be he, in bliss of birth,
Nigh to creative joy,
Ah, woe! on breast of earth
Bide we to our annoy!"

yet at the moment can only offer imperfect consolation by pointing on high: he who alone can help has gone up on the mountain! The man crouching on the ground behind him repeats his words. His gesture has the effect of a summons to the two who are slow to believe. In the centre of the composition, immediately behind the group most violently affected, a bearded man pleads in an attitude full of majesty for sympathy with sufferer and suppliants; in vain —for it is Judas towards whom he turns, Judas, who with protruded lower lip shows himself to be incapable of being affected by what is taking place either on high or in the depths.

The effect of these happenings above the earth and on it is manifestly conditioned by the all-dominating forcibleness of the line; the upper figures circle within it so that the power of the light proceeding from the Redeemer confines the hovering and the reeling figures in exactly equal measure within the line of a circle. The gesture of the arms of Christ is consummated in a round arch, with the crown of his head as centre; the same curve about the Redeemer as centre takes in the soaring feet and the fluttering garments of Moses and Elias, the awakening, unsteady figures of Peter and John as they start back. With him, the heavenly sphere comes down to earth, compelling the chosen followers to conform with its law. Gravity gives place to easy poise, and transfixed between the two, the three favourite disciples can only reel as in a stratum above the ground. But within the sphere of the picture the same law is communicated also to the figures bound to the soil in the dark vale of earth. Like a forecourt to a domed building streaming with light and soaring into the beyond, the groups below are disposed almost in an ellipse, so that they reach forward towards the two wings;—and so their lines bend round in the figure of Andrew and in the line of the father as segments about the two lower angles. By this device also height and depth, remaining inseparable in an inner, poetic union, are bound together. Indeed, this union has so strong an effect on the eye that, in conformity with the great laws of pattern that, deriving from Gothic, are still vitally operative in Raphael, one might be tempted to think of an upper termination in a semi-circle to round off the groups in the lower angles. It would fit in with the dynamic effect of the supernatural circle of light; indeed, it would perhaps intensify it, because then the empty corners would be eliminated. But we are immediately bound to admit that if there were a complete semi-circle above—as for example is shown by the great design for the RESURRECTION, at Bayonne (Plate 97, $R. Z.$, VIII, 387), it would be impossible to say anything in favour of such an extension of the picture upwards, above the figure of the Redeemer So we come back repentant to the form we have before us, satisfied with the thought that there is inherent precisely in this sphere of light descending on Mount Tabor, with no round upward termination, a dynamic tension of its own. We are allowed to witness its appearance, and as it subsides yieldingly upon the summit of the mountain, this state of still incomplete attainment—a truly Raphaelesque *ritardando*—creates in us, all the more, a presentiment of its approach in all completeness.

Here artistic media are brought into play that are without parallel in that and in any period; a new poetry thus broke forth in painting which was re-echoed in Titian alone—a jealous fate caused it to cease and withheld from us its ultimate expression, colour. It can only be conjectured that the same transforming spirit that found, for its sublime sermon upon earth, coming out of the beyond, such lines as we have here, and these heroic forms, must of necessity have moved freely in light and colour.

We felt how from the period of the Second Stanza onward, Raphael was seeking pictorial expression along new paths. In the Repulse of Attila he gave a diagonal direction to the colour symmetry, an audacity as unexpected for Central Italian art as the local colouring resolved in reflections and brought into harmony. These last examples of fresco-painting by Raphael's own hand were followed next by the mosaics of the Chigi Chapel, that have been preserved in the colouring originally intended, and by the tapestries. In both cases his desire is to obtain harmony by means of reflected high lights. In the tapestries, as a development of the weaving technique, lights in gold were intended to provide a splendid transition between the deliberately chosen light tones of the weaving; in the Galatea, amidst all the refreshing sea-green and whitish-blue lightness of the sea with its creatures, silvery lights, arbitrary in colour but striking as in music a necessary note, play over her red mantle.

§ Colour

| Here, in the Transfiguration, a poetical quality in the painting was the natural outcome of the very wording of the Gospels—the concourse of restless figures on earth seeking to extricate themselves from this valley of shadow in their helpless vacillations; their garments of many varied hues, yet all in common caught in the half darkness round them and the half light that flits over their bodies, heads and limbs. Pose as well as colour tells of bondage, unredeemed; there above is utmost clearness—every colour of an earthly sort dies away in light, and all human heaviness rises soaring aloft—and even on Tabor the three figures, earthbound though elect, are constrained within the sphere of this radiance. |

The storm in which Moses and Elias seem to have been wafted down from Sinai and Carmel, has darkened the firmament with bluish-black clouds. The tops of the trees sway with the tempest, and as it passes on to the garments of the two witnesses, they remain all the time, even in their ecstasy, human beings borne up in the wind; only the Transfigured Lord soars wafted on his own breath as Creator—creative in his creation. He only is at one with the light of Transfiguration, so white that no fuller could give a lighter colour to his garments. The shimmer from this silvery light glides over the figures of the witnesses as they are wafted near; the garments of Elias flutter in its reflection against the stormy sky and the bright cloud, a quiet harmony of terracotta shot with olive, and the shimmering bluish-pink robe, lifted high by the blast, and olive and terracotta cape of Moses—in colour they are in a wonderful, magic harmony with the atmosphere behind, with the vitality of which they seem to accord as they fly. The head of Moses (Plate 272) is set down in a sketchy manner against the clouds, as if in a tempest, with an expression depicting exactly the fulfilment of the promise of the Lord (*Exodus* xxxiii, 19): "I will make all my goodness pass before thee." The touch of the master's hand here convincingly holds our sympathetic interest; in the principal figure, that of the Redeemer, the power lies in the incomprehensible nature of the gesture; in the face, the extreme, supernatural force seems to be obscured by the hand of a pupil. The three disciples on the mountain fit in harmoniously with the turf on the ground: James is in a greenish gold cloak over a robe of shimmering olive-green and terracotta; Peter, in cool blue, sinks back on his cloak, which is shot with orange-yellow, whilst John is in soft pinkish-violet, his fair, golden locks waving in light and wind above his temples—so bold is the motive to express an indescribable state of dazzlement, so impetuous, here also, is the graphic expression of mortal man caught up into Transfiguration, as the brush tempestuously limned the abounding light that glances over the scene, the golden shimmer of the waving locks. The two martyr deacons, in gold and green brocade, are withdrawn out of the circle of light, in shadow against the tree as a foil.

The earthly scene, in the twilight of the unredeemed, formerly, before the yellow varnish of centuries had given everything the notorious academic golden tone, had certainly the aspect of a diminution of colour in gradually increasing coolness, so as to enhance the light, upon the reflections of which Raphael certainly depended, in this part of the picture also, for colour. Everywhere the draperies gleam out in broad surfaces or sink into half shadow. From the grey-haired Andrew in the foreground to the horror-stricken group of an old and a young man in the middle, everything seems still to be reduced to the same key of colour, carefully calculated around the central idea of the cold, earthly vale harrowed by perplexity and distraction. And yet, on the opposite side of the picture, in the crowd of the populace, a phlegmatic, plastic play of colour makes itself obtrusively felt, extending to the cherry-red and bronze flesh-tones of the shouting boy; in colour and form, and even in details like zig-zag edges to the drapery, we have the entire gamut of *bravura* and triviality of Giulio Romano's own pictures, in the Anima and San Prassede.

§ Raphael's own Share in the Painting

Certainly it is not to be doubted that the principles of composition dominating this portion also are those of Raphael, that the group demanding help was intended to obtrude itself into the light, that the magnificent young mother is made to speak for them against the leaderless Apostles;—but it remains equally certain that the hand that carried out the work placed burdens on the figures instead of giving them wings. And if this may be said also of several figures in the group of Apostles, in the main they bear the marks of Raphael's most personal touch. Each of the figures has perceptibly its surrounding spatial sphere, with its own individuality, being set off against the others in an *aura* of its own atmosphere. And the hand of the busy artist was still able, with animating effect, to run over many portions that he was obliged to leave to assistants. The St Andrew in the foreground (Plate 273) we must regard as almost entirely his work; the sweeping, impetuous touches of his hand are here triumphant beyond anything to be found in the division of labour in the workshop. There is heroic landscape in this head full of traces of the severest trials (Plate 274); the manner in which the locks surge like agitated waves round the magnificently-formed head was conceived, drawn and painted, as regards colour and movement and originality alike, in one single instant. The figure with its oblique movement is dashed in so directly under the impulse of its passion—the curves that indicate the locks of hair being laid quite thinly over the ground—that we fancy we can see the actual dots made by tracing from the cartoon, or at least their lines taken up by the stroke of the brush. On this point we get enlightenment from the glorious though too much worked-up drawing in the British Museum (Plate 275), an intermediate study, coming after the cartoon and before the final carrying out. It was no longer understood by the draughtsman who worked over the drawing in the seventeenth century, otherwise he would surely have carried his pencil along the merely dotted lines; so they remained unimpaired. We find these very dotted lines again in the painting of the TRANSFIGURATION, in the locks of hair which, after the manner of Leonardo, suggest by their waving the temperament of the figure; and this is in the very portion where traces still remain of Raphael's most personal participation. Such participation was the rule, when the master had reached his maturity, with the heads of men—above all, of old men—or may it be that the fateful affection of later generations of over-painters concerned itself especially with the young men of Raphael? We can judge conclusively the loss thereby entailed from the last large drawing known to us, at Oxford: the heads and hands for the group, in sympathetic horror, of the young Apostle and his older companion, in an attitude of aversion, in the centre (Plates 276, 277). In such intermediate studies after the finished cartoon, before the execution of the figures in the picture, the master, on his own account and perhaps also for the benefit of the pupils entrusted with the work, occasionally took up chalk and charcoal once again and made himself responsible for the final touches of profound expression he wished to put before the eyes of the worshipper. There the contours are—in the dots produced by tracing the cartoon, and now the chalk plays its part, with broad, uncrossing, simple passages of shading, at the same angle, in the same direction, in which the figures bend forward; it shapes them, rounds them off, and gives them movement by means of the lights, all in the same stroke of a single application, between which the gleaming light is indicated by leaving the ground of the paper in reserve. This supreme miracle of the art of drawing and of psychological interpretation shows only the heads and hands, but from these details one can recognise that the whole figure strives to attain the goal of its aspiration, appearing to be swept along in the current of its impulsive feelings.

In the picture, the grey-haired Apostle, like the figure of St Andrew, has retained this elemental heroic quality even beneath disfiguring layers of pigment; the youthful figure, in expression and form, in face and hair, is smothered in swollen masses of oil and varnish. He too, like the others, may have been one of the victims of Giulio Romano, the master of all Mannerists and Academic painters and thus of restorers.

For the martyrdom undergone by Raphael's last and sublimest pictorial conception of the beyond had already begun at the moment when the work was in progress. It ought to have remained impossible, from the first sketch to the final pictorial idea, to think of any other initiating force than that of Raphael himself, which ever sought new paths, planning, constructing, breaking forth out of the chaos of creative sensibility, to find its goal here. If none of the preparatory drawings, not even the constructional sketches for the composition of the upper part, at Chatsworth, can safely be assigned to Raphael, if they must with tolerable certainty be attributed to the pupils who carried out the work, particularly the *Fattore*, yet the conception and a great part of the work speak again and again for Raphael. In the upper part, the light region in front of the stormy sky, with Moses and Elias, is his work throughout, certainly also the reeling figure of St John on Tabor, which in painting is entirely in keeping with the heavenly region above the St Cecilia. The Apostle Andrew, and the heads of old men in the middle plane still bear traces of his hand. In a picture in which the workshop and, unfortunately, later centuries co-operated, it is hardly possible any longer to disentangle what Raphael left to his pupils to set down and execute, with the intention of yet taking a hand himself.

§ Division of Labour between Master and Pupils

Perhaps, under stress of necessity, Raphael was the inventor of the system of setting up in his studio an organised division of labour of which the most celebrated example was later provided by Rubens. In this case, the pupils seem actually to have prepared in studies the individual figures and groups. But already at this stage, in these early studies on paper, we must think of the master as intervening with his animating impulse. The Louvre drawing, with the forward-stooping young man and the man pointing upward, might serve as an example of his correcting, with his creative invention, the pupil's laborious earthbound study from the model (Plate 271). It seems that such preliminary working-up of details was left to the tractable *Fattore*. To seek to define the shares taken in the picture by Giulio Romano and Penni, where so many hands have been at work, would be rash and, in every sense of the word, thankless. Knowledge concerning such sublime matters should not be encumbered with the concerns of petty underlings employed upon them, where supreme value is so obvious and manifest. The gulf between teacher and pupil cannot be bridged; indeed, it does not seem too daring to find it in the space dividing the group of Apostles from those seeking their aid. For everywhere in the group on the left atmospheric space is the rule between the figures; by virtue of it every figure is free, in a marvellous state of detachment, their heads are set off from those of their neighbours and also from their own arms, their highly expressive gestures oscillate in movement through the small space which forms a perceptible atmosphere round each figure; this airy *aura* is Raphael's customary element. Perhaps, on the opposite side of the picture, it is only the kneeling woman who can still breathe thus freely—but she also, the loveliest of compositions, has been obliged to suffer submergence in layers of colour of a kind devoid of spiritual feeling at the hands of Academicians; a similar fate has befallen the sister, full of the sympathy she is demanding of others, with her insensitive bulging eyes, in which the iris is fixed and immovable, instead of convincing us by their flashing glance; her nostrils show no emotion, her lips are anything but sensitive. The lunatic boy, as a nude, has an effect not so much of painful suffering as of painstaking in the rendering of his figure; only the father represents again some advance in spiritual quality beyond the unsympathetic drawing of the nude in the Ambrosiana. The man to the left of him, in an attitude of entreaty, with the youth on his right, as if reminiscent of Leonardo's EPIPHANY, shows still, in treatment, the pulsing vitality of the original composer. The shouting figure with uplifted hand seems, with the accompanying heads that fill the gap, to appear on the scene as a harbinger of the decline of which Giulio was the leader. But here also the great new, or rather revived, eternal laws remain perceptible, in conformity with which the sublime, predicatory style on the heroic plane discloses itself in this latest work of the master. From the gleaming, light-toned foot and the puffed-out folds of the falling cloak of the father, to the yellow light on the green shoulder of the young Apostle and the bright reflection on the hand and book of St Andrew, a geometrical and at the same time a spiritual connection is set up. A streak of light springing from the illuminated forehead of the Apostle on the left behind passes across the upward-pointing hand of the figure seen from behind below him, to the forelock of Andrew and his light-suffused fingers, which form the transition to the opposite side of the composition. These are the methods of late Northern Gothic; in Hugo van der Goes and Justus van Gent these pictorial-structural links are to be found, as the linear, almost musical, consistent repetition of the arresting pattern. Here the lower groups also fit in, as a refrain, with the great circle above, in disguised symmetry, in front of the angles; in his latest as in his first work the master showed himself devoted to that poetry of which the means of expression had been provided in advance by Gothic for every interpretation of the Beyond.

This language which speaks through the essential is here heard once again before it came to its end, as the swan-song of the Sublime Style, in the painting of Central Italy, to proclaim abroad great religious poetry to contemporaries and posterity alike, as a heritage of the most sublime of spirits—

"et moriente mori".

XVI

PERSONALITY

WE seem to lack documents for the comprehension of Raphael's personality. His nature moved about the world with less friction than that of Michael Angelo. There was much less occasion for a deposit of records embodied in official documents; nor was it given to him, as it was to Leonardo, to explore creation and to commit his knowledge to the pen, nor to grow old enough to reflect upon himself. The written authorities we possess for Raphael's life range between the opposite poles of sober business and mystic admiration. Little transpires from the letters written by him and about him—so far as they are genuine at all; the amorous contents of the sonnets he shares, of course, with many of his age and period—we have hardly any disclosures made by Raphael himself as to the course of his development—his only *confessions* are his works.

And yet—we believe we know that, as a human being, he attracted the love of the world; and it is known how his astounding wealth of activities and endeavours at the moment of his death were already recognised as not of this world. Such a phenomenon will leave behind it when it disappears a lustre of which the light must needs become ever more radiant from generation to generation. Scanty tradition will become pious legend.

§ Vasari as Source: Mysticism in Vasari

Vasari still, in his day, knew Raphael's intimate friends and immediate pupils, he was familiar with the artistic and intellectual heritage. This sufficed to bring the biographer, from whom otherwise any kind of romantic disposition was far removed, under the influence of this personality, as if he had to bear witness to a power from beyond the grave. When as a professional he discusses the works, he speaks in tones that are often full of understanding, but frequently narrow-minded and even overweening; but the *human* element puts Vasari, who has to write first and foremost, and with a sense of responsibility, about Raphael, completely under his spell. The information he had been able to gather personally from men like Altoviti, Giulio Romano, and Giovanni da Udine, who had still been in close association with the artist, is enough to lend to his words a rapturous touch. From the enthusiastic witnesses of Raphael's own time, therefore, the figure soars aloft of the darling of the gods, early snatched away, whose activities and aspirations, incomprehensible and unbounded as they were, could only be experienced as "divino"—"thou that art from Heaven". "Il grazioso", the lovable, blest spirit, "il graziosissimo", he that is endowed with all the gifts of grace, are phrases often used almost without preliminaries in the *Vite* where Raphael is spoken of; a life full of abounding love towards mankind and from them towards him, whose magic influence continues beyond the bourn of death, for whose consecrated creations even the elements show respect: his masterpiece the *Spasimo* is miraculously rescued from shipwreck between Civita Vecchia and Palermo and brought undamaged to Genoa; it afterwards arrives at the place for which it is destined and becomes in Sicily a "greater wonder, and more renowned, than Etna". And the tidings of his death are interwoven with the report that the Vatican Palace threatens to collapse— "when beggars die, there are no comets seen".

As early as Vasari therefore his course is followed with amazement, he is seen performing great things and planning greater, and everything is esteemed great that has to do with him who instigated so many and so much; this was so even when his gaze, sweeping beyond the limits of his country, followed the Antique to its land of origin, and when he maintained draughtsmen working for him in Greece, "tanta era la grandezza di questo uomo". There must have been something in him, something must have gone out from him, that stimulated to the utmost the instincts of his contemporaries. It was not admiration of his works alone—the source whence they came was regarded by his own age and by futurity with veneration, tenderness and emotion—they loved him out of sheer good will towards him.

§ "Felice e beata Anima"

Whence came this phenomenon, that has never repeated itself with any great men, however closely, deeply and intimately their communities may have felt themselves attached to them? Here the influence was operative of a power derived from the past and the beyond, that can only be explained as arising out of that sense for the beauty of tragedy by which myth lives: the glorious youth, ordained to die, whose pure nature reflects his divine origin, who came to reveal himself to the world only briefly, to turn once again to his true home: "Ora pro nobis", sighs Pope Leo X, feeling the shallowness of his own nature, on hearing the tidings of the decease of the man of genius. And Vasari, who may have known of this, when he relates Raphael's death, breaks out into the words: "Quite surely this pure soul, who was able by his gifts to spread beauty around him here below, will now be himself an adornment for Heaven also . . . 'O felice e beata anima' . . . O, thou happy blessed spirit, everyone speaks of thee with love and celebrates thy deeds and admires every drawing thou hast left behind! Well might Painting herself also prepare to die when this noble artist died; for when he closed his eyes, she was left as good as blind. . . . Yet over and above the gifts our art owes to him as its promoter, he always taught us through his life how one should behave amongst men of every kind, the great ones of the world, those of middle rank, and simple folk. And in truth, among all his outstanding gifts, one strikes me as of such especial value that I can never cease to wonder at it: all artists—not merely subordinates, but also those who really aspired to greatness, were overcome by such a spirit of unity and harmony when they worked together with him and under him, that all ill humour was as if extinguished under his eyes, and not the slightest trace of petty or envious feeling could arise. Such concord was seen only in his time, never again. It arose solely from the spell he cast on all, through his art as through his courtesy; but they were constrained even more by the genius of his happy nature—for his heart was so full of friendliness towards all the world and so overflowing with goodness that not merely men but animals also came trustingly to him. . . . Truly thou mayst count thyself fortunate, sublime art of painting, to call such an artist thine; he has through his great gifts and his pure character exalted thee above all others."

§ Art and Character as well: "Mortal God"

"Nature gave him to the world when she felt herself excelled by the great art of Michael Angelo and desired now to be surpassed by Raphael in art *and* character as well. In Raphael the rarest gifts of the soul were resplendent, in union with charm, zeal, beauty, humility of character, and all the best qualities such as would have caused one to forget quite serious defects. We may therefore boldly aver that one possessed of such rare gifts in such abundance as they were in Raphael is hardly any longer to be counted merely among men; one may well call him a mortal god."

§ The "Divine Son of Urbino"

Ever since Raphael was thus represented as a heroic figure in the first account of his life, he has gone on his way through the centuries as "the Divine Son of Urbino"; he came to the fore again in the times of *Sturm und Drang*, as the vanguard of the Romantics. The earlier biographies, by Passavant and Hermann Grimm, and the most recent, by Wilhelm Stein, continue in this strain. Goethe held himself in solitary aloofness with the expression of his admiration: he was conscious of the "dæmonic" nature in Raphael, as in Mozart, and extols the manifestation of it as "masculine". This verdict is reached through observation of the unity in Raphael's creation. Evidence of this are his works and many of the opinions of his time. They sound a less emphatic note than Vasari's panegyrics, and it was possible for their silent importunacy to fail in making itself heard, even where they were known. Perhaps they lack also the effect of remoteness. For they come from independent and free spirits who do not look up to him as disciples; but they had seen him in Roman society and at his astoundingly multifarious work, and so were stirred to the very depths by his nature.

§ Opinions of the Period

Under the immediate impression of Raphael's death the distinguished Venetian MARCANTONIO MICHIEL writes to a friend: "That most amiable and most excellent painter Raphael has died, to the sorrow of everyone; most of all, scholars have cause to lament him, for now his book, *The Restoration of Ancient Rome*, remains unfinished. The Pope himself feels inordinately distressed; during the fortnight for which the artist lay ill he enquired after him some six times and sent messages of consolation. During those days the Papal palace threatened to collapse, so that His Holiness was obliged to move to the apartments of Cardinal Cibò. People say that the cause of the fissure is not that the lower foundations were too weak to bear the load of the upper Loggie, but that it was a miraculous sign due to the decease of him who gave to the Loggie their decoration. And truly a man whose like cannot be found has been snatched from us. . . . He has been laid to rest in the Pantheon, whither he was carried in a cortège of honour. And without doubt his soul has entered to behold the glory of the heavenly dwelling where all suffering has an end; but his memory and his name will endure here below and long live on in the thoughts and hearts of good men."

§ Commendation by Celio Calcagnini

And the letter written by a humanist in Rome to Basle, to a Swiss kindred spirit, that of Celio Calcagnini to Jacob Ziegler,[1] reads as follows: Raphael of Urbino, a man of great wealth, in peculiar favour with the Pope, distinguished in the years of his youth by his noble disposition and wonderful intellect, perhaps the king amongst painters; this holds good equally of his thought and of his achievements. But as architect his aspirations and energy are such that he undertakes and carries through what even the boldest spirits would never have taken upon themselves. Vitruvius he knows by heart; he matches himself against him, he refutes him. He is Superintendent of the Works of St Peter's. In addition to this, he cherishes into the bargain a plan for reviving the ancient city, its former aspect, its extent and the beauty of its lay-out; he has already made a beginning with this, and can show in advance a large part of it; with this in view he has compared the excavations and the finds from them with the descriptions of the Ancients. With all these talents his bearing is far removed from any kind of arrogance; indeed, his behaviour is friendly and courteous, nor does he reject any advice, or refuse to listen to an expression of opinion—rather he rejoices in every objection—for *he holds learning and teaching to be the highest and most advantageous things in life*—"docerique ac docere vitae praemium putet".

[1] Quoted by Vincenzo Golzio, *Raffaello*, Città del Vaticano, 1936, p. 281.

No praise is more weighty than this—"summa bonitas" set beside "admirabile ingenium". For he who wrote these words was counted among the most exacting intellects of humanist Italy—CELIO CALCAGNINI of Ferrara, at that time Papal Protonotary, after service with Maximilian, Julius II and Alfonso d'Este; he was a man in whose presence the highly versatile Erasmus had to confess himself to be as if "exlinguis", tonguetied, when Celio welcomed him to Ferrara in Latin, in the most honourable terms, with fluent eloquence. If such a practised intelligence found occasion to acknowledge in the artist precisely his intellect, his admiration was certainly not limited merely to his capability; it must have applied to the man of all-round perfection, the truly cultured nature,—in fact, the seldom realised ideal of humanism. The words "doceri ac docere"—"learning and the capacity for intellectual leadership are the reward of life"—commendatory beyond every kind of praise, are a splendid reflection, truly worthy of humanity, of this conscious growth, self-control and readiness to help others.

§ Raphael's Role in Intellectual Society

This was the attitude of mind which Raphael was observed to take towards the fastidious society of Rome—"in the arena of talents"—with equal demands upon himself and others. He had been accustomed to life at this high state of tension since his youthful days in Urbino. Beside the Arno he had sought it himself in the *bottega* of Baccio d' Agnolo, and there he was "il primo di costui . . ." Now in Rome the liveliest and choicest intellects from the palace at Urbino met him again; on his repeated visits to his birthplace he must have come across them. Bembo, then in his youth, had his portrait painted by Raphael; the painter's St GEORGE is connected with Castiglione's mission to England; Bibbiena, Giuliano de' Medici—they all found their way repeatedly to the Papal Court, the chosen nucleus about which an exalted society formed itself in the freest intellectual atmosphere.

§ Julius II as Maecenas and the Medici Legend

It was Rome, not the Pope, that brought them together. More and more the legend evaporates of the success of a Medici as Maecenas at the Court of Leo; what there took shape was no more than had already been brought together under the great Della Rovere Pope—and anyone like Erasmus and Ariosto who at any time sojourned as guest among this society and later became separated from it by life or his own resolve, like Sadolet, longed to be back again amid the scintillating excitements and agreeable formalities of its intercourse. "For everything converges on this soil as in a theatre . . . lesser minds have their place everywhere, but Rome is the home of all men of true culture—it maintains and promotes them." In these terms CARDINAL RIARIO pleads for the return of Erasmus in his pressing letter of invitation—

and they are echoed in the scholar's reply: "Nothing can ever extinguish in me the longing to return to Rome"!—he always retained a recollection of "the freedom and the agreeable formalities of the cultured society, of the rich treasure-store of books, of intercourse with all those *literati*, of the ancient monuments, of so much light focussed on a single point in the world". And all this had already been provided by the *milieu* in the capital of Julius II that Erasmus had visited in 1506 and Raphael had entered at the age of twenty-five.

§ Raphael and Julius II

Perhaps the Pope had made Raphael's acquaintance through his relatives, the ducal family, when he visited Urbino in 1506—what is certain is that three years later the artist was entrusted by the noble-hearted Pontiff, the most ardent Maecenas of his age, with the control of the painting of vast wall-surfaces —in fact, of the greatest themes of human knowledge. On the 14th October, 1509, a Papal *motuproprio* confers upon "Raphael Johannis de Urbino scolari Urbinatensi pictori in palatio" . . . "pupil of his father Giovanni Santi, painter of Our palace", in order to provide more conveniently for his maintenance, the office just vacant of a Scrittor de' Brevi, "scriptor brevium apostolicorum". The young man of twenty-six thus becomes one of the officials of the Papal palace, with few duties, but with freedom to see the world and life from a position in close proximity to the Apostolic hierarchy, and to step forth on the road pointed out to him by another Power as poet of the higher revelations and inter-preter of the beyond.

§ Raphael's Independence

All that Rome and the Papal Court have to offer, all that gravitates ever around this centre of ecclesiastical and intellectual life, came also within the field of operations of his dynamic spirit; seeming to attract what may serve the purpose he has once recognised as his, he forms the centre of a new, purer world, moved by intellectual and spiritual forces, that withdraws on courses of its own from the confusingly multifarious courses taken by others, to circle in the clear atmosphere above it. It is his *daimonion* that impels him; and we may believe that it was this that those who met him divined, and that became woven like rays into a legendary nimbus about his appearing. For from many circles and classes of society came this echo: true poets, and those who, in close contact with his personality, believed themselves to be poets, because like him they were engaged in higher things, bore testimony to him and acknowledged something about him as a phenomenon evading all definition.

§ Intercourse with Poets

There was a complete understanding between the poet-painter and them. The greatest of poets, Dante, he acknowledged from his youth up, because he knew how much he was indebted, to him in particular, for his own art. Now he met in Ariosto the living spokesman of the new outlook in his own generation. Threads of intercourse had been woven between them since Urbino days—legend tells of a lost letter to Ariosto in which Raphael asked his advice about the persons who should find a place in the fresco of the *DISPUTA*. A poetical programme in the painting may raise in us expectations or not—of more essential importance remains the fact that Raphael could in any case have given concrete shape to such advice only as something that vitally affected him, not as something prescribed. But even if the vision of the *DISPUTA* as a picture was already familiar to him from the *Divina Commedia* in a light that is not of this earth, for the great theological, philosophical, humanistic implications of the Renaissance the young man of twenty-six obviously needed the experience of a tutored mind at his side. Whether that person could have been LUDOVICO ARIOSTO is not certain—but it would be quite possible that there was some small grain of truth in that legend of a letter; not Ludovico, but the poet's brother GALASSI ARIOSTO might very well have played the part of adviser, as a learned cleric of wide culture, the familiar of Cardinal Girolamo Riario, the Papal Chamberlain. Yet Messer Ludovic will engage our attention in quite another context as he crossed the path of Raphael. We come across traces of him twice in the First Stanza. They must have met one another; in 1506 Ariosto gave a reading of some songs from the *Orlando* before Ottavio Fregoso. At the time when Raphael was at work on his painting in the First Stanza the poet appeared some five times in Rome, as agent for his master Cardinal Ippolito d'Este, who is presumed to be the subject of Raphael's portrait at Madrid; at that time Julius II threatened to have the undesired envoy thrown in the Tiber. He returned again in the company of Alfonso I, when the Duke incurred the violence of the resentful Pope. It was during an unpleasantly long absence of his lord in the palace that the young Federigo Gonzaga, whose portrait Raphael was then engaged upon, conducted the waiting suite through the Stanze. Ariosto then fled, incognito and adventurously, with his Duke, the "nobil mascherato", before the unreliably volcanic temper of Julius II. Raphael was witness of the dénouements of this star performance; twice over in the First Stanza we come across the traces of the interesting stranger in Rome: according to a tradition which does not go back to Vasari, he is to be found in the PAR-NASSUS, standing among the modern poets; but which could be he? Hardly a single one of the bearded heads but has been suspected of representing the singer of "donne e cavalieri", yet the beardless figure in the foreground, with his finger on his lips, alone bears the unmistakable profile of Ariosto, with the aquiline nose that Titian has handed down to us, accompanied by a beard and with thinner hair on the temples—and the slight cast in the eye that otherwise twinkles dæmoniacally in "charming madness" but also with furtive irony (Plates 280, 281). If Ariosto must be dismissed as scientific adviser, Raphael was not shut off from the appeal of this poet's world. No illustrator could have conceived a more congenial embodiment of Ariosto's virago, Angelica or Bradamante, than this *FORTITUDO*, armed and rejoicing in the fray, on the fourth wall of the *Jurisprudence*, an illustration in the truest sense (Plate 279). She threw light on the verses of the singer even before they were printed, and her figure was to float before the eyes of every reader between the verses of Ariosto's rolling stanzas as a witness to the style of his fancy—a confession, in common, as it were, between comrades, of that admired ideal of powerful womanhood. That masculine period gladly looked upon this ideal as heroic, whether embodied in actual life or in poetry.

It was no more than was due between such kindred spirits that Ariosto should dedicate, over his grave, to the friend who died thus early, an elegy after his manner—"ch' onora Urbino"; all poets felt themselves affected by this loss, especially those nearest him, of his circle. Raphael had deserved this of Antonio Tebaldeo; the portrait in which he captured Tebaldeo's features stirred his friends to enthusiasm. Bembo writes to Cardinal Bibbiena that it surpasses even the portrait of Count Castiglione—"it is more like our Tebaldeo than he is himself; I never saw such a speaking likeness; I am quite envious, and I hope he will paint my portrait also". Unfortunately our curiosity as to this miraculous work is merely aroused and not satisfied by the old copy in the portrait-gallery of the Uffizi corridor between the Palazzo Pitti and the Uffizi. We may grant that it allows us to get an inkling of the monumental stylisation that everything assumed in Raphael's eyes in these last five years; but if we may believe Vasari, Tebaldeo is also represented in the fresco of the PARNASSUS, about eight years younger, among Muses and poets (Plate 82). Perhaps it is his head that looks down on us from the top of the mount, beside the laurel-tree. This face seems as it were to tolerate poetry; it is he to whom we should soonest attribute Tebaldeo's own epitaph:

> "Cunctarum ignarus rerum vixi, *una poesis*
> Atque amor: illa parum nota mihi, hic nimium."

> "In ignorance of all things have I lived
> *Save poesy* and love; of poesy
> My knowledge was too slight, of love too great."

Probably the famous epitaph in the Pantheon was not Bembo's composition, but it was Tebaldeo who epitomised the veneration and sorrow of the world and of the age:

> "Ille hic est Raphael timuit quo sospite vinci
> Rerum magna parens et moriente mori."

> "Raphael lies here; whilst he survived,
> The great All-mother feared to be excelled,
> But with him dying feared herself to die."

PIETRO BEMBO was certainly of such a disposition towards Raphael as might have prompted him to compose this rare eulogy above his grave; Raphael was well-known to him ever since his days in Urbino, between 1506 and 1508, when as confidant of the Ducal house and enthusiastic participant in the *Cortegiano* discussions, he already gave the young portrait-painter and interpreter of men opportunities for proving his talents. At a later date, as a Cardinal with long white beard as he was painted by Titian, he still preserved in his house at Padua a small portrait from the days of his youth in Urbino that were so dear to him. He shared with the artist an intimacy with TADDEO TADDEI, Raphael's friend and host in Florence, with the circle of Giuliano de' Medici, the *"Magnifico"*, as he was called when an exile at Urbino, and with Raphael's inseparable friend, Bibbiena. Once, in Rome, when Taddei was writing to Bibbiena, who had meanwhile become a Prince of the Church and Secretary of State, Raphael entered and dictated to him a request for themes for the pictures in the Cardinal's bathroom, in the upper storey of the Vatican, next to the Loggie, "of which a beginning is to be made in a few days". As *scrittor de' brevi* Raphael will also have been in immediate personal touch with Bembo and Sadolet, as Apostolic Secretaries under Leo X. An intellectual interchange took place between the refined stylist and the explorer of sublime style; in 1516 they made an excursion together in company with Castiglione and the Venetian friends Beazzano and Navagero, to visit the monuments at Tivoli, the Temple of the Sibyl, the Egyptian telamons, and the tripod candelabrum for the *"triangolo"* which is to-day in the Doge's Palace, with the Grimani antiques. NAVAGERO took with him to his new post in Venice as Librarian of San Marco impressions of this journey. He left his friend BEAZZANO behind as Bembo's secretary. The evidence of their intimacy, the double portrait in the Doria Gallery, belonged to Bembo; after Navagero's death he gave it to the surviving friend. Even without knowing these two men, we could not fail to perceive in this group of friends evidence of that society of strenuous activity in research and poetical composition of which the artist was able to feel himself an effective member; for in his creative work he succeeded in giving shape to something which it was granted to but few amongst them to achieve in their lives—harmony of endowments and character. In this pair, at one with each other yet so diverse in nature, he felt how opposites complement one another to produce the much-desired equilibrium—"the presence of so many men of letters together, the agreeable formalities of a cultured sociability", to which Erasmus was able to testify in such high terms.

Such was the wide compass of the human scale of which Raphael had the skill to awaken the strains, so complex in its harmonies was the milieu in which it was granted him to find—and to dispense—stimulus and exaltation; and among those "agreeable formalities of cultured sociability" were the *Orti Letterari* of Rome, a network of villas spread over the hills and valleys of the city, charming as scenery and of antiquarian attractiveness, in which stood fragments of Antiquity scattered amongst grottoes and arbours, little groves and vistas; their best adornment was the spirit which the master of the house was able to conjure up in them because he was conscious of the *genius loci*. SADOLET had his villa on the Quirinal; he thought of it with homesickness in his banishment. ANGELO COLOCCI, in the same official circle in the Vatican with Raphael, Secretary of the Correspondence, had his "hortulus" beside Sant' Andrea delle Fratte, near the Palazzo del Bufalo, by the arches of the Aqua Vergine; among creeper-clad fragments of architecture and statues was couched a sleeping nymph, above the outflow of the spring, hallowed of old—its genius:

> "Hic genii locus est, genii una cura voluptas;
> Aut genii vivas legibus, aut abeas."

> "This is the place of the genius, whose only care
> Is pleasure; live by its laws, or else go hence."

Such were the lines placed below by the Papal Secretary, Abbreviator, Procurator and Notary of the Camera. In contrast with many of his contemporaries, his genius seems to have abandoned him; he provided Erasmus with an object of biting invectives, and also JAN GORITZ, the prelate of Luxemburg, from 1512 onwards Papal Protonotary, who was perhaps his competitor in conviviality. His garden by the Forum of Trajan, at the foot of the Capitol, seemed to attract the most select minds, as did the master of the house himself. "Father of all delights", "a man pure in heart", Erasmus calls him— "Corycius senex" was his name among his Roman friends, after the pattern of dignified cheerfulness in Virgil's *Georgics* (IV, 127). "What good use you have made of your more than limited means; you have thereby won for yourself the best of names and everlasting remembrance." Thus a friend writes to him, the poet BLOSIO PALLADIO, when he sets up a literary monument to him. It is the preface to a remarkable anthology of the most outstanding Roman poets and men of letters who were guests of the Luxemburger. The occasion seems sufficiently worthy of remark: "Paucissimis divitiis"—out of the very limited means of his Vatican office Goritz understood how to play the Maecenas in a noteworthy manner. A kind of chapel was erected by him in Sant' Agostino; at the third pillar he erected an altar—the much admired group of St Anne with the Virgin and Child by Andrea Sansovino stood there; above, Raphael painted the Prophet Isaiah as most passionate witness for the birth of the Messiah. The inner connection between the group of two mothers and the foreteller of the Divine Child is to-day destroyed by the removal of the sculpture into a side-chapel. The festival at the consecration of this altar speaks for the value of its dedication to the donor and his circle of friends. On the day of his patroness St Anne there was a gathering around Corycius at Sant' Agostino. Each of his friends laid on the table that there stood ready a poem extolling the founder of the altar and his pious work. In the evening they met again in his garden in the solemn precincts of Trajan, by the steps leading up to the Campidoglio. New verses were pinned to the trees; after the banquet there was a reading of these tributes, and others were improvised. The poet Blosio Palladio, a friend of Ariosto and intimate of the house of Chigi and also of Raphael, secretly collected these poetical presents from the guests as a surprise for Goritz and published them as "Coryciana" with that dedication.

Those who can overcome the sense of aversion and boredom induced by Latin verse exercises of intellectual Humanists and turn over the leaves of this volume, will come across proud names like those of Castiglione, Bembo, Sadolet, Vida, Beroaldo, with others less distinguished, following a scheme of artificial verses. But suddenly there is, as it were, a rush of wings above these pages of exercises, and a sweep in the Latin strophes of which the others had not the slightest conception; amid all the scansion of these versifiers a young poet, never failing and with a graceful irony at his own expense, craves inspiration of his Muse: "Da mi musa aliquid novum . . ." (Plate 282.) For

> "Many as blades in spring that are sown over the fields
> Many as blossoms that later adorn the earth
> Many as bees that Hybla feeds
> Many as flakes that winter strews
> Many as stars that beam from the poles of North and South
> Many as clusters that vintage in autumn yields
> Many as grains at harvest in Libya's acres reaped
> Many as in the forest green there are leaves on the trees
> Many as fishes in ocean depths
> Many as birds that flit through the air—
> To count them were vain, as to count
> The lines on Father Corycius' altar."

Even before he has uttered his petition, the Muse has already caught his voice, among the many that must have wearied her, and bestows on him her blessing, the genuine poet, "Huldericus Huttenus Eques Germanus" (ULRICH VON HUTTEN).

Even though the painter of the Isaiah is not mentioned by name, and besides Sansovino only "Apelles" is spoken of, he must have moved among the company gathered for the solemnity—in the guise in which his figure appears in the SCHOOL OF ATHENS or on the wall of the HELIODORUS (Plates 285, 286). It is tempting to fancy that the inspired and armoured German devotee of humanism and the true portrayer of his ideals here encountered one another, and to picture to one's self how, "exlingues" perhaps, they yet had intercourse, amidst the Latin and Greek orations of the *literati*, in the language of creative imagination, and understood one another. Even though this may not appear in the "acts", yet it may be counted among the facts. The horizon of the Urbino master was wide enough; not much later his relations began with Dürer, whose creative work was familiar to him since his Perugian days, and whose engravings spoke to him from the walls of his studio.

Thus the poetically creative imagination and passion of the North gained access to him for a second time, a passion to which he showed himself as a painter as susceptible as to the austere contemplativeness and otherworldly rapture of the Middle Ages. To the official humanists, even including the Apostolic Chancellery, "Dante's language" seemed "obscure, Cicero's crystal-clear"—they regarded the Middle Ages as barbaric; only the truly creative spirits, Raphael and Michael Angelo, were capable of a discerning glance at the elemental, spiritual forces in that epoch, and of opening themselves to their influence, to the benefit of their own and coming ages. Yet something of this must have reached the consciousness of Raphael's entourage. Colocci was made, at least æsthetically, a partisan in spirit by his concern with the Troubadours and early Italian poetry. But in the villa of Raphael's friend, the Papal Grand Datario, BALDASSARE TURINI, on the Janiculum, the medallions of a ceiling by Giulio Romano are said to be decorated with portraits of poets:[1] beside Dante, Petrarch and Marsilio Ficino, the "poet-painter"—*not* Ariosto—is seen as fourth, with the bearded features of the enigmatic self-portrait in the Louvre; and this tribute in the decade after Raphael's death came from those near him in time and human relationship. We may recall that Giulio was his pupil, the master of the house his executor, and that the latter had acquired, out of respect for Raphael's memory, for the church of his own native town of Pescia, the unfinished altarpiece of the Dei, the MADONNA DEL BALDACCHINO.

In these circles, then, he was thought something of! And it appears that he possessed other friends to whom he did not merely present this or that aspect of his nature and ideas, but who understood and comprehended him as a man also more profoundly. Relations grew up between him and the noble BALDASSARE CASTIGLIONE as early as his Urbino days; the "Formator del Cortegiano" is already alluding to the established conception of Raphael's grace when, in his dialogues, he represents Count CANOSSA as being chaffed on account of his peculiar affection for the "*graziosissimo*" among the painters. (*Cortegiano*, I, 2.) At an early stage Castiglione may have found it worth while to contribute furtherance, rather than knowledge, out of the abundance of his own aristocratic breeding to this fine culture so different in kind. That the Count should have had a share, as regards its style, in the drafting of the memorial

[1] The room is inaccessible, so it is not possible to say whether this sentimental juxtaposition is old or modern.

on Ancient Rome—if Raphael was its author—is as probable as their correspondence. Even if the oft-cited writing addressed to him by Raphael must be taken as an invention, it contains nothing, particularly as to the "certa idea", that could not have been discussed between them, in view of the aims of the artist and the knowledge of the Count. To both of them Plato was ever present, in their leaning towards Antique art, directing them, as it were, and dedicating them to a lifetime of productivity. The portrait of Castiglione represents a culmination in Raphael's painting, and stands as a beautiful testimony to their mutual understanding. That the man of the world felt himself to be the recipient of a tribute may be inferred from the delicacy of the sonnet already referred to: the dialogue of the spouse with the portrait of her absent one betrays the deep impression made by this art on the life of the noble pair. We like to picture to ourselves the two men, the scholar and the artist, on their visit together to the monuments in Rome and Tivoli, and we understand all the more readily the complaint of Castiglione in his letter to Maria Aloisa Gonzaga: "I feel tolerably well, but it is as if it were not Rome where I am since my poor Raphael ('il mio poveretto Raphael') no longer dwells in the land of the living; God in His mercy receive his soul!"

A worldwide horizon opened before the artist in his intercourse with AGOSTINO CHIGI. Nothing worked with such stimulating effect on his creative talent as the cult of the Antique and the astrological beliefs of the "magnanimo" of the world of commerce. From his personality, with his enterprise in matters of finance and his wide intelligence, embracing heights and depths and stirring the minds of men, an energy must have gone forth which in the fascination it exercised on the imaginative faculty may be compared, distantly perhaps, with the dæmonic force of Julius II. In their intercourse "one paid with his wealth, the other with his genius"—that is the view of the matter-of-fact Aretino. But if Chigi "was a merchant in acquiring, a king in giving", Aretino was precisely in a position to know it; so much was it also characteristic of this prince that he knew how to gather men of talent round his throne. After the centripetal force of this system of planets, this was certainly the peculiar attraction of the house for Raphael. Chigi's collections—his antiques and gems—were superintended and added to by a learned priest. The printing press in his house brought out the first Greek editions of PINDAR'S "Odes of Victory" (Plate 226) and of the idylls of THEOCRITUS. Probably it was Raphael who designed the spirited Byzantine double eagle for the device of the Cretan printer Zacharias Calergi, quite in the style of his mythological monster for Chigi's dishes. It is impossible that his easily-kindled spirit should have allowed such poetic treasures to pass by him unnoticed, even if Greek was a closed book to him; for whom, if not for him, was this cult favoured by the great-hearted master of the house? Their intercourse, their mutual give-and-take, have become legendary in a few anecdotes. A conflict threatened with regard to the SIBYLS between Raphael and Chigi's cashier, who refused to pay more than 500 guilders; the artist proposed as arbitrator Michael Angelo, who is supposed to have valued the head of a single Sibyl at 100 guilders. On his return from a journey Agostino heard of this, and "although Raphael makes no demand, because he was in no way inferior to him in delicacy of feeling", he assigned him 100 guilders for every head in the picture and impressed upon his cashier that he must "be nice to him, so that he may be content with this payment; for if he insisted on the draperies of his figures being paid for, it would be the ruin of us". The other story—of the Fornarina who was to chain the painter to his work by being kept a prisoner in the Villa, seems to have been invented to apply rather to intercourse with strangers than with a friend. The great calculator seems this time to have calculated wrongly; the pictures are the work of pupils!

The perpetual goings and comings of artists certainly had also a stimulating effect on Raphael. As a master of building PERUZZI remained on intimate terms with him for his own architectural activities also; SEBASTIANO DEL PIOMBO communicated to him some notion of an art that was poles apart from him, and perhaps of music also—it was really for the sake of his lute-playing that Chigi had brought Sebastiano with him from Venice. They lived, as it seems, side by side in a kind of reciprocity, especially as portrait-painters, until in the senseless competition for Narbonne the rivalry between Raphael and Michael Angelo was involved; they became opponents at least, if not enemies. All this has been handed down to us is carping criticisms of the Venetian in the letters to Michael Angelo and Raphael's proud words: "If Sebastiano allows himself to be helped by Michael Angelo, my victory will be all the greater."

The scene of the peaceful activity of all these artists in the "viridarium" or "suburbanum" of Chigi, the Vigna outside the Porta Settimaniana in the Trastevere—later famous under the name of the "Farnesina"—was described by the poet BLOSIO PALLADIO before it was quite finished. We may safely assume that he understood what he was talking about; his own villa, up the hill behind St Peter's, was famous through the setting here provided for himself and his guests by the intelligence of this witty and cultivated man. "Blosii villula ter quaterque felix"—Ariosto longs for his daily intercourse with him and with Bembo, Sadolet and Giovio, and is thinking of him when he praises an unpretentious and tranquil way of living (*Satira* V). "Blosius meus Palladius Romanae urbis delitiae", the humanist writes of him. The "ornament of Rome" had in its garden a fountain with marble benches and laurel hedges behind; there was a path leading uphill through a fragrant grove to the place where Blosio entertained his friends at table; beside a spring with water from Tibur a miniature temple surrounded by lemon-trees with a little fountain served as sideboard, and pillars "in the manner of a theatre" carried a pergola of vines affording shade. The dwelling with its wealth of art was reached through a laurel grove to provide berries for the birds to find. Where Raphael makes his appearance amongst the company, Blosio is to be met with; at Chigi's house he plays the part of herald of the household; at the celebration of the appointment of Giuliano de' Medici as a *Patricius*, on the Capitol, it was Blosio who composed the festal ode; at the solemnities in Sant' Agostino it is he who collects the poetical tributes of the guests as "*Coryciana*"; even the renowned IMPERIA was the subject of an encomium that was much remarked, and of a salutation over the tomb:

"Di duo magna duo tribuerunt munera Romae
Imperium Mavors, et Venus Imperiam."

("Two mighty gifts two gods to Rome did give—
The empire Mars, Venus Imperia.")

For, as Beroaldo relates, in the temple precincts of this "god-bestowed," finely-cultured lady also, the sybaritic humanists Colocci and Blosio Palladio met one another, together with the great personages of the Vatican, Cardinal Giuliano de' Medici, Sadolet and Fedra, with their handsome presents—excelled, of course, by the prodigal whims of the "gran mercante di christianità".

We trace something of the spirit pervading Chigi's circle, in which life was lived with the gods, in freedom, when they were conjured to his festivities. It was FILIPPO BEROALDO who conjured them, by translating Apuleius; he thus made the master of the villa, and what was more important, his painter, familiar with the charm of the fable of Cupid and Psyche. Where Venus rides over the waves the picture of Galatea immediately comes to mind. Beroaldo was one of Raphael's first friends in Rome, even before Castiglione, Bembo and Bibbiena arrived there—"spirito arguto e faceto", "a man of keen and ready wit", the *Cortegiano* calls him; as secretary he was in the service of Cardinal Giovanni de' Medici, and even before the Papacy of Leo X he was very likely weaving threads of intercourse between the house of Medici, once more coming to the fore, and the artist. At Urbino Beroaldo kept up relations with the ruling house and their faithful supporters, and he defended Francesco Maria against the anger of Julius II; and Bembo came thence to visit him, Sadolet and Inghirami. Together with them, he was one of the *Prelati Domestici* under Leo X, and afterwards he became Inghirami's successor as Prefect of the Vatican Library. But he died a tragic humanist's death through vanity, because he thought his merits inadequately regarded by the moody Pope whom he served. Many a one might have taken the same course if there had been a more wide-spread disposition to take anything to heart in the Rome of Leo X.

RAPHAEL

§ Aretino on Leo X

"For Leo's nature had a way of swinging from one extreme to the other; it would be difficult to say what gave him greater joy, the talents of men of culture or the foolish antics of the *buffoni*; otherwise he could not have given such rich rewards to both." This was the judgment of one in closest relationship with him and in the circle of Chigi, who understood how to give correctly— even if in princely fashion. PIETRO ARETINO was attached to Chigi's palace in Raphael's last years. It was frequently recounted that he was dismissed from the house on account of a theft, but in the annals of the Chigi family he is called an "eruditus homo, vir acerrimi judicii", and he himself always recalled thankfully these very days that he spent there with Bembo and Bibbiena. His culture and his keen critical sense gave him in those years a position in relation to Raphael also, if we may believe his own words. Without the exalted schooling of the humanism of the period, which was passed on from generation to generation, he appears as a magnificent upstart who was not impressed by the versifying grammarians. "Strive to be sculptors of sense, not miniaturists of words," he writes to Dolce. This striking metaphor makes us understand how rightly he could claim, among so many men of letters, that he was not *without eyes*—it seems, he himself painted—and that Raphael and Sebastiano as well as Titian often relied upon his judgment; indeed, in the Dialogue with Ludovico Dolce he asserts that Raphael showed almost every one of his works to him first before making them public; Aretino must as a matter of fact have had experience of Raphael's working at close quarters to be in a position to know of Dürer's engravings on the walls in his studio, and to be able to weigh the great artists so understandingly one against another: "Until you see the nudes of Michael Angelo you do not understand the sublime grace of Raphael; it wins you by the charm of his invention—Michael Angelo appears unsurpassed in drawing, but in Raphael everything is seen combined." He was present at the scene, at the Pope's table, of the burning of the reconstruction of Rome, and possessed an instinct for propriety and decorum, even if this instinct did not always tempt him to follow its guidance.

In such moments the painter, with his emotional temperament, as unlike Aretino as could possibly be, may have allowed himself, with his "bee's instinct", to take a pleasure in this liveliest of intelligences, all the more when he saw how that intelligence was included within the wide horizon of Chigi's house and style of living.

§ Widened Horizon of Life in Chigi's Circle

For, as regards the company that frequented it, the house of this ordinary citizen had broken down its social limitations, and Raphael could there meet with the Court in the intimacies it indulged in outside the walls of the Vatican; he may have witnessed or heard how Julius II tauntingly asked the owner of the Farnesina whether his palace would become as magnificent as that of Cardinal Riario over the way (on the site of the present Palazzo Corsini) and received the answer that the stables, built by Raphael, were more splendid than the Cardinal's dining-room. He may also have been a witness of the convulsions in the State and in private life when the Pope pawned the Triple Crown with Agostino for 40,000 florins, and then had it demanded back with threats and without payment—and perhaps the subjects of the COUNCIL and the BANQUET OF THE GODS first acquired a meaning for Raphael after he had seen the Pope and his Cardinals sitting at table and feasting underneath them, in this garden pavilion, with the same simple irresponsibility. Here he met the historian and collector of portraits PAOLO GIOVIO, future Bishop of Como, Cardinal BIBBIENA, BEMBO, the man of present enjoyments, but also such a man of the future, as GIOVAN MATTEO GIBERTI.

§ Raphael in the Vatican: Attitude of Julius II towards him and Impression upon Raphael

For the Urbino master, who came from a cultured Court in his native city, "quel nido di gentilezza", from the cradle of all forms of distinguished sentiment, and had quickly obtained a footing in the Vatican, the Papal Palace was more than a mere scene of his labours. To him, as poetical interpreter of life and men, it must have seemed like a stage on which the great played their part in world events. We possess no observations of Julius II about the painter, but we can imagine how this stormy personage perceived the imperturbability and free incorruptibility that were part of the charm of the young man's nature, and how the ruler contemplated enlisting in the service of his world-system and his high intentions one so readily swayed; and Raphael's answer may be read from the portrait of the Pope, who "was never seen" by his trusty Master of the Household "to joke"—he at least never observed it—we may read it also from the air of veneration that dominates the BESTOWAL OF THE DECRETALS, from the imposing power with which the Pope triumphs in the HELIODORUS, or from the manner in which the Rock upon which the Church is founded takes part in the MASS OF BOLSENA. Yet the influence of this mighty personality forced its way more profoundly still into the sphere of the artist's imagination; it introduced to his experience the tottering of a world and the dramatic act of its rescue—and the man who controlled this tremendous event awakened, by his commissions and by the spectacle of his own life, the still slumbering powers in the painter; indeed, the mere existence of this patron, his *terribiltà*, to which Michael Angelo also was obliged to do homage, in his MOSES, caused Raphael to mature into a creator of monumental figures and to surpass himself as the dramatist of the historical paintings. Never did a Maecenas exercise by his mere nature so profound an influence as this Pope, whose—always grandiose—will afforded no room for rest to the artists and no relaxation for himself. This was also the truth which his overmastering feeling for power may have discovered in wine. His mode of recreation seemed to the world remarkable enough. The unlearned man who did not wish to hold a book in his hand, and cried out to Michael Angelo "Give me a sword", in the critical moment of his life, a month before he forced his way on a ladder through the breach at Mirandola, and shortly before he thundered out to the world his Bull against simony, sat evening by evening with Bramante and made him read aloud and expound Dante to him. "Every day our Sovereign makes progress" are the words of December, 1510; "it seems he yet intends to become a learned Dante scholar"— "parmi si voglia far docto in Dante". A remarkable picture—the two old firebrands, men of action who were in such haste to be building, deep in a book, the poetry of the other world, at the very time when Raphael was interpreting, in the DISPUTA, the serenity of the *Paradiso*, when the architect of the cupolaspace of St Peter's was striving to achieve the final transfiguration, and the great Viceroy of Christ was planning to set on foot the new triumph of ecclesiastical power.

§ The Character of Leo X: Disillusionment

This imposing unity and consistency of aims appeared to be endangered by a papacy whose holder had cried out to his people, at the moment of his elevation: "Godiamoci il papato poichè Dio ci lo ha dato", "let us enjoy the Papacy, since God has given it us". As echo came back, from his jesters, the words: "Yes, *babbo Santo*, little Holy Father, let us live, all else is but nonsense"— "viviamo babbo Santo che ogni altra cosa è burla".

Praised as much as blamed, the pontificate of Leo X continued, so far at any rate as cultural things are concerned, the great movements that had already come into prominence with the Della Rovere Pope. The majority of the leading spirits had already set foot in Rome at an earlier date, and now derived no advantage, even though respected and employed by Leo. Bembo, Sadolet— both *Secretarii Papali*—quitted Rome, Bembo under a subterfuge and complaining of ten years thrown away, Sadolet in voluntarily chosen exile: they wished to live for themselves instead of the Court—"this Court". The Ferrarese Ambassador reports to his Duke: "Raphael assures me over and over again how much sooner he would serve Your Excellency than *this* Court." By degrees many came to think so, even the most intimate. During a mission in France in 1519, Bibbiena commended to his friend Bembo the interest of the King, Francis I, in poetry; and Bembo answered: "In this epoch of low breeding and paltriness no Prince will tolerate about him a truly cultured man who might be able to direct him upwards out of vulgarity. We will therefore set our hopes on King Francis, and I know I shall have experiences I have never had before." And this, written on the steps of the throne, comes from the immediate entourage of Leo, the renowned Maecenas. Under him, too, the illustrious son of the great Laurentius, the laurel (synonymous with the reputation of his father) was found to be lying in the mire—"il lauro giacente nel fango". At least no-one saw the Pope making the right use of it; high praise for him was mostly attuned to the expectation of reward—reproof came from the disillusioned, and what persons of significance and higher feeling were not included among them?

ARIOSTO, with his longing for the spirit of Rome and unsatisfied with his Ferrarese relationships, had hastened to Rome upon Leo's elevation; he came, with a sense of his friendly offices on behalf of the House of Medici in the years of their banishment, "to kiss the red slippers of the new Pope". But being inwardly too aristocratic to sneak prebends and outwardly "left by Apollo and the Sacred College of Muses without a decent mantle", he was hardly noticed, and went back disillusioned (*Satire* IV). Nor was the laurel wreath kept in reserve by the Pope even for him. Raphael, who had already crowned him with it in the PARNASSUS, was his witness in this experience; he may well have seen, and with similar sensations, how the office of *Piombatore de' Brevi*, which had been held by Bramante, his teacher and guide in the high realms of architectural thinking, passed to the special favourite of the Pope, his talented jester FRA MARIANO, who now took possession of the Appartamento of Innocent. in the immediate proximity of his master. Mariano was part of the old family belongings of the Medici, and had already served Lorenzo as barber. Moreover, he may have been "a fellow of inexhaustible humour"—even Cardinal Bibbiena was quite ready to compete with him, and his garden by the monastery on the Quirinal could be counted among the "orti letterari". The artist frequently had dealings in financial matters with SERAPICO, the powerful and unscrupulous Papal Private Secretary, formerly Master of the Hounds with the Pope's hunting-companion, Cardinal Sanseverino. The Court became more and more democratic, the more the Church got out of touch with the people. Raphael saw this crowned and boasted magnificence at close quarters without withdrawing from it. He produced settings for Fra Mariano's *Capricci* exactly as he did for Ariosto's *Suppositi*. When the deplorable foolery was over, he was obliged to perpetuate in a picture on the wall of the gate-tower of the Palace the elephant Annone (Hanno), a gift to the Pope from the King of Portugal, on which the vainglorious poet BARABALLO rode in triumphal procession. His friend, the Chamberlain Battista Branconio d'Aquila, was installed as keeper of the precious animal, and could feel himself continually reminded of his own woes and of the whim of his Papal master, in his dwelling opposite to the palace built by Raphael.

§ Friendship with Bibbiena

The spiritual bridge to this so often unspiritual Court was, for the artist, the Cardinal of Santa Maria in Portico, DOVIZI DA BIBBIENA, an old adherent of the Medici House; he was, with the banished Giuliano, among the

Cortegiani at Urbino, and doubtless was then already acquainted with the talents of Raphael. With his wit and intelligence he may have responded to Raphael's sense for the gracious in that somewhat massive, materially over-weighted society; and the mutual understanding of the artist and the finely-polished ironist can still be recognised in the old copy of his missing portrait and in the playfully frivolous gracefulness of the decoration in his bathroom. There were men of many grades with whom the Madonna-painter himself had friendly intercourse. An instinct for summing-up, habit, and a genuine affinity at heart, may have combined to weave such a web of friendship; a painting on canvas of the Madonna by Raphael that served the Cardinal as a domestic altarpiece in his bedroom was bequeathed by him to Count Castiglione, and we can assume that the Secretary of State, long so powerful, played the part of the painter's protector, when he betrothed his niece to him. This life also, dedicated to the Medici Pope, was to have a tragic ending close beside Raphael.

§ Raphael's Betrothal : Rumours of a Cardinalate for Raphael: Social Standing

To what extent Raphael was interested at heart in this betrothal it will never be possible to discover; we might rather believe Vasari's assertion that he withdrew ever further from its fulfilment. But we may reflect on the light thrown by it on his social standing: at a time when every red hat could be converted overnight for its wearer into the Triple Crown, the most powerful Cardinal and diplomat desired to take the artist into close relationship with himself. The supposition that Raphael himself was selected by the Pope to be a Cardinal because that was the only way to satisfy the extravagant demands of the artist does not sound quite reconcilable with the accustomed practices of the Church, even at that time almost unshaken. The strict Spanish Cardinal Ximenes, for one, would certainly have expressed himself unfavourably concerning such a profanation of a consecrated office; he died shortly before Leo's great creation of Cardinals, but would have been in a position to receive previous intelligence of this intention. Only one thing remains finally well-founded: Raphael's still outstanding claims on the Pope can hardly have been so excessive; we have receipts preserved dating from his last years for large sums paid to him out of the Vatican chest. It will nevertheless seem a characteristic fact that already in Vasari's time such a profanation of the Church, or such an exaltation of the artist, was held to be possible without misgivings. Such was the mythical height attained by the relief in his unbounded ascendancy with the contemporary world. For he departed this life with this great reputation. Artistic worth had been transformed into a position of social and economic standing that was unheard of before him and remained unattainable after him save by few artists, and then not always by the great. He had known instinctively how to suit the framework of his life to the circle in which he operated, before whose eyes his immense activity played its part. His attachment to the Palace, the office of *Cubiculario*—Gentleman of the Bedchamber—of which Vasari speaks, the big receipts from his multifarious Roman works and from foreign commissions ranging from Naples to Fontainebleau, his relations with princely houses and the Patriciate of Florence and Rome, his dwelling on the Piazza Scossacavalli and his *palazzo* with studios on the Piazza of St Peter's, his plots of land and vineyards in various localities of Rome—all this caused him to pass for a "homo praedives", a man of great wealth. His estate was valued after his death at 16,000 ducats, of which 5,000 were to be divided among friends and servants, in addition to his house of the value of 3,000 ducats, which he had bequeathed to Cardinal Bibbiena. His style of living had a truly princely appearance—"da principe".

§ Raphael's Superhuman Activity: his Pupils as Friends

He presented to his age the entirely new spectacle of an unbounded spirit of enterprise. The number of works he took on hand at once, from his thirtieth year onwards, tasks of which every single one amounted to a bold enterprise, seemed to exceed all human power—the Vatican Stanze, the Loggie, the tapestry cartoons, the office of architect to St Peter's, the superintendence of ancient monuments, the reconstruction of Ancient Rome, the laying-out of new avenues of traffic as *Maestro delle Strade*, the palace buildings and villas for distinguished members of Roman society. "He always keeps innumerable people at work for him," says Vasari; a kind of family connection formed itself around him—Perino del Vaga married a sister of Penni, Giulio Romano's sister became the wife of Lorenzetti. His studio, his body of pupils and the number of his assistants grew with the commissions; with his feeling of responsibility not only for their work but also for their development, he took an interest in them by example and instruction, and "affectionately, as if they were not artists but his own sons".

§ Widespread Influence: Diffusion of Raphael's Ideas by Graphic Art

From his studio threads were spun far and wide: the draughtsmen in Greece were put under his care; but what a strong, if not also beneficent, influence was exercised by his tapestry cartoons in Brussels: and he himself was alive to the diffusion of his influence. MARCANTONIO RAIMONDI and UGO DA CARPI—the one in engravings, the other in chiaroscuro cuts—were made to spread throughout the world knowledge of his great, new motives and his painter's manner of draughtsmanship; the prints of DÜRER, with which he was familiar, and the consciousness of a style of his own, may have brought him to this, as they did later Rubens. In any case, this gave rise to relations between him and the Nuremberg master that helped to strengthen Raphael's "evangelistic" seriousness at the moment of the tapestry designs, and brought about a kind of friendly exchange between North and South; Thomas Vincidor was his advocate with the weavers in the Netherlands, Baviera was representative of the North with him. All this was accomplished with Italian publicity before the eyes of his contemporaries. Far-embracing energies and inexhaustibly fertile ideas, inspired groups and vast numbers were seen to be brought into play, a mighty organism called into being and kept in motion by the will of a single individual. The essential, from the artistic point of view, was invention; this was the foundation of everything and gave life to the execution, even if the latter was left to the labours of assistants. The master made designs, directed, set forces to work, assisted, intervened, went over what was being done, and his name, even on works by pupils, offered the guarantee that these works in the new style could not originate from any other source than from him.

In the same manner Rubens built up his workshop eighty years later, when he came from Italy. In Rome he had stood, admiring and copying, before the tapestries, the PROPHETS, the SIBYLS, and the Farnesina ceiling; in Mantua, on the track of Giulio Romano and in the presence of the heritage left by Raphael, he could feel the great tradition in the air about him; from the engravings and woodcuts he learned Raphael's message; in this also, Raphael had set up for him to follow an example, of an intelligent industry, which is inseparably connected with the fashioning of his mode of life. The "King of Painters and Painter of Kings" felt himself to be a disciple, and followed entirely in the steps, of the painter of Popes, who as the leading artist lived "da principe".

§ Raphael's Prestige: his Horse

Raphael could be counted on to adapt himself to every advancement in standing. "He never appeared on the way to the Vatican without an escort of 50 artists," who—if we may believe Vasari— were always only waiting to leave their work and walk behind him to do him honour. Only duns, as the Ferrarese documents show, found difficulty in meeting him—then he had gone out riding; accounts for deliveries of hay, for a horse, have been preserved; perhaps this horse was one of the animals that did honour to him—"l'onoravano"—"just like human beings", as Vasari says. On this point, the exactitude of our Goethe researches need no longer awaken a blush in art historians, any more than the adherents of the "divino", in representing him in the saddle. For his journeys from Florence to Urbino, from Rome in the suite of the Pope to Florence and perhaps also to Bologna, were certainly made on horseback. And if this looks like a digression, we may remind ourselves that the superiority of art of the past in its feeling for bodily physique is actually derived from such necessary activities, which were indeed taken for granted. We actually possess a picture of Michael Angelo on his old man's pony. To the man who was endowed with an abundance of feeling for the vitality of the limbs, this form of movement also meant buoyancy in creative composition. Where there was a lack of creative sense in general, even with a horse to ride on one could become a tedious academic mannerist. Creativeness depends upon a consciousness of the physical frame, and Raphael still continued to step along the hilly streets of his birthplace with the same feeling of buoyancy in the knees which he gives to his figures as they stride.

§ Social Aptitudes: Women: Vasari's Allusions: Romantic Legends

He was the freeborn man, and introduced this quality also into his art as into the circles that admitted him on account of his art and ended by learning to appreciate him for the sake of his character, counting him altogether as one of themselves. For his social gifts were as winning as his art. He can dare to keep waiting the Duke of Ferrara, and to strain the patience of his envoy to the utmost, and finally the envoy himself advises courteous formality towards him, because he is completely under the spell of his character. His works bespeak a breadth of culture that could never be a hindrance to him, because it was on a higher plane than knowledge and science. The portraits breathe a knowledge of man and the world, and every likeness must have been arrived at through an inner, sympathetic participation in the destiny, or rather, in the aptitude for destiny, of the human being before him; there was no limit to the degree of differentiation that his own fine feeling was capable of perceiving; it carries him into the select and limited ranks of the few real "painters of women". Legend has caused many a womanly figure to pass within the effective range of this richly-endowed being—a love-demanding and love-bestowing throng; the DONNA VELATA at least, and the FORNARINA, and his bride Maria Bibbiena, seem to have documentary backing, either in pictures or by report. Yet that enigmatic apparition after sundown, the lady to whom the DISPUTA sonnets are addressed, might, as a fair unknown, bring on the scene a company to which fancy sets no limits, that floated hither and thither above the path of the "graziosissimo", now beneficent, now fatefully fraught with destiny. As to all this, and its effect on his life and death, we have no information but what Vasari gives us—in much-quoted, much-credited and disputed suggestions as to the causes of his death (in these most intimate of matters there is entire lack of confirmation or of proof to the contrary).

Nothing is known about the famous baker's daughter from Trastevere whose features are supposed to be perpetuated in the VELATA and the FORNARINA; her house is reputed still to be in existence, near the Palazzo Corsini. Her entry into a convent after Raphael's death is said to have documentary support, if she really was named *Margherita*, whereas from the pictures of her with the wheel she was surely called *Caterina*.

We had no need to be assured by Vasari, in the most trivial of terms, that the "man of all-embracing vision", with his instinct for elemental life in every form, "whom even animals approached with confidence", possessed a frank, enquiring, always insatiable sense for the inscrutability of woman's nature;

nor can this fact be disputed, passed over in silence, or censured. Of this susceptibility his pictures give evidence. What souls—according to the doctrine of the prophet—would those lovely creatures have had to require of their painter who, in the HELIODORUS, throng around the portable chair of the Pope? It was in the period of his *DISPUTA* sonnets to his nameless nightly companion that the conception dawned upon him of the wealth to be found in the region of woman's soul—in the most gracious of Madonnas and in the three female figures symbolising Fortitude, Prudence and Temperance, and soon after, in the Sibyls and the goddesses of the Farnesina ceiling—from the Psyche received on the threshold of the hall of the gods to the Proserpine beside the gloomy Hades in the Olympian wedding feast.

§ Raphael's Answer

Raphael gives in advance his answer to the gossip about him gathered together by Vasari: the *VELATA* radiates over the world the happiness of profoundest joy in created things; in the SISTINE MADONNA he raises this joy to the level of entire devotion in the presence of the mystery of what is purest and holiest in all womanhood. He had long before expressed a presentiment of this in his Madonnas—the *MADONNA DEL GRANDUCA* in her unapproachableness, the quiet aloofness of the VIRGIN IN THE MEADOW, the majesty of the MADONNA WITH THE FISH, St Margaret's virgin entry on the scene. Raphael thus belongs to those rarest interpreters of the mystery of woman, and proclaims it in a profound, popular fashion. Possibly that child of the world Heinse was right, by social standards: "his women would not have been able to capture the heart of Alcibiades", but so far as the melancholy lady robed in green is concerned, she remains the unique witness to the truly well-bred character of her painter; his instincts and sensibilities in the presence of unusual emotion were ordered and grouped in this tranquillity of outline, this breathing quietness, this harmony of the colours with her complexion. In the *DONNA VELATA*, whatever the sentiments may have been that associated him with her in real life, the joyously sensuous impression offers an interpretation of the profoundest depths in a child of the people such as—once again—could be achieved only by one able to control and purify the chaos within himself. From this point up to the heads of the Church, with their so various aspects, and then down again to their servants and diplomats, the humanists and men of the world, every manifestation struck a related chord in his inner being; and understanding all, thanks to the ordered wealth within him, he becomes thus as of right the trained painter and interpreter of the society to which they belonged. In his way of living as in his art, he associates with them in accordance with the prompting of his all-controlling inner nature.

§ Readiness of Wit

How well he could speak, even by the standard of the lofty demands of the

Florentines, we have already learned from the "dispute" at the house of Baccio d'Agnolo. Anecdotes were current of his ready wit. Michael Angelo, who must have been uncouth rather than fluent of speech towards others, meets him coming along in the midst of his crowd of pupils: "You go about like the Saviour." "And you alone, like the *sbirro*." When two Cardinals objected to the strong red in the flesh-tones of the Princes of the Apostles in the ATTILA fresco, his answer was: "Could they help blushing, when they see their Church led by priests like you?" Such an answer was held to be possible within the hierarchy, because it was thought to be deserved; for the "graziosissimo" the phrasing seems somewhat severe; it has already been suggested that he would rather have clothed what he felt impelled to express in an allusion to the words of Peter in Dante's verse.

§ Humour

In the pre-eminence of his character amid such diverse types among those who met him, a quality is expressed that is as a rule to be found only in those of full-blooded nature: it is called "humour" and signifies the opposite of dullness and asceticism; even the painter of Madonnas was far removed from these last qualities, to say nothing of the mature master who found nothing, from great historical subjects to the idyllic, from the Christian vision to Olympus, that would have remained foreign to the healthiness of his nature. Perhaps the question of his humour will seem as much out of place as the spectacle of his horse-riding.

But anyone who, like Raphael, all through his life strove out of a heart full of love for mankind to talk in the presence of the people in *their* accents, could scarcely do so otherwise than with that sacred absorption in the very essence of life to which every expression of feeling, even the unforeseen and homely, is of itself sacred. How should his mothers and children, even more, the groups of mother and child, be represented except with that smile that is so near to emotion? The helplessness of the *bambino* who feels his way round the knees of his mother towards the little St John provided the motive for the greatest diversity of sketches; the most pious devotional picture of his period of travels, the *MADONNA DEL GRANDUCA*, with her delicate hand round the plump figure of the Child, is filled with this almost painful sense of emotion in happiness; the *SPOSALIZIO* is dominated by the true, popular, full-blooded atmosphere of the mystery-plays, in the side-play of the companion beside the Virgin: she strokes her still vacant ring-finger and looks enquiringly along the row of rejected suitors. And with it all, temple and light-flooded landscape breathe a vitality of sportiveness and youth and of pentecostal joy to be felt in every pore. Raphael was bestowed on us, like Dante's angel, to soar jubilant through space in "baldezza e leggiadria". It is entirely in keeping with Dante's sublime vision, with his attitude of sympathetic humour towards mankind and life, compatible

313

as they are with a profound reverence before the grandeur of God in nature, when Raphael, on the Second Day of Creation, in the Loggie, makes the earth look almost like a plaything:

"l'aiuola che ci fà tanto feroci . . ."

"This plot of ground that maketh us all so fierce."

With the growth of his knowledge of the world and humanity his social superiority increased. A poet even in his architecture, he shows himself a man of a thousand conceits. What but humour is the transition, in the Palazzo Pandolfini, from the display on the exterior to the quiet serenity of the garden front (Plates 176, 177)? And in his masculine consciousness of seeing to the deepest depths of life, he ventures, and ventures successfully, on truly Shakespearean touches even in the story of the Apostles—humour even when the power of the other world is revealed in this one. How the old fisherman Peter, regardless of the spoils of his calling in the boat—still merely a poor sinner—throws himself on his knees before the Lord! How the Roman State, in the person of its deputy, totters at the punishment of Elymas the Sorcerer! And what is it but humour that provides the setting of the SACRIFICE AT LYSTRA, when the rough temple-attendant and the cultivated physician sink to the same level of incomprehension? The learned man with beautifully curled beard, a man of fashion from the fold of his cloak to his sandals, becomes a foolish and grudging doubter in the presence of the miracle and, as for the man of the people, his comprehension is at a standstill; for what kind of gods are these, if they wish for no sacrifice? This—to be familiar with heights and depths—is certainly the part of the "divine" Raphael—as also his ability to smile!

§ Raphael's Attitude towards his Time: Leo's Humours conducive to his Development

This pre-eminence concealed within it also the capacity for the deepest seriousness in his latest creative work. How often a quality which we possess only fluctuatingly, an undeveloped propensity, is confirmed by its opposite, which asserts itself in us in our daily experience. This may have been the effect, on a profound nature like Raphael's, that feels impelled to express itself, of this Papal Court and of the disintegrated Roman life under Leo X. The moody demands of the Pope in matters of art have been criticised; there has been a suggestion that self-reproach can be heard in his sighs over Raphael's death. It seems to have been reserved for Leo to liberate positive forces, in art also, as in the history of the Church, through exaggerations of his own failings. As a personality or in character he was not so essential in this artist-life, called as it was from the outset to the highest revelations. But the Pope seemed to have been destined by the irony of fate for a special task: his uncertain humours and precipitate wishes were compelled by their abundance to serve one purpose alone, to assist the birth in Raphael of his superhuman creative capacity.

§ Power of Seclusion

Only this dæmonic being, conscious of his mission, could succeed among such associates in talking their language, taking part in their festivities, fulfilling their wishes, in displaying the superiority in intellect and outward show as regards style of living demanded by this society, and could, at the same time, muster the mysterious potentiality for seclusion and the strictest self-composure; he only could set his energy and the inspired strength of his will in opposition to an apparent dependence and a limitation by factors other than those of his very own choice. In externals, he may have raised himself above the limits prescribed for an artist and, whilst appearing to provide society with what befitted it, in reality he cast his spell over it and reserved what belonged peculiarly to the very depths of his nature for a circle and an age of whose coming power, so utterly different in kind, he must have had a presentiment. As the noblest spokesman of his time he took upon himself the martyrdom of being "too early"; he lent expression and voice to what was still unconsciously slumbering in his generation. *He made an epoch!*

§ Attitude towards Reform

It is thrilling to picture to one's self how, in the midst of all the unreflecting activity, one solitary man forced himself to attain a tremendous capacity for self-reflection; how, with an irresistible power of conviction, he created anew those essential formulas of belief, the need for which the rest, by virtue of their office more responsible than he, saw inescapably coming, but were compelled to forego, in their limitation, with their petty resources, to the temporal sphere. "Sal igitur infirmatum est"—"the salt, then, has lost its virtue", are the words in a complaint about Leo and his circle. It was of course inevitable, before the conclusion of the Lateran Council, that a noble mind like GIAN FRANCESCO PICO DELLA MIRANDOLA should compose an address to the Pope: "Ad Leonem ... de reformandis moribus ecclesiae"—on the moral reformation of the Church; he wrote of it to WILLIBALD PIRCKHEIMER, and we may imagine how Dürer, also stirred by this voice coming from Rome, was already meditating on his figures of the Apostles at the very time when Raphael was illustrating this pronouncement in his portrait of Leo X with his nephews, (at the same time however the wrathful VISION OF EZEKIEL and the TRANS-FIGURATION on Tabor, above the sufferings and doubts of mankind, were presenting themselves before his mind). In the highest grades of society he had opportunities of convincing himself of the rottenness that was weakening the Church: Cardinal Giuliano de' Medici, who commissioned the TRANSFIGURATION, at that time owner of the villa on the Monte Mario (the Villa Madama), scarcely four years later, when he was Clement VII, the "Pope of the Fall" and witness of deepest degradation, thus expressed himself to an episcopal friend: "I have my friends in the pictures from Ovid's *Metamorphoses* in my villa on Monte Mario—le cose del Testamento vecchio bastino alla Loggia di nostro Signore—let the things from the Old Testament suffice for the Loggia of His Holiness." And Bembo, the author, faultless in style, of so many Papal briefs, writes from the immediate neighbourhood of the Holy See to the Duchess of Urbino: "You are anxious on my behalf, as to whether I also am occupied with the thought of another world— No, it has never really occupied me much; now it has ceased to occupy me at all."

§ Profanation of Religion

In reality, acquiescence and approval in religious matters coming from this circle have an even more damaging effect. When Vida and Sannazaro, incited by the Pope, beg their Latin Muse to turn her attention to Christian subjects, this is the praise bestowed by competent humanists on Leo: "So at last, O Leo, under thy rule, Sacred Poetry, hitherto familiar only with Christian themes and hardly accessible to the laity, lifts her radiant locks above the stars." In Sannazaro's *De partu Virginis*—"The Birth of the Virgin", and in Vida's *Christiade*, men believed, when the most sacred figures were treated in the same manner as the divinities of the Ancients, that they were turning over something like a new page in the book of ancient mythology. They had a comfortable feeling that in this heathen dress Christianity was really for the first time becoming fit for presentation at Court in the circle of the cultured; it lost for them something at least of its menacing hostility. "The opponents of Luther praised Jupiter, Minerva, Venus. . . . The ancient gods that had once been thrown headlong from their power, returned to the Christian Heaven." Erasmus found that "the Roman See has only the friends of profane literature to thank for its calamities; they have less Christianity in them than those whose books they condemn!" For this epoch was no longer so "created and disposed for serenity" as Sadolet still pictured it to himself at a later date, in the yearning reminiscences of exile—any more than its great painters. Out of the inner religiousness of their time, a religiousness that transcended denominational bounds, they had quite other truths to proclaim to the world than the writers of Papal briefs and bulls. For whilst rolling thunder was already beginning to peal from beyond the Alps, in serious-minded circles within the Church that silent, unexpressed conspiracy of like-minded men was taking place which, prepared as it was generations before in advance, possessed the power of giving the lead, out of its own ranks, to internal reform at the very moment when the leaders of the Church defaulted and the deepest humiliation lay in store for their weakness. For Raphael these conceptions were not new. The unfulfilled demands of SAVONAROLA were still effectively alive in his instinct. In the midst of all humanistic surroundings, he bore "the Gospel with him", according to

316

the meaning of the preacher and martyr—not the book, but the spirit of the Gospel; for "if thou hast not the Spirit of Grace, though thou carry with thee the whole book, it would profit thee nothing". "The true books of Christ are the Apostles and Saints." After his experiences and endeavours how deeply he must have been moved by the words: "The more spiritual a sovereignty is, the better and stronger will it be; for the more nearly it approaches the divine, the nearer it comes to perfection and immutability." And so Raphael gave Savonarola a place among the true advocates of the Holy Scriptures in the DISPUTA, behind Augustine, Buonaventura and Dante—and the monk stood even now, purged from his political errors, exhorting and assenting, at the head of that group which was striving in quiet concord after a new deepening of religion; it was their aim to be indispensable to devout natures amid the convulsions of the time. Ideas of reform that NICOLAUS CUSANUS had already endeavoured to realise half a century earlier were then awakening to new power. His spirit, equally at home on both sides of the Alps, and never forgotten by men of insight, found vital expression again for the first time with the printing of his works in 1514, as if of set purpose, to generate a spiritual revival. It was *this* generation that first succeeded in imbuing once more with sublime humanity the humanism that had become futile. Men no more trusted to the intelligence in order to attain to "the Tree of Life", and built upon "justification" through that faith which was preached by CONTARINI as it had been once by Cusanus.

§ Oratorio del Divino Amore: Raphael Member of the Brotherhood of Corpus Domini at Urbino

This was the way of thinking in that "secreta, spirituale e christianissima compagnia" of the Oratorio del Divino Amore—that secluded, spiritual, above all Christian community of the Oratory of the Divine Love, to which in its quiet but irresistible energy an almost legendary influence was attributed. In fact men of the approaching Counter-Reformation were preparing themselves here, in noble absorption and still without political aims, for their future tasks. Giovan Pietro Caraffa, the later Paul IV, was one of these; Sadolet and Gian Matteo Giberti were in a position to instruct Raphael as to these endeavours; in the houses of Sadolet, Bembo and Castiglione the artist had opportunities of meeting Gian Francesco Pico della Mirandola, Alberto Pio da Carpi, Gaetano Thiene. We must suppose him to have been familiar by his own natural disposition, in the depths of his heart, with the sentiments which gave this circle a new lease of life. Such spiritual threads were not inevitably woven into the social web with which he was surrounded. From March, 1514, onwards, for the last six years of his life, he belonged to the old Brotherhood of the Corpus Domini at Urbino. It was a foundation centuries old of pious men for keeping up the devotion to the Sacrament and for perpetual and active service of a God actually experienced. On their altar stood the LAST SUPPER of Justus van Gent; Raphael, as we know, from his youth up beheld with deep emotion of his own this group, full of profound feeling, of kneeling Apostles in the vaulted chamber around the figure, gliding like a spirit, of the Saviour. Certainly, when visiting his home in maturer years, he must have felt ever more profoundly, even if unconsciously, the seriousness that had guided the thoughts of this painter from the country of the Brethren of the Common Life, the contemporary of Nicholas of Cusa, in his austere and pious work. He himself had a similar experience when he immersed himself in the Gospel narrative in his search for subjects from the ACTS OF THE APOSTLES; his heroes had been changed from the *Cortegiano* into the *Apostle*, from the knightly cavalier into the man of the people, "him that is lowly and of no account, but elect", full of the Spirit. They had put on the "new man". He himself once felt constrained to liken himself to the Apostle Paul, who could not speak of "the unutterable things that met him", in a trance-like rapture, "in the seventh heaven" of which the love-abounding sonnet on the *DISPUTA* sketch bears witness (Plate 89). In feeling he was always near to the great traveller and preacher of Conversion,[1] as if in his own perpetual "die to live" he were of the blood of the Apostle. In such periods, when he underwent the stirring of the spirit within him, he might well feel as a happiness not free from pain his loneliness in the midst of the world; he sets it resolutely and almost bitterly against the outward duties which thronged about him—the happiness of conversion and withdrawal in this manner from an earth-imprisoned society when that society thought to possess him. Anyone who came within the range of his companionable graciousness might believe himself to have penetrated within the outer walls of this fastness, but would have found the citadel impregnable. "Like blessed spirits in the skies that float And crown and kingdoms hold in deep disdain."

§ The Man of Melancholy

This was certainly not the least of the charms of this personality, and finer natures surely had an inkling of the remoteness of those regions out of which he condescended to come for intercourse with the everyday world; they felt themselves attracted within his sphere without coming nearer to him. The Ferrarese Ambassador, who would certainly have had reason, like his Duke, to feel Raphael's charms, nevertheless proposes "rather to deal with him with befitting courtesy"; and respect, as well as a certain awe of the incomprehensible, is the note of his words: "homini di questa excellentia sentono tutti de melencolico"—"in men so highly gifted there is usually to be felt a strain of melancholy". One may not intrude upon their state; they seem to be hallowed.

Would the "serene" Raphael thus have turned into a man of melancholy? Yes, surely, for to select spirits of his age such as Marsilio Ficino the word

[1] "Wanderer und Wandler"; the play on words cannot be satisfactorily rendered in English —*Translator.*

"malinconico" implies admiration almost. Melancholy—as Dürer knew, and Giorgione—was the best "complexion" for serious endeavour, penetrating deeply into the foundations of things; it is a qualification for the noble intellectualism of the man of Platonic temperament. It comes from Saturn, who thus becomes not a bringer of misfortune but a dispenser of noble gifts, purchased by purification.

§ The latest Self-portrait: The marginal Note on Vitruvius: Prescription against Phthisis

In addition to a thought-provoking testimony like this from a contemporary, dating from the master's last years, we have that other, even more enigmatic, document, his late portrait of himself—the bearded Raphael—with his friend so unlike him, in the Louvre. Because we know that this was his appearance as he went about, we fix our gaze with pious eyes on this face as if it were his "last dying look" (Plate 287). The enigma is increased by the fact that there hovers round this presentment the conception of the darling of the gods who dies in his youth, of the "grazioso", of the "serene" and serious-minded creator, like the Greeks and Mozart. And we find a *man* whose melancholy is familiar with sufferings and who bears them with an uncanny *insouciance*, if not ease—a man of maturity, with clear yet not unclouded brow and the wrinkles that come of strenuous endeavour; the right eye (his left eye in the self-portrait) still gazes forth enquiringly, deliberately, the other with a spiritual look, and as if troubled and sorrowful; and the mouth also, perhaps accentuated by the shadow of the beard, does not display that mobility which once pursed up those full lips charmingly and proudly also. Fringed round by the brown abundance of the locks and beard, this head would seem to be offering itself with an almost uncanny resignedness, as if for a sacrifice, were it not for the supple tension in the neck, the infinite easiness in the genial movement towards the shoulders of his friend, and a suspicion of irony about the mobile nostrils—still a remnant, therefore, of the graciousness we expect and seek out almost, as if we missed it sadly. Is that marginal note, written in his hand, in the Munich Vitruvius manuscript of Fabio Calvi, one of his few spontaneous confessions (Plate 283)? Where the Roman architect speaks of the properties of building-timbers, against the larch, the following words are written in Raphael's hand: "la ragia delo arice e bona al mal del tisicho"—the resin of the larch is good for phthisis. Had he, the "vir gracilis et procerae staturae", reason for allowing himself to be distracted by this prescription from his thoughts about building to other shores?

§ Literary Portrait: Autobiography in Painting

"Vir gracilis et procerae staturae omnibus amabilis perspicacis ingenii—a man of balanced suppleness and fine build, of great amiability towards everyone and of profound understanding—so he is called in the letter of a contemporary,

319

the literary portrait, of his latest period, side by side with these very last words of his own! And the spiritual likeness is provided by his works, his only confessions. They also express what his features bespeak; first and foremost, his own portraits as autobiography: the serious, enquiring boy of scrutinising instincts and noble character, in the Oxford drawing of his twelfth or fourteenth year (Plate 1); the ardent and yet, again, so clear-sighted youth in his period of travel—he bears in himself the touchstone for the purity and genuineness of everything he meets with, his all-embracing gaze knows how to select and weigh, and he knows his own place in the firmament, whence the things of the world are displayed to the view in the Divine ordering—one of the elect who can behold and interpret. In the SCHOOL OF ATHENS, his place is where those mighty figures with the features of the thinker and inventor are intent on geometry (Plate 285); in the HELIODORUS (Plate 286), he stands beside the Pope, matured by responsibility, yet with a new glow in his eyes that almost seems painfully to sear him—and now here, hallowed with the gift of deep-penetrating, grave endeavour, called by his destiny to ever new gifts, acquired ever anew at the price of purification, conscious of upheaval within him, with uncertainty ahead of him; thus with his inborn pride he fixes his eye on his high calling and the world that disturbs it. In the attempt at a sonnet on the *DISPUTA* drawing at Montpellier he has jotted down a few lines:

> O fatiche euoi famosi afanni
> (r)isvegliate el pensier che inotio giace
> (m)ostrateli quel cole alto che face
> (s)alir da bassi aipiu sublimi scanni
> (u)oler se quita la nostra stella . . . " [1]

In these unique lines he gives information about himself and his desires in life; and glancing once more at his latest painted self-portrait, we find both—glorious anguish seems to have become for him an element that he loved, inseparable from his creative nature, the *Purgatorio* through which he finds, along new paths, purification and freedom; he peers intensely and penetratingly before him, the "manly" Raphael. Only Goethe had an inkling of "the fearful conditions under which alone even those most resolute by nature can rise to the utmost attainable success".

§ On the Brink of Chaos

The latest portrait charms us as if we felt ourselves in the presence of the painter of the ACTS OF THE APOSTLES and the TRANSFIGURATION, the seer of his

[1] "Ye labours and ye tribulations famed,
Awaken ye the thought that idle lies,
Disclose to it that summit high which calls
Us from below its topmost heights to scale."

final visions on the brink of chaos, to which it was his desire to give the shape of something tragically incomplete. Thus his contemporaries felt his end to be the last day of art—all their sublime skill must needs die with him, "morienti mori". His life, his wishes and his deeds seemed to them to be beyond all comprehension and not of this world—

DIVINO.

XVII

AFTER-ECHOES OF RAPHAEL

"Of the merits we know how to appreciate the germ is within ourselves."

GOETHE, *Zum Shakespearestag.*

OPINIONS must be weighed, not counted.

Anyone who surveys the gigantic following that for generations marched in the track of Raphael will soon learn to sift those who range themselves in his train at the dictates of fashion, from those who, often at wide distances of time and space, acknowledge his leadership in that accord of secret understanding which at the turning-points of time unites kindred spirits. The value of the echo that answers to his call or reverberates through the centuries is not determined by numbers. An essential part of his validity also rests on the foundation of the spiritual impetus and fire of the strong personalities that came after him; his nature is effective even for us, as if the torch of enthusiasm that *he* carried in the van of his epoch had been continually passed on and held aloft by worthy hands right down to us.

§ Pupils: After-effects of the Chigi frescoes: Free Followers

His pupils handed down only a soulless semblance of his forms and therefore desecrated them. In these earliest Mannerists and in the Eclectics his beautifully draped men stream through the sacred scenes, his women sway buoyantly, as they walk or kneel; but they obeyed only the artist who had created them for his sublime emotions, and remain, in the hands of Giulio Romano, the Caracci, Guido Reni, Poussin and their international academic following, nothing but superficial pattern; the immediate, profound seriousness, the magnetic and compelling austerity of profession, which is owed solely to the inner struggles and conversions of their creator, must of necessity be lacking in them. Only where these forms were enlisted in the service of Ancient mythology, where the world of the gods enlivens with their superhuman power the zone beyond reality, did Raphael find true pupils; these pupils he found not in Giulio Romano, whose unspiritual coarseness drags down to earth everything even out of this sphere, but in each one of the truly creative talents. In the frescoes of the CARACCI for the Farnese Gallery with subjects from the lives and loves of the gods (Plate 288), in the AURORA of GUIDO (Plate 289), his free Roman style reverberates, that

322

style which alone is able to make credible the Olympians; it is as if Raphael had created for Agostino Chigi these beings on clouds in the blue air, in the mosaics of the sepulchral chapel and in the Farnesina, expressly to be an example for these artists to follow.

It was precisely for this upward soaring in air and sunshine that the painter won for himself a following of his own more worthy than the trivial successors of his studio. In the forefront of all, CORREGGIO gave evidence of his rapturous enthusiasm for him as painter of the beyond. There is no surer evidence of his sojourn in Rome, about 1518, than in the ever-recurring acknowledgments of indebtedness to the works done by Raphael for Chigi; the mosaics of the cupola found their first echo in this painter from Upper Italy. Here Raphael, as true heir of Melozzo da Forlì, was able to exercise an influence across the Appenines and, thanks to Correggio, through the centuries. The angel above the Artemis in the PLANETS mosaic (Plate 290), with his bearing of heavenly unrestraint and his sweeping glance over his shoulder towards the heights, passed on a greeting to Parma, to the CORONATION OF THE VIRGIN in San Giovanni. We meet with him on the right, behind the Baptist from the *DISPUTA*, and even more distinctly in the youthful St Thomas on the cloudy cornice in the dome (Plate 291). The Rising Saviour, with his outspread arms, traverses and dominates the circle just as the figure of the Almighty divides and fills the *opaion* in Santa Maria del Popolo; and the ecstatic turning of the Prophet Jonah, in Santa Maria della Pace, recurs in the Cathedral at Parma in the head of the St Andrew beneath the upward-pointing *putto*, and in the *grisaille* of Aaron on the soffit of the arch under the pendentive.[1] Even the angel above Raphael's Cumaean Sibyl floats before Correggio's memory, down to the period of his MARTYRDOM OF SS. PLACIDUS AND FLAVIA.

It is as if Correggio was of the opinion that this motive of the glance over the shoulder had been invented by Raphael specially for him and not for Agostino Chigi. On Correggio alone the peculiar enchantment of these cupola-pictures dawned as a vision of the beyond, an enchantment that he could not find in Mantegna; he met with this experience at the psychological moment shortly before his great commission for Parma at the beginning of the 1520s. Then he lost himself, on a path of his own, in heights to which he had been shown the way by the great exemplar from the Marches, in Rome.

The energies diffused by these cupola mosaics continued to exercise a powerful influence; the last century was able to pass by, without noticing it, the poetry of their invention, but RUBENS must have been brought into the closest possible contact with them. It fell to him to deliver copies of them[2] as a gift to Philip III when travelling on the embassy of 1603, and probably he had to make good some damages in them. Whether accidental or predestined, it was like a personal arrangement between two men of equally lofty intellect. They

[1] Gronau, *Klassiker der Kunst—Correggio*, pp. 64, 79, 80.
[2] Now in the Prado, Madrid, Nos. 306–312.

understood one another regarding the unapproachable powers that point out to life its course beneath the sway of the All-high. For both, these gods moved and had their being in the air above, deep-breathing and free—gleaming figures set against the blue of the firmament. The Jupiter, the Mercury, the Helios of the cupola—they "drink the air" like Ariel. Sitting and reclining, they are still "veinless", at one with the blue æther that once enveloped them on the Farnesina ceiling, like Melozzo's celestial orchestra, as still shown by the archangels of the Loggie and by the mosaics—gleaming bodies in gleaming light, and borne along with it by the bright æther, in all their power and splendour, as by a mighty breath. Raphael could have found no more devoted disciple, none with a more docile understanding, than the artist from the North, Rubens, the greatest of all who gave movement to form, whatever the confusions on this point in which belated worshippers of a Nazarenised Raphael may have been involved. In this instinctive feeling for divine freedom and the humanly triumphant, to which feeling alone the essential character of Ancient mythology discloses itself, the two humanists among the painters were on common ground. In the cosmic expanses of the world of the ancient gods the fabulous element, that which is born of the imagination of the common people, was revealed to them in equal vitality. Rubens had only to carry on the style of the Farnesina a hundred years later in order to transmit the classical myth to his native country. For this he took with him over the Alps the chief groups of Raphael's gods and from them composed anew a story of Psyche in the wide universe high above earth and sea; the Graces, the car drawn by doves with its fair, radiant driver, above all, the upward sweep of Mercury with Psyche, seem only to have been slumbering a few generations in order to be reanimated by his breath and move afresh in a second life (Plate 292). One of Raphael's souls seems to have been pleased to migrate into Rubens, but the other seems to have determined to part company with it on this passage. When sacred motives stray within the range of the great Fleming, the beautiful forms and draperies remain empty; the barytone pathos of the new school is incapable of filling them or of setting them in motion at all (Plate 298). Only in a copy of the DAVID AND DANIEL, that sublime conception of Raphael's carried out in poor school fashion probably by Giulio Romano, above the SIBYLS of Santa Maria della Pace, does Rubens feel the strong pulse-beats of the standing prophet (Plate 191); he bestows on it, in his red chalk sketch, something of that peculiar primitive force derived from the people that had once given irresistible power to the figures of Claus Sluter.

He must have penetrated into the intimacy of Raphael's drawings; the sketch for Marcantonio's JUDGMENT OF PARIS (Plate 294) has been preserved for us only in a copy, in the Louvre (Plate 295a);—the Venus, haltingly advancing, as if self-absorbed—or perhaps the delicate study for this figure, at Budapest (Plate 295b), recurs as a bashful Angelica in the rescue of her by Ruggero, in Berlin. And as Raphael shares with Ariosto this motive of masculine superiority, viewed almost with a feeling of triumph, so it is now introduced into the scene of the formidable victor confronting the maiden who stands helpless on the cold rock, warmly glowing against the cool background (Plate 296). It recurs once more in the radiant FALL in the Mauritshuis (Plate 297); in the Adam we have a revival of the sunny freedom of the royal shepherd-boy of Ida, as in the unbridled Ixion before Juno; indeed, for Rubens, throughout his life, a breath of Olympian vitality sweeps straight from the mighty, relaxed back and pairs of figures leaning one against another of the FEAST OF THE GODS in the Farnesina—elemental power that no-one *before* Raphael, and *after* him only the great Fleming, knew how to conjure up. The figure of a Triton seen from behind, amid the whirl of billows and sea-monsters in the design for the rim of a dish, for Agostino Chigi (Plate 300), is transported into the sport of Nereids around the corpse of Leander (in Dresden, Plate 293), and the wave-pattern composed of tossing sea-horses, in the same original, is repeated in the London *grisaille* and is converted back again into the design for a dish with the BIRTH OF VENUS (Plate 301).

§ Raphael's Example in his Manner of Life: *Castiglione* copied by Rubens and Rembrandt

Yet more of Raphael's essential character may have been revealed to Rubens between Mantua and Rome. Living with the Gonzagas and producing for them, he was entirely under the spell of Giulio Romano, who was his predecessor. He certainly still heard and saw much of the tradition of the triumphant and widely influential Urbino master. The employment of a multitude of capabilities for manifold purposes, the opportunities given to men of talent to circle in the orbit of his own driving energy, the tested division of labour—this entirely new element in art seems to have made such a strong impression on Rubens when at Mantua, that on his return home he established his workshop on similar principles. His own power was multiplied, as it were, to make itself master of the abundance of invention, and gave to all a forward impulse, designing, suggesting, co-operating, painting over, completing. The new *cortegiano* among painters may secretly have set up his forerunner as his ideal; amongst kindred or adopted traits we find also the greatest, that is, his planning of his time; open to every stimulus, his mind seeks improvement, even while he is painting, by being read aloud to over his work, just as tradition relates of Raphael. They were the humanists of two different generations and of two different climates who here met, to create for the artist an entirely new social status. And as the ideal of social behaviour the courtier of Urbino and Mantua, the "Cortegiano", continued to show himself again and again. Thus it was something more than a coincidence in the field of art when Rubens copied for himself Raphael's portrait of Castiglione (Plate 121) This act of homage is especially valuable for us: the copy still gives the hands of the Count at the correct distance from the lower frame; in the presence of this great silhouette we experience more strongly than in the shortened original in the Louvre the original, full, breathing freedom of the picture.

The lofty character of the painter and his model met with an even more honourable acknowledgment at almost the same period. REMBRANDT was a competitor for the Castiglione when he saw it at the auction sale of Lucas van Uffelen in Amsterdam in 1639. The cool golden harmony of colour was after his own heart and, inseparable from it, the monumental outline that held this harmony together. As he had to yield the picture to a wealthier competitor, the magnificently executed outline remained sufficiently alive in his mind; he was able to fix it in a rapid reed-pen sketch (in the Albertina) and he "would not let it go except it blessed him"; the etched self-portrait of 1639 (B.21), the proud portrait of himself belonging to the National Gallery, of 1640, with its look of sublimity, are echoes of the great Italian melody awakened by the avowal of his very deepest aspirations. This was not the only testimony of his veneration. He would not have spoken like a modern Impressionist from whom, in the presence of the MASS OF BOLSENA, was wrung the avowal: "I undervalued it." Great men, as a rule, never remain so estranged from one another as their followers. Rembrandt kept in his house, by Raphael, a Madonna composition, a portrait, and four volumes with engravings by Marcantonio and others after him. When there is a meeting of such polar opposites, it is interesting to enquire what are the forces that have brought them together over space and time. It was the *heroic*. Of this, in Holland, only just liberated and resting from its struggles, Rembrandt felt himself to have a unique call to be the interpreter. This was the emotion aroused in him by the primitive maternal, animal-like turn in the MADONNA DELLA SEDIA, which he made note of in a sketch (at Dresden); the world-wide majesty of bearing in Marcantonio's PIETÀ resounds as the leading voice in the choir of lamentation around the DEATH OF THE VIRGIN (B.99); from the series of Apostles after Raphael the ST MATTHEW supplies to the PROPHET ELISHA[1] the dignity of step in the great fold of the mantle.

Rembrandt must have been especially deeply affected by the power with which, in Raphael, sensibility unburdens itself in gestures—in fact, in entire groups of figures possessed. We do not know how much of Raphael's work he owned, but the paintings of the Second Stanza were familiar to him. The arm of the heavenly avenger brandishing a rod was taken from the HELIODORUS, and its effect transferred to the figure of Christ in the CLEANSING OF THE TEMPLE, as early as 1635 (B.69), and Rembrandt was acquainted with the composition of the ATTILA; a drawing in the Berlin Kabinett (Plate 299)[2] shows the tumult round the King of the Huns hastily sketched in red chalk, with bistre washes, and vigorously

[1] In the Hermitage; Valentiner, *Zeichnungen Rembrandts*, No. 438.
[2] *Katalog der Zeichnungen*, 13733.

326

drawn over again with penstrokes of the 1650s; many of the more ordinary warrior figures of Raphael became more "horsemanlike" by this working-over with a view to emphasis; the heroicised grey on the right was converted into a "primeval horse", the antique visor, difficult to make out, on Attila's helmet, on the fist of his armour-bearer in the middle of the fresco, became a new hero, the "Man with the Golden Helmet", Rembrandt's brother, about 1650.

§ Raphael's and Rembrandt's last Style in Composition

The change, in Raphael's late works, to a free mobility of space, monumentality by means of contrasted proximity and distance, must in particular have filled Rembrandt with enthusiasm. The tapestry of St Paul preaching in Athens sets the apostle on steps, exalted above space and multitude, and this vision became for the etcher the leading idea for the Christ Preaching ("petite tombe", B.67); an ever-welcome motive for dramatic effects, the appearance of the principal personage on a terrace, figures emerging at the foot of the steps, the figures standing out in all the grandeur of their drapery against the recession of the ground, in the Healing of the Lame Man (B.94)—these are elements from Raphael's maturest period which, for Rembrandt in particular, fitted in, as if they were his own, in his monumental conceptions in the last decade and a half. In drawings of this late period the dynamic rhythms will continually be heard re-echoing from Raphael's tapestries, in the alternation of energetic perpendiculars and violent diagonals. The diametrical opposite of the Italians in the North is more closely akin, in architecturally constructive, inescapable power and evangelic force, to their greatest master than to his own fellow-countrymen.

In former times many an inspiring appeal had made its way southwards from Northern Gothic over the Alps, to find an echo in the young Umbrian alone. Now, in the most independently developed master of the North, Southern expression became a new power in his poetic language, as the only echo of equal standing and worth, an echo more essential than any contribution from the South by Mannerists and Romanists! Rembrandt's contact with Raphael had an effect that was "inspiring"—*begeisternd*—in the truest sense of the word. . . .

§ Raphael's Influence as Painter

How little on the other hand does it signify when "Classical ideology" borrows ever again and again from Raphael, when Eclectics and Academics, from the Caracci by way of Poussin right down to Mengs, Guérin and Regnault, mingle Raphael's motives in their bloodless compositions! Borrowings are not the mark of the true follower. *It was as painter that Raphael stood at the head of the three great masters*, Correggio, Rubens, Rembrandt; if he was acclaimed by such masters of light and colour, it was Raphael the painter that they acknowledged, not the draughtsman, who alone almost was still found worthy of commendation by Academic generations.

RAPHAEL

§ Classicistic and Classical Appreciation: *Sturm und Drang*

But this veneration becomes comprehensible in the presence of his *form*. So long as the society continued to exist for whose adherents the *Cortegiano*-ideal was created and given visible shape by Raphael, and so long as it continued to hold fast to this beautiful vision, his figures were as it were the expression of their heroic aspirations. After new strata had forced themselves upwards, towards the time of the French Revolution, and the bourgeoisie had asserted themselves, such aristocratic forms could not but lose much of the strength of their convincingness. No exclusive ideal figure was needed by the new popular powers for their turbulence, nor by the national forces in their federation. The young selfconsciousness sought expression for what was coming into existence, and found it less in art than in language. Here the really constructive powers forced their way to the top, and in the new poetical language of *Sturm und Drang* Raphael found an echo that could do him greater honour than the acknowledgments of bloodless Classicism and of Romanticism with its lack of vitality.

The great creators and masters of language, poets and thinkers, Janusheaded in their wide outlook on tradition and future, raised their voice, and never, not even in his own epoch, were weightier things said of Raphael's art, never was his nature in all its elemental power more devotedly comprehended, or from more varied standpoints, than in our Classical epoch. The great thinkers really showed themselves here also as "classical", in accordance with the naïve French *mot*, "because they all had good ideas and found the right words for them". Whilst MENGS and REYNOLDS recommended their great fellow-craftsman to the academic rising generation, not without reservations where he diverged from their combined prescriptions, there arose, in the new literature, alongside this weeping willow by the grave of Ancient art from which the blood had been drained, the high ethical claim on a work of art that it should once more provide a link between art and the soul. This link had then been lost to plastic art and had been rescued by the new creative arts of language. From this source arose a truly revived appreciation of Raphael—perhaps the proudest spiritual echo he ever found.

§ New spiritual Appreciation

WINCKELMANN may come first at the head of the series of the most influential witnesses. With his *Gedanken über die Nachahmung* ("Thoughts on Imitation"), which were intended less pedantically than they were understood, the fact that in him a mystical upward tendency guided his unparalleled sensual receptivity for every poetical art, should always have a reconciling effect. Even though he does not say so, he had before his eyes the confrontation, in a creative sphere, of the god in the Belvedere, whose "footsteps glide as if without touching the earth with his soles", with the Mother of God above clouds "in a posture of blessed repose, in that calm which the Ancients caused to dominate the figures of their divinities".[1] Only in this spiritualised form did he apprehend how the "kingly Raphael", that "Apollo of painters", attained greatness by imitation of the Ancients. "Such a beautiful soul as was his, in so beautiful a body, was required in order that, in modern times, the true character of the Ancients might begin to be appreciated." "With an eye that has learnt to perceive these beauties, with this true taste for Antiquity, their works must be approached. Then the repose and quietness of the chief figures of Raphael's ATTILA that to many seem lifeless, will be very significant and sublime.—The Bishop of Rome appears—as a venerable man who through his mere presence stills the tumult . . . the two Apostles sweep down in the clouds not like destroying angels . . . but . . . like Homer's Jupiter, who causes Olympus to shake with the blink of his eyelids."

That same sense for "the music of the spheres" which allowed Winckelmann to apprehend in the Apollo, in spite of all the weaknesses of the Late Antique marble copy, the idea of "epiphany", rare even in Antiquity, opened his eyes for the poetic invention in that one among the painters who was the poet of the beyond. He found in that fresco something more essential than later generations of his disciples in the study of art history which he founded; to those disciples this work seemed "inferior" as regards analysis of form, and of importance for style criticism only on account of the "participation of pupils". The truth is forced upon us that *we must turn back beyond the modern scientific study of art, of the last generations*, and our boldness in swimming against the stream will be rewarded if we can penetrate to sources of speculation of such an order as was the intuition of this man, of a sensibility so rare among classical scholars, who met with opposition as an enemy of art.

It is with this very abundance of vitality that HERDER takes up the workings of language and the language of art; he reproduces his impressions out of the fullness of his own nature with a plastic convincingness. Herder found prevailing that ideal of Raphael of the Academies—an ideal now become uncreative—which Reynolds extols, weighs and criticises in his celebrated pedagogic discourses. In the self-consciousness of a new bourgeois class to which he felt himself to be responsible as its leader by profession and vocation, he sets up against this ideal a Raphael he has experienced, as if Northern Protestantism were now discovering in its unexhausted spiritual powers the approach to this poet of the ancient Church. "The heavenly genius of Raphael appeared, begotten of a Greek Muse by an Angel. There resounded a song in the higher strain; a new mode of thought really began with a new age."[2]

"Through every one of the Madonnas, almost every one of the figures, of Raphael there breathes a spirit that shows on every side, even in resistance to

[1] *Gedanken über die Nachahmung*, p. 26.
[2] *Briefe zur Förderung der Humanität*. VI *Fragment*, *Werke*, ed. Suphan, Vol. XVIII, p. 73.

it, that fundamental element in human nature which has been called the *angel of man*. For light and colour bring out as it were what is spiritual in human existence; the massive and corporeal remain behind. The idea of man, his genius, becomes visible."[1]

And on "the image of devotion", the SISTINE MADONNA:

> "Erschien o Raphael, Dir auch das Bild
> der Göttin als die heilige Idee
> Dir in der Dürftigkeit der Erdenschöne
> vorschwebete? Ich seh ihr Bild, Sie wars."[2]

In opposition to this "umanissima idea divina" (to use his own words to Castiglione) which Raphael descried, Herder set up physical sensation as the source of all life, and found that Raphael's Madonnas, certainly the highest and purest of their kind, are all peasant girls, only conceived in the most fervent mood and purely idealised. "This glorious being herself who, with her Child on her arm, floats above the clouds, does not know herself and is full of mild wonder at the sublimity that has fallen to her lot."[3]

"We can render faithfully and in a truly living way those forms, and only those, which have communicated themselves to us in this manner, which live in us through the living sense." "It is well known that some of the greatest of recent painters always depicted only their lady-loves, their daughters or their wives, indisputably because nothing else possessed their hearts and senses. Raphael was rich in figures that were alive, because his disposition, his warmth of heart carried him away, and all these figures, felt and enjoyed as they were, were his own. Thus he went astray, and early ended his irreplaceable life—and many a shallow-minded person absolutely cannot understand how it was that the heavenly Raphael loved earthly maidens. Was it not from them that he got those contours, his warm living forms? He would never have come by them from heaven and cold statues alone."[4]

"Can it be that so fine a being as Raphael did not leave behind in his life more traces of fine feelings? Or are these soft touches and impressions to be found merely in his works?"[5]

Herder is here feeling how, in the Ancients, that same dynamic, "which, infused by the human soul, as into a mould, into the body created by art,

---

[1] *Kalligone, Werke*, ed. Suphan, Vol. XXII.

[2] *Werke*, ed. Suphan Vol. XXVIII, p. 194. "Did the image of the goddess appear to thee also, Raphael, as the sacred idea, did it float before thine eyes in the inadequacy of the earthly fair? I see her image, it was she."

[3] *Humanitätsbriefe, Werke*, ed. Suphan, Vol. XVII, p. 370.

[4] *Plastik, Einige Wahrnehmungen über Form und Gestalt aus Pygmalions bildende Traum, Werke*, ed. Suphan, Vol. VIII, pp. 25/6.

[5] *Werke*, ed. Suphan, Vol. VIII, p. 106.

weighed out as if on scales to every curve, every depression, every yielding or resistant form, *lives* in each one and has almost the power of transposing our soul into the identical sympathetic posture; the inscriptions of the Anthology extol this *bearing in its entirety*, this *power of coming to life through and in us*, that goes out from them". And it was to the degree of such "silent permeating sympathy" that Herder was sensible, in Raphael's creative power, of that combination of three regions of the intellect corresponding with past, present and future, the Janus-head looking three ways by which may be recognised the truly great—Homer, Sophocles, Plato, Aristotle, Archimedes, Roger Bacon, Galileo, Newton.[1]

§ Antique and Christian in Art

In such an exalted order of rank an even higher degree is implied by Herder when, in the presence of Raphael's works, he "is sensible" in his sacred figures "of a kind of spiritual grace and greatness of soul, of transcendent sublimity and devotion, of pure abstraction and awe-inspiring dignity, that maidenly devoutness, that feeling for the mother and her child, yes, one might say, that *sense of the angelic*, of which in the works of the Ancients hardly anything can actually be found save perhaps here and there a bud enveloped in sensuousness. Here this spiritual bud has broken out; it has opened in many shapes and forms."[2] And if an explanation for this height of spiritual expression in its simplicity can be found only in the nature of legend that lives on in the great artist alone, as it were from the youthful days of the new humanity, adding to the Antique an unsuspected richness, Herder knows no higher acknowledgment of such heaven-favoured operation of genius than the words of a young savage who might feel, on seeing one of Raphael's angels, that like himself he came directly from the hand of the *Great Spirit*, and might thus express his feeling: "He is one of my family."[3]

In the consecrated precincts of the new Northern cult of Raphael it may seem strange to many to meet with the sublimely profane author of *Ardinghello*, WILHELM HEINSE. But an expiatory friendship was destined ever to fall on this "Last of the Centaurs" from his friendship with Hölderlin; Hölderlin thought he had "never come across such splendid intellectual culture and so much childishness", shortly before he addressed to him his profound ode *Brot und Wein*.

> " . . . wozu Dichter in dürftiger Zeit?
> Aber sie sind, sagst Du, wie des Weingotts heilige Priester,
> Welche von Land zu Land zogen in heiliger Nacht."[4]

[1] *Zerstreute Blätter: Ueber die menschliche Unsterblichkeit, Werke*, ed. Suphan, Vol. XVI, p. 45.
[2] *Ueber die Legende, Werke*, ed. Suphan, Vol. XVI, p. 396.
[3] *Adrastea, Werke*, ed. Suphan, Vol. XXIII, p. 437.
[4] (" . . . O bard, whither in time so scant?
But they are, sayest thou, like the holy priests of the wine-god,
Who in the holy night wandered from land unto land.")

In Heinse there lived that sense for the primeval powers of creation and of art without a consciousness of which every cult of the Classical is condemned to remain academic. "Nature", invoked in many writings on æsthetics before and after him, had for him a profound significance, as of a leaven, in the creating mind: nature was for him the measure of poetic aptitude and of the ability to apprehend the beyond.

"In every work of art seek for nature first and then for art, if you wish to judge of it rightly. Those who do otherwise are going downhill in search of the source and chattering about it like fools."[1] In Raphael and his assistants, as in Rubens, he sees "plenitude and fire of the same feeling . . . absorbed into his soil and brought to birth".[2] "He was in fact a clear, still, deep water in which nature at her best was mirrored."[3] For Heinse Raphael with his intense desire for uniformity was a "poet". "Whoever discovers in what he has seen and heard a whole with all its parts, and has the power of representing it deceptively as if it were real, is a poet." Others remain at the stage of the chronicler and the writer of history.

"The most difficult thing in art is to make life perceptible, movement in full-toned unison through the entire body of the present moment; this is the function of feeling, the strong, warm feeling of a human being of the utmost sensibility and serenity".[4] "He had the absolutely good general understanding of a man of the people, and the most natural aspect of every occurrence instantly presented itself to his thoughts and perceptions, and his creative imagination and *robust style*, in which everything is complete, with nothing left out, made the whole immediately living."[5]

Such an "understanding of a man of the people" was the source out of which arose the beautiful description of the CANIGIANI MADONNA, then at Düsseldorf, entirely concentrated on the poetry of the picture: "Mary is so holy and as though in a dream; her feelings are Platonic and yet at the same time she is such a young, heart-stealing maiden that she seems as if by rights this world was no place for her to awake in. Joseph gazes with meditative brow upon the little St John, upon him and the little Jesus, like Newton on the courses of the comets."—"The beauties of Raphael, because they consist rather in spirit than in colour, call for a more practised sense and a more deeply penetrating sharpsightedness; and this is the reason why many pass on quite coldly from the latter as from something even fundamentally unimportant."

Quite apart from the effect thus produced, which derives its refreshing and convincing power from comparison with life, Heinse recognised Raphael among all great masters as "the only one who brought belief out of obscurity and set it in a

[1] *Briefe aus Düsseldorf Werke*, ed. Schüddekopf, vol. VIII, p. 121.
[2] *Ibid.*, vol. VIII, p. 341.
[3] *Italienische Reise*.
[4] From *Italienische Reise*, Werke, ed. Schüddekopf, vol. VIII, p. 510.
[5] *Briefe aus Düsseldorf, Werke*, ed. Schüddekopf, vol. VIII, pp. 265f., 301, 309, also *Ardinghello*.

heavenly light before our eyes?"[1] The fact that Pergolesi's "Ostendo Jesum" brought before him a vision of one of Raphael's Madonnas is in harmony with this frank sense for the mystical in art.

Such estimates do not lack the charm of contrast. Heinse's nature, strong and rich in inner antagonisms, does not lose itself in unconditional surrender; it traces out with exalted pretensions of its own the limitations to be found even in this sublime art: "Raphael's was the best of hearts, he was the kindliest of souls, pious and free from guilt. The vitality of the heads apparent in his works is therefore to be found chiefly in the faces of Apostles and philosophers, of which he carried his conception and feeling to the level of the ideal. His women are of an entirely simple nature, but the more intellectual and refined— heads that might captivate the heart of an Alcibiades, were foreign to him."[2]

"His failing is his agreeableness, everywhere, even where it is out of place —for instance, Attila and Heliodorus with virtuous expressions on their faces." "It seems as if he would never have been able to create an unpleasant face." The discordant peculiarities of the later works, due to pupils, did not escape this eye, with its keenness of intellectual and sensual vision. In the Farnesina ceiling "his nudes have not a pleasing effect; they have not become again that second nature, down to the arms and legs and hands and feet, which is within his power."[3] "In the Psyche there is much naïvety, as she takes the cup of nectar; but the nude is somewhat unfelt and undigested, more as if copied, even to the gracefulness in the back. The background, *blue* throughout, makes everything hard and quite unartistic."[4] In the DONNA VELATA he notes the "divine, large, serene eyes, the joyously sweet, chaste expression in the whole"—yet— "the drapery seems not to belong to her".

In all this the share of the workshop detaches itself clearly for Heinse from the highest poetry and mastery. In a hundred years style-criticism has out-stripped him only in losing sight of the master dominating all the work of his pupils. It was precisely Heinse who began to see the sublime ethos of Raphael's personality in all his creative work: "With Raphael, there is not a single work in which his life did not come into play; his highest achievements are like tutors—in them he shows himself as a noble young man who readily associates with his people."[5] "We rightly observe in the Vatican that Raphael associated with the most distinguished persons of his generation—in order to form so true a conception of high intellects, an intimate association with great men is certainly requisite."[6] "His self-portrait, although still almost childish, has the penetrating look of a genius exalted above everything, full of intelligence and

[1] *Ibid.*, p. 121.
[2] *Ibid.*, p. 199.
[3] *Italienische Reise, Werke,* ed. Schüddekopf, Vol. VIII, p. 399.
[4] *Ibid.*, p. 15; this relates to the part done by Giulio Romano and the restoration of Maratta.
[5] *Ibid.*, p. 475.
[6] *Ibid.*, p. 410.

deep sensibility, with head naturally uplifted."[1] "As painter I should like to be Titian, as man, best of all to be Raphael."

And Heinse asks himself whether Raphael would not have cast aside the brush if he had lived to grow older; and he seems to suspect that the ambition of his maturity must inevitably have risen above painting; the cardinal's hat for which he "aspired" would only need to have been replaced by the longing to be an architect.

LAVATER in his fragmentary writings on physiognomy has proved often enough by introspection and outward observation "that love is the most sharp-sighted of observers". But can we refrain from a sympathetic smile at such surrender to the worthiest object of devotion when like many in those days, he thought to recognise Raphael's traits even "to the hair" in the portrait now in the Czartoryski Collection (Plate 133),[2] and ends up with the words: "*to paint like this such features were also necessary*"? For the proposition "of the harmony of moral and bodily beauty" held good for him unshakably, and since Raphael was for him "an apostolic man", that is, "in comparison with other painters what the Apostles were as compared with the rest of mankind", so he was inwardly prepared when he was introduced to the celebrated and authenticated self-portrait in Florence (he saw it in a fine and tolerably faithful reproduction by the excellent Johann Heinrich Lips); the spirit led him to point out the truest features, that are still confirmed for us to-day by the original in Florence. "This picture—how can I look at it—can anyone—without perceiving in it—or better, feeling in it, the creator of the loveliest figures, that is, the *man of all-embracing vision*, the sensitive portrayer of what is most beautiful in nature, with but a glance at all that is common and bad? *How simple and harmonious the whole!*[3] Is it possible not to see in this face the simple lofty character of all his works? Love and sensual delight, single-heartedness and high poetic sense, are poured out over the whole face. . . . In this open, simple, innocent brow that we see before us here, is the most effortless impressionability. . . . The eyebrows are entirely those of the *poet-painter*; and the mouth—what an everlasting symbol of loving rapture and languishing singleness of heart!"

§ Antique and Christian in Art

The essential difference between Raphael and the Greeks dawned upon Lavater also, as on Herder, as something he experienced, through ordinary scholastic comparison with the Antique: "The works of Greek art are also simple—but they have not the human, intimate quality that, in spite of their sublimity, still strikes us in so many of the best compositions of Raphael. All

---

[1] *Ibid.*, p. 61.
[2] *Physiognomische Fragmente*, I, p. 117.
[3] *Physiognomische Fragmente*, I, pp. 58 ff.

his Maries, Johns, Josephs, all his figures of Jesus, have still so much of the domestic, the bourgeois about them—so much familiarity."[1]

§ Sure Eye for Style

Where has recent exact science, whose exponents feel themselves so superior to the physiognomists, shown more precise observation than Lavater, in the case of the head of the FRANCIS I MADONNA in the Louvre, which is presumably the work of Giulio Romano? His criticism takes a positive turn, with absolutely illuminating clarity: "It is not bad, although the *sharp purity of outline* is lacking in it, that *unattainable little more* that raises all the Raphael heads of his best period so far above ordinary earthliness."[2]

Lavater—the contemporary of the young Mozart—does not know "if there are Raphaels in music"—but a figure of Raphael's, a strophe of Klopstock, an air of Pergolesi, are to him, for eye, ear and heart, exaltation itself.

§ The young Goethe

The head of a monk after Raphael, over which "Goethe's effusion came nearest to the truth", must ever be allowed to stand as the loveliest testimony to the justified effort of the physiognomist (Fig. 3, p. 336). The twenty-six-year-old GOETHE, who had just made his first acquaintance at Strasburg with Raphael's tapestries, thus interprets the expression of the face:

"It seems to me to denote most of all a thinker full of sensibility, whose heart has long beaten in presentiment of a truth as to which belief and doubt have hovered by turns over his brow—and all at once there stands before him the sensual certainty of what he has been conjecturing and hoping. His eye and eyebrows are raised in a triumphant look of joy, enduring sanction rests on his brow, and his heart, now beating quite freely, presses forward towards the loving lips of the longed-for object. In short, it is for me the man who, through a sensual miracle, is rewarded for much loving, feeling and desire."

If Lavater often moves in the realm of conjecture, his collaborator here reaches with a wide and sure sweep into the region of genius, the discovery of which speaks even from the slightest reproduction. He had before him nothing but the copy of Johann Heinrich Lips after the old facsimile, by the French artist J. Bonneau, of a lost drawing; only in our time has it become known that this head of a monk appears not in the fresco, but in early studies for the *DISPUTA*, the most spiritual in a group of figures striving in common towards the goal of the Sacrament. So it is shown by the drawings in London and Paris (*R. Ƶ.*, VII, 267–68). And through the misrepresentations of the twofold copy, the eye of the true poet yet recognises the intention of the kindred spirit of the "poetical" painter. It seemed to be foreordained that they must inevitably meet in their common sphere.

[1] *Physiognomische Fragmente*, III, 60.
[2] *Physiognomische Fragmente*, IV, 402.

R.1.

Joh: H: Lips fecn

Fig. 3

AFTER-ECHOES OF RAPHAEL

In the presence of the ST CECILIA at Bologna it is borne in upon Goethe like a confession of faith that "Raphael always did what others wished to do", and the poet who in all his thinking and imagining had his eyes fixed on "the spiritual, moral nucleus as the truly effective element", takes note in Bologna of the figure of a ST AGATHA by Raphael:[1] "I will read over to her in the spirit my *Iphigenia*, and will not suffer my heroine to say anything to which this saint could not give utterance."

Raphael remained absolutely woven into his productive consciousness—even in the *Farbenlehre* ("Theory of Colours"), under the heading "Überliefertes" ("Traditional"), he describes Plato and Aristotle, in their peculiar manner of communicating their findings to the world, entirely in the language of Raphael—one might almost say, in his very words out of the SCHOOL OF ATHENS: "Plato's movements are towards the heights, in his yearning to participate once more in the origin from which he sprang. Aristotle on the other hand stands facing the world like a man, and a man who is an architect. He describes an immense circle as groundplan for his building ... whereas Plato points heavenwards like an obelisk, like a spire of flame."

In his intercourse with Heinrich Voss he often extols with pleasure Raphael's "serene figures"; "right thinking" is just what seems to him to characterise "the heaven-favoured man"; it is by this that he recognises him in everything: "Like nature, he is always right, and most fundamentally in the very things in which we comprehend them least." With these words he set up the creative idea inherent in the essential unity of the TRANSFIGURATION in opposition to the rationalistic criticism of it by reason of the alleged incompatibility of its upper and lower parts. Such creative power can only give rise to a totality in which the real and the supramundane answer one another. Sovereign poetic sway of this order over the sensual and abstract world was his conception of Raphael's mastery when the youthful impression he formed of the tapestries from the "Garde Meuble" at Strasburg was renewed and deepened in Rome before the Vatican examples. "Let us say straight out that they are all conceived in a *manly* vein; moral seriousness, an awe-inspiring grandeur are everywhere dominant"; and although "here and there mysterious" "they are yet absolutely clear to those who are sufficiently instructed in the Holy Scriptures".

And while the poet himself "undergoes renewal" on Roman soil and his mind attains to "a seriousness without dullness", a "composed character not devoid of joy"—as Tischbein depicted him in the Campagna—in the presence of this maturest of Raphael's works a presentiment came over him of the "formidable conditions under which alone even the most resolute nature can rise to the utmost possible limit of success". Already at that time he noticed with

---

[1] Bologna, 19th October, 1786; the picture has been lost, or was probably only ascribed to Raphael by the imagination of that time. The ST CATHERINE in London has also been taken into consideration in this connection.

resentment slight indications among the more recent German artists that what they observed in Raphael was rather "the talented, delicate youth who lingers over the soft, the agreeable, the natural, than the man in his consummation". And whilst, in the bloodless, superficial cult of the early style of Raphael, romance fancies itself able to weave around the artist when he grew up an imaginary picture of a revived art of mediæval piety, Goethe is ever being drawn anew, as into an abyss, towards the deep tragedy of this life cut short in the midst of its consummation; when he wanted to express what Raphael saw and half consciously recognised in that mirror-painting of himself, with its air as of spirits hovering round, the latest portrait in the Louvre, he did not greet this predestined being, chosen as it were for annihilation, with an elegiac funeral lament; no, he addressed to him a bitter dirge caught up out of the depths of his loneliness and an old man's wisdom in a mood of deliberate resignation; speaking to Eckermann of the "changes in middle life" he says:[1] "Do you know how it seems to me? Every man out of the ordinary has a certain mission which he is called to carry out. When he has performed it, he is no longer required upon earth in this shape, and Providence uses him again for something else. But since everything here below follows the course of nature, the spirits trip him up again and again until at last he is overthrown. So it happened with Napoleon and many others; Mozart died in his thirty-sixth year, Raphael at the same age, Byron only a little older. But all had completed their mission to the full, and it was indeed time they went, so that something was still left for other people to do in this world that is calculated for a long duration."

And again:[2] "When we are old we think of worldly things otherwise than when we are young. So I cannot help thinking that the spirits, in order to tease mankind and make sport of them, sometimes set up individual figures so attractive that everyone strives after them and so great that no-one overtakes them. Thus they set up *Raphael*, in whom thought and action were equally perfect; a few excellent successors came near to him, but no-one equalled him. So they set up *Mozart* as something unattainable in music. And so in poetry they set up *Shakespeare*."

For the poet, the painter Raphael stands in the uppermost human hierarchy—among the stars of the loveliest heights—SHAKESPEARE, PHIDIAS, NAPOLEON, MOZART—the great "*creative minds*". Everywhere in this exalted period poetry counted the artist Raphael amongst its own number; thus Goethe's contemporary in Italy, KARL PHILIPP MORITZ,[3] traces the sense of equality shown in the feeling with which Raphael distributed the poets in the PARNASSUS, and which must have made him sensible of his own value beside them; and FERNOW hails him precisely as a *poet* who, on the strength

[1] 11th March, 1828.
[2] 6th December, 1829.
[3] *Reisen eines Deutschen in Italien,* Berlin, 1782, p. 135.

of his *dramatic* aptitude makes of the DISPUTA, the SCHOOL OF ATHENS, and the PARNASSUS *incidents that hold one spell-bound*.[1]

The driving force is seen by this group around Goethe to lie in the strength of the emotion and of the forms given to it; Moritz establishes a kind of order of precedence in equality of rights among the great masters: "Raphael is the *clearest mirror of the soul*, Michael Angelo wraps himself in sacred gloom, Titian paints with the finger of roseate dawn."

§ Raphael and Mozart

The physiologist, physician and poetical painter KARL GUSTAV CARUS has pointed out in a stimulating and highly sympathetic manner the unique position of Raphael in the arts. In the *Picture of Pictures*, the SISTINE MADONNA,[2] he found he could follow almost step by step the great, free strokes of the brush, and one is amazed at the simplicity and sureness everywhere to be found in it: "like a sleep-walker, because a goal hovers before him in his mind which he must attain as surely, under all conditions, as the bird of passage its homeland." For the enigmatic, miracle-working power in Raphael's portrait, his power of convincing in the sphere of the other-worldly, a vision offers itself to Carus, by way of comparison, of Mozart's manner of creation—MOZART, who said of himself that his best mode of composition was that which evolved itself in him as in a dream; he overheard a piece of music in his mind not as it would of necessity be heard afterwards, that is, not one portion after another, but all simultaneously—so that he then surveyed a piece of music in his mind "all at once, like a picture or a beautiful human being, as if there were at times a possibility of freedom from the limitations of sensibility otherwise normal to us". One gifted with second sight sees far distant occurrences taking place as if going on in his actual presence; or a sinking man or one under the influence of opium beholds the history of his life passing before him as a single picture. Here we are concerned with a vision that will differ greatly from certain impressions on the senses, just as Pallas appears out of the head of Zeus; or we may call to mind the words of Goethe: "an idea stepped up to me." Thus in the SISTINE MADONNA *a mystical element* is apparent *in the abandonment of the laws of perspective; Raphael seems to be "as little bound down to those laws as Mozart, in his mental survey* of the entire inner organism of a symphony, was able to feel himself dependent on the laws of actual sequence of time in music".—Thus Raphael by virtue of three different horizons, the uppermost passing through the face of the Madonna, one through the heads of St Barbara and St Sixtus, one through the shoulders of the angels, attained a sense of omnipresence—figures stand everywhere eye to eye in front of us; immedi-

---

[1] *Römische Studien*, III, p. 73. "Ueber den Zweck, das Gebiet und die Grenzen der dramatischen Malerei."

[2] "Ueber die Sixtinische Madonna des Raphael": *Jahrbücher zur Schillerstiftung*, I, 1857, p. 3.

ately we experience freedom from the bonds of reality: "The First Picture in the World!"

In this profound comparison between Raphael and Mozart an arch spans the rivalry of the arts, as if for a token of their union; with all their diversity they seem, as it were, to participate in the same dynamic means of expression—as Nietzsche says of music that it translates the will of nature.

FRIEDRICH ROCHLITZ at that time essayed to carry through and substantiate the *parallelism between Mozart and Raphael*;[1] how high the musician sets the painter's power of expression is shown in his comparison of the SCHOOL OF ATHENS with the finale of the first act in *Don Giovanni*, and with the ghost-scene in the second. Common to both is the flow of invention in presentation of the most arresting kind, and again at the end of their days the one like the other was confronted by the vision of a "transfiguration".

§ Carus on Bourgeois and Artistic "Serenity": Raphael's Portrait

For the next following generations this profound and stimulating comparison became outworn currency, the more so as the convenient conception became diffused of the two great "serene" masters; for Carus the "serenity"[2] of Raphael lay solely in the rare, spiritualised "ether of beauty" in which the poet of the Farnesina fable and Mozart both alike live and breathe.[3] It is consistent, to his masculine sense, with the "glorious strength" of the MADONNA DEL GRANDUCA with "a beauty that I can only describe by the name of 'acerbity' ('*Herbigkeit*'),[4] and which signifies for art what the style of Dante was in poetry". This high intuition enabled him also as an exact investigator of skulls to corroborate and deepen the notions of Lavater. He sees clearly expressed in Raphael's Florentine self-portrait "the sensual, arterial and pneumatic qualities of his temperament"; Raphael's skull seems to him in its small construction to be of very harmonious proportions. "A shape of head of this order could hardly with any confidence be reconciled with the cerebral life of a scientific mind garnering up endless material in the way of ideas and objective images; on the other hand, it is entirely consistent with the cerebral life of a Raphael revealing himself in perfect beauty of form."[5]

§ The Nazarenes

Before this same portrait "*Sturm und Drang*" and the younger romantics met to do homage. It was the intention of OVERBECK, self-blest in loving devotion

---

[1] *Allgemeine musikalische Zeitung*, 12th June, 1800.

[2] "*Heiterkeit*." This word in a metaphorical sense has no precise equivalent in English; it is used of clear, unclouded skies or weather—"serenity", with an element also of cheerfulness —*Translator*.

[3] *Reise durch Deutschland, Italien, Schweiz*, 1828.

[4] *Ueber das Kind der Sixtina*.

[5] *Symbolik der menschlichen Gestalt*, 1853 (ed. Lessing), p. 196.

and imitative creation, to perpetuate it in his Triumph of Religion. The young master went in and out among his contemporaries in a mood as high-pitched as was compatible with the pious humility of an artist in the circle of the Nazarenes. Yet the dullness of the eye, the mortification expressed by the mouth, are as little suited to the selfconsciousness shown in the beautiful set of the cloak as they are to the countenance, aglow with inward fire, of the original. But this gentle youth now became an article of faith with the Romantics, in painting and doctrine; indeed, having at last attained recognition and taken possession of the direction of the academies, they almost compelled acceptance for a century of the conception of Raphael in this form, with such tenacious or-ganising energy that Goethe's word for him, "masculine", remained in oblivion even to the present day.

Originally their aim was to set up a national art of their own in opposition to the pagan and cosmopolitan cult of the Classical. Out of the consciousness of their own people, out of the depths of its soul, works were to come into being, as with the ancestral "mediæval" masters, that could not fail to go to the heart of the people and therefore could only pronounce the language of religion within the framework of the ancient Church. In the presence of nature they asserted the freshness and independence of their sensibility, especially in portraiture, often in wonderful depth and purity. In religious themes this new-created German art came with tragic weakness under the inescapable Italian spell. A new aspect was that it was the *young* Raphael who was necessarily taken as their example; to him, the pupil of Perugino, their imagination, dreaming of hier-archic expression, opened itself most willingly, and their instinct, uncertain about itself, here sensed with unusual distinctness and historical correctness how this "pupil of the Greeks" was yet all the time a devoted disciple of Gothic. That he remained so to the end of his life—indeed, that in his unwavering humanism he upheld to the very end the worth of humanity as consisting only in the unity of body and soul, their renunciation of the Classical could not admit. In fact, it is from this circle of devoted worshippers that the bitterest criticism was directed against their hero and leader.

WACKENRODER also[1] had a beautiful vision of rare historical clear-sightedness: his *Kunstliebender Klosterbruder* ("Art-loving Friar"), who loves to dwell in the realm of dreams, acknowledges that it had impressed him as wonder-ful that these two—*Dürer and Raphael*—should have had a quite peculiar kinship to his own heart. An enchanting vision in a dream at the hour of midnight shows him the great venerable masters all standing beside their works in the gallery, and he sees "*Raphael and Dürer standing hand in hand*, apart from the others, in bodily shape before my eyes and looking silently in friendly calm at their paintings hanging together. I had not the courage to speak to the divine Raphael; a secret, reverent dread closed my lips. . . ."

[1] *Herzensergiessungen eines kunstliebenden Klosterbruders im Ehrengedächtnis . . . Albrecht Dürers.*

RAPHAEL

Wackenroder's friend LUDWIG TIECK spoke in tones of similar devotion, in their common *Phantasien über die Kunst*[1] of the figures of children in Raphael's pictures: "The child is beautiful humanity itself—and these children are so truly serious and sublime . . . because they stand so near to the source of radiance that ever recedes more dimly into the distance as life advances in years."

§ Poetic Quality: Archaic Characteristics: Expression in Colour

These moderate-spoken prophets of the new Romantic painting had the wider horizon and freedom of soul in advance of their friends the artists, who watered down Raphael's early style and often acknowledged the greatness of the works of his youth in particular by mere superficial imitation. FRIEDRICH SCHLEGEL, with his all-encompassing sense, made himself the spokesman of the young Romanticism where Raphael was concerned, and his expressions of admiration or disapproval remain always the stimulating word of a productive and generous nature. For him, Raphael stands "through the profound strength of his style and of his style of thinking, through his all-embracing, as it were, all-conquering spirit" among the "*artist-heroes* of the days of old",[2] the "born poet and foremost among painters, before all others who are mere painters and no more."[3] In his creations, as, for instance, in the *Madonna della Sedia.* "Precisely what is most lovely in the modern blossoming of art and in the new refined culture coincides so nearly with the sheer simplicity and beauty of the earliest beginnings. We trace the boundaries of two great epochs."[4] "Here and there Raphael displays almost unadulterated the *style of the old school.*" In the CANIGIANI MADONNA he succeeds "as it were, without any kind of pretentiousness, in pronouncing the answer to the riddle". Schlegel perceived, for the last time for generations, the poetical expression in Raphael's colours: "Anyone who can look at the BELLE JARDINIÈRE and the MADONNA DELLA SEDIA and still think that Raphael is a bad colourist cannot have a very sensitive eye or the most impressionable of senses."[5] "Their colour-character, their glorious amplitude and cheerfulness, might be called 'gay' if we were accustomed to give to this word a more dignified meaning"; his red, white and blue are combined and contrasted, in the MADONNA DEL VELO, in the manner in which poets are accustomed to employ and interpret these colours,[6] and a construction of the colouring so much a poet's rather than a painter's, was indeed altogether peculiar to this artist. "The downright force of his green, red and white blends in the same great fundamental harmony of colour on which Dante expressly bases the more

[1] *Phantasien über die Kunst für die Freunde der Kunst*, Hamburg, 1799.
[2] *Europa*, 1803, I, Part 1, p. 136.
[3] *Ansichten und Ideen von der christlichen Kunst* (*Sämtliche Werke*, Vienna, 1846, Vol. VI, p. 111).
[4] *Europa*, II, 2, p. 26.
[5] *Ibid.*, II, 2, p. 23.
[6] *Ibid.*, I, 1, p. 150.

AFTER-ECHOES OF RAPHAEL

§ Raphael and the Primitives

INGRES celebrates his last sad farewell to Italy by making a drawing of the house at Urbino in which Raphael was born. He was occupied in making a copy of Holbein's MARY TUDOR in the house of the restorer Haro; then the admission came into his head that nothing surpasses a Holbein portrait, only Raphael's likenesses surpass everything! "Pour apprendre" he studies his works, he respects those among his productions that are "Gothic", such as the ENTOMB-MENT, and Memling, Raphael, Giotto stand for him in the uppermost zone.[1] He says to his pupils: "I do not send you to Raphael in the Louvre, to seek 'le beau idéal'; you should obtain for yourselves only 'le suc de la plante'."[2] This draughtsman much extolled as a Classicist, of them all the most sensitive to melody, combines in himself the love of Raphael with love of Memling and Mozart!

A sense for Raphael's forms came upon the youthful EUGÈNE DELA-CROIX out of his own experiences; he believed he could find the prototypes of Madonnas in the healthy strength and roughness of peasant-women of the South of France.[3] For Delacroix, Paolo Veronese "pales" before Raphael's early Peruginesque pictures. "A wonderful understanding for line gives each of his works a charm, capable of extinguishing everything one sees afterwards. Titian appears positively cold, because every sense for such a charm of line deserts him."

"Audacity and inexactitudes are found in Raphael which he commits for the sake of his style and his manner."[4] "His decorousness is a decorousness that arises, without parallel, out of restrained passion, the earthly expression of a soul that has dealings with gods.[5] In delicacy he reminds Delacroix of Chopin; his VISION OF EZEKIEL may be ranged for forcefulness above Rubens.

"Raphael's pupils almost bring us to hate the very characteristics that from his own hand would fill us with enthusiasm. It cannot be denied that a certain elegance often impairs the naturalness and even degenerates into mannerism. It is true that a great charm endures, a certain dominant something—it is as with Rossini, expression always, but before everything elegance."[6]

"With all this, Raphael's gestures are naïve, in spite of the singularity of his style—but it is hateful when stupid people imitate this style and in so doing arrive at false movements. For his charm, as often with the greatest masters, can be compared with the charm of an attractive woman who enchants us without our knowing why."

That in France an Academician like INGRES and a revolutionary like

[1] Henri Lapauze, *Ingres*, pp. 528, 553.
[2] Henri Delaborde, *Ingres*.
[3] *Briefe*, translated into German by W. Stein, I, p. 68.
[4] *Tagebuch*, p. 35.
[5] *Literarische Werke*, German translation by Julius Meier-Graefe, p. 69.
[6] *Tagebuch*, pp. 195, 244.

DELACROIX could arrive at unanimity about Raphael only proves the sway of unbroken tradition in Latin culture; it was first shattered by Impressionism, not without melancholy and ironical backward glances at the lost continuity such as Manet's *DÉJEUNER*.

§ Antagonism in the North

Yet in the North, during the distracted and contentious nineteenth century, the more the external, academic glory paled that surrounded the phenomenon of Raphael, the more antagonism grew against this art of a foreign climate and of an epoch that had become alien in soul. Differences of nationality suddenly became unconsciously more strongly felt than the "eternally uniting" element of a common humanity. And this mood ran through all forms of expression, from indifference and trivial rejection to the turn towards new, racially kindred ideals such as Rembrandt, or towards the great epochs of native art and at the same time to the clear expressive line of the Middle Ages.

Higher natures that had still grown up in reverence for the old ideal felt, with the pain of estrangement in those upper spheres, the duty of an inner vindication, when they could no more perceive in Raphael satisfaction for their profound claims.

JOHN RUSKIN, the great teacher of his nation, their guide to a reverently religious conception of art, is again becoming fruitful in the present generation, actually for the first time since he retired into the background behind his work. Out of regard for Reynolds he entered the lists for Raphael. Otherwise with his Puritanical sense he would have believed it his duty to turn aside from this mature and free art. Like the Nazarenes, he was firmly of the opinion that Raphael "painted best when he knew least" and he knew this conviction "to be shared by most of those who love Raphael truly".[1]

For painting pure and simple he establishes an order of precedence of landscape-painters: Tintoretto and Turner stand together in the first place. Raphael takes the last place but one, Perugino the last.[2] Fra Angelico, it may be said, is *glaringly conspicuous* by his absence from the list. If ever it were a question of the feeling contained in landscape for the totality of form and space, then those last in this series might easily become the first.

In the Stanze Ruskin finds nothing "likely to give anybody in a healthy state of mind . . . the slightest pleasure", with its mixture of paganism and popery.[3] As to the Loggie, Ghiberti's doors strike him as preferable. "The Book of Genesis, in all the fulness of its incidents, in all the depth of its meaning, is bound within the leaf-borders of the gates of Ghiberti. But Raphael's arabesque is mere elaborate idleness. It has neither meaning nor heart in it; it is an

[1] *Stones of Venice*, Vol. III, ch. ii, 33.
[2] *Ibid.*, Vol. I, appendix II.
[3] *Praeterita*, Vol. II, p. 48.

unnatural and monstrous abortion."[1]   Compared with genuine Gothic grotesques these arabesques are the fruit of a great mind "degraded to base objects". They are lacking in "Divine terror".[2]

Something of this sensibility seeking serious justification speaks in the words of THOMAS CARLYLE, a writer apparently unmoved by art.   At Dresden he hurried past the SISTINE MADONNA with an ill-humoured remark, and on another occasion he acknowledged to a friend: "I would rather have one real glimpse of the young Jew face of Christ than see all the Raffaelles in the world." To speak in his own words, this is "not a fact concerning Raphael, but concerning Carlyle".   Had he not been so insusceptible to art, one might have believed from this that he was ripe for Rembrandt; but in these regions, in Carlyle's case as in that of Ruskin, there is a hint of a revolutionary change of atmosphere; the clear lines of the classical landscape are darkened, fade away— their untroubled purity no longer suffices the serious sense, and to the Northerner the aspect of the conflicts of the inner man is more attractive.

Still on the threshold of these epochs of a more profound view of life, one who looks at the ground and is accustomed to intercourse with the great creative spirits of history, LEOPOLD VON RANKE,[3] acknowledges that he sees Raphael "impulsively transported to the heights of loving veneration, it is true —only not without giving expression to a self-restraining reserve, an aloofness that keeps him within bounds. He mitigates even the liveliest movement by the calmness of his figures. How a magnificent style can give rise to mannerism is demonstrated in Raphael. By the operation of his inner self he had acquired a mode of expression, similar to himself in character, that lay, so to speak, ready to hand; this continued to inhere in him even when he was designing works that are without any profound emotion, only we feel that this kind of accomplishment lies on the surface. Here also the impression remains that *we are not being introduced into the secret of a great phenomenon"*

§ New intellectual Claims: Modes and Methods antagonistic to Continuity

After many opinions of lofty minds on Raphael's character as shown in his art, this judgment of the historian cannot avail to degrade Raphael; but it causes the *researcher* to make his appearance on the high watchtower from which every great work of man demands to be viewed. A sharpened feeling of responsibility forces upon him the longing to track out the "secret of the significant phenomenon". The founders of modern art-history, a race of experts, have laid bare the "germ and unity of Raphael's influence". The noble work of

---

[1] *Stones of Venice*, Vol. III, iii, 52.
[2] *Ibid.*, Vol. III, iii, 49.
[3] *Zur Geschichte der italienischen Kunst* (*Sämtliche Werke*, 51, 52, p. 288 f). Moreover, one could not read anything more illuminating as an introduction to Raphael's spiritual character during his last years than precisely Ranke's "Analogien des Protestantismus in Italien" (in *Geschichte der Päpste*, II Buch.).

Crowe and Cavalcaselle, with its profound knowledge of the material, the work of Passavant, compiled from the Nazarene point of view and with devout, almost monastic industriousness, the pages in CARL FRIEDRICH VON RUMOHR'S *Italienische Forschungen*, have by their penetration into the region of art become indispensable for a knowledge of Raphael. But the systematised science that ensued ever sought out and produced for itself new critical and historical problems, in the thickets of which it lost from view as an entirety this art which was a matter of truly vital experience. And yet—beneath the soulless fashions of criticism and æsthetic fanaticism—the spiritual stream maintained its irresistible direction.

The *Leben Raphaels* of HERMANN GRIMM gathered together once again, before the dawn of a period with no spiritual pretensions, the inheritance of Weimar in knowledge of the sublime operations of the intellect. His phrase "*Raphael as a World Power*", at that time soon felt to be exaggerated and as reaching into the void, has ever again proved its truth; as often as there were minds that knew "how to appreciate merits" of which "the germ is within" themselves, they felt themselves brought under the compelling power of Raphael, even if in the course which they took themselves they seemed actually to avoid him. ADOLF MENZEL acknowledges: "With all his extraordinary art Raphael is nevertheless artless; a superabundant charm of free, unconstrained, fresh natural life has been poured out over his works."[1]—And if this passionate seeker after truth bows in reverence before what is elemental in Raphael's nature, DEGAS, that one and only poet and musical draughtsman among the Impressionists, makes his acknowledgments to him by what he does.[2] After the customary academic notices of the ST GEORGE, the executioners in the MASSACRE OF THE INNOCENTS, the famous Louvre drawing for the VENUS AND PSYCHE in the Farnesina, he suddenly feels himself spellbound by the "FEED MY LAMBS" tapestry. What is it that arrests this master of tranquillity? The gentleness apparent in a pair of feet, the feet of the figure of Christ who, scarcely staying on the ground, is taking his leave of the earthly!

Before one of the tapestry-compositions, the MIRACULOUS DRAUGHT OF FISHES, a more robust personality, FERDINAND HODLER, stands stirred to the very depths, when he comes across it unexpectedly in an old oleograph. He remained long standing in front of it, at first speechless; then gradually collecting himself, he said in a voice of excitement: "That is perhaps the most beautiful composition an artist ever created. And even in this mediocre reproduction, widely divergent from the original, the divine beauty so overcame me when I beheld it unexpectedly, that I had to struggle with my emotion."[3]

Amongst all Northerners it is the Swiss in whom the sense for the true

---

[1] *Briefe an C. H. Arnold*, 1836, p. 8.
[2] *Catalogue des Tableaux, Pastels, Dessins; Atelier Degas.*
[3] Fritz Widmann, *Erinnerungen an Ferdinand Hodler (Schweizer Bibliothek*, I, p. 62).

Southern values is most obvious. Hodler's great fellow-countryman, ARNOLD BÖCKLIN, even more unlike Raphael in his aspirations as a painter, spoke with the most profound understanding precisely of the monumental compositions,[1] admiring particularly the mastery of law and the freedom of its observance in the HELIODORUS. In the painter of the Stanze he saw fulfilled what he himself, true to the traditions of Basle, require of a painter, *"that he should be one of the men of culture—in the best sense—of his time"*. The unsentimental craftsmanship of the "painter-man" who characterised the epoch of Impressionism needed for his work nothing of all this. The effect was serious on scientific criticism, which having become unproductive, usually directed its attention to living art. From this quarter came the inorganic separation of Raphael into a draughtsman of genius whose "temperament-charged handwriting" could still find a place in the presence of Impressionistic pretensions, and a painter who merely filled in with colours this draughtsman's outlines and of whom therefore little was to be expected. As a result, these generations of critical observation can boast that they sought with stronger self-justification to give a correct basis to that separation of master and pupils which, in Raphael's late works, did not escape the sensitive attention of those grave observers of *Sturm und Drang* and Romanticism. But in this process of separation into drawing and painter, master and imitator, the essential thing in criticism was overlooked—*clarification*, and the critics beclouded their view of the great inventor and his essentially poetical nature; they forgot "to enquire after *logos* and *pneuma* in Raphael's art".

§ Triumph of Continuity

And yet, what passed over as a cloud in a few godless generations appears to us to-day unimportant, compared with the continuity of the *world-power* that ever asserts itself again and again in most intimately personal attitude and self-surrender; in the exponents of this power the ancient heritage of true humanism, that is to say, its human dignity, lives on and makes itself felt where the sublime theme of "Raphael" is concerned.

The immortal pages of JACOB BURCKHARDT in the earliest editions of the *Cicerone*,[2] with their spiritual fire and their sense for Raphael's ethos, have their effect ever anew in each generation that is worthy of finding its way to them. His conviction was that Italy produced in Raphael "the highest of all testimonies to herself"; and "a master who has so much significance for his own people has the same significance also for humanity as a whole".[3]

[1] Gustav Floerke: *Zehn Jahre mit Böcklin*, p. 176.
[2] Jac. Burckhardt, *Der Cicerone* (as far as the 4th edition—the latest editions inferior and deteriorated from a scientific point of view).
[3] Jac. Burckhardt, *Vorträge*, 1884–1887, "Aus grossen Kunstsammlungen", 1883, and *Beiträge zur Kunstgeschichte Italiens*.

RAPHAEL

The intellect of CARL JUSTI, sweeping on its solitary course over the period of criticism, pointed out the greatness of Raphael as poet of the beyond in the TRANSFIGURATION and the ST CECILIA.[1]

The extensive historical and æsthetic study of ROBERT VISCHER, dedicated to his father, the philosopher and poet, Friedrich Theodor Vischer, displays "a high degree of sincerity in its tense apprehension of the essential".[2] He re-establishes for himself the connection with the true, full-blooded humanists of the classical period in Germany. An ethical and æsthetic appreciation of this order remained, of course, without result in his generation and for a long period; yet inasmuch as it compares the inclination of the North towards Raphael "to the Platonic spiritual attraction towards the archetype", it leads to that *New Humanism* from which for coming generations there are hopes of a rejuvenated validity for Raphael, a less barren approach to his works. Still, in the present generation, those who look on Raphael with an instinctive gaze, as susceptible ethically as it is naïve, find in him stimulus for soul and eye; the powers still hold good as the safest guides that were most powerfully effective as mediators of this phenomenon.

§ Preservation of Tradition by Church and Humanism

Throughout the godless period of indifference or hostile rejection, *the Church and clerical science* preserved and taught, with an unshakable sense of responsibility, the lore and knowledge of those powers that were the lifelong companions of Raphael's spirit and that determined the course of all his creative activity in revealing the incomprehensible.[3] The sense for the sublime symbolism of the liturgical, the sense of being at home in this element of worship, a familiarity with the exaltation of gesture in which primeval, solemn forms of expression, consecrated throughout the history of mankind, vibrate with widening sweep, exercised their influence on his creative sense as they have, unbidden, on that of susceptible later generations; and in these circles life was pervaded with the consciousness that all spiritual activity, theological as well as secular thought, has always laid on it the responsibility of educating mankind, in the highest sense. This is what determines Raphael's creative activity, just as it is this that puts the beholder, still at the present day, under the obligation of creating Raphael's art anew in his own inner consciousness. And as something inseparable from this consciousness, a new *Humanism*—however antagonistic it might at times seem to be—that strove to build up exponents of perfect human dignity, did not, even in Raphael's time, estrange mankind in its noble representatives from the very human aptitude for reverence; it did not

---

[1] Carl Justi, *Die Verklärung Christi—eine Rede*, Leipzig, 1870.
[2] "Raphael und der Gegensatz der Style", in *Studien zur Kunstgeschichte*, Stuttgart, 1886, p. 130.
[3] Franz Xaver Kraus, *Geschichte der christlichen Kunst*, II, 1908.

confine men's upward vision, but set it free, so as to initiate many to these sublimities.

NIETZSCHE as a humanist understood Raphael, with his profound sense for mythology, which for the poetic man "transposes the horizon", and of which the figures must be the dæmonic guardians, all-present though unnoticed, under whose protection the young soul grows up, by whose signs the grown man interprets his life and his struggles.[1] For four centuries men were able to suppose that they lived in familiarity with Raphael as artist and seer. But as Nietzsche, the uncompleted teacher of coming generations, interpreted Raphael, this "natura naturans", in his truly religious paganism, this nature suddenly came to present entirely *new aspects*, of a *deeply stimulating historical truth*. The master who was perpetually subjecting himself stands for Nietzsche beside Goethe as one of the great learners who "renounced themselves" through learning:

"One must *be able* to learn.[2] In an artist opposition is frequently offered by jealousy or that pride which, on feeling something unfamiliar, immediately puts out its stings and instinctively takes up an attitude of defence instead of that of a learner. In Raphael, like Goethe, both jealousy and pride are lacking, and for that reason they were great *learners*. Raphael disappears before our eyes as one who is a learner, in the midst of his adoption of what his great rival (Michael Angelo) designated as *his* 'nature';—but before he had transferred to himself the whole of Michael Angelo, he died—and the last series of his works, as the beginning of a new course of studies, is less perfect, merely good, just because the great learner was interrupted by death in his most difficult task and took with him the final justifying purpose upon which he was directing his gaze."

§ Relation to Music

In Nietzsche's lofty survey of the arts, the words on music, in the *Geburt der Tragödie*, seem to have been spoken also of rhythm in the great dramatic painter: "music is not a reflection of phenomena, but a direct reflection of the will itself, thus presenting to everything physical in the world the metaphysical, to every phenomenon the thing in itself."[3] This allegorical character of music Nietzsche pursues into the sphere of colour: "the same princely distinction of convention shown by Raphael in the use of the simplest conventional colours" was possessed by CHOPIN, with regard however not to colours but to conventionality of melody and rhythm;[4] for Nietzsche the two coincide, even in the "highest sense for form".

[1] *Geburt der Tragödie*, 23 (ed. Musarion, III, p. 154).
[2] *Morgenröte: Gedanken über die moralischen Vorurteile*, Book V, 540 (ed. Musarion, X, p. 330).
[3] *Geburt der Tragödie*, 16 (ed. Musarion, III, p. 107 f.).
[4] *Menschliches, Allzumenschliches*, IV, 159 (ed. Musarion, IX, p. 265).

RAPHAEL

The community of impelling spiritual forces on both sides of the Alps, already constantly felt, especially in the Romantics, shows itself in Nietzsche's words: "The Renaissance displays the awakening of honesty in the South as does the Reformation in the North."[1] Raphael therefore "did not follow, for the distance of a single pace, the pretentious, ecstatic piety of many of his patrons; he preserved his honesty even in that exceptional picture, the SISTINE MADONNA. . . ." "Artists of all times, in their highest flights, have raised just these representations to the degree of heavenly transfiguration" (which at that time Nietzsche thought he recognised for religious and philosophical errors). They would have been incapable of glorifying them without believing in their absolute truth. "When once the belief in such truth declines at all . . . that art can never flourish again which presupposes—like the *Divina Commedia*, the pictures of Raphael, Michael Angelo's frescoes, and the Gothic minsters—not only a cosmic, but a metaphysical significance in the objects of art. That such an art, such faith among artists, once existed will become the subject of a moving legend."[2] Towards the end of his life Nietzsche esteemed Michael Angelo more highly than Raphael, because Michael Angelo . . . "saw the ideal of a more distinguished culture than is the Christian culture of Raphael's type, whilst Raphael only glorified faithfully and modestly the values that had been given him, and had in him no yearning instincts that sought something further"[3]—but above Raphael and Michael Angelo stands Leonardo, "thanks to his power of holding fast to an incompleted system".[4] Yet to none more deservingly than to Raphael could his words possibly be applied for lodging an appeal against romantic judgments concerning that artist's end: "Only the very rarest and best-bred attain, as is just, to the highest and most noble human joys, in which existence celebrates its own transfiguration. . . . Then an overflowing wealth of manifold powers and, at the same time, 'free will' of the most instantly adjustable force and masterly control of resources dwell together affectionately in *one and the same* human being; the spirit is then on as familiar terms with the senses, as much at home with them, as the senses are familiar and at home with the spirit; and anything whatsoever has merely to be enacted in the one sphere in order to release an extraordinary happiness and activity in the other. . . . It is probable that in such perfect and consummated men the most sensual accomplishments are ultimately transfigured by an allegorising ecstasy of the highest spirituality."[5]

[1] Ed. Musarion, VI, p. 170.

[2] *Menschliches, Allzumenschliches*, IV, 220, "Aus der Seele des Künstlers. Das Jenseits in der Kunst" (ed. Musarion, VIII, p. 188).

[3] *Nachgelassene Werke*, Vol. XIV, Part III, 3—*Kunst und Künstler*, 304. (ed. Musarion XVII, p. 317).

[4] *Nachgelassene Werke*, Vol. XIII, i, 3—*Studien aus der Umwertungszeit* 1882–88, "Weltanschauung", 131. (ed. Musarion XVI, p. 51f).

[5] *Wille zur Macht*, Book IV, 1051 (ed. Musarion, XIX, p. 361).

AFTER-ECHOES OF RAPHAEL

§ An Interpretation of the Transfiguration

Moreover, interpretation of the Transfiguration places Raphael's achievement in the unapproachable, elemental sphere of supreme artistic creation; Raphael, himself one of those immortal "naïve" beings, has represented for us, in a quasi-allegorical painting, this reduction of semblance to semblance, the primal process of the naïve artist and at the same time of Apollinian culture. In his TRANSFIGURATION the lower half, with the boy possessed of an evil spirit, the despairing attendants, the Disciples in anguished perplexity, displays to us a reflection of eternal, primal suffering, the sole foundation of the world: "the 'semblance' is here a reflected semblance of eternal opposition, the father of all things. Out of this semblance now rises up, like an ambrosial vapour, a vision-like new world of semblance of which those who are involved in the first semblance see nothing—a radiant floating in purest joy and contemplation free from suffering, beaming from wide-open eyes. Here we have before our gaze, in highest art-symbolism, that Apolline world of beauty and its underground counterpart, the terrible wisdom of Silenus; and we apprehend, by intuition, their mutual inevitability. . . ."[1] Of the three grades into which the artist has here divided humanity—the perplexed sufferers, the bewildered dreamers, and those in heavenly ecstasy, Nietzsche discovered later that "we no longer look out on the world *in this manner, nor would even Raphael be free to do so* any longer. He would behold with his eyes a new Transfiguration".[2]

To-day, after half a century, the one truth in such a pronouncement deserves still to be taken to heart and firmly established: the way to this greatest of plastic poets and interpreters of earth and the beyond can only lead through our own spiritual life; for humanity and for time his art offers a mirror and a measure, and his creation has to be measured by the richness of its vitality; this is the eternal, sublime claim to which Nietzsche gave validity anew. And therewith his audacity has induced in the beholder an exaltation that forbids him any more to enter the sanctuary of this art except as one consecrated to an act of self-surrender.

As an addition to the ancient ecclesiastical tradition, the academic cult, that astonishing Protestant deepening of appreciation in the Classical period, and the Catholic revival in the age of Romanticism, Nietzsche was able to leave behind him, as a heritage to the generations after him, now without a leader, a renewed sense for the true values of Humanism, with which to find again the way into Raphael's world also. It thus became possible to succeed in effacing completely the immediate past, with its spiritual emptiness, and to bring ourselves into association with the nobler preceding age, to knit up once again the seemingly broken tradition.

---

[1] *Geburt der Tragödie*, 4 (ed. Musarion, III, p. 36).
[2] *"Morgenröte"*, I, 8 (ed. Musarion, X, p. 15).

353

RAPHAEL

§ Revival of Reverence

If these men contributed, to the great tradition in which they lived, each time and every one from out of himself, a content of their own, and brought into effect for it a newly founded justification, it is a spectacle worthy of admiration; *a greater blessing* for us is the fact that, after a long desolation and a period lacking in reverence, this heritage that has come down to us has a new validity, now that it has been approached with self-surrender, and the sublime has been allowed once more to be counted among the stars of our existence.

§ Sense for the Ethical in Raphael

Uncontested through the void of criticism and formalism, friends of art with a *sense for the ethical side of creative genius* have drawn up a secular Book of Saints in which Raphael's name stands beside that of Goethe. It was love that sought out the spirit and character in his ideal figures, finding it essential to enquire into the sources of a culture that made that spirit capable of such high achievement. A new conscientiousness was awakened in research. Thus a foundation, as it were, was provided—and an outline, within which the structure could be carried further.[1]

§ Influence emanating from Raphael's Figure as a Youth

There arose, from the circle of those who in aloofness preserved the heritage of Nietzsche to the *Universitas* against the ban of the universities, and strove by their priestly attitude to increase that heritage, a new appreciation of Raphael's youthful figure in the midst of the brotherhood inspired by him, an appreciation of which the rays could not fail to penetrate into the higher realms of feeling of the period. Romanticism and Hellenism agree to unite in devotion to this harmony, in Raphael, of soul and phenomenon.

The figure of the artist in all the beauty of youth, captivating and "working upon" the period and the world about him, as the centre of his enraptured circle of friends, is pointed out as "passing by" among supporters and opponents, until in its maturity it seems to grow dim to the affectionate gaze and pass away.[2]

§ New View of Raphael's Form

Even for the *consistency* displayed by the course of this life, as short as it was rich in transformations, our vision had to be set free anew. It means much if,

[1] Oscar Ollendorf, *Raphael-Studien: der Cortigiano-Typus, eine Studie über Raphaelische Charaktere* 1896.—*Ueber Raphaels Wissen,* 1913.
[2] Wilhelm Stein, *Raffael (Blätter der Kunst,* 1923).

after a long, mechanically thoughtless idealisation of the conception of Raphael emphasis can once more be laid on the fact that his "*form* in its inmost vitality is something *very personal*". This individual form is explained only by the sense for unity in Raphael's manner of working; in subservience to the whole, in feeling for space and framework, each of his figures takes on that *character of pattern* which is peculiar to Raphael alone. This differentiates his creations finally from the Antique, which is always being compared to him. "*Our veneration for Raphael is liberated from the force of example and norm.*" [1]

And yet, the "compelling force of example" obtrudes itself on us again and again within the range of Raphael's spell, and will not be denied. His lofty spirit, holding sway over all art, never abandoned him. With one of his breeding it could not be otherwise. With the *Timaeus* under his arm, Plato strides into the hall of the SCHOOL OF ATHENS, directing towards heaven the assembled learning of earth; on the facing wall, the great, universal picture of the *DISPUTA* —Platonic, Biblical, Dantesque—"that eternal threefold stratification of the animate universe; at the apex, the Creator, with the orb in his hand; on the plane of the clouds, those that have become divine, Christ and the Saints; and on the earth, the congregation, filled with the heavenly spectacle. And *Plato's sublime figure re-unites the two pictures with the only-begotten eternal universe*". [2]

§ Raphael's Drawings the Key to the Indivisibility of his Character

After renewed, profoundly penetrating humanism of such an order, it might seem almost like an anticlimax if the collecting of Raphael's drawings were made the occasion of adding once more to the mass of material. Yet these half thousand drawings are not without their sanction—that of unity. We behold a world taking shape in ferment, on a higher plane; an imagination welling forth inexhaustibly comes wildly streaming in, and is duly relegated ever anew to its appointed end: ideas of colour and light, apparently unrestrained, group themselves in lovely constraint around a centre; on the wings of a free-soaring power of presentation the legitimate, architectonic work of art comes into being.

Thus enriched, the vision may be stimulated, through the multitude of inspired ideas on paper which are those of a painter, to rediscover, in the picture also, the *painter*, and thus to approach more nearly the imperative duty of venerating the essential indivisible unity in the elemental energy of a heaven-graced, creative nature.

In the foregoing pages it has been the writer's desire to set down something of the superhuman working of Raphael's imagination, some glimpses of the foundations of his character, of the dæmonic forces that urged him on to become

[1] Theodor Hetzer, *Gedanken um Raffaels Form*, 1932.
[2] Kurt Hildebrandt, *Uebertragungen der Schöpfungsgeschichte in Platons Timaios* (Handpresse Burg Giebichenstein, Halle, 1925).

the leader, into depths that were his own and into undreamt-of heights, of his own and later ages. It is his hope

> "che una scintilla sol della tua gloria
>   possa lasciare alla futura gente"

> "that he may to the future race bequeath
>   a spark, no more perchance, of thy renown."

CATALOGUE RAISONNÉ

A.D.

Circa 1497.   *Self-portrait*, chalk drawing. Oxford, Ashmolean Museum. (*R.Z.*, I, 1.*)

1499.   *Banner*. Città di Castello, Pinacoteca Comunale.

   Drawing for the Almighty: Oxford, Ashmolean Museum. (*R.Z.*, I, 2).

Madonna with children, pen drawing (on the *verso* of the preceding drawing) (*R.Z.*, I, 3).

Warriors, pen drawing. Paris, Louvre (Fischel, *Zeichnungen der Umbrer*, fig. 137).

Kneeling youth (for the *Transfiguration* in the Cambio?), pen drawing, on the *verso* of the preceding drawing. (*Zeichnungen der Umbrer*, fig. 136.)

1500.   Details for Perugino's *Assumption of the Virgin* (Florence, Uffizi): Angel with harp, head of the flying angel, to the left below, St. Michael and St. Augustine, cherub head above.

Details for the *Cambio frescoes*, Perugia: Fortitudo, head of King Solomon.

John the Evangelist, after Donatello, pen drawing. Paris, Louvre (*R.Z.*, I, 10).

Jousting Putti, chalk cartoon. Chantilly, Musée Condé. (*R.Z.*, I, 42.)

Coronation of St. Nicholas of Tolentino. Fragments at Brescia, Pinacoteca Martinengo, and Naples, Museo Nazionale.

   Drawings at Lille, Musée Wicar (*R.Z.*, I, 5–6) and Oxford, Ashmolean Museum (*R.Z.*, I, 7–8).

The Knight's Dream. London, National Gallery. The cartoon (*R.Z.*, I, 40) also in the National Gallery.

The Three Graces. Chantilly, Musée Condé.

The Virgin reading, with Child, pen drawing. Paris, Louvre (*R.Z.*, I, 43).

Madonna with St. Jerome and St. Francis. Berlin, Kaiser-Friedrich-Museum.

   Study for St. Jerome, chalk drawing. Lille, Musée Wicar (*R.Z.*, I, 44).

Diotalevi Madonna. Berlin, Kaiser-Friedrich-Museum.

Solly Madonna. Berlin, Kaiser-Friedrich-Museum.

   Sketches of the Madonna for the *Virgin at a Window*: (1) Entire composition and Child, pen drawing. Oxford, Ashmolean Museum (*R.Z.*, I, 46). (2) Nude study for the Virgin, silverpoint. Lille, Musée Wicar (*R.Z.*, I, 50). (3) Head of the Virgin, silverpoint, London, British Museum (Malcolm Collection) (*R.Z.*, I, 51).

Conestabile Madonna. Leningrad, Hermitage.

St. George (with sword). Paris, Louvre. Drawing for the same: Florence, Uffizi (*R.Z.*, I, 57).

St. Michael. Paris, Louvre.

1502.   *Youth with Cap*, chalk drawing. Formerly Locker Lampson Collection. (*R.Z.*, I, 14.)

Christ in Benediction. Brescia, Pinacoteca Martinengo.

St. Sebastian. Bergamo, Accademia Carrara.

St. Sebastian, pen drawing. Lille, Musée Wicar. (*R.Z.*, I, 13.)

*These references are to the eight volumes of the Author's *Raphaels Zeichnungen*, G. Grote Verlag, Berlin, 1913–1941.

Madonna with St. Sebastian and St. Roch, pen drawing. Paris, Louvre. (*R.Z.*, I, 45.)

1502/3.
Crucifixion. London, National Gallery (Mond Bequest).
Predella paintings: (1) *St. Jerome punishing the heretic Sabinianus.* Lisbon Gallery. (2) *Cyrillus brings back to life three corpses with the garment of St. Jerome.* Richmond, Cook Collection.

Nude study for St. Francis, pen drawing. London, British Museum. (*R.Z.*, I, 55.)

Portrait (presumed to be *Perugino*). Rome, Borghese Gallery.

The Holy Family. Tondo (panel). Sir Edward Mountain, Bt. (*Burlington Magazine*, vol. 86, 1945, p. 82.)

Coronation of the Virgin from Città di Castello. Rome, Vatican.
Predella paintings: (1) *Ave Maria, Presentation in the Temple, Adoration of the Magi.* Rome, Vatican. (2) Drawings for the same (*R.Z.*, I, 15–32; *Burlington Magazine*, vol. 71, 1937, p. 167).

Kneeling Saint, Silver-point drawing. Oxford, Ashmolean Museum. (*R.Z.*, I, 41.)

1503.
Portions by Raphael in Pinturicchio's frescoes in the Libreria, Siena.
Drawings for the same. Florence, Uffizi (*R.Z.*, I, 60–62). (1) *Marriage of Frederick III.* Florence, Conte Contini (formerly Perugia, Casa Baldeschi) (*R.Z.*, I, 65). (2) Central Group of the *Coronation of Pius II.*

Portrait, Francesco Maria della Rovere. Florence, Pitti Palace.

St. Mary Magdalene and St. Catherine, cartoons for a lost painting. Berlin (Kupferstich-Kabinett) and Paris (Edmond de Rothschild) (*R.Z.*, I, I, 56, 56a; *Jahrbuch der Königl. Preuss. Kunstsammlungen*, vol. 36, 1915, p. 92).

1504.
Sposalizio. Milan, Brera.
Drawings for the same (*R.Z.*, I, 35–36).

Portrait of a Young Man. Budapest, Museum of Fine Arts.

1504/5.
St. George. Washington, National Gallery of Art (Mellon Collection). Formerly in the Hermitage, Leningrad.

Circa 1505.
Duke of Terranuova Madonna. Berlin, Kaiser-Friedrich-Museum.
(1) Drawing of the composition. Lille, Musée Wicar (*R.Z.*, I, 54). (2) Fragment of cartoon for the head of the Virgin. Berlin, Kupferstich-Kabinett (*R.Z.*, III, 104).

Ansidei Madonna. London, National Gallery.

St. John the Baptist preaching. Bowood, Lord Lansdowne.

Madonna della Malagrana, chalk drawing. Vienna, Albertina (*R.Z.*, I, 53).

Circa 1504.
Madonna painted for the nuns of Sant' Antonio, Perugia. New York, Metropolitan Museum.
Predella paintings: (1) *Christ on the Mount of Olives.* New York, Metropolitan Museum. A much discussed replica in private possession. (2) *Pietà.* Boston, Gardner Museum. (3) *Procession to Calvary.* London, National Gallery. (4, 5) *St. Francis* and *St. Anthony.* Dulwich Gallery.

Florence
Circa 1505.
Madonna del Granduca. Florence, Pitti Palace.
Sketch in the round and with landscape, chalk. Florence, Uffizi (*R.Z.*, III, 105).
Sketch-books: Green (*R.Z.*, II, 74–77); Grey (*R.Z.*, II, 68–73); Large (pen-drawings). (*R.Z.*, II, 81 sqq.)

Casa Tempi Madonna. Munich, Alte Pinakothek.

Madonna (the *Small Cowper Madonna*). Philadelphia, Widener Collection. Replica, under-painting, in the market, America (from the Peruzzi Collection).

Madonna in the Meadow. Vienna, Kunsthistorisches Museum.
Studies for the same: Oxford, Ashmolean Museum (*R.Z.*, III, 118) and Vienna, Albertina (*R.Z.*, III, 115–116).

Madonna del Cardellino. Florence, Uffizi.
Drawings for the same: Oxford, Ashmolean Museum (*R.Z.*, III, 112–113).
Madonna with Beardless St. Joseph. Leningrad, Hermitage.
Orleans Madonna. Chantilly, Musée Condé.
Holy Family with the Palm-tree. London, Bridgewater House.
Sketch for the same, on pink-ground paper. Paris, Louvre (*R.Z.*, III, 139).
Portraits of Angelo and Maddalena Doni. Florence, Pitti Palace.
Young Girl at a Window, pen drawing. Paris, Louvre. (*R.Z.*, II, 80.)
The *Donna Gravida.* Florence, Pitti Palace.
Lady in Green. Formerly Florence, Uffizi, now Urbino, Ducal Palace.

1505/7. The *San Severo Trinity.* Perugia, San Severo.
Sheet of studies for the same, with the group of horsemen of the *Battle of Anghiari.*
Oxford, Ashmolean Museum (*R.Z.*, IV, 210).
Holy Family, from the Casa Canigiani. Munich, Alte Pinakothek. The
   cherub heads, now missing in the original, can be seen in the copies
   in the Palazzo Rinuccini and in the Sacristy of San Frediano, Florence.
Drawings at Chantilly, etc. (*R.Z.*, III, 130 sqq.); heads of children, Hamburg,
Kunsthalle (*R.Z.*, III, text fig. 140, 142).
Madonna with Lamb, with entirely original portions, presumed to be at
   Siena, mentioned by Vasari.
Esterhazy Madonna. Budapest, Museum of Fine Arts.
Sketch cartoon. Florence, Uffizi (F. III, 126).
Holy Family with the Lamb. Madrid, Prado.
Old replica in the possession of Lord Lee of Fareham, Richmond (*Burlington
Magazine,* vol. 64, 1934, p. 14 and 242).
Belle Jardinière. Paris, Louvre.
Sketch, studies, cartoon, in the Louvre, Chantilly, Oxford, Holkham Hall (*R.Z.*,
III, 119–125).

1507. *Entombment.* Rome, Borghese Gallery.
Predella-panels. Rome, Pinacoteca Vaticana. (1) Ornamental intermediate
panels of the predella. Perugia, Pinacoteca. The Almighty, Perugia, after design
by Raphael, Lille, Musée Wicar (F.IV, 180). (2) Sketches and studies in Paris,
London, Oxford, etc. (*R.Z.*, IV, 164–186).

Circa 1507. *St. Catherine.* London, National Gallery.
Sketch and studies. Chatsworth, Duke of Devonshire, and Oxford, Ashmolean
Museum (*R.Z.*, IV, 204–206).
Bridgewater Madonna. London, Bridgewater House.
Sketches Vienna, Albertina. Paris, Louvre. London, British Museum (*R.Z.*, III,
108–111; *Burlington Magazine,* vol. 74, 1939, p. 187).
Madonna of the Casa Colonna. Berlin, Kaiser-Friedrich-Museum.
Pen drawing for the same. Vienna, Albertina. (*R.Z.*, III, 10.)
The red-stained sketchbook. Bayonne, Musée Bonnat; Vienna, Albertina;
   Stockholm, National Museum; Oxford, Christ Church. (*R.Z.*, III,
   150–158.)

1508. The *Large Cowper Madonna.* Washington, National Gallery of Art (Mellon
   Collection). (O. Fischel, in *Das unbekannte Meisterwerk,* hrsg. v. W. R.
   Valentiner, 1930, p. 20).
Contemporary replica with slight alterations. Florence, Private Possession.
Madonna del Baldacchino. Florence, Palazzo Pitti.
Sketch and studies at Chatsworth, Duke of Devonshire; Paris, École des Beaux
Arts; Florence, Uffizi; Lille, Musée Wicar (*R.Z.*, III, 140–148).
Combat-scenes, pen drawings. Oxford, Ashmolean Museum (*R.Z.*, IV, 193–
   195.)

359

Hercules with the Lion, pen drawing. Windsor, Royal Library. (*R.Z.*, IV, 190.)
Playing Putti, pen drawing. Vienna, Albertina. (*R.Z.*, IV, 202.)
Adam, pen drawing, employed by Marcantonio in *The Fall.* Oxford, Ashmolean Museum (*R.Z.*, IV, 201; *Old Master Drawings,* vol. 13, 1938–39, p. 50).
Landscape with Bridge, pen drawing. Weimar, Museum (*R.Z.*, IV, 203.)

Rome

1508.   The Pink Sketchbook, with designs for the Bridgewater Madonna, the Madonna with the Sleeping Child, the Child awakening, the Aldobrandini Madonna, the Mackintosh Madonna, the *Madonna della Sedia,* the *Madonna Alba.* (*R,Z.*, VIII; *Burlington Magazine,* vol. 74, 1939, p. 181.)
Madonna with the Carnation. Examples in Lucca (Count Spada), Alnwick Castle, Lützschena, without claims to originality.
Child's head, on a page from the Pink Sketchbook. Basle, R. von Hirsch Collection. (*Burlington Magazine,* vol. 74, 1939, p. 186; *R.Z.*, VIII, 354.)

1509.   Stanza della Segnatura:
Ceiling-paintings: Roundels:
  Jurisprudence.
  Poetry.
(1) Sketch. Chalk drawing. Windsor, Royal Library (*R.Z.*, V, 228). (2) Fragment of cartoon, of the putto with tablet on the right. Chalk drawing. London, British Museum (*R.Z.*, V, 229). (3) Study for a mask on the throne of "Poetry". Silver-point. Lille, Musée Wicar (*Burlington Magazine,* vol. 74, 1939; *R.Z.*, VIII, 345, p. 180).
  Philosophy.
  Theology.
Sketch of the figure, pen drawing. Oxford, Ashmolean Museum (*R.Z.*, V, 225).
Ceiling-paintings: Square panels:
  Punishment of Marsyas.
  The Fall.
Studies for Adam, pen and red chalk. Paris, Louvre (*R.Z.*, V, 224).
  Judgment of Solomon.
(1) Sketch, silver-point. Oxford, Ashmolean Museum (*R.Z.*, V, 230). (2) Study for the executioner, with kneeling mother, pen and chalk drawings. Vienna, Albertina (*R.Z.*, V., 231–232).
  Astronomy.
Sketch, pen drawing. Vienna, Albertina (*R.Z.*, V., 237).
Massacre of the Innocents.
(1) Red chalk. Windsor, Royal Library. On the back, design for a dish, combat of Tritons (*R.Z.*, V, 234–235). (2) Red chalk and pen, retouched by another hand. London, British Museum (*R.Z.*, V, 233). (3) Executioner and fleeing mother, red chalk. Vienna, Albertina (on the back of the sketch for the Astronomy) (*R.Z.*, V, 236).
Assumption of the Virgin, pen drawing. Oxford, Ashmolean Museum. (On the back of the study for the Theology.) (*R.Z.*, V, text fig. 212.)
Assumption of the Virgin, pen drawing. Stockholm, National Museum. (*R.Z.*, V, text fig. 198.)

1509.   *Disputa.*
(1) Sketches and studies (*R.Z.*, VI, 258–303). (2) Study for the *Birth of Venus,* pen drawing. Florence, Uffizi (*R.Z.*, VI, 264). (3) Study after the *Belvedere Apollo* on the back of the study for the Adam in the *Disputa* (*R.Z.*, VI, 249). (4) Sketch of a *Triumphal Car* with Julius II as Mars, pen drawing. Budapest, Museum of Fine Arts (*R.Z.*, VI, 302). (5) Sketch for *Prudence,* on sheet with drawing for the

newly converted youth, pen and chalk drawing. Oxford, Ashmolean Museum (*R.Z.*, VI, 280). (6) Drafts for *Sonnets*: Oxford, Ashmolean Museum (*R.Z.*, VI, 277, 279, 280); Vienna, Albertina (*R.Z.*, VI, 283); Montpellier, Musée Fabre (*R.Z.*, VI, 287).

1509.
Parnassus.
(1) Sketch in copy. Oxford, Ashmolean Museum (*R.Z.*, V, 237a). (2) Sketch-fragment in copy of the right half. Paris, Louvre (*R.Z.*, V, 238). (3) Study for one of the Muses, chalk drawing. Captain Norman Colville Collection (*Burlington Magazine*, vol. 71, 1937, p. 167).
School of Athens.
(1) Cartoon without architecture. Milan, Ambrosiana (*R.Z.*, VII, 313–344). (2) Sketches, studies (*R.Z.*, VII, 305–312a; *Burlington Magazine*, vol. 74, 1939, p. 187). The first sketch for the *Madonna on Clouds*, chalk drawing. Frankfort, Staedelsches Institut (on the back, copy of a red chalk study for the figure of Zoroaster in the *School of Athens*) (*R.Z.*, VII, text fig. 271).
Justinian delivering the Pandects.
Study washed in bistre. Frankfort, Staedelsches Institut (*R.Z.*, V, 255).

1511.
Gregory IX delivering the Decretals.
Study for the group on the right, pen drawing. Frankfort, Staedelsches Institut (*R.Z.*, V, 256).
Putti on the keystones of the framing arches, Stanza della Segnatura.
Chiaroscuri on the window-jambs of the Stanza della Segnatura after Raphael's designs, amongst which the judge Zaleucus is by his own hand.
Adoration of the Child in the Stable. Small cartoon, silver-point, heightened with white, on grey prepared paper. Florence, Uffizi (*R.Z.*, VIII, 356).
Studies for the awakening Child. Basle, Hirsch Collection, from the Pink Sketchbook (*Burlington Magazine*, vol. 74, 1939, p. 187; *R.Z.*, VIII, 354).
Mary and Joseph with the Awakening Child.
Completed work missing, old replica in the storeroom of the Uffizi. Composition handed down in two drawings, one by Penni in the Albertina, the other Oxford, Ashmolean Museum (from the Locker-Lampson Collection) (*Old Master Drawings*, vol. 2, 1927/28, pl. 3).
Adoration of the Shepherds, with Julius II as Donor.
Pen drawing. Oxford, Ashmolean Museum *Bolletino d'Arte*, vol. 28, 1934, p. 196; *R.Z.*, VIII, 361).
Madonna del Velo. Paris, Louvre (for the most part by Penni).
Madonna di Loreto, missing, handed down in several not original examples. Paris, Louvre. A fragment with the Child from a contemporary replica in the Galleria Corsini, Rome.
(1) Head of the Madonna, chalk cartoon fragment. London, British Museum (*R.Z.*, VIII, text, fig. 286). (2) The awakening Child, silver-point on pink prepared paper. Lille, Musée Wicar, from the Pink Sketchbook. (*Burlington Magazine*, vol. 74, 1939, p.187; *R.Z.*, VIII, 351.)
Madonna studies: Bridgewater Madonna, Madonna with the Child in the act of benediction, Madonna with children on the ground, the blessing Child sitting. Leaves from the Pink Sketchbook. See also above. (Uffizi, Albertina, Lille) (*Burlington Magazine*, vol. 74, 1939, p. 181.)
Group of the *Madonna with the Child on the ground*, with Joseph and Angel, red chalk. Cambridge, Fitzwilliam Museum. (*R.Z.*, VIII, 357.)
Alba Madonna. Tondo. Washington, National Gallery of Art (Mellon Collection) (formerly in the Hermitage. Leningrad).
(1) Old replica, frequently cited, rectangular, with misunderstood alterations. (2)

Sketch with studies, beside it design for the *Madonna della Sedia*. Red chalk. Lille, Musée Wicar (*R.Z.*, VIII, 364). (3) Study for the kneeling St. John as a boy. Silver-point. Haarlem, Koenigs Collection (*Burlington Magazine*, vol. 74, 1939, p. 187; *R.Z.*, VIII. 355).

Madonna seated on the ground in the attitude of the Prudentia, with the child St. John, pen drawing, copy of a lost design. Milan, Brera.

Madonna with sleeping Child and laughing St. John, kneeling: early Roman composition, original lost or only carried out by pupils. Munich; London, Duke of Westminster; Neuwied; Budapest.

Coronation of the Virgin, with aureole of angels, pen drawing. Bayonne, Musée Bonnat (*R.Z.*, VIII, 382).

Coronation of the Virgin, on throne, small sketch and large sketch for composition in a throne-recess. Bayonne, Musée Bonnat (*R.Z.*, VIII, 383).

Resurrection. (*Jahrbuch der Preussischen Kunstsammlungen*, vol. 46, 1925, pp. 191 sqq.; *R.Z.*, VIII, 387–395.)

(1) Large sketch, pen drawing. Bayonne, Musée Bonnat. (2) Sketch for the lower part, pen drawing. Oxford, Ashmolean Museum. (3) Studies for the groups of terror-stricken guards, pen drawing. Oxford, Ashmolean Museum. (4) Separate studies for the guards, in chalk. Oxford, Ashmolean Museum; Windsor, Royal Library; Chatsworth, Duke of Devonshire; London, British Museum. (5) Standard-bearer, engraving by Marcantonio, B.481.

Portrait of a man with long hair, cap and *lucco*. London, Agnew (formerly in the Whitney Collection, New York). Of the transitional period or the very beginning of the Roman period.

Circa 1510/11   *Portrait of a young Cardinal*. Madrid, Prado. The person represented, wrongly called Bibbiena, sometimes Schinner or Trivulzio, appears to be Cardinal Ippolito d'Este.

Cardinal Alessandro Farnese (later Paul III). Naples, Museo Nazionale. Formerly called Cardinal Passerini. Copy, presumably Florentine (by Bacchiacca?), with alteration of the original format.

Julius II. Florence, Uffizi. Difficult to judge.

(1) Version with divergences. London, National Gallery. (2) Red chalk study for the head. Chatsworth, Duke of Devonshire (*R.Z.*, V, 257). (3) The example in the Pitti Palace is Titian's copy made for Guidobaldo II of Urbino.

Stanza of Heliodorus:

1511.   *Ceiling-paintings* carried out by Raphael in tapestry style with golden high lights. The plaster ground disintegrated and the colour scheme falsified by Maratta.

(1) *God's Command to Noah*. (2) *Jacob's Dream* of the Ladder to Heaven. (3) *Moses and the Burning Bush*. Sketch for the figure of the Almighty, with angels. Oxford, Ashmolean Museum. (4) *The Sacrifice of Abraham*.

Expulsion of Heliodorus.

(1) Studies for the group of kneeling women, chalk drawings. Oxford, Ashmolean Museum. (2) Study for the kneeling mother, chalk drawing. Zurich, Art Society (*Burlington Magazine*, vol. 46, 1925, p. 134). (3) Fragments of cartoon: two angelheads to the right. Paris, Louvre. (4) Fragment of cartoon, horse's head. Oxford, Ashmolean Museum.

Mass of Bolsena.

(1) Sketches of the composition and architecture handed down only in workshop drawings. Oxford, Ashmolean Museum. (2) Nude study of a kneeling woman, red chalk. Chatsworth, Duke of Devonshire.

Deliverance of St. Peter.

Sketch, pen drawing with wash, heightened with white, damaged. Florence, Uffizi.

Encounter of Leo I with Attila. Original, apart from a few heads inserted on the right, behind.

(1) Workshop sketch, pen drawing, with wash, heightened with white. Paris, Louvre. (2) Poor copy of an early stage of the composition, with Julius II and Cardinal Federigo Gonzaga. Oxford, Ashmolean Museum. (3) Study for the horseman on the right of Attila, silver-point on grey ground, heightened with white. Frankfort, Staedelsches Institut. (4) Drawing after the relief of horsemen on the attic of the Arch of Constantine, silver-point, grey ground, heightened with white. Munich, Kupferstichkabinett. From the same sketchbook as that used for the horseman on the right.

Chiaroscuri in the window-jambs, presumably early works of Giulio Romano?

Putto with the Medici ring in the ceiling-pendentive above the Attila fresco, to the right, *grisaille* by Penni.

Original sketch by Raphael, chalk. Haarlem, Teyler Museum (Plate 99).

1511/12. *Madonna di Foligno.* Rome, Vatican. Original, and as far as the crudely restored nimbus in the upper part, well preserved, also in the *putto* below. The landscape in the middle background of a strange, Ferrarese character, has suggested the collaboration of Dosso Dossi, for which otherwise there is no evidence. St. John and St. Francis almost without a trace of Raphael's own hand, the right-hand group better preserved. The tablet held by the *putto* presumably bore an inscription.

(1) First idea of the appearance on clouds on a sheet with a drawing for the *School of Athens*, chalk. Frankfort, Staedelsches Institut (*R.Z.*, VII, text fig. 271; see also above, p. 361). (2) The Virgin on clouds with the Child in the act of benediction, chalk. Chatsworth, Duke of Devonshire (*R.Z.*, VIII, 369). (3) The same motive, varied, together with a study after an antique kneeling nymph. Old copy of a lost original. Florence, Uffizi. (4) The Virgin in the same pose as in the painting, the Child still sitting, chalk. Chatsworth, Duke of Devonshire. (5) Engraving by Marcantonio after a lost study for the Madonna, diverging from the painting.

Circa 1512. *Isaiah*, fresco. Rome, Sant' Agostino. Defaced beyond recognition by old over-painting.

Putto with oak-wreath, fragment of fresco. Rome, Accademia di San Luca. By Raphael's own hand.

Mackintosh Madonna. London, National Gallery. In its present condition difficult to judge.

(1) Cartoon, undoubtedly genuine, in the British Museum (*R.Z.*, VIII, 362). (2) Studies at Lille, Musée Wicar, and for the heads of the Virgin and Child in the British Museum; both from the Pink Sketchbook (*Burlington Magazine*, vol. 74, 1939, p. 182; *R.Z.* VIII, 347, 349).

1513. *Sistine Madonna*, on canvas. Dresden, Gemäldegalerie. Probably intended as a wall-painting for the funeral velarium of Julius II, subsequently taken to Piacenza. Preservation good in essential parts, apart from the head of St. Barbara; in the angels and in St. Sixtus, excellent. No preliminary studies as those for the *Madonna di Foligno*.

Donna Velata, canvas. Florence, Pitti Palace. Near in date to the *Sistine Madonna*, and to be regarded as a model for that painting. The Magdalen in the picture of St. Cecilia (1514) shows the features already less pure and fresh. On the left side, over-paintings on the shapeless veil; the original condition was shown by the lost replica in the Arundel Collection perpetuated by the engraving by Hollar (see Plate), with the attributes of St. Catharine. The same features in the portrait at Hanover (Kestner Museum), and in a less refined version in the picture ascribed to Penni, also, with the attributes of St. Catherine, at Strasburg.

Circa 1513.

Madonna with the Fish. Madrid, Prado. (Gronau 108.)
(1) First study for the composition, after models, red chalk. Florence, Uffizi (*R.Z.*, VIII, 371). (2) Sketch of the composition, brush drawing, bistre heightened with white. London, Capt. Colville (*R.Z.*, VIII 372). (3) Angel's head in black chalk and white, damaged, attributed to Fra Bartolommeo, perhaps for this stage of the composition. Berlin, Kupferstichkabinett.
Madonna with the Candelabra. Formerly London, Sir Charles Robinson. Not original apart from the head of the Virgin; probably by Giulio Romano.
Madonna dell' Impannata. Florence, Pitti Palace. Composition by Raphael, perhaps intended as a *tondo* or octagonal, disfigured by the window; executed by Penni.
(1) Sketch of the composition by Raphael's own hand, silver-point on brown-ground paper, heightened with white. Windsor, Royal Library (*R.Z.*, VIII, 373). (2) Study for the Child and the St. John, in similar technique, original. Berlin, Kupferstichkabinett (*R.Z.*, VIII, 374).
Madonna sitting on the ground with a book, two cherub-heads above, pen drawing (Plate 139). Vienna, Albertina (*R.Z.*, VIII, 354). On a sheet with a design for the *Disputa*, with sonnet: *Lingua or di parlar.* (*R.Z.*, VI, text fig. 257.)

1514.

Galatea, fresco. Rome, Farnesina.
Prophets and Sibyls. Rome, Santa Maria della Pace.
(1) Sketch of the whole wall, preserved only as copied drawing. Stockholm, National Museum. (2) The Prophets, pen drawing (lost) marked out in squares, from the de Triqueti (?) Collection. Giulio Romano. (3) Prophet Daniel and study for the angel behind him, red chalk. Florence, Uffizi. (4) Studies for the angel of the Cumaean Sibyl, red chalk. Vienna, Albertina. (5) Study for the the upper part of the body of the same angel and for the arm of the Cumaean Sibyl. Oxford, Ashmolean Museum. On the back the leaning *putto*, damaged. (6) Study for the Phrygian Sibyl on the arch to the left, in varied attitude. Oxford, Ashmolean Museum. (7) Study for the Tiburtine Sibyl, red chalk. Vienna, Albertina.

Circa 1514.

Portrait of a woman unknown—the Fornarina(?). Cracow, Czartoryski Gallery. A most finished painting, as regards colour, of the period of the *Attila*. Engraved by Pontius as a portrait of Raphael, copied by Van Dyck in the Chatsworth sketchbook (at that time the right hand was still fully visible).

Circa 1514.

Portrait of Tommaso ("Fedra") Inghirami. Florence, Pitti Palace. Second example from the Palazzo Inghirami at Volterra, in the possession of Mrs. Gardner, Boston. The example in the Pitti Palace has the good qualities, in the application of the pigments, of the fresco heads in the Second Stanza; the picture at Boston shows the head less strongly fore-shortened.

1514/15.

St. Cecilia. Bologna, Pinacoteca.
Studies for the drapery of St. Paul, Haarlem, Teyler Museum. Copy after a lost drawing.

1514/15.

Madonna della Sedia. Florence, Pitti Palace. A work by Raphael's own hand of the period of the *Mass of Bolsena*, and the design for the Chigi Chapel.
(1) Study for the Madonna—Nude. From the Pink Sketchbook. Basle, Hirsch Collection (*Burlington Magazine*, vol. 74, 1939, p. 187; *R.Z.*, VIII, 354). (On the same sheet as the Head of a Child, and the studies for an Awakening Child; see above.) (2) Study for the composition on the sheet with the *Alba Madonna*. Lille, Musée Wicar (see above).

Circa 1515.	*Portrait of Bindo Altoviti.* Washington, National Gallery of Art (Kress Collection). Formerly in the Alte Pinakothek, Munich. (Gronau, 125.) In spite of good authentication of pedigree and subject not convincing in composition or in the manipulation of the colouring. Mannered in structure, harsh brownish-red in the flesh-tones, and cold in colouring.
Circa 1515.	*Portrait of Count Baldassare Castiglione.* Paris, Louvre. The painting splendidly preserved; the composition shortened below, as can be seen from the copy by Rubens, in private possession in Vienna, and from Rembrandt's drawing in the Albertina.
Circa 1515.	*Portrait of Giuliano de' Medici Duke of Nemours.* New York, Jules S. Bache. Formerly Berlin, Huldschinsky Collection. Head and composition at least designed by Raphael; the defective sense of space justifies considering only a pupil such as Giulio Romano as the painter.
	Madonna della Tenda. Munich, Alte Pinakothek. In spite of all attributions to Giulio Romano, Penni or Alfano, a marvellously authentic work by Raphael's own hand of his freest period. Old replica at Turin.
1515/16.	*The Tapestry Cartoons.* London, Victoria and Albert Museum. Much overpainted at a later time. In large portions the artist's own work, in the freest style of the latest frescoes in the Vatican, particularly the *Mass of Bolsena.* Raphael's own brushwork has been preserved in its entirety in the "*Feed my Lambs*", and in the *Punishment of Ananias*; in the subsidiary figures in the middle of the *Healing of the Lame Man*, in the young man in the *Miraculous Draught of Fishes*, in St. Paul and the sacrificing attendant in the *Sacrifice at Lystra.*
	(1) Original design for the "*Feed my Lambs*", red chalk. Windsor and Paris. (2) Study for the St. Paul at Lystra, silver-point heightened with white, on grey paper. Chatsworth, Duke of Devonshire. (3) Other drawings only studio works.
1515.	*Cupola* of the Chigi Chapel at Santa Maria del Popolo, Rome.
	(1) Designs for the mosaics carried out in 1516 by Alviso della Pace—*The Almighty*, and the *Planets accompanied by Angels.* (2) Red chalk drawings at Oxford and Lille (*Vasari Society*, 2nd series, XI, Nos. 5 and 6).
1516.	*Double portrait of Navagero and Beazzano.* Rome, Doria Gallery. Entirely original work of Raphael's own hand, possibly composed of two separate pictures combined, formerly with landscape background.
1514–17.	Frescoes of the Stanza dell' Incendio. *The Fire in the Borgo.* Raphael was still perhaps the designer of the first ideas for the middle of the composition. Execution by Giulio Romano, with background by Penni. All the drawings by Giulio.
	The Battle of Ostia. By Giulio Romano, entirely without Raphael's participation.
	Coronation of Charlemagne. The composition, as somewhat novel, may have been indicated by Raphael.
	Drawings at Düsseldorf and in the Albertina, by Penni.
	The Purificatory Oath of Leo III. Sketch of the composition by Penni. Florence, Horne Collection.
1517.	*Lo Spasimo di Sicilia.* Madrid, Prado. Composition of the lower part by Raphael himself, altered upward by pupils. Christ, Joseph of Arimathaea and the Virgin show traces of Raphael's most individual touch.
	Drawings in the Uffizi and Albertina.

1517.

Pope Leo X with Cardinal Giulio de' Medici and Ludovico de' Rossi. Florence, Pitti Palace. (Gronau, 156.) Authentic in essentials; the share taken according to Vasari (ed. Milanesi, V, 41) by Giulio Romano not identifiable.

(1) Copy by Andrea del Sarto, Naples. (2) Copy in the Corsini Gallery (by Bugiardini?).

Circa 1518.

Vision of Ezekiel. Florence, Pitti Palace. Composition by Raphael himself, carried out in the studio by Giulio Romano and perhaps by Thomas Vincidor.

Circa 1518.

Portrait of Joanna of Aragon. Paris, Louvre. According to Vasari by a pupil, presumably Giulio Romano; in any case no part of the execution by Raphael.

Circa 1518.

Ceiling of the Garden Saloon in the Villa Farnesina. *Story of Psyche.* Frescoes. Carried out after Raphael's designs mostly by his pupils Giulio Romano and Penni.

(1) Original design only for *Venus and Psyche*, pen and red chalk. Oxford, Ashmolean Museum. (2) Corrections by Raphael's own hand in Giulio's red chalk drawing for this, in the figure of Psyche, and in the Three Graces for the picture of the *Wedding Feast*.

Circa 1518.

The Francis I. Holy Family. Paris, Louvre. Painting in all essentials by Giulio Romano and Penni, the head of Joseph carried out by Raphael himself in the style of the authentic portions of the *Transfiguration*.

(1) The cartoon fragment with Joseph, at Bayonne, Musée Bonnat, and St. Anne with St. John and the Child Christ, in Melbourne ? by the hand of Giulio. (2) Replica of the Madonna with the Child, dated (? old) 1517, presumably with the use of the same cartoon by Penni.

1518.

St. Michael overcoming Satan. Paris, Louvre. Design by Raphael, carried out by Giulio Romano, not without Raphael's participation in the arm and head of the Angel and of Satan, and in the landscape.

St. Margaret. Paris, Louvre. Executed by Giulio Romano from a composition by Raphael.

The so-called "La Perla" Holy Family. Madrid, Prado. Hardly anything of the composition or execution by Raphael himself, but almost entirely by Giulio Romano.

(1) Fragment of cartoon for the head, much worked over. Lille, Musée Wicar (*R.Z.*, VIII, 379). (2) A large drawing of the entire composition in London appears to be by Penni.

Circa 1518.

The Holy Family under the Oak-tree (also *The Madonna with the Lizard*, which however occurs only in the replica in the Pitti Palace). Madrid, Prado. The bold grouping in the novel landscape may possibly be traceable to Raphael himself. Execution by Giulio Romano and Penni. The two circular buildings on the eminence are the Temple of Minerva Medica and the former Capella Santa Maria della Febbre near St. Peter's. The antique base to the right is the Triangolo Grimani, then at Tivoli, now in the Ducal Palace at Venice.

Circa 1518.

Madonna with the Rose. Madrid, Prado. (Gronau, 170.) May possibly go back to an elder design by Raphael. Execution by Giulio Romano and Penni.

The small *Holy Family* known as the "*Madonna piccola Gonzaga*". Paris, Louvre. (Gronau, 171.) Composition and execution by a pupil, probably Penni.

(1) Replica at Nanterre. (2) Red chalk drawing of the entire composition at Windsor, Royal Library, by an artist near to Giulio Romano.

Circa 1518.   *Madonna del Divino Amore*. Naples, Museo Nazionale. Design and execution by Penni.
(1) Cartoon by him at Naples; fragment of another cartoon in London, British Museum. (2) Red chalk drawing for the St. Joseph (inspired by the statue of Aeschines), Vienna, Albertina, probably by Penni (*R.Z.*, VIII, text, fig. 303).

Circa 1519.   *The Visitation*. Madrid, Prado. (Gronau, 173.) Composition from older motives of Raphael and execution by Penni.

Circa 1518.   *The youthful John the Baptist in the Wilderness*. Florence, Uffizi. Probably after Raphael's design by Penni.

?1518–19.   *The Loggie*. Vatican. Architectural decoration composed by Raphael. The only original works by his own hand among the paintings are a few lozenges in the first vault with Cherubim and Seraphim. After his design probably the figures of the Almighty in the *Story of the Creation, God appearing to Isaac, Jacob's Ladder, Joseph's Dream, Moses on Sinai*. The execution by Giulio Romano, Penni, Perino del Vaga, and Polidoro. The drawings are by Giulio and Penni; occasionally— *e.g.* in *Jacob's Ladder*—over a preliminary drawing by Raphael.

Circa 1517–20.   *The Transfiguration*. Rome, Vatican. (Gronau, 202.) The design certainly by Raphael alone, but the preparatory work for the execution left to pupils, particularly Penni: red chalk sketch with nudes for the upper part, Chatsworth. A number of intermediate cartoons for the heads below partly on the base of the cartoon-tracings by Penni (Chatsworth, Vienna); also the nude drawings for the groups below (Vienna, Milan, Chatsworth). The retouched head of Andrew, and the heads of the old and young Apostle in the centre, drawn by Raphael himself. In the picture, Elijah and Moses with clouds behind them, the Apostles on Tabor, the heads and figures of Andrew in the foreground on the left and of the old Apostle in the centre may also be recognised as by his hand; the others executed by Giulio Romano and (mostly) by Penni. The head of Christ, obviously not quite finished, completed by Penni.

1520–24.   *Sala di Constantino* (Sala dei Papi). The idea of dividing the walls by introducing figures enthroned and tapestries is perhaps still owed to Raphael. In the composition, not to speak of the execution, there is no longer any trace of his work, but that of Giulio Romano and Penni.

BIBLIOGRAPHY OF RECENT LITERATURE

O. Fischel: "Due ritratti di Giulio II." *Bollettino d'Arte*, XXVIII (1934), 194–197.

O. Fischel: "Raphael's Auxiliary Cartoons." *Burlington Magazine*, LXXI (1937), 167–168.

G. Glück: "Ein wenig beachtetes Werk Raffaels." *Jahrbuch der kunsthistorischen Sammlungen in Wien*, N.F., X (1936), 97–104 (Ste Margarete, Vienna).

V. Golzio: *Raffaello nei documenti, nelle testimonianze dei contemporanei e nella letteratura del suo seculo.* Città del Vaticano, 1936.

G. Gronau: "Some portraits by Titian and Raphael." *Art in America*, XXV (1937), 93–104.

F. Hartt: "Raphael and Giulio Romano. With notes on the Raphael School." *The Art Bulletin*, XXVI (1944), 67–94.

U. Middeldorf: "Raphael's Drawings." New York, 1945, review by A. E. Popham, *Burlington Magazine* (June, 1946), 155–156.

A. P. Oppé: "Right and Left in Raphael's Cartoons." *Journal of the Warburg and Courtauld Institutes*, VII (1944), 82–94.

K. T. Parker: "Observations on the Oxford Raphaels." *Old Master Drawings*, XIV (1939–40). (*Last Supper*, early drawing. Study for the Magdalene in the National Gallery *Crucifixion*. The Large Florentine Sketchbook.—Combat of Nude Men, used for the painted relief in the *School of Athens*.—Old copy of the *School of Athens* without the figure of Heraclitus.)

A. E. Popham: "An unnoticed drawing by Raphael." *Old Master Drawings*, XII (1937–38), 45–46. (Cartoon for the Vatican *Coronation of the Virgin*, Windsor Castle.)

A. E. Popham: "Raphael, Standing Figure with Hands Joined in Prayer." *Old Master Drawings*, XIV (1939–40), 50. (Ottawa, National Gallery of Canada. According to O. Fischel a study for the St. John in the Mond Crucifixion.)

D. Redig de Campos: *Raffaello e Michelangelo.* Rome, 1946.

I. A. Richter: "A contribution to the understanding of Raphael's art: The Drawings for the *Entombment*." *Gazette des Beaux Arts*, ser. 6, XXVIII (1945), 335–356.

W. E. Suida: *Raphael.* London, 1941.

E. Wind: "Platonic Justice, designed by Raphael." *Journal of the Warburg Institute*, I (1937), 69–70.

INDEX

INDEX

371

INDEX

INDEX

INDEX

INDEX

379

INDEX

INDEX

INDEX

PLATES

See pages 25, 320.

1. Self-portrait.   Oxford, Ashmolean Museum.

See page 4.   *Photo Alinari.*

2A. PIERO DELLA FRANCESCA. Landscape. Florence, Uffizi.

See page 4.   *Photo Arceci.*

2B. Street in Urbino.

See page 4.   *Photo Arceci.*

2C. Raphael's Birthplace, Urbino.

See page 25.

3. Coronation of St. Nicholas of Tolentino. Lille, Musée Wicar.

See pages 8, 222.

4. JUSTUS VAN GENT. Dante. Urbino, Ducal Palace.

See page 14.

5. **MARTIN SCHONGAUER.**   The Temptation of St. Anthony.

See pages 21, 196, 231.

6. PERUGINO.   The Assumption of the Virgin.   Florence, Academy.

ee page 22.

7. **PINTURICCHIO.**   The Coronation of Pope Pius III.   Siena, Cathedral.

See pages 21, 231.

Photo Alinari.

8.　The Assumption of the Virgin (detail).　Florence, Academy.

pages 21, 231.

9A, B. The Assumption of the Virgin (details). Florence, Academy.

See page 21.

10.   Horatius Cocles.   Perugia, Cambio.

See pages 35, 224.

11. St. Sebastian. Bergamo, Gallery.

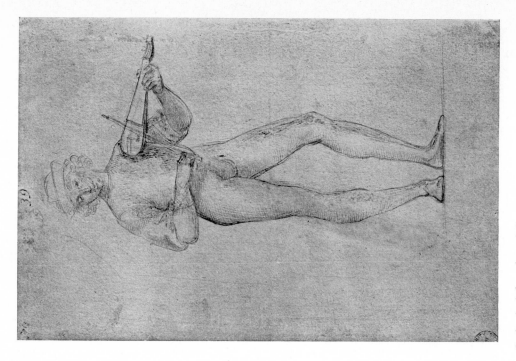

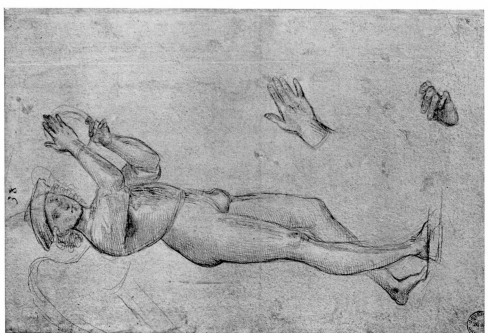

See page 27. 12A, B. Studies for *The Coronation of the Virgin.* Oxford, Ashmolean Museum.

13.   The Adoration of the Magi.   Stockholm, National Museum.

See page 27.

14.   St. Thomas.   Study for *The Coronation of the Virgin*.   Lille, Musée Wicar.

See page 27.

15. St. James. Study for *The Coronation of the Virgin*. London, British Museum.

See page 27.

16. Angel. Study for *The Coronation of the Virgin*. London, British Museum.

See page 28.

17A.   Head of the Virgin.
Study for *The Annunciation*.   London, British Museum.

See pages 28, 231.

17B.   The Annunciation.   Rome, Vatican.

See page 28.

18. The Knight's Dream.   London, National Gallery.

See page 33.   *Photo Alinari.*

19.   *Pax vobiscum.*   Brescia, Gallery.

See pages 31, 194.

20. St. George. Paris, Louvre.

Photo Alinari.

21. St. Michael. Paris, Louvre.

See pages 36, 225.

22. The Coronation of the Virgin. Rome, Vatican.

See page 37.

23. *Lo Sposalizio.*   Milan, Brera.

See page 44.   *Photo Hanfstaengl.*

24. The Diotalevi Madonna.   Berlin, Kaiser Friedrich-Museum.

See page 45.

25.   The Solly Madonna.   Berlin, Kaiser Friedrich-Museum.

See pages 45, 54.   *Photo Hanfstaengl.*

26.   The Conestabile della Staffa Madonna.
Formerly in the Hermitage, Leningrad.

See page 53.   *Photo Mansell.*

27.   The Holy Family with the Palm.
London, Bridgewater House, Lord Ellesmere.

The painting bears the inscription: SALVE·MATER·CHRISTI

See page 46.

Photo Hanfstaengl.

28.   The Ansidei Madonna.   London, National Gallery.

See page 67.

29.   The Madonna of the Baldacchino.   Florence, Pitti Palace.

See page 47.   *Photo Anderson.*

30.   The *Madonna del Granduca*.   Florence, Pitti Palace.

See page 47.

Photo Anderson.

31. The *Madonna del Granduca* (detail). Florence, Pitti Palace.

See page 49.

32. The *Madonna del Cardellino*. Florence, Uffizi.

See pages 64, 194.

33. St. Catherine. London, National Gallery.

See pages 50, 226.

34.   The Madonna in the Meadow.   Vienna, Kunsthistorisches Museum.

See page 51.

35. *La Belle Jardinière.* Paris, Louvre.

See page 51.

36. The Holy Family with the Lamb. Madrid, Prado.

See page 54.

37.   St. George.   Washington, National Gallery of Art (Mellon Collection).

See pages 52, 234.

38. Woman walking.   Oxford, Ashmolean Museum.

See page 63.

39. St. Mary Magdalen. Study for *The Entombment*. Haarlem, Lugt Collection.

See page 53.

40.   The Tempi Madonna.   Munich, Alte Pinakothek.

See page 66.   *Photo Hanfstaengl.*

41. The Colonna Madonna. Berlin, Kaiser-Friedrich Museum.

See page 54.

42. The Small Cowper Madonna. Philadelphia, Widener Collection.

See page 68.

43. Study of drapery for the *Madonna of the Baldacchino.*
Paris, École des Beaux Arts.

See page 60.

44.   Self-portrait.   Florence, Uffizi.

See page 56.

45.   Portrait, presumed to be of Perugino.   Rome, Borghese Gallery.

See page 57.

46.   Angelo Doni.   Florence, Pitti Palace.

See page 57.

47. Maddalena Doni. Florence, Pitti Palace.

See page 59.

48.   The *Donna Gravida*.   Florence, Pitti Palace.

See pages 59, 234.   *Photo Hanfstaengl.*

49.   The Lady in Green.   Urbino, Ducal Palace.

See page 68.

50B. The Virgin and Child.
Bayonne, Musée Bonnat.

See page 66.

50A. The Virgin and Child with St. John.
Florence, Uffizi.

See page 68.

51. Studies of Children. Paris, École des Beaux Arts.

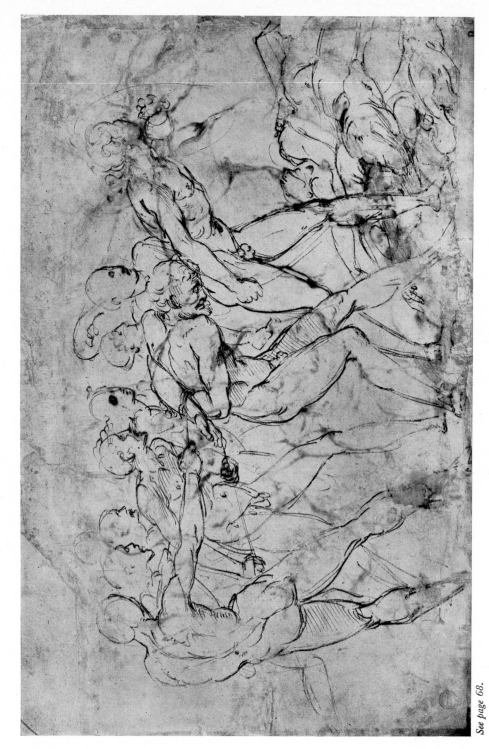

See page 68.

52. Combat. Oxford, Ashmolean Museum.

See page 60.

53. St. Placidus and other Studies. Oxford, Ashmolean Museum.

54.   Stanza della Segnatura, Rome: The *Disputa* and *Justitia.*

See page 73.

See page 73.

55. Stanza della Segnatura, Rome: Parnassus and The School of Athens.

See page 76.

56.   Theology.   Oxford, Ashmolean Museum.

See page 74.

57. Poetry. Windsor, Royal Library.
By gracious permission of H.M. The Queen.

See page 77.

58.   The Massacre of the Innocents.   Engraving by Marcantonio Raimondi.

See page 77.

59.   Studies for *The Massacre of the Innocents.*   Vienna, Albertina.

See pages 76, 194.

60.   The Judgment of Solomon.   Rome, Stanza della Segnatura.

See page 76.

61. Study for *The Massacre of the Innocents*.   Oxford, Ashmolean Museum.

See page 80.

62. The *Disputa.* Rome, Stanza della Segnatura.

63.   The *Disputa* (detail).   Rome, Stanza della Segnatura.

See pages 81, 231.

64.   Study for the *Disputa*.   Windsor, Royal Library.

By gracious permission of H.M. The Queen.

65.   Study for the *Disputa*.   London, British Museum.

See page 82.

66. Study for the *Disputa.*   Oxford, Ashmolean Museum.

See page 82.

67. Study for the *Disputa*. Chantilly, Musée Condé.

See pages 198, 232.

68.   St. Stephen. Study for the *Disputa*.   Florence, Uffizi.

See page 82.

69. Christ. Study for the *Disputa*. Lille, Musée Wicar.

See pages 84, 232.

70.   St. Paul, and the leg of Adam.   Studies for the *Disputa*.   Florence, Uffizi.

See pages 84, 198.

71. The Belvedere Apollo. Rome, Vatican.

See pages 85, 144.

72. The School of Athens. Rome, Stanza della Segnatura.

See page 88.

73. Parnassus. Rome, Stanza della Segnatura.

See page 83.

74. Study for the *Disputa*.   London, British Museum.

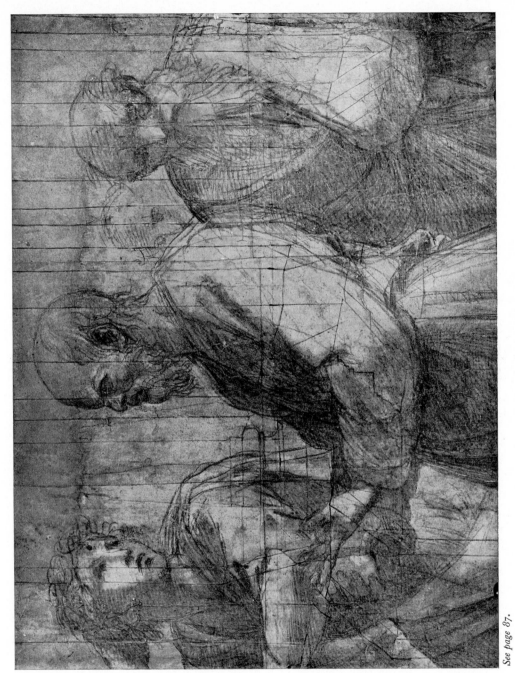

See page 87.

75. Socrates. Milan, Ambrosiana.

See page 87.

Photo Paoletti.

76. Anaxagoras. Milan, Ambrosiana.

See page 87.

77.   Zoroaster and Ptolemy.   Milan, Ambrosiana.

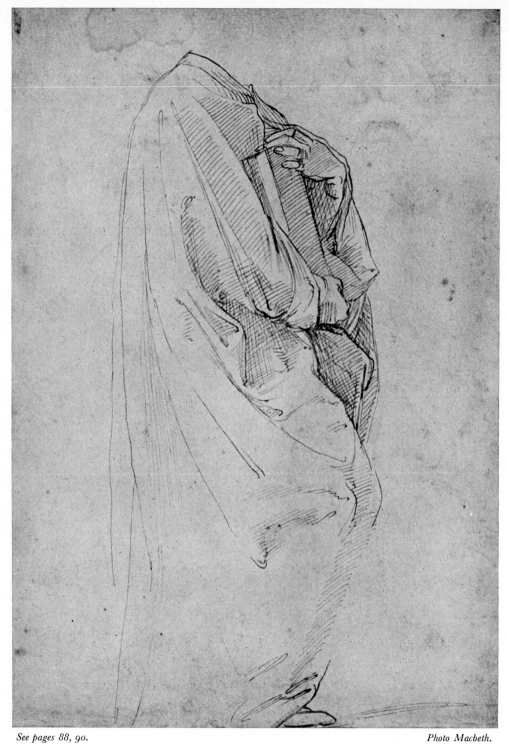

See pages 88, 90. *Photo Macbeth.*

78. Dante. Study for *Parnassus*. Windsor, Royal Library.
By gracious permission of H.M. The Queen.

See pages 89, 90.

79. Melpomene. Study for *Parnassus*. Oxford, Ashmolean Museum.

See pages 89, 191.

80. Achilles in Scyros. Graeco-Roman sarcophagus relief. Paris, Louvre.

See pages 89.

81. Muses. Detail of *Parnassus*. Rome, Stanza della Segnatura.

See pages 88, 296.

82.   Tebaldeo.   Detail of *Parnassus*.   Rome, Stanza della Segnatura.

See page 91.

83. Ariosto. Detail of *Parnassus*. Rome, Stanza della Segnatura.

See page 91.

84. *Putto.* Detail of *The Judicial Virtues.* Rome, Stanza della Segnatura.

Photo Archivio Fotografico, Gallerie Pontificali.

See page 91.

85. Prudence. Detail of *The Judicial Virtues.* Rome, Stanza della Segnatura.

See page 91.

86. The Judicial Virtues. Rome, Stanza della Segnatura.

See page 112.

87.   Group of Cardinals.   Detail of *Gregory IX delivering the Decretals.*
Rome, Stanza della Segnatura.

See page 90.

88.   Dante, Homer and another. Studies for *Parnassus*.
Windsor, Royal Library.

See page 248.

89. Sonnet with Figures. Study for the *Disputa*.
Oxford, Ashmolean Museum.

See page 93.

90.   Pope Julius II.   Chatsworth, Duke of Devonshire.

See page 93.

91.   Pope Julius II.   London, National Gallery.

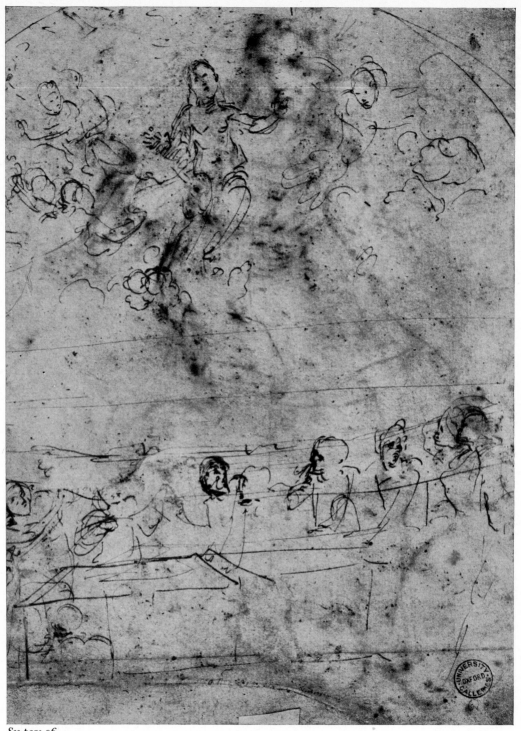

See page 96.

92. The Assumption of the Virgin. Oxford, Ashmolean Museum.

See page 97.

93. Studies for *The Resurrection*.   Oxford, Ashmolean Museum.

See page 96.

94. The Glorification of the Virgin. Stockholm, National Museum.

See pages 96, 97, 103, 197.

95. The Resurrection. Oxford, Ashmolean Museum.

See pages 103, 227.

96. Studies for *The Expulsion of Heliodorus*.
Oxford, Ashmolean Museum.

See pages 96, 282.

97. The Resurrection. Bayonne, Musée Bonnat.

See page 104.

98.   Study for *The Mass of Bolsena*.   Chatsworth, Duke of Devonshire.

See pages 193 note, 363.

99. *Putto* with the Medici ring. Haarlem, Teyler Museum.

See page 99.

100.   God's Command to Noah.   Rome, Stanza of Heliodorus.

See page 100.

101.   Moses and the Burning Bush.   Rome, Stanza of Heliodorus.

See pages 102, 145, 228.

102.   The Expulsion of Heliodorus.   Rome, Stanza of Heliodorus.

See pages 102, 197.

103. The Expulsion of Heliodorus (detail). Rome, Stanza of Heliodorus.

Photo Hanfstaengl.

104.   The Mass of Bolsena.   Rome, Stanza of Heliodorus.

See page 104.

See pages 107, 194.

105. Attila. Rome, Stanza of Heliodorus.

See page 104.

106.   The Mass of Bolsena (detail).   Rome, Stanza of Heliodorus.

See pages 105, 106.

107.   The Mass of Bolsena (detail).   Rome, Stanza of Heliodorus.

See page 105.

Photo Anderson.

108.   The Mass of Bolsena (detail).   Rome, Stanza of Heliodorus.

See page 105.

109.   The Mass of Bolsena (detail).   Rome, Stanza of Heliodorus.

See pages 65, 106.   110.   The Deliverance of St. Peter.   Rome, Stanza of Heliodorus.

See page 106.

111.   Study for *The Deliverance of St Peter*.   Florence, Uffizi.

See page 108.

112. Attila (detail). Rome, Stanza of Heliodorus.

See page 106.

113.   The Deliverance of St. Peter (detail).   Rome, Stanza of Heliodorus.

See page 102.

114.   Fragment of Cartoon for *The Expulsion of Heliodorus*.   Paris, Louvre.

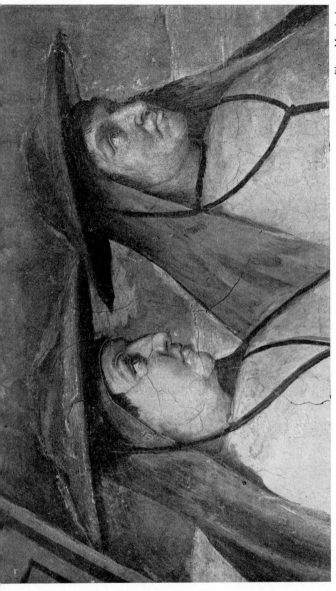

See page 109.

Photo Moscioni.

115A. Attila (detail). Rome, Stanza of Heliodorus.

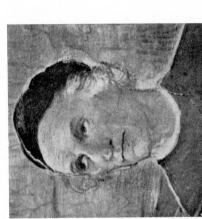

Photo Moscioni.

See page 108.

115B. Attila (detail).
Rome, Stanza of Heliodorus.

See page 56.

116.   Portrait of a Humanist.   Budapest, Museum of Fine Arts.

See page 112.

117.   Portrait of a Cardinal.   Madrid, Prado.

See page 112. *Photo Hanfstaengl.*

118. Tommaso Inghirami ("Fedra"). Florence, Pitti Palace.

See page 122.

119A.   Valerio Belli.   London, Sir Kenneth Clark.

See page 117.   *Photo Anderson.*

119B.   Andrea Navagero and Agostino Beazzano.   Rome, Doria Gallery.

See page 115.

120. Castiglione. Paris, Louvre.

See pages 116, 325.

121. RUBENS. Copy of Raphael's *Castiglione*. Vienna, Private Collection.

See page 118.

122. Andrea Navagero (detail).   Rome, Doria Gallery.

See page *118*.

123.   Agostino Beazzano (detail).   Rome, Doria Gallery.

See page 119.

124. Raphael and his Fencing-master. Paris, Louvre.

See page 119. *Photo Giraudon.*

125.   Raphael's Fencing-master (detail).   Paris, Louvre.

See page 119.

126. Raphael. Engraving by Marcantonio Raimondi.

RAPHAEL D'VRBIN

Ipfe Raphael, pinxit   W. Hollar fecit. 1651   F. van den Wyngarde excudit.

See page 119.

127. Self-portrait. Engraving by Wenzel Hollar after Raphael.

See page 120.

128. Leo X with Cardinals Ludovico de' Rossi and Giuliano de' Medici.
Florence, Pitti Palace.

See page 120.

129.   Leo X (detail).   Florence, Pitti Palace.

See page 123.

130. The *Donna Velata*. Florence, Pitti Palace.

See page 124.

131. The *Donna Velata*. Engraving by Wenzel Hollar after Raphael.

See page 123.

132. The *Donna Velata* (detail). Florence, Pitti Palace.

See page 124.

133. Portrait of a Woman. Cracow, Czartoryski Gallery.

See page 127.   *Photo Cooper.*

134. The Bridgewater Madonna.
London, Bridgewater House, Lord Ellesmere.

See page 129.

135. The Mackintosh Madonna. London, National Gallery.

See page 127.

136. Studies for the *Bridgewater Madonna*. Florence, Uffizi.

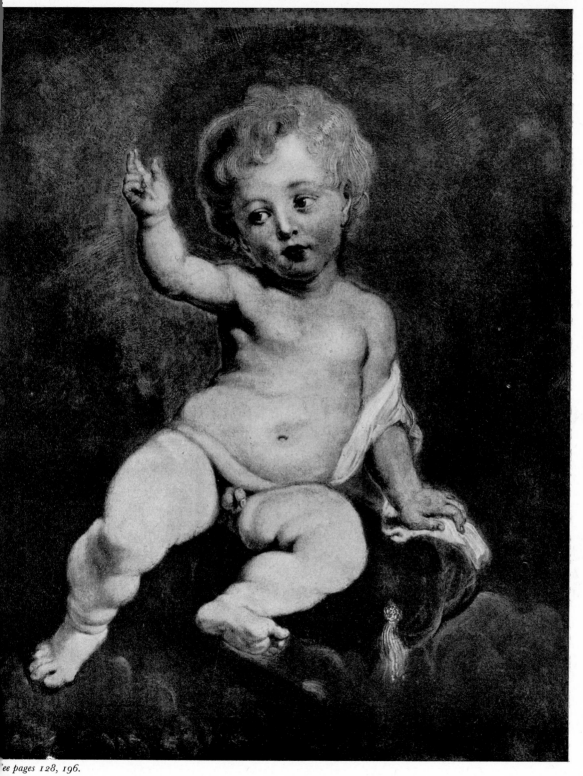

ee pages 128, 196.

137. RUBENS. The Child Christ. Amsterdam, Goudstikker Collection.

See page 129.

138A. Study for the *Mackintosh Madonna.*
London, British Museum.

See page 130.

138B. Study for the *Madonna della Sedia.*
Basle, Hirsch Collection.

See page 364.

139.   The Virgin and Child.   Vienna, Albertina.

See page 129.

140. Cartoon for the *Mackintosh Madonna*.
London, British Museum.

See pages 134, 244.

141. Study for the *Madonna of Foligno*. Chatsworth, Duke of Devonshire.

See page 131.

142.   The *Madonna della Sedia*.   Florence, Pitti Palace.

See page 132.

143. The Alba Madonna.
Washington, National Gallery of Art, Mellon Collection.

See page 132.

144.   Studies for the *Alba* and *Della Sedia Madonnas*.
Lille, Musée Wicar.

See page 133.

145. Study for the *Madonna of Foligno*. Frankfort-on-the-Main, Städelsches Institut.

See page 133.   *Photo Anderson.*

146.   The Madonna of Foligno.   Rome, Vatican.

147.   The Sistine Madonna.   Dresden, Gemäldegalerie.

See page 132.

148. The *Madonna della Tenda*. Munich, Alte Pinakothek.

See page 139.

149. The Madonna with the Fish. Madrid, Prado.

See page 139.

150.   Study for the *Madonna with the Fish*.   Florence, Uffizi.

See page 140.

151.   Study for the *Madonna with the Fish*.   London, Captain Colville.

See page 143.

152.   Detail of the *Sposalizio*.   Milan, Brera.

See page 146.

153A. MARTEN VAN HEEMSKERCK. St. Peter's under construction.
Berlin, Kupferstichkabinett.

See page 146.

153B. MARTEN VAN HEEMSKERCK. St. Peter's under construction.
Berlin, Kupferstichkabinett.

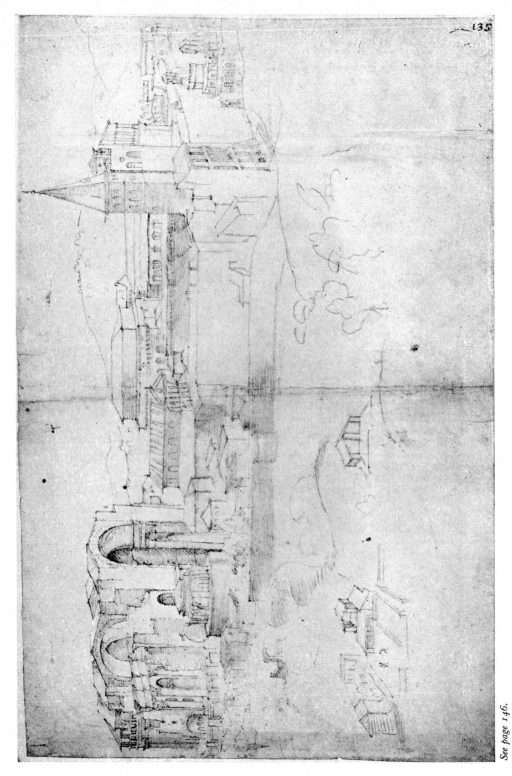

See page 146.   154.   MARTEN VAN HEEMSKERCK.   St. Peter's under construction.   Berlin, Kupferstichkabinett.

See page 146.

155. Study for *The Mass of Bolsena*. Oxford, Ashmolean Museum.

See page 147.

156.   Sant' Eligio degli Orefici, Rome.

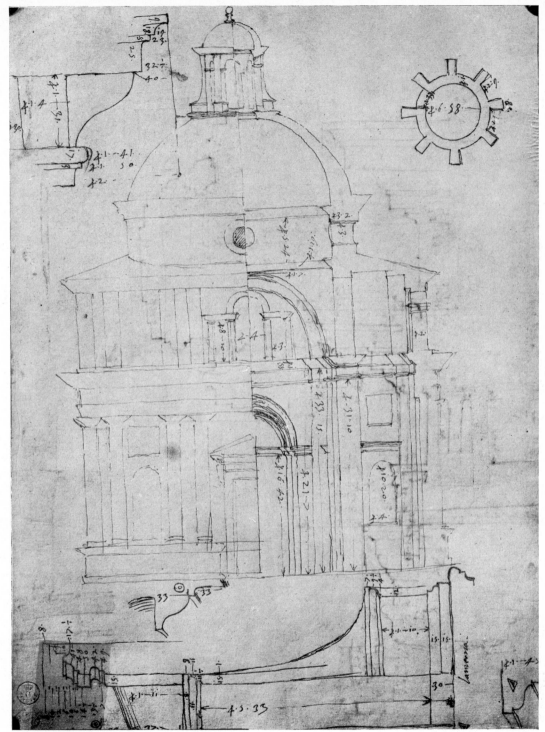

See page 148.

Photo R. Soprintendenza, Florence.

157. Designs for Sant' Eligio degli Orefici, Rome. Florence, Uffizi.

See page 148.   *Photo Fototeca Italiana, Florence.*

158.   Designs for Sant' Eligio degli Orefici, Rome.   Florence, Uffizi.

See page 148.

159.   Design for Sant' Eligio degli Orefici, Rome. Florence, Uffizi.

See page 149.

160.   Chigi Chapel, Santa Maria del Popolo, Rome.

See pages 149, 151.   *Photo Anderson.*

161. Chigi Chapel, Santa Maria del Popolo, Rome.   Interior of Dome.

See pages 153, 255.

162. The Almighty. Study for the Chigi Chapel. Oxford, Ashmolean Museum.

See page 153.

163. Angel. Study for the Chigi Chapel. Oxford, Ashmolean Museum.

See page 153.

164. Mars. Study for the Chigi Chapel. Lille, Musée Wicar.

See page 181.

165. Daniel. Study for Santa Maria della Pace. Florence, Uffizi.

See page 148.

166.   Sant' Eligio degli Orefici, Rome.   Interior of Dome.

See page 155.

167.   The Loggie of the Vatican.   Vault of the First Bay.

See page 153.

Photo Alinari.

168.   The Loggie of the Vatican, Rome.

See page 153.

Photo Archivio Fotografico, Gall. e Musei Vaticani.

169.   The Loggie of the Vatican (detail).

See page 157.   170.   God dividing the Light and Darkness.   Rome, Loggie of the Vatican.

See page 158.

171.   God dividing the Dry Land from the Waters.   Rome, Loggie of the Vatican.

See page 158.   *Photo Archivio Fotografico, Gall. e Musei Vaticani.*

172A. Detail of Vault. Rome, Loggie of the Vatican.

See page 156.

172B. Detail of Vault. Rome, Loggie of the Vatican.

See page 158.

173A, B. Details of Vault. Rome, Loggie of the Vatican.

See page 161.

174.   Palazzo Vidoni, Rome.

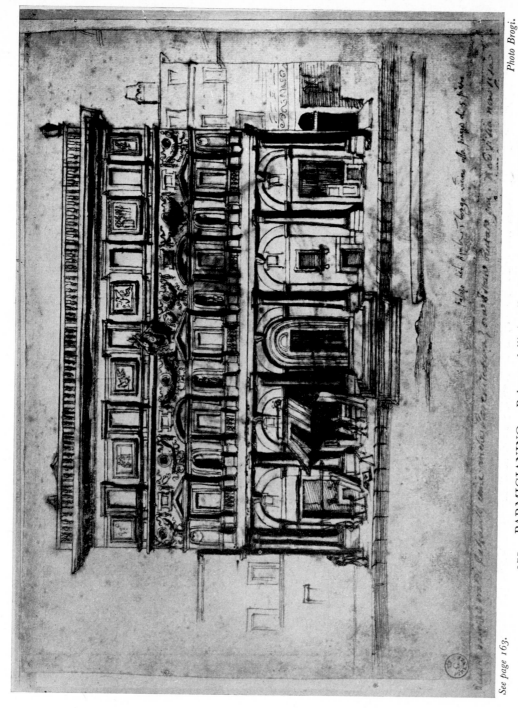

175. PARMIGIANINO. Palazzo dell' Aquila, Rome. Florence, Uffizi.

See page 163.

See pages 162, 314.

Photo Bicchierai.

176. Palazzo Pandolfini, Rome. Street Front.

See pages 162, 314.

Photo Bicchierai.

177. Palazzo Pandolfini, Rome. Garden Front.

See page 162.

Photo Moscioni.

178.   Palazzo Antonio da Brescia, Rome.

See page 163.

179A.   MARTEN VAN HEEMSKERCK.
Palazzo Antonio da Brescia.   Berlin, Kupferstichkabinett.

See pages 163, 195.   *Photo Macbeth.*

179B.   Cupid with the Eagle.   London, British Museum.

180. Villa Madama, Rome. Exterior.

See page 164.

181.   Villa Madama, Rome.   Interior.

See page 165.

See page 165.

182. Villa Madama, Rome. Interior.

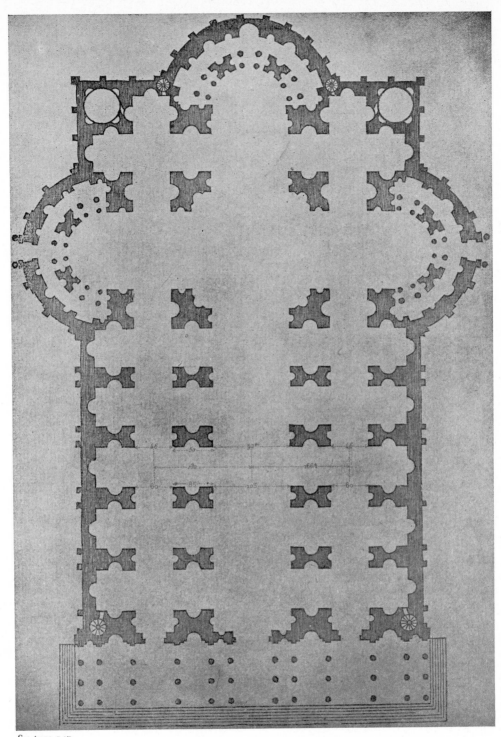

See page 147.

183.   Raphael's Plan for St. Peter's, Rome (after Serlio).

See page 165.

184A. LOUIS CHAYS. Villa Madama, Rome. Berlin, Kupferstichkabinett.

Grundriß, Aufriß und Durchschnitte von der Villa Madama.

See page 166.

184B. Villa Madama, Rome. Detail of Engraving after Gutensohn-Thürmer.

See page 165.

185A, B. MARTEN VAN HEEMSKERCK. Garden of the Villa
Madama, Rome. Berlin, Kupferstichkabinett.

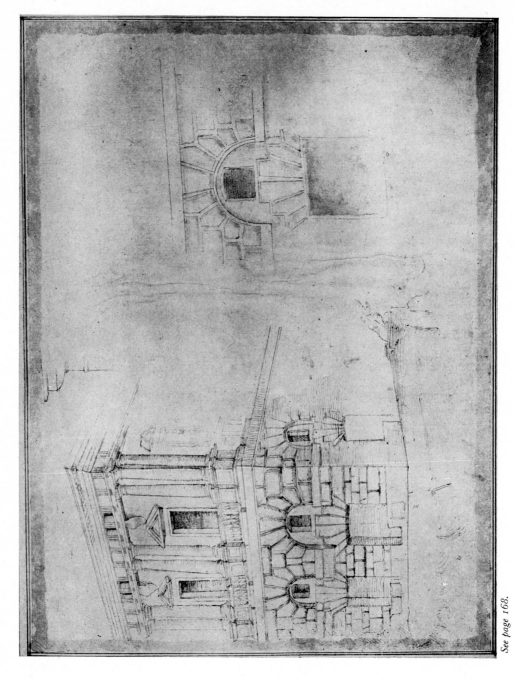

186.   PALLADIO.   Raphael's Palace, Rome.   London, Royal Institute of British Architects.

See page 212.

187. BALDASSARE PERUZZI. Stage Design. Florence, Uffizi.

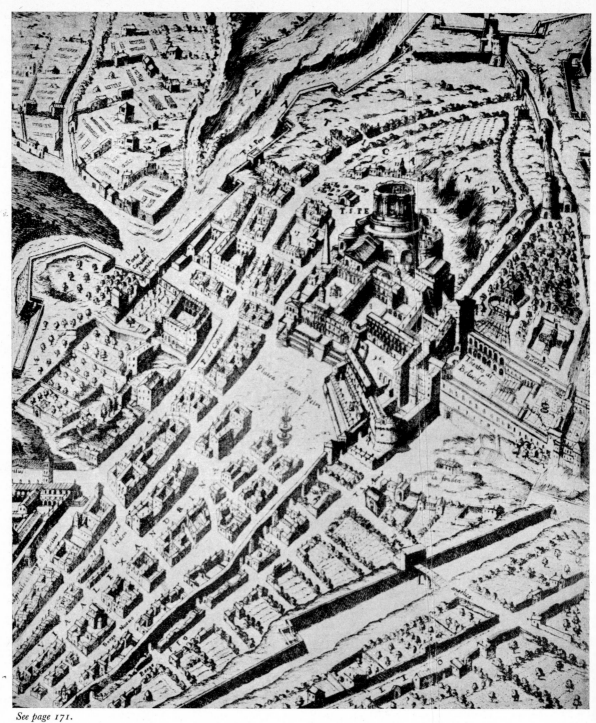

See page 171.

188. LAFRERI. Plan of Rome, 1577. Detail showing the Borgo and
St. Peter's under construction.

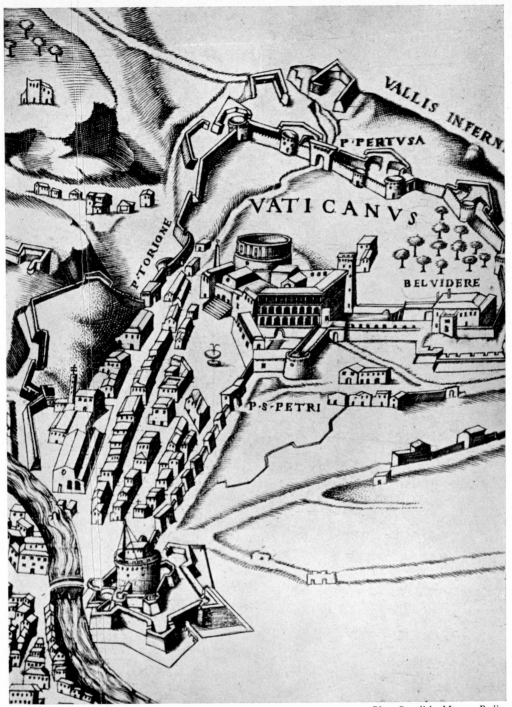

VALLIS INFERN.

P. PERTVSA

VATICANVS

BELVIDERE

P. TORIONE

P·S·PETRI

See page 172.

189. SEBASTIAN DEL RÈ. Plan of Rome. Detail.

See page 177.

190. Design for a Dish. Windsor, Royal Library.
By gracious permission of H.M. The Queen.

See pages 181, 324.

191. RUBENS (after Raphael). David and Daniel. Amsterdam, Regteren-Altena Collection.

See pages 182, 228.

192. Santa Maria della Pace, Rome. Diagram.

See page 181.

193. Santa Maria della Pace, Rome; Prophets and Sibyls. Sketch.
Copy after Raphael. Stockholm, National Museum.

See page 181.

194A, B.   The Prophets, Santa Maria della Pace, Rome.
Engraving by Giovanni Battista Volpato after Raphael.

See pages 181, 228.

194C.   The Sibyls, Santa Maria della Pace, Rome.
Engraving by Giovanni Battista Volpato after Raphael.

See pages 179, 183.

Photo Alinari.

195. *Putto*. Detail of Fresco. Rome, Santa Maria della Pace.

See pages 178, 182.

196.   The Prophets.   Rome, Santa Maria della Pace.

See page 178.

197.   The Sibyls.   Rome, Santa Maria della Pace.

See page 178.   *Photo Alinari.*

198.   The Cumaean Sibyl (detail).   Rome, Santa Maria della Pace.

See page 178.

199.   The Phrygian Sibyl (detail).   Rome, Santa Maria della Pace.

See page 178.

200. Study for the *Persian Sibyl*. Oxford, Ashmolean Museum.

See page 178.

201. Studies for the *Sibyls* fresco.   Oxford, Ashmolean Museum.

See page 178.

202. Studies for the *Sibyls* fresco. Vienna, Albertina.

See page 180.

203.   Angel of the Persian Sibyl (detail).   Rome, Santa Maria della Pace.

See page 186.

204.   Galatea.   Rome, Farnesina.

See pages 166, 184.

205.   Mercury and Psyche.   Rome, Farnesina.

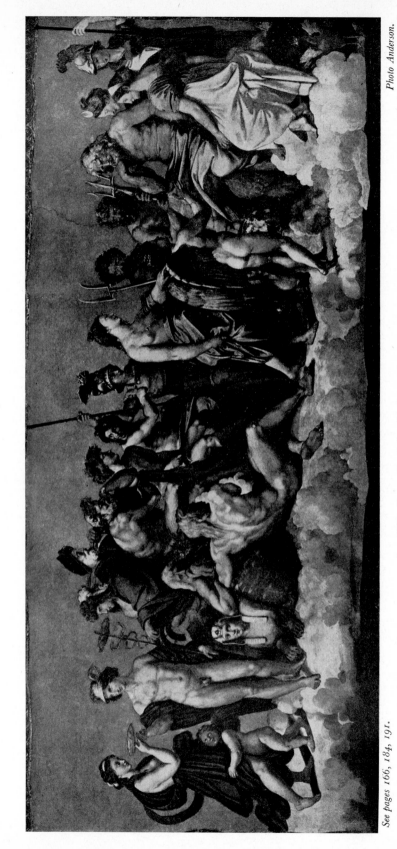

See pages 166, 184, 191.

206.   The Council of the Gods.   Rome, Farnesina.

207.   The Wedding Feast of Cupid and Psyche.   Rome, Farnesina.

See pages 185, 192.

See pages 167, 184.

208. Venus in her Car; Venus and Jupiter. Rome, Farnesina.

See pages 166, 167.

209. *Putti with Attributes.* Rome, Farnesina.

See pages 166, 184.

210. Mercury. Rome, Farnesina.

See page 166.

211.   Venus and Cupid.   Rome, Farnesina.

See page 185.

212.   Mercury and Psyche.   Study by a pupil of Raphael.
Chatsworth, Duke of Devonshire.

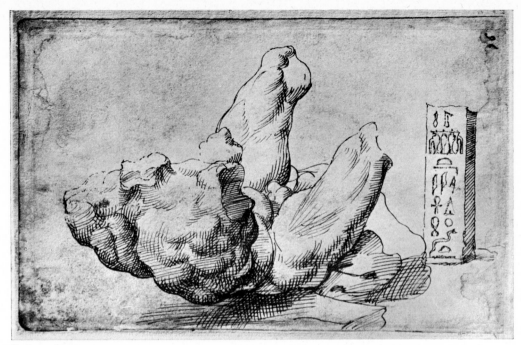

See page 185.

213A. MARTEN VAN HEEMSKERCK.
Antique Sculptures at the Casa Galli, Rome.   Berlin, Kupferstichkabinett.

See pages 186, 192, 198.

213B. MARTEN VAN HEEMSKERCK.
The Belvedere Torso.   Berlin, Kupferstichkabinett.

See page 185.

214.   The Three Graces.   Study for *The Wedding Feast of Cupid and Psyche.*
Windsor, Royal Library.

By gracious permission of H.M. The Queen.

See page 184.

215. Venus and Psyche. Study for the Farnesina fresco. Paris, Louvre.

216.   Relief on the attic of the Arch of Constantine, Rome.

See page 194.

217. Relief on the Arch of Constantine. Munich, Kupferstichkabinett.

See page 195.

218A.   Boy with Goose.
Ancient Roman.
Rome, Museo delle Terme.

See page 196.

218B.   Sarcophagus with Relief of the Four Seasons.   Ancient Roman.

See page 192.

219A. The *Triangolo Grimani.*
Part of an engraving by Hieronymus Cock after Heemskerck.

See page 196, 274.

219B. Nike sacrificing a Bull. Ancient Roman.
London, British Museum.

See page 197.

220.   The Charge to the Apostles.   Mosaic.
Rome, Santa Maria Maggiore.

Photo Alinari.

221.   The Battle of Joshua.   Mosaic.   Rome, Santa Maria Maggiore.

See page 198.

222. *"Quos ego"*. Engraving by Marcantonio Raimondi after Raphael.

See pages 195, 197, 272. *Photo Hanfstaengl.*

223.   The Vision of Ezekiel.   Florence, Pitti Palace.

See pages 156, 167, 198.

224.   Angels.   Detail of vault painting.   Rome, Loggie of the Vatican.

225. Victories. Mosaic. Ancient Roman. Rome, Museo delle Terme.

See page 198.

ΠΙΝΔΑΡΟΥ,

ΟΛΥΜΠΙΑ. ΠΥΘΙΑ.
ΝΕΜΕΑ. ΙΣΘΜΙΑ.

Μετὰ ἐξηγήσεως παλαιᾶς πάνυ ὠφελί
μου, καὶ σχολίων ὁμοίων.

Impressi Romæ per Zachariam Calergi Cretensem, per
missu S. D. N. Leonis. X. Pont. Max. ea etiam condi
tione, ut nequis alius per quinquennium hos imprimere,
aut uenundare Libros possit: utq̃ qui secus fecerit, is ab uni
uersa dei Ecclesia toto orbe terrarum expers excommunica
tusq̃ censeatur.

See page 176, 301.

226. Title-page. Pindar, 1515.

See page 215.

227.   Plato and Aristotle.   Detail of *The School of Athens*.
Rome, Stanza della Segnatura.

See pages 7, 221, 227.

228. **JUSTUS VAN GENT.** The Last Supper. Urbino, Ducal Palace.

See page 266.   *Photo Kunstgeschichtliches Seminar, Marburg.*

229A.   NIKOLAUS GERHAERT.
Bärbel.
Strasburg, Museum.

See page 226.

229B.   The Virgin.
Detail of the *Madonna in the Meadow*.
Vienna, Kunsthistorisches Museum.

See page 221.

229C.   The Procession to Calvary.   London, National Gallery.

See pages 222, 227.

230. ROGER VAN DER WEYDEN. The Entombment. Florence, Uffizi.

See page 227.

231.   The Expulsion of Heliodorus (detail).
Rome, Stanza of Heliodorus.

See pages 34, 224.   *Photo Metzger.*

232. MARTIN SCHONGAUER. The Last Judgment (detail).
Breisach, Domkirche.

See page 221.

233.   The Procession to Calvary (detail).   London, National Gallery.

See pages 29, 226.

234. The Three Graces. Chantilly, Musée Condé.

See page 226.

235. MEISTER GERHAERT VON LEIDEN.   The Virgin and Child with St. Anne.
Berlin, Deutsches Museum.

See pages 228, 278.

236.   The Transfiguration (detail).   Rome, Vatican.

See page 229.

Photo Alinari.

237. TADDEO GADDI. The Transfiguration. Florence, Academy.

See page 233.

238.   The Madonna in the Meadow (detail).
Vienna, Kunsthistorisches Museum.

See page 233.

239. St. Catherine (detail). London, National Gallery.

See page 237.

Photo Archivio Fotografico, Gall. e Musei Vaticani.

240.   The Transfiguration (detail).   Rome, Vatican.

See page 261.

241.   The Death of Ananias (detail).   London, Victoria and Albert Museum.

By gracious permission of H.M. The Queen.

See pages 68, 232.

242. Study for the *Colonna Madonna*. Paris, Louvre.

See page 68.
243. St. Bruno. Study for the *Madonna of the Baldacchino.* Florence, Uffizi.

See pages 124, 148, 244.

244. St. Cecilia. Bologna, Pinacoteca.

See page 246.

245.   St. John.   Detail of *St. Cecilia*.   Bologna, Pinacoteca.

Photo V. and A. Museum.

246.   "Feed my Lambs".   London, Victoria and Albert Museum.
By gracious permission of H.M. The Queen.

See page 257.

See page 256.

247.   Study for *"Feed my Lambs"*.   Windsor, Royal Library.
By gracious permission of H.M. The Queen.

See page 257.

248. Christ. Detail of "*Feed my Lambs*". London, Victoria and Albert Museum.
By gracious permission of H.M. The Queen.

See page 257.

249.   Christ.   Detail of "*Feed my Lambs*".   London, Victoria and Albert Museum.
By gracious permission of H.M. The Queen.

See page 259.

250.   The Miraculous Draught of Fishes.   London, Victoria and Albert Museum.

251.   The Death of Ananias.   London, Victoria and Albert Museum.
By gracious permission of H.M. The Queen.

See pages 197, 261.

See page 258.

252.   Head of a Disciple.   Detail of *"Feed my Lambs"*.
London, Victoria and Albert Museum.

See page 255.   *Photo V. and A. Museum.*

253. Head of Ananias.   Detail of *The Death of Ananias*.   London, Victoria and Albert Museum.

See page 262.

254.   Group of Disciples.   Detail of *The Death of Ananias*.   London, Victoria and Albert Museum.

By gracious permission of H.M. The Queen.

255. Two Disciples. Detail of *The Death of Ananias*. London, Victoria and Albert Museum.
By gracious permission of H.M. The Queen.

See page 263.

256.   The Healing of the Lame Man.   London, Victoria and Albert Museum.
By gracious permission of H.M. The Queen.

See pages 192, 263.

Photo V. and A. Museum.

257.   The Blinding of Elymas.   London, Victoria and Albert Museum.

By gracious permission of H.M. The Queen.

See page 266.

I. SERGIVS PAVLVS
ASIAE. PROCOS:
CHRISTIANAM FIDEM
AMPLECTITVR.
SAVLI PREDICATIONE

See page 264. Photo V. and A. Museum.

258. Heads of Onlookers. Detail of *The Healing of the Lame Man*.
London, Victoria and Albert Museum.
By gracious permission of H.M. The Queen.

See page 264.

259.   Mother and Child.   Detail of *The Healing of the Lame Man*.
London, Victoria and Albert Museum.
By gracious permission of H.M. The Queen.

See page 268.

260.   The Sacrifice at Lystra.   London, Victoria and Albert Museum.
By gracious permission of H.M. The Queen.

Photo V. and A. Museum.

261.   St. Paul at Athens.   London, Victoria and Albert Museum.

By gracious permission of H.M. The Queen.

See page 271.

See page 259.

262. Two Disciples. Detail of *The Miraculous Draught of Fishes.*
London, Victoria and Albert Museum.
By gracious permission of H.M. The Queen.

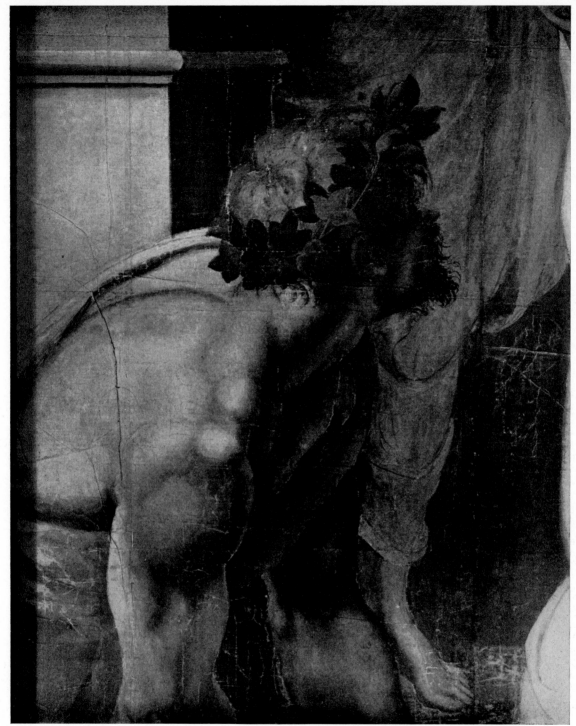

See page 269.

263. Sacrifice Attendant. Detail of *The Sacrifice at Lystra*.
London, Victoria and Albert Museum.
By gracious permission of H.M. The Queen.

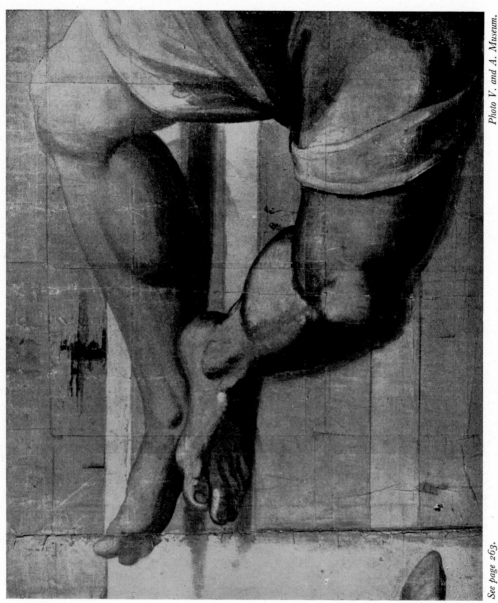

264. Legs of Ananias. Detail of *The Death of Ananias.*
London, Victoria and Albert Museum.
By gracious permission of H.M. The Queen.

See page 263.

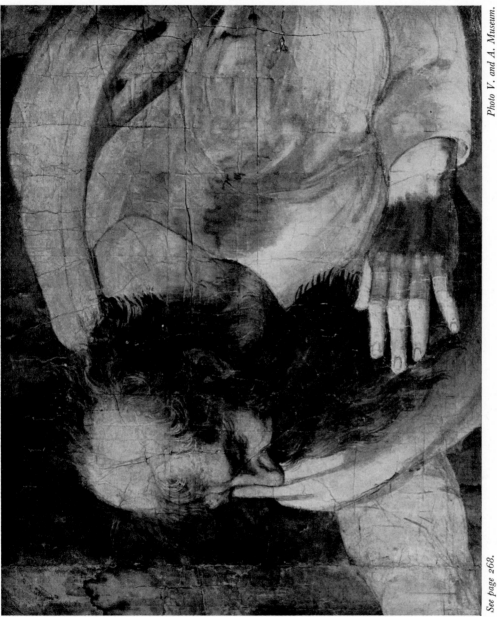

See page 268.

265. Head of the Physician. Detail of *The Sacrifice at Lystra.*
London, Victoria and Albert Museum.
By gracious permission of H.M. The Queen.

See page 268.

266. Head of Priest. Detail of *The Sacrifice at Lystra*.
London, Victoria and Albert Museum.
By gracious permission of H.M. The Queen.

See page 276.

267.   The Bearing of the Cross (*Lo Spasimo di Sicilia*).   (Detail.)   Madrid, Prado.

See pages 228, 278.

268.   The Transfiguration.   Rome, Vatican.

See page 280.

269. St. John. Detail of *The Transfiguration*. Rome, Vatican.

See page 256.

270.   Study for "*Feed my Lambs*".   Paris, Louvre.

See page 286.

271. Study for *The Transfiguration*. Paris, Louvre.

See page 284.   *Photo Anderson.*

272.   Moses.   Detail of *The Transfiguration*.   Rome, Vatican.

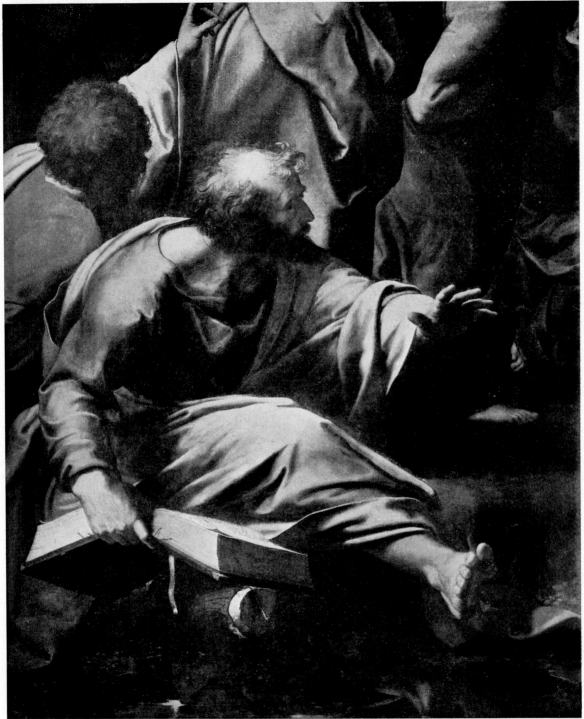

See page 285.

273. St. Andrew. Detail of *The Transfiguration*. Rome, Vatican.

See page 285.

274. St. Andrew.   Detail of *The Transfiguration*.   Rome, Vatican.

See page 285.

275.   St. Andrew.   Study for *The Transfiguration*.   London, British Museum.

See page 285.

276.   The Transfiguration (detail).   Rome, Vatican.

See page 285.

277.   Study for *The Transfiguration*.   Oxford, Ashmolean Museum.

278. St. Cecilia (detail). Bologna, Pinacoteca.

See page 245.

See page 296.

279. Fortitude.   Rome, Stanza della Segnatura.

See pages 91, 295.

280.   Ariosto.   Detail of *Parnassus*.   Rome, Stanza della Segnatura.

See pages 91, 295.

281. TITIAN. Ariosto. Ferrara, Casa Oriani.

Ut vultus hos esse suos didicere, vicissim
 Effigies proprias marmor habere probant
Lumina cum satiasset opus, mirata profantur,
 Quis putet humanas hoc potuisse manus?
Nos homines nobis similes produximus olim
 Assimulant nobis marmora nunc homines
Quod si vocales valuissent fingere, quis non
 Crederet et magnos progenuisse Deos?

Huldericus Huttenus Eques Germanus
Certum est Corycii patris Sacellum,
 Quod fecere alii prius pöete,
 Non libo colere, aut mola recenti,
 Nec caeso boue, victima cruenta,
 Sed versu ingeniòsq, qualecunq est,
 Da mi musa aliquid nouum, dedisti
 Quod non his alijs prius pöetis,
 Consumpta est ait, ut nihil supersit.
 Omnis copia tot prius pöetis,
 Iuuat me tamen, et iuuabit vsq,
 Quae sors cunq feretur, experiri
 Quiddam ad Corytij patris sacellum.

See page 299.

282.   Page from *Coryciana*.

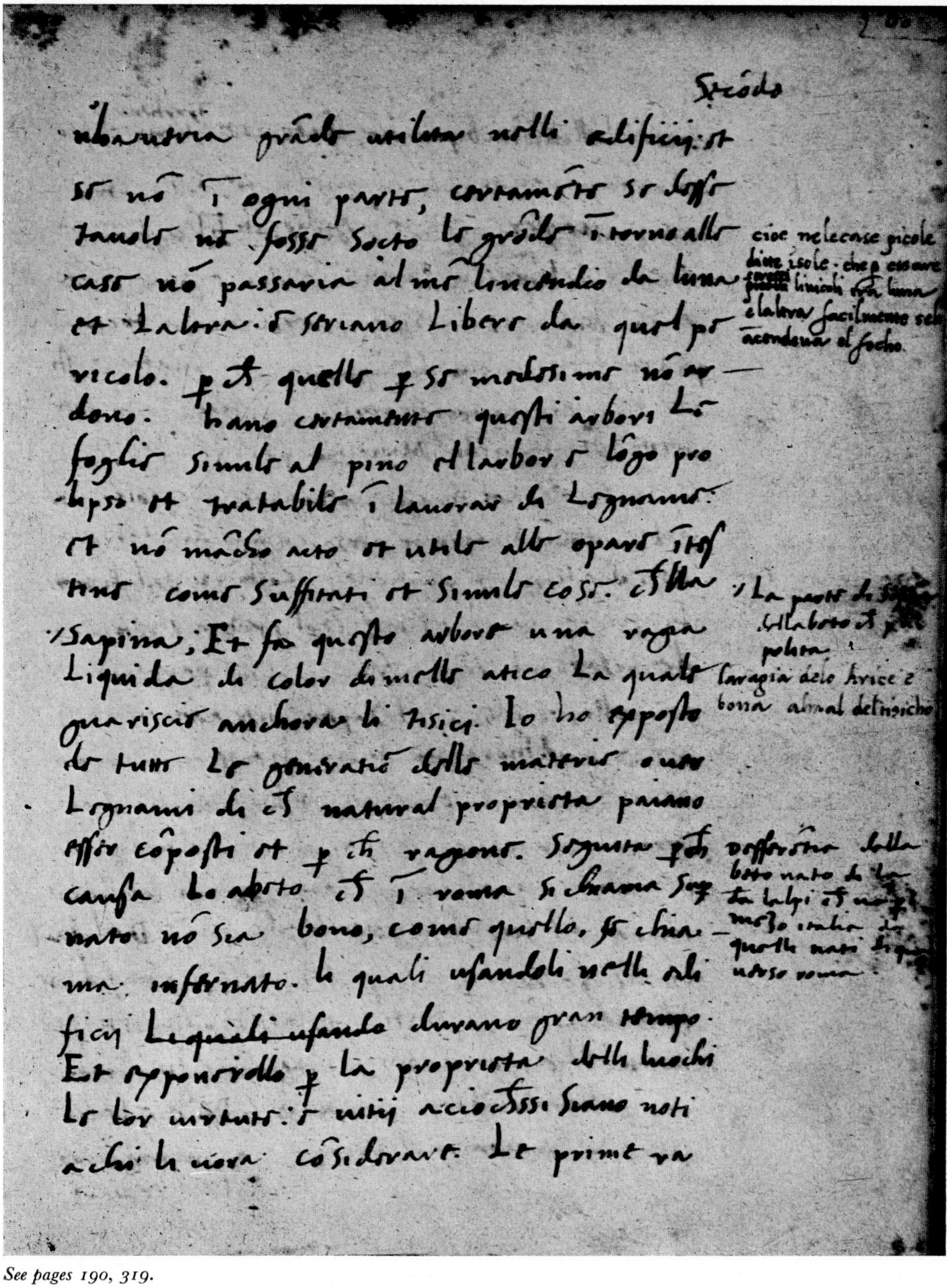

See pages 190, 319.

283. MS. of Vitruvius, translated by Fabio Calvi, with marginal notes in the hand of Raphael. Munich, Staatsbibliothek.

See page 23.

284. PINTURICCHIO.
Portrait of Raphael (detail of *The Coronation of Pius III*).
Siena, Cathedral.

See pages 61, 88, 299, 320.   *Photo Alinari.*

285. Self-portrait. Detail of *The School of Athens*.
Rome, Stanza della Segnatura.

See pages 103, 299, 320.

286.   Self-portrait.   Detail of *The Expulsion of Heliodorus*.
Rome, Stanza of Heliodorus.

See page 319.

287. Self-portrait. Detail of *Raphael and his Fencing-master*. Paris, Louvre.

Photo Anderson.

See page 322.

288. AGOSTINO CARACCI. Galatea. Rome, Farnese Palace.

289. GUIDO RENI. Aurora. Rome, Rospigliosi Gallery.

See page 322.

See pages 151, 323.

290. Chigi Chapel, Santa Maria del Popolo, Rome.   Detail of Dome.

See page 323.

291.   CORREGGIO.   St. Thomas.   Detail of *The Coronation of the Virgin.*   Parma, San Giovanni.

See pages 167, 324.

292.   RUBENS.   The Story of Cupid and Psyche.   Potsdam, Sanssouci.

293.   RUBENS.   The Death of Leander.   Dresden   Gemäldegalerie.

See page 325.

See page 324.

294.   The Judgment of Paris.   Engraving by Marcantonio Raimondi after Raphael.

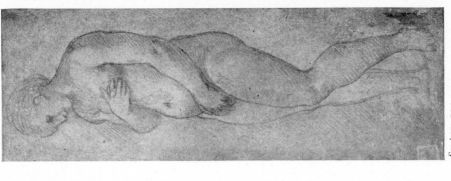

See page 324.

295B.   Venus.
Study for *The Judgment of Paris.*
Budapest, Museum of Fine Arts.

See page 324.

295A.   The Judgment of Paris.   Copy of Raphael.   Paris, Louvre.

296.   RUBENS.   Ruggero and Angelica.   Berlin, Kaiser Friedrich Museum.

See page 325.

297. RUBENS. The Fall. The Hague, Mauritshuis.

See page 325.

298. RUBENS.   The Miraculous Draught of Fishes.   London, National Gallery.

See page 324.

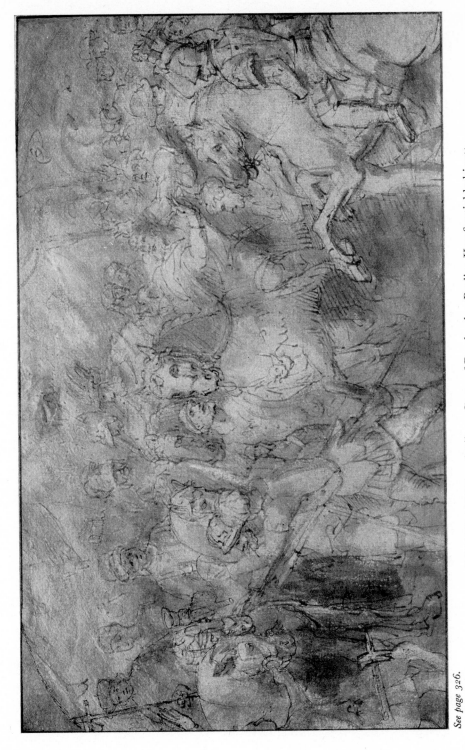

See page 326.

299. REMBRANDT. Attila. Copy of Raphael. Berlin, Kupferstichkabinett.

See pages 177, 325. 300. Design for a Dish. Oxford, Ashmolean Museum.

See page 325.　　301.　RUBENS.　The Birth of Venus.　Design for a Dish.　London, National Gallery.

See pages 149, 201, 213.

302.   The *opaion* of the Pantheon, Rome.